Show Me Microsoft® Office PowerPoint 2003

Steve Johnson

Perspection, Inc.

Que Publishing
800 East 96th Street
Indianapolis, IN 46240 USA

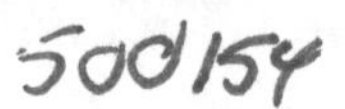

Show Me Microsoft® Office PowerPoint 2003

International Standard Book Number: 0-7897-3009-X

Library of Congress Catalog Card Number: 2003108683

Printed in the United States of America

First Printing: September 2003

06 05 04 03 4 3 2 1

Que Publishing offers excellent discounts on this book when ordered in quantity for bulk purchases or special sales. For information, please contact:

U.S. Corporate and Government Sales

1-800-382-3419

corpsales@pearsontechgroup.com

For sales outside the U.S., please contact:

International Sales

1-317-428-3341

International@pearsontechgroup.com

Trademarks

All terms mentioned in this book that are known to be trademarks or service marks have been appropriately capitalized. Que cannot attest to the accuracy of this information. Use of a term in this book should not be regarded as affecting the validity of any trademark or service mark.

Microsoft and the Microsoft Office logo are a registered trademarks of Microsoft Corporation in the United States and/or other countries.

Warning and Disclaimer

Every effort has been made to make this book as complete and as accurate as possible, but no warranty or fitness is implied. The authors and the publishers shall have neither liability nor responsibility to any person or entity with respect to any loss or damage arising from the information contained in this book.

Publisher
Paul Boger

Associate Publisher
Greg Wiegand

Managing Editor
Steve Johnson

Author
Steve Johnson

Project Editor
Melinda Lankford

Technical Editor
Holly Johnson

Production Editor
Beth Teyler

Page Layout
Kate Lyerla
Joe Kalsbeek
Ryan Suzuki

Interior Designers
Steve Johnson
Marian Hartsough

Indexer
Katherine Stimson

Proofreaders
Melinda Lankford
Beth Teyler

Team Coordinator
Sharry Lee Gregory

Acknowledgements

Perspection, Inc.

Show Me Microsoft Office PowerPoint 2003 has been created by the professional trainers and writers at Perspection, Inc. to the standards you've come to expect from Que publishing. Together, we are pleased to present this training book.

Perspection, Inc. is a software training company committed to providing information and training to help people use software more effectively in order to communicate, make decisions, and solve problems. Perspection writes and produces software training books, and develops multimedia and Web-based training. Since 1991, we have written more than 60 computer books, with several bestsellers to our credit, and sold over 4.5 million books.

This book incorporates Perspection's training expertise to ensure that you'll receive the maximum return on your time. You'll focus on the tasks and skills that increase productivity while working at your own pace and convenience.

We invite you to visit the Perspection Web site at:

www.perspection.com

Acknowledgements

The task of creating any book requires the talents of many hard-working people pulling together to meet impossible deadlines and untold stresses. We'd like to thank the outstanding team responsible for making this book possible: the writer, Steve Johnson; the editor, Melinda Lankford; the technical editor, Holly Johnson; the production team, Kate Lyerla, Joe Kalsbeek, Ryan Suzuki, Matt West; the proofreader, Beth Teyler; and the indexer, Katherine Stimson.

At Que publishing, we'd like to thank Greg Wiegand for the opportunity to undertake this project, Sharry Gregory for administrative support, and Sandra Schroeder for your production expertise and support.

Perspection

Dedication

Most importantly, I would like to thank my wife Holly, and my three children, JP, Brett, and Hannah, for their support and encouragement during the project. I would also like to thank Sarah Bartholomaei for her tender loving care and dedication towards our children during the deadline times.

About The Author

Steve Johnson has written more than twenty books on a variety of computer software, including Microsoft Office XP, Microsoft Windows XP, Macromedia Director MX and Macromedia Fireworks, and Web publishing. In 1991, after working for Apple Computer and Microsoft, Steve founded Perspection, Inc., which writes and produces software training. When he is not staying up late writing, he enjoys playing golf, gardening, and spending time with his wife, Holly, and three children, JP, Brett, and Hannah. When time permits, he likes to travel to such places as New Hampshire in October, and Hawaii. Steve and his family live in Pleasanton, California, but can also be found visiting family all over the western United States.

We Want To Hear From You!

As the reader of this book, *you* are our most important critic and commentator. We value your opinion and want to know what we're doing right, what we could do better, what areas you'd like to see us publish in, and any other words of wisdom you're willing to pass our way.

As an associate publisher for Que, I welcome your comments. You can email or write me directly to let me know what you did or didn't like about this book—as well as what we can do to make our books better.

Please note that I cannot help you with technical problems related to the topic of this book. We do have a User Services group, however, where I will forward specific technical questions related to the book.

When you write, please be sure to include this book's title and author as well as your name, email address, and phone number. I will carefully review your comments and share them with the author and editors who worked on the book.

Email: feedback@quepublishing.com

Mail: Greg Wiegand
Que Publishing
800 East 96th Street
Indianapolis, IN 46240 USA

For more information about this book or another Que title, visit our Web site at *www.quepublishing.com.* Type the ISBN (excluding hyphens) or the title of a book in the Search field to find the page you're looking for.

Contents

Introduction xiii

1 Getting Started with PowerPoint 1

Starting PowerPoint 2
Viewing the PowerPoint Window 3
Using Task Panes 4
Choosing Menu Commands 5
Working with Toolbars 6
Choosing Dialog Box Options 8
Choosing the Best Method to Start a Presentation 9
Creating a Blank Presentation 10
Creating a Presentation Using Suggested Content 11
Creating a Presentation Using a Template 12
Opening a Presentation 13
Finding a File or Contents in a File 14
Arranging Windows 15
Understanding PowerPoint Views 16
Browsing a Presentation 18
Getting Help While You Work 20
Getting Help from the Office Assistant 22
Saving a Presentation 24
Getting PowerPoint Updates on the Web 26
Upgrade Recovering a Presentation 27
Detecting and Repairing Problems 28
Closing a Presentation and Quitting PowerPoint 30

2 Developing Presentation Content 31

Creating New and Consistent Slides 32
Working with Objects 34
Developing Text 36
Entering Text 38
Editing Text 40

Resizing Text While Typing 41
Correcting Text While Typing 42
Changing Text Alignment and Spacing 44
Finding and Replacing Text 45
Inserting Research Material 46 New!
Finding the Right Words 47
Inserting and Developing an Outline 48
Moving and Indenting Text 50
Setting Tabs 52
Formatting Text 54
Modifying a Bulleted List 56
AutoFormatting Text and Numbered Lists 58
Creating a Text Box 60
Rearranging Slides 62
Using Slides from Other Presentations 64

3 Designing a Look 65

Applying a Design Template 66
Making Your Presentation Look Consistent 67
Viewing Masters 68
Controlling Slide Appearance with Masters 70
Controlling a Slide Background with Masters 72
Inserting the Date, Time, and Slide Numbers 74
Adding a Header and Footer 76
Understanding Color Schemes 77
Viewing and Choosing a Color Scheme 78
Creating a Color Scheme 80
Adding Colors to a Presentation 82
Adding and Modifying a Slide Background 83
Saving a Template 84

4 Drawing and Modifying Shapes 87

Drawing and Resizing Shapes 88
Inserting AutoShapes from the Clip Gallery 90
Drawing Lines and Arrows 92
Creating and Editing Freeforms 94
Modifying a Freeform 96
Copying and Moving an Object 98
Choosing Shape Colors and Fill Effects 100

Applying Fill Effects 102
Creating Shadows 104
Aligning Objects to Grids and Guides 106
Aligning and Distributing Objects 108
Connecting Shapes 110
Changing Stacking Order 111
Adding 3-D Effects to a Shape 112
Rotating and Flipping a Shape 114
Grouping and Ungrouping Shapes 116
Adding a Shape to the Clip Organizer 118

5 Inserting Pictures and Media 119

Inserting Media Clips 120
Adding and Removing Clips 121
Locating and Inserting Clip Art 122
Organizing Clips into Categories 124
Accessing Clip Art on the Web 126
Inserting a Picture 128
Modifying a Picture 130
Recoloring a Picture 132
Cropping a Picture 134
Creating WordArt Text 136
Modifying WordArt Text 138
Applying WordArt Text Effects 140
Inserting Movies and Sounds 142
Recording Sounds 144
Playing Movies and Sounds 145 New!

6 Inserting Charts and Related Material 147

Sharing Information Among Documents 148
Inserting a Graph Chart 149
Opening an Existing Graph Chart 150
Selecting Graph Data 151
Importing Data 152
Entering and Formatting Graph Data 154
Editing Graph Data 156
Modifying the Datasheet 158
Selecting a Chart Type 160
Formatting Chart Objects 162
Choosing Advanced Graph Options 164

Creating an Organization Chart 165
Structuring an Organization Chart 166
Formatting an Organization Chart 168
Inserting a Microsoft Excel Chart 170
Inserting a Microsoft Word Table 172
Inserting a Table 173
Formatting a Table 174
Copying and Pasting Objects 176
Embedding and Linking an Object 178
Modifying Links 180
Creating a Diagram 182

7 Finalizing a Presentation and Its Supplements 183

Creating a Summary Slide 184
Working with Fonts 185
Changing Page Setup Options 186
Preparing Handouts 188
Preparing Speaker Notes 190
Customizing Notes Pages 192
Changing Text to a Language 194
Exporting Notes and Slides to Word 195
Working with Outlines 196
Saving Slides in Different Formats 197 New!
Checking Spelling 198
Checking Presentation Styles 200
Documenting Presentation Properties 202
Previewing a Presentation 204
Printing a Presentation 206
Printing an Outline 208

8 Creating a Web Presentation 209

Using Web Templates 210
Adding Actions Buttons 212
Adding Hyperlinks to Objects 214
Creating Hyperlinks to External Objects 216
Inserting Hyperlinks 218
Using and Removing Hyperlinks 220
Creating a Web Page 222
Changing Web Page Options 224
Opening a Web Page 225

Previewing a Web Page	226	
Using the Web Toolbar	228	
Adding a Digital Signature	230	
Accessing Office Information on the Web	232	
9 Preparing a Slide Show	**233**	
Setting Up a Slide Show	234	
Creating a Custom Slide Show	236	
Creating Slide Transitions	238	
Adding Animation	240	
Using Specialized Animation	242	
Coordinating Multiple Animations	244	
Adding Slide Timings	246	
Recording a Narration	248	
Creating a Self-Running Presentation	250	
10 Presenting a Slide Show	**251**	
Starting a Slide Show	252	
Navigating a Slide Show	254	New!
Annotating a Slide Show	256	New!
Using Presenter View with Multiple Monitors	258	
Packaging a Presentation on CD	259	New!
Using the PowerPoint Viewer	260	New!
11 Reviewing and Sharing a Presentation	**261**	
Adding Comments to a Presentation	262	
Adding Password Protection to a Presentation	264	
Restricting Presentation Access	266	New!
Sending a Presentation for Review Using E-Mail	268	
Tracking Changing in a Presentation	270	
Comparing and Merging Presentations	272	
Broadcasting a Presentation	274	
Collaborating in an Online Meeting	276	
12 Working Together on Office Documents	**279**	
Viewing SharePoint Team Services	280	New!
Administering SharePoint Team Services	282	New!
Storing Documents in the Library	284	New!
Viewing Team Members	285	New!
Setting Up Alerts	286	New!

Assigning Project Tasks 287 New!
Creating an Event 288 New!
Creating Contacts 290 New!
Holding Web Discussions 292 New!
Working with Shared Workspace 293 New!
Installing Windows 2003 and SharePoint Server 2003 294

13 Customizing the Way You Work 295

Setting PowerPoint Options 296
Customizing the Way You Perform Commands 298
Simplifying Tasks with Macros 300
Controlling a Macro 302
Assigning a Macro to a Toolbar or Menu 304
Customizing the Way You Create Objects 305
Controlling PowerPoint with Your Voice 306
Executing Voice Commands 308
Dictating Text 309
Handwriting Your Text 310 New!
Using Smart Tags 312 New!
Using Multiple Languages 314

Microsoft Office Specialist *315*
New Features *319*
Troubleshooting *321*
Index *327*

Introduction

Welcome to *Show Me Microsoft Office PowerPoint 2003*, a visual quick reference book that shows you how to work efficiently with Microsoft Office PowerPoint 2003. This book provides complete coverage of basic and intermediate PowerPoint 2003 skills.

How You'll Learn

Find the Best Place to Start

What's New

How This Book Works

Step-by-Step Instructions

Real World Examples

Troubleshooting Guide

Show Me Live Software

Microsoft Office Specialist

Find the Best Place to Start

You don't have to read this book in any particular order. We've designed the book so that you can jump in, get the information you need, and jump out. However, the book does follow a logical progression from simple tasks to more complex ones. Each task is no more than two pages long. To find the information that you need, just look up the task in the table of contents, index, or troubleshooting guide, and turn to the page listed. Read the task introduction, follow the step-by-step instructions along with the illustration, and you're done.

What's New

If you're searching for what's new in PowerPoint 2003, just look for the icon: New! The new icon appears in the table of contents so you can quickly and easily identify a new or improved feature in PowerPoint 2003. A complete description of each new feature appears in the New Features guide in the back of this book.

How This Book Works

Each task is presented on no more than two facing pages, with step-by-step instructions in the left column and screen illustrations in the right column. This arrangement lets you focus on a single task without having to turn the page.

Step-by-Step Instructions

This book provides concise step-by-step instructions that show you "how" to accomplish a task. Each set of instructions include illustrations that directly correspond to the easy-to-read steps. Also included in the text are timesavers, tables, and sidebars to help you work more efficiently or to teach you more in-depth information. A "Did You Know?" provides tips and techniques to help you work smarter, while a "See Also" leads you to other parts of the book containing related information about the task.

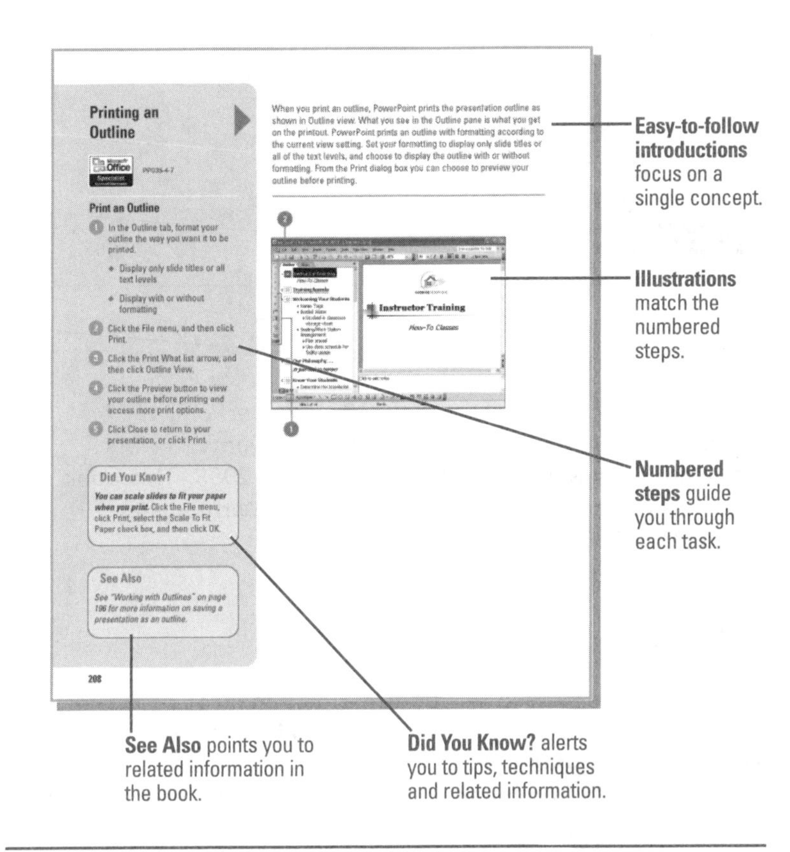

Real World Examples

This book uses real world examples to help convey "why" you would want to perform a task. The examples give you a context in which to use the task. You'll observe how *Home Sense, Inc.*, a fictional home improvement business, uses PowerPoint 2003 to get the job done.

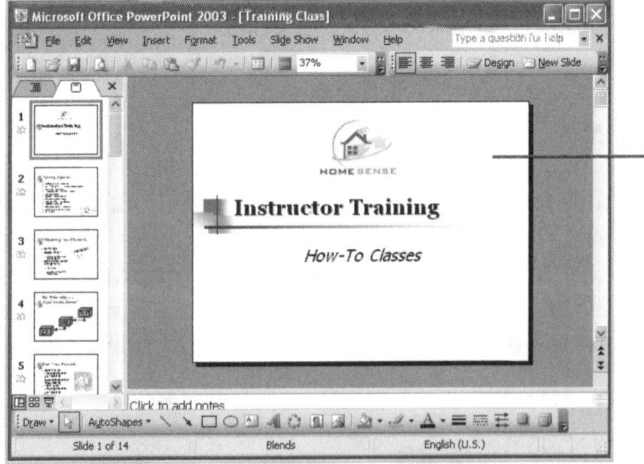

Real world examples help you apply what you've learned to other tasks.

Troubleshooting Guide

This book offers quick and easy ways to diagnose and solve common PowerPoint 2003 problems that you might encounter. The troubleshooting guide helps you determine and fix a problem using the task information you find. The problems are posed in question form and are grouped into categories that are presented alphabetically.

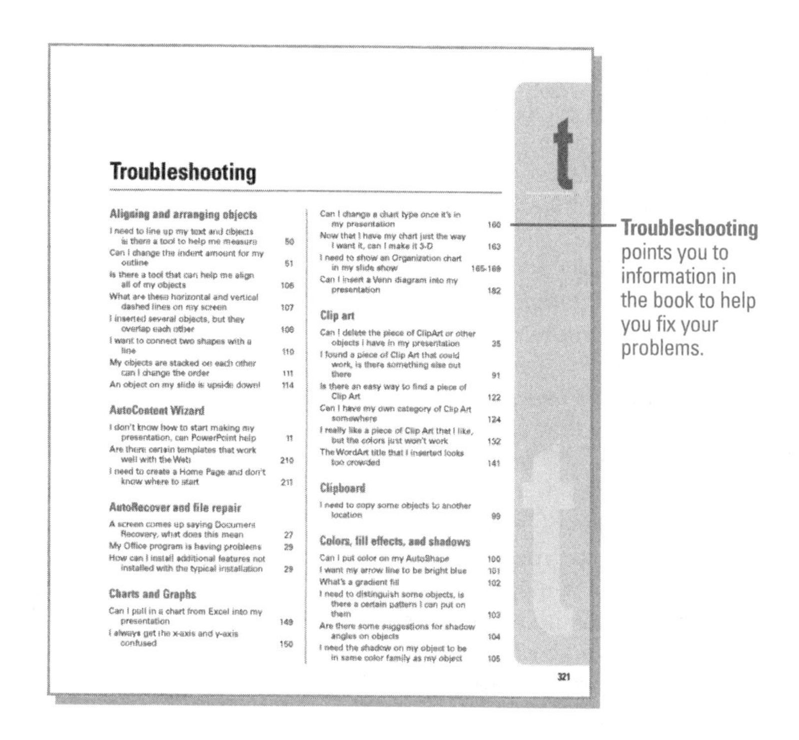

t

Troubleshooting

Aligning and arranging objects

I need to line up my text and objects is there a tool to help me measure 50
Can I change the indent amount for my outline 51
Is there a tool that can help me align all of my objects 106
What are these horizontal and vertical dashed lines on my screen 107
I inserted several objects, but they overlap each other 108
I want to connect two shapes with a line 110
My objects are stacked on each other can I change the order 111
An object on my slide is upside down! 114

AutoContent Wizard

I don't know how to start making my presentation, can PowerPoint help 11
Are there certain templates that work well with the Web 210
I need to create a Home Page and don't know where to start 211

AutoRecover and file repair

A screen comes up saying Document Recovery, what does this mean 27
My Office program is having problems 29
How can I install additional features not installed with the typical installation 29

Charts and Graphs

Can I pull in a chart from Excel into my presentation 149
I always get the x-axis and y-axis confused 150
Can I change a chart type once it's in my presentation 160
Now that I have my chart just the way I want it, can I make it 3-D 163
I need to show an Organization chart in my slide show 165-169
Can I insert a Venn diagram into my presentation 182

Clip art

Can I delete the piece of ClipArt or other objects I have in my presentation 35
I found a piece of Clip Art that could work, is there something else out there 91
Is there an easy way to find a piece of Clip Art 122
Can I have my own category of Clip Art somewhere 124
I really like a piece of Clip Art that I like, but the colors just won't work 132
The WordArt title that I inserted looks too crowded 141

Clipboard

I need to copy some objects to another location 99

Colors, fill effects, and shadows

Can I put color on my AutoShape 100
I want my arrow line to be bright blue 101
What's a gradient fill 102
I need to distinguish some objects, is there a certain pattern I can put on them 103
Are there some suggestions for shadow angles on objects 104
I need the shadow on my object to be in same color family as my object 105

321

Troubleshooting points you to information in the book to help you fix your problems.

Show Me Live Software

In addition, this book offers companion software that shows you how to perform most tasks using the live program. The easy-to-use VCR-type controls allow you to start, pause, and stop the action. As you observe how to accomplish each task, Show Me Live highlights each step and talks you through the process. The Show Me Live software is available free at *www.perspection.com or www.quepublishing.com/showme.*

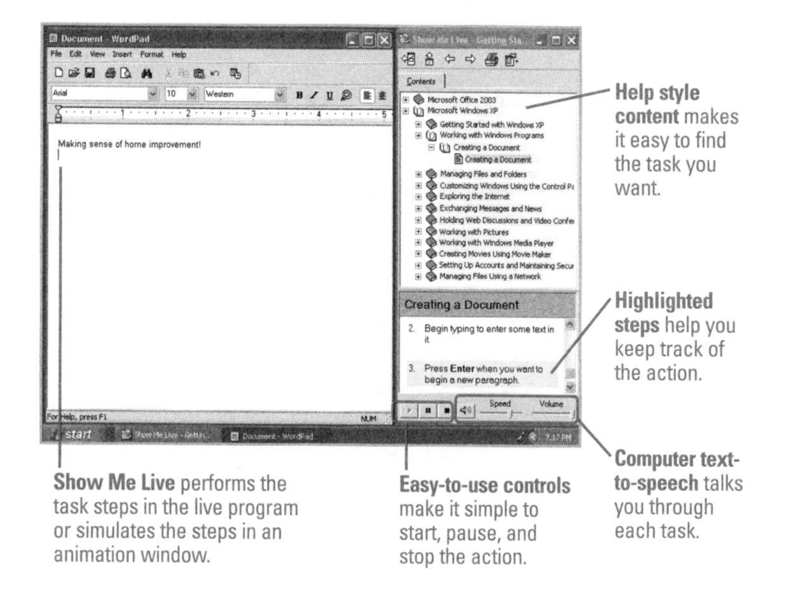

Help style content makes it easy to find the task you want.

Highlighted steps help you keep track of the action.

Computer text-to-speech talks you through each task.

Show Me Live performs the task steps in the live program or simulates the steps in an animation window.

Easy-to-use controls make it simple to start, pause, and stop the action.

Microsoft Office Specialist

This book prepares you fully for the Microsoft Office Specialist exam at the specialist level for Microsoft Office PowerPoint 2003. Each Microsoft Office Specialist certification level has a set of objectives, which are organized into broader skill sets. To prepare for the certification exam, you should review and perform each task identified with a Microsoft Office Specialist objective to confirm that you can meet the requirements for the exam. Throughout this book, content that pertains to an objective is identified with the Microsoft Office Specialist logo and objective number next to it.

Microsoft Office Specialist

About the Microsoft Office Specialist Program

The Microsoft Office Specialist certification is the globally recognized standard for validating expertise with the Microsoft Office suite of business productivity programs. Earning an Microsoft Office Specialist certificate acknowledges you have the expertise to work with Microsoft Office programs. To earn the Microsoft Office Specialist certification, you must pass one or more certification exams for the Microsoft Office desktop applications of Microsoft Office Word, Microsoft Office Excel, Microsoft Office PowerPoint, Microsoft Office Outlook, or Microsoft Office Access. The Microsoft Office Specialist program typically offers certification exams at the "specialist" and "expert" skill levels. (The availability of Microsoft Office Specialist certification exams varies by program, program version, and language. Visit *www.microsoft.com/officespecialist* for exam availability and more information about the program.) The Microsoft Office Specialist program is the only Microsoft-approved program in the world for certifying proficiency with Microsoft Office programs.

What Does This Logo Mean?

It means this book has been approved by the Microsoft Office Specialist program to be certified courseware for learning Microsoft Office PowerPoint 2003 and preparing for the certification exam. This book will prepare you fully for the Microsoft Office Specialist exam at the specialist level for Microsoft Office PowerPoint 2003. Each certification level has a set of objectives, which are organized into broader skill sets. Throughout this book, content that pertains to a Microsoft Office Specialist objective is identified with the Microsoft Office Specialist logo and objective number below the title of the topic:

PP03S-1-1
PP03S-2-2

315

Logo indicates a task fulfills one or more Microsoft Office Specialist objectives.

Getting Started with PowerPoint

1

Introduction

Whether you need to put together a quick presentation of sales figures for your management team or create a polished slide show for your company's stockholders, Microsoft Office PowerPoint 2003 can help you present your information efficiently and professionally.

PowerPoint is a **presentation graphics program**—software that helps you create a slide show presentation. A slide show presentation is made up of a series of slides that can contain charts, graphs, bulleted lists, eye-catching text, multimedia video and sound clips, and more. PowerPoint makes it easy to generate and organize ideas, and it provides tools for creating the parts of an effective slide show. PowerPoint also makes it easy to create slide show supplements, such as handouts, speaker's notes, and transparencies.

Using the AutoContent Wizard, you can put together a quick presentation for a staff meeting. PowerPoint also provides a selection of professionally designed slide templates that can be used for all your business needs. When it comes time to develop your presentation, PowerPoint offers a selection of views and panes—Normal view, Slide Sorter view, and Slide Show view. Normal view is helpful for working on individual slides and notes, while Slide Sorter view helps you organize all of your slides and add transition elements. The Slide Show view pulls it all together, allowing you to view your slide show on your computer monitor for fine tuning. When building your presentation, or doing a lot of adjusting to your presentation, you might find the Outline and Slides pane to be a quick way to accomplish your presentation changes.

There are a variety of tools that PowerPoint provides for packaging your presentation. You can save your presentation on a CD for clients, view it at the office, send it through e-mail, or even broadcast your presentation over the Internet.

What You'll Do

Start PowerPoint

View the PowerPoint Window

Use Task Panes

Choose Menu Commands

Work with Toolbars

Choose Dialog Box Options

Create a Blank Presentation

Create a Presentation Using Suggested Content

Create a Presentation Using a Template

Open a Presentation

Find a File or Contents in a File

Understand PowerPoint Views

Get Help

Save a Presentation

Get PowerPoint Updates on the Web

Recover a Presentation

Detect and Repair Problems

Close a Presentation and Quit PowerPoint

Starting PowerPoint

The two quickest ways to start PowerPoint are to select it on the Start menu or double-click a shortcut icon on the desktop. By providing different ways to start a program, Office lets you work the way you like and start programs with a click of a button. When you start PowerPoint, a program window opens, displaying a blank presentation, where you can create a new presentation or open an existing one.

Start PowerPoint from the Start Menu

1. Click the Start button on the taskbar.
2. Point to All Programs.
3. Point to Microsoft Office.
4. Click Microsoft Office PowerPoint 2003.

   The first time you start Office, an Activation Wizard opens; follow the instructions to activate the product.

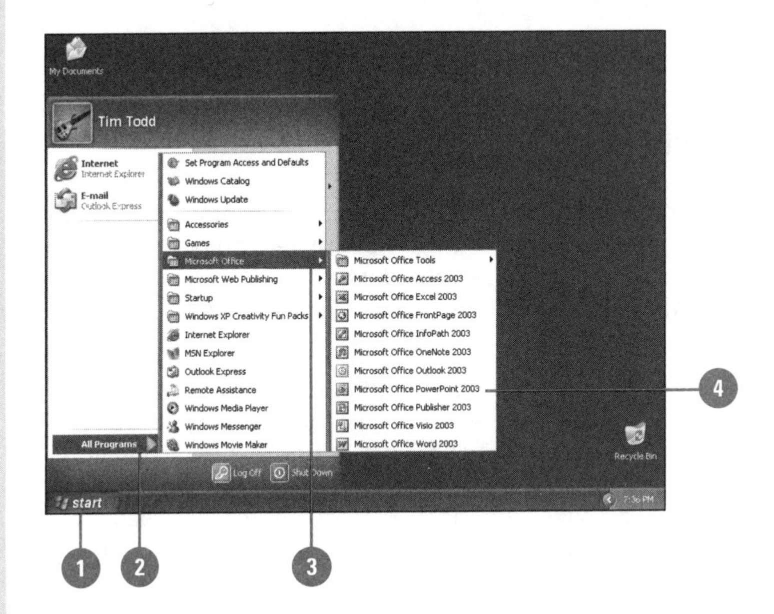

Did You Know?

You can create a program shortcut from the Start menu to the desktop. Click the Start menu, point to All Programs, point to Microsoft Office, right-click Microsoft Office PowerPoint 2003, point to Send To, and then click Desktop (Create Shortcut).

You can start PowerPoint and open a presentation from Windows Explorer. Double-clicking any PowerPoint presentation icon in Windows Explorer opens that file and PowerPoint.

Viewing the PowerPoint Window

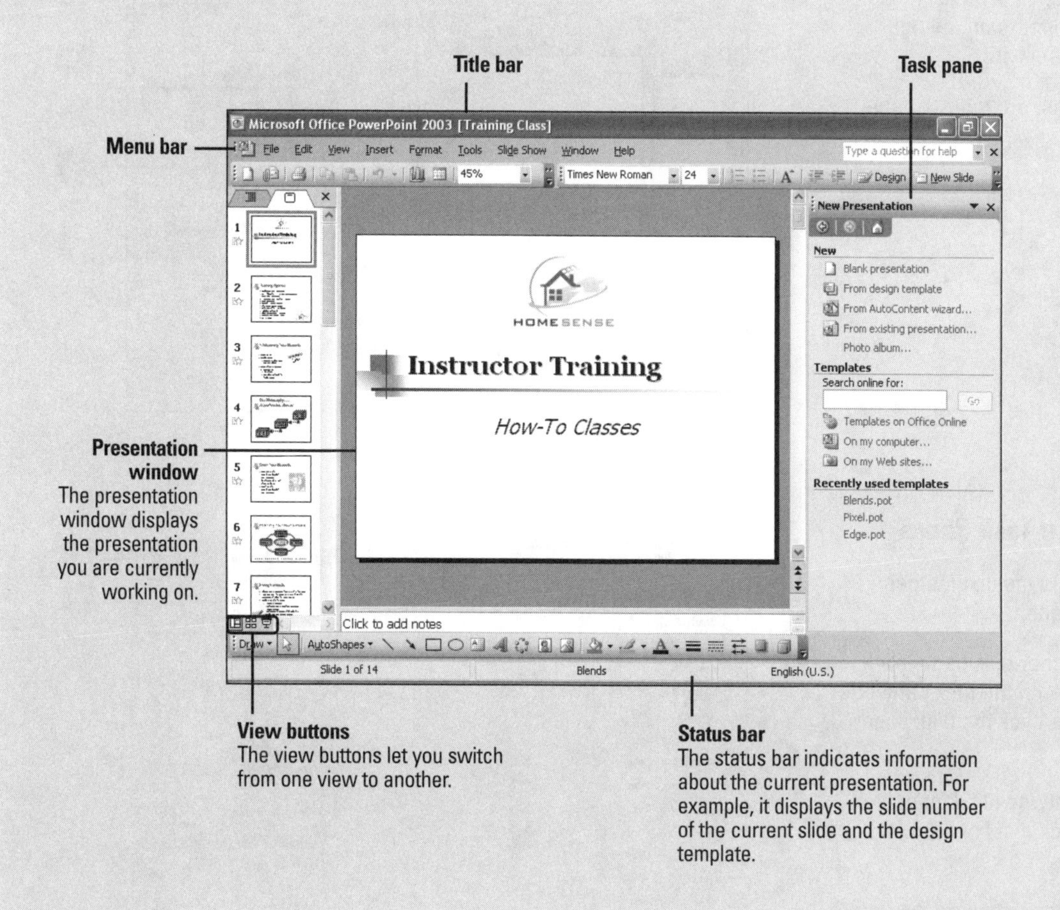

Presentation window
The presentation window displays the presentation you are currently working on.

View buttons
The view buttons let you switch from one view to another.

Status bar
The status bar indicates information about the current presentation. For example, it displays the slide number of the current slide and the design template.

Using Task Panes

When you start PowerPoint, a task pane appears by default on the right side of the program window. The task pane displays various options that relate to the current task. There are several types of options available on the task pane. You can search for information, select options, and click links, like the ones on a Web page, to perform commands. You can also display different task panes, move back and forth between task panes, and close a task pane to provide a larger work area.

Use the Task Pane

1. When you start PowerPoint, the task pane appears on the right side of your screen.
2. Click an option on the task pane.

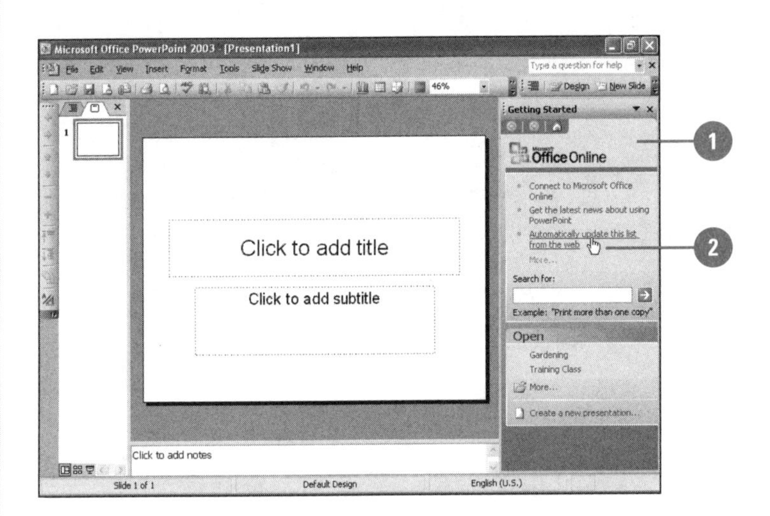

Open and Close Task Panes

1. Click the View menu, and then click Task Pane.
2. To open another task pane, click the list arrow on the task pane title bar, and then click the task pane you want.
3. To switch between task panes, click the Back and Forward task pane buttons.
4. Click the Close button on the task pane.

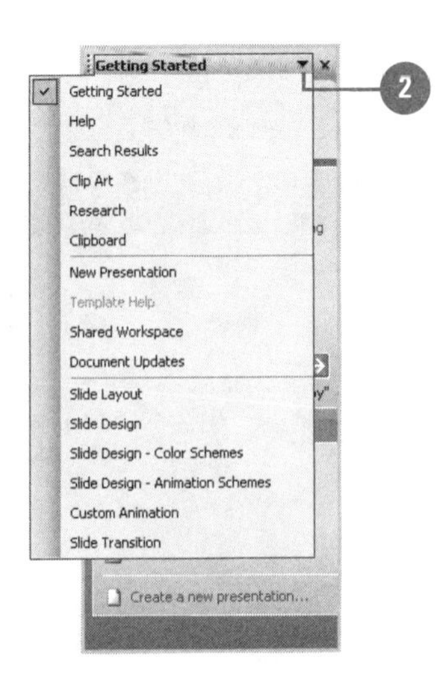

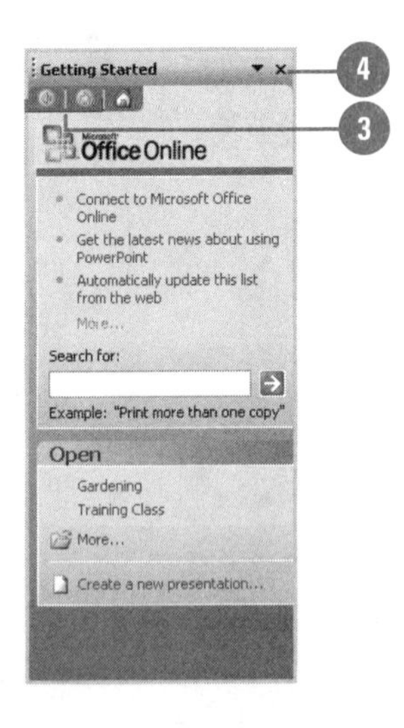

Choosing Menu Commands

The PowerPoint commands are organized in menus on the menu bar. The menus are personalized as you work—when you click a menu name, you first see the commands you use most frequently. After a few moments, you see the entire list of commands. You can also open a **shortcut menu**—a group of related commands—by right-clicking a PowerPoint element.

1

Choose a Command from a Menu

1. Click a menu name on the menu bar.
2. If necessary, click the double-headed arrow to expand the menu, or wait until the expanded list of commands appears.
3. Click the command you want. If the command is followed by an arrow, point to the command to see a list of related options, and then click the option you want.

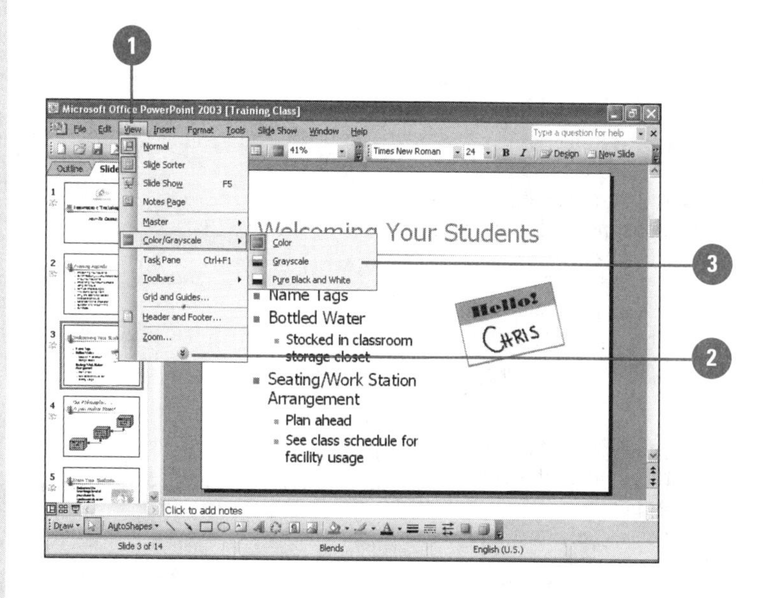

Choose a Command from a Shortcut Menu

1. Right-click an object (a text or graphic element).
2. Click a command on the shortcut menu. If the command is followed by an arrow, point to the command to see a list of related options, and then click the option you want.

TIMESAVER *You can use a shortcut key to choose a command. Press and hold down the first key and then press the second key. For example, press and hold the Ctrl key and then press S to select the Save command.*

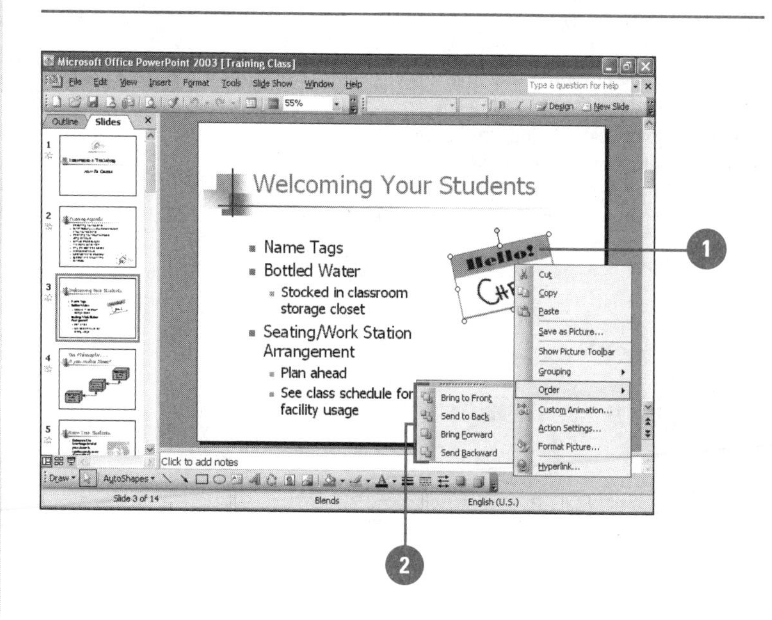

Working with Toolbars

PowerPoint includes its most common commands on toolbars. Click a toolbar button to choose a command. When PowerPoint starts, the Standard and Formatting toolbars are at the top of the window aligned on a single bar, and the Drawing toolbar is at the bottom, unless you've changed your settings. The toolbars are personalized as you work, showing only the buttons you use most often. Additional toolbar buttons are available by clicking the Toolbar Options list arrow at the end of the toolbar. You can hide or display any toolbar, and you can move a toolbar around the screen so it's right where you need it.

Choose a Command Using a Toolbar Button

1. If you are not sure what a toolbar button does, point to it to display a ScreenTip.
2. To choose a command, click the button or click the Toolbar Options list arrow, and then click the button.

   When you select a button from the Toolbar Options drop-down list, the button appears on the toolbar, which shows only the buttons you use most often.

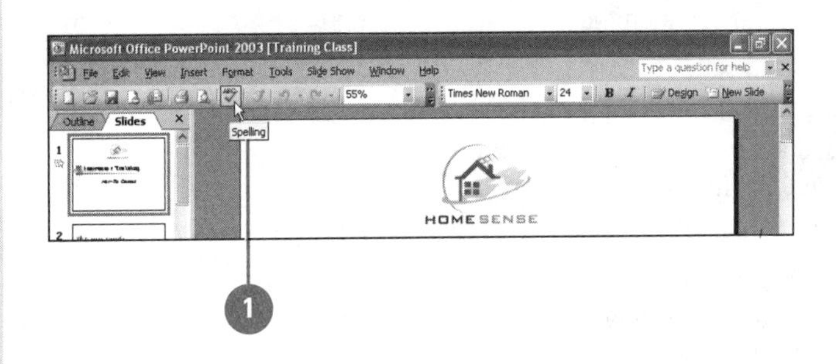

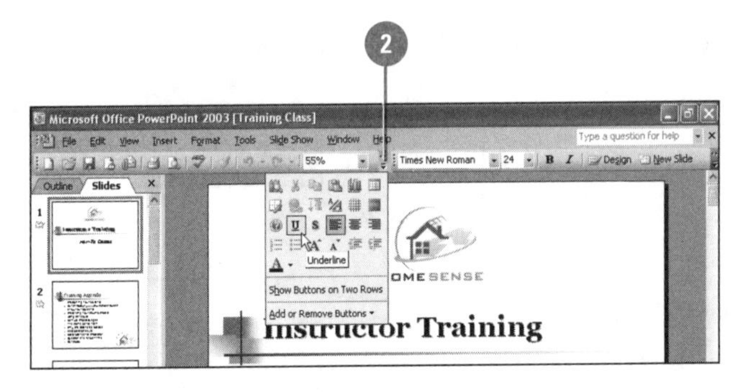

Did You Know?

You can choose a toolbar quickly. To quickly display the list of available toolbars, right-click a toolbar and then click the toolbar you want to use.

Display or Hide a Toolbar

1. Click the View menu, and then point to Toolbars.
2. Click the toolbar you want to display or hide.

   A check mark next to the toolbar name indicates that it is currently displayed on the screen.

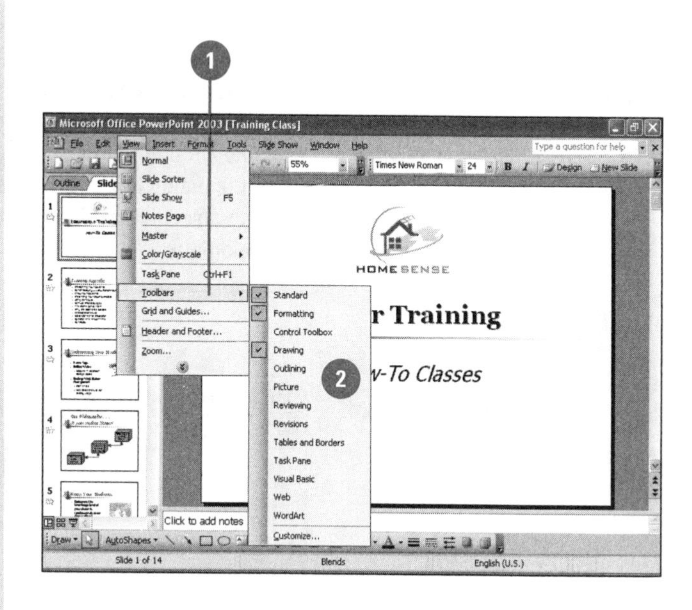

Move and Reshape a Toolbar

- To move a toolbar that is docked (attached to one edge of the window) or floating (unattached) over the window, click the gray dotted edge bar on the left edge of the toolbar, and then drag it to a new location.
- To move a toolbar that is floating (unattached) over the window, drag the title bar to a new location.
- To return a floating toolbar to its previously docked location, double-click its title bar.
- To change the shape of a floating toolbar, drag any border until the toolbar is the shape you want.

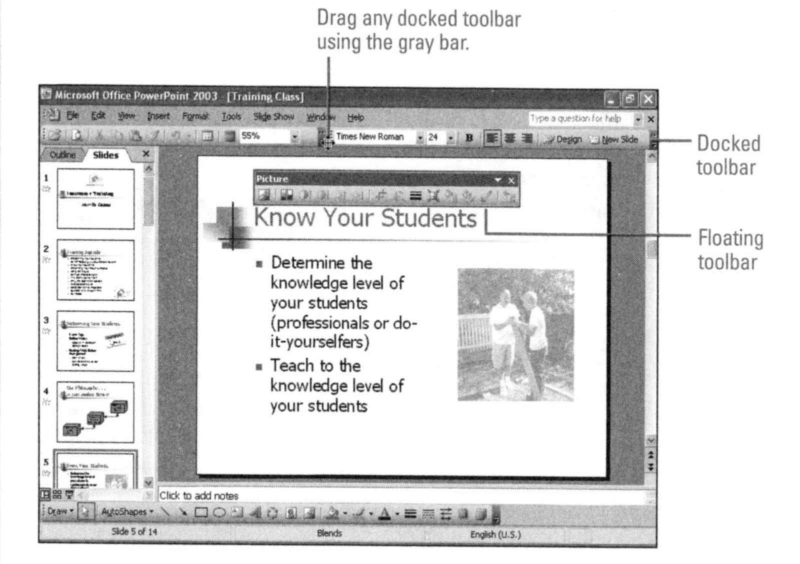

Choosing Dialog Box Options

A **dialog box** is a window that opens when you choose a menu command followed by an ellipsis (. . .). The ellipsis indicates that you must supply more information before the program can carry out the command you selected. After you enter information or make selections in a dialog box, click the OK button to complete the command. Click the Cancel button to close the dialog box without issuing the command. In many dialog boxes, you can also click an Apply button to apply your changes without closing the dialog box.

Choose Dialog Box Options

All dialog boxes contain the same types of options, including the following:

- **Tabs.** Click a tab to display its options. Each tab groups a related set of options.
- **Option buttons.** Click an option button to select it. You can usually select only one.
- **Up and down arrows.** Click the up or down arrow to increase or decrease the number, or type a number in the box.
- **Check box.** Click the box to turn on or off the option. A checked box means the option is selected; a cleared box means it's not.
- **List box.** Click the list arrow to display a list of options, and then click the option you want.
- **Text box.** Click in the box and type the requested information.
- **Button.** Click a button to perform a specific action or command. A button name followed by an ellipsis (...) opens another dialog box.
- **Preview box.** Many dialog boxes show an image that reflects the options you select.

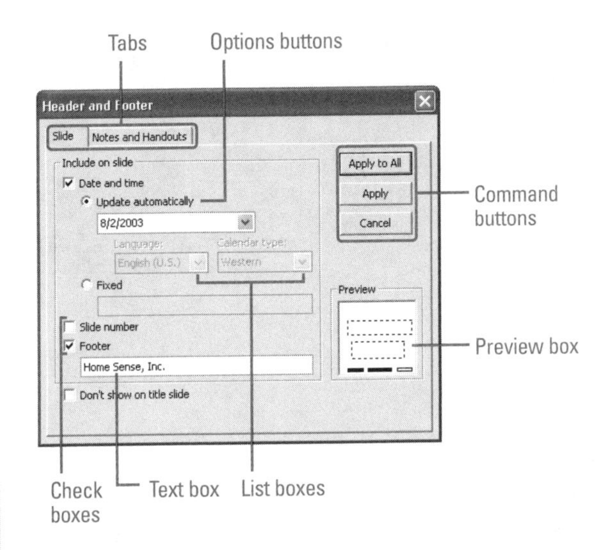

For Your Information

Navigating a Dialog Box

Rather than clicking to move around a dialog box, you can press the Tab key to move from one box or button to the next. You can also use Shift+Tab to move backward, or Ctrl+Tab and Ctrl+Shift+Tab to move between dialog box tabs.

Choosing the Best Method to Start a Presentation

To begin working with PowerPoint, you can create a new presentation or you can open one that you've already worked on. You can use the New Presentation task pane as your starting point. The option that you choose on the task pane depends on how you want to start a presentation. If you need help with content and a presentation look, choose the From AutoContent Wizard option. If you have content ready but need help with a presentation look, choose the From Design Template option. If you have content ready and have a design in mind, choose the Blank Presentation option. If you have an existing presentation and want to make design and content changes to it for a new presentation without altering the original, choose the From Existing Presentation option. The following table describes the methods available to you when you start or open a presentation from the New Presentation task pane.

New Presentation Task Pane Options

Click	To
From AutoContent Wizard	Create a new presentation using the AutoContent Wizard, which prompts you for a presentation title and information about the presentation. After you choose a presentation style and type, PowerPoint provides a basic outline to help you organize the content into a professional presentation.
From Design Template	Create a new presentation based on a design template, which is a presentation with predefined slide colors and styles. After you click this option, the Slide Design task pane appears, in which you can choose a template.
Blank Presentation	Create a new, blank presentation. After you click this option, the Slide Layout task pane appears with 27 predesigned slide layouts from which you can choose to create a new slide.
From Existing Presentation	Create a copy of an existing PowerPoint presentation in order to make design and content changes to it for a new presentation, without changing the original presentation. After you click this option, the New From Existing Presentation dialog box appears, from which you can browse to find the presentation that you want to open.

Creating a Blank Presentation

If you are not sure how you want your presentation to look, you can start a new presentation from scratch. You can create a blank presentation when you first start PowerPoint or after you have already started PowerPoint. Either way, a blank presentation appears, ready for you to use.

Start a Blank Presentation

1. Start PowerPoint.
2. A blank presentation is displayed when you first open PowerPoint.

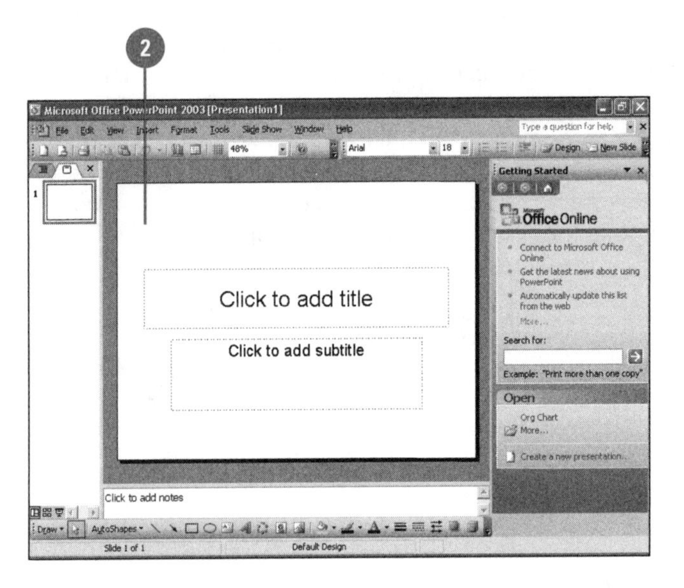

Start a Blank Presentation Within PowerPoint

1. Click the File menu, and then click New.
2. In the New Presentation task pane, click Blank Presentation.

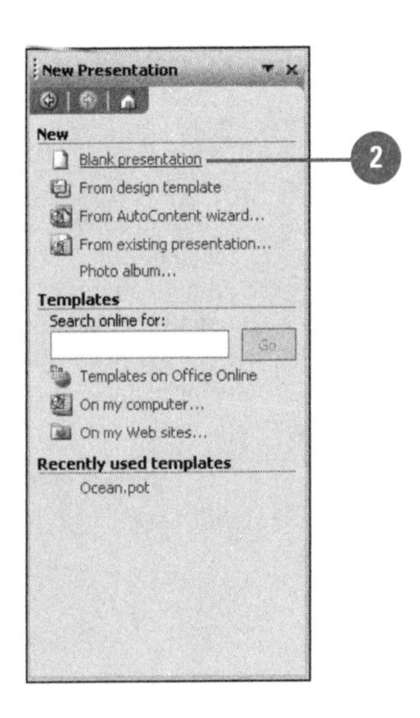

Did You Know?

You can display the New Presentation task pane. Click the File menu, and then click New. In a task pane, select the Other Task Panes list arrow, and then click New Presentation to return to the New Presentation task pane.

Creating a Presentation Using Suggested Content

PP03S-1-1

Often the most difficult part of creating a presentation is knowing where to start. PowerPoint solves this problem for you. Use the AutoContent Wizard to help you develop presentation content on a variety of business and personal topics. An AutoContent presentation usually contains 5 to 10 logically organized slides. Edit the text as necessary to meet your needs. Many AutoContent presentations are available in Standard and Online formats. You can use the AutoContent Wizard anytime, while in PowerPoint, to create a new presentation by clicking New on the File menu.

Create a Presentation Using the AutoContent Wizard

1. Start PowerPoint, click Create A New Presentation in the task pane, and then click From AutoContent Wizard.
2. Read the first Wizard dialog box. Click Next to continue.
3. Click the appropriate category button.
4. Click the presentation type you want, and then click Next.
5. Click the presentation style you want to use. Click Next to continue.
6. Enter a presentation title and any items you want to include on each slide.
7. If you want, enter a presentation footer.
8. Select or clear the Date Last Updated check box.
9. Select or clear the Slide Number check box.
10. Click Next to continue.
11. Read the last Wizard dialog box, and then click Finish.

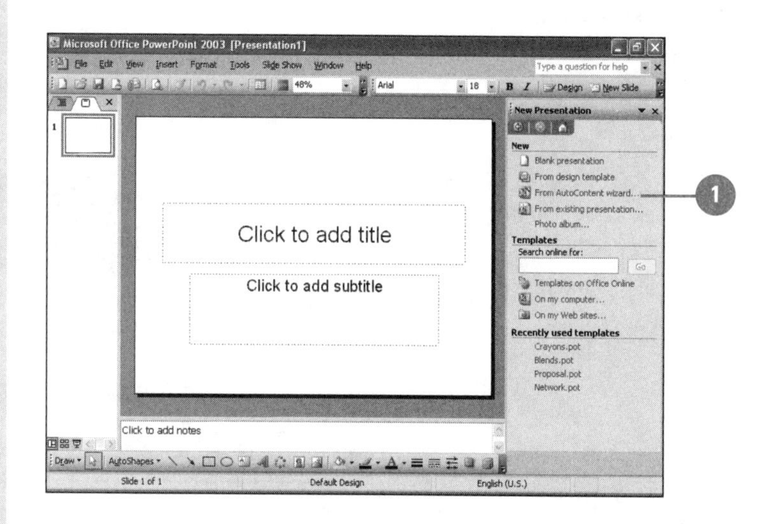

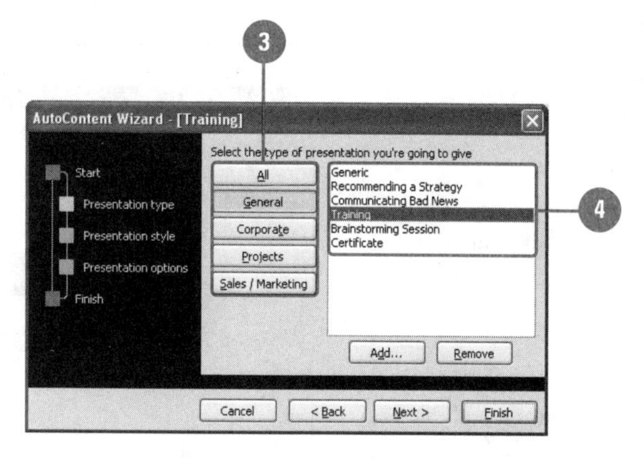

Creating a Presentation Using a Template

PP03S-1-1, PP03S-2-3

PowerPoint provides a collection of professionally designed templates that you can use to create effective presentations. Start with a template when you have a good idea of your content but want to take advantage of a template's professional design and formatting. Each template provides a format and color scheme so you only need to add text. You can choose a new template for your presentation at any point, when you first start your presentation or after you've developed the content. Select Additional Design Templates or Design Templates on Microsoft Office Online to view more templates.

Create a Presentation with a Template

1. Start PowerPoint or click the File menu, and then click New.
2. Click Create A New Presentation on the task pane, and then click From Design Template.
3. Click the template you want to apply to your slide.

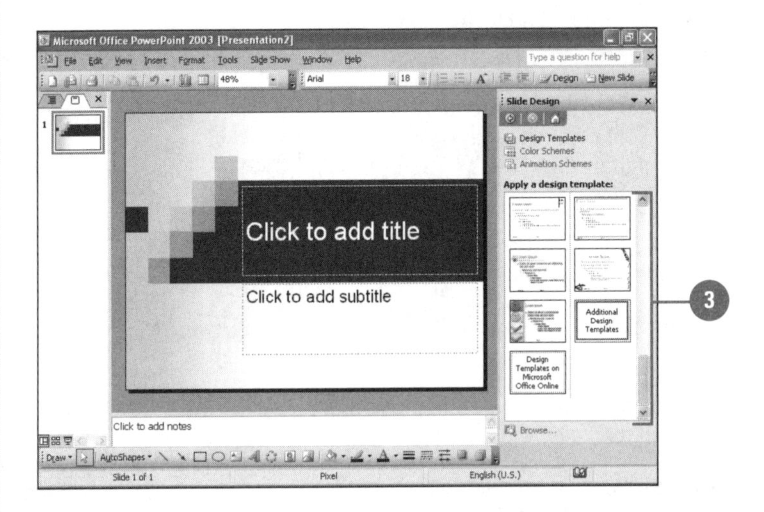

Apply a Template to an Existing Presentation

1. Click the Slide Design button on the Formatting toolbar, or click the Format menu, and then click Slide Design.
2. Point to the template you want to apply to your slides.
3. Click the list arrow, and then click Apply To All Slides or click Apply To Selected Slides.

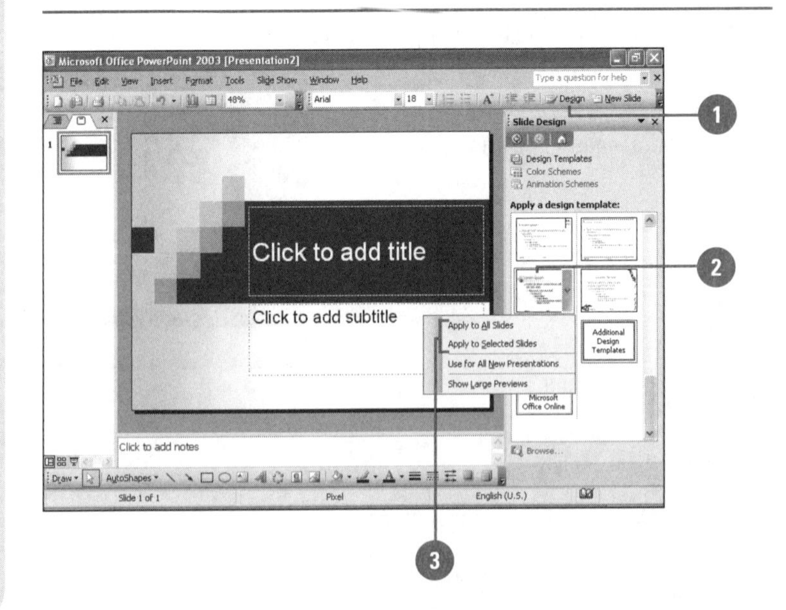

Opening a Presentation

You can open an existing presentation from the Getting Started task pane you see when you first start PowerPoint or by navigating to this task pane at any point. You can also open an existing presentation by clicking Open on the File menu, or by using the Open button on your toolbar. If you are not sure where a file is stored, you can search for it.

1

Open a Presentation

1. Start PowerPoint.
2. In the Getting Started task pane, click a recent presentation under Open, or click More.
3. Click one of the icons on the Places bar for quick access to an often-used folder.
4. If the file is located in another folder, click the Look In list arrow, and then navigate to the file you want to open.
5. Double-click the file.

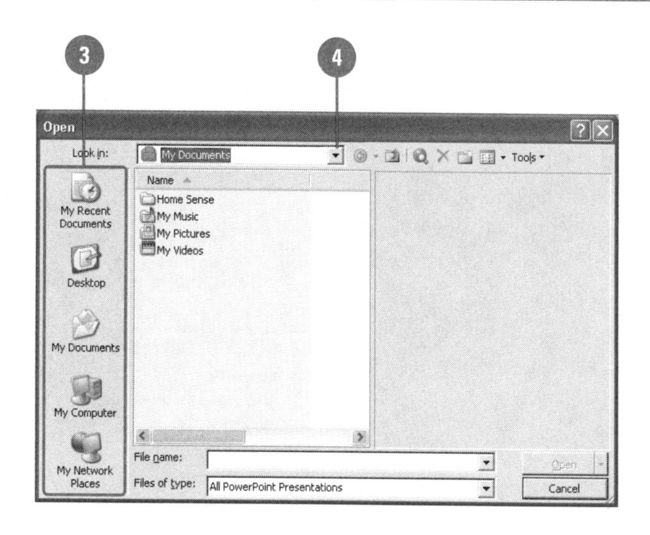

Find a Presentation

1. Click the Open button on the Standard toolbar.
2. Type as much of the filename as you know. PowerPoint tries to match those characters.
3. Click the Tools list arrow, and then click Search.
4. If necessary, type the file name in the Search Text box.
5. Click Go.
6. Double-click the file you want to open, and then click Open.

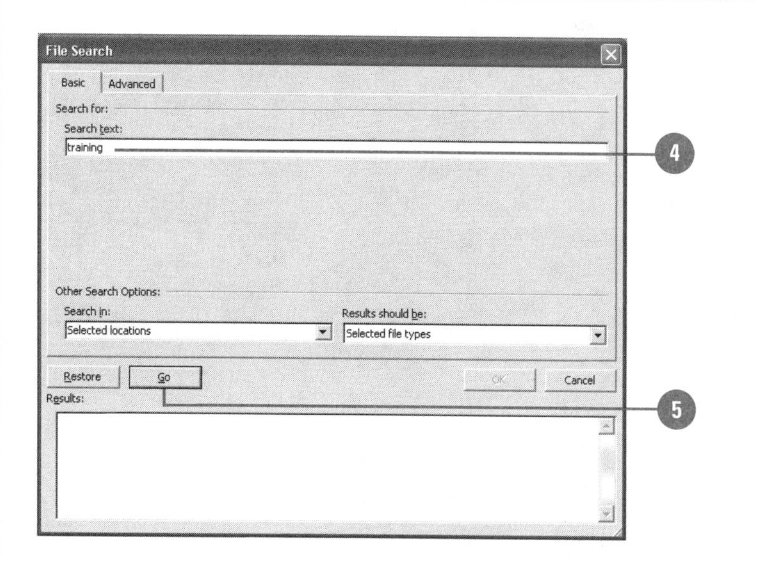

Finding a File or Contents in a File

The search feature available in the Open dialog box is also available using the Search task pane. You can use the Search task pane to find a file's name or location as well as search for specific text or property in a presentation. This becomes handy when you recall the content of a presentation, but not the name. When you perform a search, try to use specific or unique words to achieve the best results.

Find a File or Contents in a File

1. Click the File menu, and then click File Search.
2. Type the name of the file you are looking for or any distinctive words or phrases in the presentation.
3. Click the Search In list arrow, and then select or clear the check boxes to indicate where you want the program to search.

   Click the plus sign (+) to expand a list.
4. Click the Results Should Be list arrow, and then select or clear the check boxes to indicate the type of files you want to find.
5. Click Go.
6. To revise the find, click Modify.
7. When the search results appear, point to a file, click the list arrow, and then click the command you want.
8. When you're done, click the Close button on the task pane.

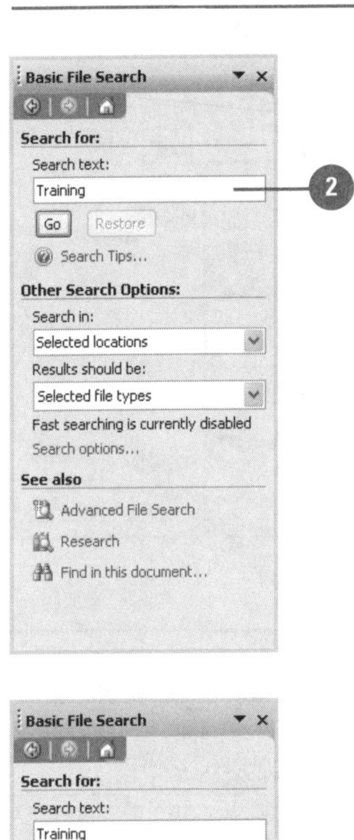

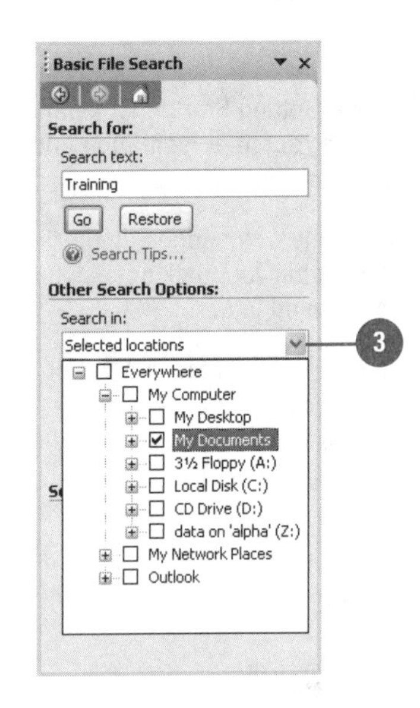

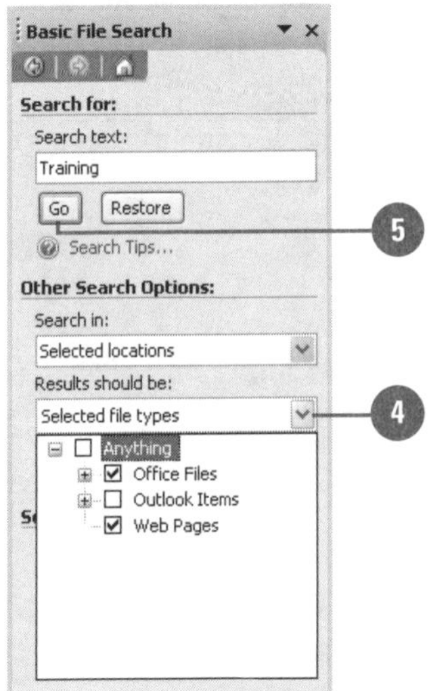

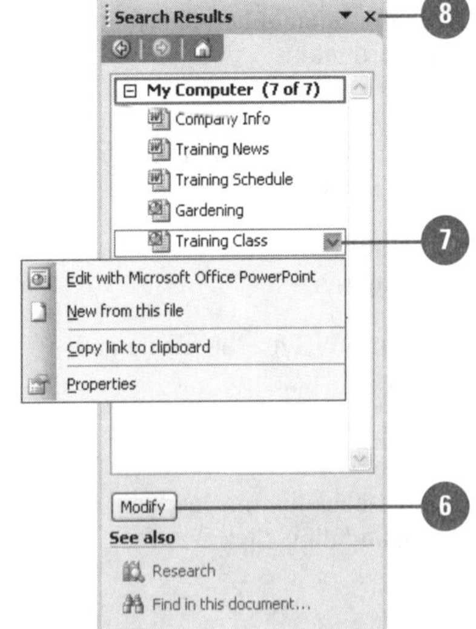

Did You Know?

You can use wildcards to search for file names. When you recall only part of the file name you want to open, type a question mark (?) for any one unknown character or an asterisk (*) for two or more unknown characters.

Arranging Windows

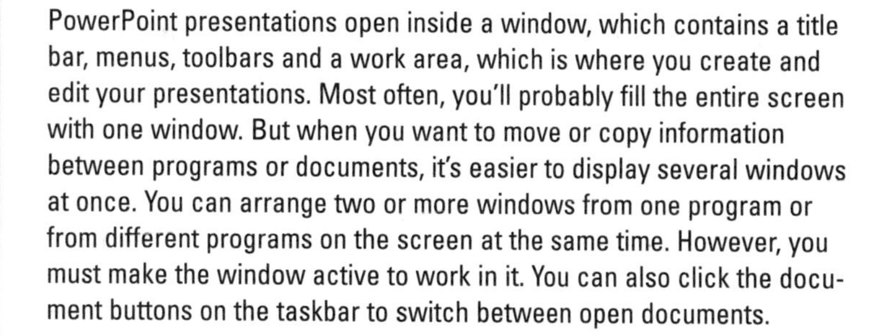

PowerPoint presentations open inside a window, which contains a title bar, menus, toolbars and a work area, which is where you create and edit your presentations. Most often, you'll probably fill the entire screen with one window. But when you want to move or copy information between programs or documents, it's easier to display several windows at once. You can arrange two or more windows from one program or from different programs on the screen at the same time. However, you must make the window active to work in it. You can also click the document buttons on the taskbar to switch between open documents.

Resize and Move a Window

All windows contain the same sizing buttons:

- **Maximize button.** Click to make a window fill the entire screen.
- **Restore Down button.** Click to reduce a maximized window to a reduced size.
- **Minimize button.** Click to shrink a window to a taskbar button. To restore the window to its previous size, click the appropriate taskbar button.
- **Close button.** Click to shut a window.

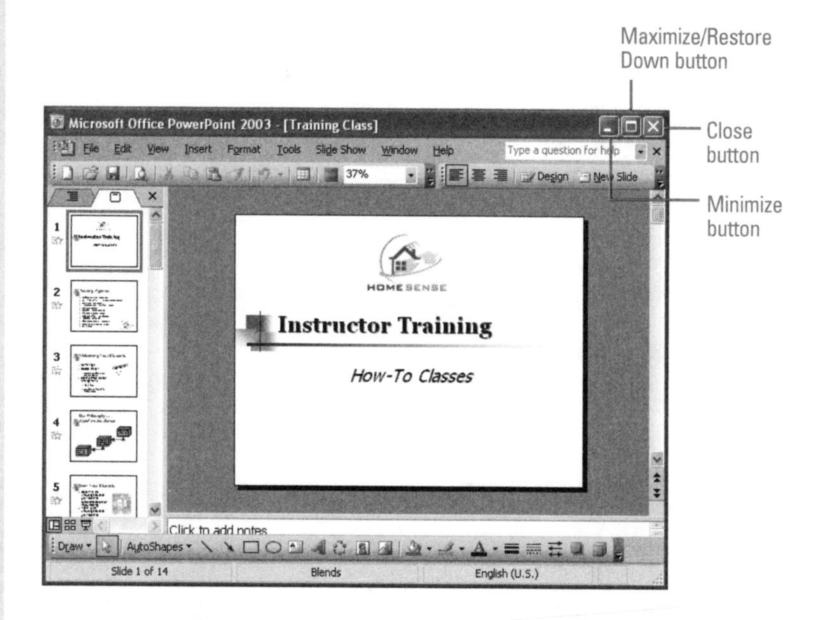

Arrange or Switch Between Windows

1. Open the presentations you want to arrange or switch between.
2. Click the Window menu.
3. Click a window command:
   - The presentation name you want.
   - Arrange All to fit the windows on the screen.

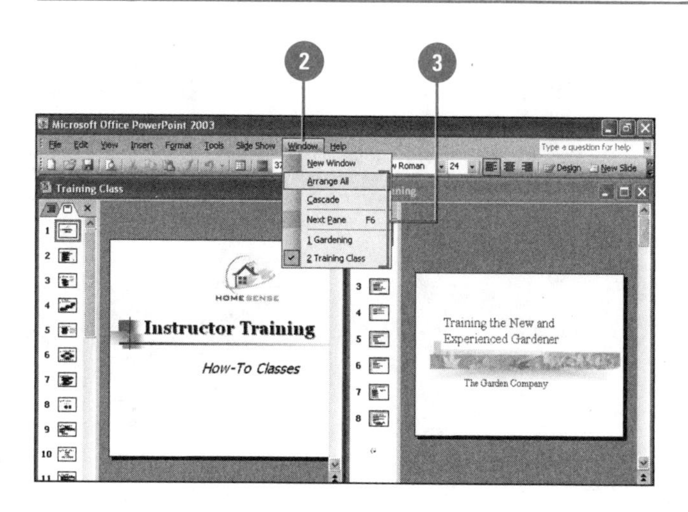

Understanding PowerPoint Views

PP03S-4-1

To help you during all phases of developing a presentation, PowerPoint provides three different views: Normal, Slide Sorter, and Slide Show. You can switch from one view to another by clicking a view button located next to the horizontal scroll bar. In any view, you can use the Zoom feature on the Standard toolbar to increase and decrease the page view size and display the slide to fit the screen.

Normal view

Use the Normal view to work with the three underlying elements of a presentation—the outline, slide, and notes—each in its own pane. These panes provide an overview of your presentation and let you work on all of its parts. You can adjust the size of the panes by dragging the pane borders. You can use the Outline pane to develop and organize your presentation's content. Use the Slide pane to add text, graphics, movies, sounds, and hyperlinks to individual slides, and the Notes pane to add speaker notes or notes you want to share with your audience.

Outline pane

Use the Outline pane in Normal view to develop your presentation's content. Individual slides are numbered and a slide icon appears for each slide.

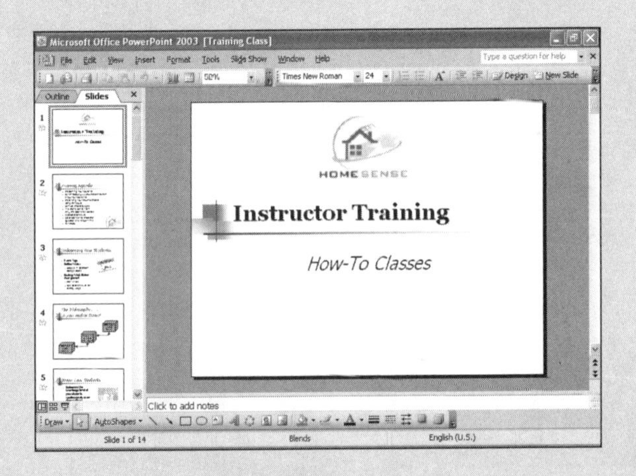

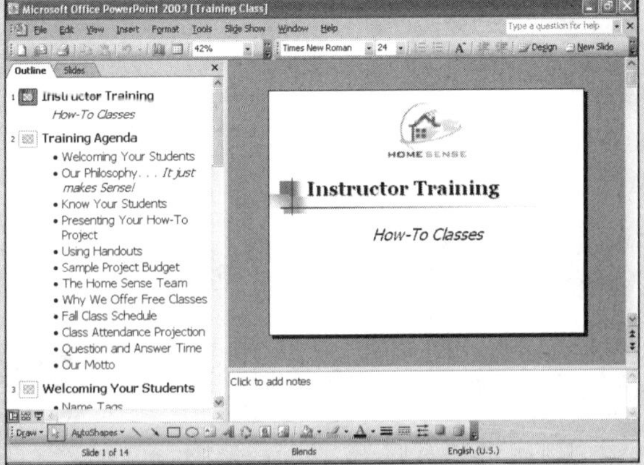

Slides pane

Use the Slides pane in Normal view to preview each slide. Click the slide you want to view. You can also move through your slides using the scroll bars or the Previous Slide and Next Slide buttons. When you drag the scroll box up or down on the vertical scroll bar, a label appears that indicates which slide will be displayed if you release the mouse button.

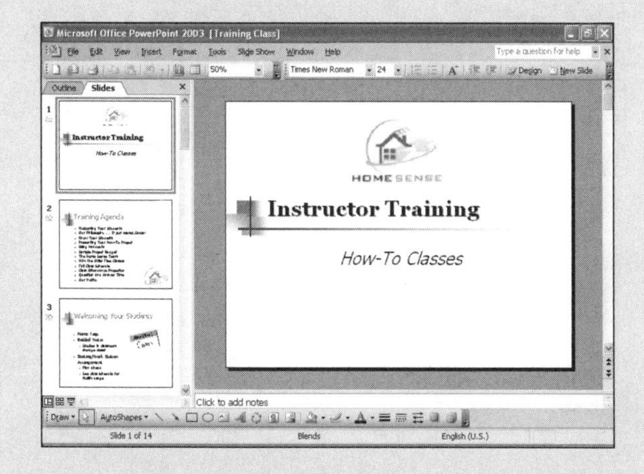

Slide Sorter view

Use the Slide Sorter view to organize your slides, add actions between slides—called slide transitions—and apply other effects to your slide show. The Slide Sorter toolbar helps you add slide transitions and control your presentation. When you add a slide transition, you see an icon that indicates an action will take place as one slide replaces another during a show. If you hide a slide, you see an icon that indicates the slide will not be shown during the presentation.

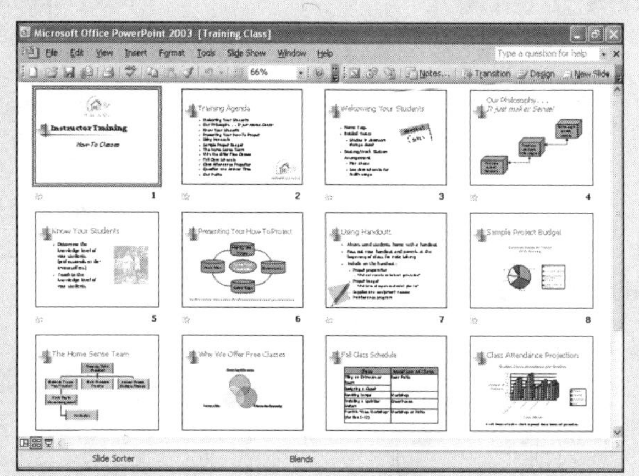

Slide Show view

Slide Show view presents your slides one at a time. Use this view when you're ready to rehearse or give your presentation. To move through the slides, click the screen, or press Enter to move through the show.

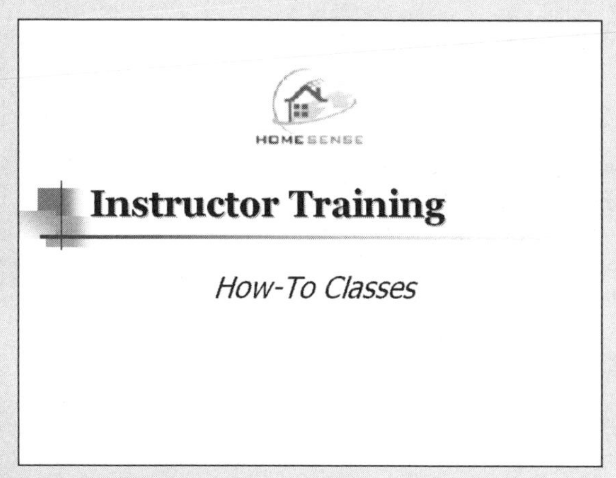

Browsing a Presentation

You might want to browse through a completed presentation to view the contents and design of each slide and to evaluate the types of slides in a presentation in several ways. When a slide doesn't fit the screen, you can click the scroll arrows to scroll line by line or click above or below the scroll box to scroll window by window and move to another slide. To move immediately to a specific slide, you can drag the scroll box. In Slides pane, you can click the Next Slide and Previous Slide buttons, which are located at the bottom of the vertical scroll bar, to switch between slides in a presentation.

Browse Through a Presentation

- Click the Up scroll arrow or Down scroll arrow to scroll line by line.

  When you scroll to the top or bottom of a slide, you automatically move to the previous or next page.

- Click above or below the Scroll box to scroll window by window.
- Drag the Scroll box to move immediately to a specific slide.

  As you drag, a slide indicator box appears, telling you the slide number and title.

- Click the Previous Slide or Next Slide button.

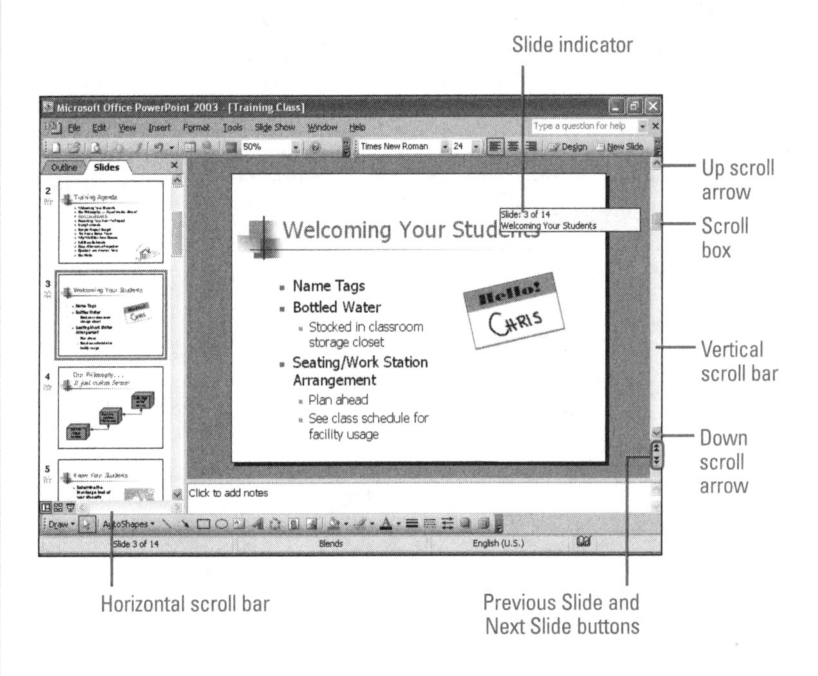

Did You Know?

You can use the keyboard to browse slides. Press the Page Up or Page Down key to switch between slides. If you use these keys, the slides in the Slides pane will change also.

Browse Through Slides or an Outline

1. In Normal view, click the Outline or Slides tab.
   - Click the Up scroll arrow or Down scroll arrow to scroll line by line.

     The slide doesn't change as you scroll.
   - Click a slide icon or slide miniature to display the slide.

Slide icon

Change Presentation View Size

1. Click the Zoom list arrow on the Standard toolbar.
2. Click the view percentage you want or click Fit to size the slide to the size of your screen.

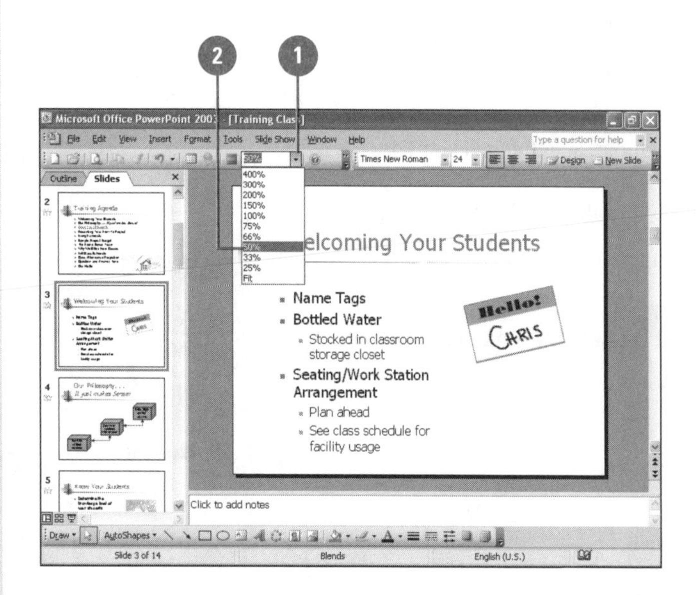

Getting Help While You Work

At some time, everyone has a question or two about the program they are using. The Office Online Help system provides the answers you need. You can search an extensive catalog of Help topics using a table of contents to locate specific information, or you can get context sensitive help in a dialog box. You can also ask your question in the Type A Question For Help box located on the right side of the menu bar. When you use any of these help options, a list of possible answers is shown to you in the Search Results task pane, with the most likely answer to your question at the top of the list.

Get Help Without the Office Assistant

1. Click the Help button on the Standard toolbar.
2. Locate the Help topic you want.
   - Type one or more keywords in the Search For box, and then click the Start Searching button.
   - Click Table Of Contents, and then click a topic.

   The topic you want appears in the right pane.
3. Read the topic, and then click any hyperlinks to get information on related topics or definitions.
4. When you're done, click the Close button.
5. Click the Close button on the task pane.

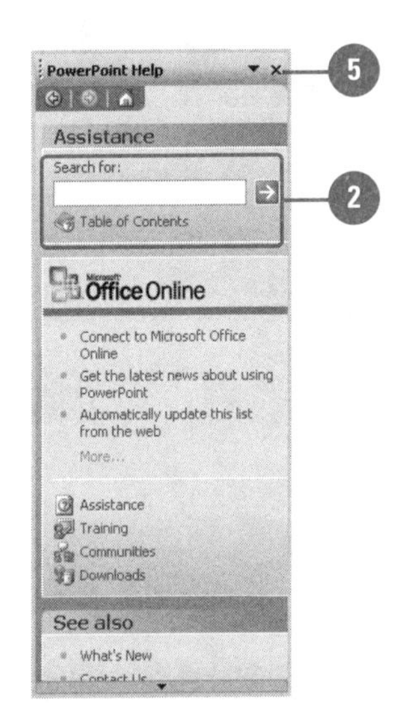

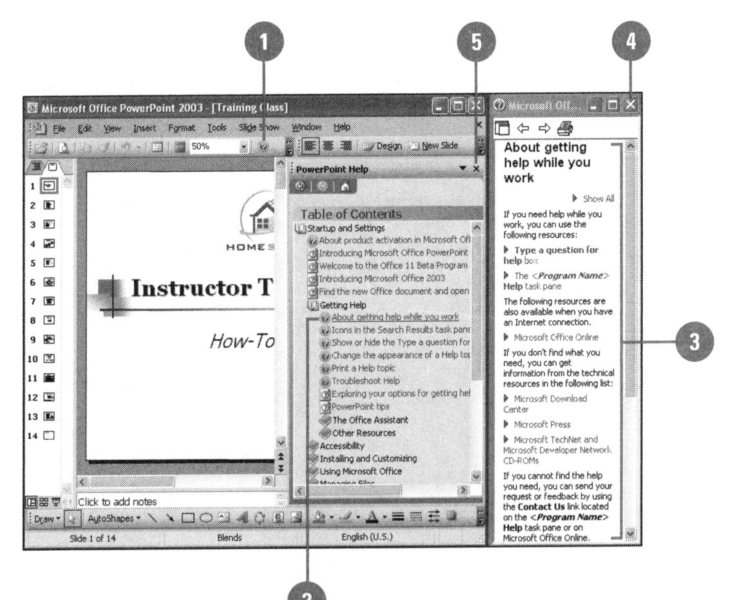

Get Help While You Work

1. Click the Type A Question For Help box.
2. Type your question, and then press Enter.
3. Click the topic that you want to read about.
4. When you're done, click the Close button on the task pane.

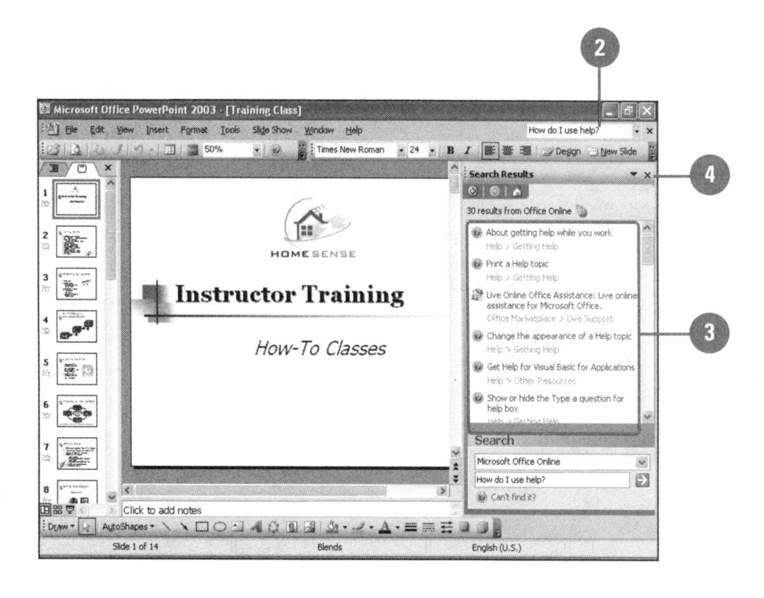

Get Help in a Dialog Box

1. Display the dialog box in which you want to get help.
2. Click the Help button.
3. Read the information in the Help window, and then click any links to display additional information.
4. When you're done, click the Close button.

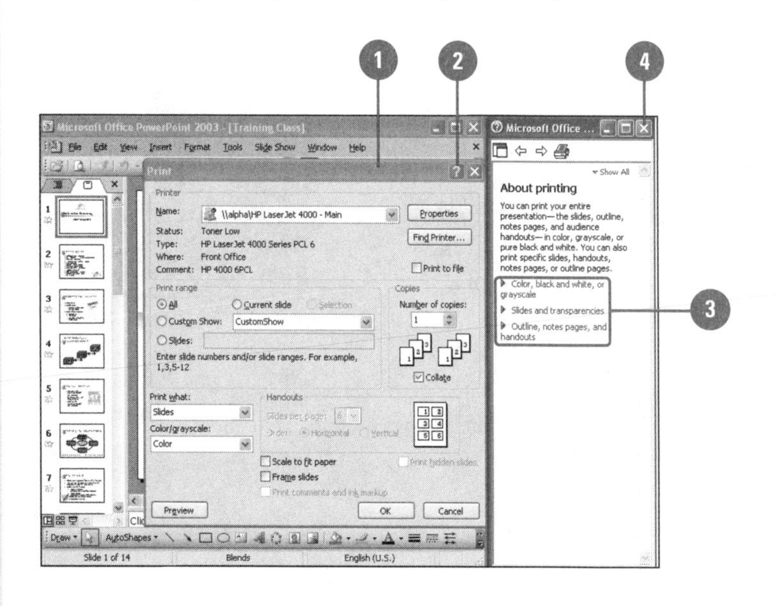

Getting Help from the Office Assistant

Often the easiest way to learn how to accomplish a task is to ask someone who knows. Now, with Office, that knowledgeable friend is always available in the form of the Office Assistant. The **Office Assistant** is an animated Help feature that you can use to access information that is directly related to the task you need help with. Using everyday language, just tell the Office Assistant what you want to do and it walks you through the process step by step. You can turn this feature on and off whenever you need to. If the personality of the default Office Assistant—Clippit—doesn't appeal to you, choose from a variety of other Office Assistants.

Ask the Office Assistant for Help

1. Click the Help menu, and then click Show Office Assistant.
2. Click the Office Assistant, if necessary, to display the help balloon.
3. Type your question about a task you want help with.
4. Click Search.
5. Click the topic you want help with, and then read the information.
6. After you're done, click the Close button.
7. To refine the search, click the Search list arrow, select a search area, and then click the Start Searching button.
8. When you're done, click the Close button on the task pane.
9. Click the Help menu, and then click Hide The Office Assistant.

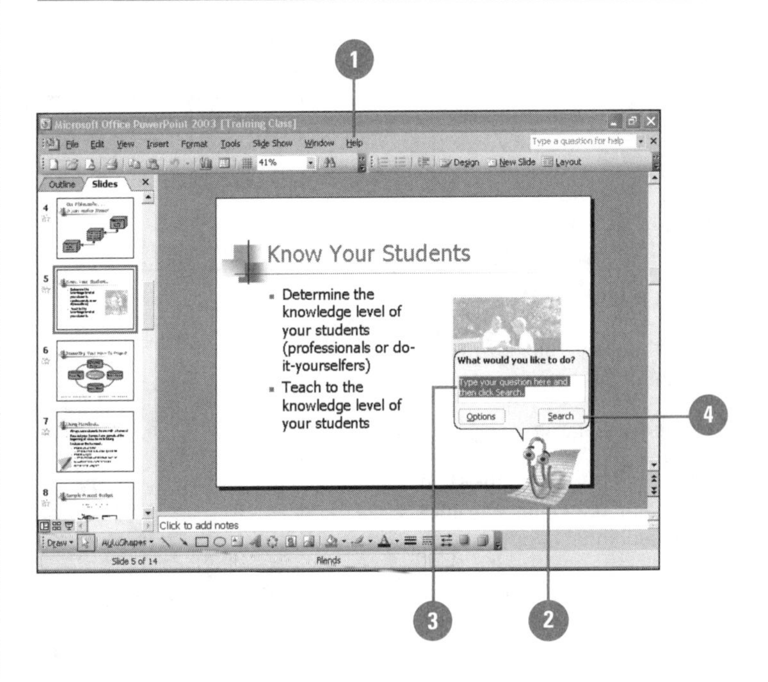

Hide the Office Assistant

1. Right-click the Office Assistant.
2. Click Hide.

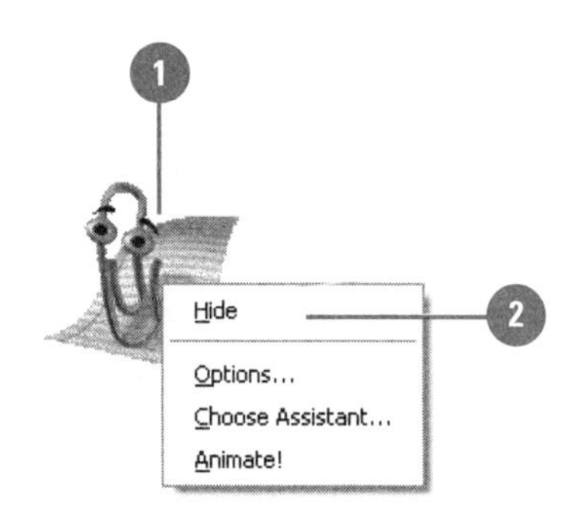

Turn Off the Office Assistant

1. Right-click the Office Assistant and then click Options, or click the Options button in the Assistant window.
2. Click the Options tab.
3. Clear the Use The Office Assistant check box.
4. Click OK.

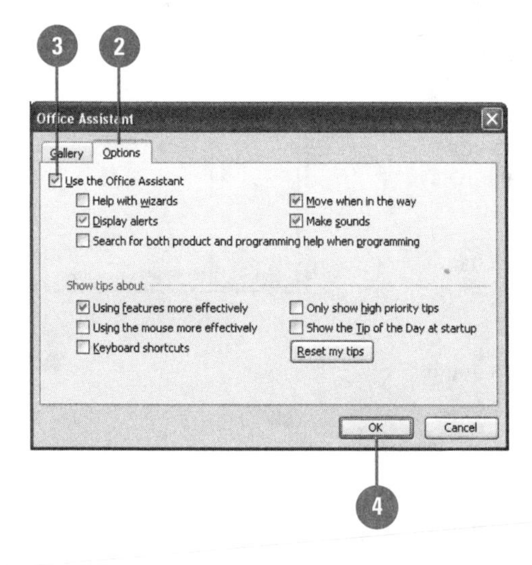

Did You Know?

You can change the Assistant character. Right-click the Assistant, and then click Choose Assistant. Click the Next and Back buttons to view the available Assistants, and then click OK. You might be asked to insert the original installation CD.

Saving a Presentation

PP03S-4-6

When you create a PowerPoint presentation, save it as a file on a disk or on your computer's hard disk so you can work with it later. When you save a presentation for the first time or if you want to save the file with a new name, use the Save As command. When you want to save your changes to an open presentation, use the Save button on the Standard toolbar. You can also create and name a new folder to save your presentations in.

Save a Presentation for the First Time

1. Click the File menu, and then click Save As.
2. Click one of the icons on the Places bar to select a location to save the presentation file.
3. If necessary, click the Save In list arrow, and then select the drive and folder where you want to save the presentation file.
4. Type the new presentation name.
5. Click Save.

   The new filename appears in the title bar.

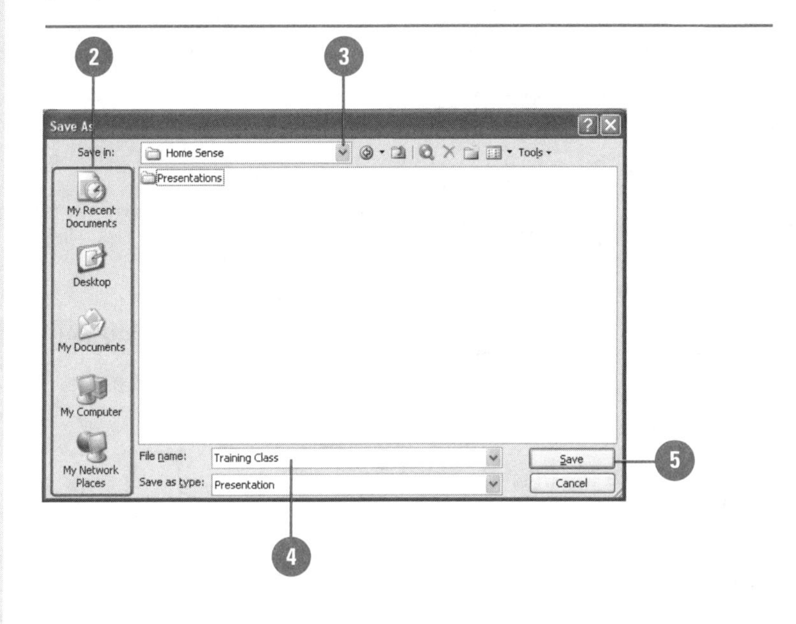

Save a Presentation in a New Folder

1. Click the File menu, and then click Save As.
2. Locate and select the drive and folder where you want to create the new folder.
3. Click the Create New Folder button.
4. Type the new folder name, and then click OK.
5. Type the new presentation name.
6. Click Save.

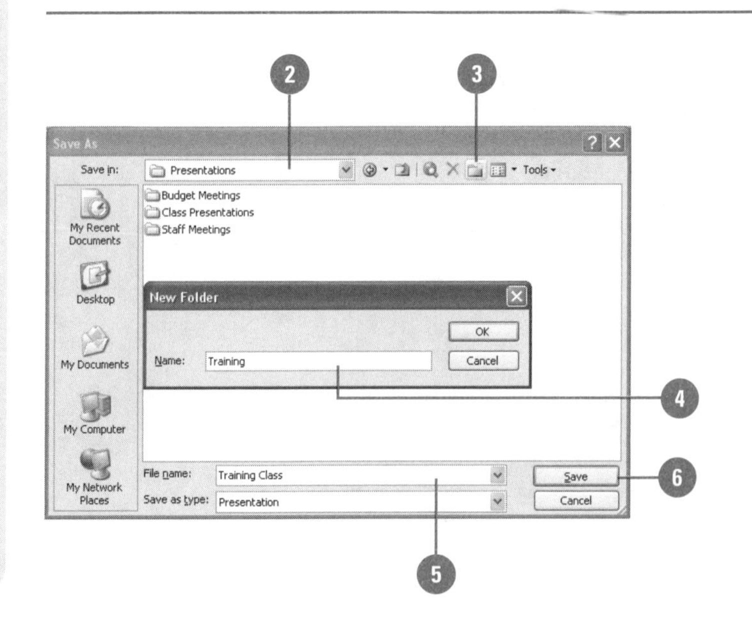

Save a Presentation with Another Name

1. Click the File menu, and then click Save As.
2. Click an icon on the Places bar or click the Save In list arrow, and then click the drive or folder where you want to save the file.
3. Type a new filename.
4. Click Save.

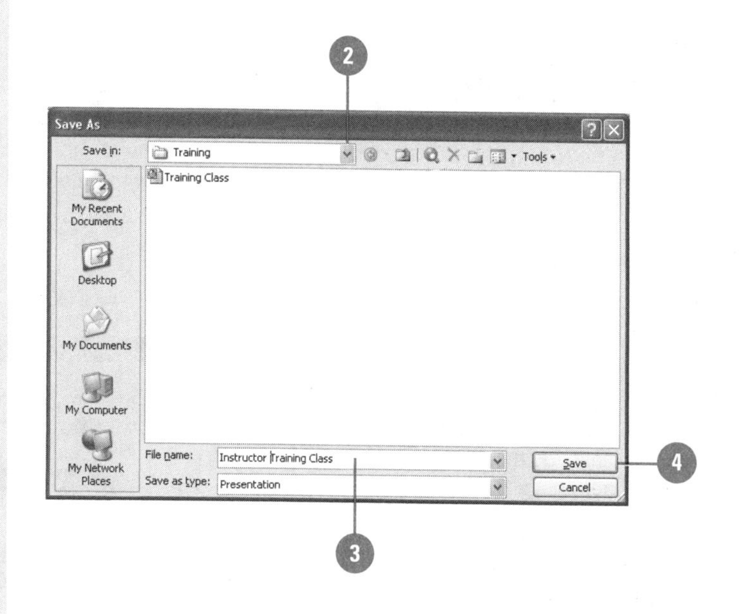

Save an Existing Presentation

1. Click the Save button on the Standard toolbar.

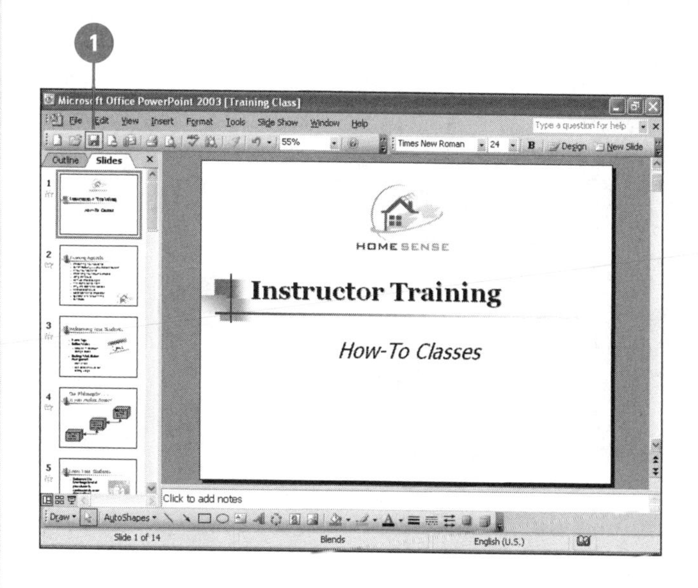

Did You Know?

Your presentation is automatically saved. Although you should save your changes frequently to avoid losing any work from a power failure or computer error, PowerPoint does save a temporary file of your presentation at timed intervals.

You can change your save options. To modify your default save settings, click the Tools menu, click Options, click the Save tab, click the save options you want, and then click OK.

Getting PowerPoint Updates on the Web

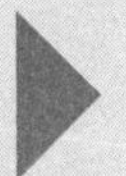

PowerPoint offers a quick and easy way to update PowerPoint with any new software downloads that improve the stability and security of the program. From the Help menu, simply select the Check For Updates command to connect to the Microsoft Office Online Web site to have your computer scanned for necessary updates, and then choose which Office updates you want to download and install.

Get PowerPoint Updates on the Web

1. Click the Help menu, and then click Check For Updates.

   The Microsoft Office Online Web site opens, displaying the Downloads page.

2. Click Check For Updates to find out if you need PowerPoint updates, and then choose the updates you want to download and install.

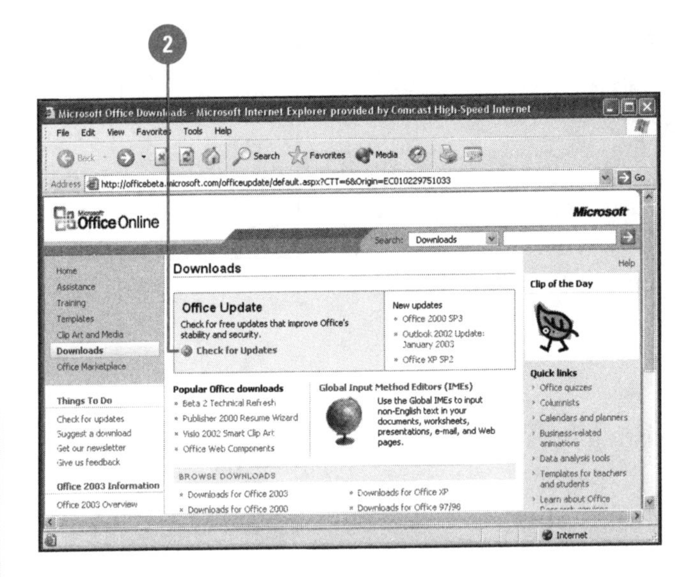

Recovering a Presentation

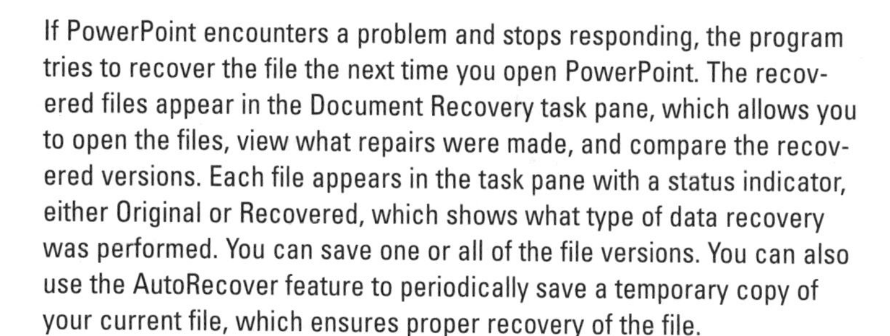

If PowerPoint encounters a problem and stops responding, the program tries to recover the file the next time you open PowerPoint. The recovered files appear in the Document Recovery task pane, which allows you to open the files, view what repairs were made, and compare the recovered versions. Each file appears in the task pane with a status indicator, either Original or Recovered, which shows what type of data recovery was performed. You can save one or all of the file versions. You can also use the AutoRecover feature to periodically save a temporary copy of your current file, which ensures proper recovery of the file.

Recover a Presentation

1. When the Document Recovery task pane appears, click the list arrow next to the name of each recovered file, and then perform one of the following:
   - Click Open to view the file for review.
   - Click Save As to save the file.
   - Click Delete to close the file without saving.
   - Click Show Repairs to find out how PowerPoint fixed the file.
2. When you're done, click the Close button.

Use AutoRecover

1. Click the Tools menu, and then click Options.
2. Click the Save tab.
3. Select the Save AutoRecover Info Every check box.
4. Enter the number of minutes, or click the up and down arrows to adjust the minutes.
5. Click OK.

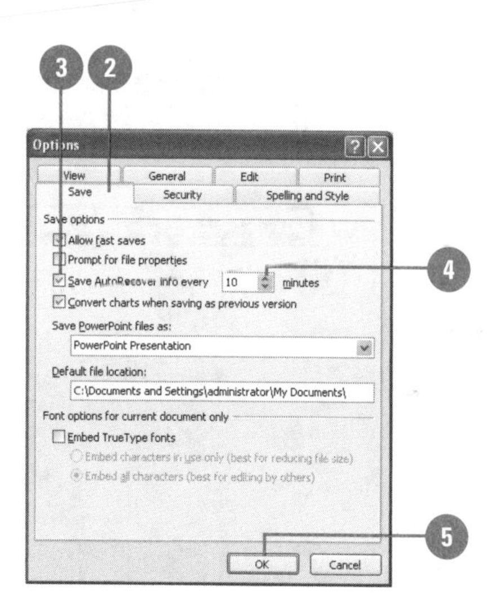

Detecting and Repairing Problems

At times you may determine that PowerPoint is not working as efficiently as it once did. This sometimes happens when you install new software or move files into new folders. Use the Detect And Repair command to improve performance by repairing problems such as missing files from setup and registry settings. Note that this feature does not repair personal files such as your presentations. If the Detect And Repair command does not fix the problem, you might have to reinstall PowerPoint. If PowerPoint doesn't respond and close, you can use Microsoft Office Application Recovery to exit the program. If you need to add or remove features, reinstall PowerPoint, or remove it entirely, you can use Office Setup's maintenance feature.

Detect and Repair Problems

1. Click the Help menu, and then click Detect And Repair.
2. Click Start.

   If prompted, insert the PowerPoint or Office CD in your drive.
3. If necessary, click Repair Office, and then click the Reinstall Office or Repair Errors In Your Office Installation option.
4. Click OK.

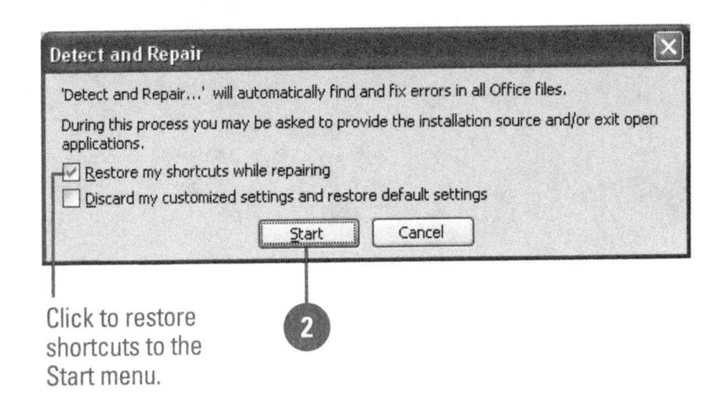

Click to restore shortcuts to the Start menu.

Recover an Office Program

1. Click the Start button on the taskbar, point to All Programs, point to Microsoft Office, point to Microsoft Office Tools, and then click Microsoft Office Application Recovery.
2. Select the application you want to recover.
3. Click Recover Application or End Application.

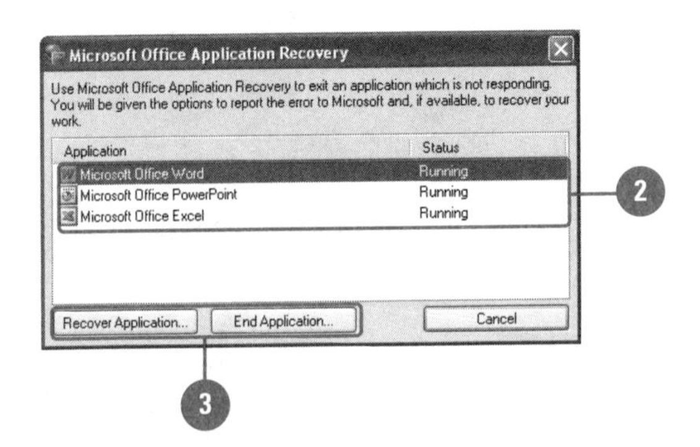

Perform Maintenance on Office Programs

1. Insert the PowerPoint or Office CD in your drive.
2. In Windows Explorer, double-click the Setup icon on the PowerPoint or Office CD.
3. Click one of the following maintenance buttons.
   - Add Or Remove Features to change which features are installed or remove specific features.
   - Reinstall Or Repair to reinstall or repair Microsoft Office 2003 to its original state.
   - Uninstall to uninstall Microsoft Office 2003 from this computer.
4. Click Next, and then follow the wizard instructions to complete the maintenance.

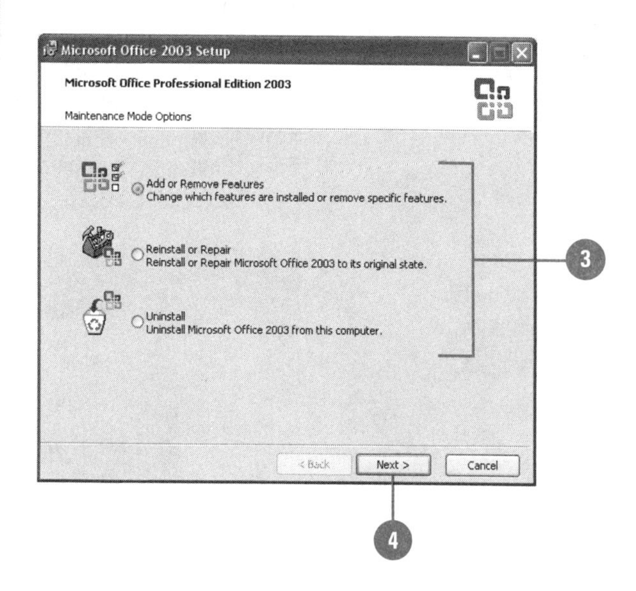

1

Closing a Presentation and Quitting PowerPoint

After you finish working on a presentation, you can close it. Closing a file makes more computer memory available for other activities. Closing a presentation is different from quitting PowerPoint; after you close a presentation, PowerPoint is still running. When you're finished using PowerPoint, you can quit the program. To protect your files, always quit PowerPoint before turning off the computer.

Close a Presentation

1. Click the Close Window button on the presentation window, or click the File menu, and then click Close.
2. If you have made changes to any open files since last saving them, a dialog box opens, asking if you want to save changes. Click Yes to save any changes, or click No to ignore your changes.

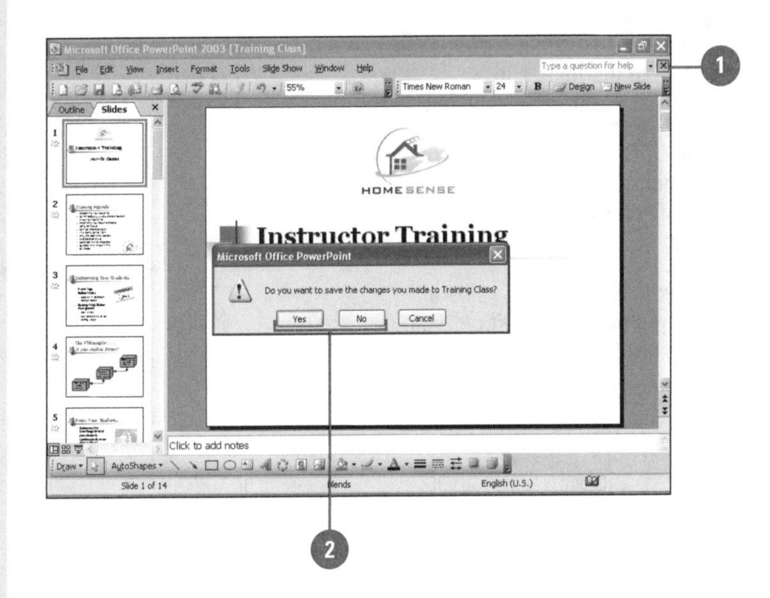

Quit PowerPoint

1. Click the Close button on the PowerPoint window, or click the File menu, and then click Exit.
2. If you have made changes to any open files since last saving them, a dialog box opens asking if you want to save changes. Click Yes to save any changes, or click No to ignore your changes.

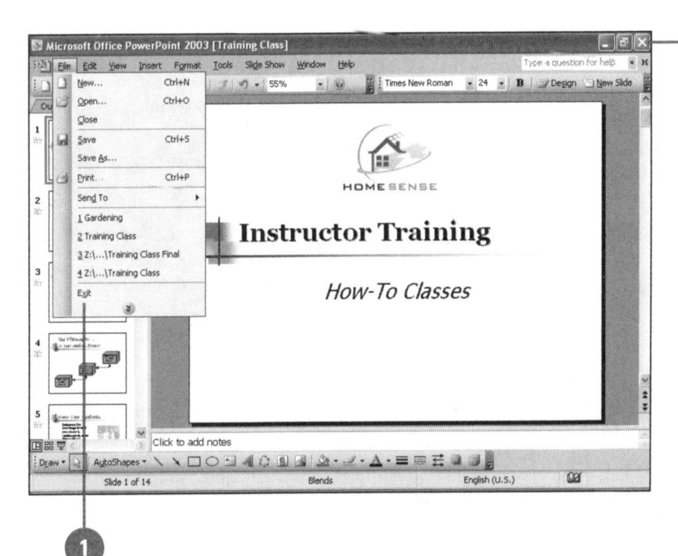

Developing Presentation Content

2

Introduction

When creating a new presentation, there are things to consider as you develop your content.Microsoft Office PowerPoint 2003 can help you with this process.There are various elements to a presentation that make looking at your slides interesting. Bulleted lists, the use of clip art, charts and diagrams, organization charts and tables, and media clips or pictures. All of these items are considered graphic objects, and are separate from the text objects that you enter. Objects can be moved from one part of a presentation to another.You can also resize, move, and delete them.

As you develop your presentation, there are a few things to keep in mind—keep the text easy to read and straight to the point, make sure it isn't too wordy, and have a balance of text and graphics.Too much text can lose your audience while too many graphics can distract their focus on your presentation.

PowerPoint offers many tools to help you develop your text. Using the AutoCorrect feature, text is corrected as you type. A build-in Thesaurus is always a few keystrokes away, and a research option that allows you to look for information is available in PowerPoint or has links to the Web.

Once you've begun to enter your text, you can adjust the spacing, change the alignment, set tabs, and change indents. You can also format your text by changing the font style or its attributes such as adding color to your text. If you decide to enter text in outline form, PowerPoint offers you the Outline pane to jot down your thoughts and notes. If bulleted or numbered lists are your preference, you can enter your ideas in this format. Should you need to rearrange your slides, you can do this in various PowerPoint views.

What You'll Do

Create New and Consistent Slides

Work with Objects

Develop, Enter, and Edit Text

Resize Text While Typing

Correct Text While Typing

Change Text Alignment and Spacing

Find and Replace Text

Insert Research Material

Find the Right Words

Insert and Develop an Outline

Move and Indent Text

Set Tabs

Format Text

Modify a Bulleted List

AutoFormat Text and Numbered Lists

Create a Text Box

Rearrange Slides

Use Slides from Other Presentations

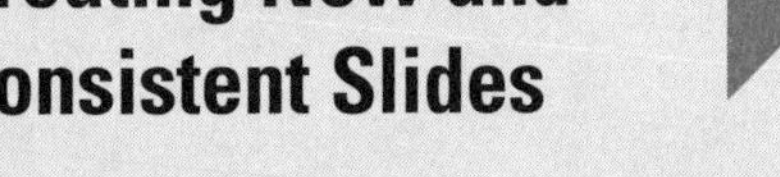

Creating New and Consistent Slides

PP03S-2-3, PP03S-4-1

You need to arrange the objects on your slides in a visually meaningful way so that others can understand your presentation. PowerPoint's AutoLayout feature helps you arrange objects on your slide in a consistent manner. When you create a new slide, you can apply one of the AutoLayouts. You can also apply an AutoLayout to an existing slide at any time. When you change a slide's AutoLayout, you keep the existing information. PowerPoint applies the new AutoLayout, and you can arrange the placeholders the way you want them.

Insert a New Slide

1. Click the New Slide button on the Formatting toolbar.
2. In the Slide Layout task pane, click the Slide Layout you want to use.

Did You Know?

You can insert a new slide from the slide layout task pane. Point to the layout you want the slide to have, click the list arrow, and then click Insert New Slide.

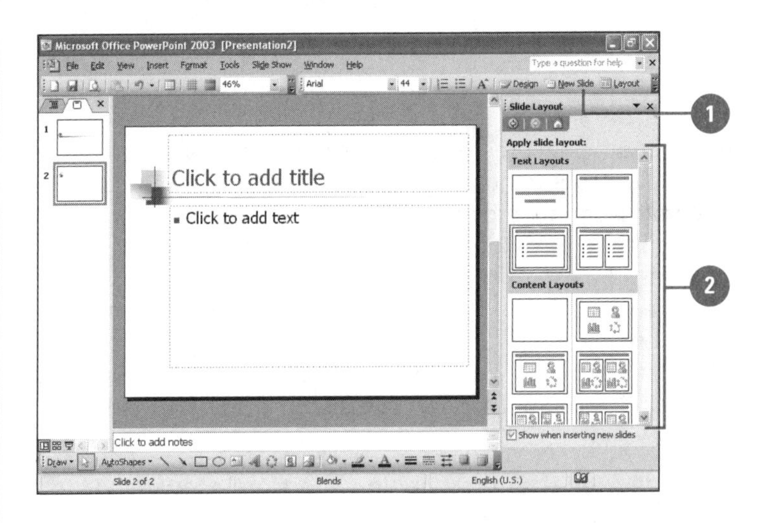

Apply an AutoLayout to an Existing Slide

1. In Normal view, display the slide you want to change.
2. Click the Slide Layout button on the Formatting toolbar if displayed, or click the Other Task Panes list arrow and select the Slide Layout task pane.
3. Click the Slide Layout you want to use.

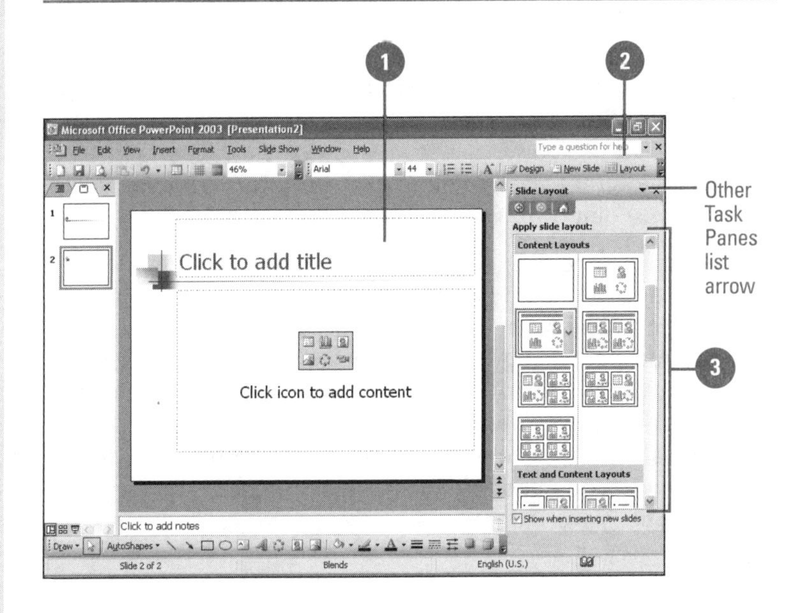

Enter Information in a Placeholder

- For text placeholders, click the placeholder, and then type the text.
- For other objects, click the placeholder, and then work with the accessory that PowerPoint starts.

Did You Know?

You can use placeholders to enter information efficiently. When you apply an AutoLayout to a slide, an arranged group of placeholders appears—one placeholder for each object on the slide. The placeholders include instructions for entering object contents.

You can delete a slide quickly. In Outline or Slides pane or Slide Sorter view, select the slide you want to delete, and then press Delete.

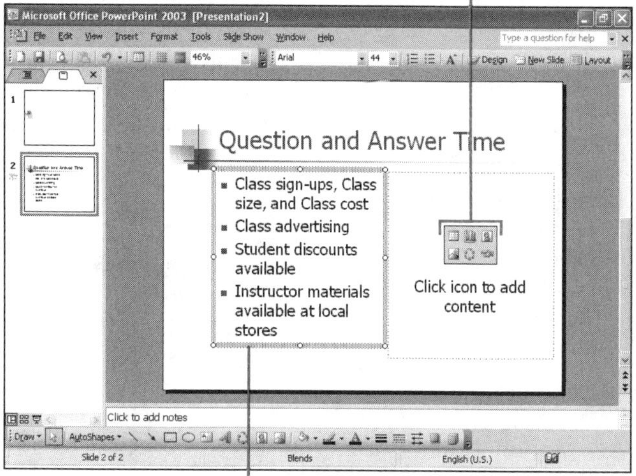

AutoLayout Placeholder

A placeholder is a border that defines the size and location of an object.

AutoLayout Placeholders

Placeholder	Description
Bulleted List	Displays a short list of related items
Clip Art	Inserts a picture from the Clip Organizer
Chart	Inserts a chart
Diagram or Organization Chart	Inserts an organizational chart
Table	Inserts a table from Microsoft Word
Media Clip	Inserts a music, sound, or video clip
Picture	Inserts a picture from a file

Working with Objects

PP03S-2-2

Once you create a slide, you can modify any of its objects, even those added by an AutoLayout. To manipulate objects, use Normal view. To perform any action on an object, you first need to select it. When you select a text object, the text is surrounded by a rectangle of gray dots called a **selection box**. When you select a graphic object, the graphic is surrounded by sizing handles (small white circles). You can resize, move, delete, and format selected objects.

Select and Deselect an Object

- To select an object, move the pointer (which changes to a four-headed arrow) over the object, and then click to select.
- To select multiple objects, press and hold Shift as you click each object or drag to enclose the objects you want to select in the selection box.
- To deselect an object, click outside its border.
- To deselect one of a group of objects, press and hold Shift, and then click the object.

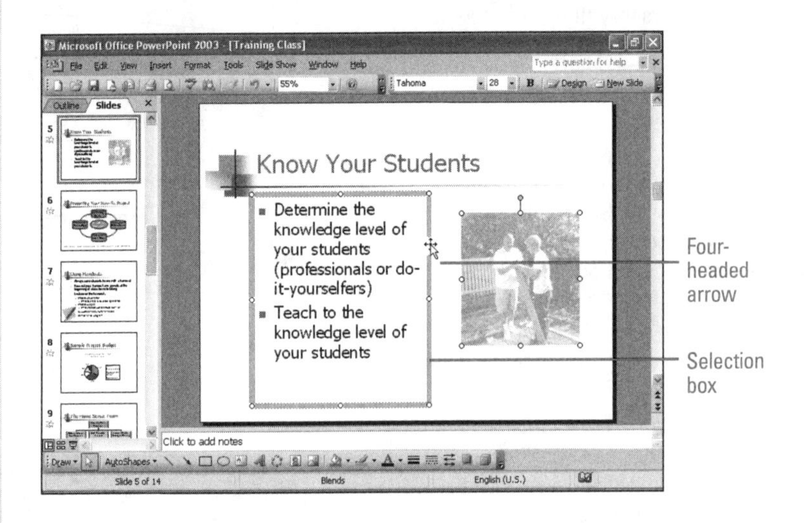

Resize an Object

1. Move the pointer over a sizing handle.
2. Drag the sizing handle until the object is the size you want.

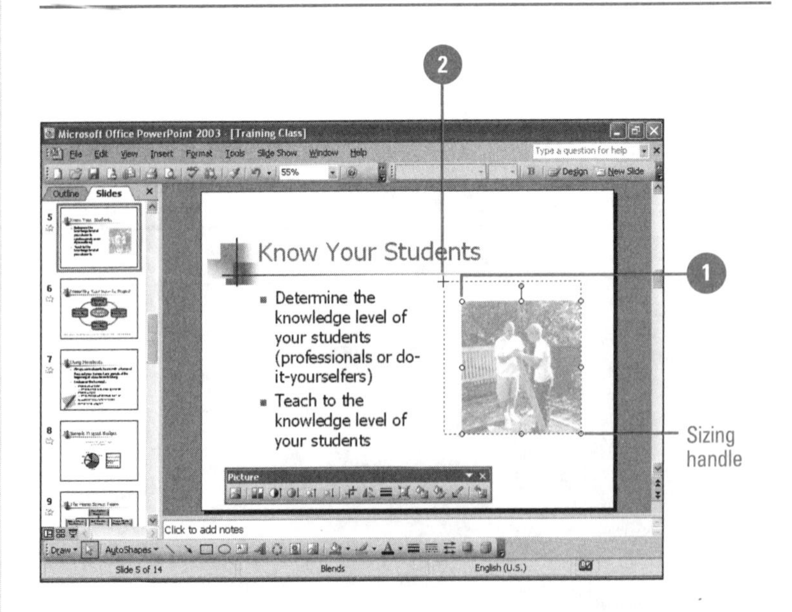

Did You Know?

You can use a corner sizing handle to create proportional objects. Press and hold Shift as you drag a corner sizing handle in a diagonal direction. This is useful when you are resizing a picture or clip art where changing the proportions might distort the picture.

Move an Object

- **Using the mouse**. Move the pointer (which changes to a four-headed arrow) over the object, and then drag it to the new location. To move unfilled objects, drag the border. You can move an object in a straight line by pressing Shift as you drag the object.
- **Using the keyboard**. Click the object, and then press the arrow keys to move the object in the direction you want.

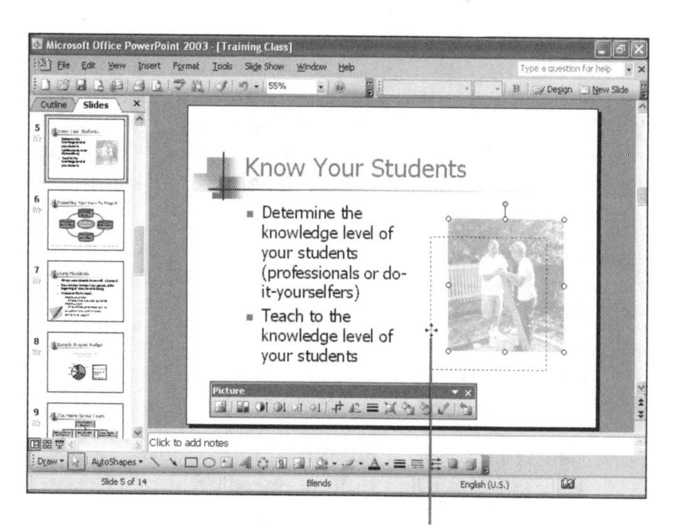

Use the four-headed arrow to drag the object to a new location.

Did You Know?

You can use keyboard shortcuts to cut, copy, and paste objects. To cut an object from a slide, select the object and then press Ctrl+X. To copy an object, select the object, and then press Ctrl+C. To paste an object on a slide, press Ctrl+V.

Delete an Object

1. Click the object you want to delete.
2. Press Delete.

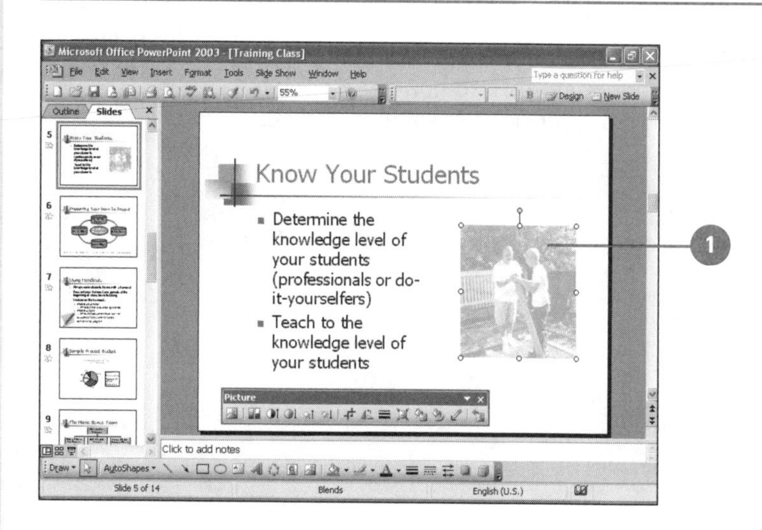

Did You Know?

You can use the Tab key to select hard-to-click objects. If you are having trouble selecting an object that is close to other objects, click a different object and then press Tab until you select the object you want.

You can select all objects on a slide. Click the Edit menu, and then click Select All.

2

Developing Text

Your presentation's text lays the foundation for the presentation. Keep these basic presentation rules in mind when developing your text.

- Keep it simple.
- If you plan to present your slides to a large group, think about the people at the back of the room and what they can see.
- Keep the text to a minimum with no more than five bullets per slide and no more than five words per bullet.
- If you find a graphic that illustrates your point in a memorable way, use it instead of a lot of text.

PowerPoint provides several views that can help you organize your text. You can work with text and other objects one slide at a time in Normal view or, by clicking the Outline tab, you can work with all the presentation text on all slides at once.

PowerPoint also offers many text formatting features traditionally associated with word processing software. You can apply fonts and text attributes to create the look you want. You can set tabs, indents, and alignment. Finally, you can edit and correct your text using several handy tools, including style, grammar, and spelling checkers.

PowerPoint includes three types of text objects.

- **Title text objects**. Presized rectangular boxes that appear at the top of each slide—used for slide titles and, if appropriate, subtitles
- **Bulleted list objects**. Boxes that accommodate bulleted or numbered lists.
- **Text box objects**. Boxes that contain non-title text that you don't want to format in bulleted or numbered lists—often used for captions.

The first slide in a presentation typically contains title and text and a subtitle. Other slides often start with a title and then list major points in a bulleted list. Use text boxes only occasionally—when you need to include annotations or minor points that don't belong in a list.

When to Enter Text on a Slide

Use the slide pane of Normal view to enter text when you are focusing on the text or objects of one slide at a time.

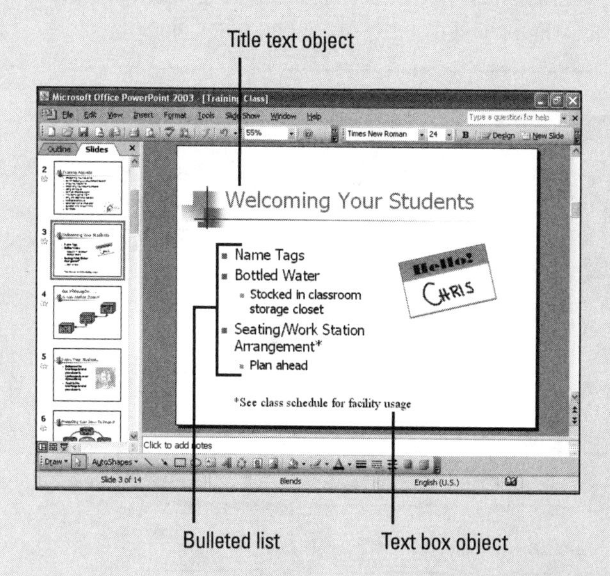

When to Enter Text in an Outline

If you are concentrating on developing presentation content, but not on how the text looks or interacts with other objects on the slide, use the Outline tab in Normal view. This view lets you see the titles, subtitles, and bulleted text on all your slides at a single glance.

The outline tab in Normal view is particularly useful for reorganizing the content of your presentation and ensuring that topics flow well from one to the next. You can easily move presentation topics up and down the outline.

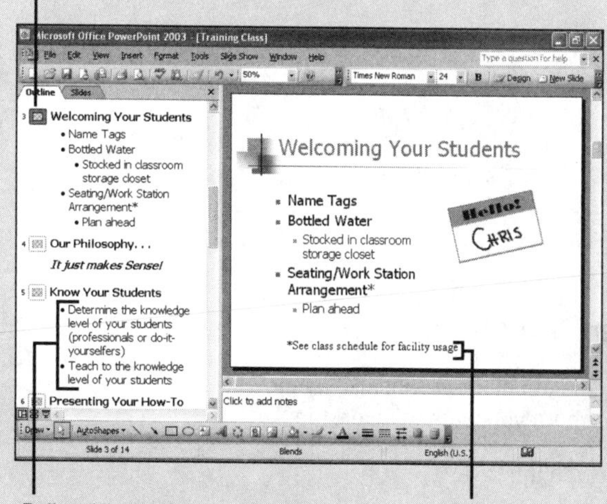

2

Entering Text

PP03S-1-2

In Normal view, you can type text directly into the text placeholders. A **text placeholder** is an empty text box. If you type more text than fits in the placeholder, the text is automatically resized to fit on the slide. You can also manually increase or decrease the line spacing or font size of the text. The insertion point (the blinking vertical line) indicates where text will appear when you type. To place the insertion point into your text, move the pointer over the text. The pointer changes to an I-beam to indicate that you can click and then type. When a selection box of slanted lines appears, your changes affect only the selected text. When a dotted selection box appears, changes apply to the entire text object.

Enter Text into a Placeholder

1. In Normal view, click the text placeholder if it isn't already selected.
2. Type the text you want to enter.
3. Click outside the text object to deselect it.

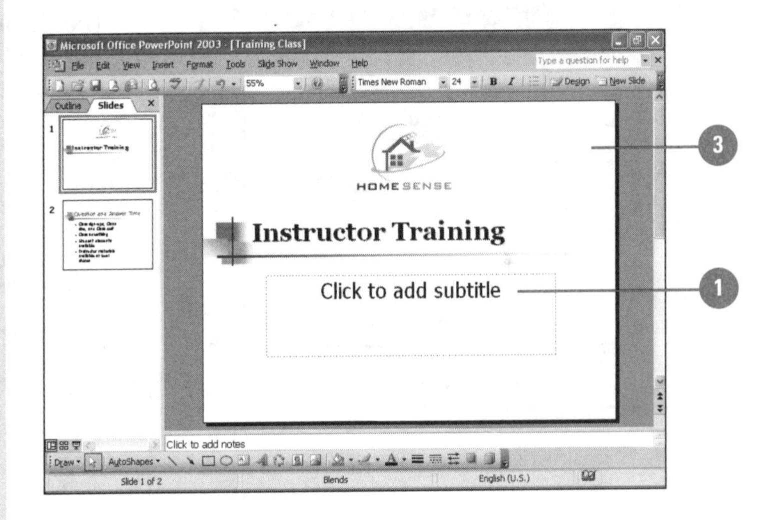

Insert Text

1. Click to place the insertion point where you want to insert the text.
2. Type the text.

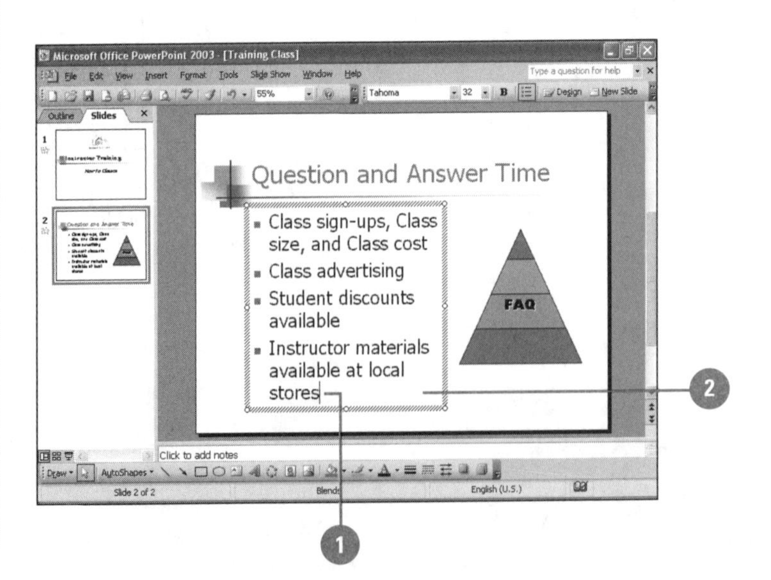

Enter Text in a Bulleted List

1. In Normal view, click the bulleted text placeholder.
2. Type the first bulleted item.
3. Press Enter.
4. Type the next bulleted item.
5. Repeat steps 3 and 4 until you complete the list.

Did You Know?

You can use the insertion point to determine text location. When entering bulleted text, be sure the insertion point is at the beginning of the line, and then press Tab to indent a level or press Shift+Tab to move back out a level.

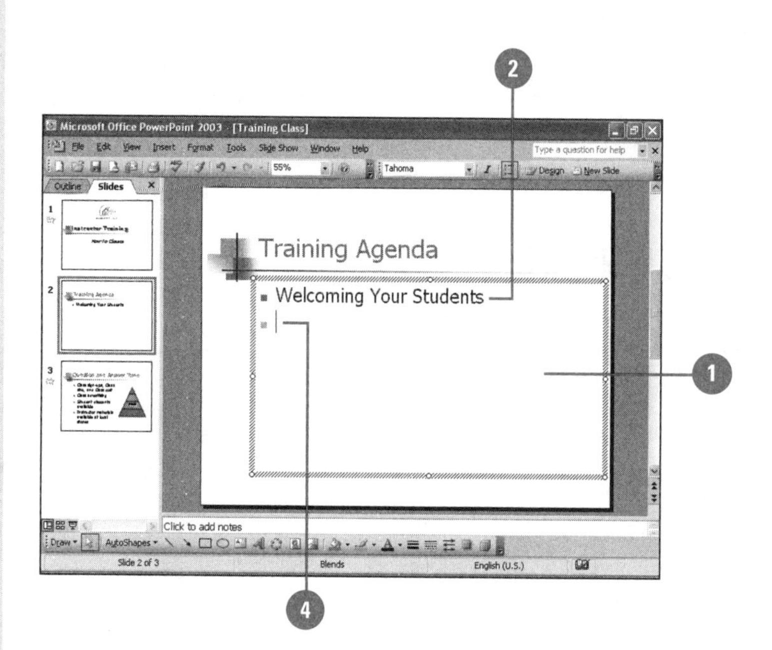

Adjust Paragraph Line Spacing

1. Click anywhere in the paragraph you want to adjust.
2. Click the Format menu, and then click Line Spacing.
3. Set the spacing options that you want.
4. Click OK.

Did You Know?

You should use caution when you adjust line spacing. When you decrease paragraph spacing, make sure you leave enough space for the height of each entire letter, including extenders such as the bottom of "p" and the top of "b."

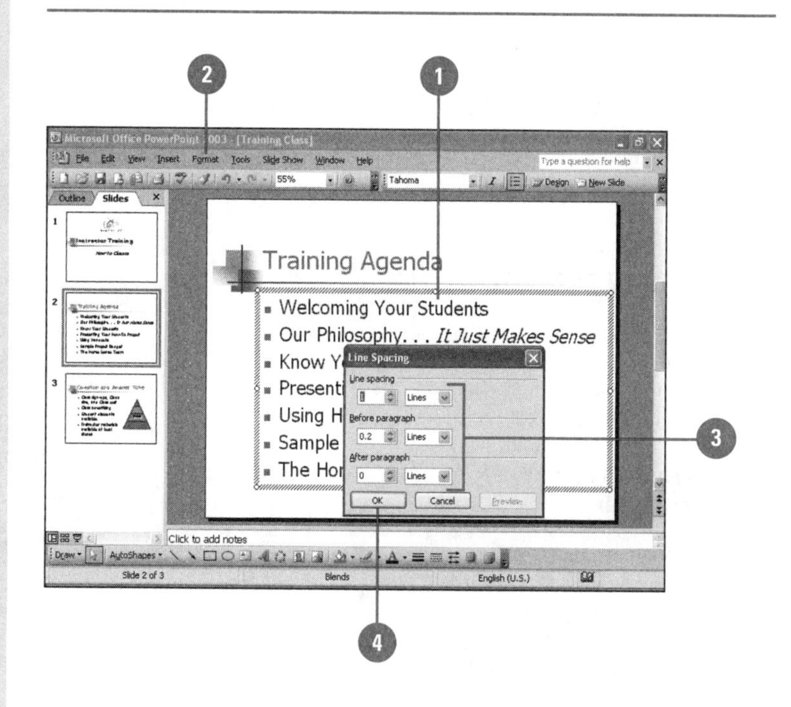

Editing Text

PP03S-1-2

If you are familiar with word processing programs, you probably already know how to perform most text editing tasks in PowerPoint. You can move, copy, or delete existing text; replace it with new text; and undo any changes you just made. Some of the editing methods require that you select the text first. When you select text, the text is surrounded by a rectangle of gray slanted lines, indicating you can now edit the text.

Select and Modify Text

1. Position the mouse pointer to the left of the text you want to highlight.
2. Drag the pointer over the text—just a few words, a few lines, or entire paragraphs.
3. Release the mouse button when you have selected all the text you want.
4. Modify the text the way you want.
   - To delete text, press Delete.
   - To replace text, type your new text.

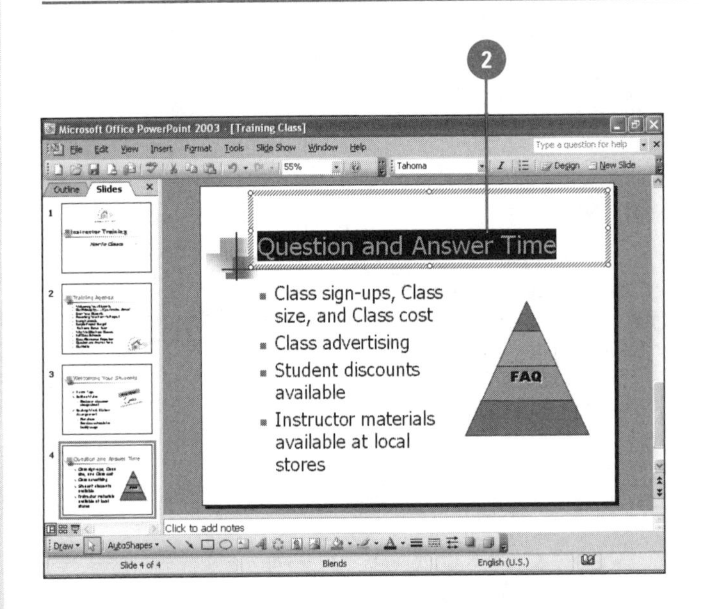

Move or Copy Text

1. Select the text you want to move or copy.
2. Move or copy the text the way you want.
   - To move text short distances in the outline tab or on a slide, drag the text to the new location. To copy text, press and hold the Ctrl key as you drag the text.
   - To move or copy text between slides, click the Cut or Copy button on the Standard toolbar, click where you want to insert the text, and then click the Paste button.

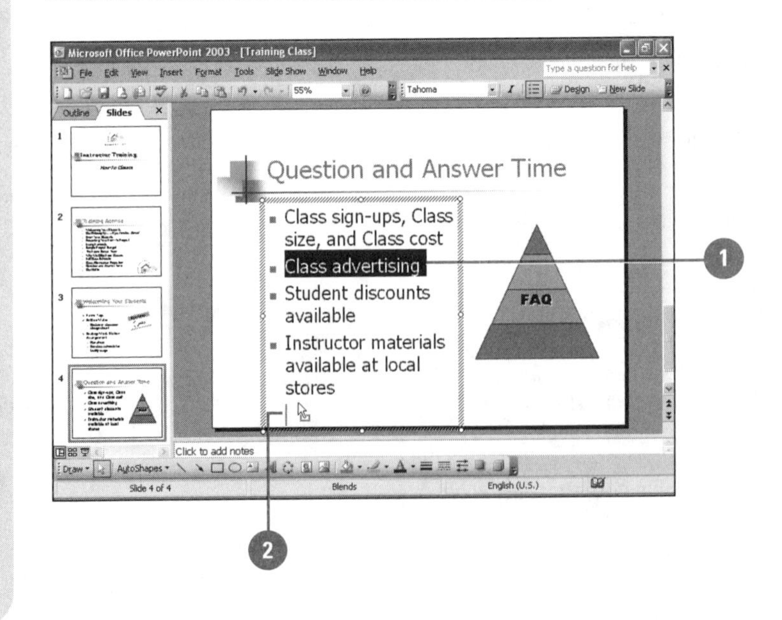

Resizing Text While Typing

If you type text in a placeholder, PowerPoint uses AutoFit to resize the text, if necessary, to fit into the placeholder. The AutoFit Text feature changes the line spacing—or paragraph spacing—between lines of text and then changes the font size to make the text fit. The AutoFit Options button, which appears near your text the first time that it is resized, gives you control over whether you want the text to be resized. The AutoFit Options button displays a menu with options for controlling how the option works. You can also display the AutoCorrect dialog box and change the AutoFit settings so that text doesn't resize automatically.

Resize Text as You Type

1. If the AutoFit Options box appears while you type, click the AutoFit Options button to select an option, or continue typing and PowerPoint will automatically adjust your text to fit.
2. If you click the AutoFit Options button, click the option you want to fit the text on the slide.

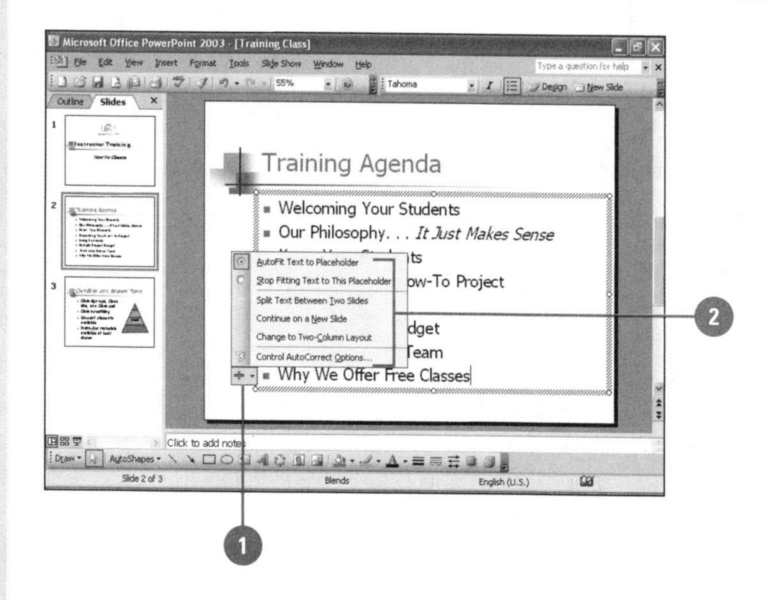

Turn Off AutoFit

1. Click the Tools menu, and then click AutoCorrect Options.
2. Click the AutoFormat As You Type tab.
3. Clear the AutoFit Title Text To Placeholder and AutoFit Body Text To Placeholder check boxes.
4. Click OK.

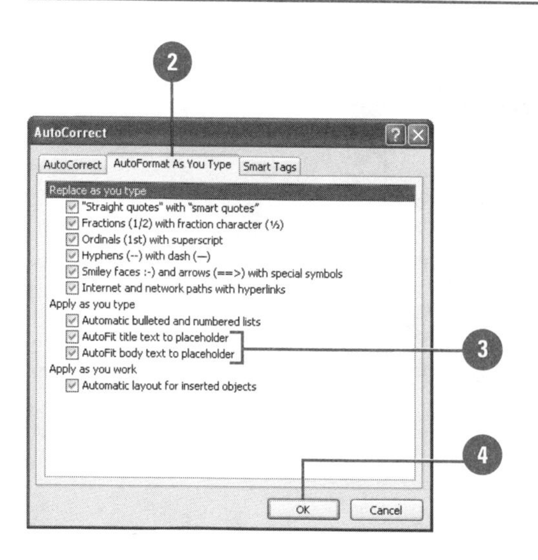

Correcting Text While Typing

PP03S-1-2

With AutoCorrect, PowerPoint corrects common capitalization and spelling errors as you type. You can customize AutoCorrect to recognize or ignore misspellings that you routinely make or to ignore specific text that you do not want AutoCorrect to change. When you point to a word that AutoCorrect changed, a small blue box appears under the first letter. When you point to the small blue box, the AutoCorrect Options button appears. The AutoCorrect Options button gives you control over whether you want the text to be corrected. You can change text back to its original spelling, or you can stop AutoCorrect from automatically correcting text. You can also display the AutoCorrect dialog box and change AutoCorrect settings.

Add an Entry to AutoCorrect

1. Click the Tools menu, and then click AutoCorrect Options.
2. Click the AutoCorrect tab.
3. Select the check boxes of the AutoCorrect features you want to enable.
4. Type the abbreviation or misspelling you want to add to the list of AutoCorrect entries in the Replace box.
5. Type the replacement text for your AutoCorrect entry in the With box.
6. Click OK.

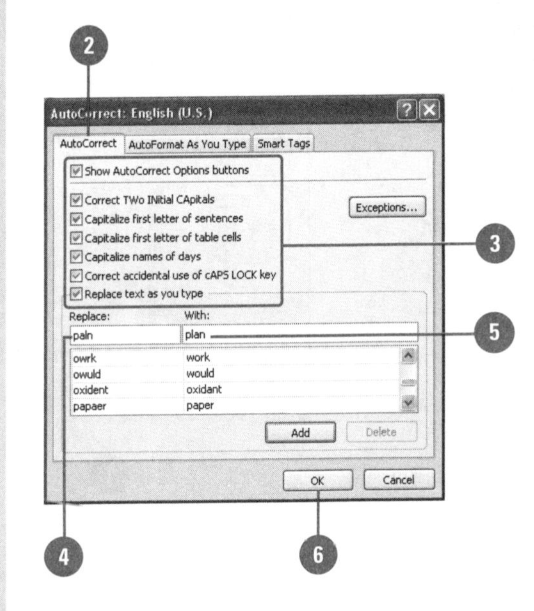

Did You Know?

You can use AutoCorrect to recognize abbreviations or codes. Use AutoCorrect to recognize abbreviations or codes that you create to automate typing certain text. For example, you can customize AutoCorrect to type your full name when you type in only your initials.

Correcting Text as You Type

1. If you misspell a word that PowerPoint recognizes, it will correct it and the AutoCorrect button will appear.
2. Point to the small blue box under the corrected word, and then click the AutoCorrect Options button list arrow to view your options.
3. Click an option, or click a blank area of the slide to deselect the AutoCorrect Options menu.

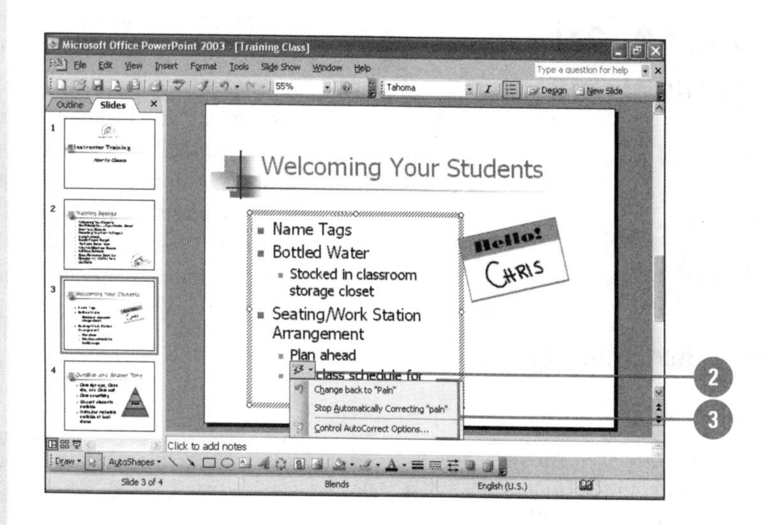

Undo an Action

- To undo an action, click the Undo button on the Standard toolbar; click it repeatedly to undo previous actions.
- To undo multiple actions, click the Undo list arrow on the Standard toolbar to view a list of the most recent changes, and then click the actions you want to undo.

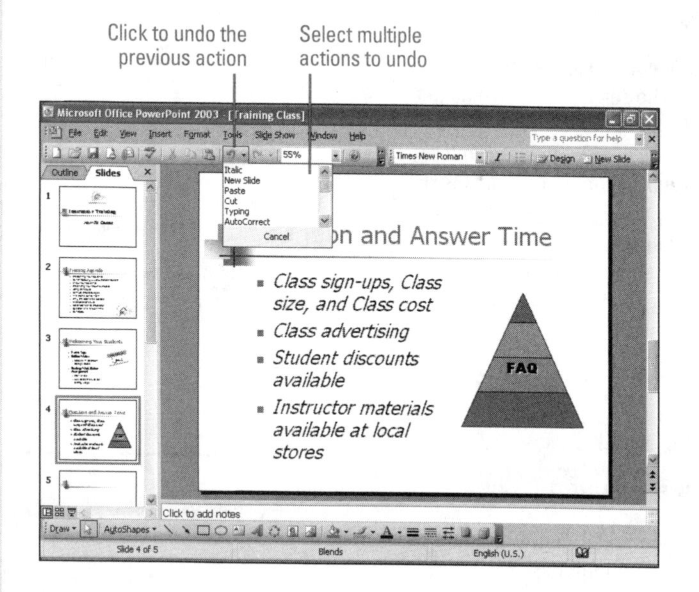

Did You Know?

You can use ScreenTips to help undo actions. Position the pointer over the Undo or Redo button to display a ScreenTip identifying the action.

You can redo one or more actions you just undid. Click the Redo button on the Standard toolbar to redo one action. Click the Redo button list arrow on the Standard toolbar, and then click the actions you want to redo.

2

Changing Text Alignment and Spacing

PP03S-2-1

PowerPoint enables you to control the way text lines up on the slide. You can align text to the left or right or to the center in a text object. You can also adjust the alignment of text in an object by selecting the object, and then clicking an alignment button (Align Left, Center, or Align Right) on the Formatting toolbar. Adjust the vertical space between selected lines and the space before and after paragraphs by selecting the object, and then clicking a line spacing button (Increase Paragraph Spacing or Decrease Paragraph Spacing) on the Formatting toolbar or by using the Line Spacing command on the Format menu.

Change Text Alignment

1. Select the text box.
2. On the Formatting toolbar, click an alignment button (Align Left, Center, or Align Right).

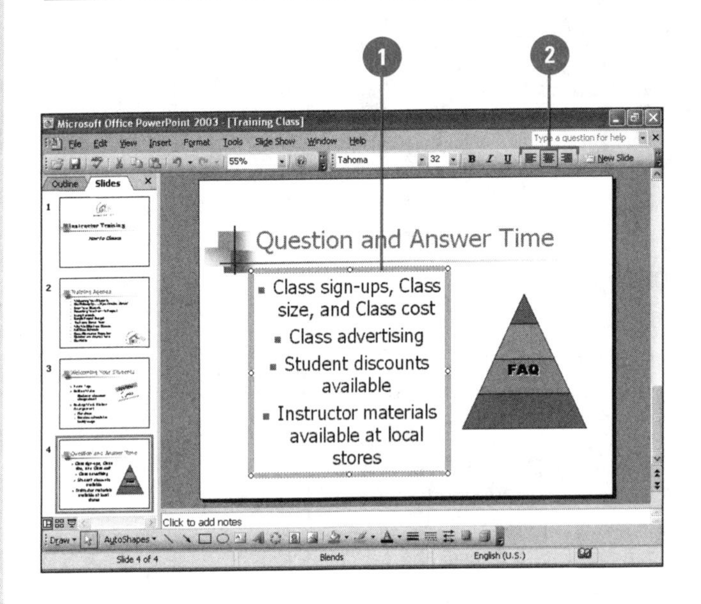

Did You Know?

You can choose the appropriate alignment. The Align Left button aligns text evenly along the left edge of the text box and is useful for paragraph text. The Align Right button aligns text evenly along the right edge of the text box and is useful for text labels. The Center button aligns text in the middle of the text box and is useful for titles and headings.

Adjust Line Spacing

1. Select the text object with the dotted selection box.
2. Click the Format menu, and then click Line Spacing.
3. Click the Line Spacing,Before Paragraph, or After Paragraph list arrows to select a setting.
4. Click OK.

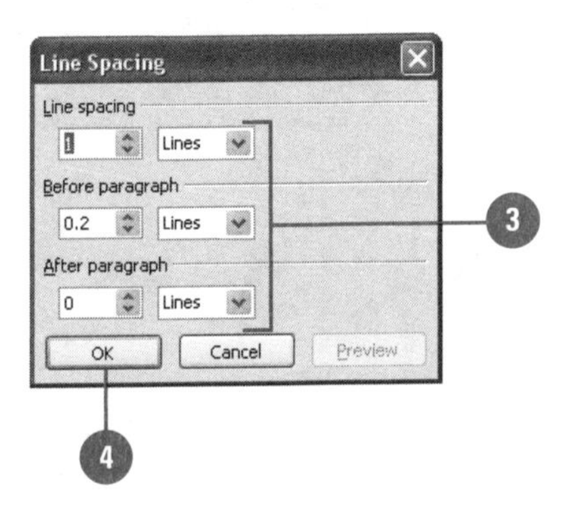

Finding and Replacing Text

PP03S-2-1

The Find and Replace commands on the Edit menu allow you to locate and change specific text in a presentation. Find helps you locate each occurrence of a specific word or set of characters, while Replace locates every occurrence of a specific word or set of characters and replaces it with a different one. You can change every occurrence of specific text all at once, or you can accept or reject each change individually.

Find and Replace Text

1. Click the Edit menu, and then click Replace.
2. Click the Find What box, and then type the text you want to replace.
3. Click in the Replace With box, and then type the replacement text.
4. Click one of the following buttons.
   - Click Find Next to find the next occurrence of the text.
   - Click Replace to find and replace this occurrence of the text.
   - Click Replace All to find and replace all occurrences of the text.
5. Click OK, and then click Close.

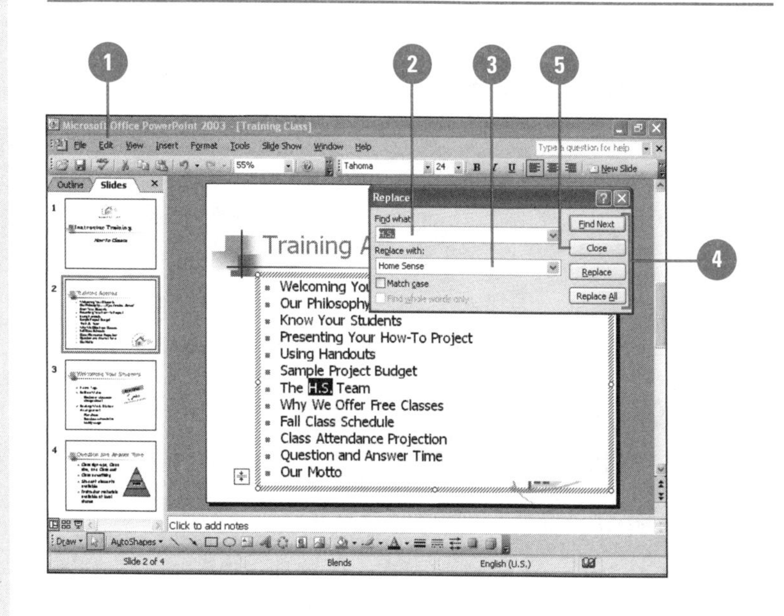

Did You Know?

You can use the Find command to search for text. To find text in your presentation, click the Edit menu, click Find, type what you want to find, and then click Find Next.

Inserting Research Material

PP03S-1-2

With the new Research task pane, you can access data sources and insert research material right into your text without leaving your PowerPoint presentation. The Research task pane can help you to access electronic dictionaries, thesauruses, research sites, and proprietary company information. You can select one reference source or search in all reference books. This new feature allows you to find information and incorporate it into your work quickly and easily.

Research a topic

1. Click the Tools menu, and then click Research.
2. Type the topic you would like to research.
3. Click a reference source, or select All Reference Books.
4. Click the Start Searching button (green arrow).
5. Point to the information in the Research task pane that you want to copy.
6. Click the list arrow, and then click Copy.
7. Paste the information into your presentation.
8. When you're done, click the Close button on the task pane.

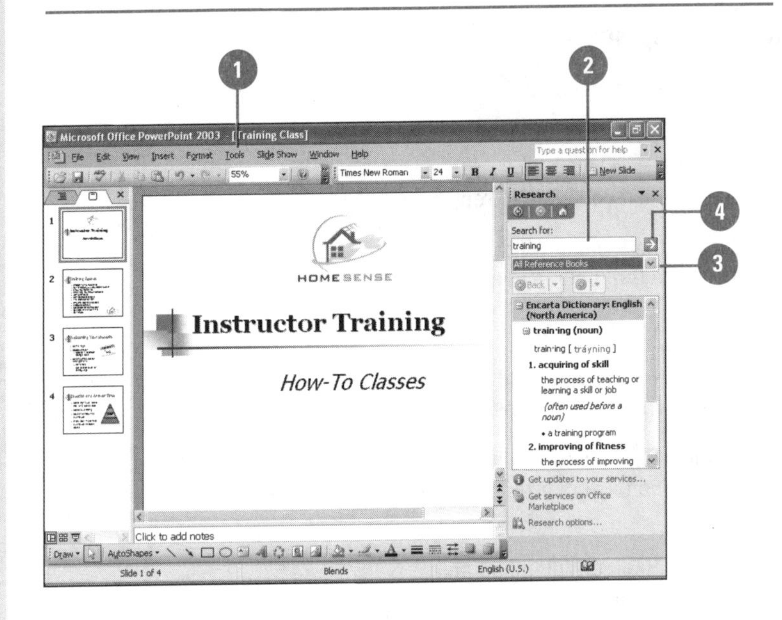

Finding the Right Words

PP03S-1-2

Repeating the same word in a presentation can reduce a message's effectiveness. Instead, replace some words with synonyms or find antonyms. If you need help finding exactly the right words, use the short-cut menu to look up synonyms quickly or search a Thesaurus for more options. This feature can save you time and improve the quality and read-ability of your presentation. You can also install a Thesaurus for another language. Foreign language thesauruses can be accessed under Research Options on the Research task pane.

Use the Thesaurus

1. Click the Tools menu, and then click Research.
2. In the Search For list, select a Thesaurus.
3. Press and hold down the Alt key, and then click a word you want to look up.

   TIMESAVER *Right-click the word you want to look up, click Synonyms, and then click Thesaurus.*

4. Point to the the word in the Research task pane.
5. Click the list arrow, and then click one of the following:
   - Click Insert to replace the word you looked up with the new word.
   - Click Copy to copy the new word and then paste it within the presentation.
6. When you're done, click the Close button on the task pane.

Did You Know?

You can search for more related words. In the Research task pane, click one of the words in the list of results.

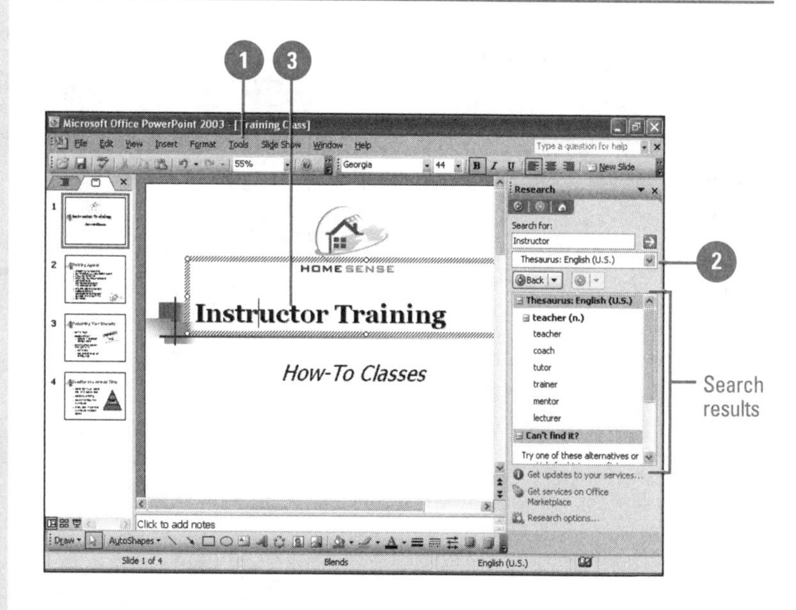

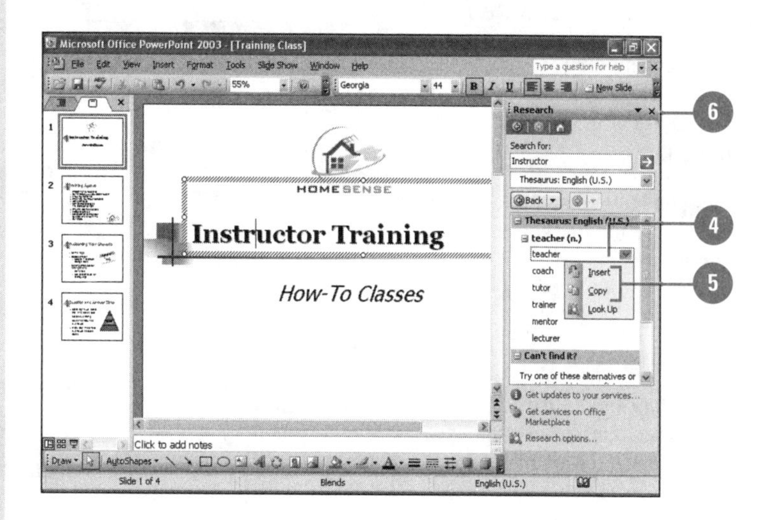

Inserting and Developing an Outline

PP03S-1-2

If you create your presentation using an AutoContent Wizard, PowerPoint generates an outline automatically. If you prefer to develop your own outline, you can create a blank presentation, and then type your outline in the Outline pane of Normal view. As you develop an outline, you can add new slides and duplicate existing slides in your presentation. You can also insert an outline you created in another program, such as Microsoft Word. Make sure the document containing the outline is set up using outline heading styles. When you insert the outline in PowerPoint, it creates slide titles, subtitles, and bulleted lists based on those styles.

Enter Text in the Outline Pane

1. In the Outline pane of Normal view, click to place the insertion point where you want the text to appear.
2. Type the text you want to enter, pressing Enter after each line.

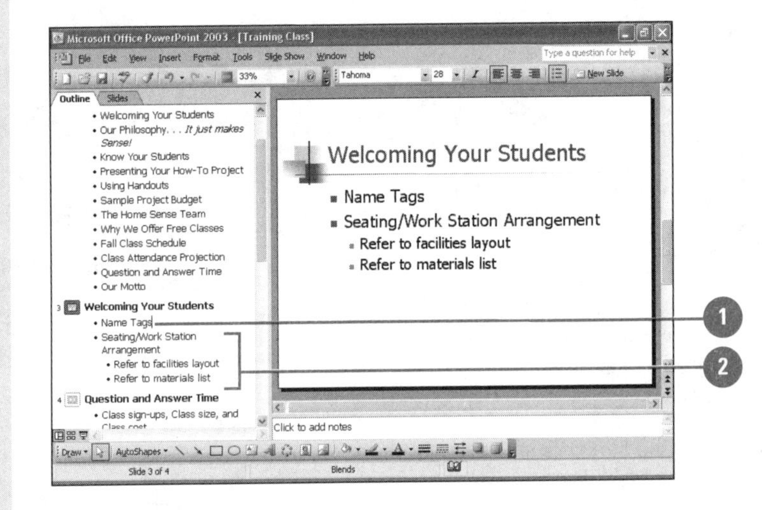

Add a Slide in the Outline Pane

1. In the Outline pane of Normal view, click at the end of the slide text where you want to insert a new slide.
2. Click the New Slide button on the Formatting toolbar and then click a layout.

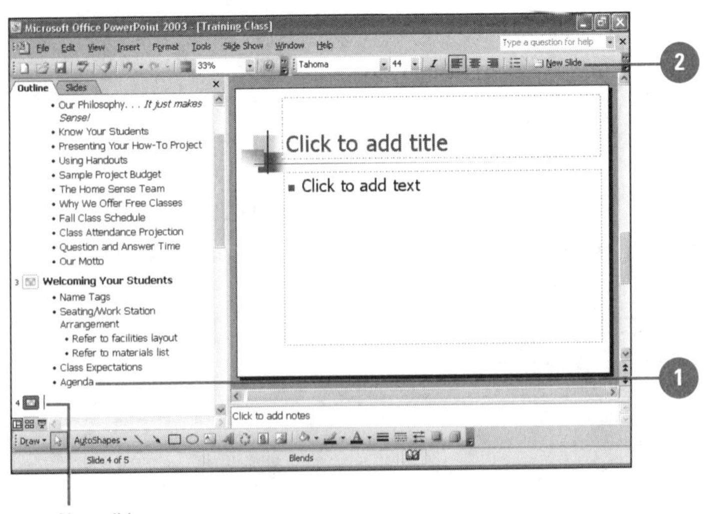

New slide

Did You Know?

You can delete a slide. In the Outline or Slides pane or in Slide Sorter view, select the slide you want to delete. Press Delete, or click the Edit menu, and then click Delete Slide.

Duplicate a Slide

1. In the Outline pane of Normal view, click the slide you want to duplicate.
2. Click the Edit menu, and then click Duplicate.

   The new slide appears directly after the slide duplicated.

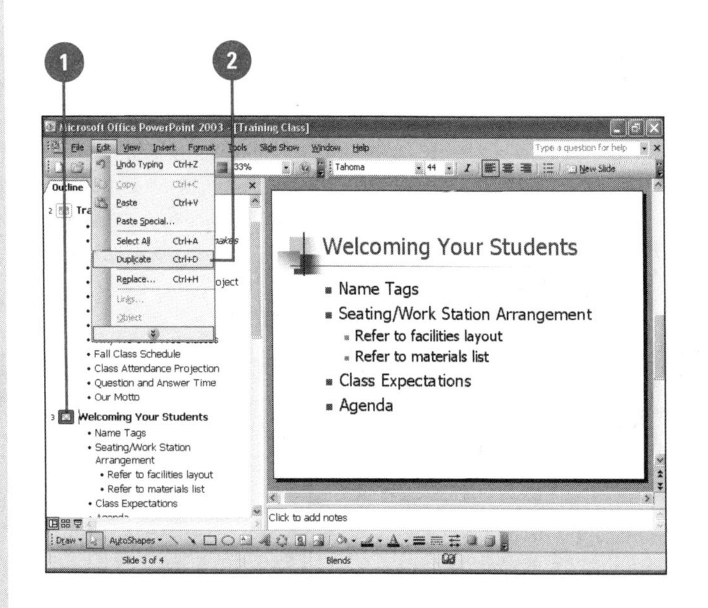

Did You Know?

You can change the display view size. Click the Zoom list arrow on the Standard toolbar, and then select a view size.

Insert an Outline from Another Program

1. In the Outline pane of Normal view, click the slide after which you want to insert an outline.
2. Click the Insert menu, and then click Slides From Outline.
3. Locate and select the file containing the outline you want to insert.
4. Click Insert.

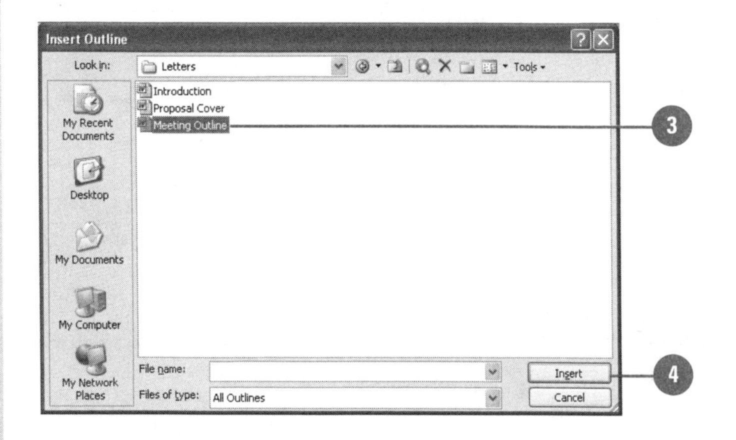

Did You Know?

You can open an outline from another program in PowerPoint. Click the Open button on the Standard toolbar, click the Files Of Type list arrow, click All Outlines, and then double-click the outline file you want to open.

Moving and Indenting Text

PP03S-2-1

Title text is usually the most prominent text object on a slide; next is subtitle text, and then body text, which you can indent or to which you can add bullets. You can indent paragraphs of body text up to five levels using the Promote and Demote buttons on the Formatting toolbar. In an outline, these tools let you demote text from a title, for example, to bulleted text. You can view and change the locations of the indent markers within a text object using the ruler.

Change the Indent Level

1. In Normal view, click the line of text you want to indent.
2. Click the Promote button on the Outlining toolbar to move the line up one level (to the left).
3. Click the Demote button on the Outlining toolbar to move the line down one level (to the right).

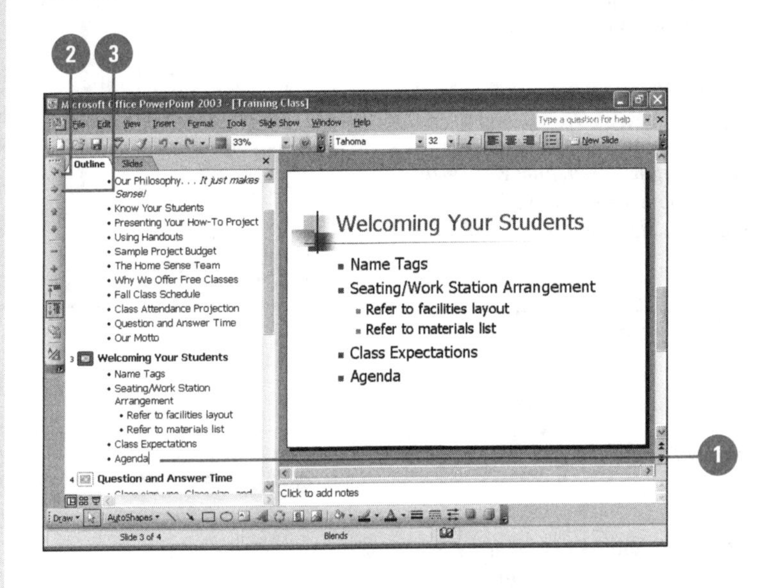

Did You Know?

You can display the Outlining toolbar. If the Outlining toolbar is not visible, right-click a visible toolbar, and then click Outlining.

Display the Ruler

1. In Normal view, click the View menu, and then click Ruler.

   To hide the ruler, click the View menu, and then click Ruler again.

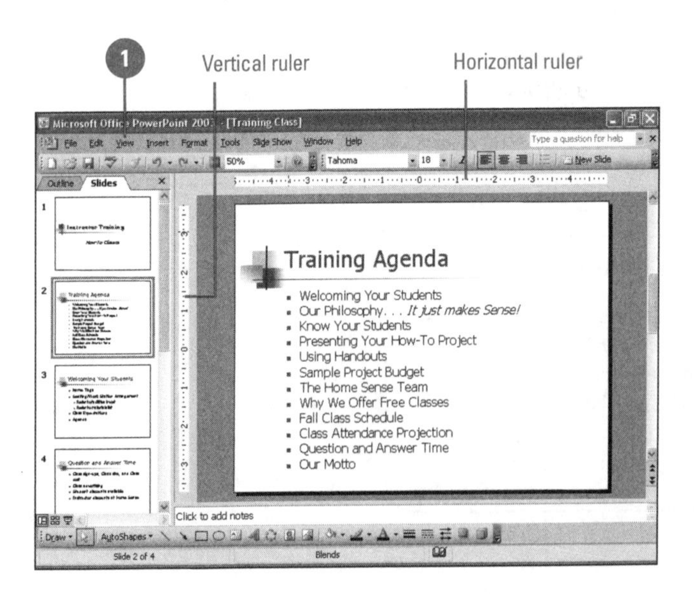

Did You Know?

You can Show or Hide formatting in Outline view. Click the Show Formatting button on the Outlining toolbar to show or hide formatting.

Change the Indent

1. Display the ruler.
2. Select the text for which you want to change the indentation.
3. Change the indent level the way you want.
   - To change the indent for the first line of a paragraph, drag the first-line indent marker.
   - To change the indent for the rest of the paragraph, drag the left indent marker.
   - To change the distance between the indents and the left margin, but maintain the relative distance between the first-line and left indent markers, drag the rectangle below the left indent marker.

Did You Know?

You can use the mouse to promote or demote text. Move the mouse pointer over the bullet you want to promote or demote, and then when it changes to a four-headed arrow, drag the text to the left to promote it or to the right to demote it.

You can operate the Ruler feature. When you select a text object and then view the ruler, the ruler runs the length of just that text object, and the origin (zero point) of the ruler is at the box borders, starting with the upper left. When you select an object other than text, the ruler runs the length of the entire slide, the origin is at the center, and then measurements appear for the entire slide.

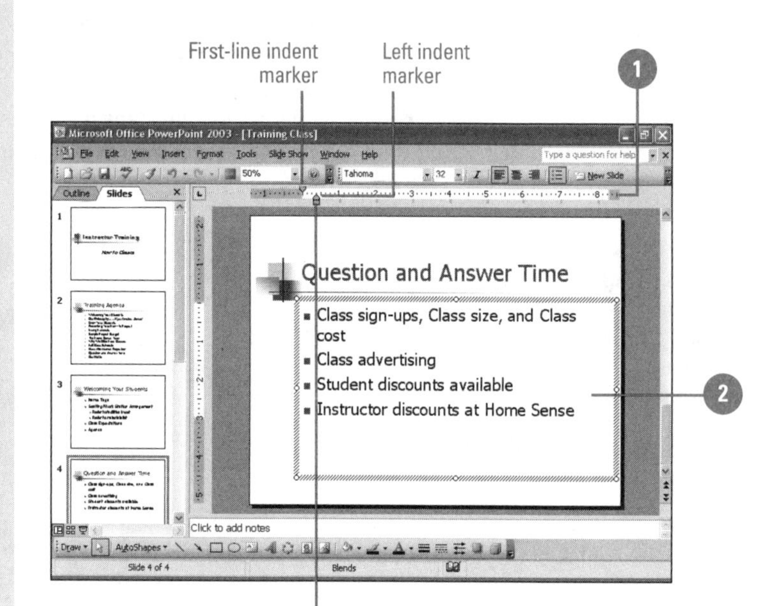

2

Setting Tabs

PowerPoint includes default tab stops at every inch; when you press the Tab key, the text moves to the next tab stop. You can control the location of the tab stops using the ruler. When you set a tab, tab markers appear on the ruler. Tabs apply to an entire paragraph, not a single line within that paragraph. You can also clear a tab by removing it from the ruler.

Set a Tab

1. Click the paragraph or select the paragraphs whose tabs you want to modify. You can also select a text object to change the tabs for all paragraphs in that object.
2. If necessary, click the View menu, and then click Ruler to display the ruler.
3. Click the Tab button at the left of the horizontal ruler until you see the type of tab you want.
4. Click the ruler where you want to set the tab.

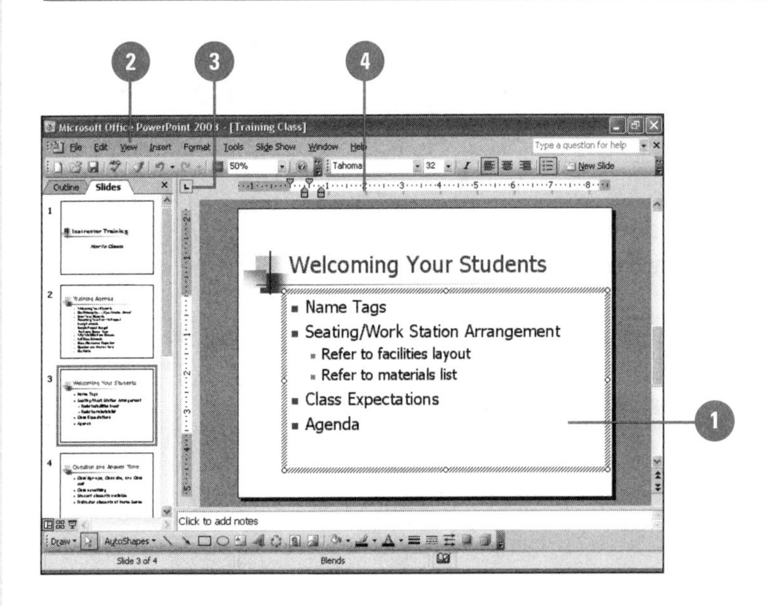

Tab Button Alignments

Tab Button	Aligns Text with
└	Left edge of text
┴	Center of text
┘	Right edge of text
┴.	Decimal points in text

Change the Distance Between Default Tab Stops

1. Select the text object in which you want to change the default tab stops.
2. If necessary, click the View menu, and then click Ruler to display the ruler.
3. Drag any default tab stop marker to a new position.

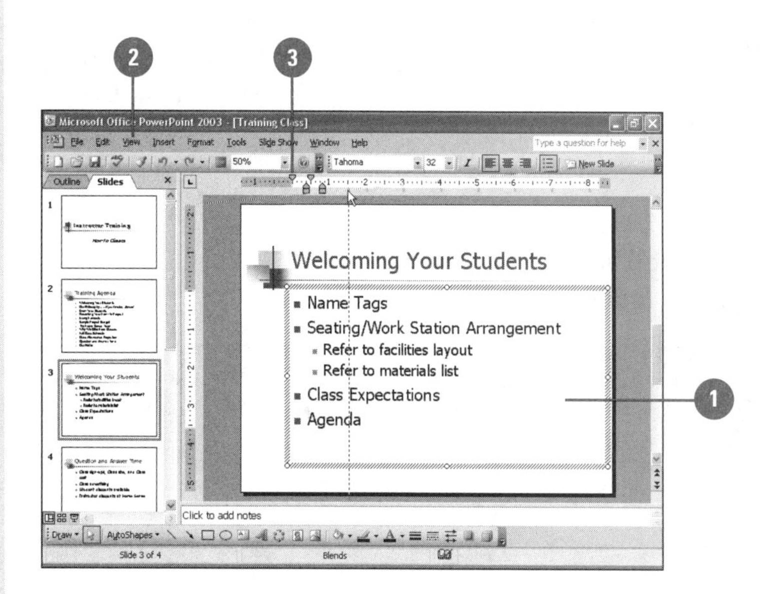

Clear a Tab

1. Drag the tab marker off the ruler.

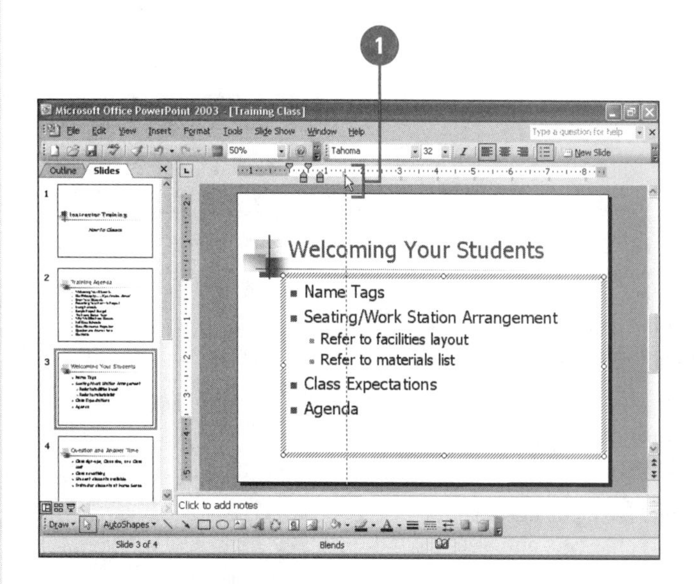

Did You Know?

You must use caution when you change a default tab. When you drag a default tab marker to a new location, the spaces between all the tab markers change proportionally.

Formatting Text

PP03S-2-1

Although PowerPoint's templates provide preformatted styles for text objects, you can change the formatting or add extra emphasis to a word or text object. The four most basic formats you can apply to text are bold, italic, underline, and shadow. Each has its own button on the Formatting toolbar. You can format a single letter, a word, a phrase, or all the text in a text object. You can also align text to make it stand out.

Format Text Using the Formatting Toolbar

1. Select the text you want to format, or click the selection box of a text object to format all the text in the box.
2. Click one or more of the formatting buttons on the Formatting toolbar: Bold, Italic, Underline, or Shadow.

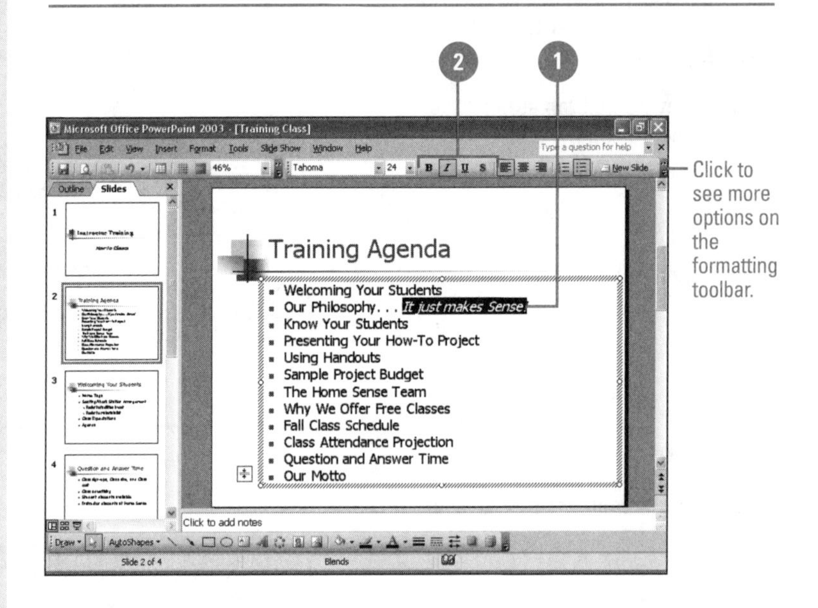

Click to see more options on the formatting toolbar.

Format the Text Font

1. Select the text you want to format, or click the selection box of a text object to format all the text in the box.
2. Click the Format menu, and then click Font.
3. Make any changes you want to the Font, Font Style, and Size.
4. Make any changes you want to the Effects.
5. If you want, click the Color list arrow, and then click a color.
6. Click OK.

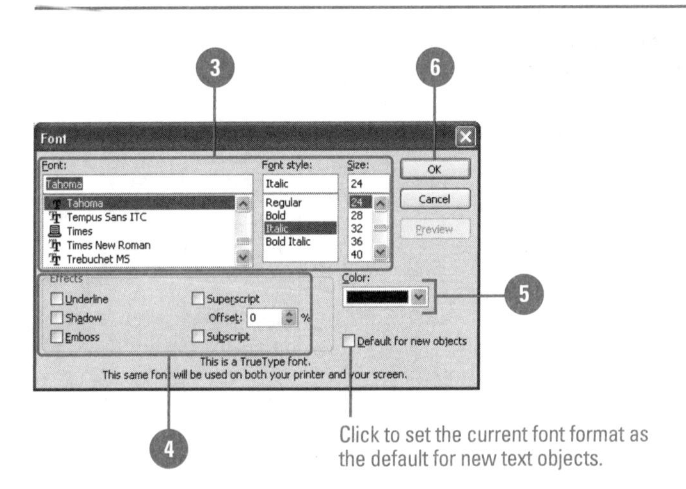

Click to set the current font format as the default for new text objects.

Change the Font Using the Formatting Toolbar

1. Select the text or text object whose font you want to change.
2. Click the Font list arrow on the Formatting toolbar.
3. Click the font you want.
4. Click the Font Size list arrow on the Formatting toolbar.
5. Click the font size you want.

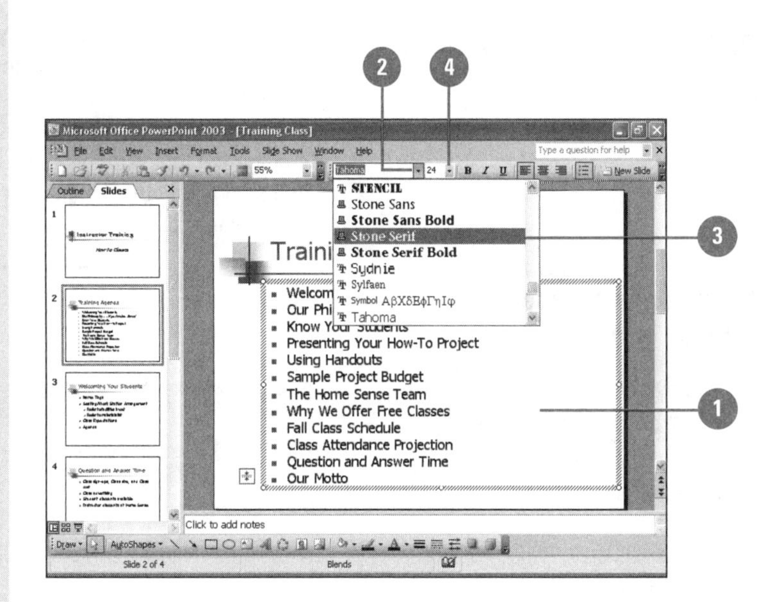

Align Text

1. Select the text or text object you want to align.
2. Click one of the alignment buttons on the Formatting toolbar—Align Left, Center, or Align Right—to align the text to the left margin, center, or right margin of the selection box border, respectively.

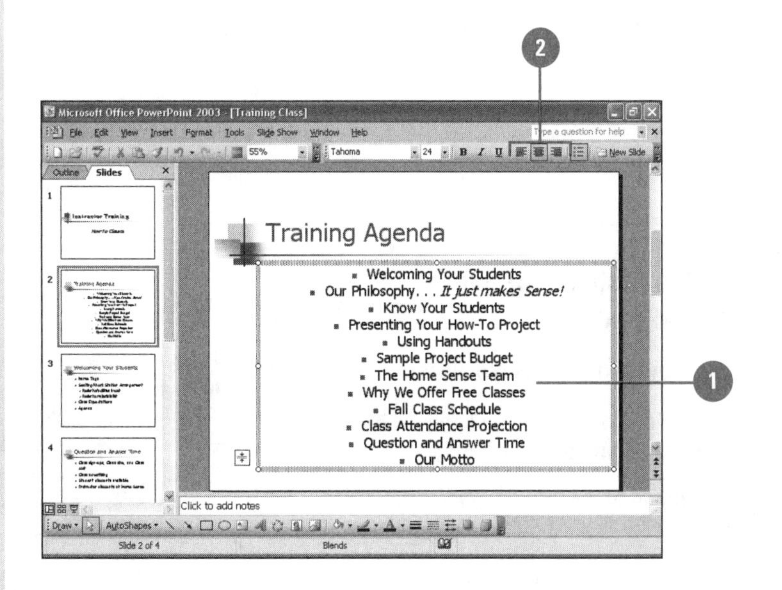

Did You Know?

You can pick up and apply a style using the Format Painter. The Format Painter lets you "pick up" the style of one section of text and apply, or "paint," it to another. Select the word or text object whose format you want to pick up. Click the Format Painter button on the Standard toolbar, and then drag to select the text to which you want to apply the format.

Modifying a Bulleted List

When you create a new slide, you can choose the bulleted list AutoLayout to include a bulleted list placeholder. You can customize the appearance of your bulleted list in several ways. You have control over the appearance of your bullets, their size, and their color. You can change the bullets to numbers or import pictures to use as bullets. You can also adjust the distance between a bullet and its text using the PowerPoint ruler.

Add and Remove Bullets from Text

1. Click anywhere in the paragraph in which you want to add a bullet.
2. Click the Bullets button on the Formatting toolbar.
3. Click anywhere in the paragraph from which you want to remove the bullet.
4. Click the Bullets button on the Formatting toolbar.

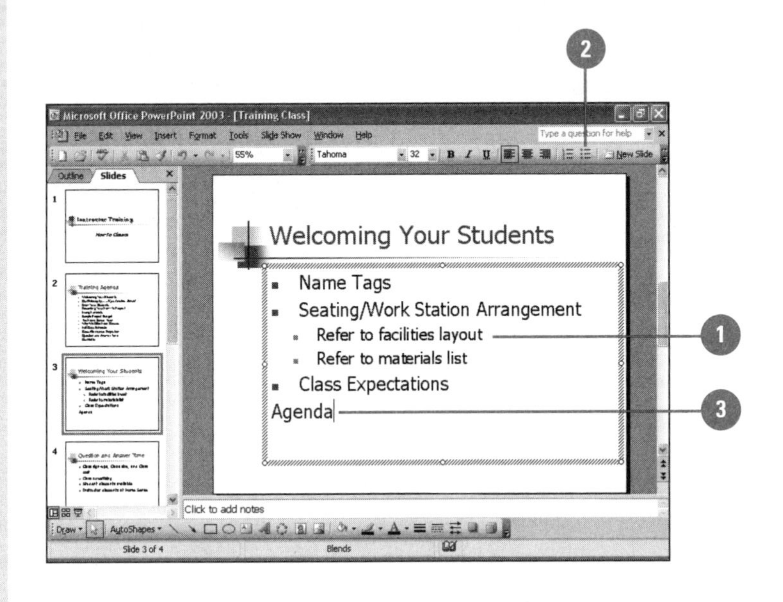

Change the Distance Between Bullets and Text

1. Select the text you want to indent.
2. If the ruler isn't visible, click the View menu, and then click Ruler.
3. Drag the indent markers on the ruler.

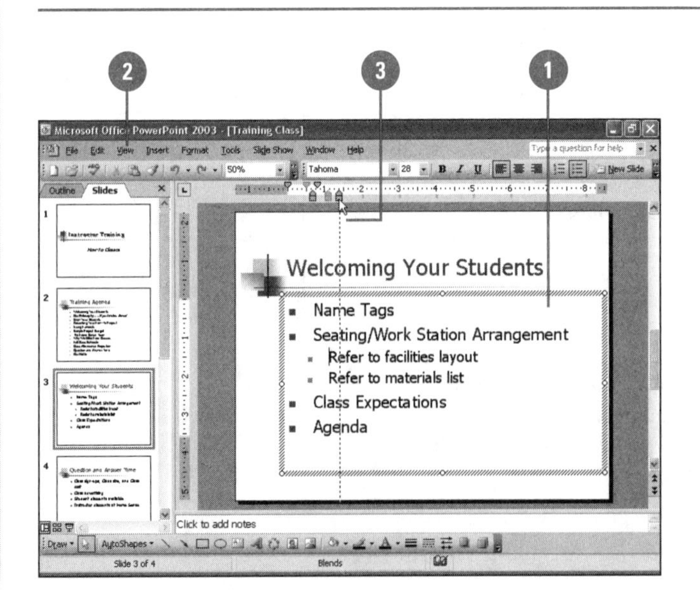

Did You Know?

You can create numbered bullets. To change bullets to numbers, select the bulleted text, and then click the Numbering button on the Formatting toolbar.

Change the Bullet or Number Character

1. Select the text or text object whose bullet character you want to change.
2. Click the Format menu, and then click Bullets And Numbering.
3. Click the Bulleted or Numbered tab.
4. Click one of the predefined styles or do one of the following:
   - Click Customize, and then click the character you want to use for your bullet character.
   - Click Picture, and then click the picture you want to use for your bullet character.
5. To change the bullet or number's color, click the Color list arrow, and then select the color you want.
6. To change the bullet or number's size, enter a percentage in the Size box.
7. Click OK.

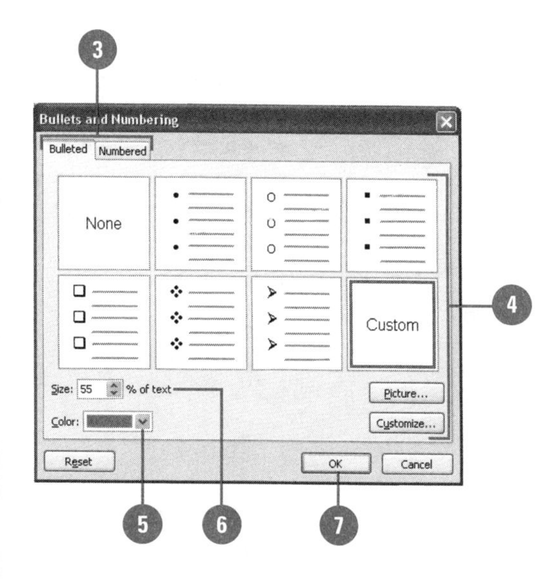

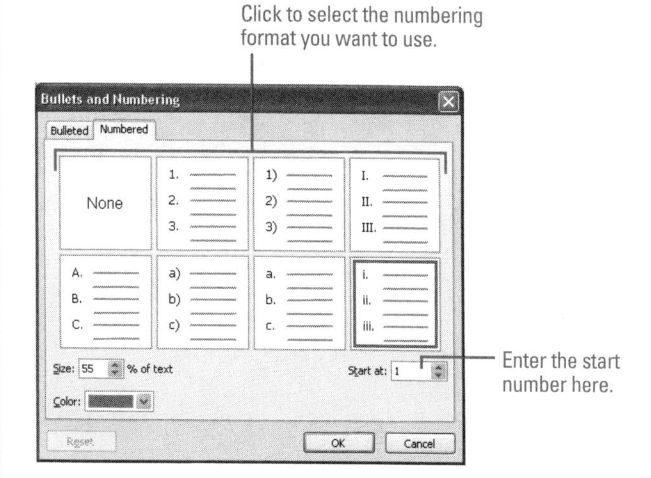

2

AutoFormatting Text and Numbered Lists

PowerPoint recognizes ordinals, fractions, em-dashes and en-dashes, formatted AutoCorrect entries and smart quotes followed by a number, and formats them as you type. For example, if you type 1/2, PowerPoint replaces it with ½. You can also automatically number a list. PowerPoint recognizes your intent; when you enter a number followed by a period and a space, PowerPoint will format the entry and the subsequent entries as a numbered list. If you insert a new line in the middle of the numbered list, PowerPoint automatically adjusts the numbers.

AutoFormat Text as You Type

1. In Normal view, click to place the insertion point in the text where you want to type.
2. Type text you can AutoFormat, such as 1/2, and then press the Spacebar or Enter.

   PowerPoint recognizes this as a fraction and changes it to ½.

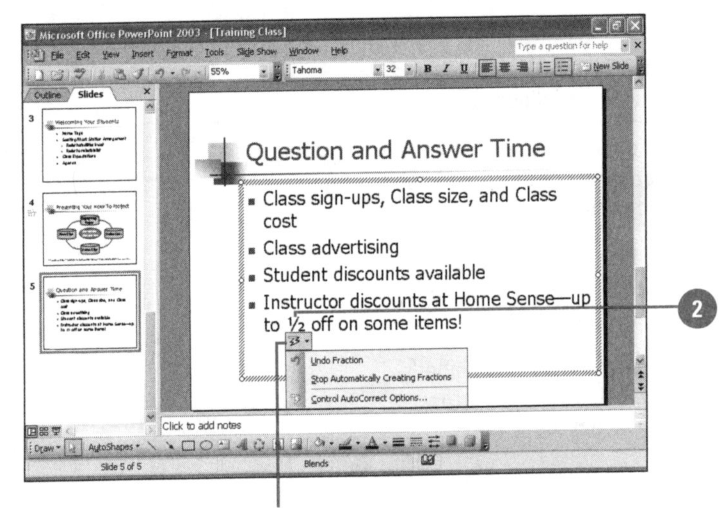

Click to undo automatic fraction or stop automatically creating fractions.

Did You Know?

You can use the AutoCorrect Options button to undo automatic numbering or fractions. Click the AutoCorrect Options button that appears when you begin numbering or type a fraction, and then click Undo Automatic Numbering or Undo Fraction.

AutoNumber a List as You Type

1. In Normal view, click to place the insertion point in the text at the beginning of a blank line where you want to begin a numbered list.
2. Type *1.*, press the Spacebar, type text, and then press Enter.

   PowerPoint recognizes this as a numbered list and displays the next number in the list in gray.
3. Type text, and continue until you complete the list.

Did You Know?

You can select bulleted or numbered text. Position the mouse pointer over the bullet or number next to the text you want to select; when the pointer changes to the four-headed arrow, click the bullet.

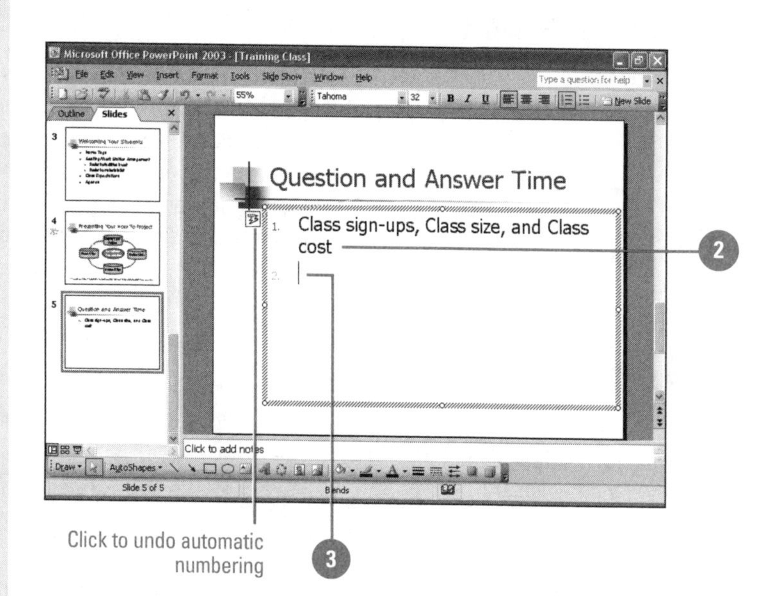

2

Creating a Text Box

Usually you use the title, subtitle, and bulleted list placeholders to place text on a slide. However, when you want to add text outside one of the standard placeholders, such as for an annotation to a slide or chart, you can create a text box. Text boxes appear in all views and panes, except in the Outline pane. Your text box doesn't have to be rectangular—you can also use one of PowerPoint's AutoShapes, a collection of shapes that range from rectangles and circles to arrows and stars. When you place text in an AutoShape, the text becomes part of the AutoShape. You can also orient text in text boxes, table cells, and AutoShapes vertically instead of horizontally.

Create a Text Box

1. In Normal view, click the View menu, point to Toolbars, and then click Drawing if necessary.
2. Click the Text Box button on the Drawing toolbar.
3. To add text that wraps, drag to create a box, and then start typing. To add text that doesn't wrap, click and then start typing.
4. Click outside the selection box to deselect the text box.

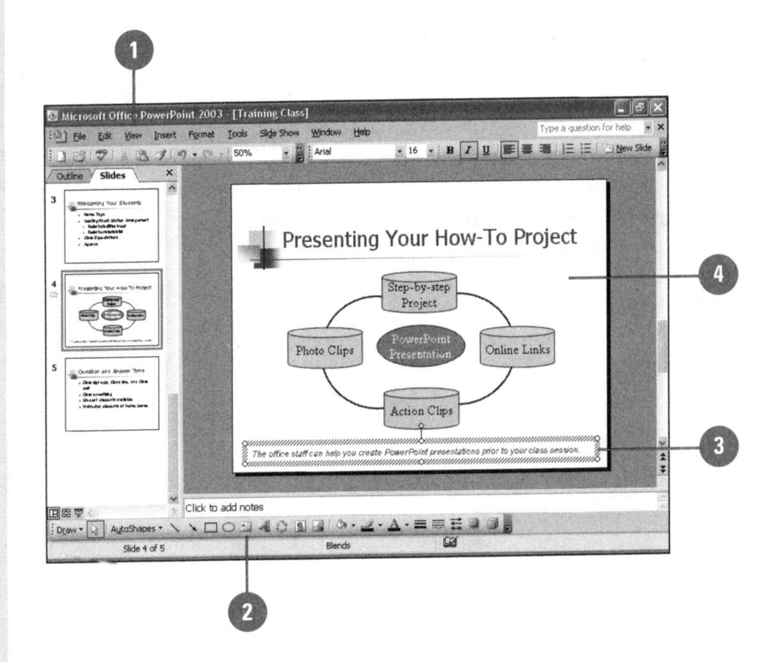

Did You Know?

You can use the sizing handles to adjust text boxes. If you create a text box without word wrapping and then find that the text spills over the edge of your slide, use the sizing handles to resize the text box so it fits on your slide. The text then wraps to the size of the box.

You can edit a text box. Click the text box, and then select the text you want to edit. Edit the text, and then click outside the text box to deselect it.

Add Text to an AutoShape

1. Click the AutoShapes button on the Drawing toolbar.
2. Point to the shape category you want to use.
3. Click the shape you want.
4. Drag to draw the shape on your slide.
5. Type your text.

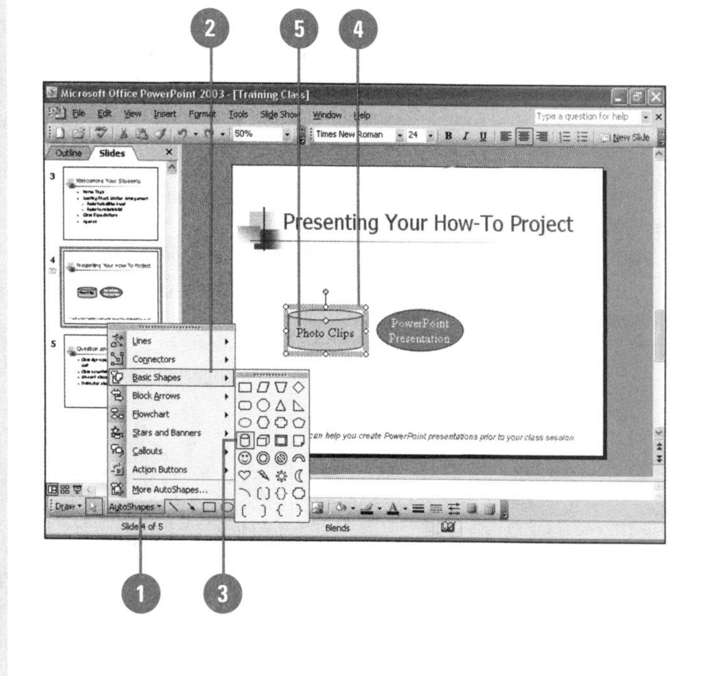

Change Text Orientation

1. In Normal view, select the text box, AutoShape, or table cell you want to change.
2. Click the Format menu, and then click Text Box, AutoShape, or Table.
3. Click the Text Box tab.
4. To change orientation, select the Rotate Text Within AutoShape By 90° check box.
5. To change the way text appears in a shape, select the Word Wrap Text In AutoShape check box or the Resize AutoShape To Fit Text check box.
6. Click OK.

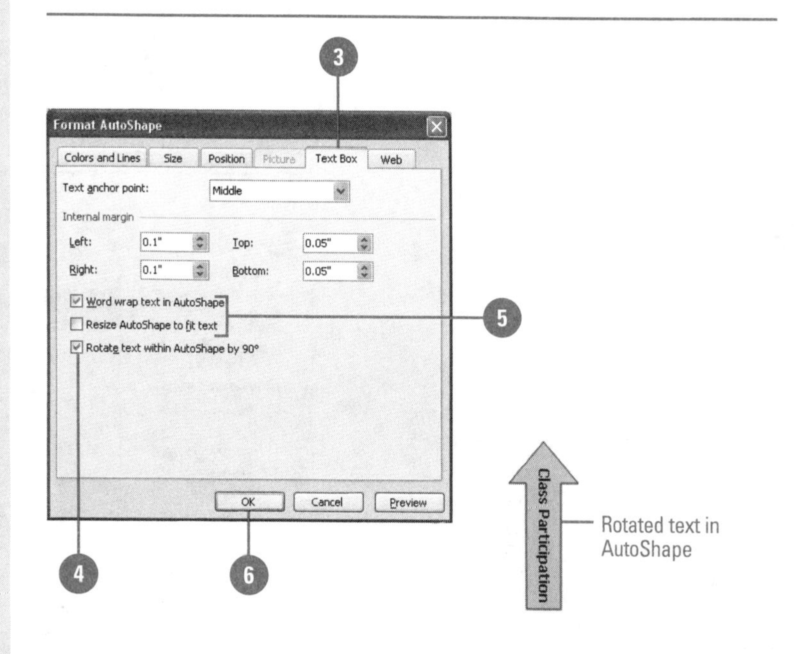

Rearranging Slides

PP03S-4-1

You can instantly rearrange slides in Outline or Slides pane or in Slide Sorter view. You can use the drag-and-drop method or the Cut and Paste buttons to move slides to a new location. In Outline pane of Normal view, you can use the Move Up and Move Down buttons to move selected slides within the outline. You can also collapse the outline to its major points so you can more easily see its structure.

Rearrange a Slide in Slide Pane or Slide Sorter View

1. Click Slides pane in Normal view or click the Slide Sorter View button.
2. Select the slide(s) you want to move.
3. Drag the selected slide to a new location. A vertical bar appears where the slide(s) will be moved when you release the mouse button.

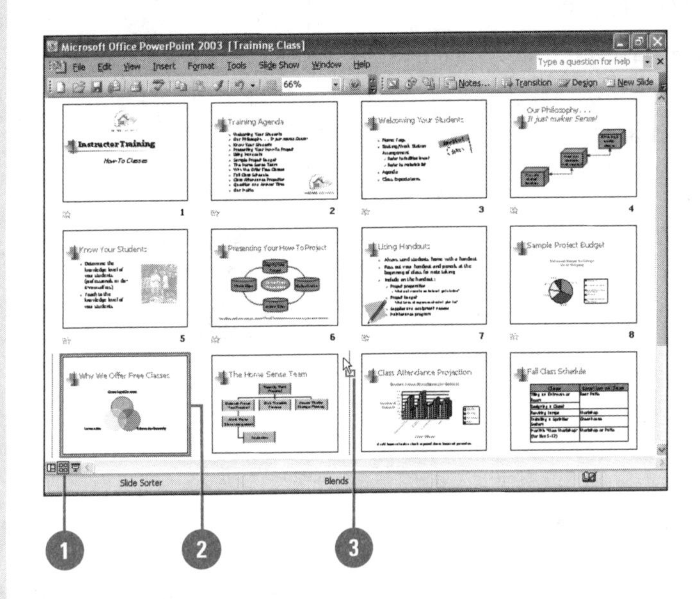

Rearrange a Slide in the Outline Pane

1. In the Outline pane in Normal view, click the slide icon you want to move.

   TIMESAVER *Drag the slide up or down to move it in Outline pane.*

2. If necessary, click the View menu, point to Toolbars, and then click Outlining to display the Outlining toolbar.
3. Click the Move Up button, or click the Move Down button.

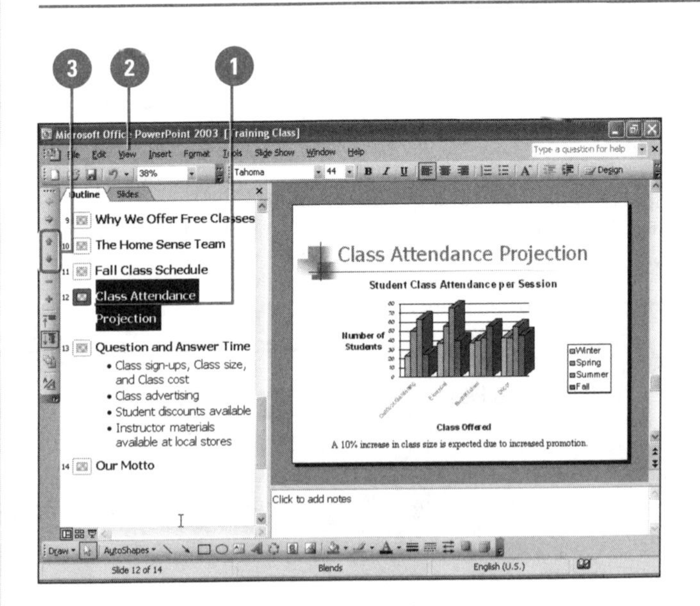

Move a Slide Using Cut and Paste

1. In the Outline or Slides pane or in Slide Sorter view, select the slide(s) you want to move.
2. Click the Cut button on the Standard toolbar.

   The Clipboard task pane might open, displaying items you have cut or copied.
3. Click the new location.
4. Click the Paste button on the Standard toolbar.

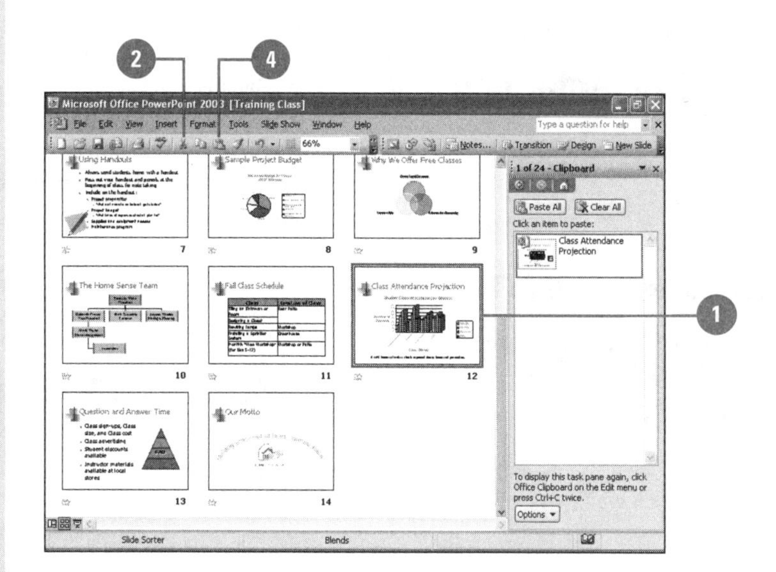

Collapse and Expand Slides in the Outline Pane

1. In the Outline pane in Normal view, select the slide you want to work with, and then click the button you want.
   - To collapse the selected slides, click the Collapse button.

     A horizontal line appears below a collapsed slide in Outline view.
   - To expand the selected slides, click the Expand button.
   - To collapse all slides, click the Collapse All button.
   - To expand all slides, click the Expand All button.

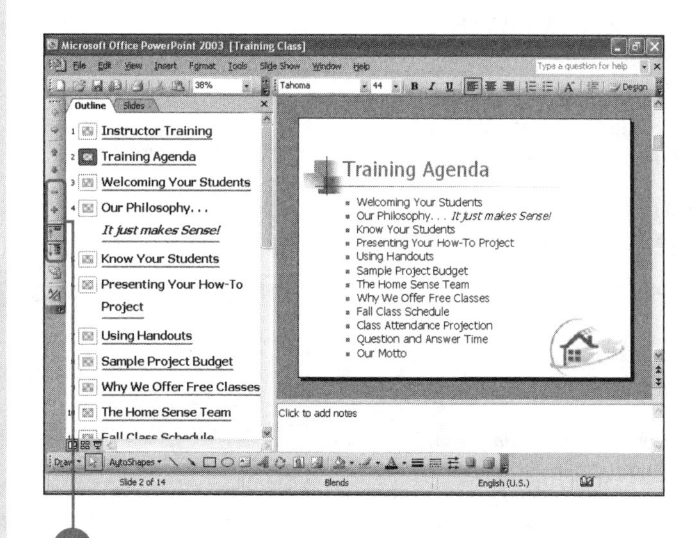

Using Slides from Other Presentations

PP03S-4-1

To insert slides from other presentations in a slide show, you can open the presentation and copy and paste the slides you want, or you can use the Slide Finder feature. With Slide Finder, you don't have to open the presentation first; instead, you can view a miniature of each slide in a presentation and then insert only the ones you select. With Slide Finder, you can also create a list of favorite presentations you can use as source material for future slide shows.

Insert Slides from Slide Finder

1. Click the Insert menu, and then click Slides From Files.
2. Click the Find Presentation tab.
3. Click Browse, locate and select the file you want, and then click Open.
4. Select the slides you want to insert.
   - To insert just one slide, click the slide, and then click Insert.
   - To insert multiple slides, click each slide you want to insert, and then click Insert.
   - To insert all the slides in the presentation, click Insert All.
5. Click Close.

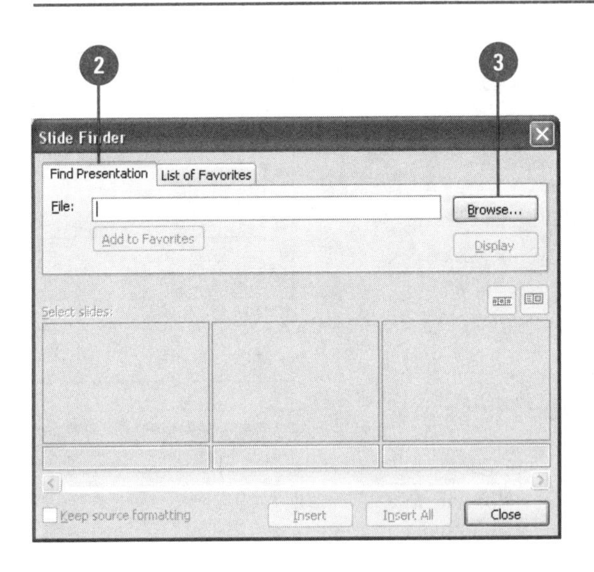

Click to display only the slide miniatures.

Click to display only the slide titles.

Slide Finder

Find Presentation | List of Favorites

File: tor\My Documents\Home Sense\Presentations\Gardening.ppt

Browse... Add to Favorites Display

Select slides:

4. Know your Students | 5. Using Available Resources | 6. Providing Key Information

Keep source formatting | Insert | Insert All | Close

4

5

Did You Know?

You can add or remove a slide presentation from your list of favorites. Click the Insert menu, click Slides From Files, locate the presentation you want to add, click Add To Favorites, and then click OK. Click the List Of Favorites tab, select the presentation you want to remove, and then click Remove.

Designing a Look

3

Introduction

As you develop your presentation, an important element needs to be considered: the look of your slides. The design of your presentation is just as important as the information that it contains. A poorly designed presentation, without the eye-catching design elements will lose your audience, and then what your presentation has to say won't really matter.

Microsoft Office PowerPoint 2003 has professionally designed templates available to you. To make your presentation consistent, masters are available. Masters are templates that contain all of the properties of your PowerPoint presentation—background color, text font style and color, date and time, and graphic placement, are all examples of properties that will be placed on each of your slides. Using the Title and Slide Masters, you can set up your presentation to have the dynamic details that will make your slide show a success.

Besides the text and graphics that you place on your slides, another important part of a presentation is the use of color. Color schemes are used throughout your PowerPoint slides—the background, text, graphics, shapes, and shadows. All of the colors need to work together. Not everyone has an eye for color, and pulling it all together can be daunting. PowerPoint uses eight preset colors that are included in color schemes to help you design your presentation faster. You can add other custom colors to your scheme using hues, saturation, and luminosity.

Once you've set up your masters to be exactly the way you want them, you can save it as a new master. Company specific styles, graphics such as logos, colors schemes and other elements, can now become a new template to be used with other presentations in the future.

What You'll Do

Apply a Design Template

Make Your Presentation Look Consistent

View Masters

Control Slide Appearance with Masters

Control a Slide Background with Masters

Insert the Date, Time, and Slide Numbers

Add a Header and Footer

Understand Color Schemes

View and Choose a Color Scheme

Create a Color Scheme

Add Colors to a Presentation

Add and Modify a Slide Background

Save a Template

Applying a Design Template

PP03S-2-3

PowerPoint design templates feature customized color schemes, slide and title masters, and fonts that come together to create a particular impression. You can apply a design template to a presentation at any time—even if you created the presentation with a different template. When you apply a design template to a presentation, the masters and color scheme of the new template replace the original ones. You can conveniently view design templates in the Slide Design task pane.

Apply a Design Template

1. Click the Format menu, and then click Slide Design to open the Slide Design task pane.
2. Locate and click the design template you want to apply.

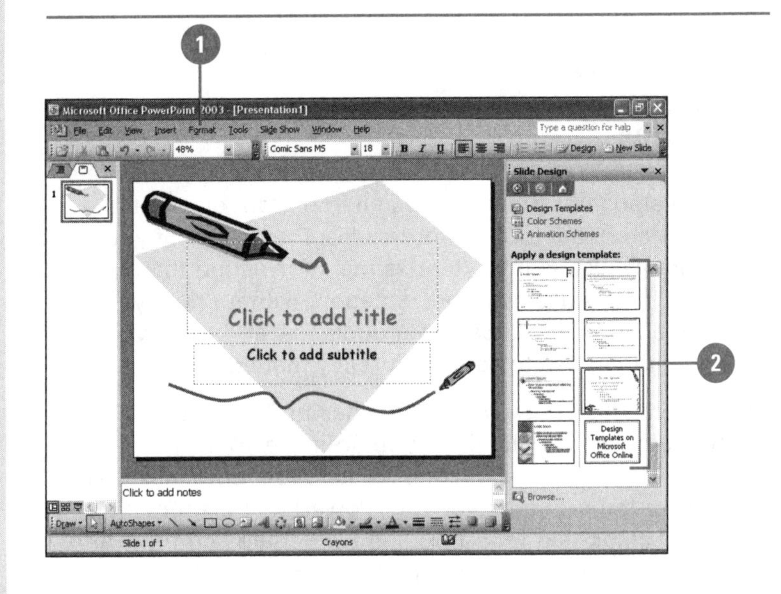

Did You Know?

You can use a toolbar button to apply a design template. Click the Slide Design button on the Formatting toolbar, click Design Templates if necessary, and then click the template you want.

Apply a Design from an Existing Presentation

1. Click the Format menu, and then click Slide Design to open the Slide Design task pane.
2. At the bottom of the Slide Design task pane, click Browse to open the Apply Design Template dialog box.
3. Click the Files Of Type list arrow, and then click Presentations And Shows.
4. Locate and select the presentation whose design you want to apply.
5. Click Apply.

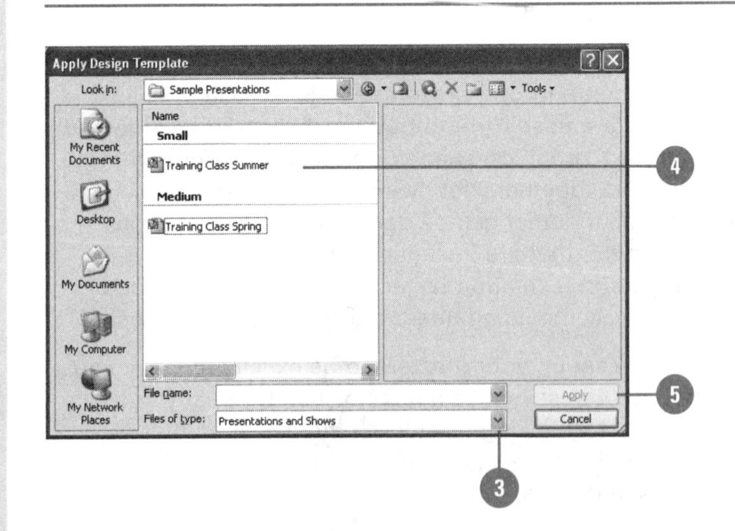

Making Your Presentation Look Consistent

PP03S-2-7

PowerPoint comes with two special slides called masters–Slide Master and Title Master. The Slide Master and Title Master for a template are called a slide-title master pair. You can create more than one Slide Master or Title Master within a presentation. This is useful for creating separate sections within the same presentation. To create multiple masters in a presentation, you can insert a new Slide Master and Title Master in a presentation or apply more than one template to your presentation.

The **Slide Master** controls the properties of every slide in the presentation. All of the characteristics of the Slide Master (background color, text color, font, and font size) appear on every slide in the presentation. When you make a change on the Slide Master, the change affects every slide. For example, if you want to include your company logo, other artwork, or the date on every slide, you can place it on the Slide Master. The Slide Master contains master placeholders for title text, paragraph text, date and time, footer information, and slide numbers. The master title and text placeholders control the text format for every slide in a presentation. If you want to make a change throughout your presentation, you need to change each slide master or pair of masters. For example, when you change the master title text format to italic, the title on each slide changes to italic to follow the master. If, for a particular slide, you want to override the default settings on the Slide Master, you can use the commands on the Format menu. For example, if you want to omit background graphics on a slide, you can use that option in the Background dialog box for the selected slide.

The title slide has its own master, called the **Title Master**. Changes that you make to the Title Master affect only the title slide of the presentation. Like the Slide Master, the Title Master contains placeholders. The main difference between the Slide Master and the Title Master is the Title Master's use of a master subtitle style instead of the master text style. The Slide Master and Title Master appear together in Slide Master view. You can select either master as a slide miniature in Slide Master view to make changes to it. When you view a master, the Master toolbar appears. This toolbar contains the Close Master View button, which returns you to the view you were in before you opened the Master. The Master toolbar also contains several buttons to insert, delete, rename, duplicate, and preserve masters. When you preserve a master, you protect it from being deleted.

Each master contains placeholders. Background objects, such as text and graphics that are entered into placeholders will appear on every page associated with that master. Examples of objects that you may want to include are your company name, logo, or product name. You can modify and arrange placeholders on all of the master views for the date and time, footers, and slide numbers, all of which appear on the Slide Master in the default position. You can also customize the position of the placeholders. PowerPoint also comes with a Handout Master and a Notes Master, where you can add text and graphics.

Viewing Masters

If you want to change the appearance of each instance of a slide element, such as all the title fonts or all the bullet characters, you don't have to change every slide individually. Instead, you can change them all at once using a **Master**. PowerPoint updates the existing slides, and then applies your settings to any slides you add. Which master you open depends on what part of your presentation you want to change. The **Slide Master** controls all slides that do not use the Title Slide AutoLayout, while the **Title Master** controls the look of your title slide.

View the Slide Master

1. Click the View menu, point to Master, and then click Slide Master.
2. Click the Close Master View button on the Slide Master View toolbar.

TIMESAVER *You can view a master quickly. Press and hold the Shift key, point to a view button to determine the master, and then click a view button to go to a master view.*

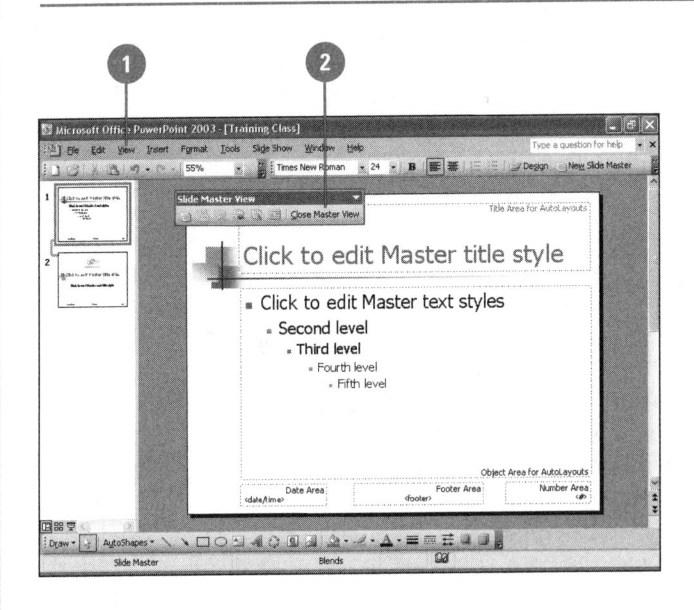

View the Title Master

1. Click the View menu, point to Master, and then click Slide Master.
2. Click the slide miniature of the Title Master.
3. Click the Close Master View button on the Slide Master VIew toolbar.

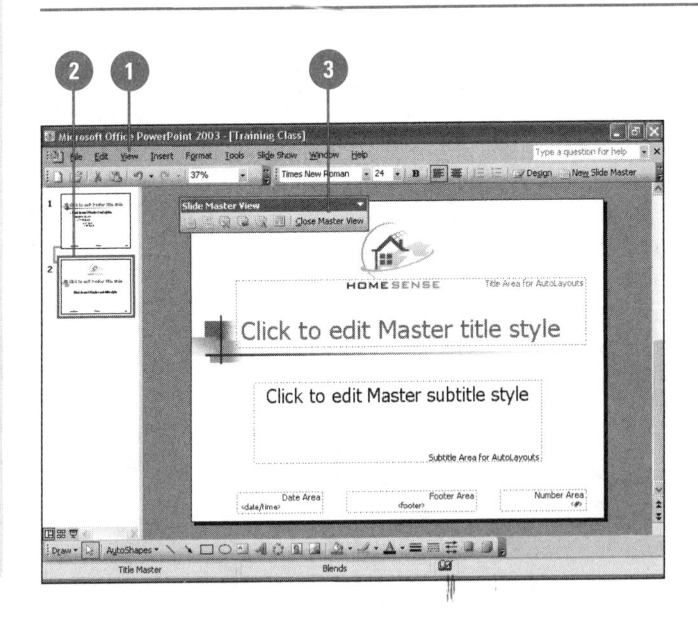

View the Notes Master

1. Click the View menu, point to Master, and then click Notes Master.

   The Notes Master controls the look of your notes pages.

2. Click the Close Master View button on the Notes Master View toolbar.

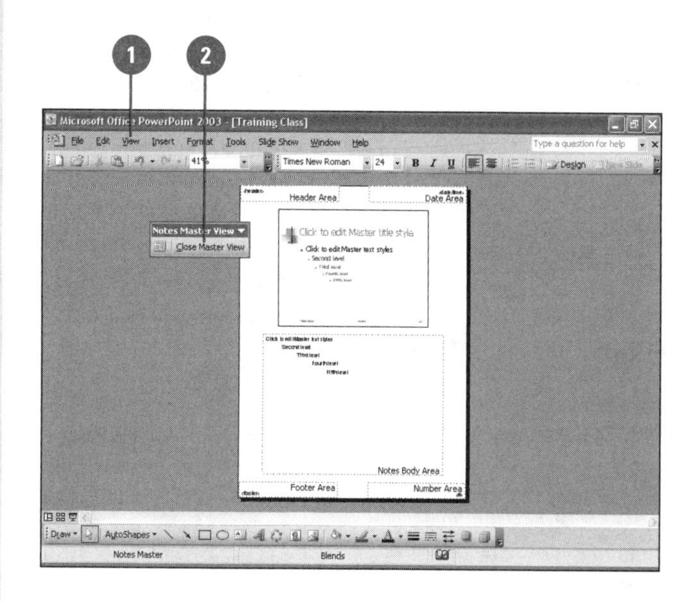

View the Handout Master

1. Click the View menu, point to Master, and then click Handout Master.

   The Handout Master controls the look of your handouts.

2. Click the button on the Handout Master View toolbar with the number of slides you want on your handout pages: one, two, three, four, six, or nine.

3. Click the Show Positioning Of Outline button to set how the outline appears.

4. Click the Close Master View button on the Handout Master View toolbar.

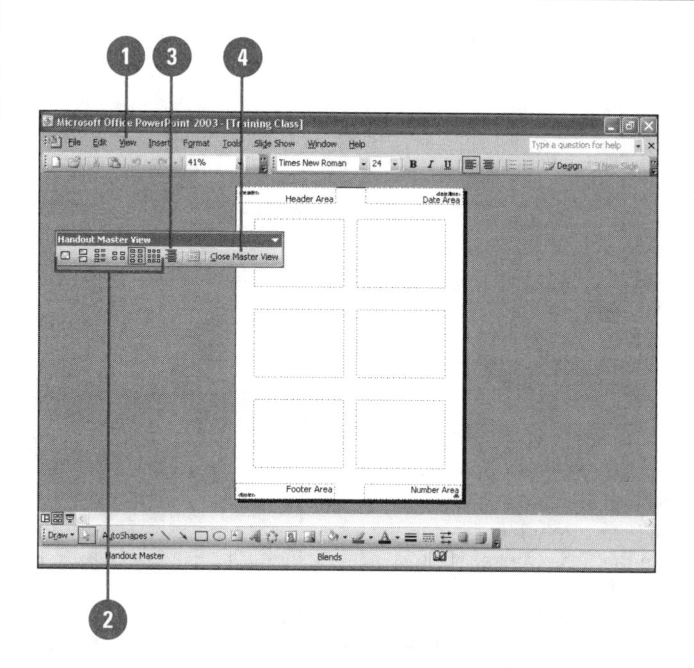

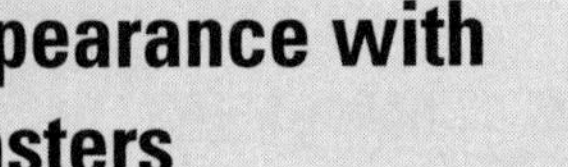

Controlling Slide Appearance with Masters

PP03S-2-7

If you want an object, such as a company logo or clip art, to appear on every slide in your presentation (except the title slide), place it on the **Slide Master**. All of the characteristics of the Slide Master (background color, text color, font, and font size) appear on every slide. The title slide has its own master, called the **Title Master**. You can also create unique slides that don't follow the format of the masters or apply a design template to a master. The Slide Master View toolbar contains several buttons to insert, delete, rename, duplicate, and preserve masters. When you preserve a master, you protect it from being deleted.

Include an Object on Every Slide

1. Click the View menu, point to Master, and then click Slide Master.

   TIMESAVER *Press and hold Shift, and then click the Normal view button to view the Slide Master.*

2. Add the object you want, and then modify its size and placement.
3. Click the Close Master View button on the Slide Master View toolbar.

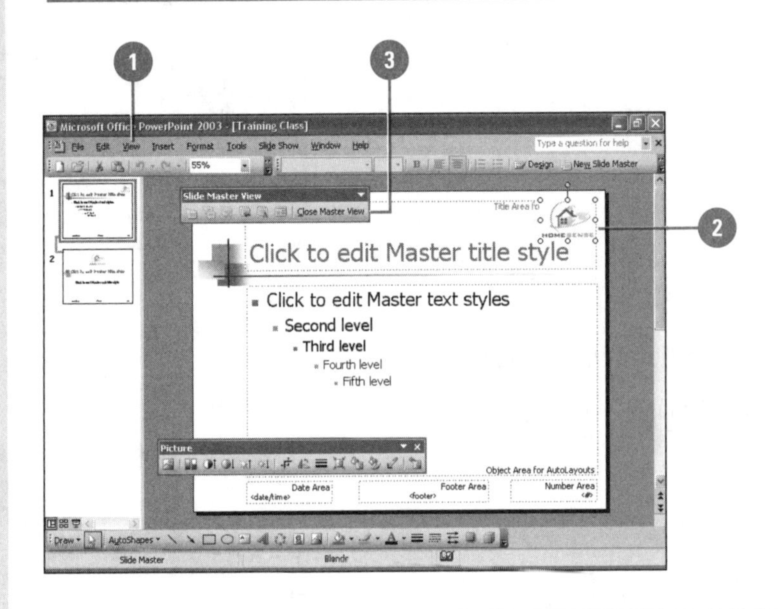

Insert a New Master

1. Click the View menu, point to Master, and then click Slide Master.
2. To insert a new master, click the Insert New Slide Master button, or click the Insert New Title Master button on the Slide Master View toolbar.
3. Click the Close Master View button on the Slide Master View toolbar.

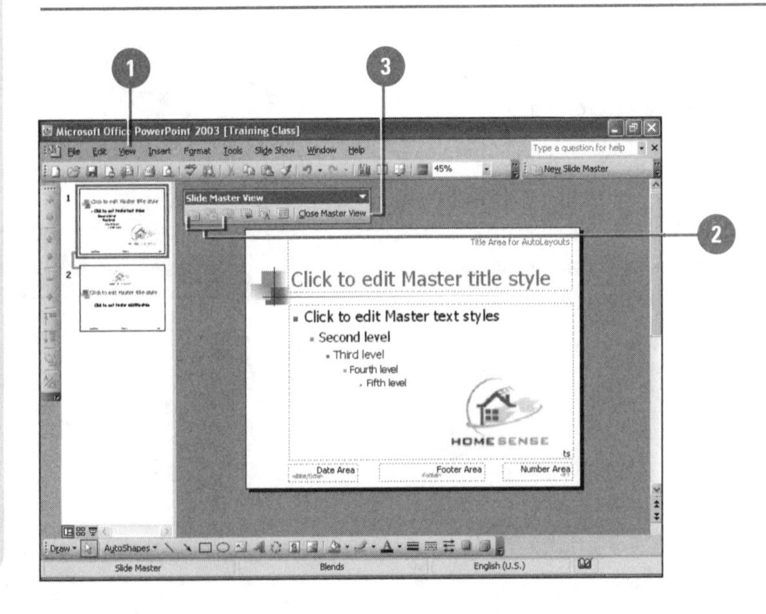

Apply a Design Template to a Master

1. Click the View menu, point to Master, and then click Slide Master.
2. Select the master slide you want to apply a design.
3. Click the Slide Design button on the Formatting toolbar.
4. Point to the design you want, click the list arrow, and then click Replace Selected Designs.
5. Click the Close Master View button on the Slide Master View toolbar.

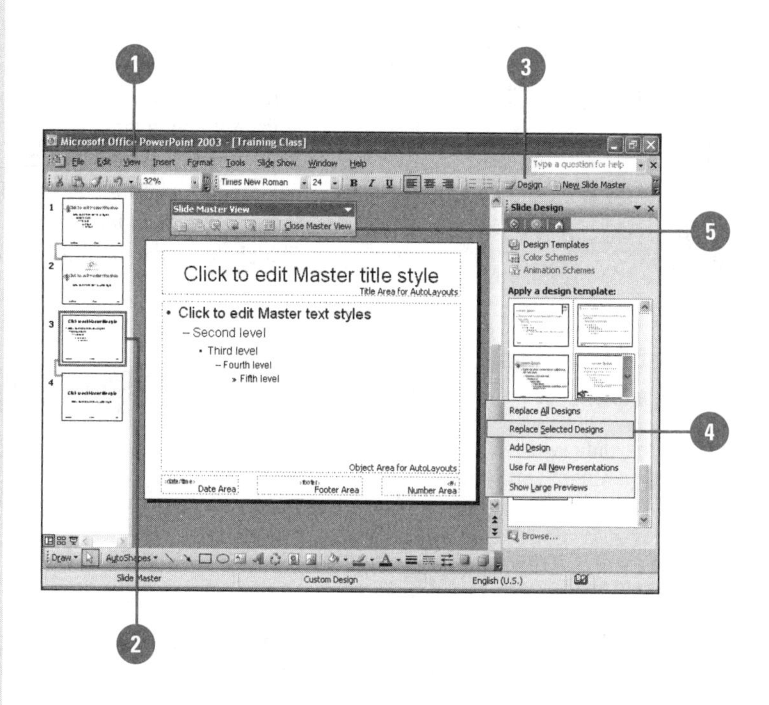

Preserve a Master

1. Click the View menu, point to Master, and then click Slide Master.
2. Click the master that you want to preserve.
3. To lock a master, click the Preserve Master button on the Slide Master View toolbar.

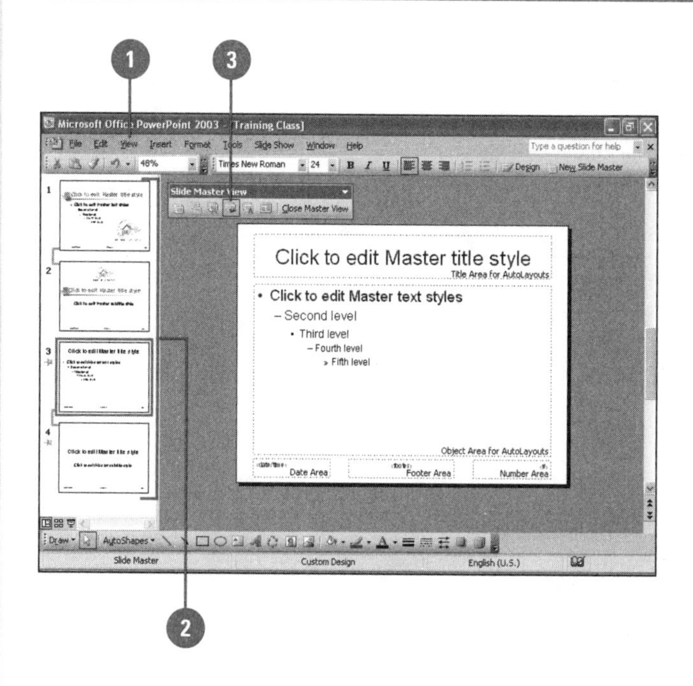

Controlling a Slide Background with Masters

PP03S-2-7

You may want to place an object onto most slides, but not every slide. Placing the object on the Slide Master saves you time. Once an object is placed on the Slide Master, you can hide the object in any slide you want. You can even choose to hide the object on every slide if needed. Each master contains placeholders. You can modify and arrange placeholders for the date and time, footers, and slide numbers. You can also format a placeholder using the formatting tools on the Formatting toolbar. Placeholders can be removed or added back in from the Master Layout dialog box.

Hide Master Background Objects on a Slide

1. Display the slide whose background object you want to hide.
2. Click the Format menu, and then click Background.
3. Select the Omit Background Graphics From Master check box.
4. Click Apply.

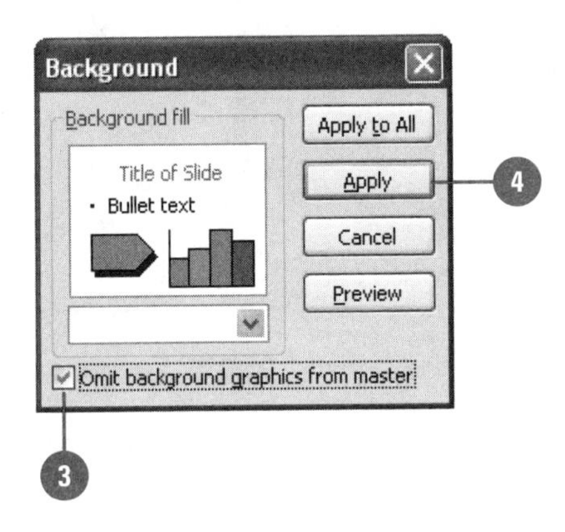

Did You Know?

You can make changes to more than one slide. If you change a slide and want the change to apply to all slides, click Apply To All instead of Apply.

Modify Placeholders

1. Click the View menu, point to Master, and then click Slide Master.
2. Select the master slide with the placeholder you want to change.
3. Select the placeholder you want to change.
4. To format the placeholder, use the formatting tools on the Formatting toolbar.
5. To delete the placeholder, press the Delete key.
6. To add placeholders, click the Master Layout button on the Slide Master View toolbar, select the check boxes with the placeholders you want to add, and then click OK.
7. Click the Close Master View button on the Slide Master View toolbar.

Did You Know?

You can change the master layout. In any Master view, click the Master Layout button on the Master View toolbar, click the check boxes for the options you want, and then click OK. You cannot deselect placeholders in this option box.

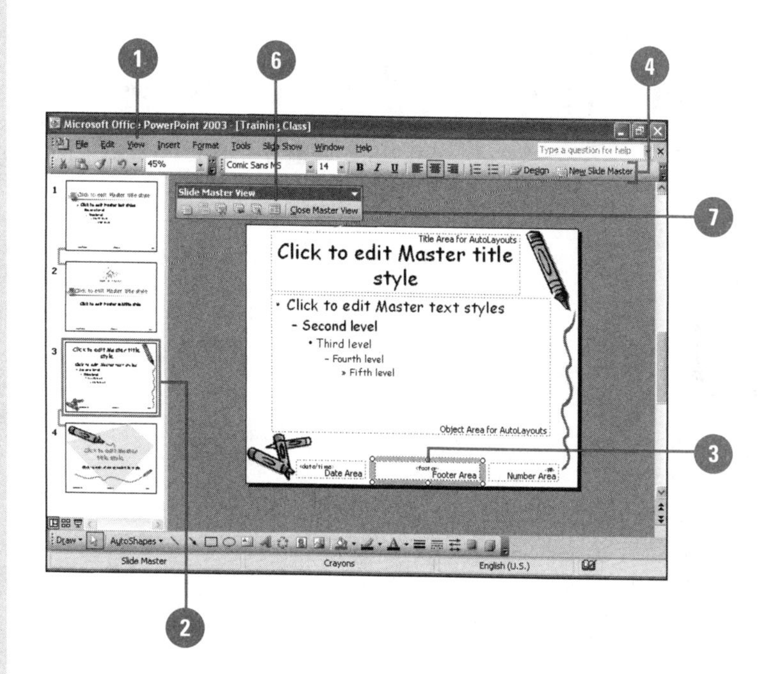

3

Inserting the Date, Time, and Slide Numbers

You can insert the date, the time, and slide numbers into the text of your presentation. For example, you might want today's date to appear in a stock market quote. Dates and times come in two formats: as a field or as text. If you insert the date as a field, PowerPoint inserts a code for the date and then every time you open the presentation, it automatically updates the date from your computer's clock. If you insert the date as text, the date remains the same until you change it. When you insert slide numbers, PowerPoint keeps track of your slide numbers for you. You can even start numbering with a number other than one. This is useful when your slides are a part of a larger presentation.

Insert the Date and Time

1. Click to place the insertion point in the text object where you want to insert the date or time.
2. Click the Insert menu, and then click Date And Time.
3. Click the date or time format you want.
4. Click Apply to apply your selections to the current slide, or click Apply To All to apply the selections to all slides.

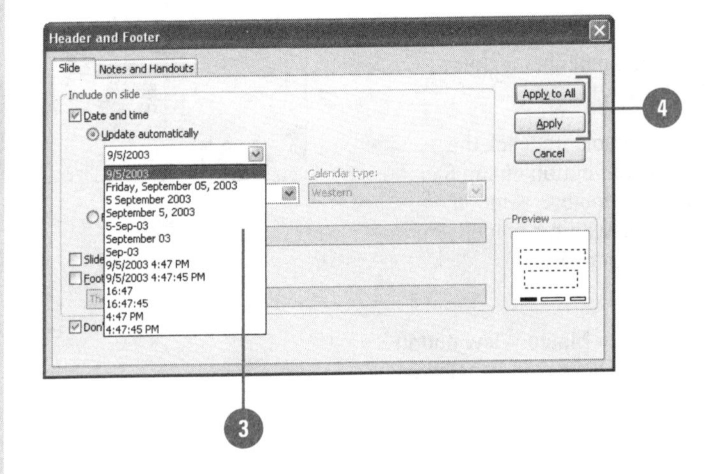

Insert Slide Numbering

1. Click to place the insertion point in the text object where you want to insert the current slide number.
2. Click the Insert menu, and then click Slide Number.
3. Select the Slide Number check box.
4. Click Apply to apply your selections to the current slide, or click Apply To All to apply the selections to all slides.

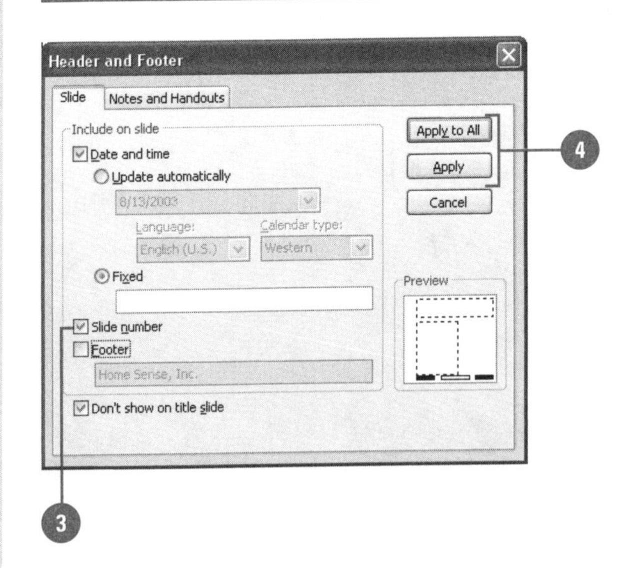

Start Numbering with a Different Number

1. Insert the slide number if you need one on the slide or slide master.
2. Click the File menu, and then click Page Setup.
3. Click the Number Slides From up or down arrow to set the number you want.
4. Click OK.

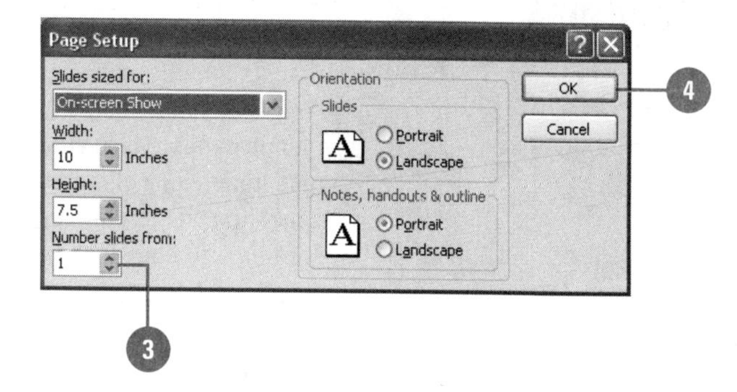

See Also

See "Adding a Header and Footer" on page 76 for information on adding the page number to a slide.

3

Adding a Header and Footer

PP03S-2-7

Headers and footers appear on every slide. You can choose to not have them appear on the title slide. They often include information such as the presentation title, slide number, date, and name of the presenter. Use the masters to place header and footer information on your slides, handouts, or notes pages. Make sure your header and footer don't make your presentation look cluttered. Their default font size is usually small enough to minimize distraction, but you can experiment by changing their font size and placement to make sure.

Add a Header and Footer

1. Click the View menu, and then click Header And Footer.
2. Click the Slide or Notes And Handouts tab.
3. Enter or select the information you want to include on your slide or your notes and handouts.
4. Click Apply to apply your selections to the current slide (if available), or click Apply To All to apply the selections to all slides.

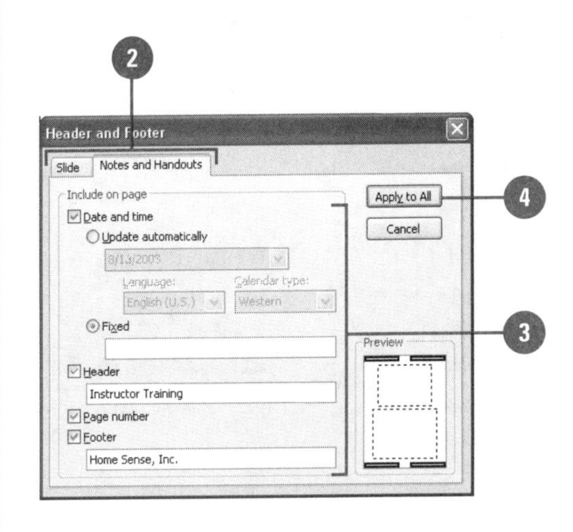

Change the Look of a Header or Footer

1. Click the View menu, and then point to Master.
2. Click the master you want to change.
3. Make the necessary changes to the header and footer. You can move or resize them or change their text attributes.
4. Click the Close Master View button on the Slide Master View toolbar.

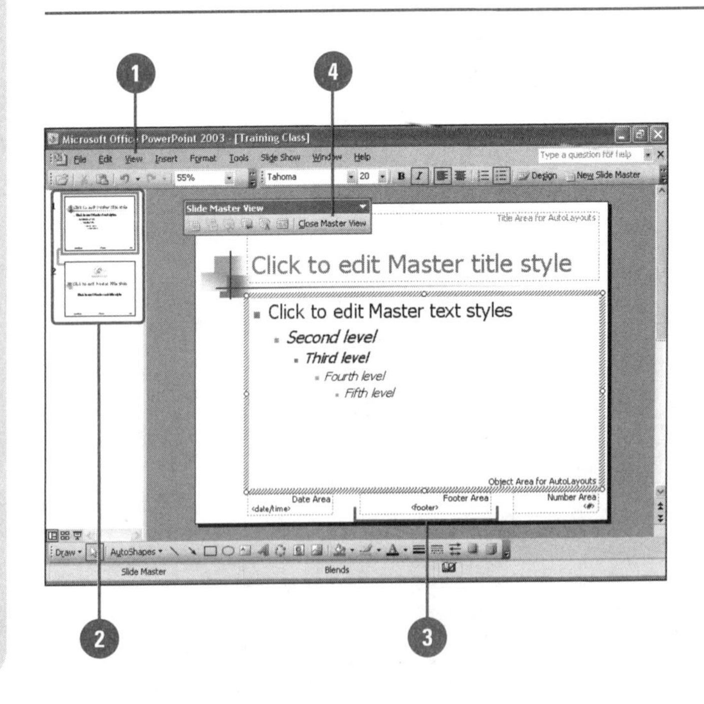

Understanding Color Schemes

Every presentation has at least one color scheme. A presentation with more than one set of slide masters can have more than one color scheme. A color scheme can be a set of custom colors that you choose, or it can be the default color scheme. Understanding color schemes helps you create professional-looking presentations that use an appropriate balance of color for your presentation content.

The default color schemes in PowerPoint are made up of a palette of eight colors. These colors appear on the menu when you click the Fill Color or Font Color button list arrow on the Drawing toolbar.

These eight colors correspond to the following elements in a presentation:

- **Background.** This color is the canvas, or drawing area, color of the slide.
- **Text and lines.** This color contrasts with the background color. It is used for typing text and drawing lines.
- **Shadows.** This color is g[illegible] darker shade of the back[illegible]
- **Title text.** This color contrasts with the background color.
- **Fills.** This color contrasts with both the Background color and the Text and lines color.
- **Accent.** This color is designed to work as a complementary color for objects in the presentation.
- **Accent and hyperlink.** This color is designed to work as a complementary color for objects and hyperlinks.
- **Accent and followed hyperlink.** This color is designed to work as a complementary color for objects and visited hyperlinks.

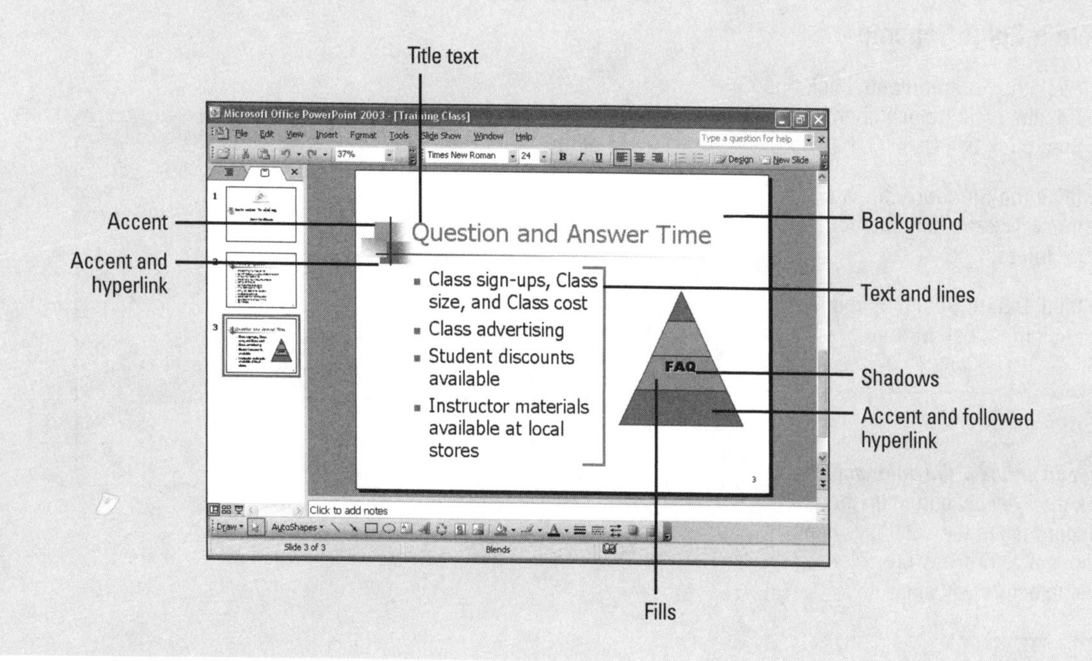

wing and Choosing a Color Scheme

You can apply a color scheme to one slide or all slides in a presentation. You can choose from one or more standard color schemes in each template. You can also create your own color schemes and save them so you can apply them to other slides and even other presentations. When you no longer need a color scheme, you can delete it from the Edit color Scheme dialog box.

Choose a Color Scheme

1. Click the Format menu, and then click Slide Design.
2. Click Color Schemes.
3. Point to the color scheme you want.
4. Click the color scheme's list arrow, and then click Apply To Selected Slides to apply the color scheme to the slide you are viewing, or click Apply to All Slides to apply the color scheme to the entire presentation.

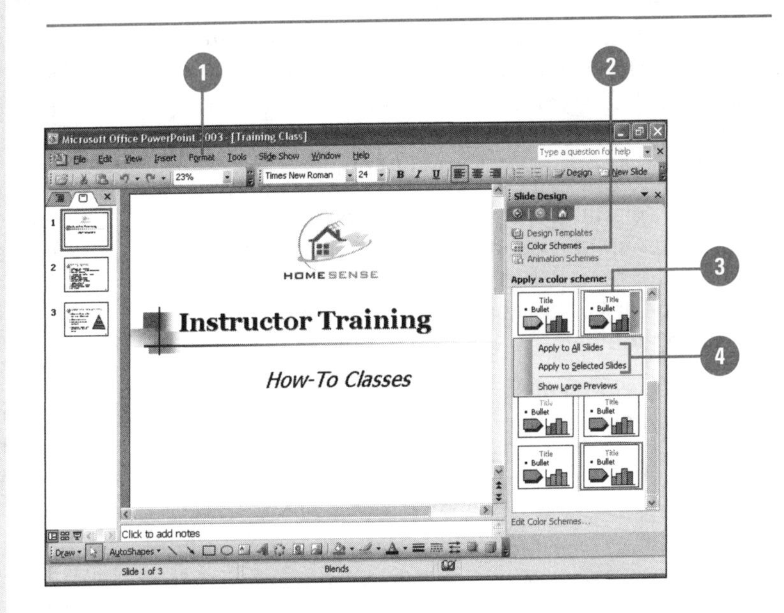

Delete a Color Scheme

1. Click the Format menu, click Slide Design, click Color Schemes, and then click Edit Color Schemes.
2. Click the Standard tab, and then click the scheme you want to delete.
3. Click Delete Scheme, and then click the Close button.

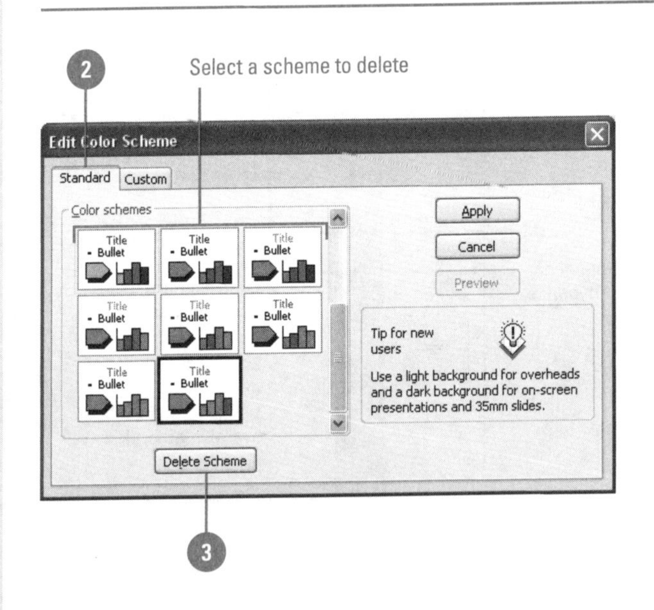

Did You Know?

You can preview the color scheme. Click the Preview button on the Standard tab of the Edit Color Scheme dialog box to preview the color scheme before you apply it.

Apply the Color Scheme of One Slide to Another

1. Click the Slide Sorter View button.
2. Click the slide with the color scheme you want to apply.
3. Click the Format Painter button on the Formatting toolbar to apply the color scheme to one slide, or double-click the button to apply the color scheme to multiple slides.
4. Click the slides to which you want to apply the color scheme. The slides can be in the current presentation or in another open presentation.
5. If you are applying the scheme to more than one slide, press Esc to cancel the Format Painter. If you are applying the scheme to only one slide, the Format Painter is canceled automatically.

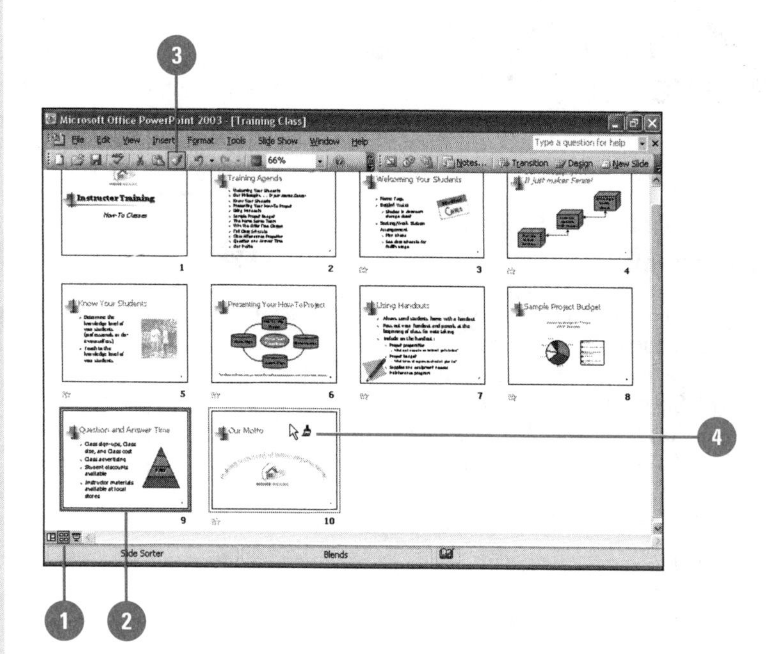

Did You Know?

What colors work better for on-screen presentations? Use dark backgrounds for on-screen presentations and 35mm slides. Use a light background for overhead transparencies.

Creating a Color Scheme

You may like a certain color scheme except for one or two colors. You can change an existing color scheme and apply your changes to the entire presentation or to just a few slides. Once you create this new color scheme, you can add it to your collection of color schemes so that you can make it available to any slide in the presentation.

Change a Color in a Standard Color Scheme

1. In Normal view, display the slide whose color scheme you want to change, click the Format menu, click Slide Design, click Color Schemes, and then click Edit Color Schemes.
2. Click the Custom tab.
3. Click the element you want to change.
4. Click Change Color.
5. Click a color on the Standard tab.
6. Click OK.
7. Click Apply.

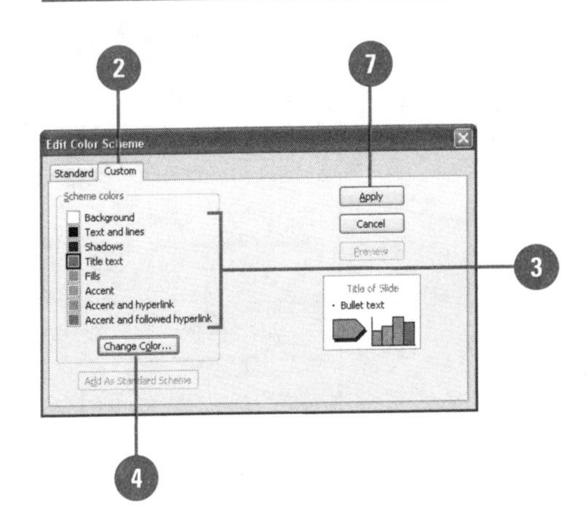

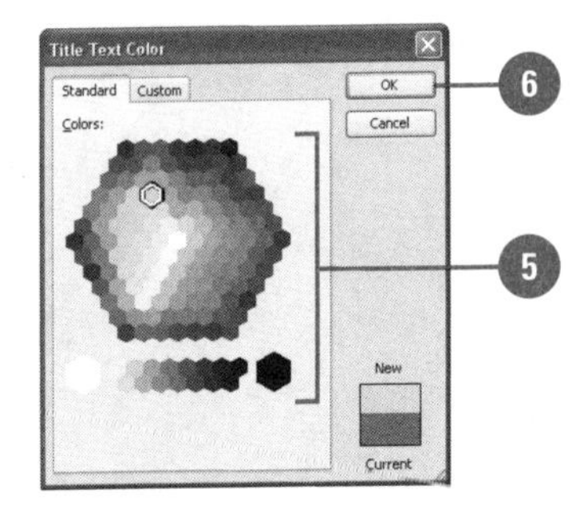

Choose a Custom Color

1. Click the Format menu, click Slide Design, click Color Schemes, and then click Edit Color Schemes.
2. Click the Custom tab.
3. Click the element you want to customize in the Scheme Colors list.
4. Click Change Color.

The Properties of Color

Characteristic	Description
Hue	The color itself; every color is indentified by a number, determined by the number of colors available on your monitor.
Saturation	The intensity of the color. The higher the number, the more vivid the color.
Luminosity	The brightness of the color, or how close the color is to black or white. The larger the number, the lighter the color.

5. Click the Custom tab.
6. Drag across the palette until the pointer is over the color you want, or choose a Color Model, and then enter the Hue, Sat, Lum, or Red, Green, and Blue values.
7. Click OK.
8. Click Apply to make the new color part of the color scheme for the selected color scheme.

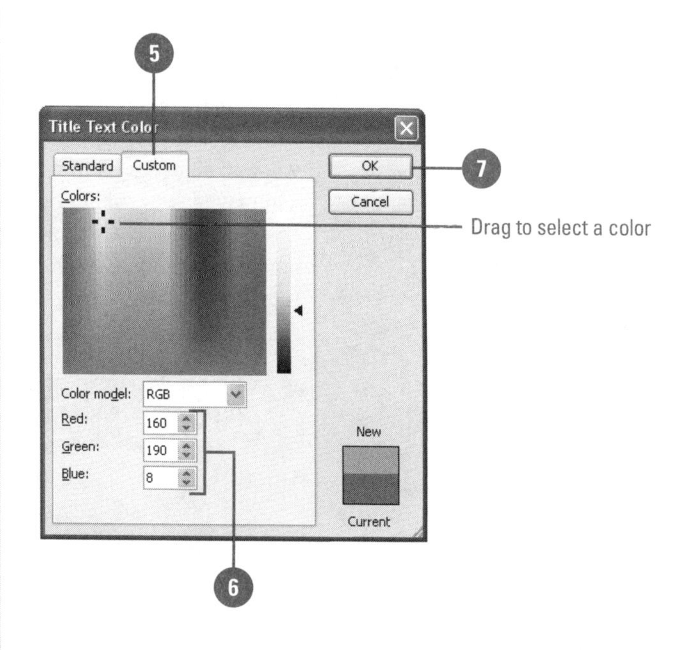

Create and Save a Color Scheme

1. Click the Format menu, click Slide Design, click Color Schemes, and then click Edit Color Schemes.
2. Click the Custom tab.
3. Change the color scheme until all eight colors are as you want them.
4. Click Add As Standard Scheme. Your new scheme now appears on the Standard tab.
5. If you want to apply the scheme, click Apply, or click Cancel to close the dialog box.

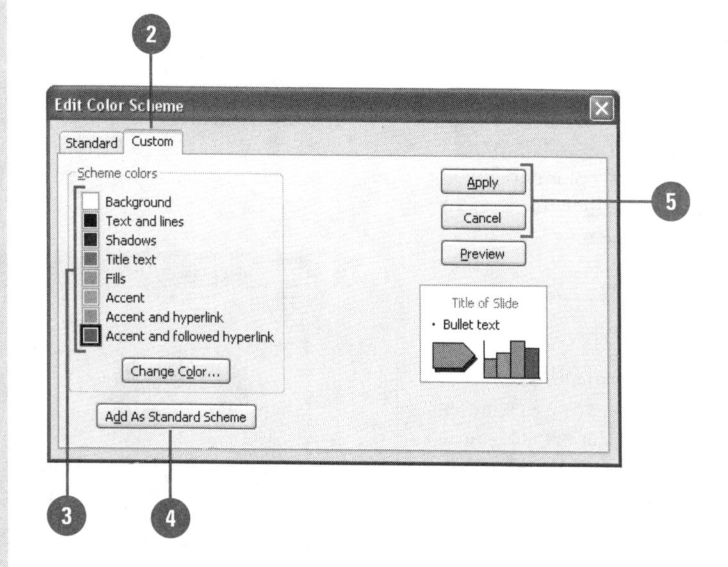

Adding Colors to a Presentation

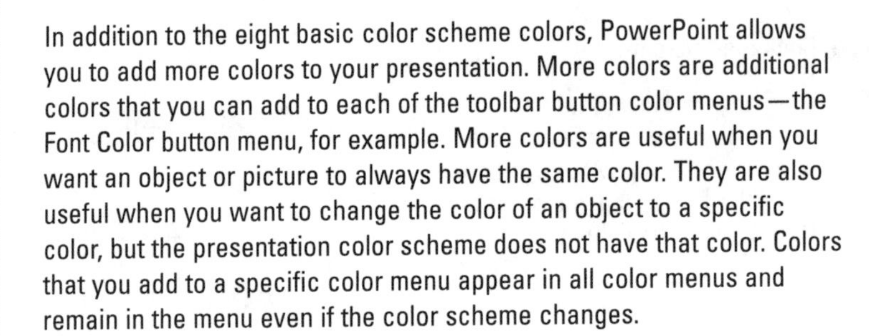

In addition to the eight basic color scheme colors, PowerPoint allows you to add more colors to your presentation. More colors are additional colors that you can add to each of the toolbar button color menus—the Font Color button menu, for example. More colors are useful when you want an object or picture to always have the same color. They are also useful when you want to change the color of an object to a specific color, but the presentation color scheme does not have that color. Colors that you add to a specific color menu appear in all color menus and remain in the menu even if the color scheme changes.

Add a Color to the Menus

1. Click the object whose color you want to change.
2. Click the Fill Color, Line Color, or Font Color button list arrow on the Drawing toolbar to change an object's color.
3. Click More Fill Colors, More Line Colors, or More Colors, and then select a color.
4. Click OK.

   The current selection is changed to the new color, plus the new color is added to the second line of color choices and is now available to use throughout the presentation.

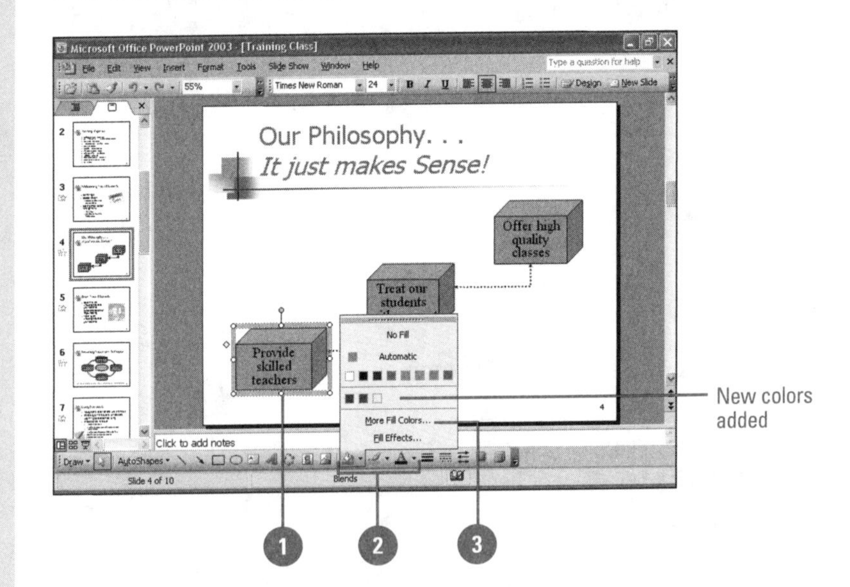

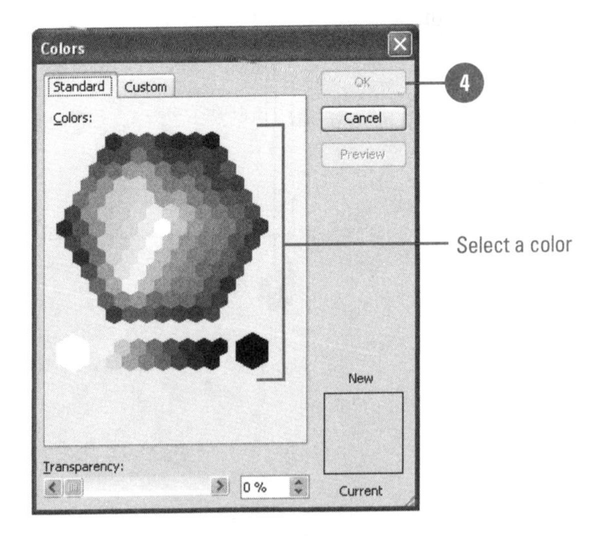

Did You Know?

You can add colors to all color menus. Any time you add a color, PowerPoint adds it to all the color menus—those that appear for text, shadows, bullets, background, and lines. PowerPoint "remembers" up to eight colors that you've added. If you add a ninth, it appears first on the palette, replacing the oldest.

Adding and Modifying a Slide Background

PP03S-2-3

In PowerPoint, you can create a special background on a slide by adding a shade, a texture, a pattern, or even a picture. A shaded background is a visual effect in which a solid color gradually changes from light to dark or dark to light. PowerPoint offers one-color and two-color shaded backgrounds with six styles: horizontal, vertical, diagonal up, diagonal down, from corner, and from title. For a one-color shaded background, the shading color can be adjusted lighter or darker, depending on your needs. You can also choose a preset color background, one of 24 professionally designed backgrounds in which the color shading changes direction according to the shading style selected. In addition to a shaded background, you can also have a background with a texture, a pattern, or a picture. PowerPoint has several different textures, patterns, and pictures that you can apply to a presentation.

Select a Background Fill Effect

1. Click the Format menu, and then click Background.
2. Click the Background Fill list arrow, and then click Fill Effects.
3. Click the Gradient, Texture, Pattern, or Picture tab to display the available fill effects.
4. Click the fill effect you want.
5. Click OK.
6. Click Apply to apply the fill effect to the current slide, or click Apply To All to apply the fill effect to all slides.

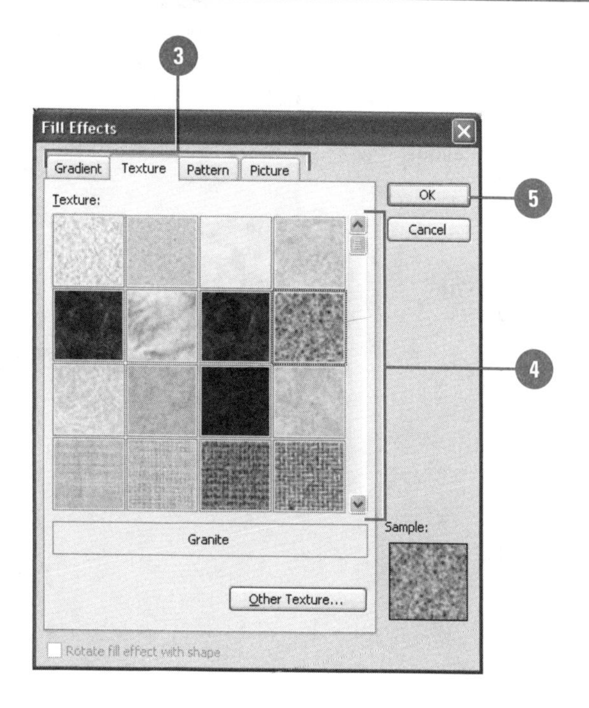

Saving a Template

PP03S-2-6

Create a Template

1. Open any presentation.
2. Click the Format menu, click Slide Design, click Color Schemes, select or create a color scheme, and then click Apply To All Slides.
3. Format the placeholders on the slide and title masters.
4. Place objects or insert pictures on the slide and title masters.
5. Add the footer and header information you want to include.
6. Click the File menu, click Save As, and then enter a name for your template.
7. Click the Save As Type list arrow, and then click Design Template.
8. Click Save.

You can save any presentation as a template. When you create a new presentation from that template, its content and design can form the basis of your next presentation. Although you can store your template anywhere you want, you may find it handy to store it in the Templates folder that PowerPoint uses to store its templates. If you store your design templates in the Presentation Designs folder and your AutoContent templates in the Presentations folder, those templates appear as options when you choose the New command on the File menu, and then click On My Computer. You can also change existing templates. For example, you can change the Blank Presentation template so that it includes your company's colors or logo.

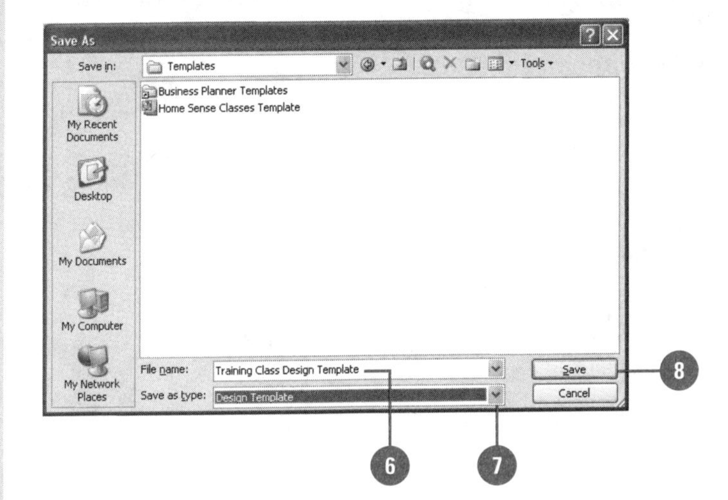

Change an Existing Design Template

1. Click the File menu, and then click Open.
2. Click the Files Of Type list arrow, and then click Design Template.
3. If necessary, click the Look In list arrow, and then select the folder containing the template you want to open.
4. Double-click the template you want to change.
5. Make your changes to the template.
6. Click the File menu, and then click Save As.
7. Click the Save As Type list arrow, and then click Design Template.
8. Click Save.
9. Click Yes to replace the existing file.

Did You Know?

You can add a template to the AutoContent Wizard. You can add a template to the AutoContent Wizard list of presentations. Click the File menu, click New, and then click From AutoContent wizard on the New Presentation task pane. Click Next, select the category where you want your template to appear, click Add, find the template, and then click OK.

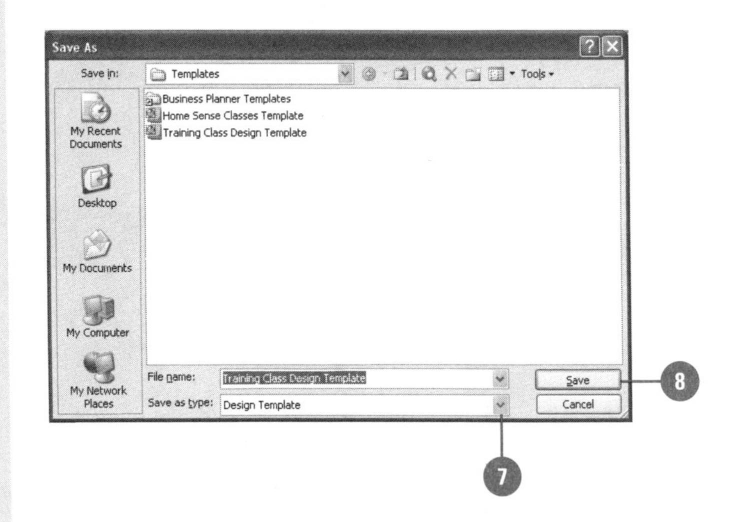

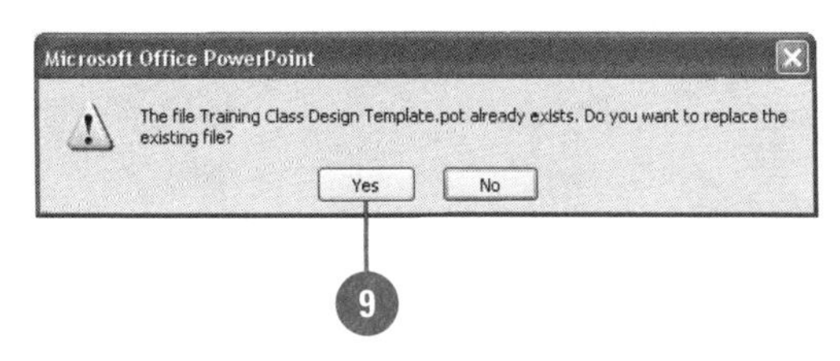

3

Drawing and Modifying Shapes

4

Introduction

When you want to add objects to your presentations, you can use Microsoft Office PowerPoint 2003 as a drawing package. PowerPoint offers a wide range of predesigned shapes, line options or freeform tools that allow you to draw, size and format your own shapes and forms.

You can add three types of drawing objects to your PowerPoint presentations—AutoShapes, lines, and freeforms. AutoShapes are preset shapes, such as stars, circles, or ovals. Lines are simply the straight or curved lines (arcs) that can connect two points or are used as arrows. Freeforms are irregular curves or polygons that you can create as a freehand drawing.

Once you create a drawing object, you can move, resize, nudge, copy or delete it on your slides. You can also change it's style, by adding color, creating a fill pattern, rotating it, applying a shadow, or 3-D effect. You can take a simple AutoShape and by the time you are done adding various effects, it could become an attractive piece of graphic art for your presentation. If you'd like to use it later, you can save it to the Clip Organizer.

Object placement on your slides is a key factor to all of your hard work. Multiple objects should be grouped if they are to be considered one larger object. Grouping helps you make changes later on, or copy your objects to another slide. PowerPoint has the ability to line up your objects with precision—rulers and guides are part of the alignment process to help you. By grouping and aligning, you are assured that your drawing objects will be accurately placed.

What You'll Do

Draw and Resize Shapes

Insert AutoShapes from the Clip Gallery

Draw Lines and Arrows

Create and Edit Freeforms

Modify a Freeform

Copy and Move an Object

Choose Shape Colors and Fill Effects

Apply Fill Effects

Create Shadows

Align Objects to Grids and Guides

Align and Distribute Objects

Connect Shapes

Change Stacking Order

Add 3-D Effects to a Shape

Rotate and Flip a Shape

Group and Ungroup Shapes

Add a Shape to the Clip Organizer

Drawing and Resizing Shapes

PP03S-1-4

PowerPoint supplies 155 different AutoShapes, ranging from hearts to lightening bolts to stars. The two most common AutoShapes, the oval and the rectangle, are available directly on the Drawing toolbar. The rest of the AutoShapes are organized into categories you can select from the AutoShapes menu on the Drawing toolbar. Once you have placed an AutoShape on a slide, you can resize it using the sizing handles. Many AutoShapes have an **adjustment handle**, a small yellow diamond located near a resize handle that you can drag to alter the shape of the AutoShape. For precision when resizing, use PowerPoint's Format command to specify the new size of the shape. In addition to drawing AutoShapes, you can insert AutoShapes, such as computers and furniture, from the Clip Art task pane.

Draw an Oval or Rectangle

1. Click the Oval or Rectangle button on the Drawing toolbar.
2. Drag the pointer on the slide where you want to place the oval or rectangle. The shape you draw uses the line and fill color defined by the presentation's color scheme.

   To draw a perfect circle or square, hold down Shift as you drag the pointer.

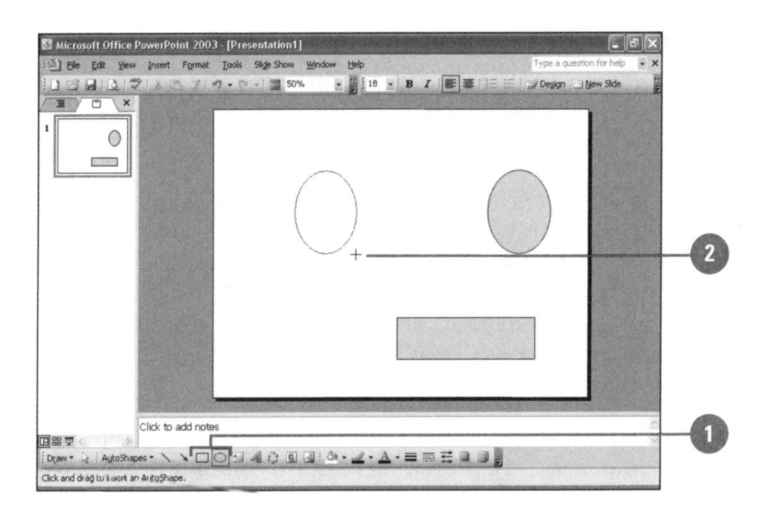

Draw an AutoShape

1. Click the AutoShapes button on the Drawing toolbar, and then point to the AutoShape category you want to use.
2. Click the symbol you want.
3. Drag the pointer on the slide until the drawing object is the shape and size that you want.

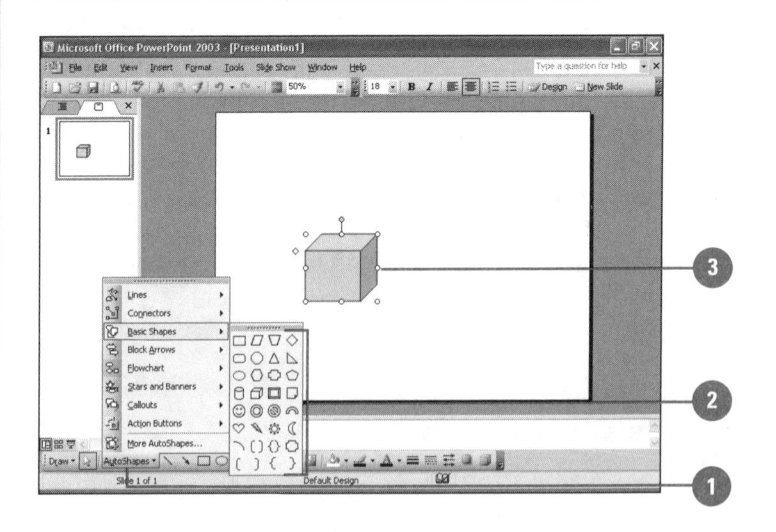

Resize an AutoShape

1. Click the object you want to resize.
2. Drag one of the sizing handles.
   - To resize the object in the vertical or horizontal direction, drag a sizing handles on the side of the selection box.
   - To resize the object in both the vertical and horizontal directions, drag a sizing handle on the corner of the selection box.

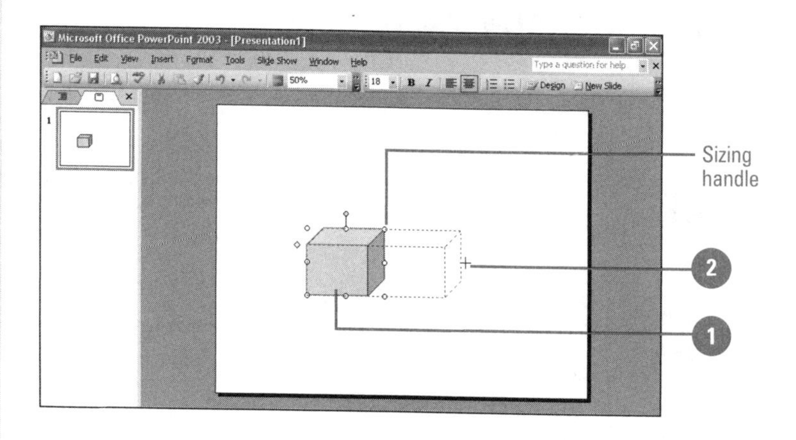

Adjust an AutoShape

1. Click the AutoShape you want to adjust.
2. Click one of the adjustment handles (small yellow diamonds), and then drag the handle to alter the form of the AutoShape.

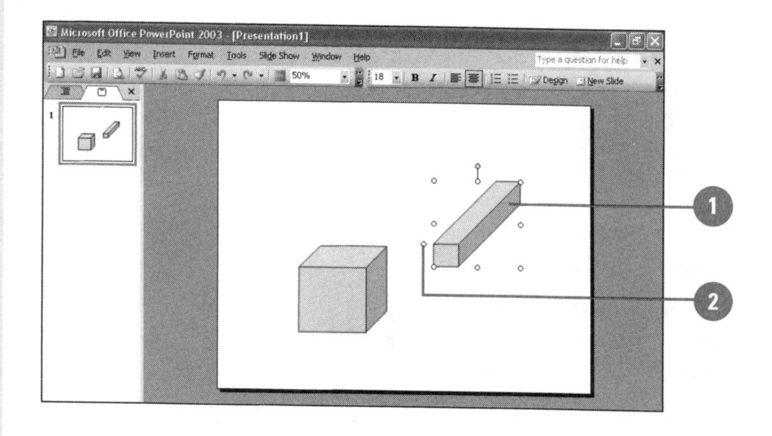

Did You Know?

You can draw a circle or square. To draw a perfect circle or square, click the Oval or Rectangle button on the Drawing toolbar, and then press and hold Shift as you drag.

You can replace an AutoShape. Replace one AutoShape with another, while retaining the size, color, and orientation of the AutoShape. Click the AutoShape you want to replace, click the Draw button on the Drawing toolbar, point to Change AutoShape, and then click the new AutoShape you want.

Inserting AutoShapes from the Clip Gallery

PP03S-1-4

In addition to drawing AutoShapes, you can insert AutoShapes, such as computers and furniture, from the Clip Art task pane. These AutoShapes are called **clips**. The Clip Art task pane gives you a miniature of each clip. You can click the clip you want to insert it onto your slide or click the clip list arrow to select other options, such as previewing the clip or searching for similar clips. After you insert a AutoShape, you can add text to it. You can format the text in an AutoShape in the same way you format text in a word processing program.

Insert an AutoShape from the Clip Gallery

1. Click the AutoShapes button on the Drawing toolbar, and then click More AutoShapes.
2. If necessary, use the scroll arrows to display more AutoShapes.
3. Click the shape you want onto your slide.
4. When you're done, click the Close button on the task pane.

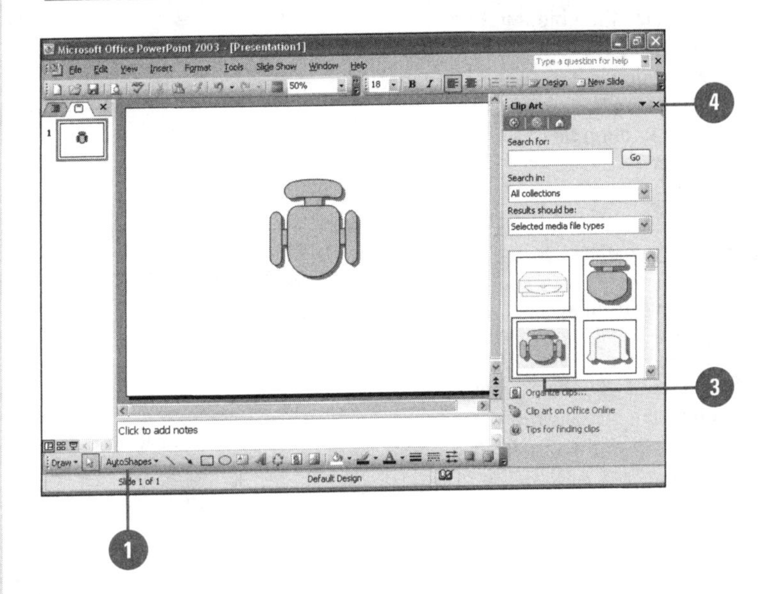

Did You Know?

You can quickly delete an AutoShape. Click the AutoShape to select it, and then press Delete.

Find Similar AutoShapes in the Clip Gallery

1. Click the AutoShapes button on the Drawing toolbar, and then click More AutoShapes.
2. Point to the AutoShape in which you want to find a similar one.
3. Click the list arrow, and then click Find Similar Style.

   The similar AutoShape styles appear in the results box.

4. When you're done, click the Close button on the task pane.

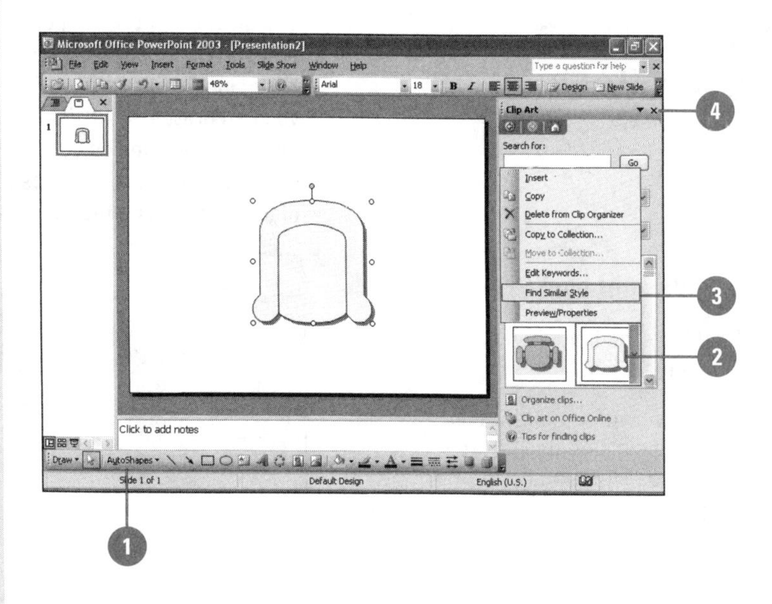

Add Text to an AutoShape

1. Click the AutoShape in which you want to add text.
2. Type the text you want.

> **Did You Know?**
>
> ***You can edit text in an AutoShape.*** Click the AutoShape to select it, click the text in the AutoShape to place the insertion point, and then edit the text.
>
> ***You can align text in an AutoShape.*** Click the AutoShape to select it, click the Format menu, click AutoShape, click the Alignment tab, select an alignment option, and then click OK.

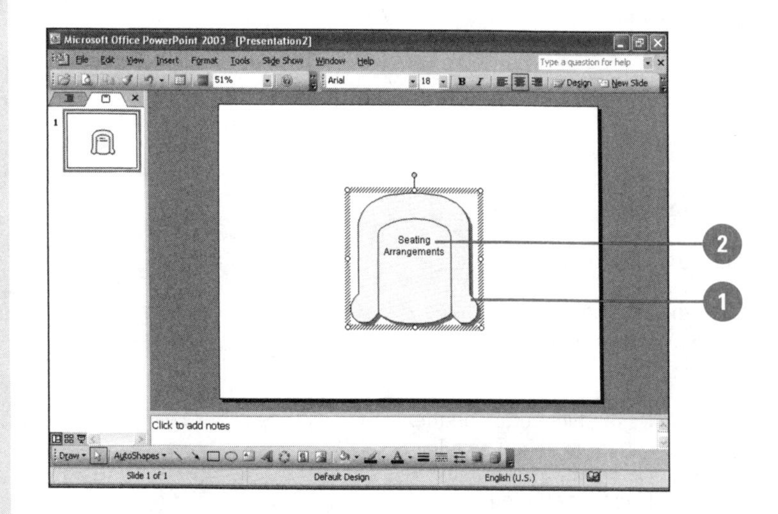

4

Drawing Lines and Arrows

PP03S-2-2

The most basic drawing objects you can create on your slides are lines and arrows. Use the Line tool to create line segments. The Drawing toolbar's Line Style and Dash Style tools let you determine the type of line you can draw—solid, dashed, or a combination. You can add arrowheads to any lines on your slide. Use the Arrow tool to create arrows that emphasize key features of your presentation. You can edit the style of the arrow using the Arrow style tool.

Draw a Straight Line

1. Click the Line button on the Drawing toolbar.
2. Drag the pointer to draw a line. The endpoints of the line are where you start and finish dragging.
3. Release the mouse button when the line is the correct length. Sizing handles appear at both ends of the line. Use these handles to resize your line or move an endpoint.

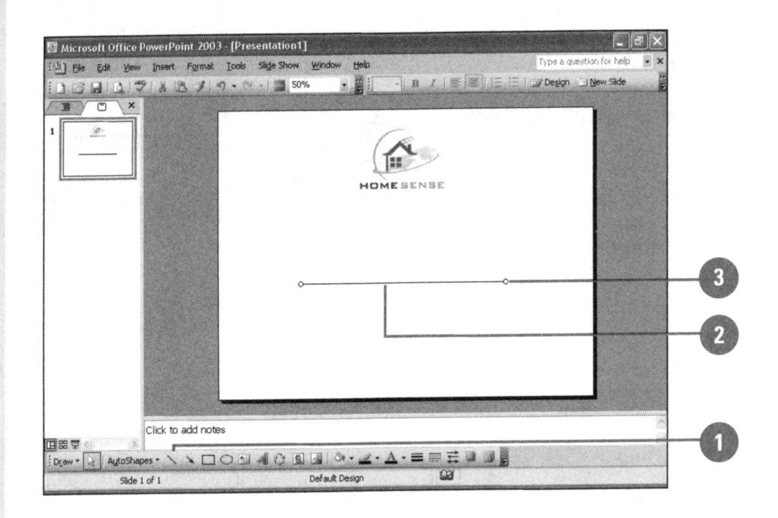

Edit a Line

1. Click the line you want to edit.
2. Click the Line Style button on the Drawing toolbar to select a line thickness.
3. Click the Dash Style button on the Drawing toolbar to select a style.
4. Click the Line Color button list arrow on the Drawing toolbar to select a color.
5. Drag a sizing handle to change the size or angle of the line.

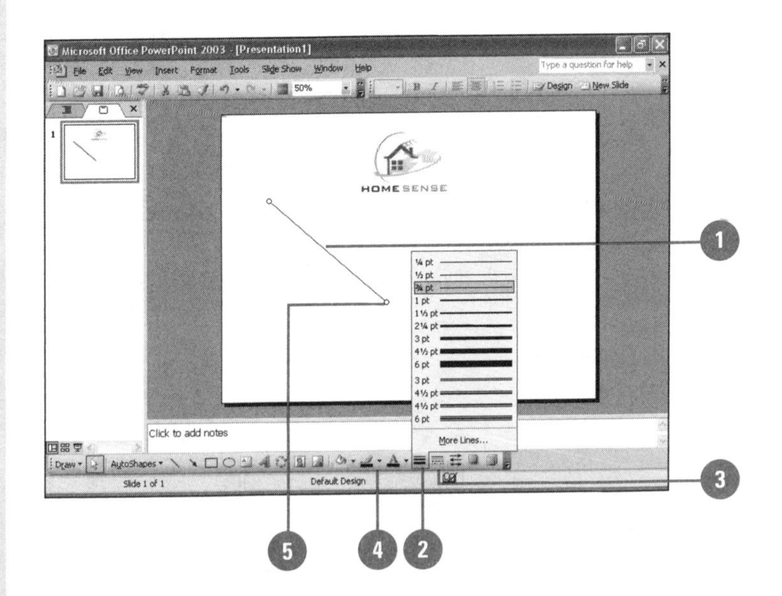

Draw an Arrow

1. Click the Arrow button on the Drawing toolbar.
2. Drag the pointer from the base of the arrow to the arrow's point.
3. Release the mouse button when the arrow is the correct length and angle.

Did You Know?

You can change the default size of an arrow. Click an arrow object, click the Arrow Style button, click More Arrows, change the line and arrow settings to the default format you want, select the Default For New Objects check box, and then click OK.

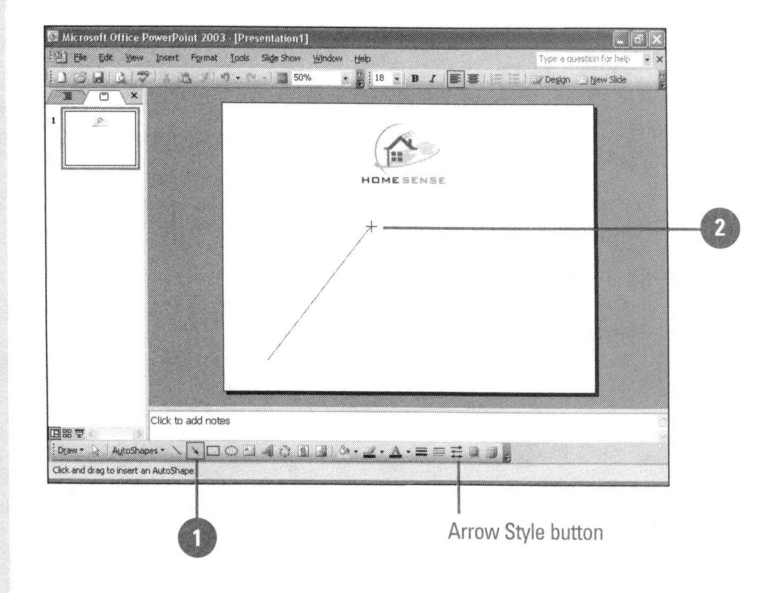

Edit an Arrow

1. Click the arrow you want to edit.
2. Click the Arrow Style button on the Drawing toolbar.
3. Click the arrow type you want to use, or click More Arrows.
4. If you click More Arrows, modify the arrow type in the Format AutoShape dialog box as necessary, and then click OK.

Did You Know?

You can increase the size of an arrow. Click the Arrow Style button, click More Arrows, and then increase the Weight setting or End Size setting.

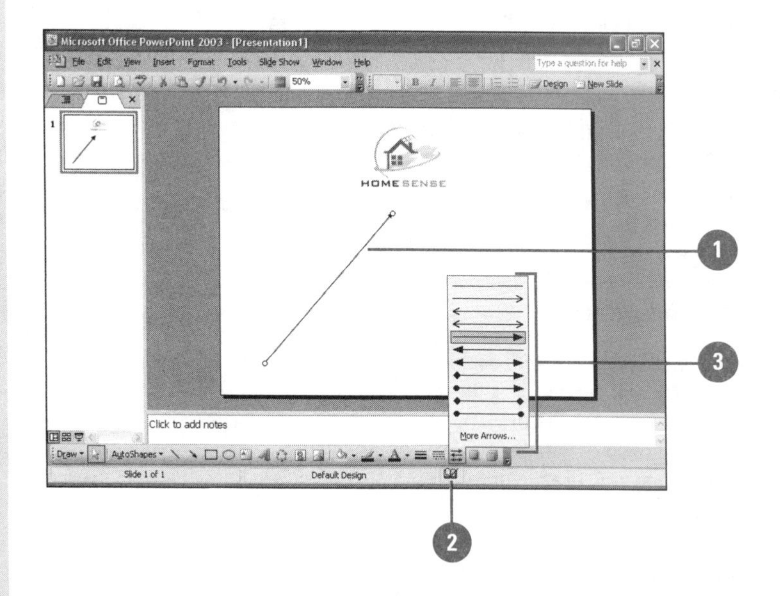

4

Creating and Editing Freeforms

When you need to create a customized shape, use the PowerPoint freeform tools. Choose a freeform tool from the Lines category in the list of AutoShapes. Freeforms are like the drawings you make with a pen and paper, except that you use a mouse for your pen and a slide for your paper. A freeform shape can either be an open curve or a closed curve. You can edit a freeform by using the Edit Points command to alter the vertices that create the shape.

Draw a Freeform Polygon

1. Click the AutoShapes button on the Drawing toolbar, and then point to Lines.
2. Click the Freeform button.
3. Click the slide where you want to place the first vertex of the polygon.
4. Move the pointer, and then click to place the second point of the polygon. A line joins the two points.
5. Continue moving the mouse pointer and clicking to create additional sides of your polygon.
6. Finish the polygon. For a closed polygon, click near the starting point. For an open polygon, double-click the last point in the polygon.

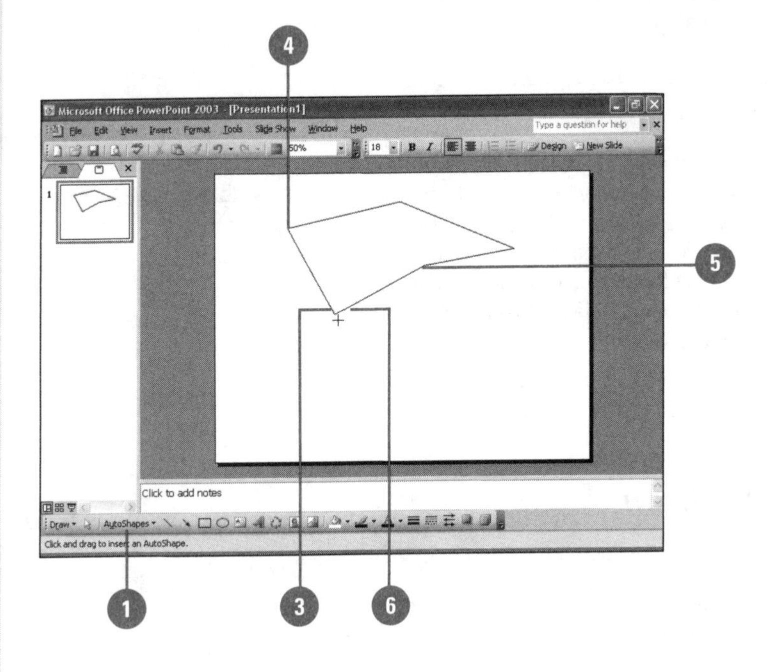

Did You Know?

You can draw an object with both straight lines and curves. Click the AutoShapes button on the Drawing toolbar, point to Lines, and then click the Freeform button. Drag to draw freehand shapes, and then click and move the mouse to draw straight lines.

You can switch between a closed curve and an open curve. Right-click the freeform drawing, and then click Close Path or Open Path.

Draw a Curve

1. Click the AutoShapes button on the Drawing toolbar, and then point to Lines.
2. Click the Curve button.
3. Click the slide where you want to place the curve's starting point.
4. Click where you want your curve to bend. Repeat this step as often as you need to create bends.
5. Finish the curve. For a closed curve, click near the starting point. For an open curve, double-click the last point in the curve.

Scribble

1. Click the AutoShapes button on the Drawing toolbar, and then point to Lines.
2. Click the Scribble button.
3. Drag the pointer across the screen to draw freehand.

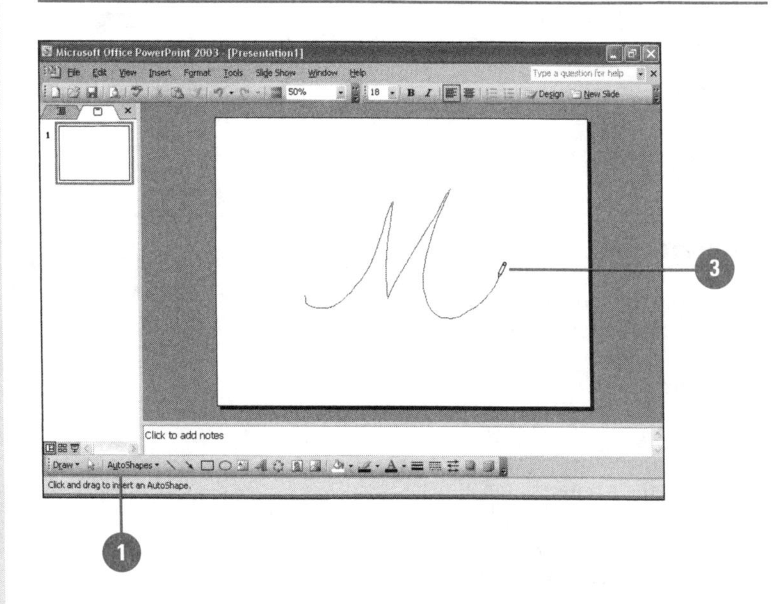

Did You Know?

You can format freeforms and curves. Enhance freeforms and curves just as you can enhance AutoShapes. For example, you can add color or a pattern, change the line style, flip or rotate them, and add shadow or 3-D effects.

Modifying a Freeform

Each **vertex** (a corner in an irregular polygon and a bend in a curve) has two attributes: its position and the angle at which the curve enters and leaves it. You can move the position of each vertex and control the corner or bend angles. You can also add or delete vertices as you like. When you delete a vertex, PowerPoint recalculates the freeform and smooths it among the remaining points. Similarly, if you add a new vertex, PowerPoint adds a corner or bend in your freeform.

Move a Vertex in a Freeform

1. Click the freeform object you want to edit.
2. Click the Draw button on the Drawing toolbar, and then click Edit Points.
3. Drag one of the freeform vertices to a new location.
4. Click outside the freeform when you are finished.

Insert a Freeform Vertex

1. Click the freeform object in which you want to insert a vertex.
2. Click the Draw button on the Drawing toolbar, and then click Edit Points.
3. Position the pointer on the curve or polygon border (not on a vertex), and then drag in the direction you want the new vertex.
4. Click outside the freeform to set the new shape.

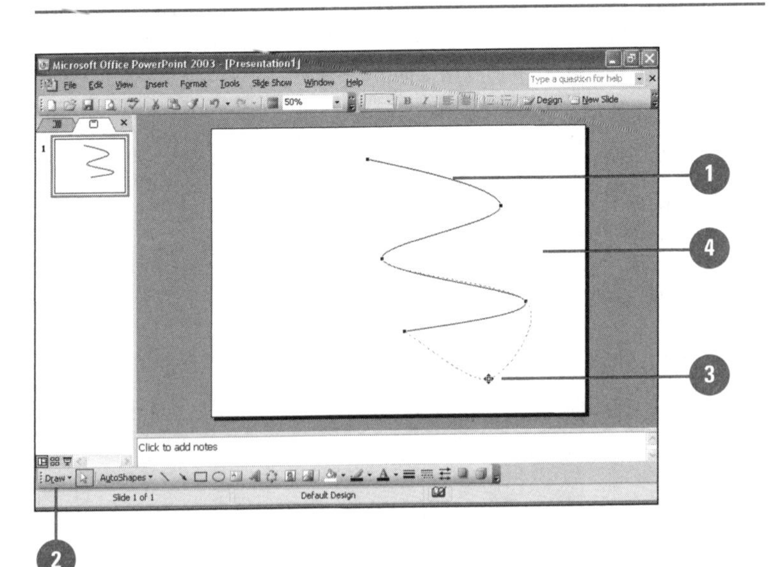

Delete a Freeform Vertex

1. Click the freeform object you want to edit.
2. Click the Draw button on the Drawing toolbar, and then click Edit Points.
3. Right click the vertex and then click Delete.
4. Click outside the freeform to set the shape of the freeform.

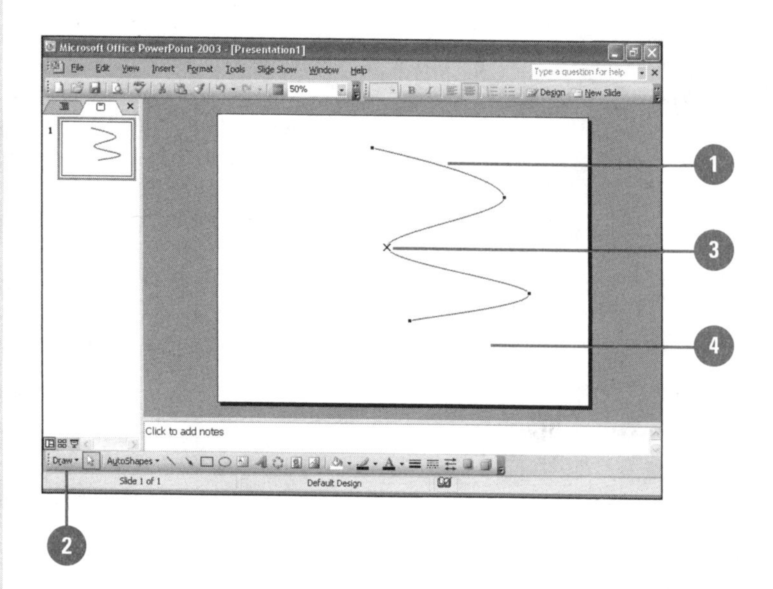

Did You Know?

You can gain control over your freeform. After you click Edit Points, right-click a vertex. PowerPoint displays a shortcut menu with options for other types of vertices you can use to refine the shape of the freeform. These commands let you specify, for example, a smooth point, a straight point, or a corner point.

Modify a Vertex Angle

1. Click the freeform object.
2. Click the Draw button on the Drawing toolbar, and then click Edit Points.
3. Right-click a vertex and click Smooth Point, Straight Point, or Corner Point. Angle handles appear.
4. Drag one or both of the angle handles to modify the shape of the line segments going into and out of the vertex.
5. Click outside the freeform to set its shape.

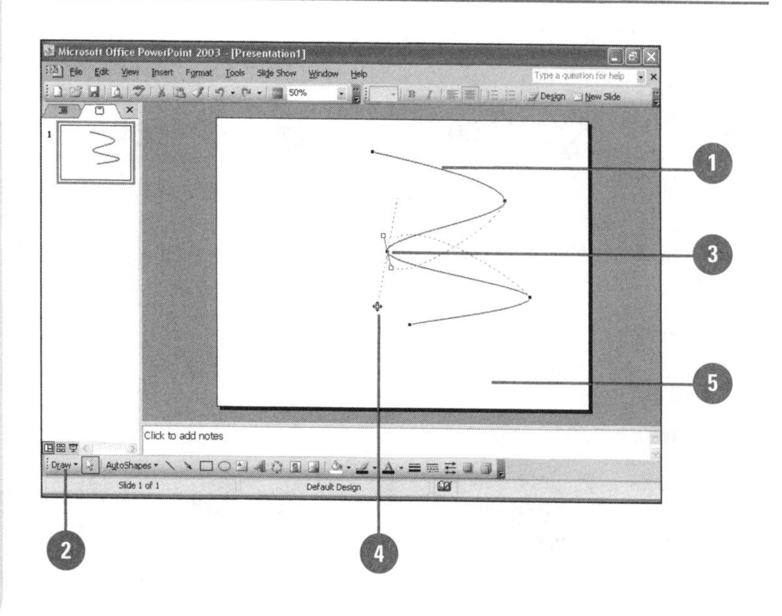

4

Copying and Moving an Object

After you create a drawing object, you can copy or move it. You can quickly move objects using the mouse, or if you want precise control over the object's new position, use PowerPoint's Format command to specify the location of the drawing object. You can also use the Nudge command to move drawing objects in tiny increments up, down, left, or right. You can copy a selected object or multiple objects to the Office Clipboard and then paste the objects in other parts of the presentation. When you copy multiple items, the Office Clipboard task pane appears and shows all of the items that you stored there. You can also copy an object to another location in a single movement by using the Ctrl key or by using the Duplicate command on the Edit menu.

Move a Drawing Object

1. Drag the object to a new location on the slide.

   Make sure you aren't dragging a sizing handle or adjustment handle. If you are working with a freeform and you are in Edit Points mode, drag the interior of the object, not the border, or you will end up resizing or reshaping the object, not moving it.

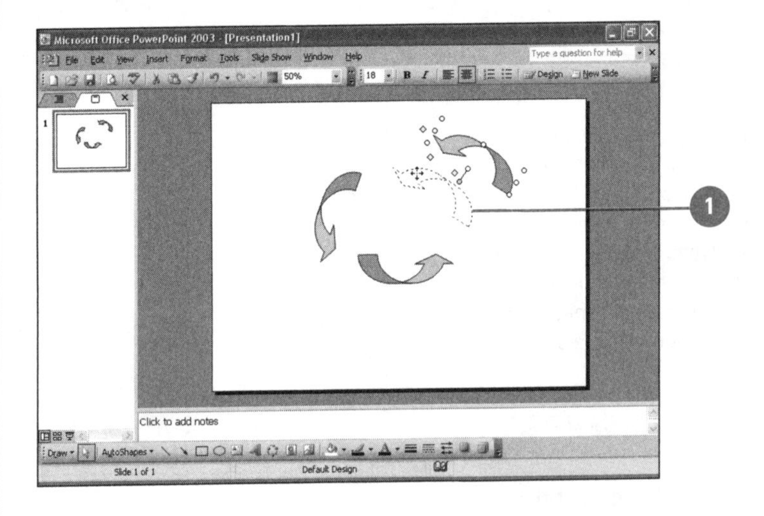

Nudge a Drawing Object

1. Click the object you want to nudge.
2. Click the Draw button on the Drawing toolbar.
3. Point to Nudge and then click Up, Down, Left, or Right.

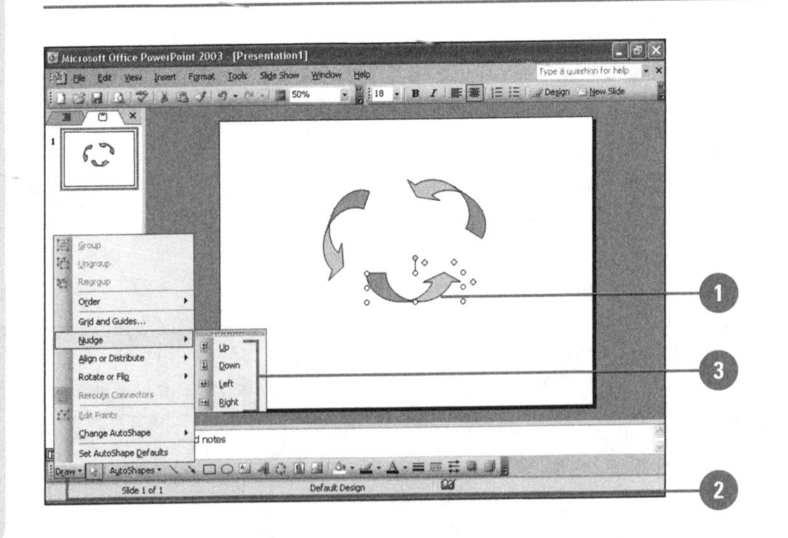

Did You Know?

You can use the keyboard to nudge a drawing object. Click the object you want to nudge, and then press the Up, Down, Left or Right arrow key.

Move an Object with Precision

1. Select the object.
2. Click the Format menu, and then click AutoShape.
3. Click the Position tab to move the object and change settings as necessary.
4. Click OK.

Did You Know?

You can copy and move an object in one step. Hold down the Ctrl key, and then drag the object.

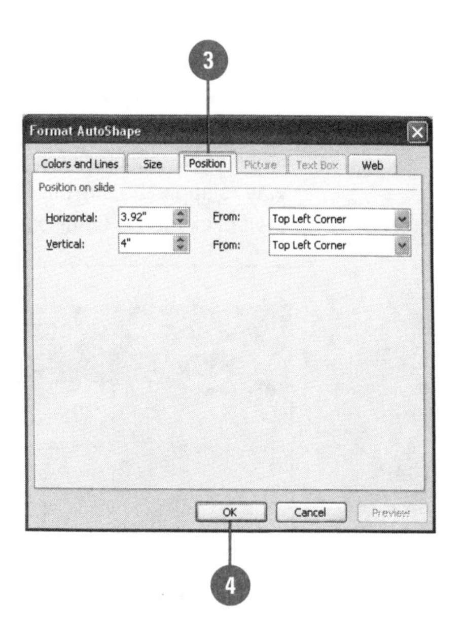

Copy Multiple Objects Using the Office Clipboard Task Pane

1. Select the multiple objects.
2. Click the Copy button on the Standard toolbar.
3. Click an item in the Clipboard task pane to paste it on the slide.

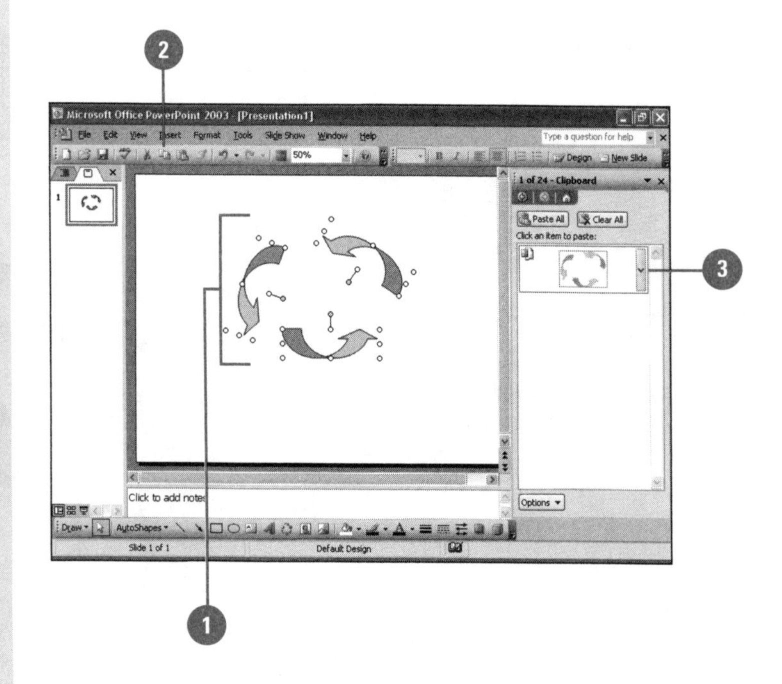

4

Choosing Shape Colors and Fill Effects

PP03S-2-2

When you create a closed drawing object such as a square, it uses two colors from the color scheme: the Fill color and the Line color. When you create a line drawing object, it uses the color scheme Line color. You can change the Fill and Line color settings for drawing objects using the same color tools for changing a slide's background or text color. An easy way to apply the current fill color to any object is to select the object and then click the Fill Color button.

Change a Drawing Object's Fill Color

1. Click the drawing object whose fill color you want to change.
2. Click the Fill Color button list arrow on the Drawing toolbar.
3. Select the fill color you want.
4. Click Fill Effects if you want to change the fill effect too.

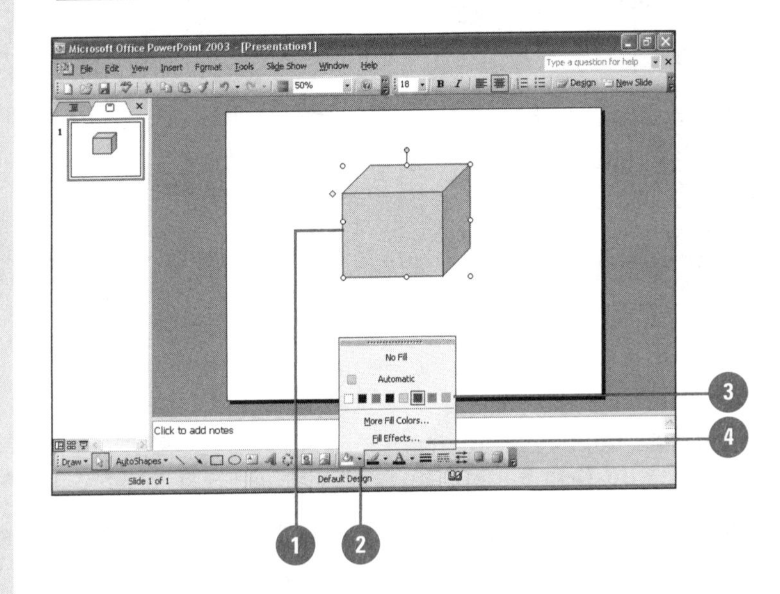

Remove a Fill

1. Click the drawing object whose fill you want to change.
2. Click the Fill Color button list arrow on the Drawing toolbar.
3. Click No Fill.

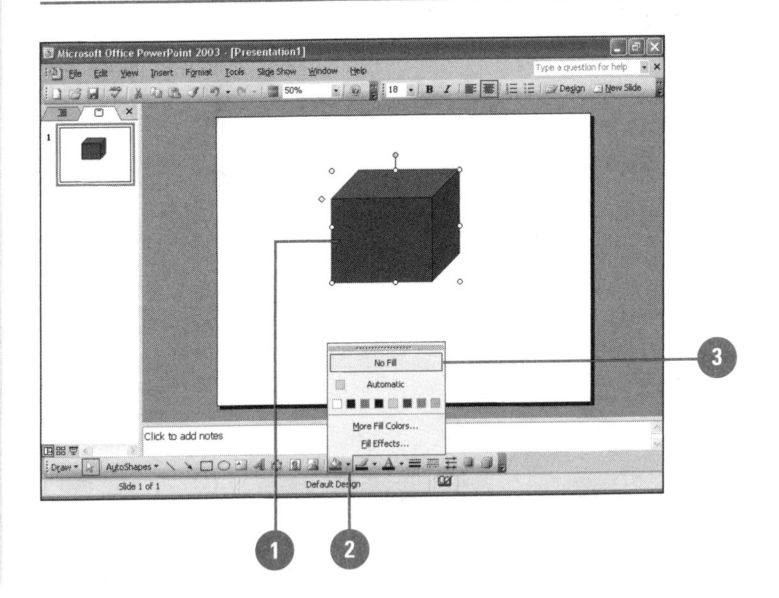

Create a Fill Pattern

1. Click the drawing object whose fill you want to change.
2. Click the Fill Color button list arrow, and then click Fill Effects.
   - Click the Gradient tab to select a gradient color and shading style.
   - Click the Texture tab to select a texture.
   - Click the Pattern tab to select a pattern, foreground,and background color.
   - Click the Picture tab to select a picture.
3. Select the fill pattern you want.
4. Click OK.

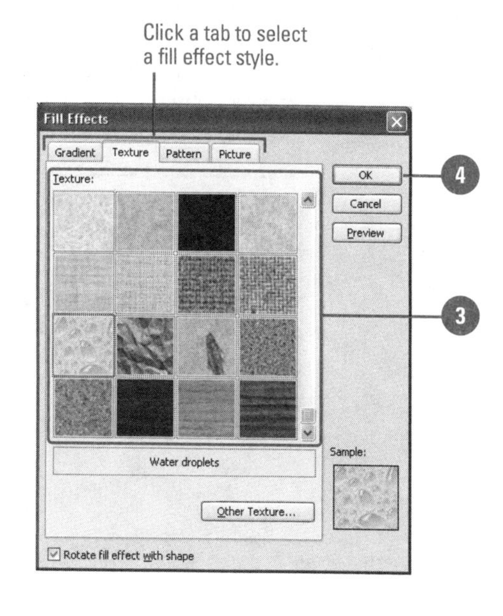

Change Colors and Lines in the Format Dialog Box

1. Click the drawing object you want to modify.
2. Click the Format menu, and then click AutoShape.
3. Click the Colors And Lines tab.
4. Set color, line, and arrow options.
5. Click OK.

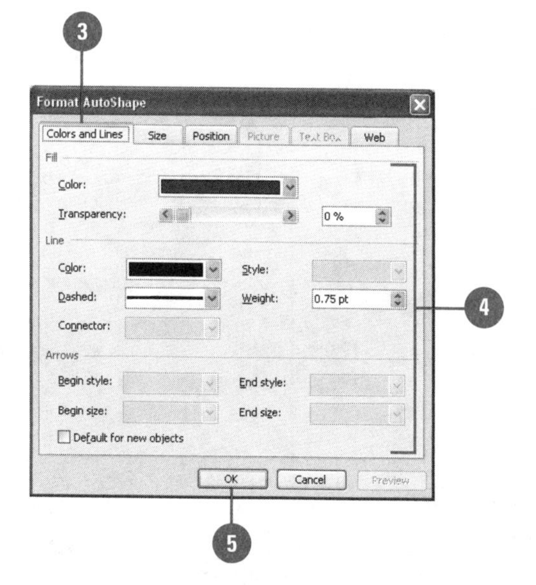

Did You Know?

You can set the color and line style for an object as the default. Right-click the object, and then click Set AutoShape Defaults. Any new objects you create will use the same styles.

4

Applying Fill Effects

Microsoft® Office Specialist Approved Courseware PP03S-2-2

Applying a fill effect to a drawing object can add emphasis or create a point of interest in your presentation. PowerPoint offers fill effects such as gradients, patterns, textures, and even clip art pictures. Spend a few minutes in the Fill Effects dialog box to create the right look for your drawing object.

Apply a Picture Fill

1. Select the object you want to fill, click the Fill Color button list arrow on the Drawing toolbar, and then click Fill Effects.
2. Click the Picture tab.
3. Click Select Picture.
4. Locate the picture you want, and then double-click it.
5. Click OK.

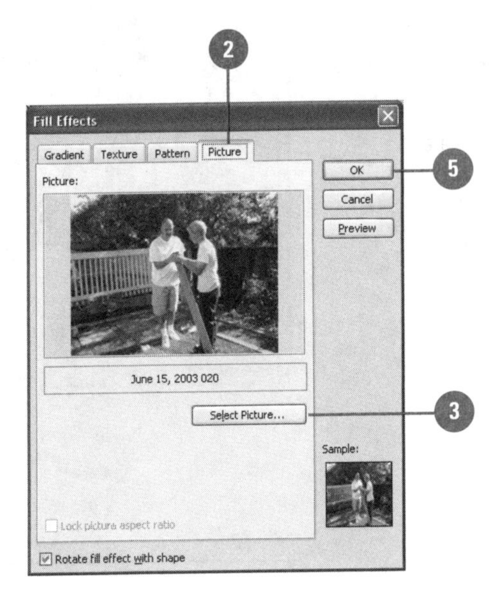

Apply a Gradient Fill

1. Select the object you want to fill, click the Fill Color button list arrow on the Drawing toolbar, and then click Fill Effects.
2. Click the Gradient tab.
3. Click the color or color combination you want.
4. Click the shading style option you want.
5. Click the variant you want.
6. Click OK.

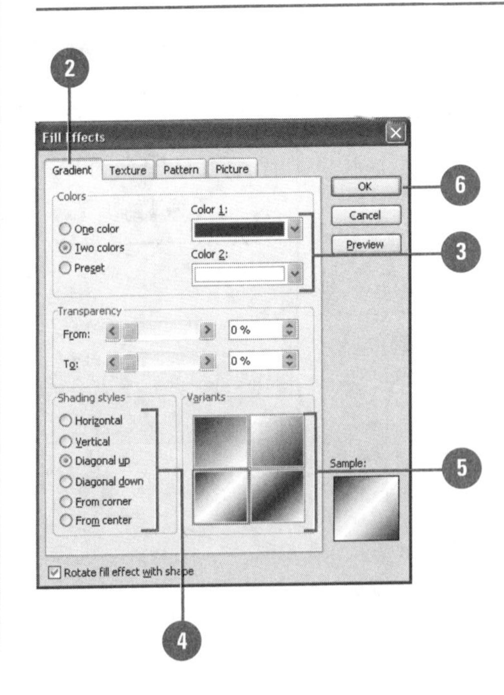

Apply a Pattern Fill

1. Select the object you want to fill, click the Fill Color button list arrow on the Drawing toolbar, and then click Fill Effects.
2. Click the Pattern tab.
3. Click the Foreground list arrow to select the color you want in the foreground.
4. Click the Background list arrow to select the color you want in the background.
5. Click the pattern you want.
6. Click OK.

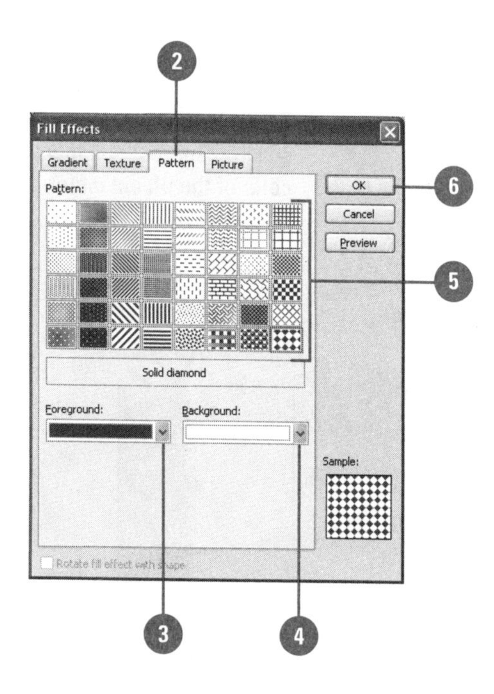

Did You Know?

You can change the fill to match the background. Select the object, click the Format menu, click AutoShape, click the Colors And Lines tab, click the Fill Color button list arrow, click Background, and then click OK.

You can set the color and line style for an object as the default. Right-click the object, and then click Set AutoShape Defaults. Any new objects you create will use the same styles.

You can apply fill effects to other objects. Apply fill effects to objects such as lines and WordArt to enhance your presentation

4

Creating Shadows

PP03S-2-2

You can give objects on your slides the illusion of depth by adding shadows. PowerPoint provides several preset shadowing options, or you can create your own by specifying the location and color of the shadow. If the shadow is falling on another object in your slide, you can create a semitransparent shadow that blends the color of the shadow with the color of the object underneath it.

Use a Preset Shadow

1. Click the drawing object to which you want to add a preset shadow.
2. Click the Shadow Style button on the Drawing toolbar.
3. Click a shadow style.

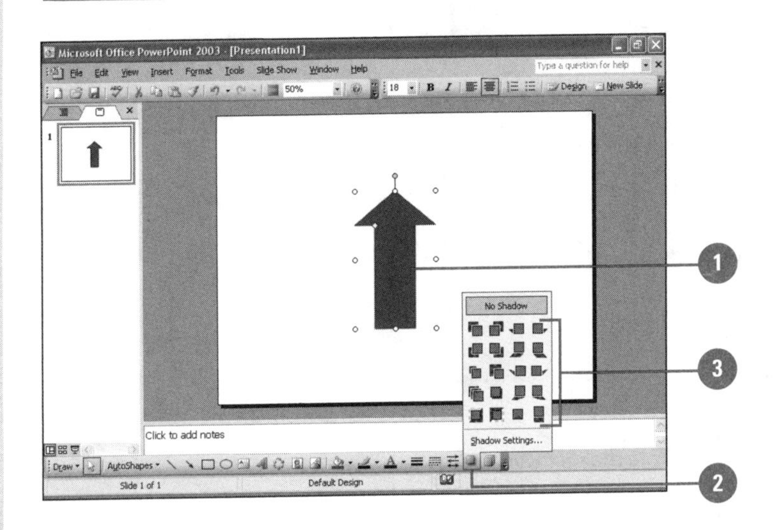

Did You Know?

You can remove a shadow. Click the drawing object with the shadow, click the Shadow button on the Drawing toolbar, and then click No Shadow.

Change the Location of a Shadow

1. Click the drawing object with the shadow.
2. Click the Shadow Style button on the Drawing toolbar, and then click Shadow Settings.
3. Click the tool that creates the effect you want. The Nudge buttons move the shadow location slightly up, down, right, or left.
4. Click the Close button on the Shadow Settings toolbar.

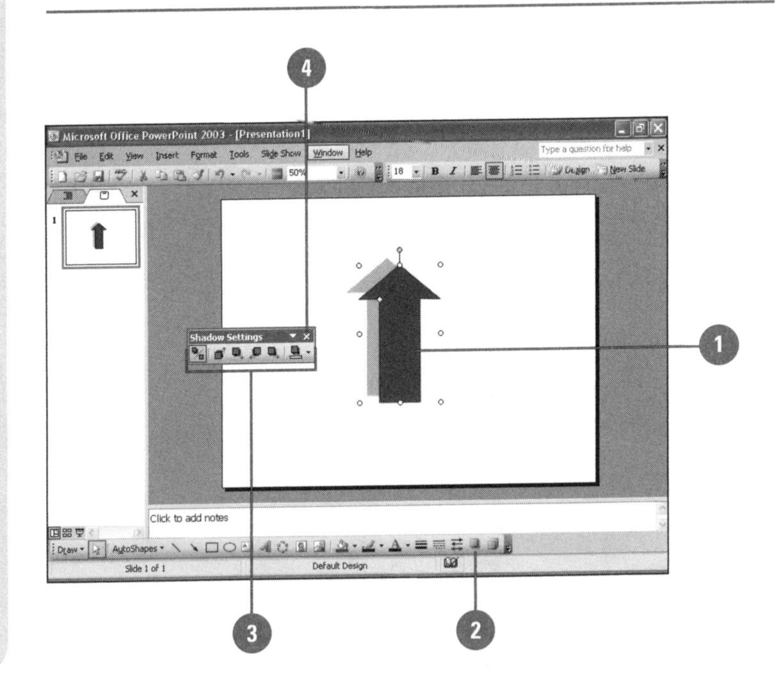

Change the Color of a Shadow

1. Click the drawing object with the shadow.
2. Click the Shadow Style button on the Drawing toolbar, and then click Shadow Settings.
3. Click the Shadow Color button list arrow on the Shadow Settings toolbar, and then select a new color.
4. Click the Close button on the Shadow Settings toolbar.

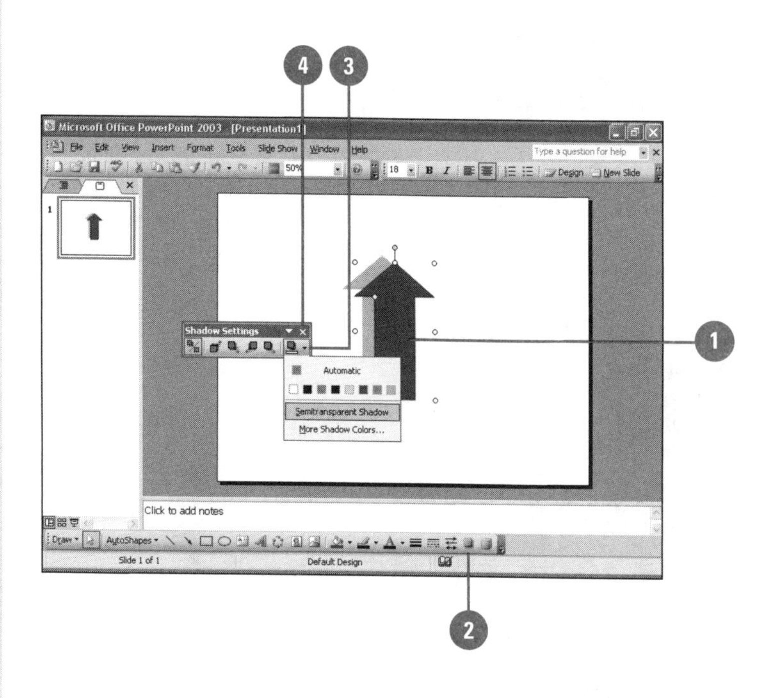

Add a Shadow to Text

1. Click the text object to which you want to add a shadow.
2. Click the Shadow Style button on the Drawing toolbar.
3. Click a shadow style.

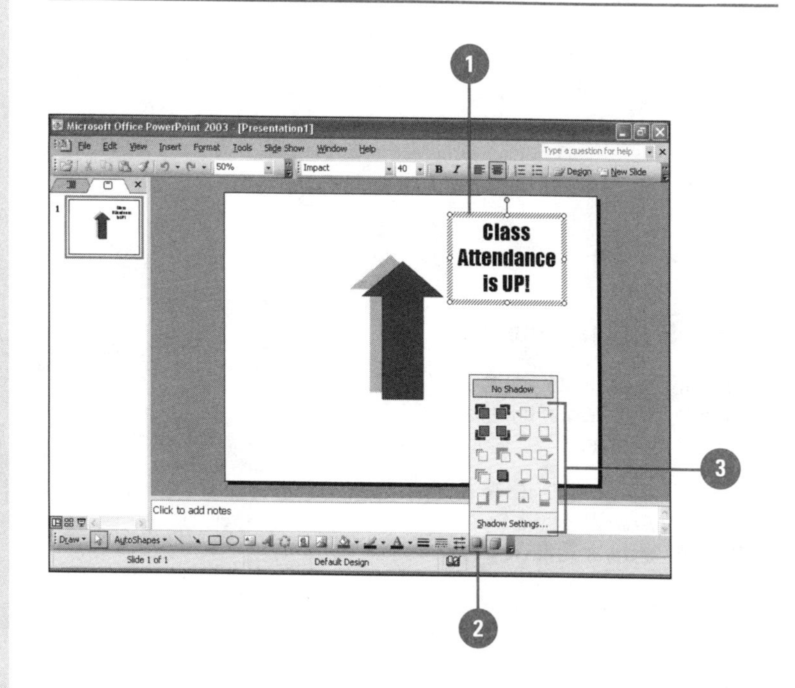

Aligning Objects to Grids and Guides

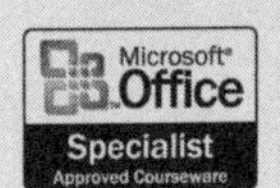

PP03S-2-2, PP03S-4-1

PowerPoint guides can align an individual object or a group of objects to a vertical or horizontal guide. Turning on the visible grid or visible guides option makes it easier to create, modify, and align a shape. Within the Grid and Guides dialog box, you can select from a variety of options, such as snapping objects to the grid or to other objects and displaying drawing guides on-screen. To align several objects to a guide, you first turn the guides on. Then you adjust the guides and drag the objects to align them to the guide.

Turn On or Turn Off the Visible Grid or Guides

1. Click the View menu, and then click Grid And Guides.
2. Select or clear the Display Grid On Screen check box.
3. Select or clear the Display Drawing Guides On Screen check box.
4. Click OK to close the Grid And Guides dialog box.

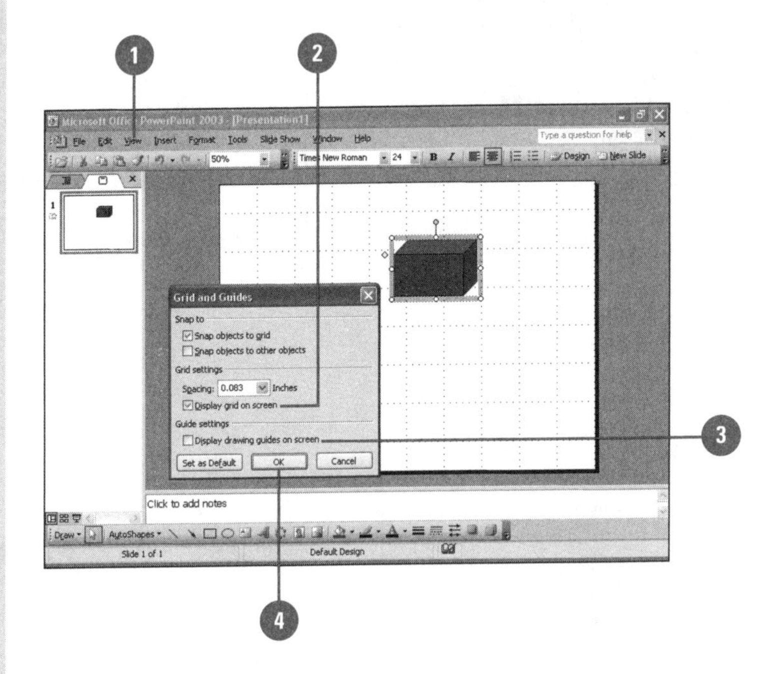

Set Objects to Snap into Place

1. Click the Draw button on the Drawing toolbar, and then click Grid And Guides.
2. Select the Snap Objects To Grid check box or select the Snap Objects To Other Objects check box.
3. Click OK.

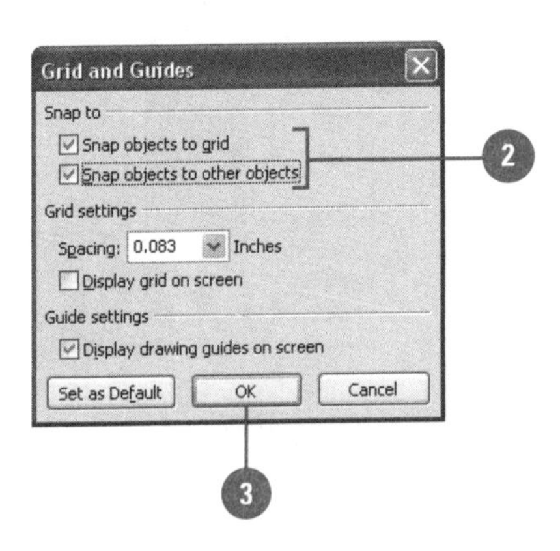

Align an Object to a Guide

1. Click the View menu, click Grid And Guides, select the Display Drawing Guides On Screen check box to display a horizontal and vertical guide, and then click OK.
2. Drag the object's center or edge near the guide. PowerPoint aligns the center or edge to the guide.

Did You Know?

You can use the keyboard to override grid settings. To temporarily override settings for the grids and guides, press and hold the Alt key as you drag an object.

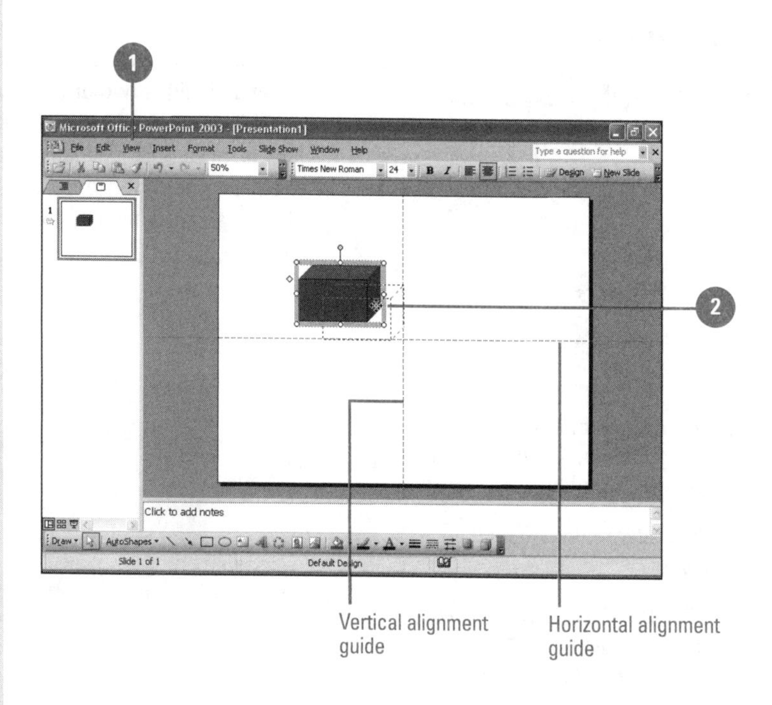

Add, Move, or Remove a Guide

- To move a guide, drag it.
- To add a new guide, press and hold the Ctrl key, and then drag the line to the new location. You can place a guide anywhere on the slide.
- To remove a guide, drag the guide off the slide. You cannot remove the original guides, they must be turned off.

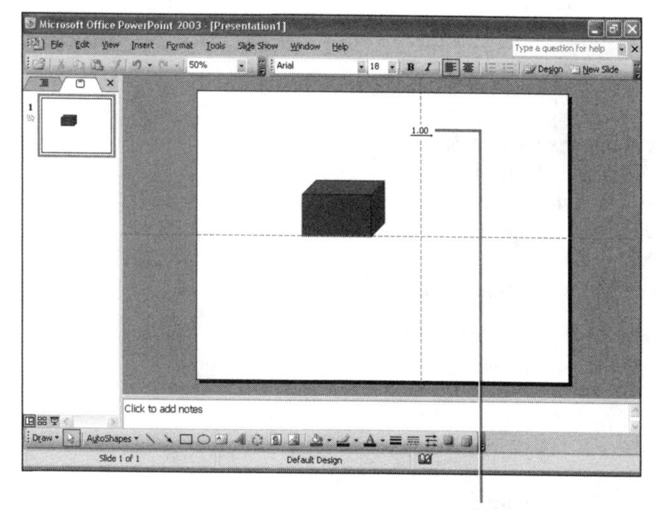

As you drag, a number appears that indicates the guide's position relative to the ruler.

4

Aligning and Distributing Objects

PP03S-2-2

In addition to using grids and guides to align objects to a specific point, you can align a group of objects to each other. The Align Or Distribute command aligns two or more objects relative to each other vertically to the left, center, or right. You can also align objects horizontally to the top, middle, or bottom. To align several objects to each other evenly across the slide, either horizontally or vertically, you select them and then choose a distribution option.

Distribute Objects

1. Select the objects you want to distribute.
2. Click the Draw button on the Drawing toolbar, and then point to Align Or Distribute.
3. Click the distribution option you want.
   - Click Distribute Horizontally to evenly distribute the objects horizontally.
   - Click Distribute Vertically to evenly distribute the objects vertically.

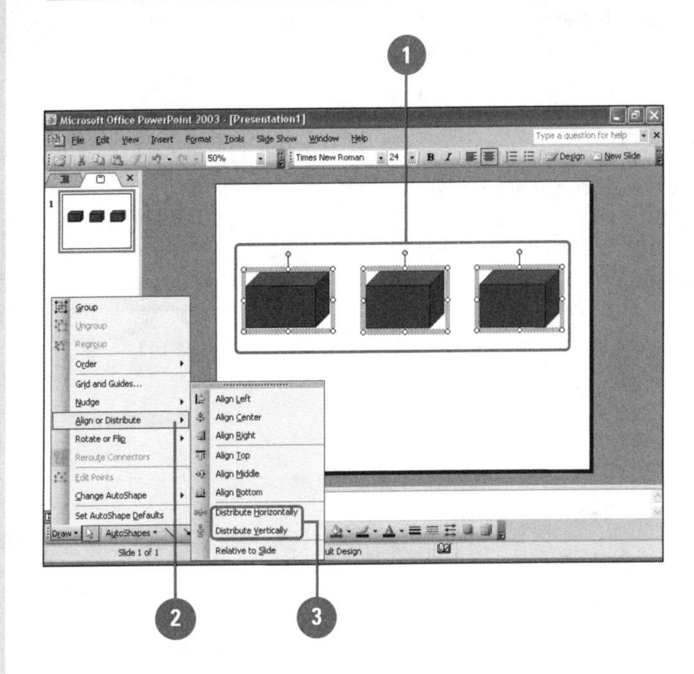

Did You Know?

You can move objects independently. Make sure Relative To Slide on the Align Or Distribute submenu isn't selected. When this command is selected, objects will move in relation to the slide as well as to other objects.

Align Objects with Other Objects

1. Select the objects you want to align.
2. Click the Draw button on the Drawing toolbar, and then point to Align Or Distribute.
3. Select Relative To Slide if you want the objects to align relative to the slide, or deselect Relative To Slide if you want the objects to align relative to each other.
4. Click the alignment command you want.
   - Click Align Left to line up the objects with the left edge of the selection or slide.
   - Click Align Center to line up the objects with the center of the selection or slide.
   - Click Align Right to line up the objects with the right edge of the selection or slide.
   - Click Align Top to line up the objects with the top edge of the selection or slide.
   - Click Align Middle to line up the objects vertically with the middle of the selection or slide.
   - Click Align Bottom to line up the objects with the bottom of the selection or slide.

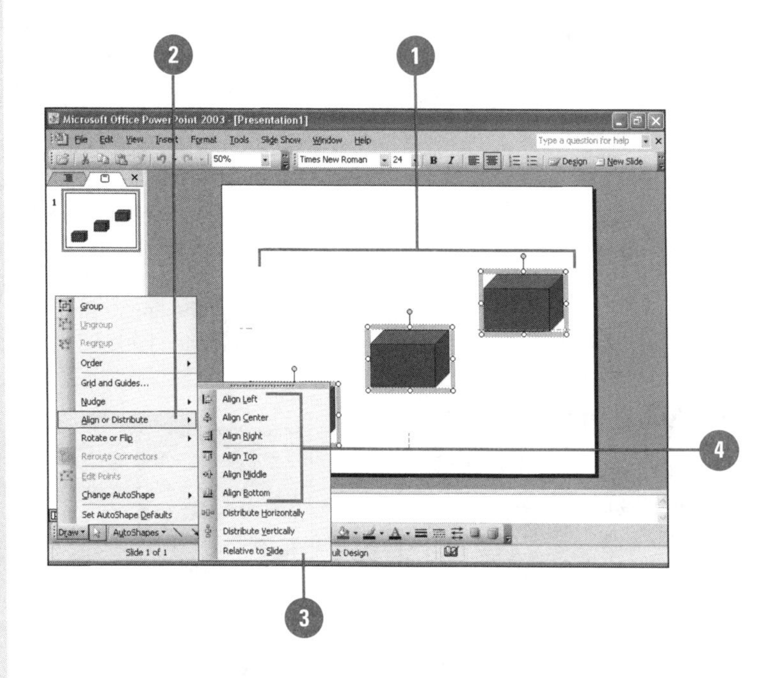

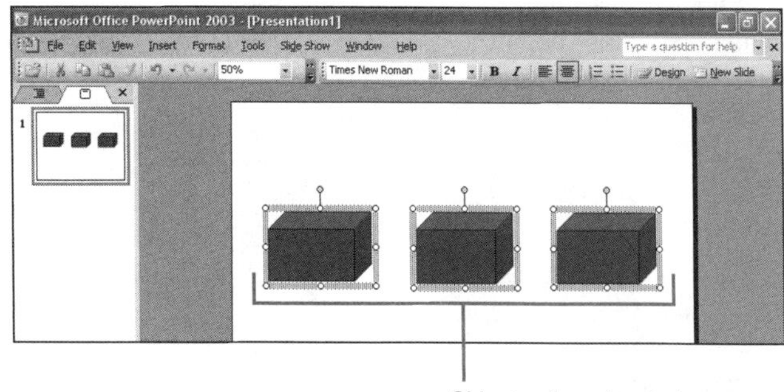

Objects aligned to their tops.

4

Connecting Shapes

PP03S-2-2

PowerPoint makes it easy to draw and modify flow charts and diagrams. Flow charts and diagrams consist of shapes connected together to indicate a sequence of events. With PowerPoint, you can join two objects with a connecting line. Once two objects are joined, the connecting line moves when you move either object. The connecting line touches special connection points on the objects. When you position the pointer over an object, small blue handles, known as connection sites, appear, and the pointer changes to a small box, called the connection pointer. You can drag a connection end point to another connection point to change the line or drag the adjustment handle to change the shape of the connection line.

Connect Two Objects

1. On the Drawing toolbar, click AutoShapes, point to Connectors, and then click a connector.
2. Position the pointer over an object handle, and then click the object to select a connection point.
3. Position the pointer over the object handle on another object, and then click the object to select another connection point.

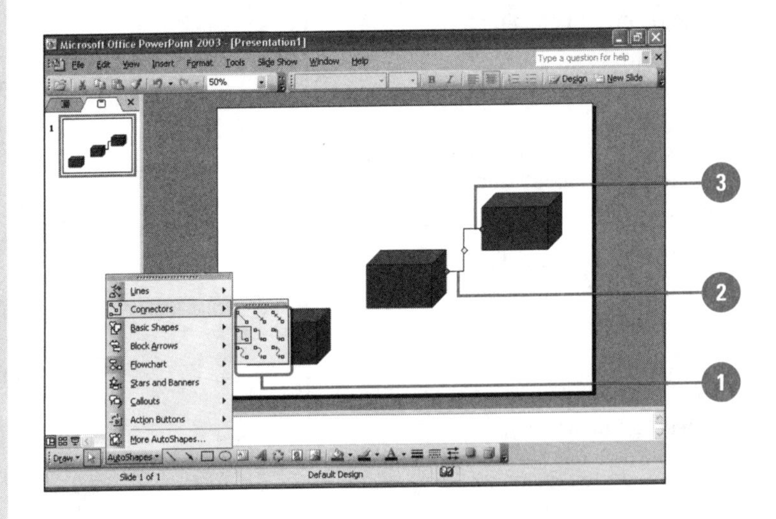

Change and Format a Connector Line

1. Click on the connector line you want to modify to select it. To select more than one line, hold down Shift, and then click all the connector lines you wish to modify.
2. On the Drawing toolbar, use buttons such as Line Style, Dash Style, and Arrow Style to modify the connector lines.

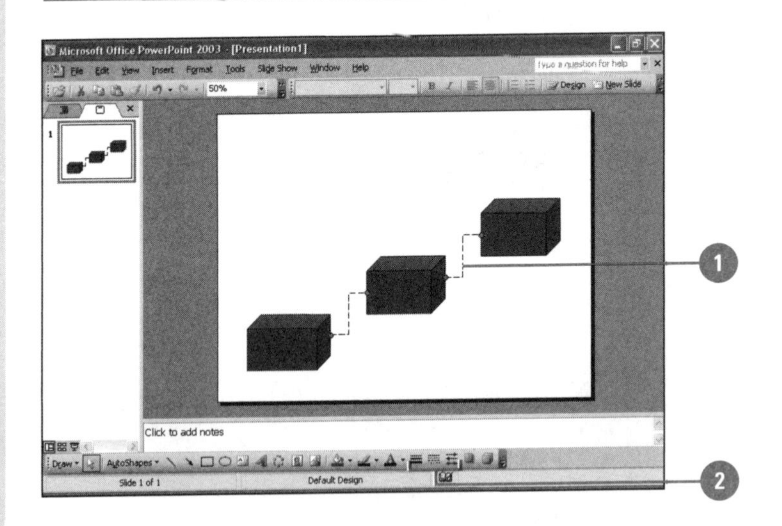

Changing Stacking Order

PP03S-2-2

When a slide contains multiple objects, the objects appear on the slide in a stacking order. Stacking is the placement of objects one on top of another. The drawing order determines the object stacking order. The first object that you draw is on the bottom, and the last object that you draw is on top. You can change the order of this stack of objects by using Bring to Front, Send to Back, Bring Forward, and Send Backward commands on the Draw menu on the Drawing toolbar.

Arrange a Stack of Objects

1. Select the object or objects you want to arrange.
2. Click the Draw button on the Drawing toolbar, point to Order, and then click the option you want.
   - Click Bring To Front or Bring Forward to move a drawing to the top of the stack or up one location in the stack.
   - Click Send To Back or Send Backward to move a drawing to the bottom of the stack or back one location in the stack.

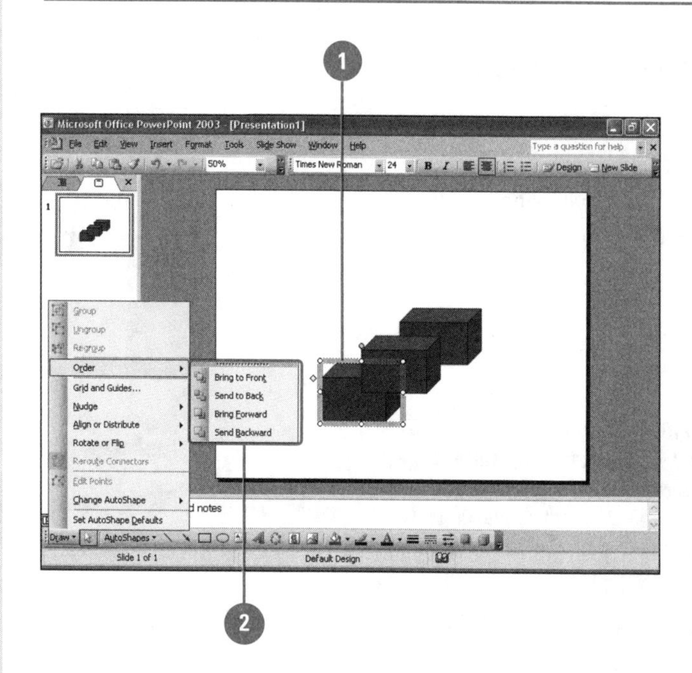

Did You Know?

You can view a hidden object in a stack. Press the Tab key or Shift+Tab to cycle forward or backward through the objects until you select the object you want.

Adding 3-D Effects to a Shape

PP03S-2-2

You can add the illusion of depth to your slides by using the 3-D tool. Although not all objects can be turned into 3-D objects, most of the AutoShapes can. You can create a 3-D effect using one of the 20 preset 3-D styles supported by PowerPoint, or you can use the 3-D tools to customize your own 3-D style. The settings you can control with the customization tools include the spin of the object, or the angle at which the 3-D object is tilted and rotated, the depth of the object, and the direction of light falling upon the object.

Apply a Preset 3-D Style

1. Click the drawing object you want to change.
2. Click the 3-D Style button on the Drawing toolbar.
3. Click a 3-D style.

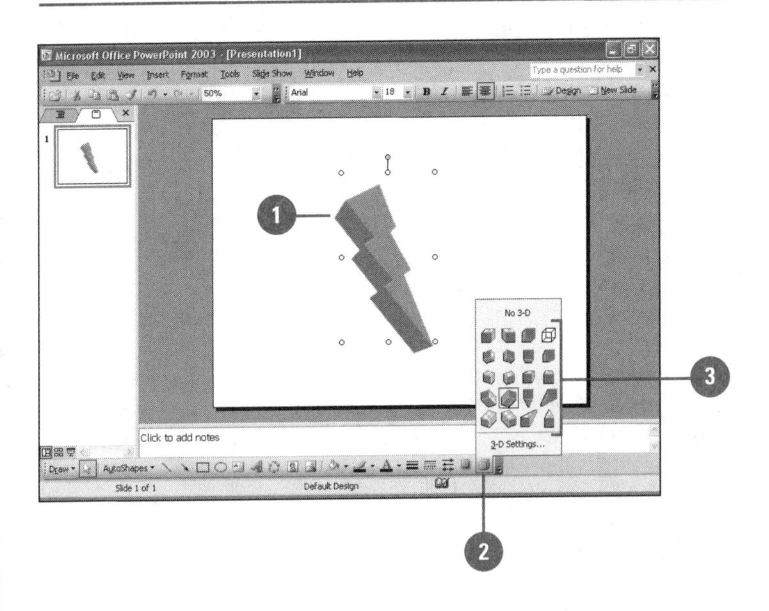

Did You Know?

You can add a different surface to your 3-D object. Apply interesting surfaces, such as wire frame, matte, plastic, or metal, to your 3-D object by clicking the Surface button on the 3-D Settings toolbar.

Tilting a 3-D Object

1. Click the 3-D object you want to change.
2. Click the 3-D Style button on the Drawing toolbar, and then click 3-D Settings.
3. Click the tilt setting you want.
4. Click the Close button on the 3-D Settings toolbar.

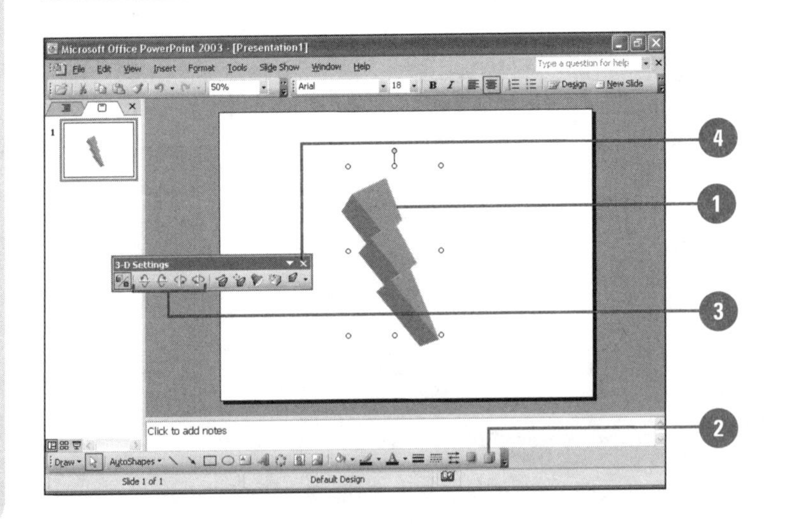

Set Lighting

1. Click the 3-D object, click the 3-D Style button on the Drawing toolbar, and then click 3-D Settings.
2. Click the Lighting button on the 3-D Settings toolbar.
3. Click the spotlight that creates the effect you want.
4. Click the Close button on the 3-D Settings toolbar.

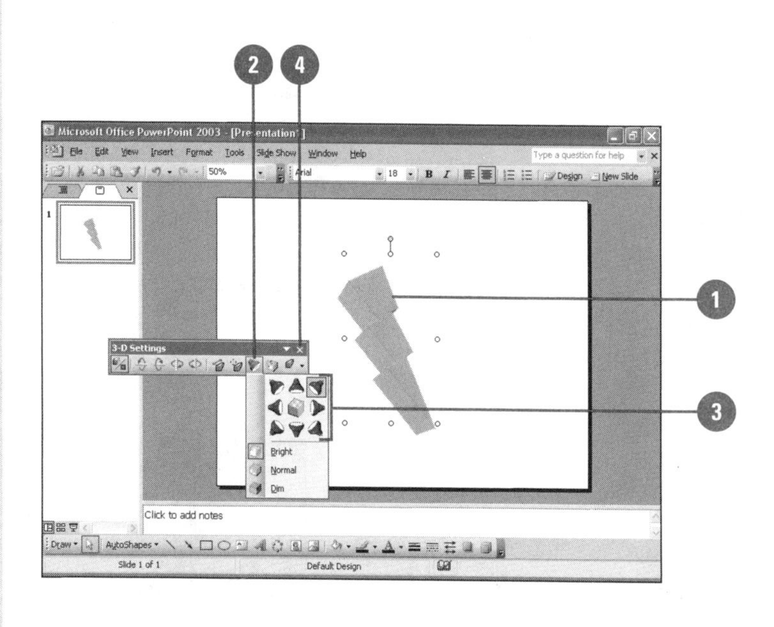

Set 3-D Depth

1. Click the 3-D object, click the 3-D Style button on the Drawing toolbar, and then click 3-D Settings.
2. Click the Depth button on the 3-D Settings toolbar.
3. Click the size of the depth in points, or enter the exact number of points you want in the Custom box.
4. Click the Close button on the 3-D Settings toolbar.

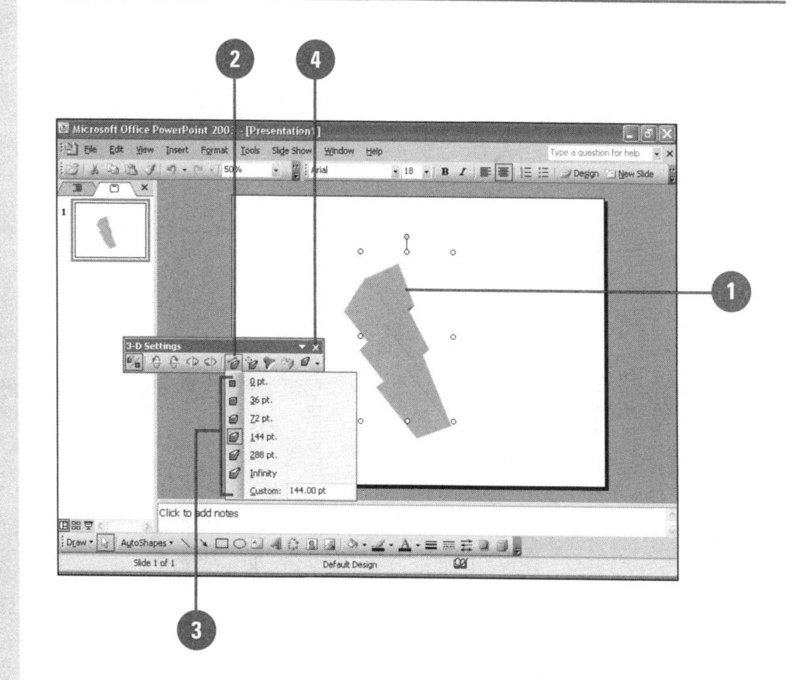

Did You Know?

You can change the direction of a 3-D object. Click the Direction button on the 3-D Settings toolbar. You can also use this button to add perspective to your objects or align them along a parallel.

4

Rotating and Flipping a Shape

PP03S-2-2

Once you create an object, you can change its orientation on the slide by rotating or flipping it. Rotating turns an object 90 degrees to the right or left; flipping turns an object 180 degrees horizontally or vertically. If you need a more exact rotation, which you cannot achieve in 90 or 180 degree increments, you can drag the green rotate lever at the top of an object to rotate it to any position. You can also rotate and flip any type of picture–including bitmaps–in a presentation. This is useful when you want to change the orientation of an object or image, such as changing the direction of an arrow.

Rotate an Object to any Angle

1. Click the object you want to rotate.
2. Position the pointer (which changes to the Free Rotate pointer) over the green rotate lever at the top of the object, and then drag to rotate the object.
3. Click outside the object to set the rotation.

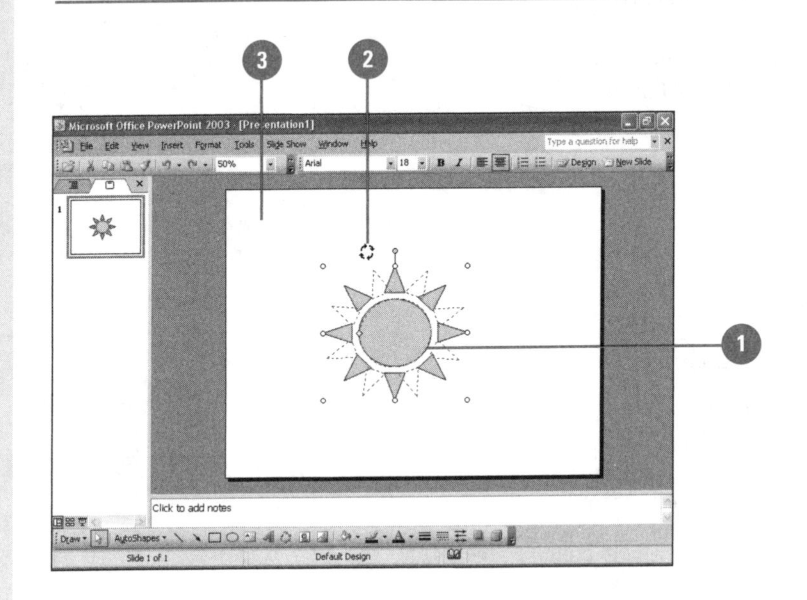

Rotate or Flip a Drawing Using Preset Increments

1. Click the object you want to rotate or flip.
2. Click the Draw button on the Drawing toolbar.
3. Point to Rotate or Flip, and then click a rotate or flip option.

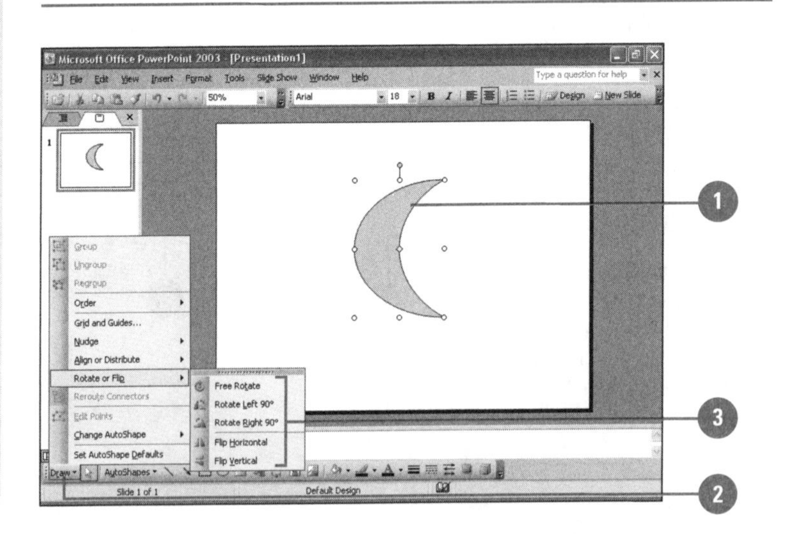

Rotate a Drawing Object Around a Fixed Point

1. Click the object you want to rotate.
2. Click the Draw button on the Drawing toolbar, point to Rotate or Flip, and then click Free Rotate.
3. Click the rotate handle opposite the point you want to rotate, and then press and hold the Ctrl key as you rotate the object.
4. Click outside the object to set the rotation.

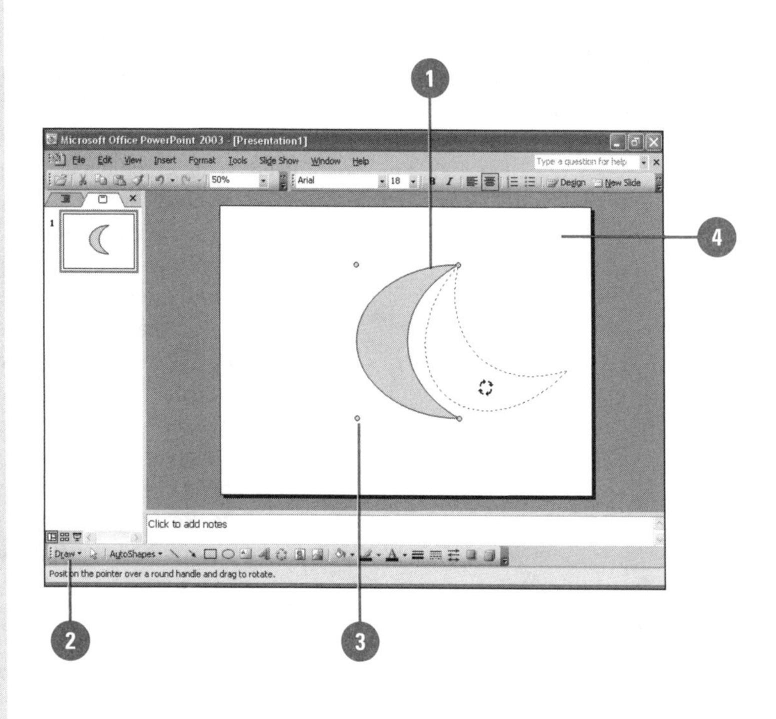

Rotate a Drawing Precisely

1. Right-click the object you want to rotate, and then click Format AutoShape.
2. Click the Size tab.
3. Enter the angle of rotation, or click the up or down arrows.
4. Click OK.

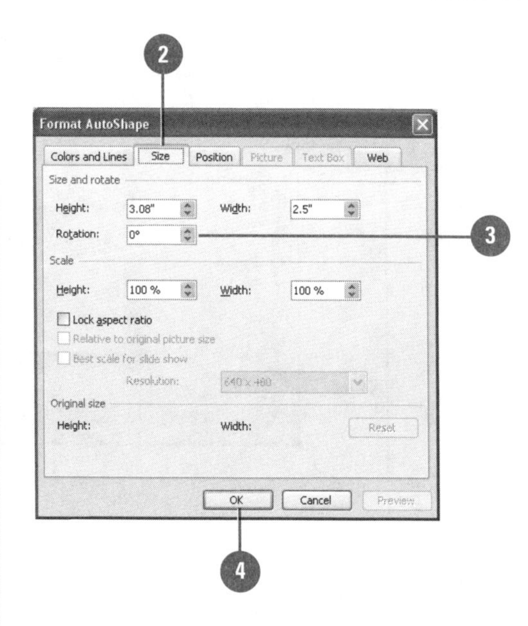

Did You Know?

You can constrain the rotation to 15-degree increments. Press and hold Shift when you rotate the object.

You cannot rotate or flip some imported objects. Not all imported objects can be rotated or flipped. By ungrouping the imported object and then regrouping its components, you might be able to rotate or flip it.

Grouping and Ungrouping Shapes

Objects can be grouped together, ungrouped, and regrouped in PowerPoint to make editing and moving information easier. Rather than moving several objects one at a time, you can group the objects and move them all together. Grouped objects appear as one object, but each object in the group maintains its individual attributes. You can change an individual object within a group without ungrouping. This is useful when you need to make only a small change to a group, such as changing the color of a single shape in the group. You can also format specific AutoShapes, drawings, or pictures within a group without ungrouping. Simply select the object within the group, change the object or edit text within the object, and then deselect the object. However, if you need to move an object in a group, you need to first ungroup the objects, make the change, and then group the objects together again. After you ungroup a set of objects, PowerPoint remembers each object in the group and in one step regroups those objects when you use the Regroup command. Before you regroup a set of objects, make sure that at least one of the grouped objects is selected.

Group Objects Together

1. Select the objects you want to group together.
2. Click the Draw button on the Drawing toolbar, and then click Group.

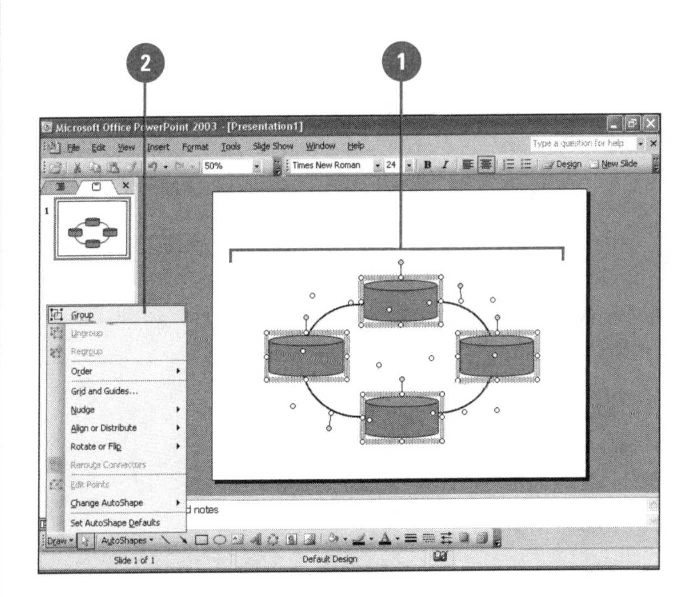

Did You Know?

You can use the Tab key to select objects in order. Move between the drawing objects on your slide (even those hidden behind other objects) by pressing the Tab key.

You can use the shortcut menu to select the Order and Grouping commands. Right-click the objects you want to group or reorder, point to Grouping or Order, and then make your selections.

Ungroup a Drawing

1. Select the grouped object you want to ungroup.
2. Click the Draw button on the Drawing toolbar, and then click Ungroup.

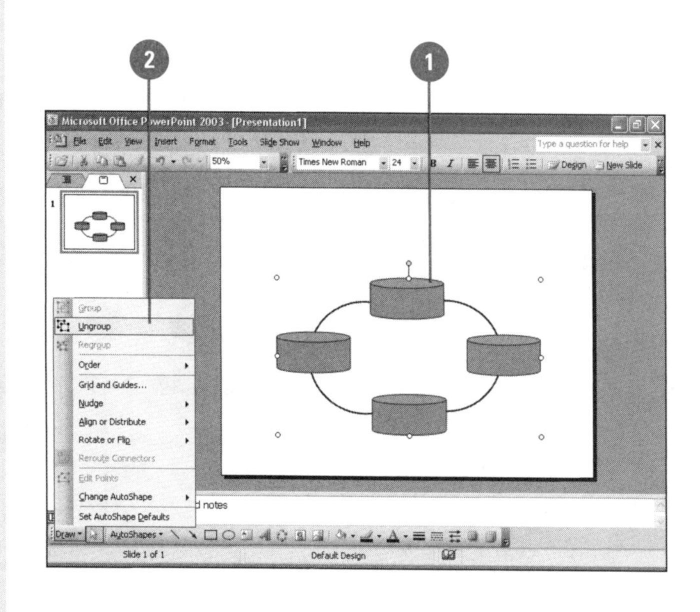

Regroup a Drawing

1. Select one of the objects in the group of objects you want to regroup.
2. Click the Draw button on the Drawing toolbar, and then click Regroup.

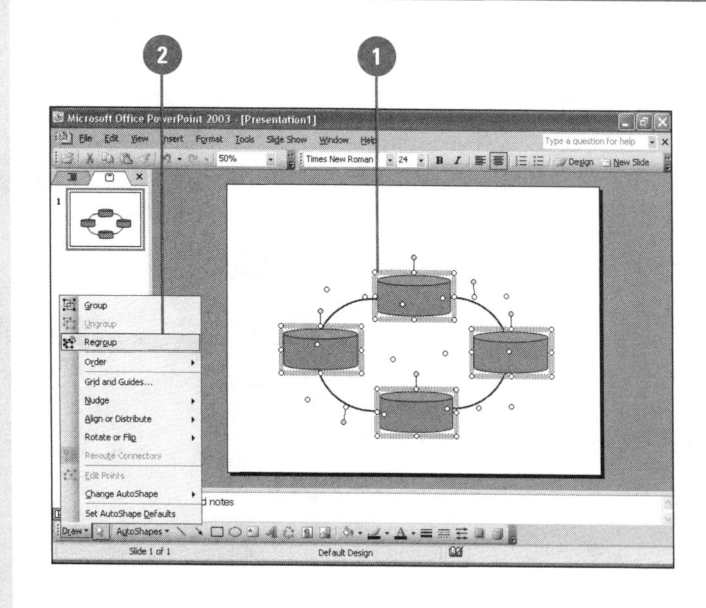

Did You Know?

You can troubleshoot the arrangement of objects. If you have trouble selecting an object because another object is in the way, try moving the first object out of the way temporarily.

Adding a Shape to the Clip Organizer

After spending time creating an object, you might want to save it for use in future presentations. You can add any object you create to the Microsoft Clip Organizer, an organized collection of clip art, pictures, videos, and sounds that come with PowerPoint. You can also find a picture in the Clip Organizer and use it as the basis for the logo for your home business. For example, you could use the basket of bread image for a home bakery.

Add Your Own Shape to the Clip Organizer

1. Select the drawing object you want to add to the Clip Organizer.
2. Click the Copy button on the Standard toolbar.
3. Click the Insert menu, point to Picture, and then click Clip Art.
4. Click Organize Clips at the bottom of the Clip Art task pane.
5. Click the collection folder you want to add the clip to.
6. Click the Edit menu in the Clip Organizer, and then click Paste.
7. Click the Close button to close the Microsoft Clip Organizer.

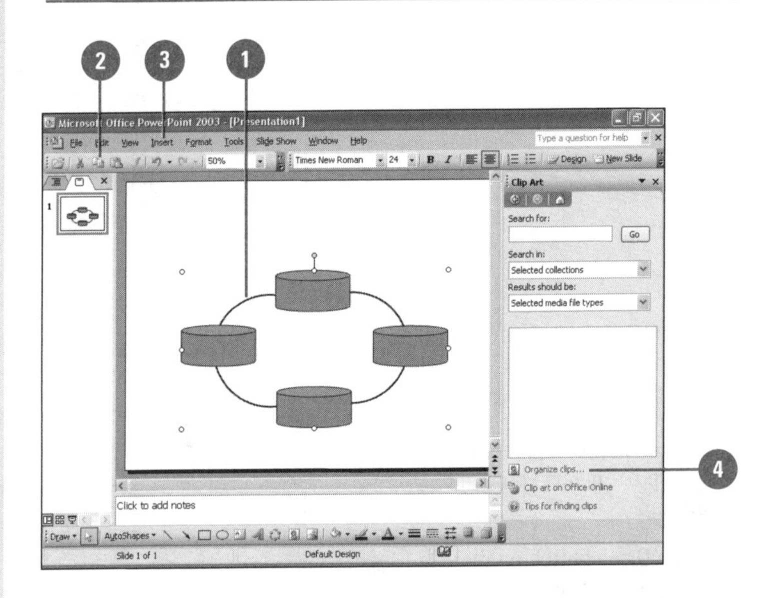

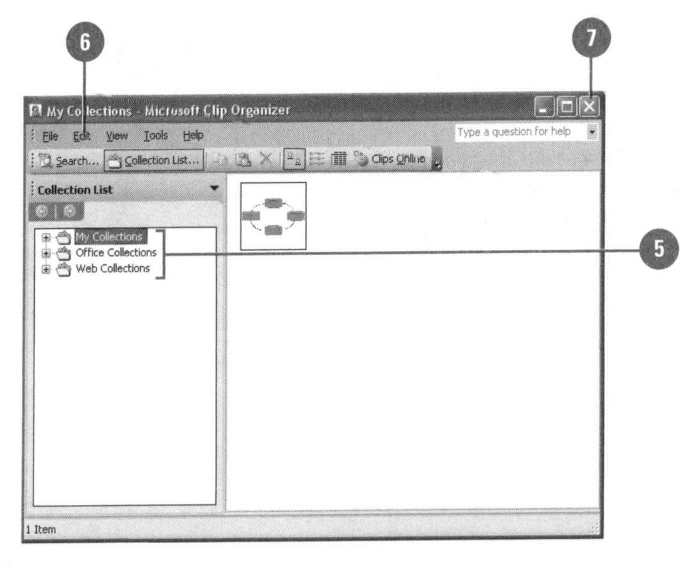

Inserting Pictures and Multimedia

5

Introduction

Although well-illustrated slides can't make up for a lack of content, you can capture your audiences' attention if your slides are vibrant and visually interesting. You can easily enhance a slide by adding a picture—one of your own or one of the hundreds that come with Microsoft Office PowerPoint 2003. If you have the appropriate hardware, such as a sound card and speakers, you can also include sound files and video clips in your presentation.

Microsoft Office comes with a vast array of ClipArt, and there are endless amounts available through other software packages or on the Web. When going online to look at clips, you can categorize them so that it's easier to find the best choice for your presentation. You can use the Microsoft Online Web site to search for and download additional clip art.

With all of your digital photos or scanned pictures, you can organize them in an album. Certain elements, such as adding text, or oval frames, make cataloging your pictures an easier process. If you need to modify your pictures, you can resize them, compress them for storage, change their brightness or contrast, recolor them, or change their shape by cropping them.

WordArt is another feature that adds detail to your slide presentation. Available in other Office applications, WordArt can bring together your slides—you can change it's color, shape, shadow, or size. Because WordArt comes with so many style choices, time spent customizing your slides is minimal.

Another element that will give your presentation a real professional look and feel is the addition of movie clips or sounds. Imagine watching a slide show presentation with music playing at key points or starting a slide show with a movie clip that loosens up the audience.

What You'll Do

Insert Multimedia Clips

Add and Remove Clips

Locate and Insert Clip Art

Organize Clips into Categories

Access Clip Art on the Web

Insert a Picture

Modify a Picture

Recolor a Picture

Crop a Picture

Create WordArt Text

Modify WordArt Text

Apply WordArt Text Effects

Insert Movies and Sounds

Record Sounds

Play Movies and Sounds

Inserting Multimedia Clips

PowerPoint provides access to hundreds of professionally designed pieces of clip art. These clips include clip art, pictures, photographs, sounds, and videos. All Office 2003 programs includes **Microsoft Clip Organizer**, which organizes these objects into categories and gives you tools to help locate the clips you need quickly. You can extend the usefulness of the Clip Organizer by importing your own objects. The Insert Clip Art task pane helps you search for clip art and access the clip art available in the Clip Organizer.

Clip Art

Clip art objects (pictures and animated pictures) are images made up of geometric shapes, such as lines, curves, circles, squares, and so on. These images, known as vector images, are mathematically defined, which makes them easy to resize and manipulate. A picture in the Microsoft Windows Metafile (.WMF) file format is an example of a vector image.

Pictures

Pictures, on the other hand, are not mathematically defined. They are **bitmaps**, images that are made up of dots. Bitmaps do not lend themselves as easily to resizing because the dots can't expand and contract when you enlarge or shrink your picture. You can create a picture using a bitmap graphics program such as Adobe Photoshop, Microsoft Paint, or Paint Shop Pro by drawing or scanning an image or by taking a digital photograph.

Sounds

A **sound** is a file that makes a sound. Some sounds play on your computer's internal speakers (such as the beep you hear when your operating system alerts you to an error), but others require a sound card and speakers. You can use the Windows accessory called **Windows Media Player** to listen to sound clips.

Videos

A **video** can be animated pictures, such as cartoons, or it can be digital video prepared with digitized video equipment. Although you can play a video clip on most monitors, if it has sound, you need a sound card and speakers to hear the clip.

Adding and Removing Clips

PP03S-1-4

You might want to add pictures and categories to the Clip Organizer for easy access in the future. You can import your own clips (pictures, photographs, sounds, and videos) into the Clip Organizer. For example, if you have a company logo that you plan to include in more than one presentation, add it to the Clip Organizer. You can also add groups of clips to the Clip Organizer. If you no longer need a picture in the Clip Organizer, you can remove it, which also saves space on your computer.

Add a Clip

1. Click the Insert Clip Art button on the Drawing toolbar, and then click Organize Clips on the Clip Art task pane.
2. Click the File menu, click Add Clips To Organizer, and then click On My Own.
3. Click the Look In list arrow, and then select the drive and folder that contain the clip you want to import.
4. Click the Files Of Type list arrow, and then select the file type.
5. Click the clip you want to import.
6. Click Add.

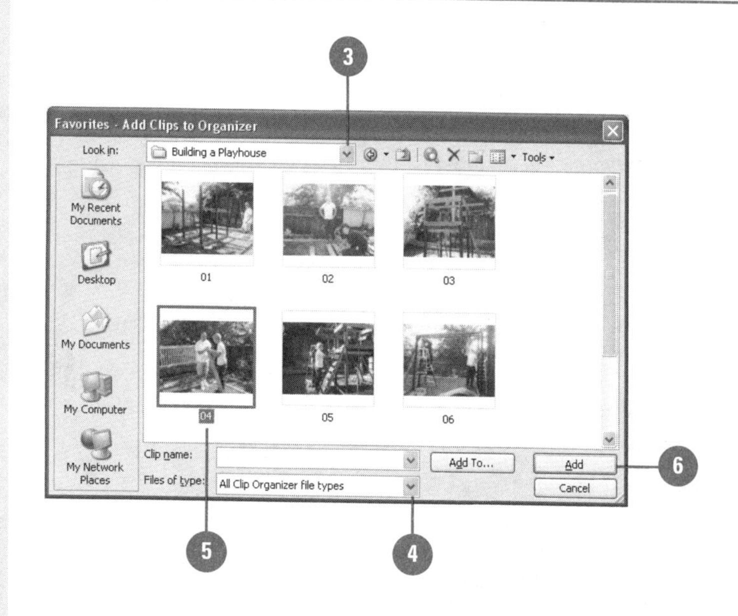

Remove a Clip

1. Click the Insert Clip Art button on the Drawing toolbar, and then click Organize Clips on the Clip Art task pane.
2. Point to the clip you want to remove, and then click the list arrow.
3. To delete the clip from all Clip Organizer categories, click Delete From Clip Organizer.

   To remove the clip from just one category, click Delete From the listed category.

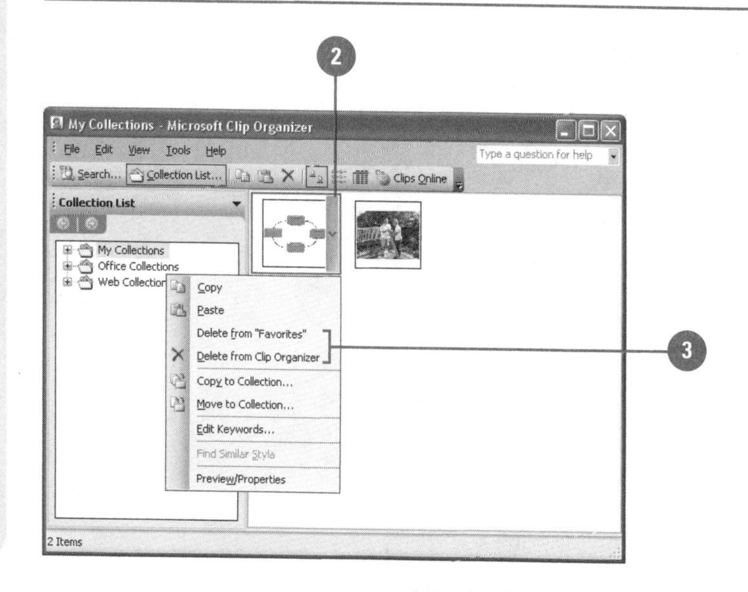

5

Locating and Inserting Clip Art

PP03S-1-4

To add a clip art image to a slide, you can use an AutoLayout with a content placeholder and simply click the Insert Clip Art icon, which opens the Select Picture dialog box. You can also click the Insert Clip Art button on the Drawing toolbar or point to Picture on the Insert menu, and then click Clip Art to open the Insert Clip Art task pane, which assists you in searching for clip art. You can limit search results to a specific collection of clip art or a specific type of media file.

Locate Clip Art by Keyword

1. Click the Insert menu, point to Picture, and then click Clip Art.
2. Type the keyword(s) associated with the clip you are looking for.

   To narrow your search, do one of the following:

   - To limit search results to a specific collection of clip art, click the Search In list arrow, and then select the collections you want to search.
   - To limit search results to a specific type of media file, click the Results Should Be list arrow, and then select the check box next to the types of clips you want to find.
3. Click Go.

   Clips matching the keywords appear in the Results list.

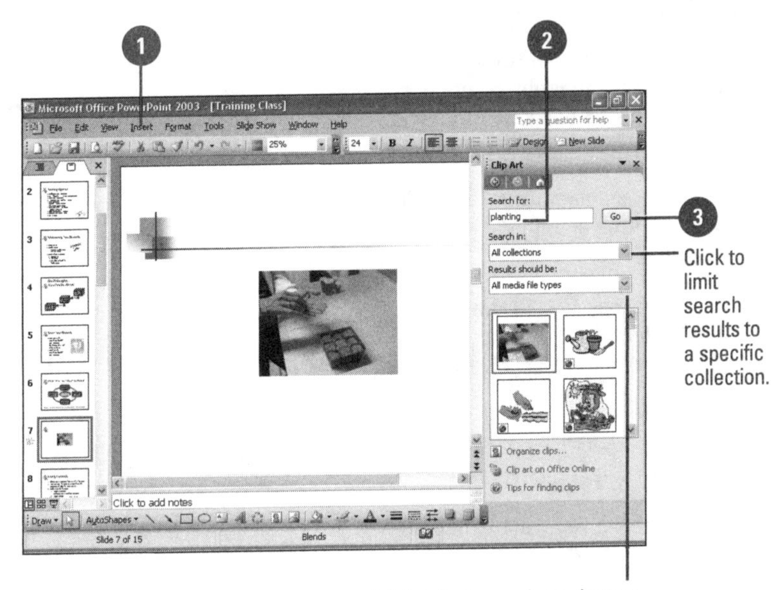

Click to limit search results to a specific collection.

Click to limit search results to a specific type of media file.

Did You Know?

You can find similar clips. In the Clip Art task pane, click the list arrow next to the clip in which you want to find similar clips, and then click Find Similar Style.

Insert a Clip Art Image Using an AutoLayout

1. Click the New Slide button on the Standard toolbar.
2. In the Slide Layout task pane, click an AutoLayout that includes the clip art content placeholder.
3. In the content placeholder, click the Insert Clip Art icon.
4. In the Select Picture dialog box, click the Search Text box, type what you want to search for, and then click Go.
5. Click the clip you want, and then click OK.

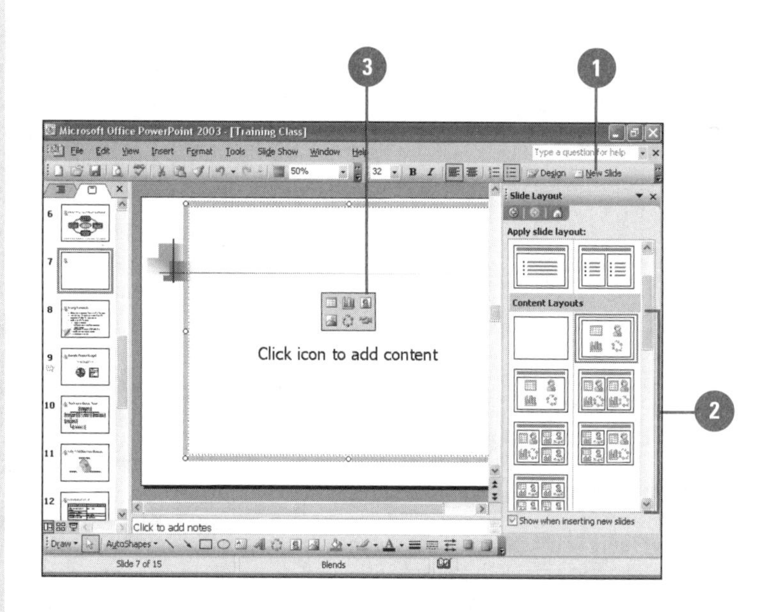

Insert a Clip Art Image Using the Insert Clip Art Task Pane

1. Click the Insert Clip Art button on the Drawing toolbar.
2. In the Clip Art task pane, click in the Search For box, type the clip you want, and then click Go.
3. Click the clip you want.
4. Click the Close button on the task pane.

Did You Know?

You can drag a picture. You can also drag a picture from the Clip Art task pane to your slide.

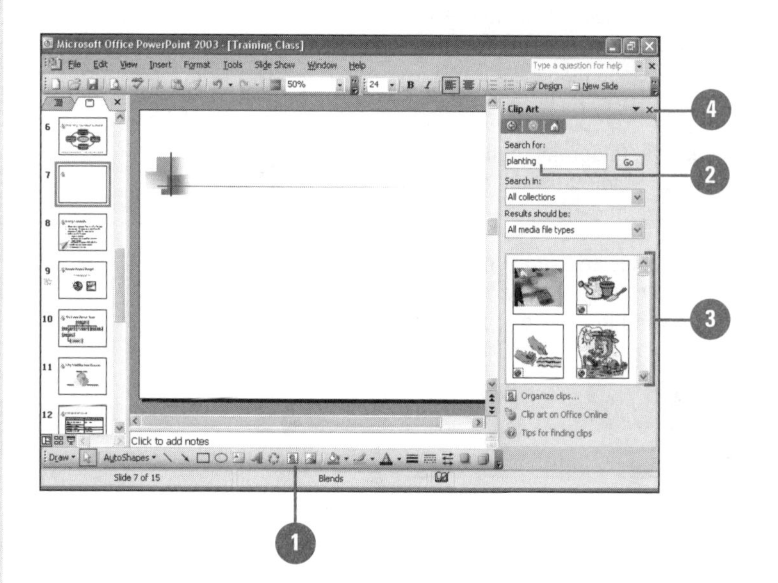

5

Organizing Clips into Categories

The clips that come with Microsoft Office PowerPoint 2003 are already organized, but if you've added clips without organizing them, it's probably hard to find what you need in a hurry. The Microsoft Clip Organizer sorts clip art images, pictures, sounds, and motion clips into categories. The Clip Organizer allows you to organize and select clips from Microsoft Office, from the Web, and from your personal collection of clips. To help you locate a clip quickly, you can place it in one or more categories. You can also assign one or more keywords to a clip and modify the description of a clip. When you add media files, Clip Organizer automatically creates new sub-collections under My Collections. These files are named after the corresponding folders on your hard disk. To help you find clips later on, Clip Organizer also creates search keywords based on the file's extension and folder name.

Categorize a Clip

1. Click the Insert Clip Art button on the Drawing toolbar, and then click Organize Clips at the bottom of the Clip Art task pane.
2. In Clip Organizer, click the File menu, point to Add Clips To Organizer, and then click On My Own.
3. Locate the folder that contains the clip you want to add, and then select the clip.
4. Click the Add To button, and then click the collection to which you want to add the clip, or click New to create a new folder. Click OK.
5. Click Add.

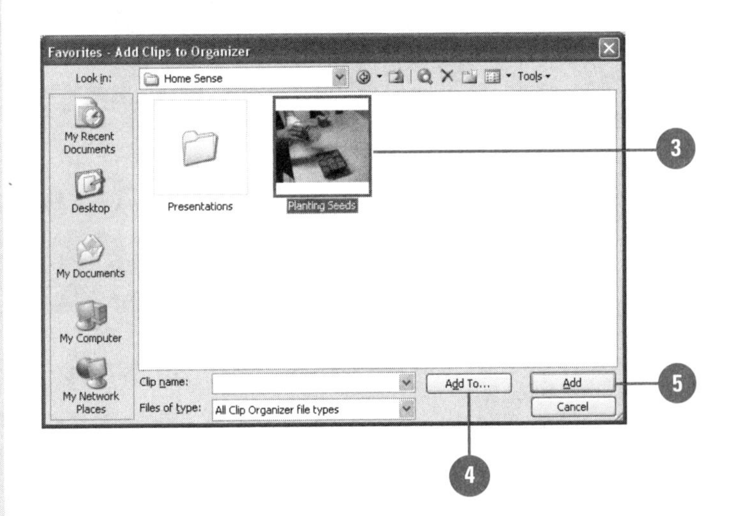

Did You Know?

You can create a new collection. In the Clip Organizer, click the File menu, click New Collection, type a new collection name, and then click OK.

Change Clip Properties

1. Click the Insert Clip Art button on the Drawing toolbar.
2. In the Clip Art task pane, click Organize Clips.
3. Find and point to the clip you want to categorize or change the properties of, click the list arrow, and then click one of the following:
   - Click Copy To Collection to place a copy of the clip in another category.
   - Click Move To Collection to move the clip to another category.
   - Click Edit Keywords to edit the caption of the clip and to edit keywords used to find the clip.
4. Click Close to close the Clip Organizer dialog box.

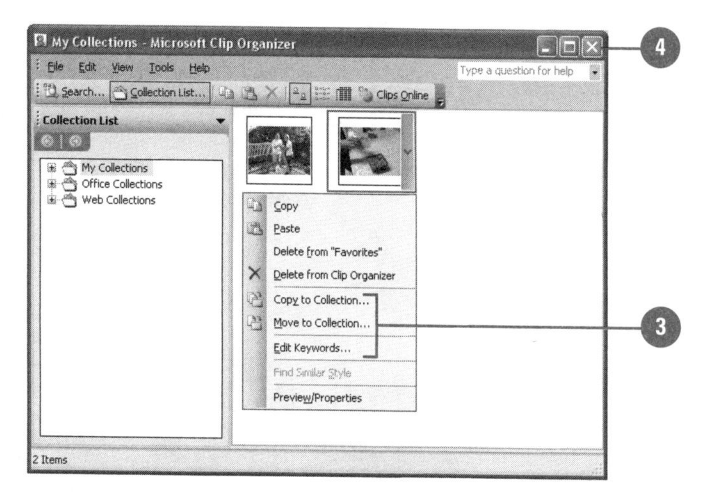

5

Accessing Clip Art on the Web

If you can't find the image that you want in the Clip Organizer, you can search for additional images in Clip art on Office Online, a clip gallery that Microsoft maintains on its Web site. To access Clip art on Office Online, you can click the link at the bottom of the Clip Art task pane or click the Clips Online button on the Clip Organizer toolbar. This launches your Web browser and navigates you directly to the Office Online Web site, where you can access thousands of free clip art images.

Open Clips Online

1. Click the Insert menu, point to Picture, and then click Clip Art.
2. Click Clip Art On Office Online
3. Establish a connection to the Internet.

   Your Web browser displays the Microsoft Office Online Clip Art and Media Home Web page.

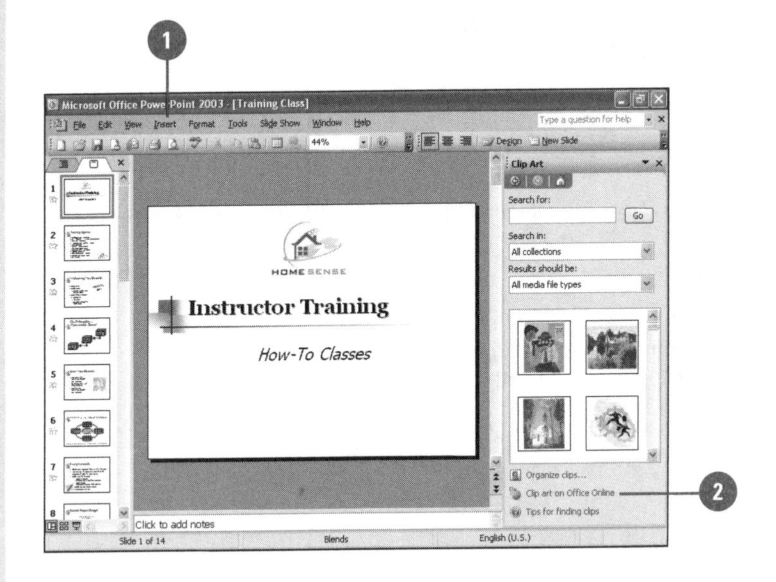

View Clips in a Category

1. If necessary, click the Accept button on the Clips Online Web page.
2. Scroll down to the Browse Clip Art And Media section, and then click the name of the category you want.

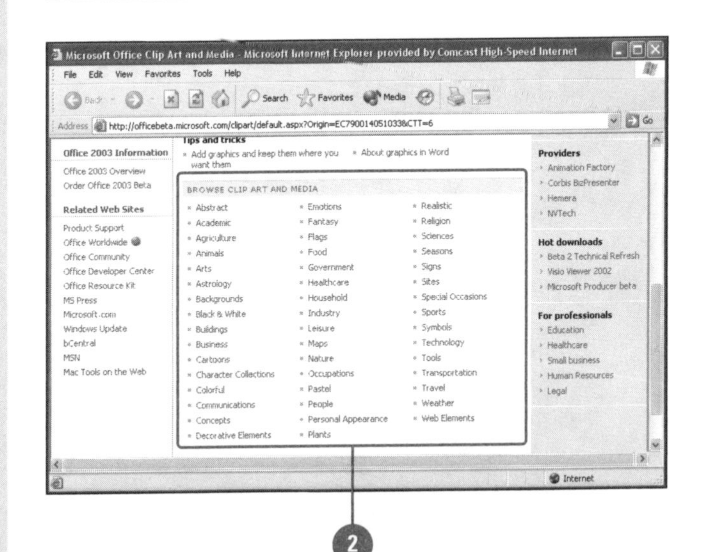

Search for a Clip

1. Click the Search list arrow on the Office Online Web page, and then select the media type you want: Clip Art, Photos, Animations, or Sounds.
2. Click the Search For box.
3. Type a keyword.
4. Click the green Click To Search arrow.

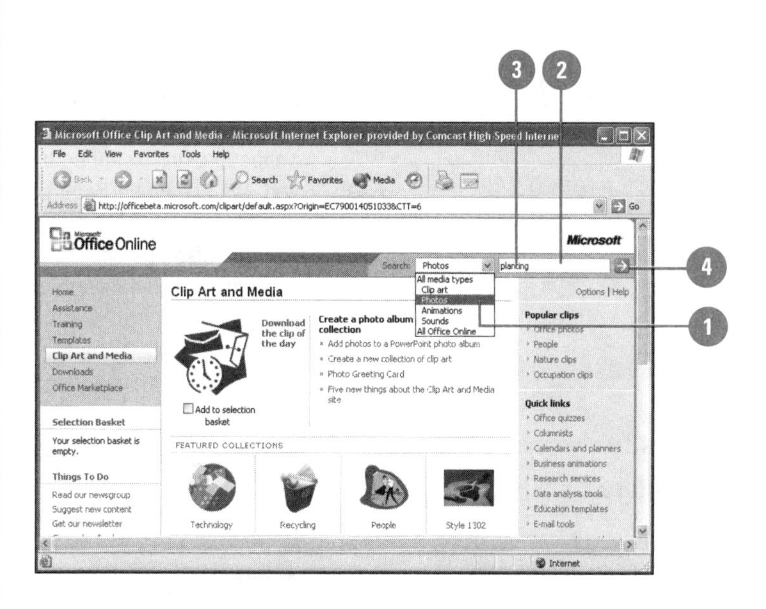

Download a Clip

1. Once you have displayed a list of clips on the Office Online Web page, select the check box below a clip to add it to your selection basket.

   You can select as many as you want. Clear the check box to deselect a clip.
2. Click Download 1 Item (will vary depending on the number of items you are downloading), review the Terms of Use, and then click Accept.
3. If a security virus warning dialog box appears, click Yes, and then click Continue.
4. Click Download Now, and then click Open.
5. The clip is stored on your hard disk and shown in your Clip Organizer where you can categorize it.

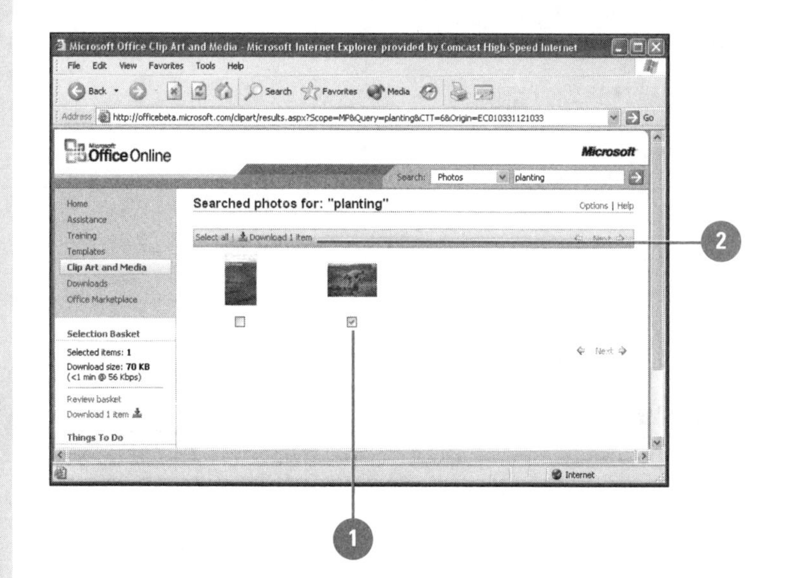

5

Inserting a Picture

PP03S-1-4

PowerPoint makes it possible for you to insert pictures, graphics, scanned photographs, art, photos, or artwork from a CD-ROM or other program into a slide. When you use the Picture submenu on the Insert menu, you specify the source of the picture–a file, Word's clip art collection, or a scanner. If you have a large collection of pictures, you can use PowerPoint to create a photo album. PowerPoint allows you to insert multiple pictures from your hard disk into your photo album. You can also customize the photo album using special layout options, such as oval frames and captions under each picture. When you insert pictures from files on your hard disk drive, scanner, digital camera, or Web camera, PowerPoint allows you to select multiple pictures, view thumbnails of them, and insert them all at once, which speeds up the process.

Insert a Picture from a File

1. Click the Insert menu, point to Picture, and then click From File.
2. Click the Look In list arrow, and then select the drive and folder that contain the file you want to insert.
3. Click the file you want to insert.
4. Click Insert.

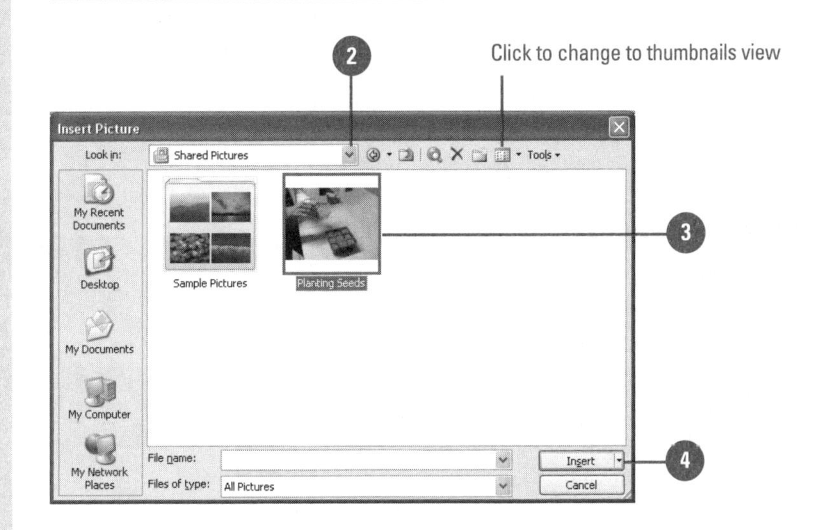

Insert a Picture from a Scanner or Camera

1. Click the Insert menu, point to Picture, and then click From Scanner Or Camera.
2. Click the Device list arrow, and then select the device connected to your computer.
3. Select the resolution (the visual quality of the image).
4. Click Insert or Custom Insert.

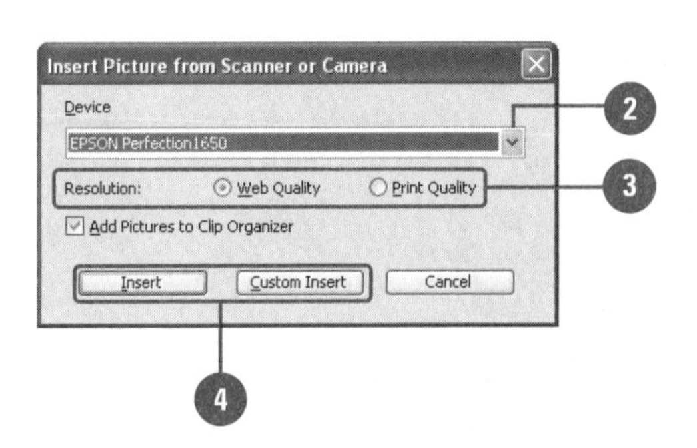

Create a New Photo Album

1. Click the Insert menu, point to Picture, and then click New Photo Album.
2. Click File/Disk.
3. Click the Look In list arrow, and then select the drive and folder that contain the pictures you want to insert.
4. Select the pictures you wish to include in the new photo album.

   TIMESAVER *Hold down the Ctrl key to select multiple pictures.*

5. Click Insert.
6. Click the Picture Layout list arrow, and then click a picture layout.
7. Click the Frame Shape list arrow, and then click a frame shape.
8. Click Create.
9. Click the File menu, click Save As, and then type a file name.
10. Click Save.

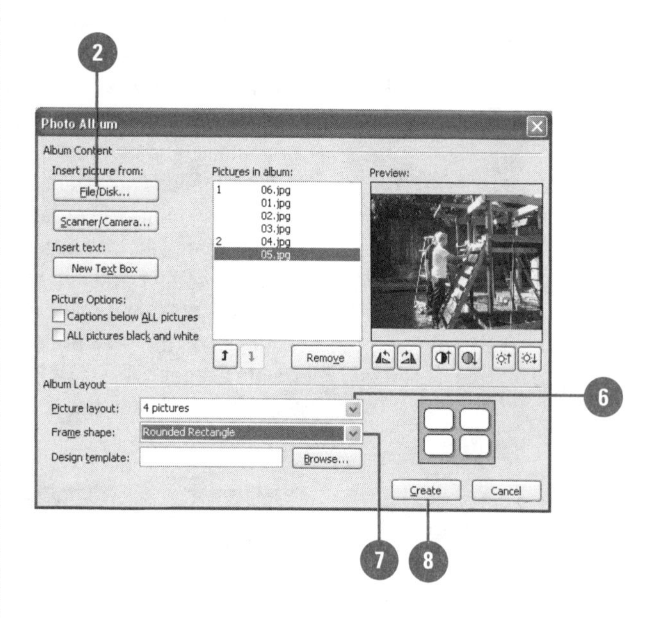

5

Modifying a Picture

PP03S-2-2

Once you have inserted clip art and other objects into your presentation, you can adapt them to meet your needs. Perhaps the clip is too small to be effective, or you don't quite like the colors it uses. Like any object, you can resize or move the clip art. You can also control the image's colors, brightness, and contrast using the Picture toolbar. You can use these same methods with bitmapped pictures. PowerPoint also allows you to compress pictures in order to minimize the file size of the image. In doing so, however, you may lose some visual quality, depending on the compression setting. You can pick the resolution that you want for the pictures in a presentation based on where or how they'll be viewed (for example, on the Web or printed), and you can set other options, such as Delete Cropped Areas Of Picture, to get the best balance between picture quality and file size.

Resize an Object

1. Click the object you want to resize.
2. Drag one of the sizing handles to increase or decrease the object's size.
   - Drag a middle handle to resize the object up, down, left, or right.
   - Drag a corner handle to resize the object proportionally.

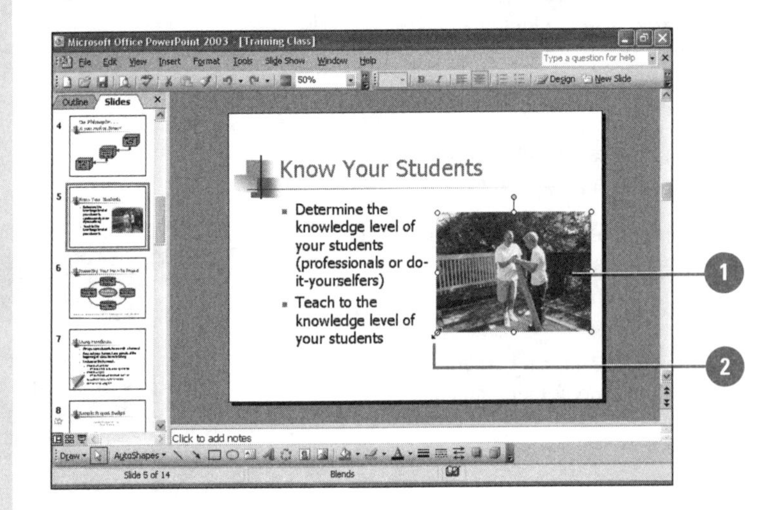

Compress a Picture

1. Click the picture you want to compress.
2. Click the Compress Pictures button on the Picture toolbar.
3. Click the compression options that you want.
4. Click OK, and then click Apply.

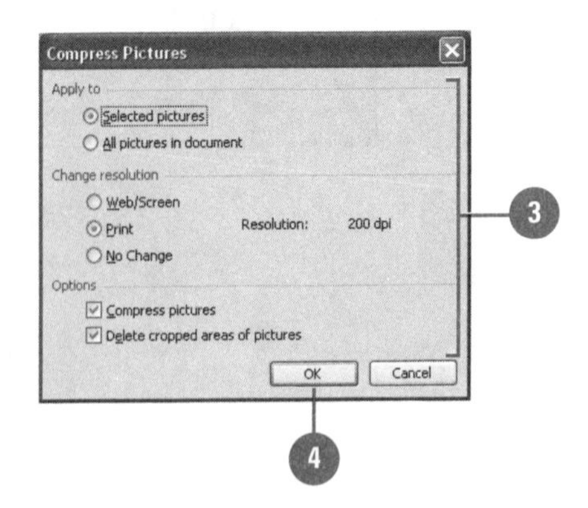

Change Brightness

1. Click the picture whose brightness you want to increase or decrease.
2. Choose the image brightness you want.
   - Click the More Brightness button on the Picture toolbar to lighten the object colors by adding more white.
   - Click the Less Brightness button on the Picture toolbar to darken the object colors by adding more black.

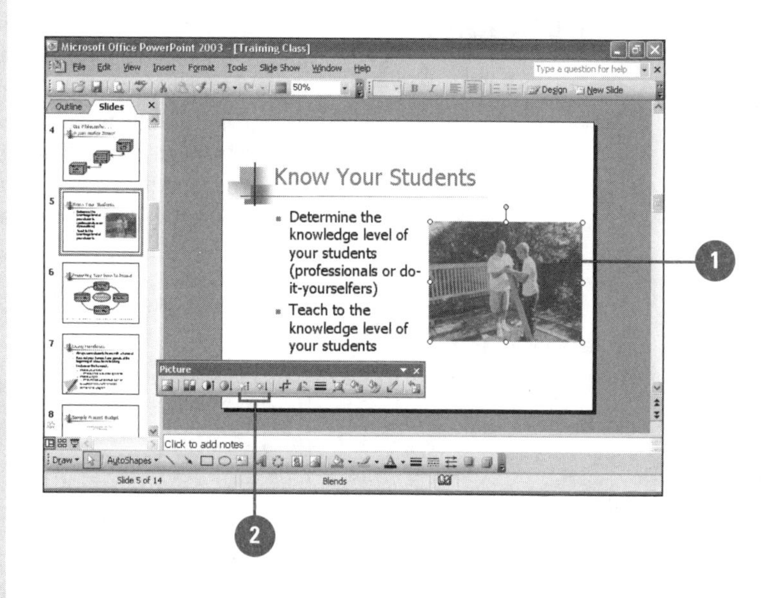

Change Contrast

1. Click the picture whose contrast you want to increase or decrease.
2. Choose the contrast you want.
   - Click the More Contrast button on the Picture toolbar to increase color intensity, resulting in less gray.
   - Click the Less Contrast button on the Picture toolbar to decrease color intensity, resulting in more gray.

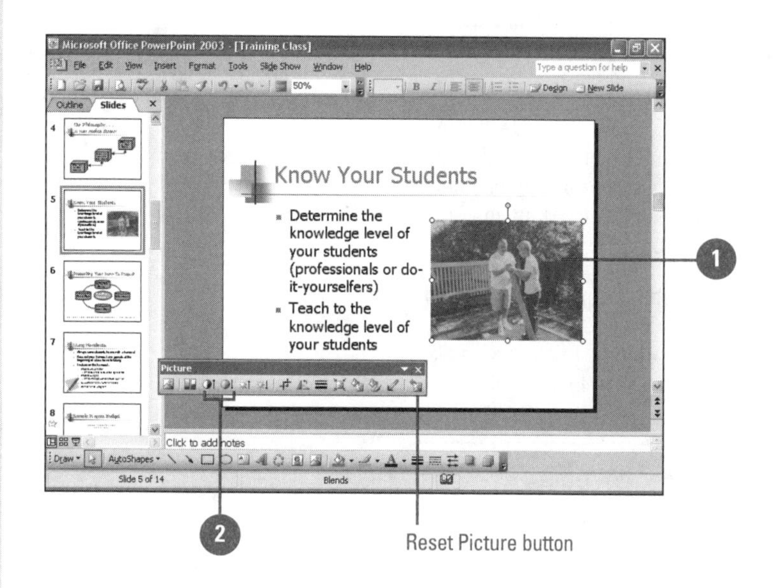

Did You Know?

You can restore a picture to original settings. Select the picture, and then click the Reset Picture button on the Picture toolbar. Resetting a picture restores its previous size and its original contrast and brightness.

Recoloring a Picture

PP03S-2-2

You can recolor clip art and other objects to match the color scheme of your presentation. For example, if you use a flower clip art as your business logo, you can change shades of pink in the spring to shades of orange in the autumn. You can also use a transparent background in your clip art to avoid conflict between its background color and your slide's background. With a transparent background, the clip art takes on the same background as your slide presentation.

Choose a Color Type

1. Click the picture whose color you want to change.
2. Click the Color button on the Picture toolbar.
3. Click one of the Color options.
    - Automatic gives the image the default coloring.
    - Grayscale converts the default coloring into whites, blacks, and grays scaled between white and black.
    - Black & White converts the default coloring into only white and black. You may lose detail in your object when you choose this option.
    - Washout converts the default coloring into whites and very light colors. This option makes a nice slide background.

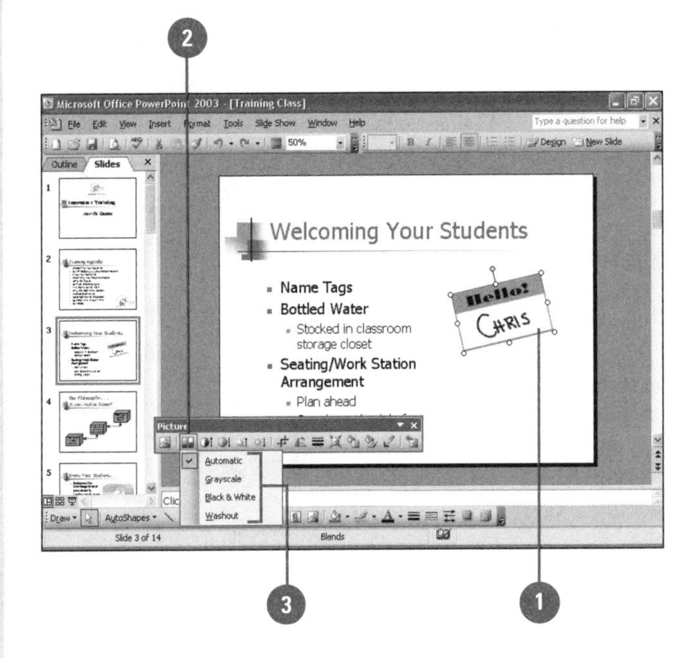

Did You Know?

You can't modify some pictures in PowerPoint. If the picture is a bitmap (.BMP, .JPG, .GIF, or .PNG), you need to edit its colors in an image editing program, such as Adobe Photoshop, Microsoft Paint, or Paint Shop Pro.

Recolor a Picture

1. Click the picture you want to recolor.
2. Click the Recolor Picture button on the Picture toolbar.
3. Click the check box next to the original color you want to change.
4. Click the corresponding New list arrow, and then select a new color.
5. Repeat steps 3 and 4 for as many colors as you want.
6. Click OK.

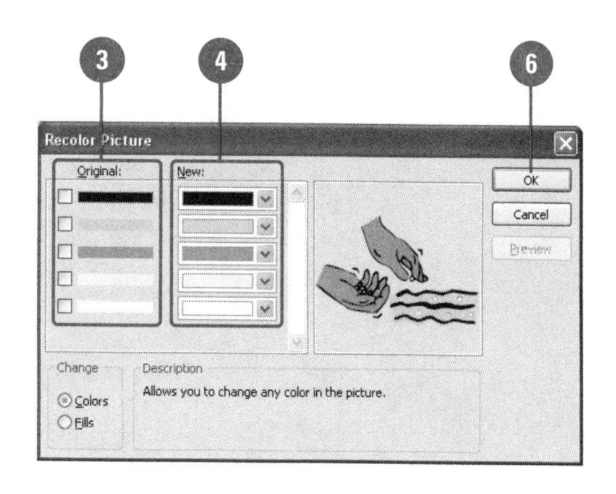

Set a Transparent Background

1. Click the picture you want to change.
2. Click the Set Transparent Color button on the Picture toolbar.
3. Move the pointer over the object until the pointer changes shape.
4. Click the color you want to set as transparent.
5. When you're done, click outside the image.

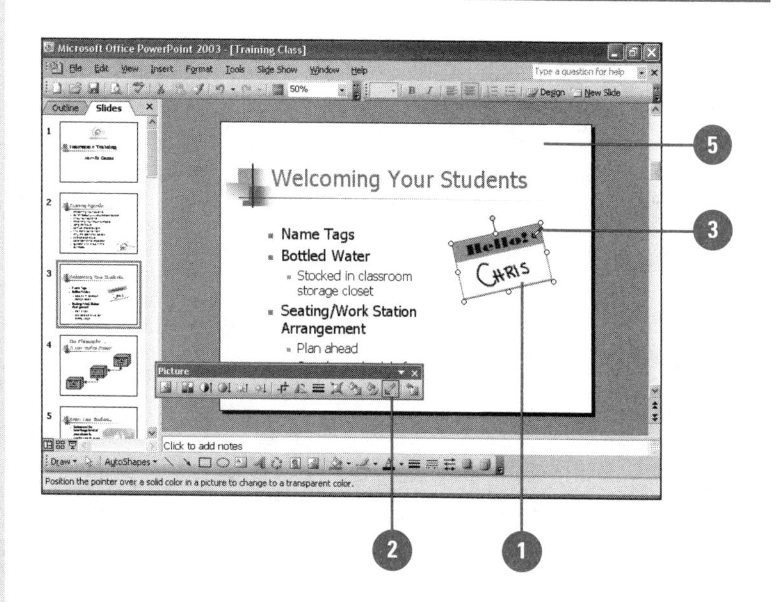

Did You Know?

Why is the Set Transparent Color button on the Picture toolbar dimmed? Setting a color as transparent works only with bitmaps. If you are working with an object that is not a bitmap, you will not be able to use this feature.

Cropping a Picture

PP03S-1-4

You can crop clip art to isolate just one portion of the picture. Because clip art uses vector image technology, you can crop, or cut out, even the smallest part of it and then enlarge it, and the clip art will still be recognizable. You can also crop bitmapped pictures, but if you enlarge the area you cropped, you lose picture detail. You can crop an image by hand using the Crop button on the Picture toolbar. You can also crop using the Format Picture dialog box, which gives you precise control over the dimensions of the area you want to crop.

Crop a Picture Quickly

1. Click the picture you want to crop.
2. Click the Crop button on the Picture toolbar.
3. Drag the sizing handles until the borders surround the area you want to crop.
4. Click outside the image when you are finished.

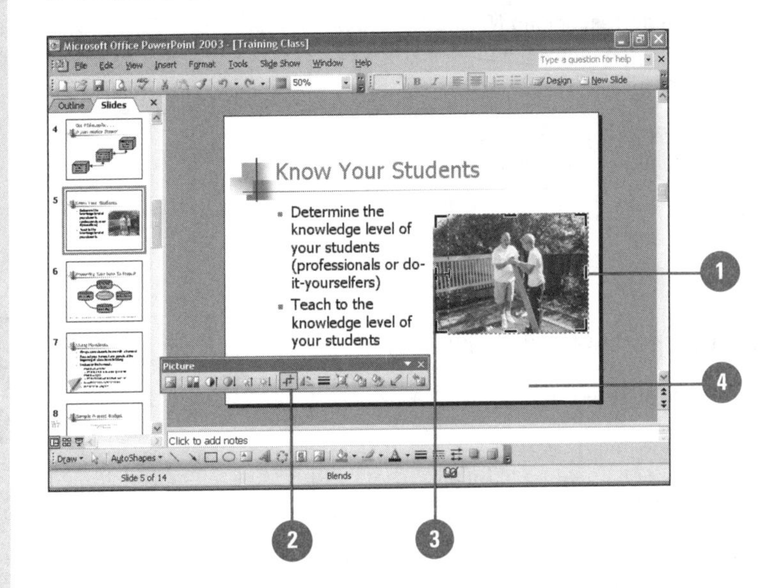

Redisplay a Cropped Picture

1. Click the picture you want to restore.
2. Click the Crop button on the Picture toolbar.
3. Drag the sizing handles to reveal the areas that were originally cropped.
4. Click outside the image when you are finished.

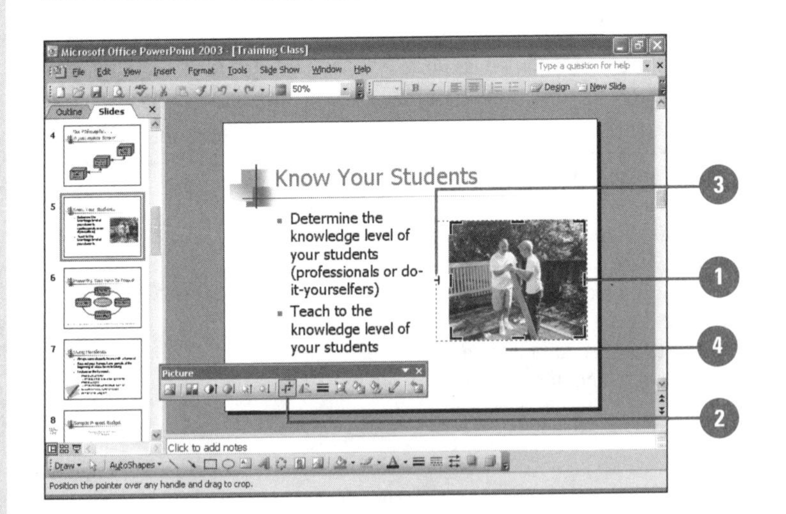

Crop a Picture Precisely

1. Right-click the picture you want to format, and then click Format Picture.
2. Click the Picture tab.
3. Adjust the values in the Left, Right, Top, and Bottom boxes to crop the image to the exact dimensions you want.
4. Click OK.

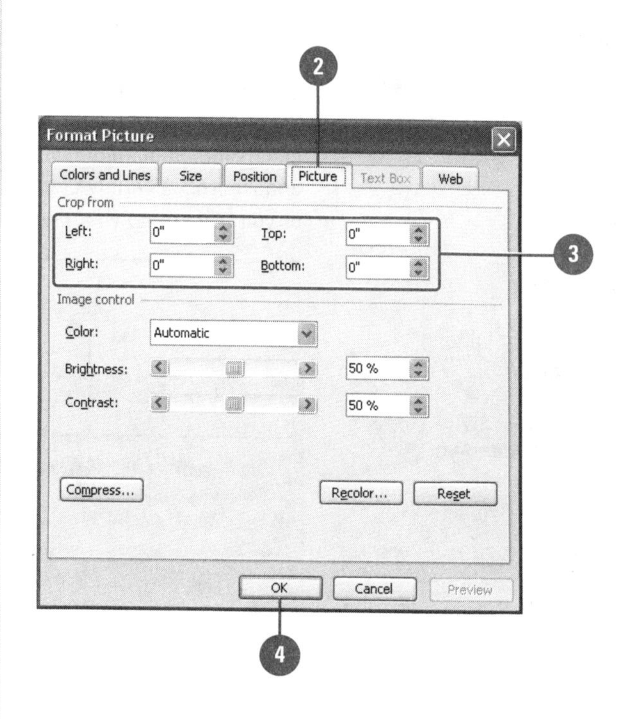

5

Creating WordArt Text

PP03S-1-4

The WordArt feature lets you create stylized text to draw attention to your most important words. Most users apply WordArt to short phrases or even just a word, such as *Making sense out of home improvement*. You should apply WordArt to a slide sparingly. Its visual appeal and unique look require uncluttered space. When you use WordArt, you can choose from a variety of text styles that come with the WordArt feature, or you can create your own using tools on the WordArt toolbar.

Insert WordArt

1. Click the Insert WordArt button on the Drawing toolbar.
2. Click one of the WordArt styles. If you want to create your own WordArt, click OK without selecting a WordArt style.
3. Click OK.
4. Type the text you want WordArt to use.
5. If applicable, use the Font, Size, Bold, and Italic options to modify the text you entered.
6. Click OK.

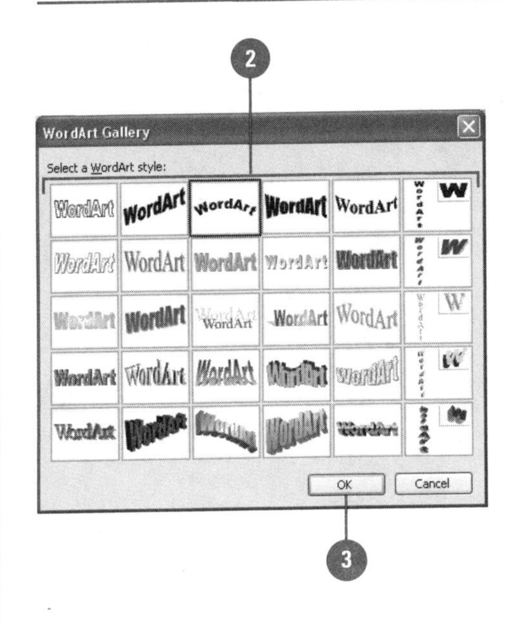

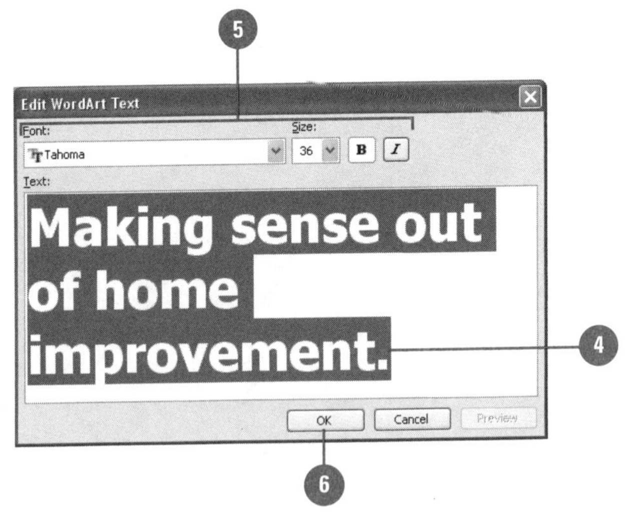

Edit WordArt Text

1. Click the WordArt object you want to edit.
2. Click the Edit Text button on the WordArt toolbar.
3. Edit the text.
4. Click OK.

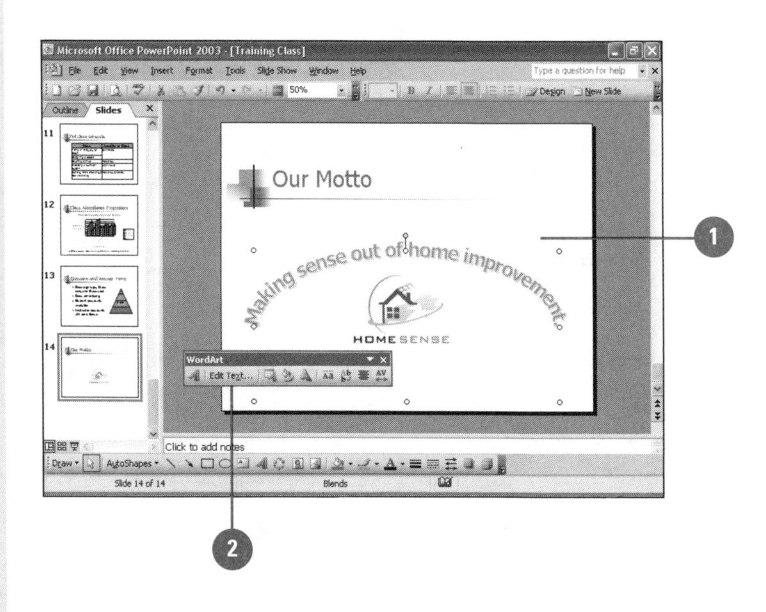

Apply a Different WordArt Style to Existing WordArt

1. Click the WordArt object whose style you want to change.
2. Click the WordArt Gallery button on the WordArt toolbar.
3. Click the WordArt Gallery style you want to apply.
4. Click OK.

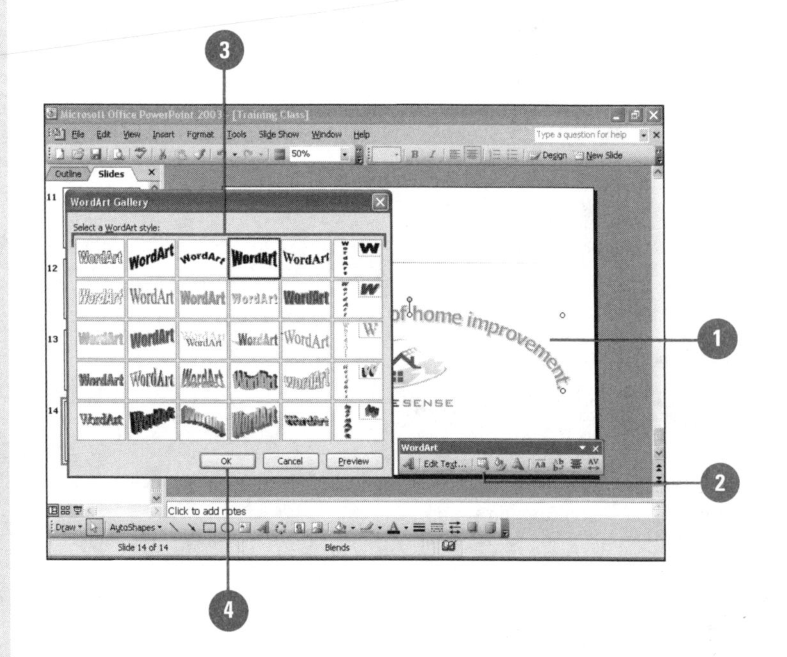

Did You Know?

You can edit WordArt text quickly. Double-click the WordArt object to open the Edit WordArt Text dialog box.

You can display the WordArt toolbar. Right-click any toolbar, and then click WordArt.

5

Modifying WordArt Text

With WordArt, in addition to applying one of the preformatted styles, you can also create your own style by shaping your text into a variety of shapes, curves, styles, and color patterns. The WordArt toolbar gives you tools for coloring, rotating, and shaping your text. You can also format your WordArt using tools on the Drawing toolbar. The Drawing toolbar makes it easy to see your format changes.

Change the Shape of WordArt

1. Click the WordArt object.
2. Click the WordArt Shape button on the WordArt toolbar.
3. Click the shape you want to apply to the text.
4. Click outside the object to deselect it.

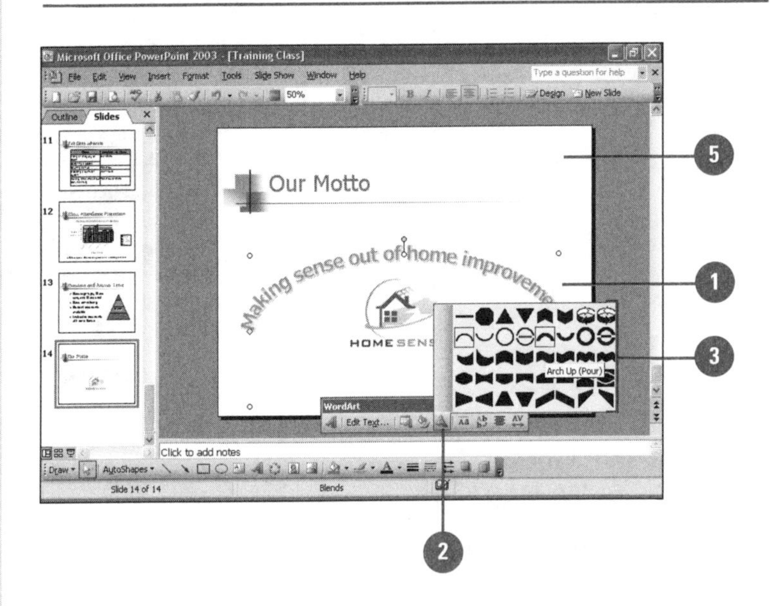

Did You Know?

You can format the WordArt text. Click the Edit Text button on the WordArt toolbar, edit the WordArt text, or click the Bold or Italic button, and then click OK.

Rotate WordArt

1. Click the WordArt object.
2. Click the Free Rotate button on the WordArt object.
3. Drag the green rotate handle to rotate the object in any direction you want.
4. When you're done, release the Free Rotate button.
5. Click outside the object to deselect it

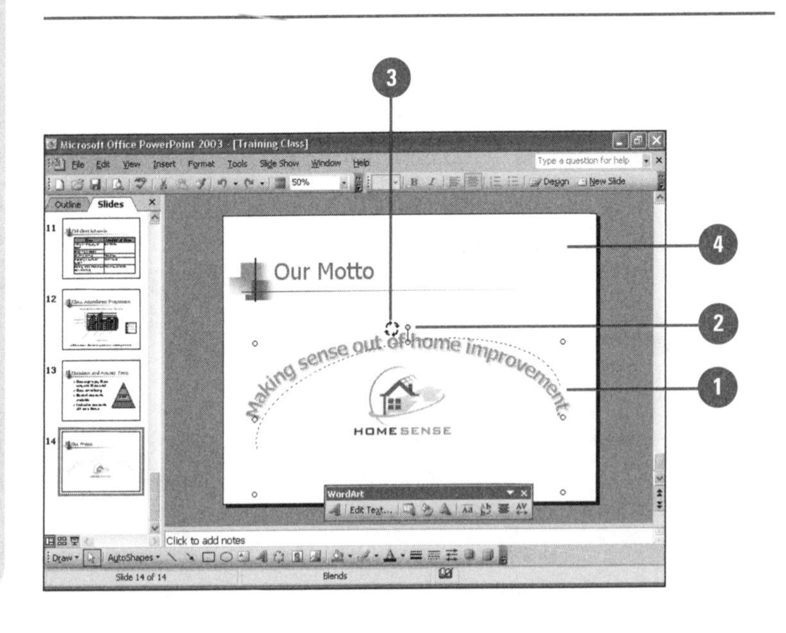

Color WordArt

1. Click the WordArt object.
2. Click the Fill Color button list arrow on the Drawing toolbar, and then click the fill color you want or click Fill Effects to apply a special effect, such as a pattern or gradient.
3. Click the Line Color button list arrow on the Drawing toolbar, and then click the line color you want.
4. Click outside the object to deselect it.

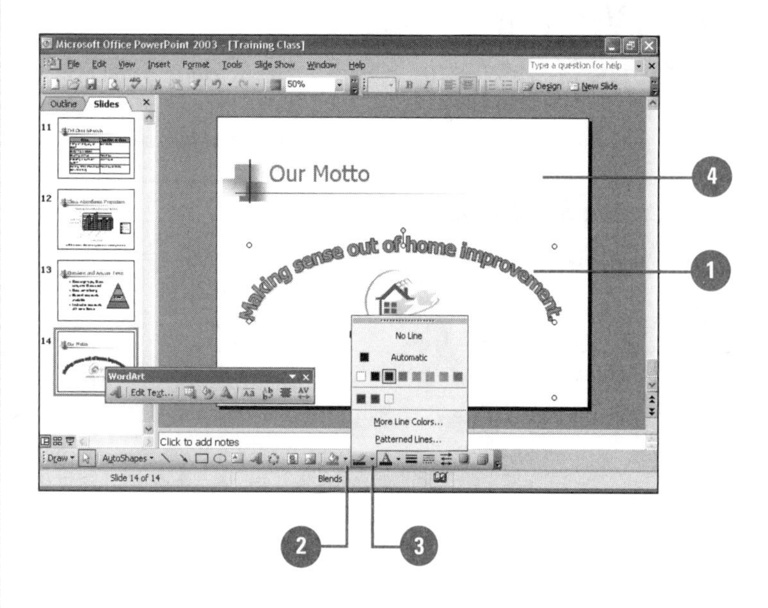

Did You Know?

You can change the WordArt fill color to match the background. Click the WordArt object, click the Format WordArt button on the WordArt toolbar, click the Colors And Lines tab, click the Fill Color button list arrow, click Background, and then click OK.

Align WordArt

1. Click the WordArt object.
2. Click the WordArt Alignment button on the WordArt toolbar.
3. Click the alignment you want.
4. Click outside the object to deselect it.

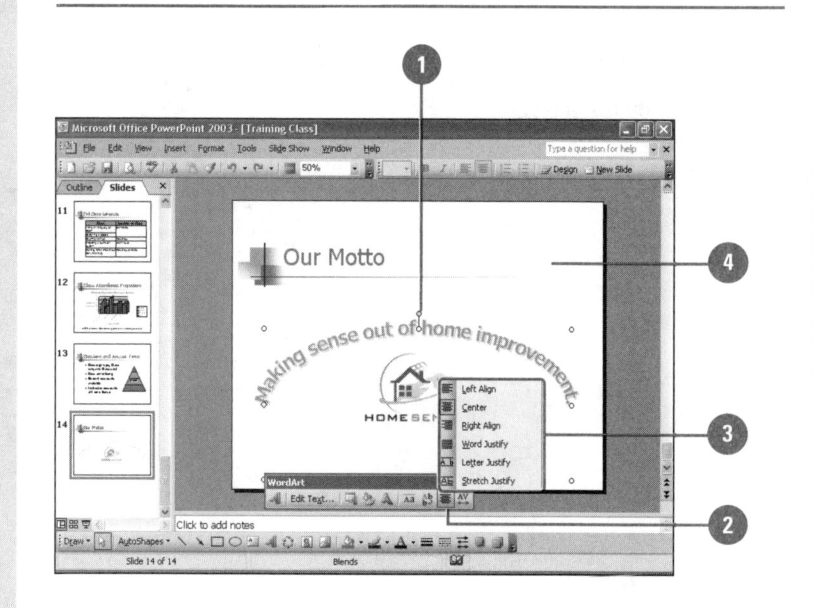

Applying WordArt Text Effects

You can apply a number of text effects to your WordArt objects that determine letter height, justification, and spacing. The effects of some of the adjustments you make are more pronounced for certain WordArt styles than others. Some of these effects make the text unreadable for certain styles, so apply these effects carefully.

Make Letters the Same Height

1. Click the WordArt object.
2. Click the WordArt Same Letter Heights button on the WordArt toolbar.
3. Click outside the object to deselect it.

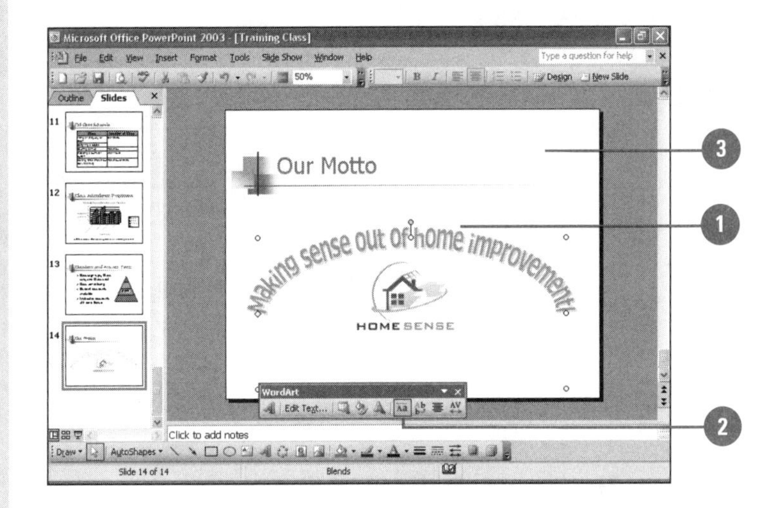

Format Text Vertically

1. Click the WordArt object.
2. Click the WordArt Vertical Text button on the WordArt toolbar.
3. Click outside the object to deselect it.

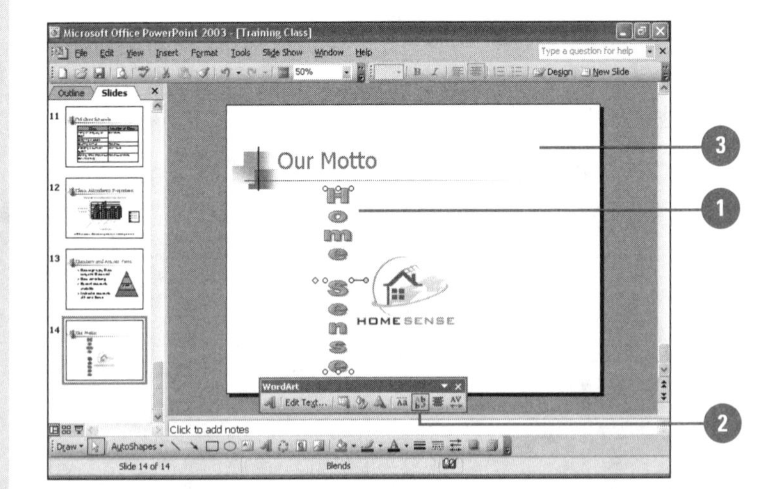

Adjust Character Spacing

1. Click the WordArt object.
2. Click the WordArt Character Spacing button on the WordArt toolbar.
3. Click a spacing setting— Very Tight, Tight, Normal, Loose, or Very Loose— to determine the amount of space between characters.
4. If you want, select or clear the Kern Character Pairs option to adjust the space between characters.
5. Click outside the object to deselect it.

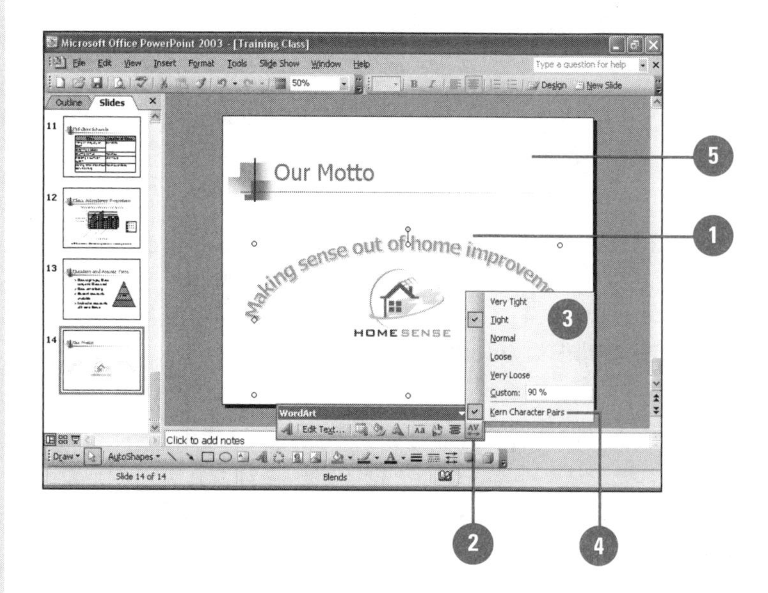

Did You Know?

You can change the WordArt size or position. Click the WordArt object, click the Format WordArt button on the WordArt toolbar, click the Size or Position tab, change the size or positioning settings, and then click OK.

You can change WordArt character spacing. Although the default spacing for the WordArt Gallery objects is usually optimal, if you change the font you might want to experiment with character spacing.

You can change WordArt text to semi-transparent. Click the WordArt object, click the Format WordArt button on the WordArt toolbar, click the Colors And Lines tab, drag the Transparency slider to make the object more or less transparent, and then click OK.

Inserting Movies and Sounds

PP03S-1-5

You can insert movies or sounds into a presentation by inserting them from the Clip Art task pane or a file. Movies can be either animated pictures, also known as animated GIFs, such as cartoons, or they can be digital videos prepared with digitized video equipment. Movies and sounds are inserted as PowerPoint objects. When you insert a sound, a small icon appears representing the sound file. When you insert a movie or sound, PowerPoint asks you how you want it to start in a slide show. You can choose to have the movie or sound play automatically or when clicked.

Insert a Clip Organizer Movie or Sound

1. Click the Insert menu, and then point to Movies And Sounds.
2. Click Movie From Clip Organizer or Sound From Clip Organizer.
3. Click the media clip you want to insert.
4. When a message is displayed, do one of the following:

   To play the media clip automatically when you go to the slide, click Automatically.

   To play the media clip only when you click it, click When Clicked.
5. When you're done, click the Close button on the task pane.

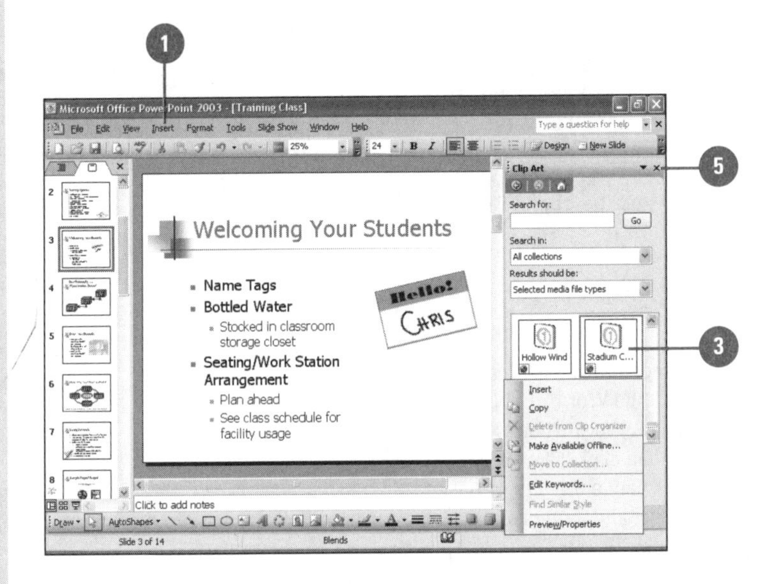

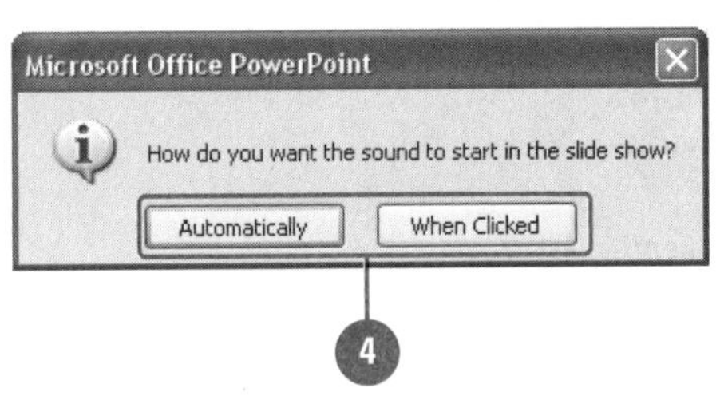

Did You Know?

You can insert movies and sounds located on your computer. Click the Insert menu, point to Movies And Sounds, click an insert command, locate and select the movie or sound, and then click OK.

Insert a Movie or Sound on a New Slide

1. Click the New Slide button on the Standard toolbar.
2. Click the Title, Media Clip and Text or the Title, Text and Media Clip AutoLayout in the Slide Layout task pane.
3. Double-click the Media Clip placeholder.
4. Click the media clip you want to insert, and then click OK.
5. When the message is displayed, click Automatically or When Clicked.
6. When you're done, click the Close button on the task pane.

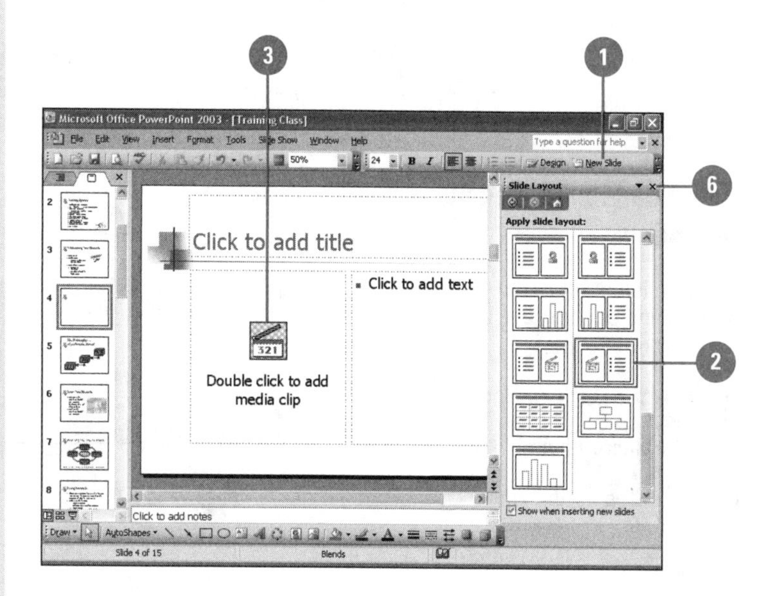

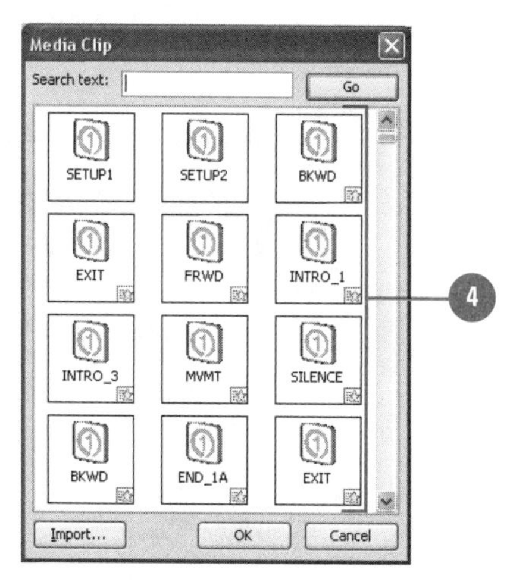

5

Recording Sounds

You can add voice narration or sound in a slide show when you are either creating a slide show for individuals who can't attend a presentation or archiving a meeting for presenters to review later and hear comments made during the presentation.

Record a Sound or Comment on a Single Slide

1. Click the Insert menu, point to Movies and Sounds, and then click Record Sound.
2. Type a name for the sound.
3. Click the Record button.
4. Click the Stop button when you are finished.
5. Click OK.

   A sound icon appears on the slide.

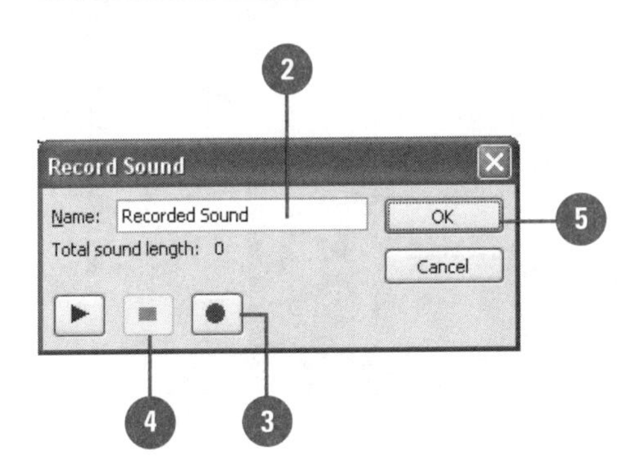

Delete a Sound or Comment on a Slide

1. Click the sound icon on the slide.
2. Click Delete.

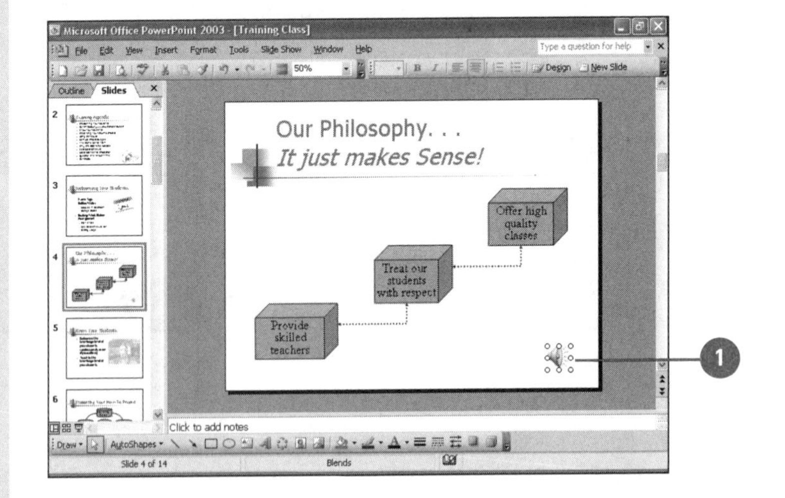

Playing Movies and Sounds

After you insert movie or sound objects, you can modify them so they play continuously or just one time. Movies and sounds can play in either Normal view or Slide Show view. You can also view and play movies using the full screen. When you install Windows Media Player 8 or later on your computer, PowerPoint supports its file formats, including ASX, WMX, M3U, WVX, WAX, and WMA. To play individual sounds, or sounds from video, you need a sound card and speakers.

Play a Movie or Sound

- To play a movie or sound in Normal view, double-click the movie object or sound icon.
- To play a movie, sound, or animated picture in Slide Show view, click the Slide Show button, and then display the slide with the media you want to play.

  Depending on your slide show multimedia options, you may need to click the movie object or sound icon to play it.

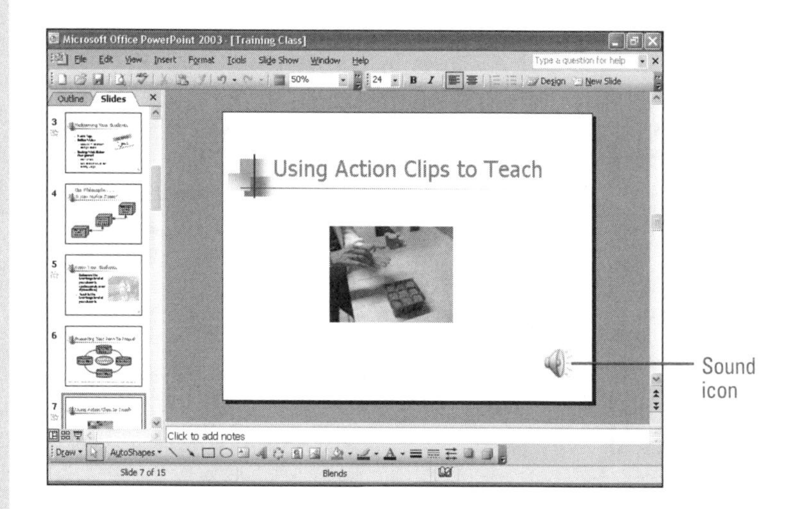

Change Play Options

1. Right-click the sound icon or movie object, and then click Edit Sound Object or Edit Movie Object.
2. Change the sound or movie settings.
   - To play continuously, select the Loop Until Stopped check box.
   - For a movie, select the Rewind Movie When Done Playing check box, or select the Zoom To Full Screen check box.
   - For a sound, select the Hide Sound Icon During Slide Show check box.
3. Click OK.

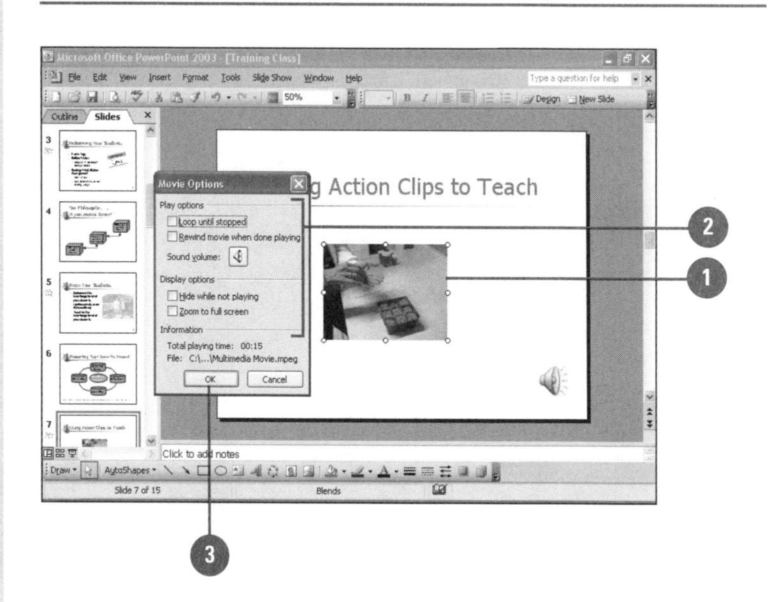

Inserting Charts and Related Material

6

Introduction

An effective presentation draws on information from many sources. Microsoft Office PowerPoint 2003 helps you seamlessly integrate information into your presentations using shared data from Office applications. In PowerPoint, you can insert an object created in another program into a presentation using technology known as **object linking and embedding** (**OLE**). OLE is a critical feature for many PowerPoint users because it lets you share objects among compatible programs when you create presentations.

When you share an object using OLE, the menus and toolbars from the program that created the object are available to you from within your PowerPoint presentation. When you want to make any changes or enhancements to the objects, you can edit the inserted object without having to leave PowerPoint.

OLE makes it easy to add graph and organization charts to present information visually. If you have information in other programs, such as Microsoft Office Word or Microsoft Office Excel, you can insert it in to your presentation with the help of OLE.

What You'll Do

Share Information Among Documents

Insert a Graph Chart

Open an Existing Graph Chart

Select Graph Data

Import Data

Enter and Format Graph Data

Edit Graph Data

Modify the Datasheet

Select a Chart Type

Format Chart Objects

Working with an Organization Chart

Insert a Microsoft Excel Chart

Insert a Microsoft Word Table

Insert and Format a Table

Copy and Paste Objects

Embed and Link an Object

Modify Links

Create a Diagram

Sharing Information Among Documents

Object linking and embedding is one of the great recent innovations in personal computing. OLE lets you insert an object created in one program into a document created in another program. Terms that you'll find useful in understanding how you can share objects among documents include:

Embedding and Linking

Term	Definition
Source program	The program that created the original object
Source file object	The file that contains the original
Destination program	The program that created the document into which you are inserting the object
Destination file	The file into which you are inserting the object

For example, if you place an Excel chart in your PowerPoint presentation, Excel is the source program and PowerPoint is the destination program. The chart is the source file; the presentation is the destination file. There are three ways to share information in Windows programs: pasting, embedding, and linking.

Pasting

You can cut or copy an object from one document and then paste it into another using the Cut, Copy, and Paste buttons on the source and destination program toolbars.

Embedding

When you **embed** an object, you place a copy of the object in the destination file, and when you activate the object, the tools from the source program become available in your presentation. For example, if you insert and then click an Excel chart in your PowerPoint presentation, the Excel menus and toolbars replace the PowerPoint menus and toolbars, so you can edit the chart if necessary. With embedding, any changes you make to the chart in the presentation do not affect the original file.

Linking

When you link an object, you insert a representation of the object itself into the destination file. The tools of the source program are available, and when you use them to edit the object you've inserted, you are actually editing the source file. Moreover, any changes you make to the source file are reflected in the destination file.

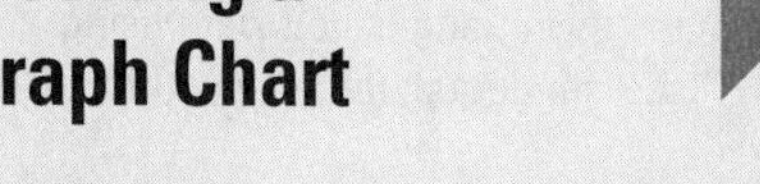

Inserting a Graph Chart

PP03S-1-3

Instead of adding a table of dry numbers, insert a Microsoft Graph chart. Charts add visual interest and useful information represented by lines, bars, pie slices, or other markers. Graph uses two views to display the information in a graph: the **datasheet**, a spreadsheet-like grid of rows and columns that contains your data, and the **chart**, the graphical representation of the data. A datasheet contains cells to hold your data. A **cell** is the intersection of a row and column. A group of data values from a row or column of data makes up a **data series**. Each data series has a unique color or pattern on the chart.

Create a Graph Chart

1. Start Microsoft Graph in one of the following ways.
   - To create a graph on an existing slide, display the slide on which you want the graph to appear, and then click the Insert Chart button on the Standard toolbar.
   - To create a graph on a new slide, click the New Slide button on the Formatting toolbar, choose a slide layout with the content or chart option from the Slide Layout task pane, and then click the chart placeholder to add the chart and datasheet.
2. Replace the sample data in the datasheet with your own data.
3. Edit and format the data in the datasheet as appropriate.
4. Click the Close button on the datasheet to close it and view the chart.
5. If necessary, change the chart type, and format the chart.
6. Click outside the chart to quit Microsoft Graph.

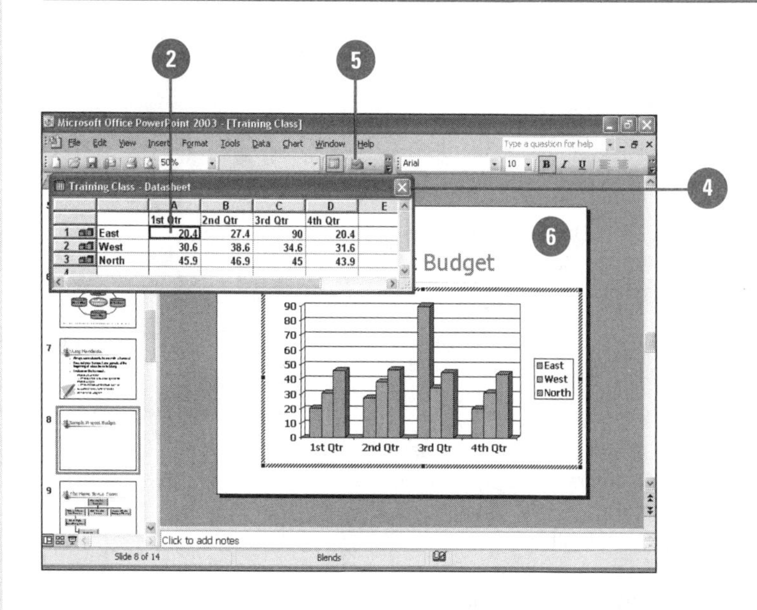

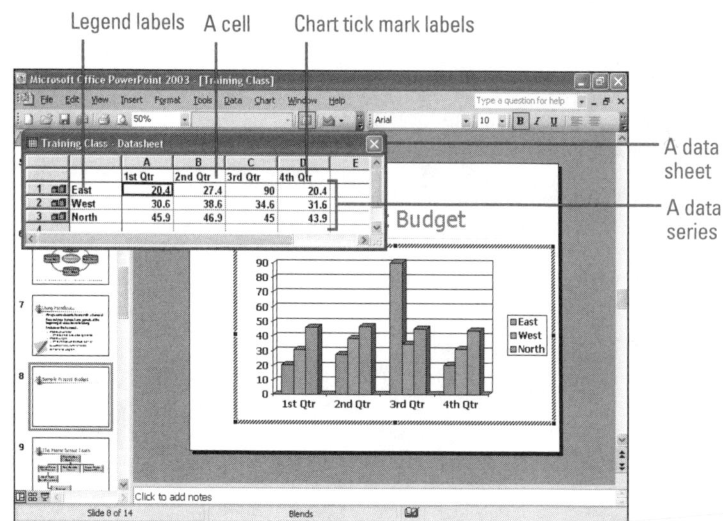

6

Opening an Existing Graph Chart

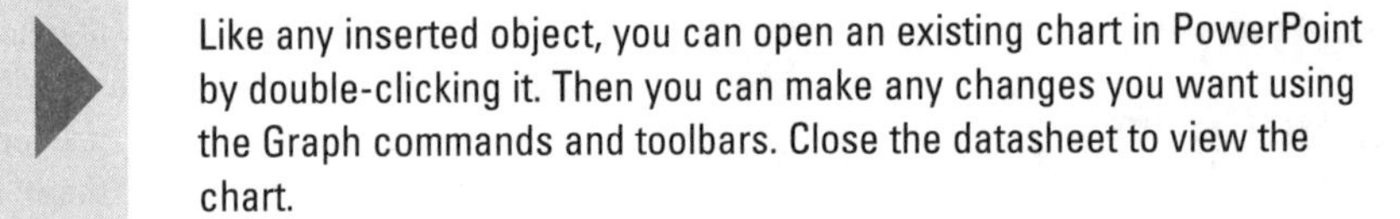

Like any inserted object, you can open an existing chart in PowerPoint by double-clicking it. Then you can make any changes you want using the Graph commands and toolbars. Close the datasheet to view the chart.

Open and View a Chart in Microsoft Graph

1. In PowerPoint, display the slide that contains the chart you want to open.
2. Double-click the chart to start Microsoft Graph.

   The Datasheet and Graph toolbars and menus appear.
3. Click the View Datasheet button on the Standard toolbar to close the datasheet.

   A chart consists of the following elements.

   - **Data markers.** A graphical representation of a data point in a single cell in the datasheet. Typical data markers include bars, dots, or pie slices. Related data markers constitute a data series.
   - **Legend.** A pattern or color that identifies each data series.
   - **X-axis.** A reference line for the horizontal data values.
   - **Y-axis.** A reference line for the vertical data values.
   - **Tick marks.** Marks that identify data increments.

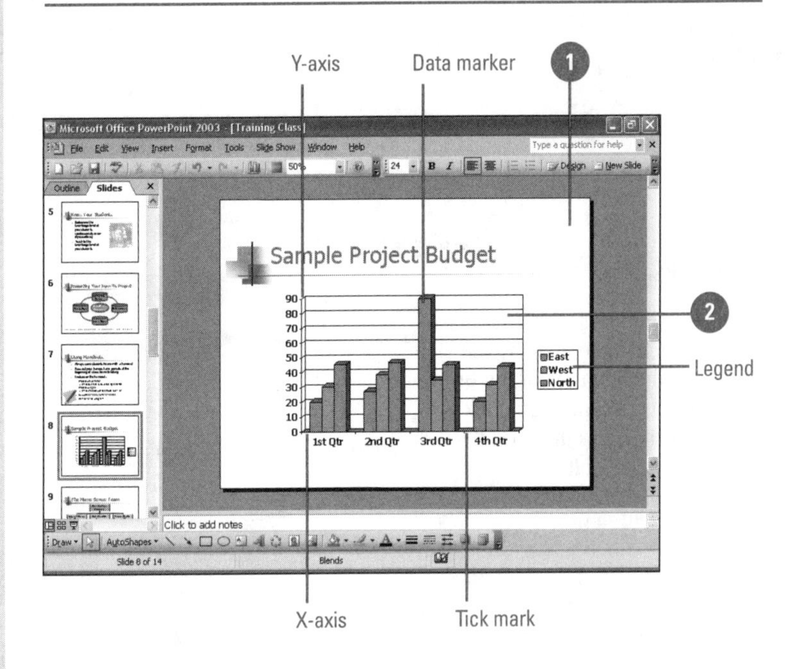

Selecting Graph Data

Use the datasheet to edit your data. Select the data first in the datasheet. If you click a cell to select it, anything you type replaces the contents of the cell. If you double-click the cell, however, anything you type is inserted at the location of the cursor.

Select Data in the Datasheet

1. In Microsoft Graph, click the View Datasheet button on the Standard toolbar.
2. Use one of the following to select a cell, row, column, or datasheet.
   - To select a cell, click it.
   - To select an entire row or column, click the row heading or column heading button.
   - To select a range of cells, drag the pointer over the cells you want to select, or click the upper-left cell of the range, press and hold Shift, and then click the lower-right cell. When you select a range of cells, the active cell has a thick border, and all other selected cells are highlighted in black.

Did You Know?

You can get help with Microsoft Graph. Get help specific to Microsoft Graph by clicking the Help button on the Graph Standard toolbar or by pressing F1 when you are in Graph.

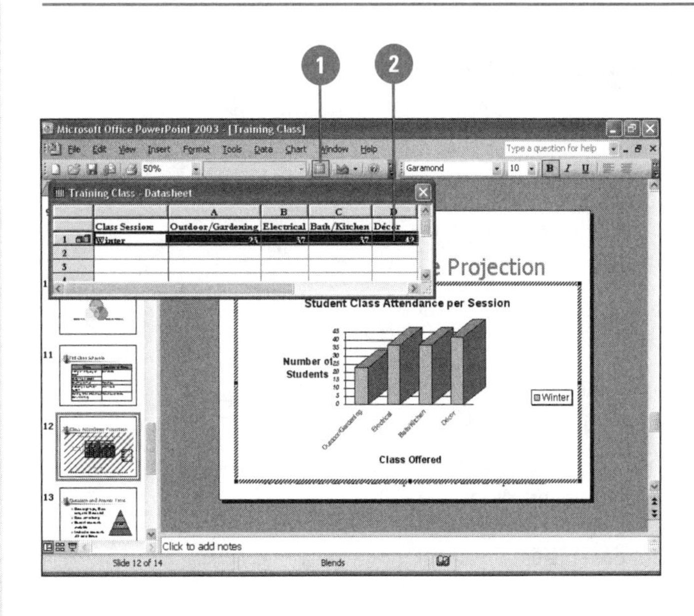

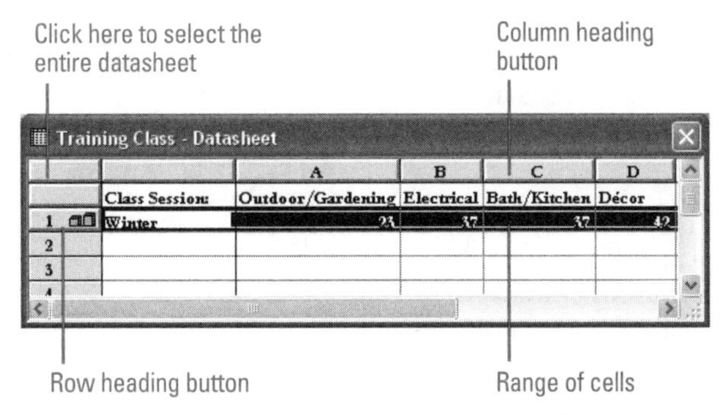

Importing Data

Microsoft Graph makes it easy to insert data from other sources, such as a plain text file or a Microsoft Excel worksheet. You have control over how much of the data in a file you want to insert, and, in the case of an imported text file, you can indicate how Graph should arrange your data once it is imported.

Import Data into the Datasheet

1. In Microsoft Graph, click the View Datasheet button on the Standard toolbar.
2. Click the cell where you want the data to begin.
3. Click the Edit menu, and then click Import File.
4. Double-click the file that contains the data you want to import.
5. If you are importing a text file, follow the Text Import Wizard steps. If you are importing Excel worksheet data, select the sheet that contains the data you want to import in the Import Data Options dialog box.
   - To import all the sheet data, click the Entire Sheet option.
   - To import only a range, click the Range option, and then type the range of data. For example, to import cells A1 through C10, type A1:C10.
   - If you selected a cell in step 2, clear the Overwrite Existing Cells check box.
6. Click OK.

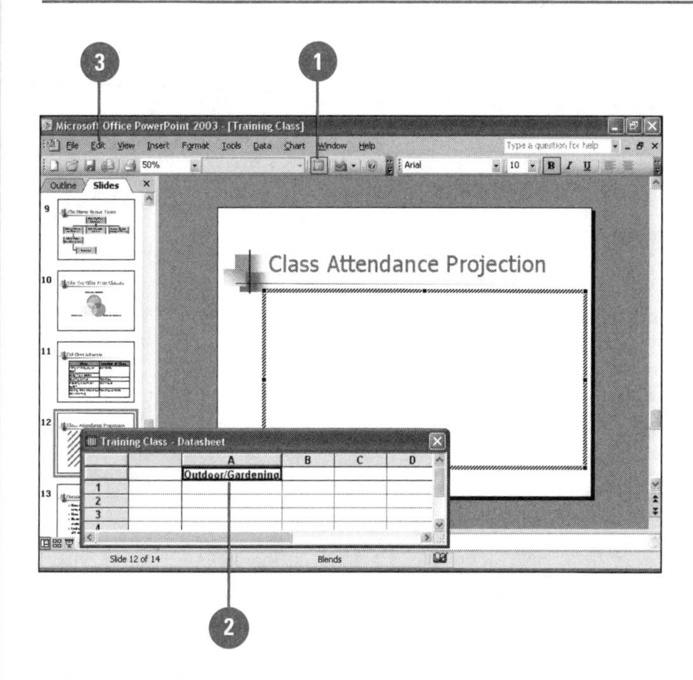

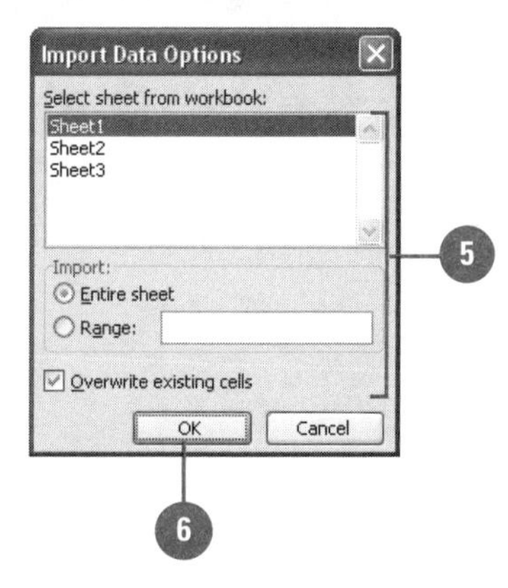

Paste Data into the Datasheet

1. In the source program, open the file that contains the data you want to paste.
2. Select the data you want to paste.
3. Click the Edit menu, and then click Copy.
4. Switch to PowerPoint, display the slide that contains the Microsoft Graph object, and then double-click the graph object.
5. If necessary, switch to the datasheet and clear its contents.
6. Paste the data into the datasheet using one of the following methods.
   - To paste the data without linking it, click the Edit menu, and then click Paste.
   - To link the data, click the Edit menu, click Paste Link, and then click OK.

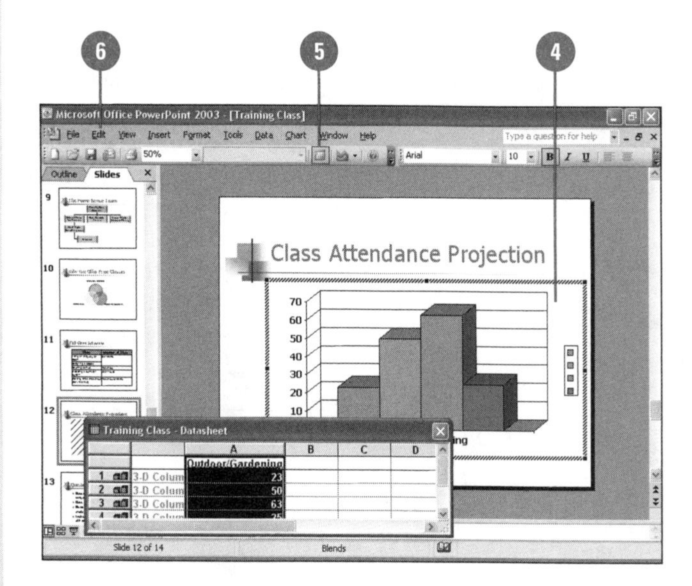

Did You Know?

You can use the first column and row to enter labels. Enter labels in the first row and column so that Microsoft Graph uses those values to label the X- and Y-axes.

You can turn on the Selection After Enter option. With this option turned on, the active cell changes after you press Enter. Click the Tools menu, click Options, click the Datasheet Options tab, select the Move Selection After Enter check box, and then click OK.

You can turn on the Cell Drag And Drop option. Click the Tools menu, click Options, click the Datasheet Options tab, select the Cell Drag And Drop check box, and then click OK.

Entering and Formatting Graph Data

You can enter graph data in the datasheet either by typing it or by inserting it from a different source. The datasheet is designed to make data entry easy, so direct typing is best when you're entering brief, simple data. For more complex or longer data, and when you're concerned about accuracy, insert and link your data to the graph object. When you first insert a graph, the datasheet contains sample labels and numbers. If you're entering data by typing, click a cell to make it the active cell, and then select the sample information and replace it with your own. You may need to reformat the datasheet itself—its size and how it displays the data—to make it easier to read. For example, you can format numbers in currency, accounting, percentage, and scientific formats. You can also change the fonts used in the graph.

Enter Data in the Datasheet

1. In Microsoft Graph, click the View Datasheet button on the Standard toolbar.
2. To delete the sample data, click the upper-left heading button to select all the cells, and then press Delete.
3. Click a cell to make it active.
4. Type the data you want to enter in the cell.
5. Press Enter to move the insertion point down one row or press Tab to move the insertion point right to the next cell.
6. Click outside the graph to return to PowerPoint.

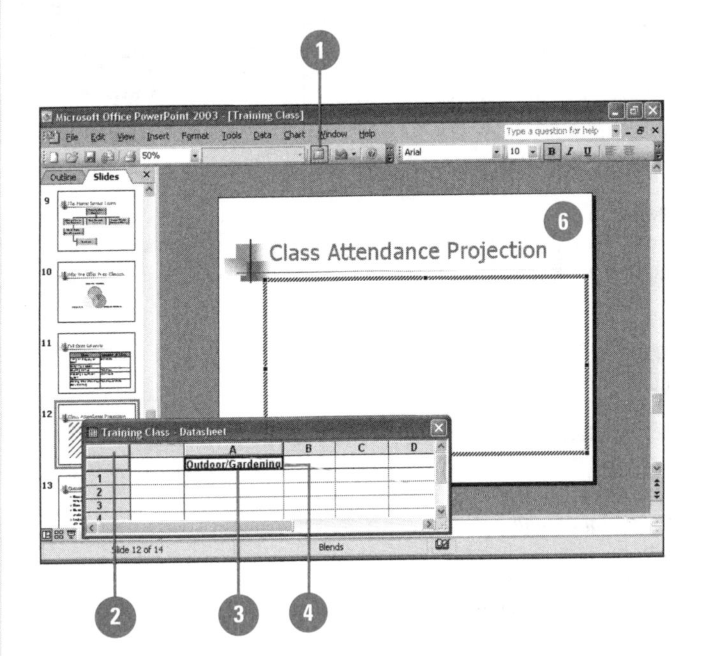

Did You Know?

You can AutoCorrect Microsoft Graph text. AutoCorrect works the same in Microsoft Graph as it does in PowerPoint. To change AutoCorrect options, click the Tools menu, click AutoCorrect Options, change the options you want, and then click OK.

Change the Datasheet Font

1. In the datasheet, click any cell.
2. Click the Format menu, and then click Font.
3. Make any changes to the font settings
   - Font, style, and size.
   - Underline and color.
   - Strikethrough, superscript, and subscript.
4. Click OK.

   Changes you make to the font affect all the data in the datasheet.

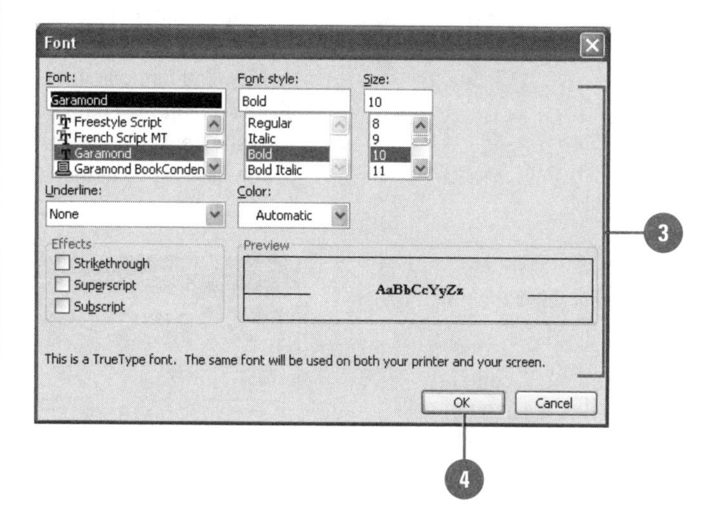

Format Datasheet Numbers

1. In the datasheet, select the data you want to format.
2. Click the Format menu, and then click Number.
3. Click the style you want to apply.
4. Select the options you want.
5. Click OK.

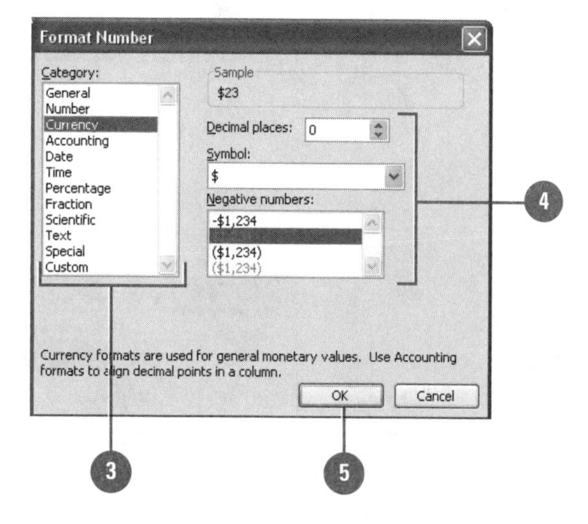

6

Editing Graph Data

Although most of the time you edit Microsoft Graph data in the datasheet, you can also change data in the chart by dragging a data marker. You can edit data one cell at a time, or you can manipulate blocks of adjacent data called **ranges**. If you are familiar with worksheets, such as Microsoft Excel, you will find that Microsoft Graph uses many of the same data editing techniques.

Edit Cell Contents

1. In the datasheet, click the cell you want to edit.
   - To replace the cell contents, type the new data into the cell. It replaces the previous entry.
   - To edit the cell content, double-click the selected cell where you want to edit.

     Press Delete or Backspace to delete one character at a time, and then type the new data.

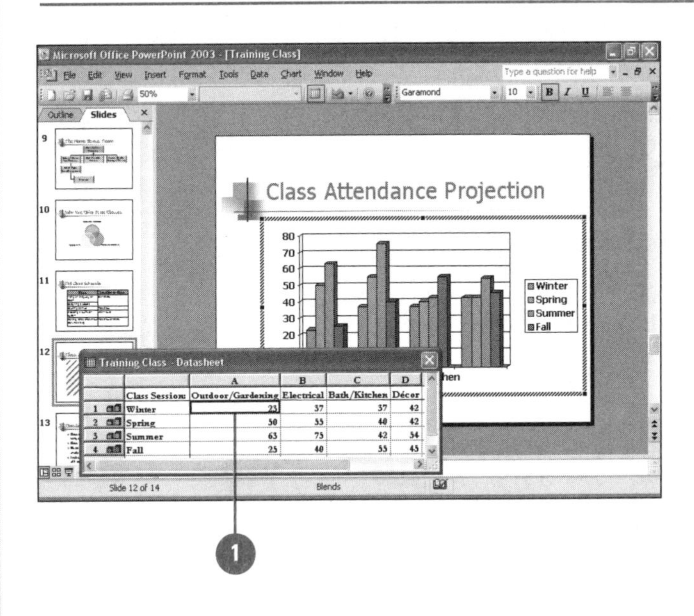

Edit Data by Dragging Data Markers

1. In the chart, click the data series that contains the data marker you want to change.
2. Click the data marker. When you select a data marker, a box appears that identifies the series and the value.
3. Drag the data marker for line or scatter plots, the top-center selection handle for bar or column charts, and the largest selection handle on the edge of a pie chart.

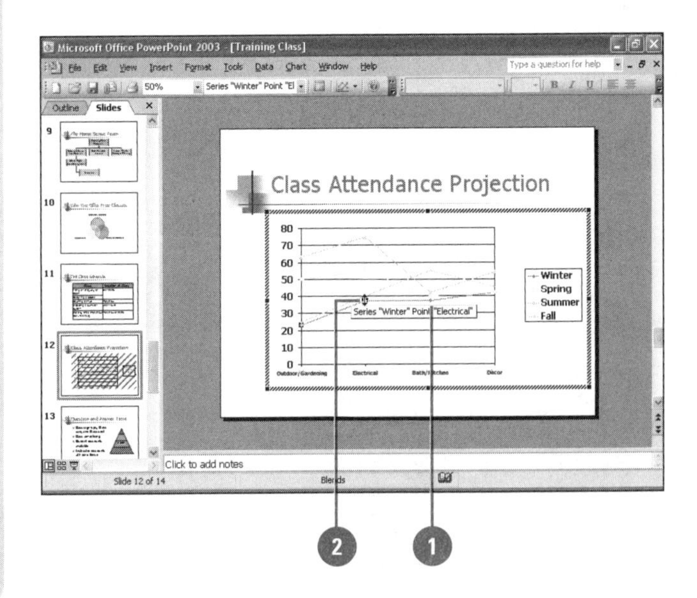

Insert Cells

1. In the datasheet, click where you want to insert cells.
   - To insert a column, click the column heading to the right of where you want the new column.
   - To insert a row, click the row heading below where you want the new row.
   - To insert a single cell, click an adjacent cell.
2. Click the Insert menu, and then click Cells.
3. Select the insert option you want.
4. Click OK.

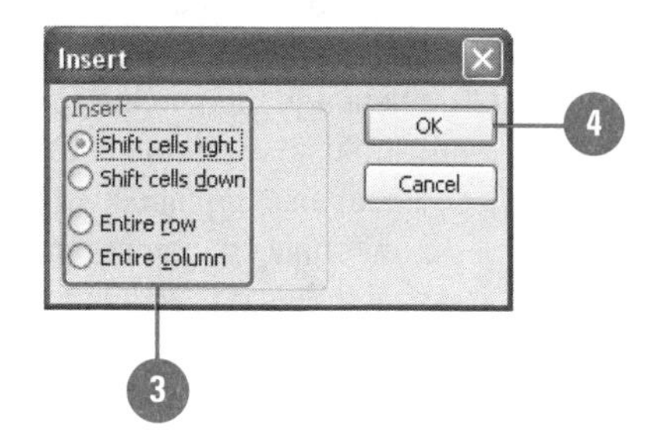

Delete Data from a Datasheet or a Graph

- Select the cell or range in the datasheet that contains the data you want to delete, and then press Delete.
- Click the data series in the graph, and then press Delete.

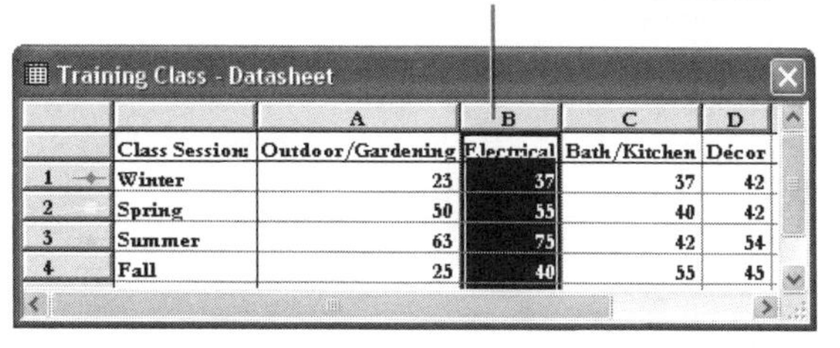

Did You Know?

You can exclude or include row or column data. Instead of deleting data, you can exclude row or column data from a graph and then include it later. Select the row or column you want toe exclude or include, click the Data menu, and then click Exclude Row/Col or Include Row/Col.

Modifying the Datasheet

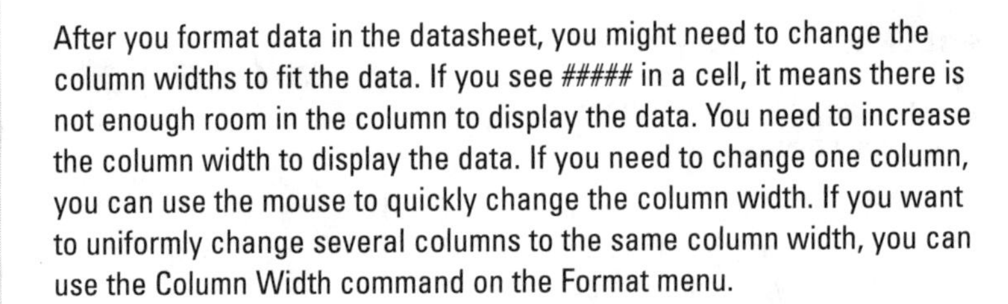

After you format data in the datasheet, you might need to change the column widths to fit the data. If you see ##### in a cell, it means there is not enough room in the column to display the data. You need to increase the column width to display the data. If you need to change one column, you can use the mouse to quickly change the column width. If you want to uniformly change several columns to the same column width, you can use the Column Width command on the Format menu.

Change the Width of a Column

- To increase or decrease the width of a column, position the pointer on the vertical line to the right of the column heading, and then drag the pointer until the column is the correct width.
- To adjust a datasheet column to display the widest data entered (also known as Best Fit), position the pointer on the line to the right of the column heading, and then double-click to adjust the column width.

  If a series of number signs (#) appears in the datasheet cell, it means the cell is not wide enough to display the entire contents of the cell. Widen the column to view the data in that cell.

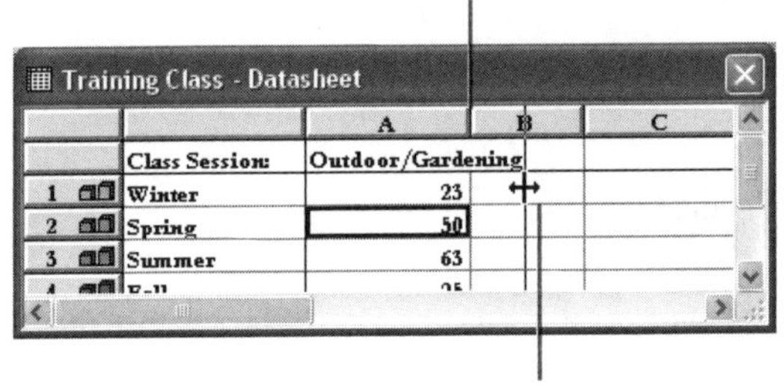

Double-click the line to the right of the column heading to resize the column to the widest entry.

Drag the pointer until the column is the correct width.

Did You Know?

You can switch the data series around. Change the data series to display by row or column. Click the Data menu, and then click Series In Row or Series In Column.

Enter a Precise Column Width

1. Click a cell in the column you want to format.
2. Click the Format menu, and then click Column Width.
3. Enter a new column width.
4. Click OK.

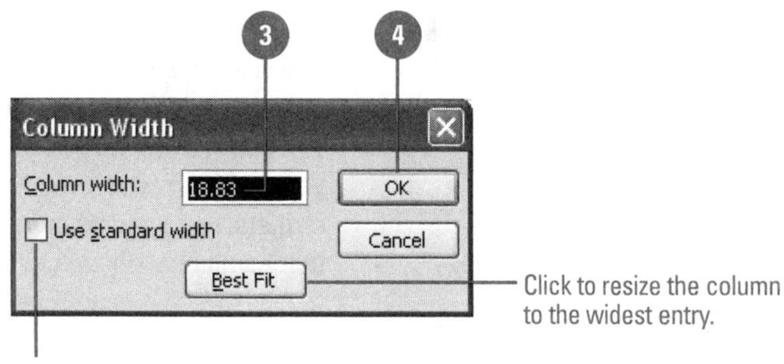

Did You Know?

You can switch the data series around. Change the data series to display by row or column. Click the Data menu, and then click Series In Row or Series In Column.

See Also

See "Entering and Formatting Graph Data" on page 154 for information on working with data in a datasheet.

Selecting a Chart Type

Your chart is what your audience sees, so make sure to take advantage of PowerPoint's chart formatting options to make the chart appealing and visually informative. You start by choosing the chart type that is suited for presenting your data. There are 18 chart types, available in 2-D and 3-D formats, and for each chart type you can choose from a variety of formats. If you want to format your chart beyond the provided formats, you can customize a chart. Save your customized settings so that you can apply that chart formatting to any chart you create.

Select a Chart Type

1. In Microsoft Graph, close the datasheet to view the chart, if necessary.
2. Click the Chart Type list arrow on the Standard toolbar.
3. Click the button corresponding to the chart type you want.

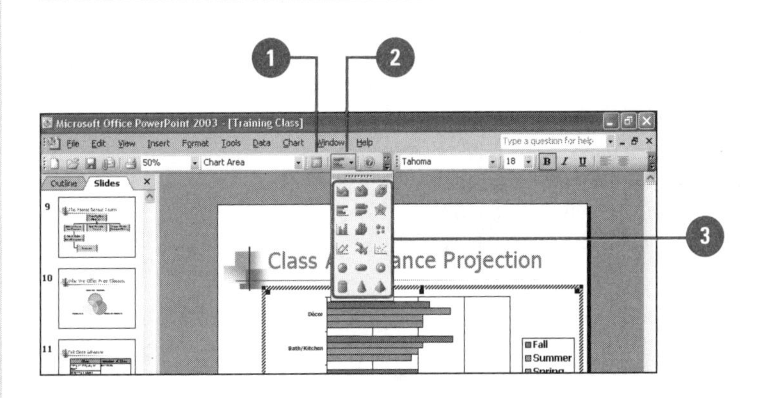

Apply a Standard Chart Type

1. Click the Chart menu, and then click Chart Type.
2. Click the Standard Types tab.
3. Click the chart type you want.
4. Click the chart sub-type you want. **Sub-types** are variations of the chart type.
5. Click OK.

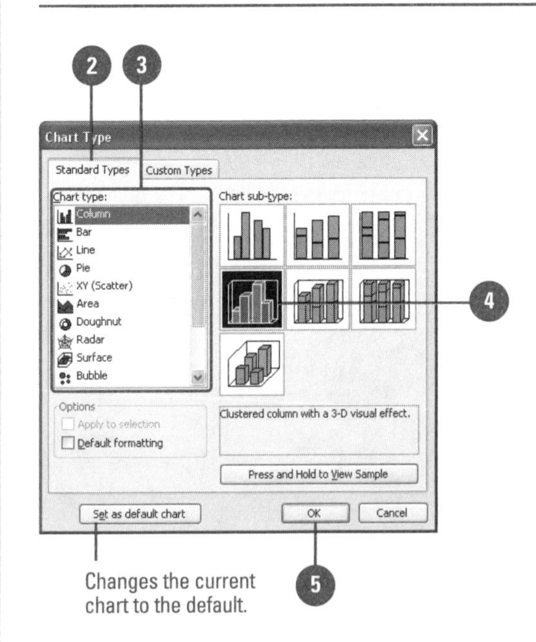

Did You Know?

Why does the Chart Type button look different? The image on the Chart Type button changes depending on which chart type is selected.

Apply a Custom Chart Type

1. Click the Chart menu, and then click Chart Type.
2. Click the Custom Types tab.
3. Click the Built-In option.
4. Click the chart type you want.
5. Click OK.

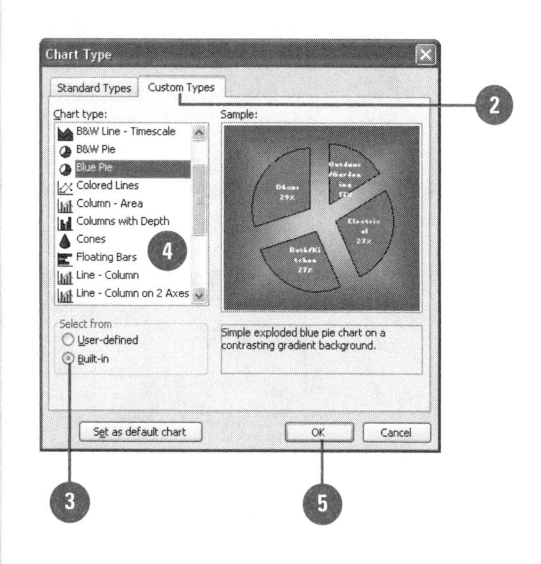

Create a Custom Chart Type

1. Select the chart you want to use to make a custom chart type.
2. Click the Chart menu, and then click Chart Type.
3. Click the Custom Types tab.
4. Click the User-Defined option.
5. Click Add.
6. Type a name and description for the chart.
7. Click OK.
8. Click OK.

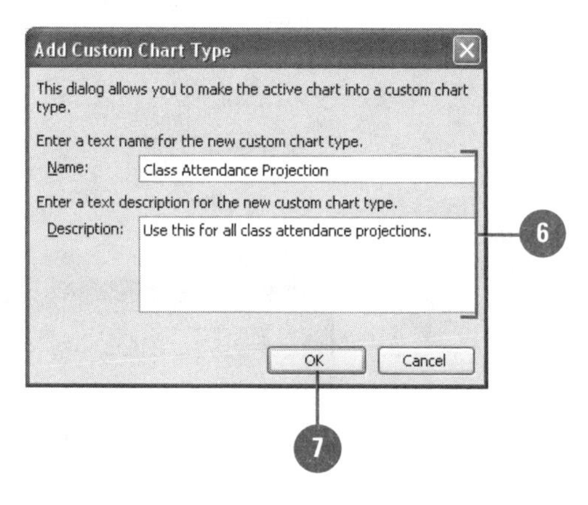

Did You Know?

You can use chart options to add a title to your chart. To add a title to your chart, click the Chart menu, click Chart Options, click the Titles tab, enter a title in the Chart Title box, and then click OK.

Formatting Chart Objects

Chart objects are the individual elements that make up a chart, such as an axis, the legend, or a data series. The **plot area** is the bordered area where the data are plotted. The **chart area** is the area between the plot area and the Microsoft Graph object selection box. As with any Microsoft add-in accessory, Graph treats all these elements as objects, so you can format and modify them individually.

Select a Chart Object

1. Click the Chart Objects list arrow on the Standard toolbar.
2. Click the chart object you want to select.

   When a chart object is selected, selection handles appear.

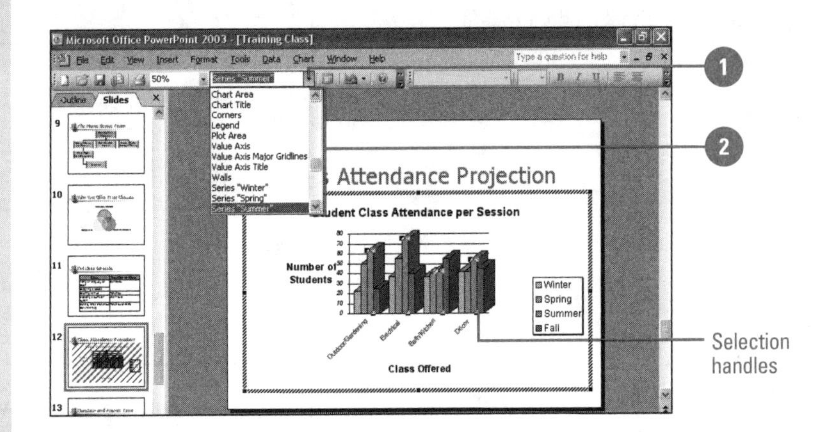

Format a Chart Object

1. Right-click the chart object you want to format, such as an axis, legend, or data series.
2. Click the appropriate Format command. For an axis, for example, the command is Format Axis.
3. Click the appropriate tab(s), and then select the options you want to apply.
4. Click OK.

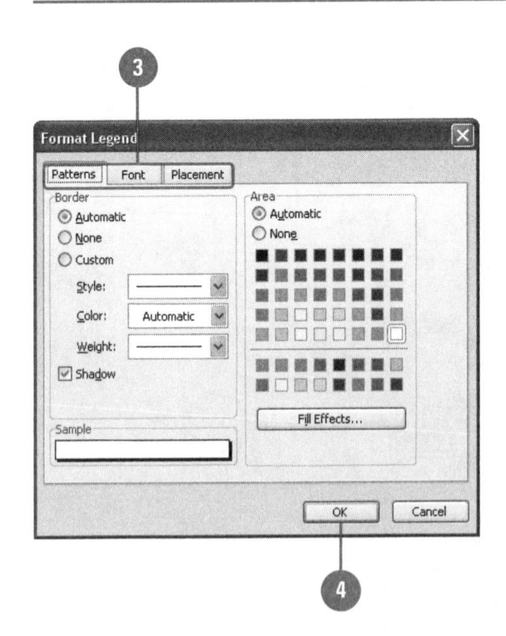

Did You Know?

You can enlarge a chart object to select it. Increase the zoom percentage to enlarge your view before using the mouse pointer to select chart objects.

Customize a Chart

1. Click the Chart menu, and then click Chart Options.
2. Click the tab corresponding to the chart object you want to customize.

   Each tab will display options that are specific to the chart object you want to customize.
3. Make the necessary changes.
4. Click OK.

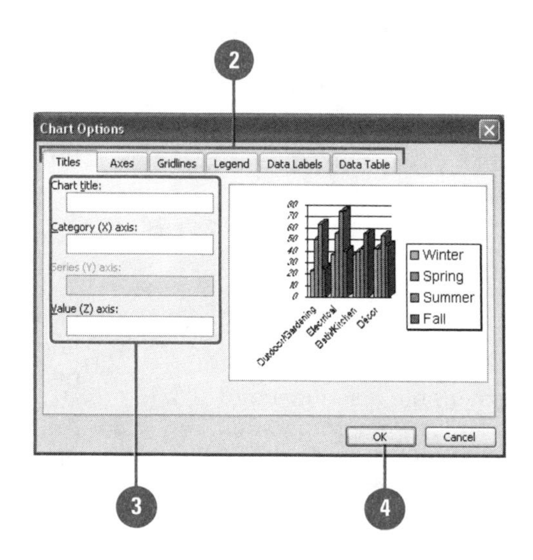

Change the View of a 3-D Chart

1. Select the 3-D chart you want to change.
2. Click the Chart menu, and then click 3-D View.
3. Click the left or right rotation button.
4. Click the up or down elevation button.
5. Click OK.

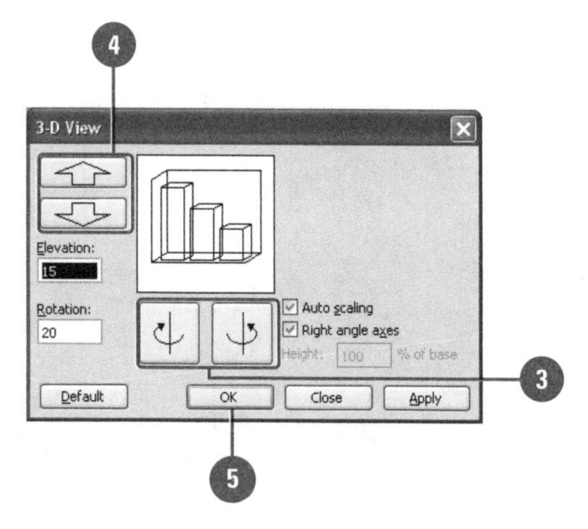

Did You Know?

You can change the placement of objects on a chart. Select the chart objects whose placement you want to change, click the Format menu, point to Placement, and then click Bring To Front, Send To Back, or Group.

You can rotate the chart axis labels. To change the angle of an axis label, right-click the axis, click Format Axis, click the Alignment tab, and then select an orientation and click OK.

6

Choosing Advanced Graph Options

Microsoft Graph offers a number of advanced graphing techniques that you can explore using the abundant information in Microsoft Graph Help. You can:

- Add trendlines derived from regression analysis to show a trend in existing data and make predictions.
- Create a moving average, a sequence of averages from grouped data points, that smooths the fluctuations in data so you can more easily identify trends.
- Add error bars that express the degree of uncertainty attached to a given data series.
- Add drawing objects, including arrows, text boxes, and pictures, to your charts.
- Fill chart elements such as bars, areas, and surfaces with textures, imported pictures, or gradient fills.
- Animate bars, data points, or other chart data for added multimedia impact.

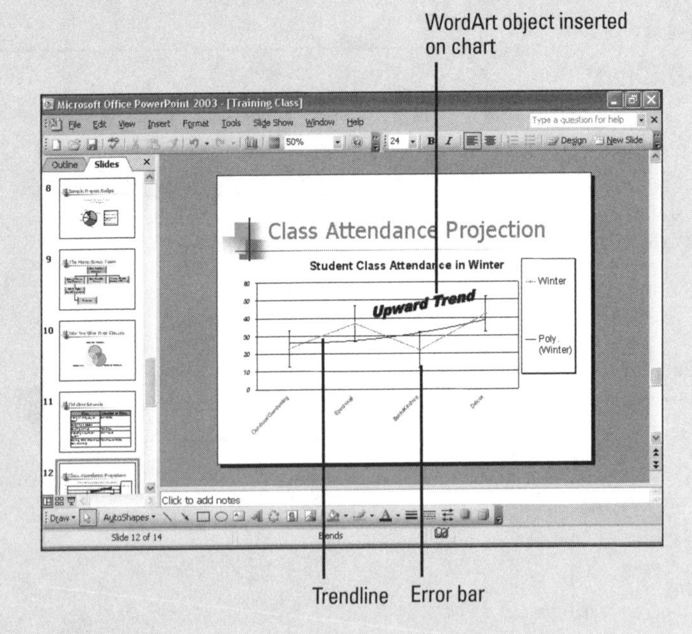

Creating an Organization Chart

PP03S-1-3

An organization chart shows the relationship between individuals in an organization. For example, you can show the relationship between a manager and employees within a company. When you create an organization chart, a sample chart appears. You can add text and format the chart boxes and connecting lines. Once you insert an organization chart, you can click the chart to edit it at any time. When you're finished working with the organization chart, you simply deselect the object. To convert an existing organization chart from a previous version of PowerPoint, simply double-click the chart, and PowerPoint converts it.

Create an Organization Chart

1. Create an organization chart in one of the following ways:
   - On an existing slide, click the Insert menu, point to Picture, and then click Organization Chart.
   - Click the New Slide button on the Formatting toolbar, click a content layout in the Slide Layout task pane, click the Insert Diagram Or Organization Chart placeholder, select Organization Chart in the Diagram Gallery dialog box, and then click OK.
2. Use the Organization Chart toolbar to design your organization chart.
3. If necessary, click a chart box in which you want to enter text.
4. Type a person's name, and then press Enter.
5. Type a person's title.
6. When you're done, click outside the chart box.
7. Click outside of the organization chart to deselect it.

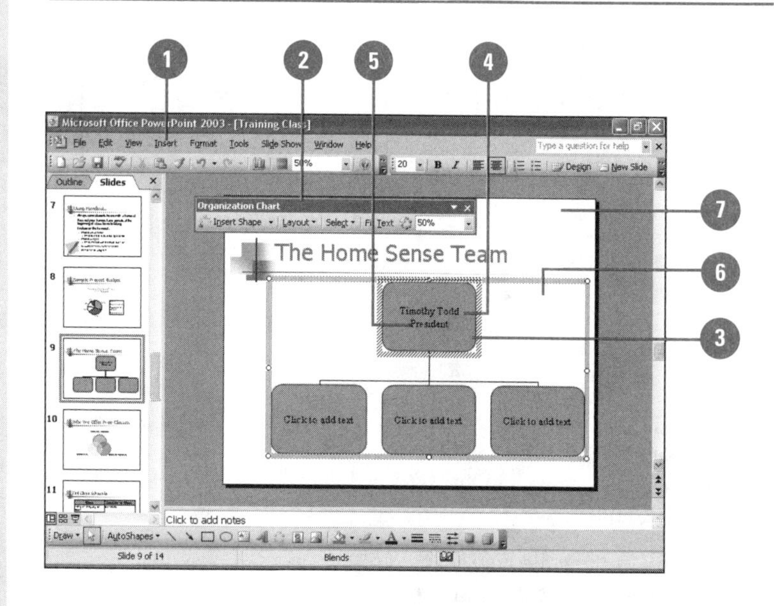

Select and Deselect Chart Boxes

To	Do this
Select a single chart box	Click a chart box using the arrow pointer
Select a set of chart boxes	Click the Select list arrow on the Organization Chart toolbar, and then click the set you want
Select one or more levels of chart boxes	Click a chart box in the level you want to select, click the Organization Chart tool bar, click Level
Deselect a chart box	Click outside the chart box

Structuring an Organization Chart

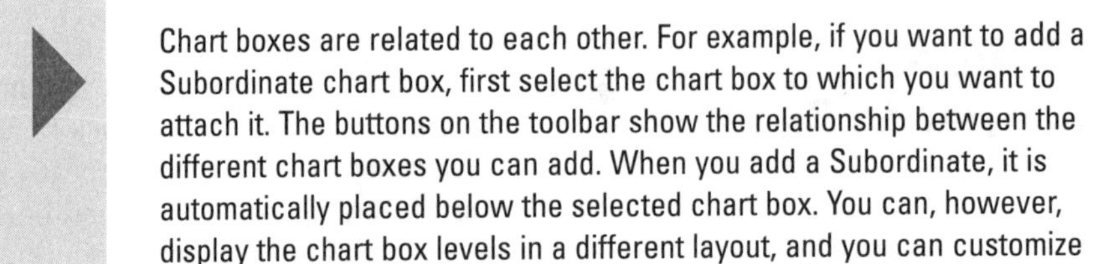

Chart boxes are related to each other. For example, if you want to add a Subordinate chart box, first select the chart box to which you want to attach it. The buttons on the toolbar show the relationship between the different chart boxes you can add. When you add a Subordinate, it is automatically placed below the selected chart box. You can, however, display the chart box levels in a different layout, and you can customize the organization chart's appearance using the formatting options.

Add a Chart Box

1. If necessary, click the org chart you want to modify.
2. Click the chart box to which you want to attach the new chart box.
3. Click the Insert Shape list arrow on the Organization Chart toolbar, and then click one or more of the following:

   Coworker–to place the shape next to the selected shape and connect it to the same manager shape.

   Subordinate–to place the new shape below the selected shape and to connect it to the selected shape.

   Assistant–to place the new shape below the selected shape with an elbow connector.
4. Enter the information in the box you just added.
5. Click outside the box.

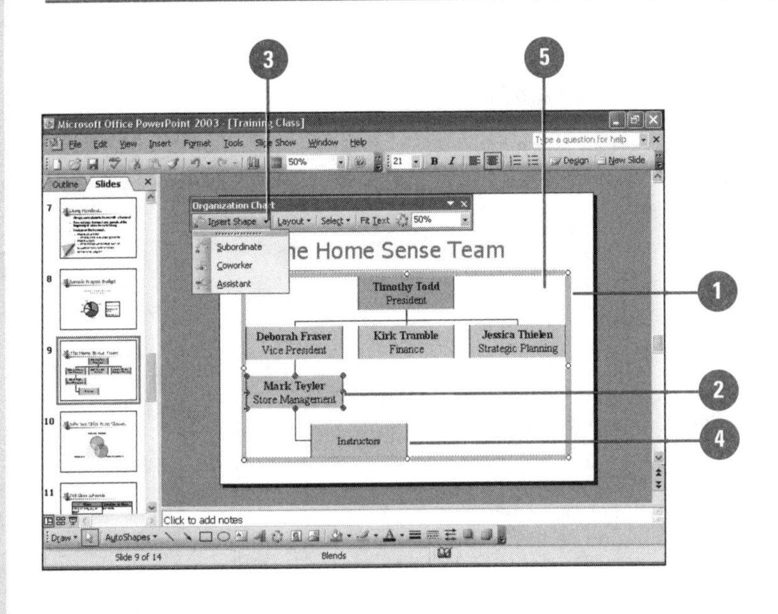

Did You Know?

You can delete a chart box. If you add a chart box in the wrong place, you can delete it by first selecting the chart box and then pressing the Delete key.

Change the Layout

1. Click the org chart you want to change.
2. Select the top chart box of the branch to which you want to apply a new layout. The chart box should have subordinates or assistants.
3. Click the Layout list arrow on the Organization Chart toolbar, and then select a new layout.

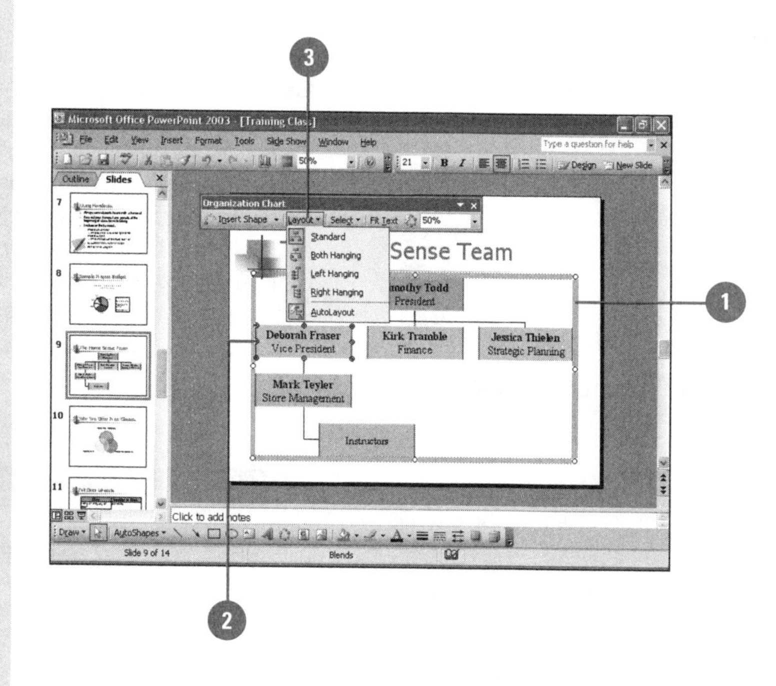

Rearrange a Chart Box

1. Click the org chart you want to change.
2. Make sure the chart box you want to move is not selected.
3. Position the mouse over the chart box you want to move. The pointer changes to a four-headed arrow.
4. Drag the chart box over an existing chart box.
5. Release the mouse button when the chart box is in the correct position.

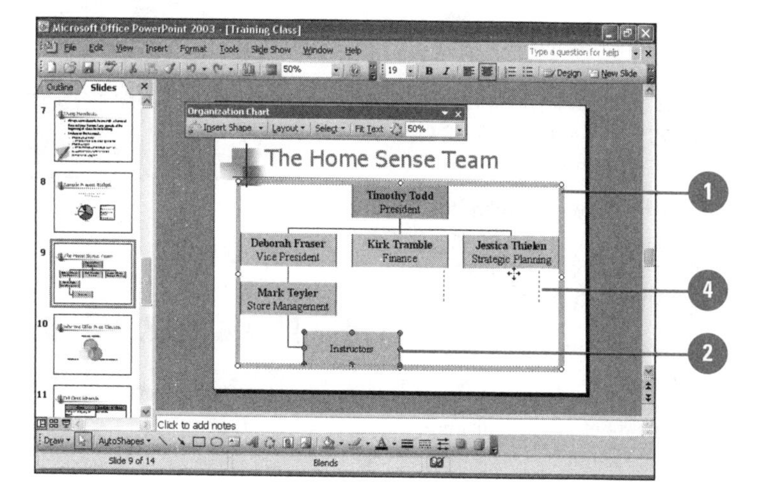

Formatting an Organization Chart

You can format the text and appearance of an organization chart with the same tools you use for other PowerPoint objects. You can change the chart style, rearrange chart boxes, or edit names in the chart boxes to match the organization of the company. The current chart type appears in the traditional style, one manager at the top with subordinates below. You can use the AutoFormat button on the Organization Chart toolbar to change the chart style. You can also change the chart box color, shadow, border style, border color, or border line style by clicking commands on the Drawing toolbar. Remember to use formatting wisely and keep in mind the overall design of your presentation.

Format an Organization Chart

1. Click the org chart you want to format.
2. Click the chart object or objects you want to format.
3. Click the button on the toolbar you want to use.
   - Use the Formatting and Drawing toolbars to format the text in a chart box.
   - Use the Drawing toolbar to change the color, shadow effect, border style, border color, and border line style of a selected chart box.
   - Use the Drawing toolbar to format the lines that connect the chart boxes, including their thickness, style, and color.
4. Make the formatting changes you want.
5. Click outside of the organization chart to deselect it.

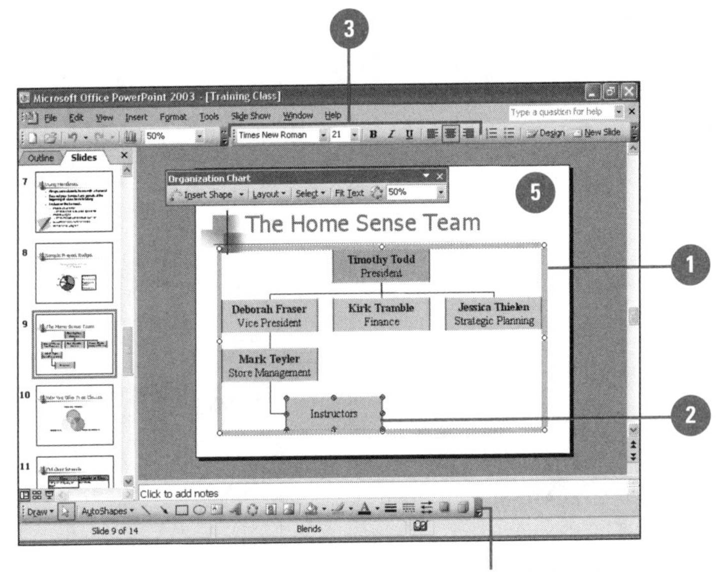

Use the Drawing toolbar to format the org chart.

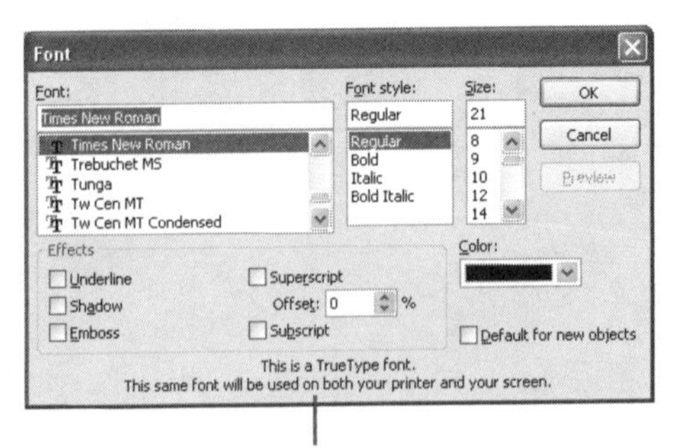

Use the Font dialog box to format an organization chart's text.

Did You Know?

You can align text in a chart box. Align the text in a chart box by selecting text in the chart box, and then clicking the Left, Center, or Right button on the Formatting toolbar.

Change the Chart Style

1. Click the org chart you want to change.
2. Click the AutoFormat button on the Organization Chart toolbar.
3. Select a Diagram Style from the Organization Chart Style Gallery.
4. Click OK.

Did You Know?

You can use the Default Chart Style when modifying. Format changes such as coloring and line style can only be made to the Default chart style, not the predesigned styles.

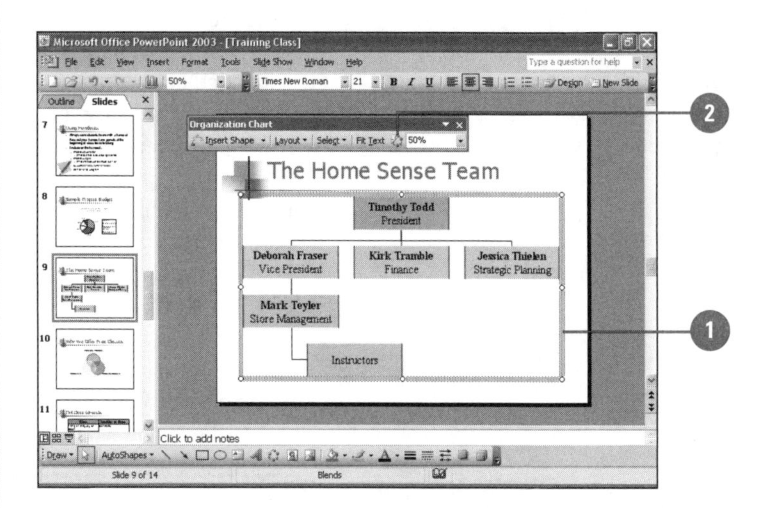

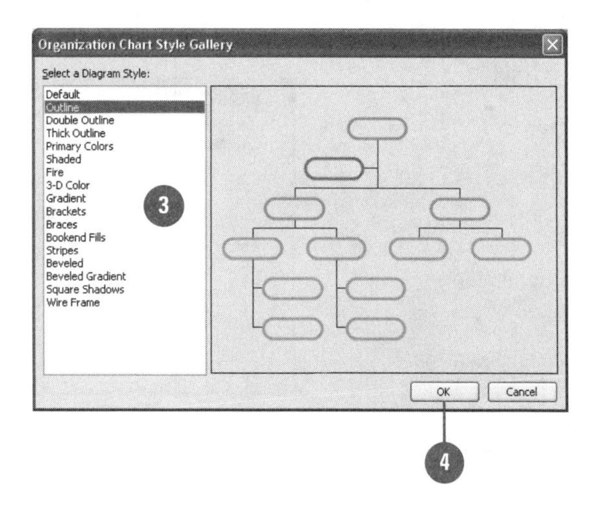

Inserting a Microsoft Excel Chart

PP03S-1-5

PowerPoint simplifies the process of inserting an Excel chart into a presentation by embedding the chart as an object in the slide. An embedded object is an object that maintains a direct connection to its original program, known as the source program. After you insert an embedded object, you can easily edit it by double-clicking it, which opens the program in which it was originally created. Embedding objects increases the file size of a presentation because the embedded object is stored in the presentation. To reduce the file size of the presentation, you can link an object instead of embedding it. A linked object appears in the slide, but it actually contains a "link" back to the original file, known as the source document. When you link an object, the original object is stored in its source document, where it was created. The presentation stores only a representation of the original. The source program will update the object when you modify the source document.

Insert a New Excel Chart

1. Click the Insert menu, and then click Object.
2. Click the Create New option.
3. Click Microsoft Office Excel Chart.
4. Click OK.
5. Use the source program tools to edit the object.
6. When you're done, click outside the object.

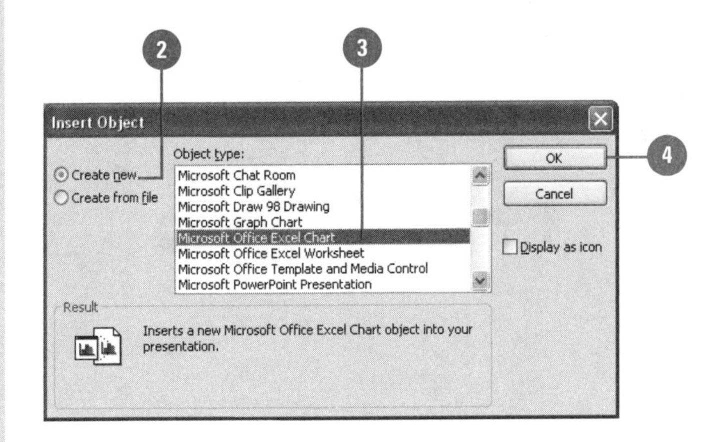

Did You Know?

You can drag a chart from Excel to PowerPoint. Open both Excel and PowerPoint, select the chart in Excel, and then drag it into PowerPoint. If the PowerPoint presentation is not visible, drag the chart to the presentation button on the taskbar to display PowerPoint.

Import a Microsoft Excel Worksheet or Chart

1. Display the slide on which you want to insert the Excel chart.
2. Click the Insert menu, and then click Object.
3. Click the Create From File option, click the Browse button, locate and select the chart you want, and then click OK.
4. To link the chart, click the Link check box.
5. Click OK.
6. If necessary, edit the worksheet using the Excel tools.
7. Click outside the worksheet when you are finished.

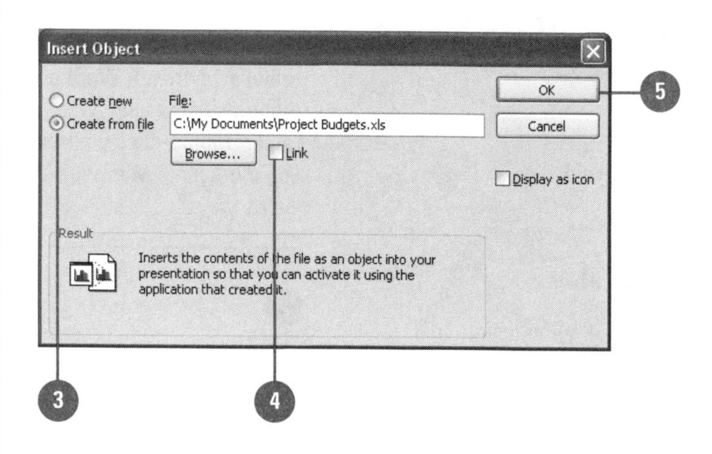

Copying and Pasting an Existing Excel Chart

1. Open the worksheet containing the chart in Excel.
2. Click the chart, and then click the Copy button on Excel's Standard toolbar.
3. Switch to PowerPoint and open the slide on which you want to add the chart.
4. Click the Paste button on the Standard toolbar.
5. Click outside the chart to deselect it.

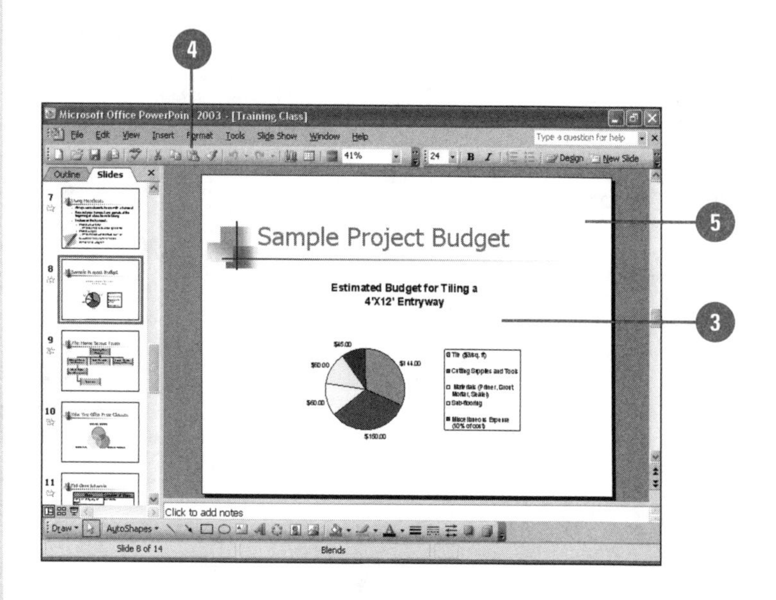

6

Inserting a Microsoft Word Table

PP03S-1-5

You can insert a Microsoft Word table into PowerPoint by inserting the table as an embedded object in a slide. When you insert a new Word table, a Microsoft Word document opens in the PowerPoint slide. A table menu will also open which assists you in creating and formatting the table. Double-click your embedded table to open Word and edit the table. You must have Microsoft Word installed on your computer to insert a Word table.

Insert a Word Table

1. Click the Insert menu, and then click Object.
2. Click the Create New option.
3. Click Microsoft Word Document.
4. Click OK.

   A Microsoft Word document opens in the PowerPoint slide.
5. Use the commands on the Table menu to create the table that you want.
6. Click outside of the table when you are finished.

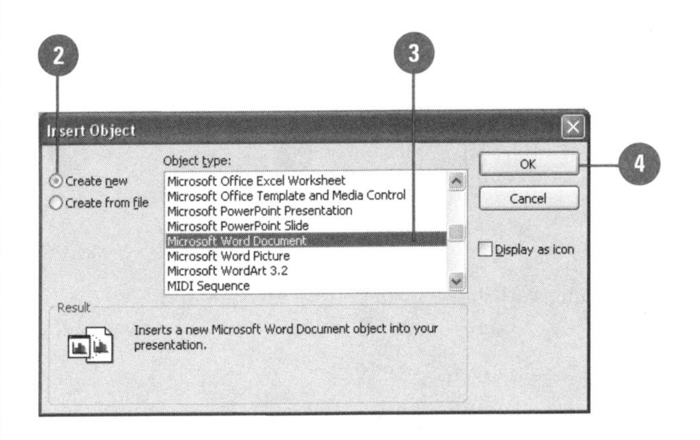

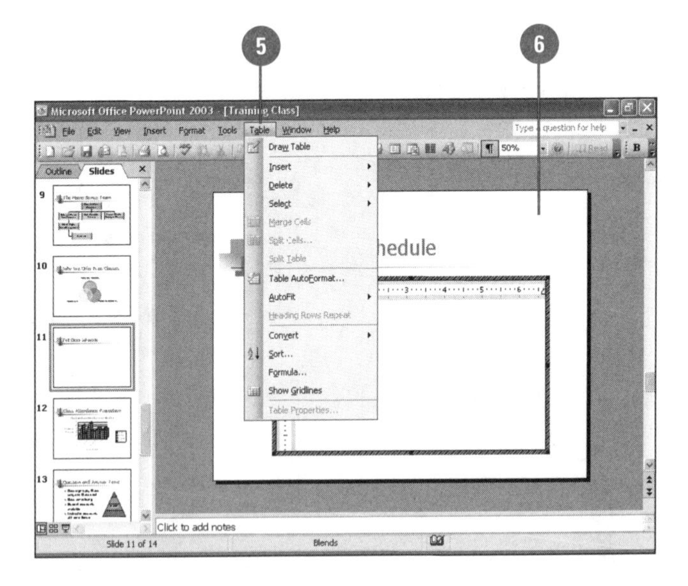

See Also

See "Sharing Information Among Documents" on page 148 for more information about an embedded object.

Inserting a Table

PP03S-1-3

A **table** organizes information neatly into rows and columns. The intersection of a column and row is called a **cell**. Enter text into cells just as you would anywhere else in PowerPoint, except that pressing the Tab key moves you from one cell to the next. PowerPoint tables behave much like tables in Word. You don't need to have Microsoft Word installed on your computer to create tables in your presentations.

Insert a Table Quickly

1. In Normal view, display the slide to which you want to add a table.
2. Click the Insert Table button on the Standard toolbar.
3. Drag to select the number of rows and columns you want.
4. Release the mouse button to insert a blank grid in the document.
5. Click outside of the table when you are finished.

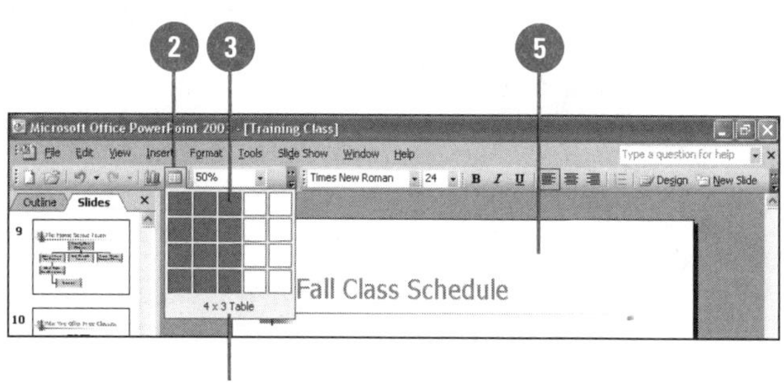

The first number indicates the number of rows. The second number indicates the number of columns.

Enter Text and Move Around a Table

The insertion point shows where text you type will appear in a table. Choose one of the following after you type text in a cell.

- Press Return to start a new paragraph within that cell.
- Press Tab to move the insertion point to the next cell to the right (or to the first cell in the next row).
- Use the arrow keys or click anywhere in the table to move the insertion point to a new location.

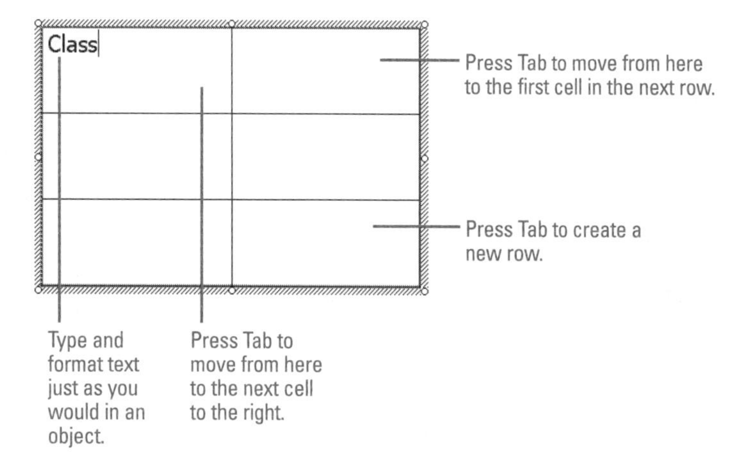

Press Tab to move from here to the first cell in the next row.

Press Tab to create a new row.

Type and format text just as you would in an object.

Press Tab to move from here to the next cell to the right.

6

Formatting a Table

After you create a table or begin to enter text in one, you might want to add more rows or columns to accommodate the text you are entering in the table. PowerPoint makes it easy for you to format your table. You can change the alignment of the text in the cells (by default, text is aligned on the left of a cell). You can also modify the appearance and size of the cells.

Insert and Delete Columns and Rows

1. Click in a table cell next to where you want the new column or row to appear.
2. Click the Table list arrow on the Tables And Borders toolbar.
3. To insert columns and rows, click one of the insert column or insert row commands.
4. To delete columns and rows, click Delete Columns or Delete Rows.

Align Text Within Cells

1. Select the text you want to align in the cells, rows, or columns.
2. Click one of the alignment buttons on the Formatting or Tables And Borders toolbar.

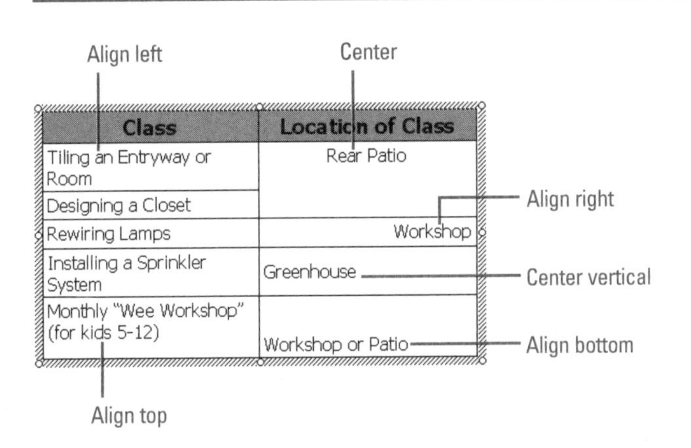

Did You Know?

You can use the pencil and eraser to add and remove cells. Click the Draw Table button on the Tables And Borders toolbar, and then drag the pencil pointer from one boundary to another to add cells. Click the Eraser button, and then click on a border to erase a cell.

Modify Cell Borders

1. Select the cells or text whose border(s) you want to modify.
2. Click the Border Style list arrow, and then select a border line style.
3. Click the Border Width list arrow, and then select a line thickness.
4. Click the Border Color button, and then select a border color.
5. Click the Borders list arrow, and then select a border style. The current border style appears selected.

TIMESAVER *When you select a new border style, width, or color in the Tables And Borders toolbar, the pointer changes to a pencil. Click the borders you want to change.*

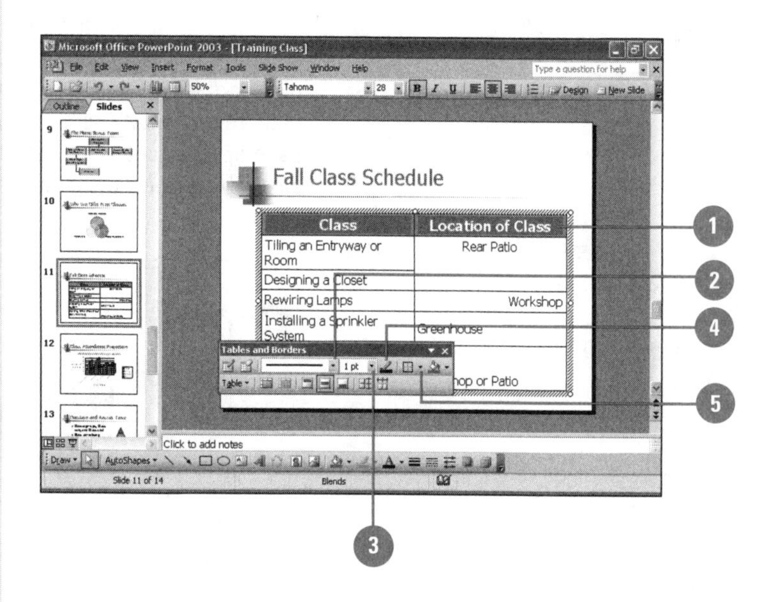

Adjust Row Height and Column Width

1. Move the pointer over the boundary of the row or column you want to adjust until the pointer changes into a resizing pointer.
2. Drag the boundary to adjust the row or column to the size you want.

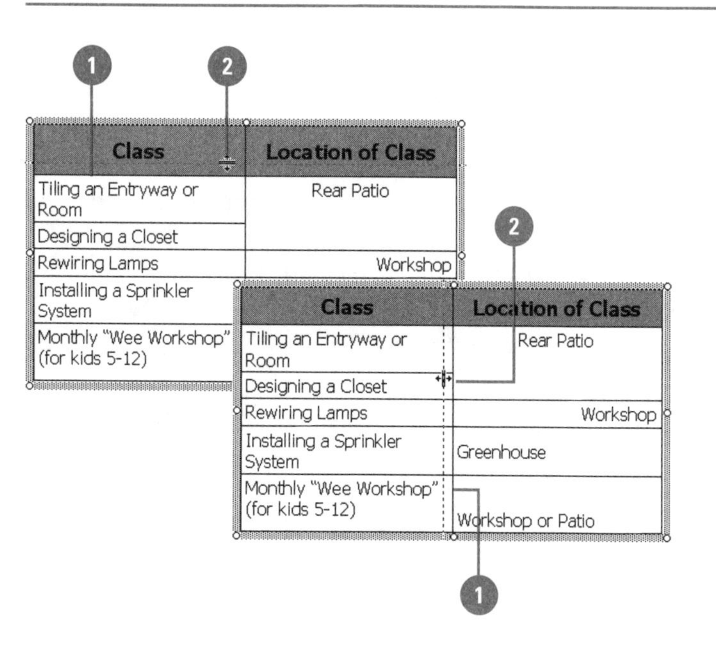

Did You Know?

You can merge or split cells. Select the cells you want to merge or the cell you want to split, and then click the Merge Cells or Split Cells button on the Tables And Borders toolbar.

6

Copying and Pasting Objects

You can copy a selected object or multiple objects to the Office Clipboard and then paste the objects in other parts of the presentation. The Office Clipboard allows you to copy multiple items of text or pictures from one or more presentations. When you copy multiple items, the Clipboard task pane appears and shows all of the items that you stored there. You can paste these items of information into PowerPoint, either individually or all at once.

Copy an Object

1. Select the object.
2. Click the Copy button on the Standard toolbar.
3. Display the slide on which you want to paste the object.
4. Click the Paste button on the Standard toolbar.

Copy and Move an Object in One Step

1. Hold down Ctrl, and then drag the object.

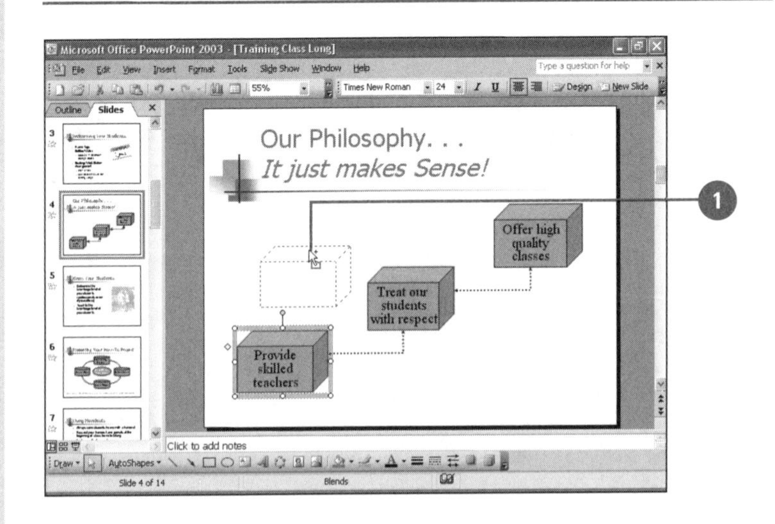

Copy Multiple Objects Using the Office Clipboard Task Pane

1. Select multiple objects you want to copy.
2. Click the Copy button on the Standard toolbar.

   The objects are copied into the Office Clipboard task pane.
3. Display the slide on which you want to paste the object(s).
4. In the Clipboard task pane, click an item to paste it on the slide.

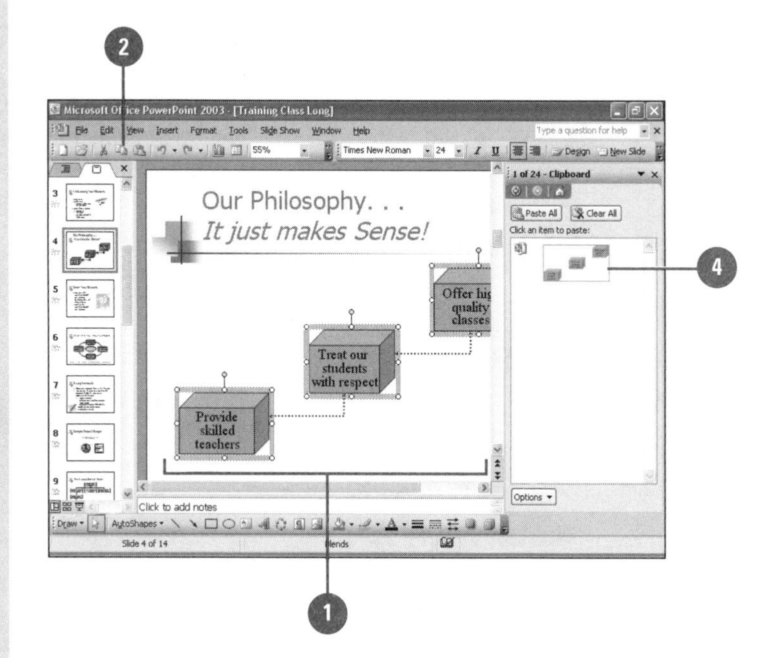

Did You Know?

You can move an object. Drag the object to another area of the slide.

You can change the Office Clipboard options. To change the way the Office Clipboard works, click the Options button at the bottom of the Office Clipboard task pane and turn on or off your preferences.

Embedding and Linking an Object

You can embed or link objects in several ways. If you are creating a new object you want to embed or link, use the Insert Object command. If you want to embed an existing file, you can also use Insert Object and specify whether you want to also link the object. If your object is already open in its source program, you can copy the object, and in some cases, paste it onto a slide, automatically embedding it. Finally, you can use the Paste Special command to **paste link** a copied object—pasting and linking it at the same time.

Insert a New Object

1. Click the Insert menu, and then click Object.
2. Click the Create New option.
3. Click the type of object you want to insert.
4. Click OK.
5. Use the source program tools to edit the object.
6. Click outside the object when you are finished.

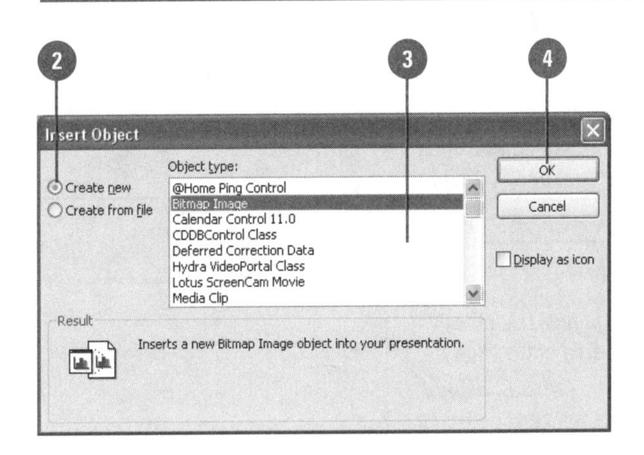

Insert a File

1. Click the Insert menu, and then click Object.
2. Click the Create From File option.
3. Click Browse.
4. Click the Look In list arrow, and then select the file you want to insert, and then click OK.
5. To embed the object, clear the Link check box, if necessary. To link it, select the Link check box.
6. Click OK.

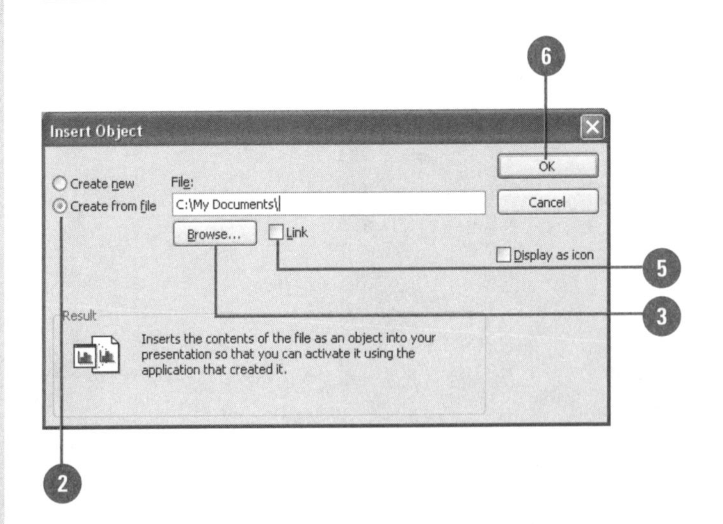

Paste Link an Object

1. In the source program, select the object you want to paste link.
2. Click the Cut or Copy button on the Standard toolbar in the source program.
3. Switch to your presentation.
4. Click the Edit menu, and then click Paste Special.
5. Click the Paste Link option.
6. Click the object type you want.
7. Click OK.

Did You Know?

You can insert objects as icons. In the Insert Object dialog box, select the Display As Icon check box. If you insert an object as an icon, you can double-click the icon to view the object. This is especially handy for kiosk presentations.

You can work with embedded objects. If you click an embedded object, you simply select it. You can then resize it in PowerPoint. If you double-click an embedded object, you activate it and the source toolbars and menus appear.

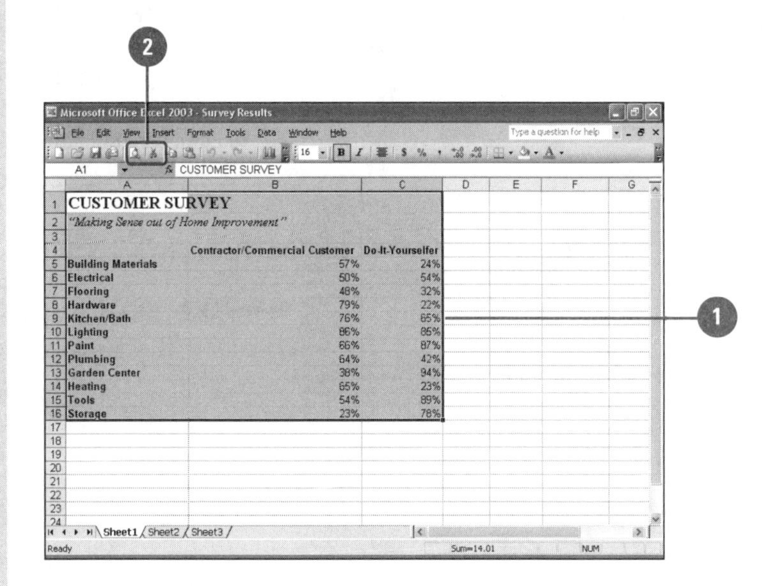

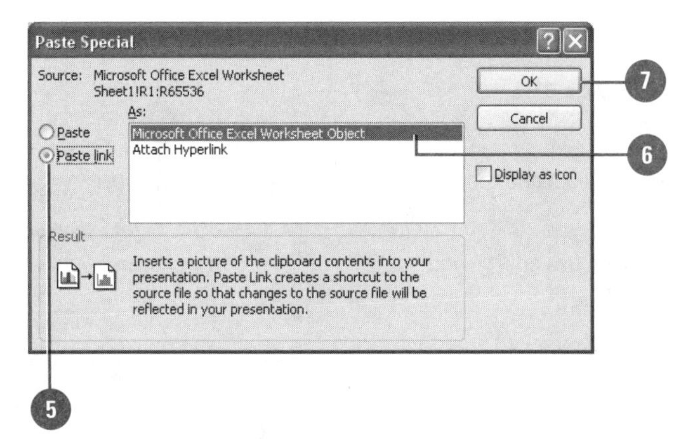

6

Modifying Links

When you modify a linked object, it is usually updated in the destination document. However, you can choose to update the link manually. All Office 2003 programs give you control over the links you have established. You can change the source file and you can break a link at any time. You can also convert a linked object to another object type.

Update Links

1. Open the presentation that contains the links you want to update.
2. Click the Edit menu, and then click Links.
3. Click the link you want to update.
4. Click Update Now.
5. Click Close.

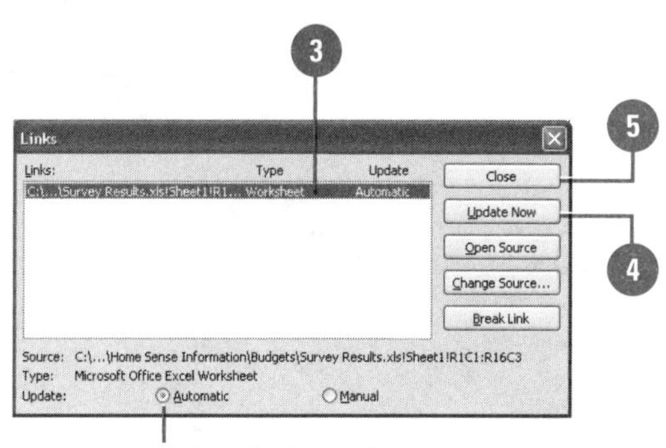

Click so that links will update automatically whenever the document is reopened.

Change the Source of a Linked Object

1. Click the Edit menu, and then click Links.
2. Click the link whose source you want to change.
3. Click Change Source.
4. Locate and double-click the new source file.
5. Click Close.

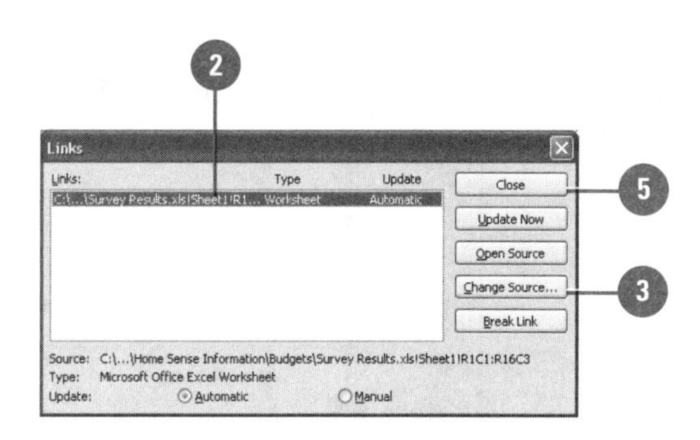

Did You Know?

You can edit an embedded object in the source program. Double-click the embedded object to open it, and make the changes you want. If you edit the object in the source program, click the File menu, and then click Exit to return to the destination file.

Break a Link

1. Click the Edit menu, and then click Links.
2. Click the link you want to break.
3. Click Break Link.

   The link no longer appears in the Links dialog box.
4. Click Close.

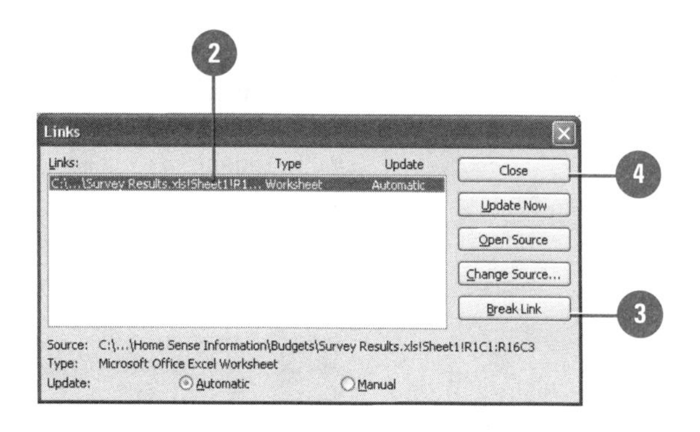

Convert a Linked Object

1. Click the linked object whose file type you want to convert.
2. Click the Edit menu, and then point to Linked Object. This command might appear as Linked Chart Object, or some other file type, depending on the object type.
3. Click Convert.
4. Click the new object type you want.
5. Click OK.

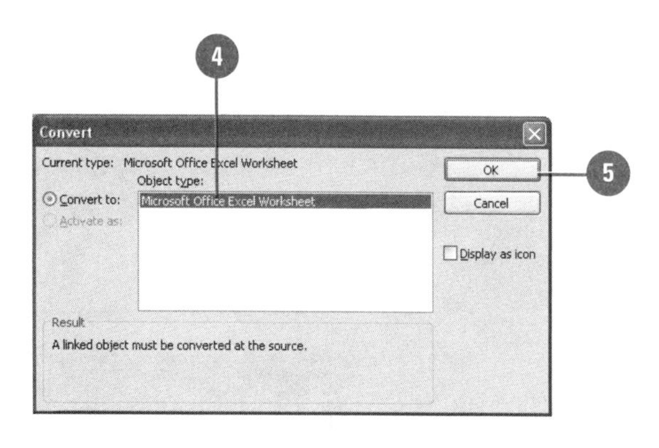

Did You Know?

You can reconnect a broken link. After you break the connection to a linked object, you must reinsert the object into your presentation to reconnect.

Creating a Diagram

PP03S-1-3

PowerPoint offers a variety of built-in diagrams from which to choose, including pyramid, cycle, radial, and Venn diagrams as well as organization charts. Using built-in diagrams makes it easy to create and modify charts without having to create them from scratch. To use the built-in diagrams, click the Insert Diagram Or Organization Chart button on the Drawing toolbar or click Diagram on the Insert menu, and then select a diagram.

Create a Diagram

1. In Normal view, display the slide to which you want to add a diagram.
2. Click the Insert Diagram Or Organization Chart button on the Drawing toolbar.
3. Select a diagram type, and then click OK.
4. Enter data into the text boxes provided.

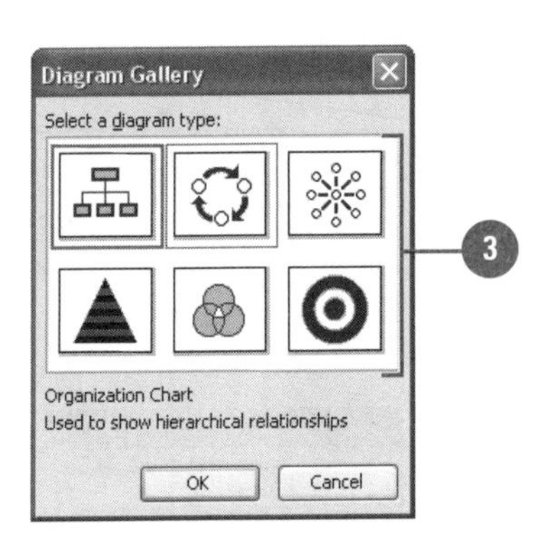

Format a Diagram

1. Click a blank area of the diagram to deselect the text box.
2. Drag a sizing handle to resize the diagram.
3. On the Diagram toolbar, click the AutoFormat button, select a style from the Diagram Style Gallery, and then click OK.

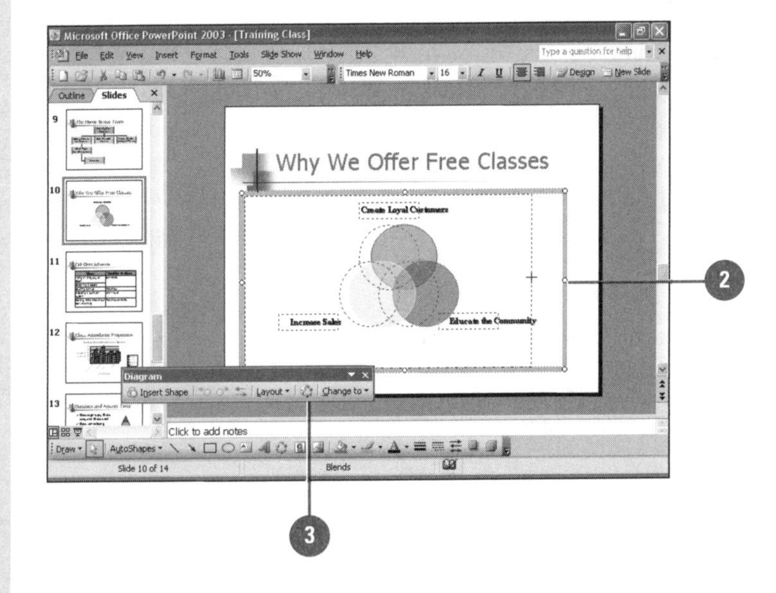

Did You Know?

You can format your diagram using the Diagram toolbar. The Diagram toolbar offers several ways to format your diagram. Use the Insert Shape button to add elements or segments, or to move them backward or forward.

Finalizing a Presentation and Its Supplements

7

Introduction

As you finish developing your presentation in Microsoft Office PowerPoint 2003, you can add some last-minute enhancements that will help with your delivery of the slide show. By creating a summary slide in the beginning of your presentation, your audience will know the scope of your presentation. Before finalizing your presentation, you should make sure that you embed true-type fonts into your presentation. This will ensure that your slide show appears correctly, regardless of the fonts installed on the various computers that you might be using.

Handouts are printed materials that you supply to your audience. Typically, handouts include an outline for the audience to follow as you speak, a copy of the slides in your presentation (printed one or more slides to a page), or a set of pages with blank lines next to reduced images of the slides for note taking. PowerPoint gives you many options for printing handouts, including editing and formatting them with the Handout Master. Most speakers feel more comfortable giving a presentation with a script in front of them, and you can easily create one in Notes Page view. With **speaker notes**, you can control the success of your presentation delivery.

As you take your presentation to various clients, it may be necessary to translate your slide show into another language. You might also want to export your notes to Microsoft Office Word to further customize them. You can save your slides in different formats—you might want to save them as part of a Web page, or maybe a different version of PowerPoint for other clients. You can also preview your presentation before printing or print as black and white or color to review your presentation in different print formats.

What You'll Do

Create a Summary Slide

Work with Fonts

Change Page Setup Options

Prepare Handouts

Prepare Speaker Notes

Customize Notes Pages

Change Text to a Language

Export Notes and Slides to Word

Work with Outlines

Save Slides in Different Formats

Check Spelling

Check Presentation Styles

Document Presentation Properties

Preview a Presentation

Print a Presentation

Print an Outline

Creating a Summary Slide

A **summary slide** is a bulleted list of titles from selected slides in your presentation. You can create a summary slide to use as an agenda slide for a presentation. To create an agenda or summary slide, you select the slides that you want to include from Slide Sorter view, and then you click the Summary Slide button on the Slide Sorter toolbar. In front of the first selected slide, PowerPoint creates a new slide that has a bulleted list with titles from selected slides.

Create a Summary Slide

1. In Slide Sorter view, select the slides you want to include on your summary slide.
2. Click the Summary Slide button on the Slide Sorter toolbar.

   A new slide appears with the title *Summary Slide* and a bulleted list of the selected slide titles.

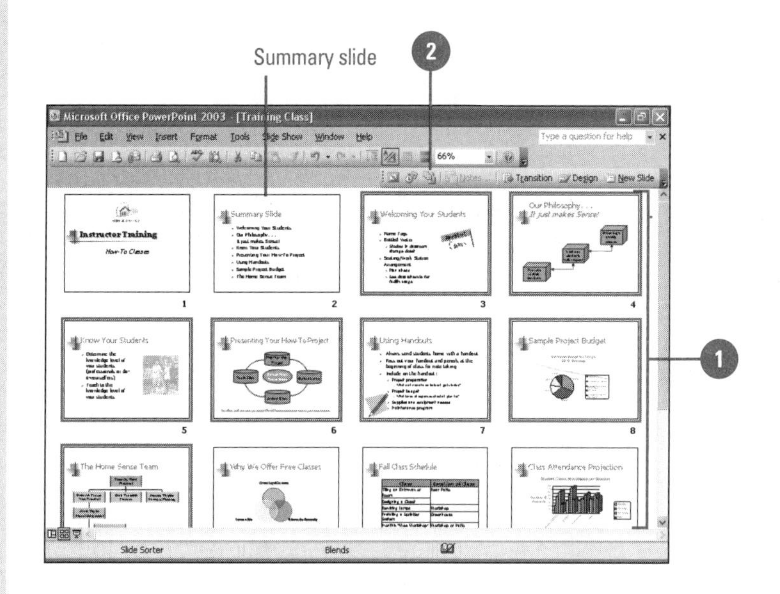

See Also

See "Adding Hyperlinks to Objects" on page 214 for more information on creating a hyperlink.

Working with Fonts

PowerPoint offers an assortment of tools for working with the fonts in your presentation. If you are using nonstandard fonts, you can embed the fonts you use so they "travel" with your presentation. Then, if the computer you use to show your presentation does not have all your fonts installed, the presentation quality will not suffer. Embedding fonts increases the size of your presentation file, however. If you decide to replace one font with another, you can easily do so with a single command.

7

Embed TrueType Fonts in a Presentation

1. Click the File menu, and then click Save As.
2. Click the Tools button, click Save Options, and then select the Embed TrueType Fonts check box. Click the option you want.
   - Click Embed Characters In Use Only (best for reducing file size)
   - Click Embed All Characters (best for editing by others)
3. Click OK.
4. If necessary, enter a file name, select a location for your presentation, and then click Save.

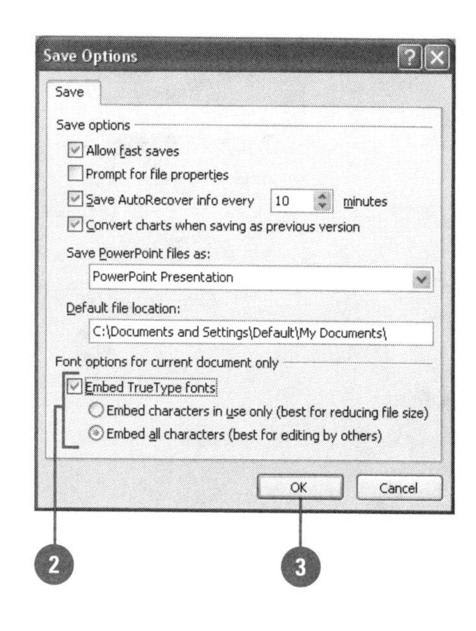

Replace Fonts

1. Click the Format menu, and then click Replace Fonts.
2. Click the Replace list arrow, and then click the font you want.
3. Click the With list arrow, and then click the font you want to substitute.
4. Click Replace, and then click Close.

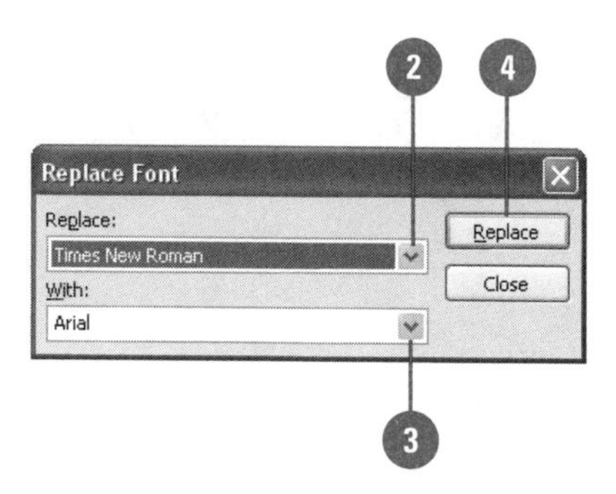

Changing Page Setup Options

PP03S-2-3

Before you print a presentation, you can use the Page Setup dialog box to set the proportions of your presentation slides and their orientation on the page. You can also control slide numbering in the Number Slides From box. For a new presentation, PowerPoint opens with default slide page settings: on-screen slide show, landscape orientation, and slides starting at number one. Notes, handouts, and outlines are printed in portrait orientation.

Control Slide Size

1. Click the File menu, and then click Page Setup.
2. Click the Slides Sized For list arrow.
3. Click the size you want.
   - Click On-Screen Show for 10-by-7.5-inch slides that fit a computer monitor.
   - Click Letter Paper for slides that fit on an 8.5-by-11-inch sheet of paper.
   - Click Ledger Paper for slides that fit on an 11-by-17-inch sheet of paper.
   - Click A3 Paper, A4 Paper, B4 (ISO) Paper, or B5 (ISO) Paper for slides that fit on international paper.
   - Click 35mm Slides for 11.25-by-7.5-inch slides.
   - Click Overhead for 10-by-7.5-inch slides that fit transparencies.
   - Click Banner for 8-by-1-inch slides that are typically used as advertisements on a Web page.
   - Click Custom to enter the measurements you want in the width and height boxes.
4. Click OK.

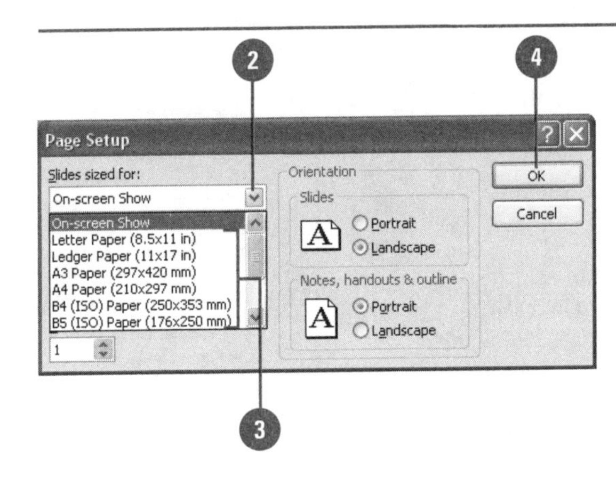

Customize Slide Proportions

1. Click the File menu, and then click Page Setup.
2. Enter a specific width in inches.
3. Enter a specific height in inches.
4. Click OK.

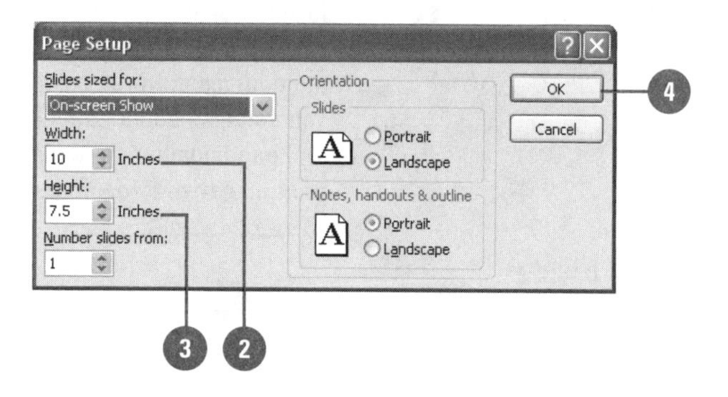

Change Slide Orientation

1. Click the File menu, and then click Page Setup.
2. To orient your slides, click the Portrait or Landscape option.
3. To orient your notes, handouts, and outline, click the Portrait or Landscape option in the Notes, Handouts & Outline area.
4. Click OK.

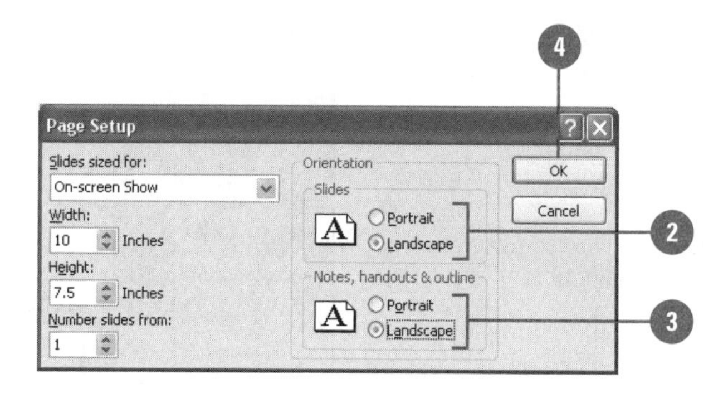

7

Preparing Handouts

PP03S-2-7

Prepare your handouts in the Print dialog box, where you can specify what to print. You can customize your handouts by formatting them in the handout master first, using the Formatting and Drawing toolbar buttons. You can also add a header and footer to include the date, slide number, and page number, for example. In the Print dialog box, you can choose to print one, two, three, four, six, or nine slides per page.

Format the Handout Master

1. Click the View menu, point to Master, and then click Handout Master.
2. Click one of the buttons on the Handout Master View toolbar to specify how many slides you want per page.
3. Use the Formatting and Drawing toolbar buttons to format the handout master.
4. If you want, add a header, footer, date, and page numbering.
5. Click the Close Master View button on the Handout Master View toolbar.

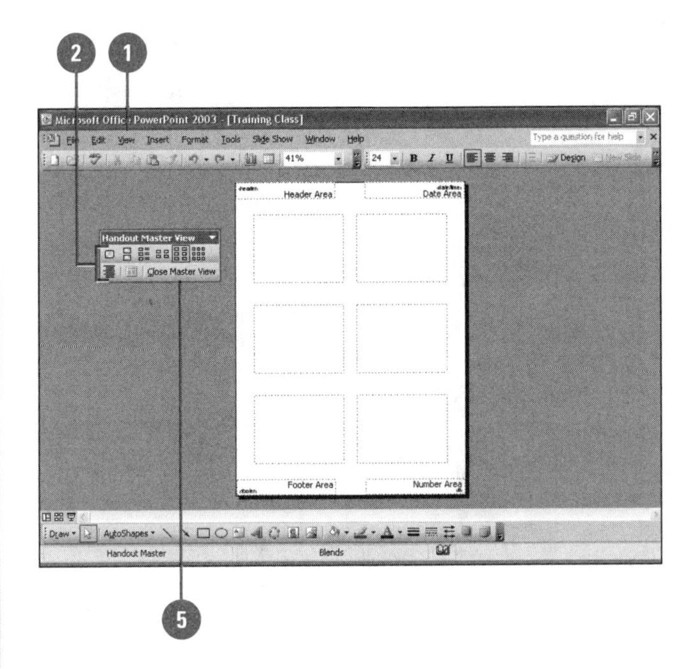

Did You Know?

What are the dotted rectangles in the handout master? The dotted rectangles are placeholders for slides and for header and footer information.

You can add headers and footers to create consistent handouts. Headers and footers you add to the handout master are also added to notes pages and the printed outline.

Add Headers and Footers to Handouts

1. Click the View menu, and then click Header And Footer.
2. Click the Notes And Handouts tab.
3. Enter the information you want to appear on your handouts.
4. Click Apply To All.

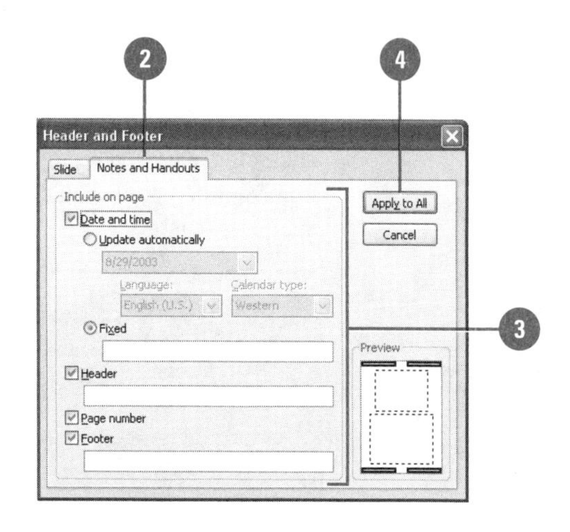

Print Handouts

1. Click the File menu, and then click Print.
2. Click the Print What list arrow, and then click the option you want.
   - Click Slides to print one slide per page.
   - Click Handouts, and then click the Slides Per Page list arrow to select one of the six options: one, two, three, four, six, or nine slides per page.
3. Click an Order option.
4. Click OK.

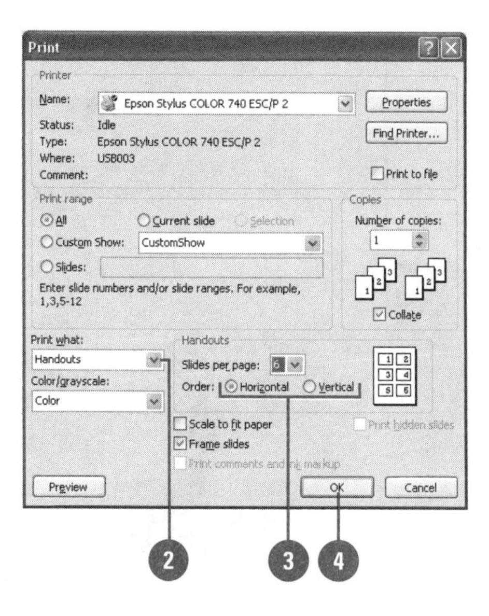

Did You Know?

You can add a frame around printed slides. Click the File menu, click Print, select the Frame Slides check box, and then click OK.

Preparing Speaker Notes

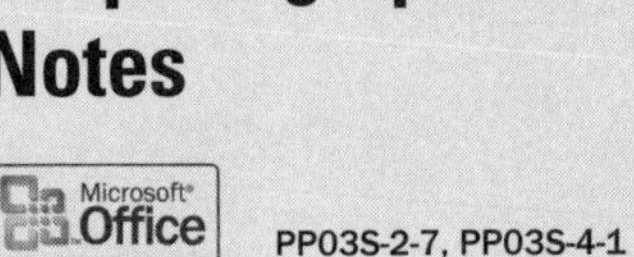

PP03S-2-7, PP03S-4-1

You can add speaker notes to a slide in Normal view using the Notes pane. Also, every slide has a corresponding **notes page** that displays a reduced image of the slide and a text placeholder where you can enter speaker's notes. Once you have created speaker's notes, you can reference them as you give your presentation, either from a printed copy or from your computer. You can enhance your notes by including objects on the notes master.

Enter Notes in Normal View

1. Switch to the slide for which you want to enter notes.
2. Click to place the insertion point in the Notes pane, and then type your notes.

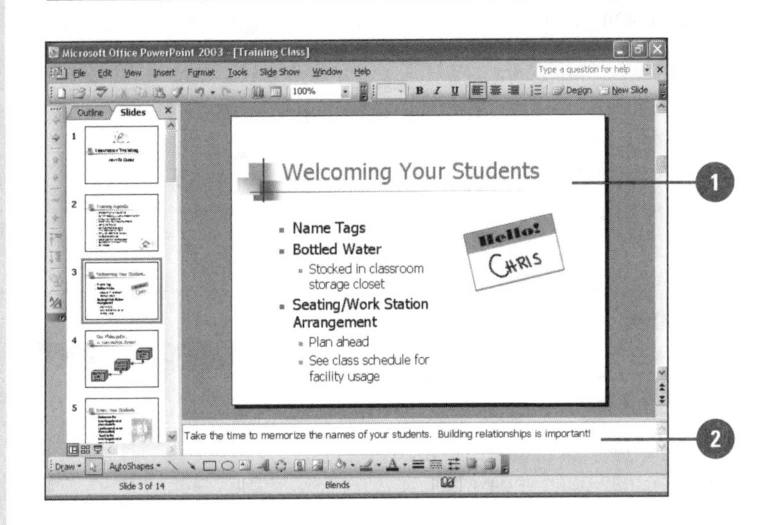

Did You Know?

You can view more of the Notes pane. To see more of the Notes pane in Normal view, point to the top border of the Notes pane until the pointer changes to a double-headed arrow, and then drag the border until the pane is the size you want.

Enter Notes in Notes Page View

1. Switch to the slide for which you want to enter notes.
2. Click the View menu, and then click Notes Page.
3. If necessary, click the Zoom list arrow, and then increase the zoom percentage to better see the text you type.
4. Click the text placeholder.
5. Type your notes.

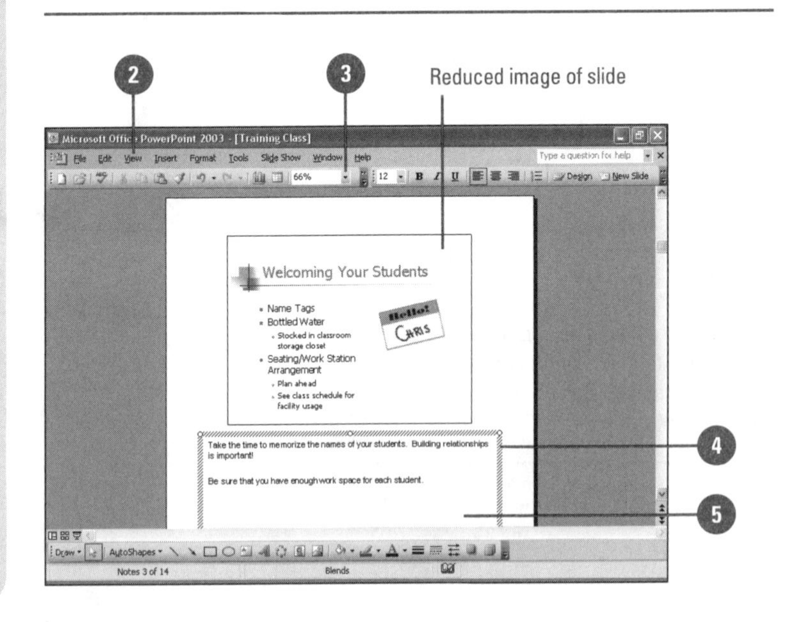

Format the Notes Master

1. Click the View menu, point to Master, and then click Notes Master.
2. Make the format changes you want.
   - You can add objects to the notes master that you want to appear on every page, such as a picture or a text object.
   - You can add a header and footer by clicking the View menu and then clicking Header And Footer.
   - You can add the date, time, or page number to your notes pages.
3. Click the Close Master View button on the Notes Master View toolbar.

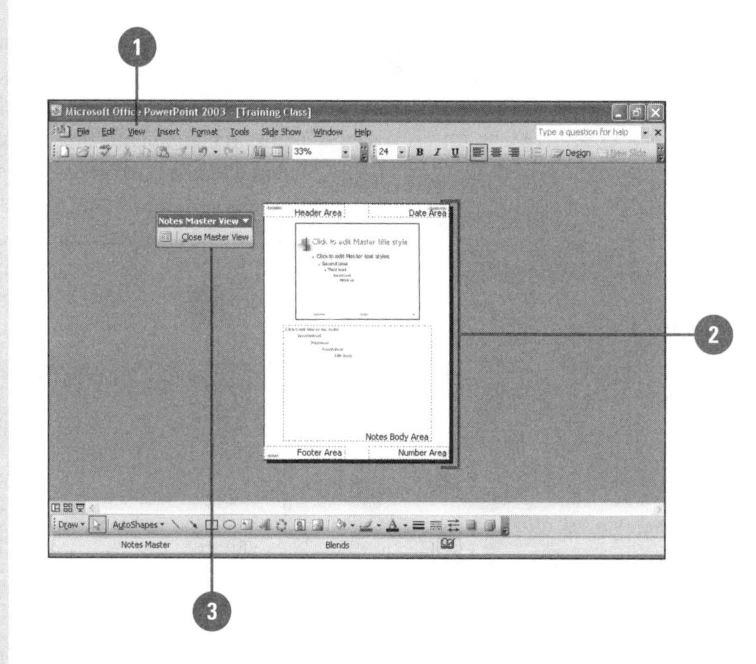

Did You Know?

Why don't the objects on the Notes master appear in the Notes pane in Normal view? The objects that you add to the Notes master will appear when you print the notes pages. They do not appear in the Notes pane of Normal view or when you save your presentation as a Web page.

You have different options to edit notes. You can edit notes in either Normal or Notes Page view using PowerPoint's text editing tools.

Customizing Notes Pages

PP03S-2-7, PP03S-4-1

You can add dates, numbering, and header and footer text to your notes pages just as you do to your slides. If you have removed objects from the master and decide you want to restore them, you can reapply any of the master placeholders (the slide image, the date, header, and so on) without affecting objects and text outside the placeholders. Moreover, if you delete the slide placeholder or text placeholder from a notes page, for example, you can easily reinsert it.

Add a Header and Footer to Notes Pages

1. Click the View menu, and then click Header And Footer.
2. Click the Notes And Handouts tab.
3. Add the header and footer information you want.
4. Click Apply To All.

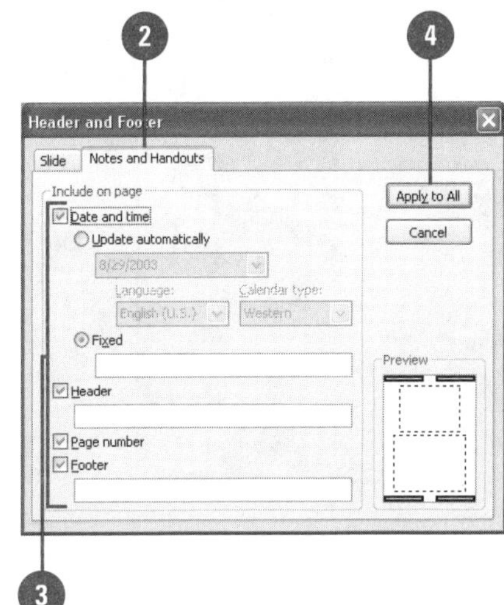

Reinsert Notes Placeholders on the Notes Master

1. Click the View menu, point to Master, and then click Notes Master.
2. Click the Notes Master Layout button on the Notes Master View toolbar.
3. Select the check boxes corresponding to the placeholders you want to reinsert.
4. Click OK.

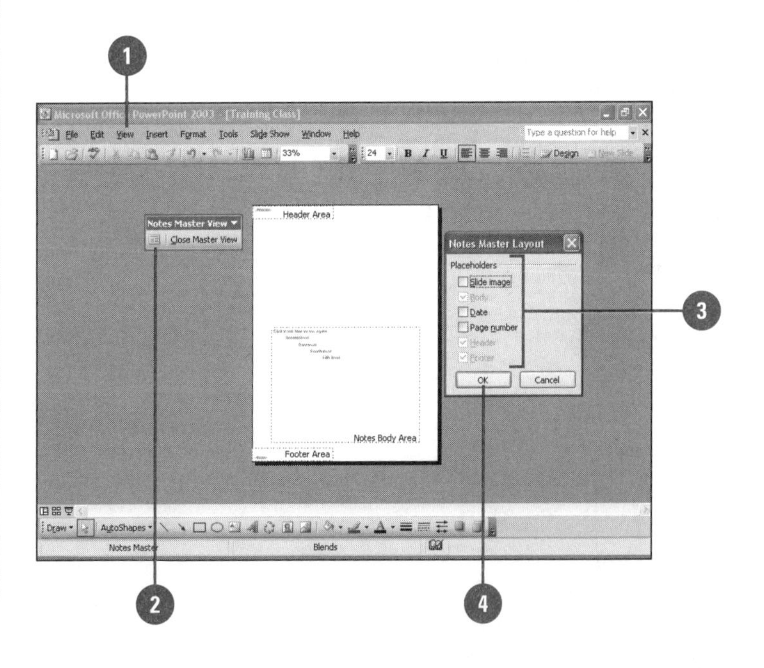

Reinsert Placeholders on an Individual Slide

1. In Notes Page view, switch to the slide whose placeholders you want to restore.
2. Click the Format menu, and then click Notes Layout.
3. Select the check boxes corresponding to the placeholders you want to reapply.
4. Click OK.

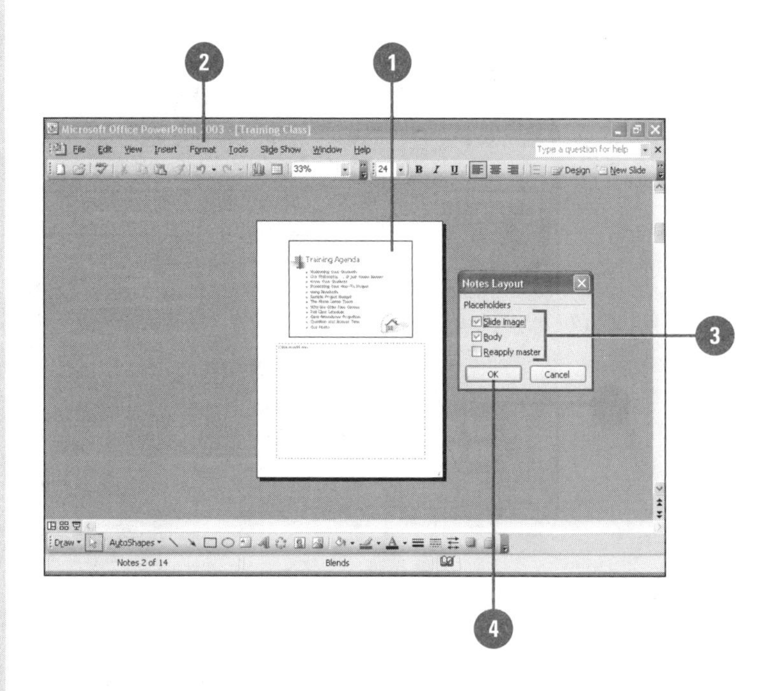

Customize Background Color of Notes Pages

1. In Notes Page view, right-click a blank area in the slide.
2. Click Notes Background to open the Notes Background dialog box.
3. Click the Background Fill list arrow, and then select a background color (a lighter color will allow you to read your notes easier).
4. Click Apply to change the selected notes page, or Apply to All to change the background of all notes pages.

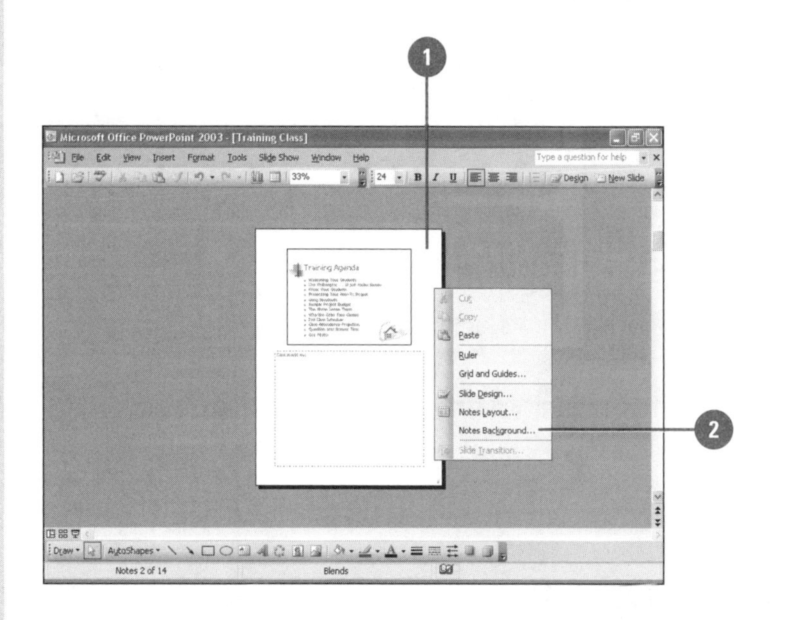

Changing Text to a Language

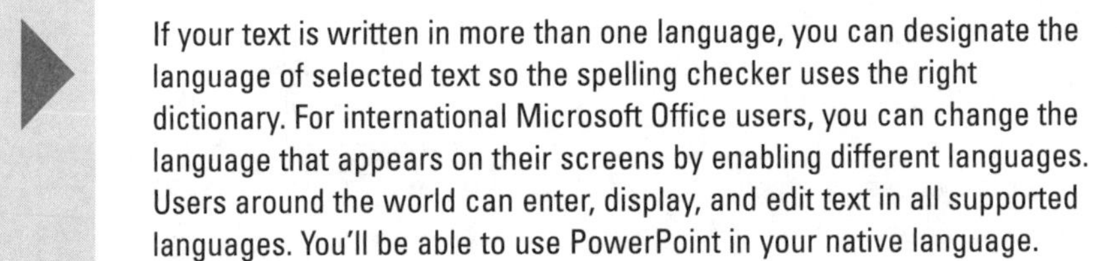

If your text is written in more than one language, you can designate the language of selected text so the spelling checker uses the right dictionary. For international Microsoft Office users, you can change the language that appears on their screens by enabling different languages. Users around the world can enter, display, and edit text in all supported languages. You'll be able to use PowerPoint in your native language.

Mark Text as a Language

1. Select the text you want to mark.
2. Click the Tools menu, and then click Language.
3. Click the language you want to assign to the selected text.
4. Click OK.

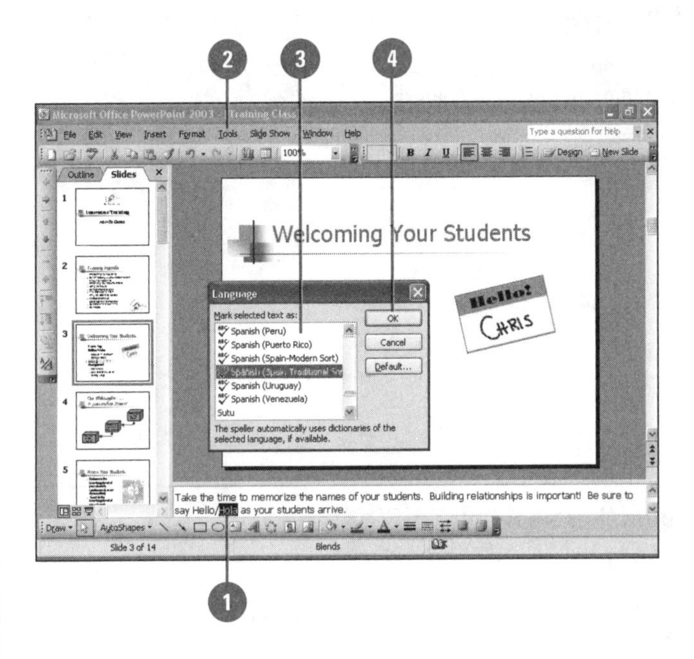

See Also

See "Using Multiple Languages" on page 314 for information on adding and enabling languages.

Did You Know?

There is a Multilingual AutoCorrect. Office supports an AutoCorrect list for each language. For example, the English AutoCorrect list capitalizes all cases of the single letter "i;" in Swedish however, "i" is a preposition and is not capitalized.

Exporting Notes and Slides to Word

PP03S-4-8

You can send both your notes and slides to Word so that you can use a full array of word processing tools. This is especially handy when you are developing more detailed materials, such as training presentations and manuals. By default, PowerPoint pastes your presentation into a Word document. If you change the presentation after sending it to Word, the changes you make to the presentation are not reflected in the Word document. If you click the Paste Link option in the Send To Microsoft Office Word dialog box, however, you create a link between the Word document and the presentation, and changes you make in one are reflected in the other.

Create Handouts in Word

1. Click the File menu, point to Send To, and then click Microsoft Office Word.
2. Click the page layout option you want for handouts.
3. To create a link to the presentation, click the Paste Link option.
4. Click OK.

   Word starts, creates a new document, and inserts your presentation slides with the page layout you selected.
5. Print the document in Word, editing and saving it as necessary.
6. When you're done, click the Close button to quit Word.

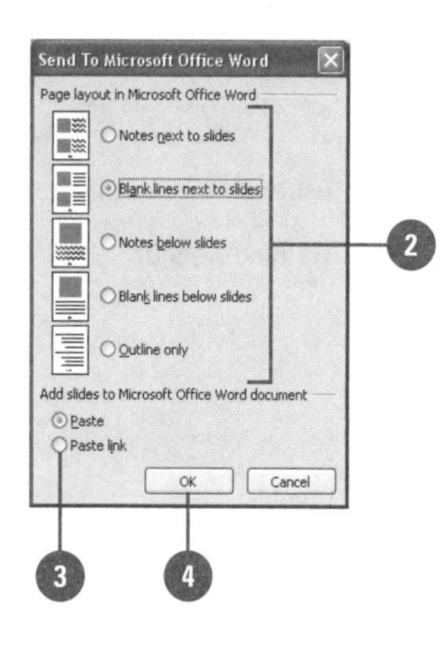

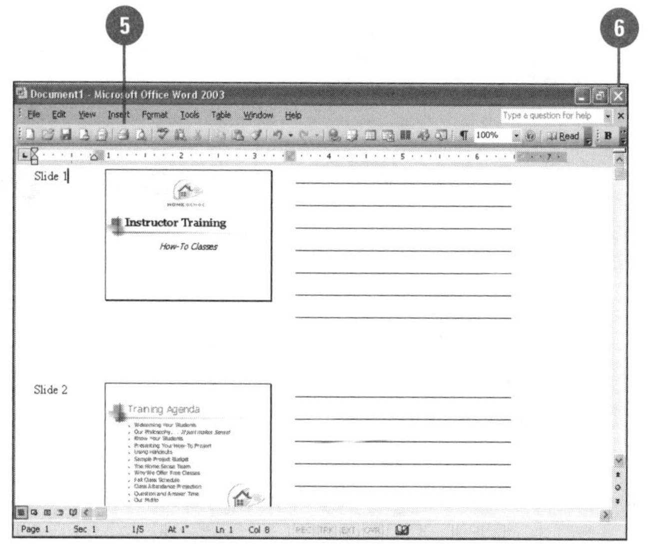

Working with Outlines

As long as Word is installed on your computer, you can export a presentation outline directly from PowerPoint into a report in Word with the Send To Microsoft Word feature. PowerPoint launches Word and sends or copies the outline in the presentation to a blank Word document. When you need the text portion of a presentation for use in another program, you can save the presentation text in a format called Rich Text Format (RTF). Saving an outline in RTF allows you to save any formatting that you made to the presentation text in a common file format that you can open in other programs.

Send a Presentation Outline to Word

1. Click the File menu, point to Send To, and then click Microsoft Office Word.
2. Click the Outline Only option.
3. Click OK.

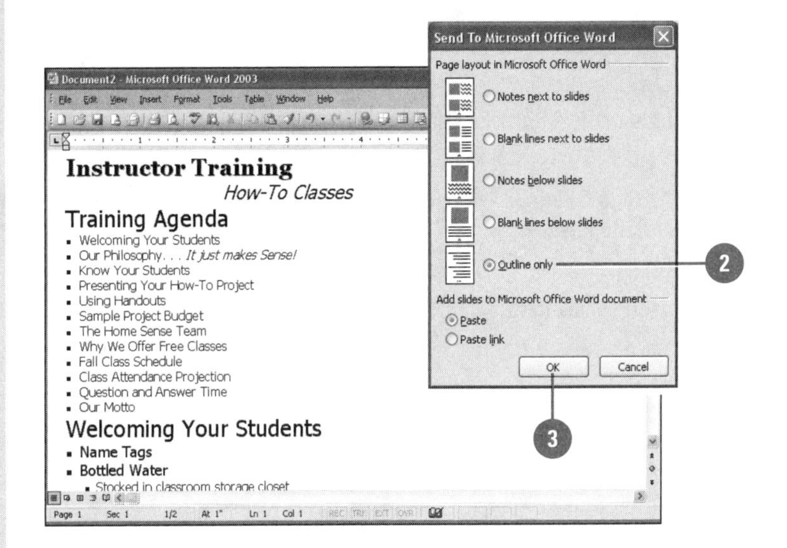

Save a Presentation as an Outline

1. Click the File menu, and then click Save As.
2. Navigate to the location in which you want to save the outline file.
3. In the File Name box, type the file name.
4. Click the Save As Type list arrow, and then click Outline/RTF.
5. Click Save.

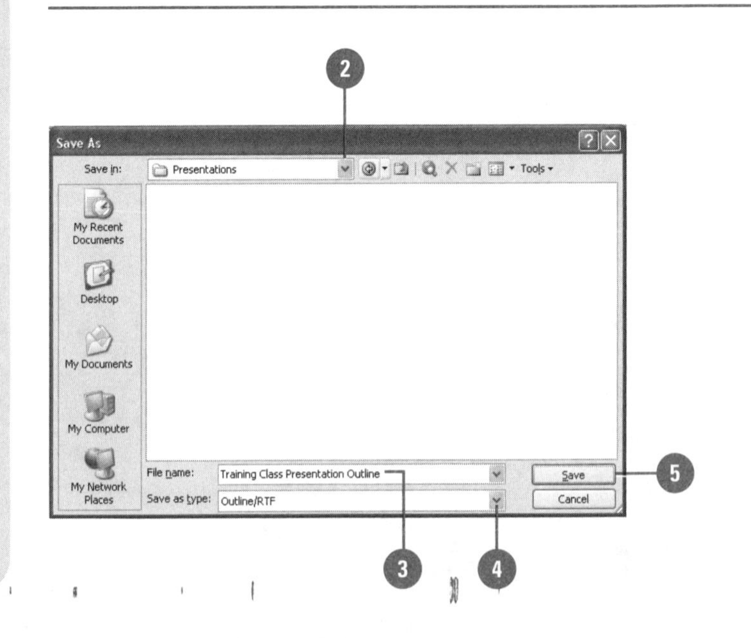

Saving Slides in Different Formats

PP03S-4-6

You can save PowerPoint presentations in a number of formats so that many different programs can access them. For example, you might want to save your presentation as a Web page that you can view in a Web browser. Or you can save a presentation in an earlier version of PowerPoint in case the people you work with have not upgraded to PowerPoint 2003. You can also save an individual slide as a graphic image that you can open in a graphics editor.

Save a Presentation in a Different File Type

1. Click the File menu, and then click Save As.
2. Click the Save As Type list arrow, and then click the format you want, such as a Web page, a previous version of PowerPoint, or an RTF (Rich Text Format) outline.
3. Type a filename.
4. Click the Save In list arrow, and then click the drive or folder where you want to save the file.
5. Click Save.

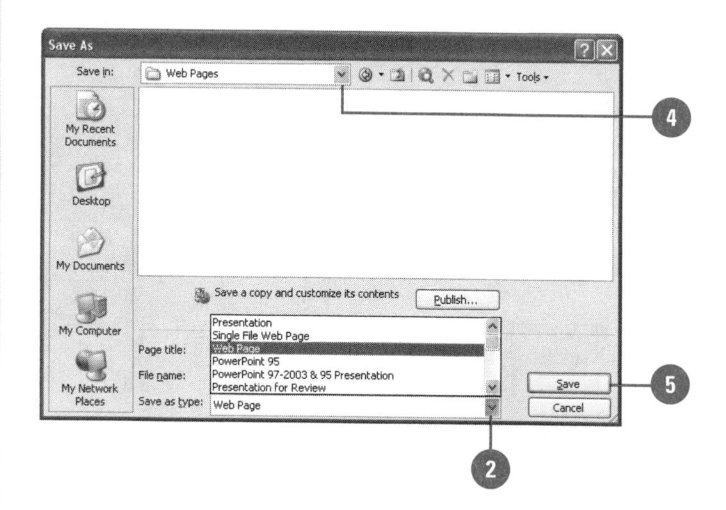

Save a Slide as a Graphic Image

1. Click the File menu, and then click Save As.
2. Click the Save As Type list arrow, and then click the graphics format you want to use (i.e. JPEG or GIF).
3. Type a filename.
4. Click the Save In list arrow, and then click the drive or folder where you want to save the file.
5. Click Save.
6. Click Every Slide to save all slides as separate graphic image files, or click Current Slide Only to save just the current slide. If necessary, click OK.

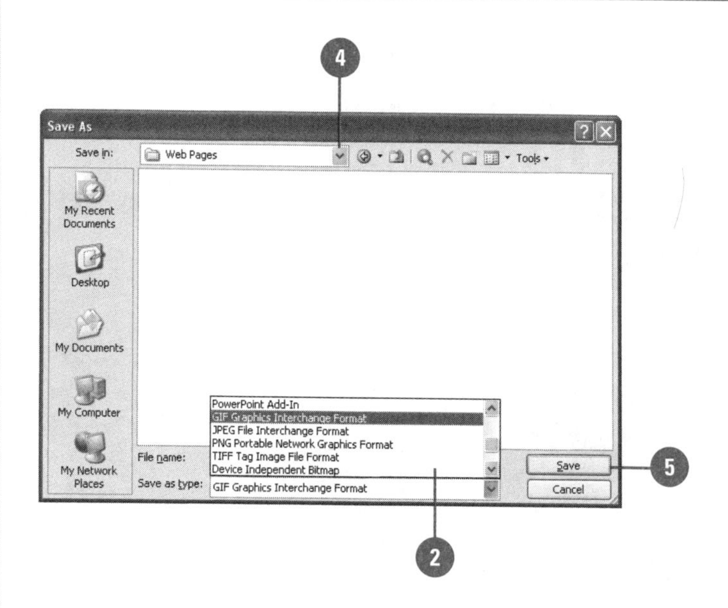

Checking Spelling

PP03S-1-2

PowerPoint's spelling checker checks the spelling of the entire presentation, including all slides, outlines, notes pages, and handout pages. To help you identify misspelled words or words that PowerPoint's built-in dictionary does not recognize, PowerPoint underlines them with a wavy red line. You can correct misspelled words in your presentation two different ways. You can use the Spelling button on the Standard toolbar to check the entire presentation using the Spelling dialog box, or when you encounter a wavy red line under a word, you can right-click the word and choose the correct spelling from the list on the shortcut menu.

Check Spelling

1. Click the Spelling button on the Standard toolbar.
2. If the Spelling dialog box opens, click Ignore if the word is spelled correctly, or click the correct spelling, and then click Change.
3. PowerPoint will prompt you when the spelling check is complete, or you can click Close to end the spelling check.

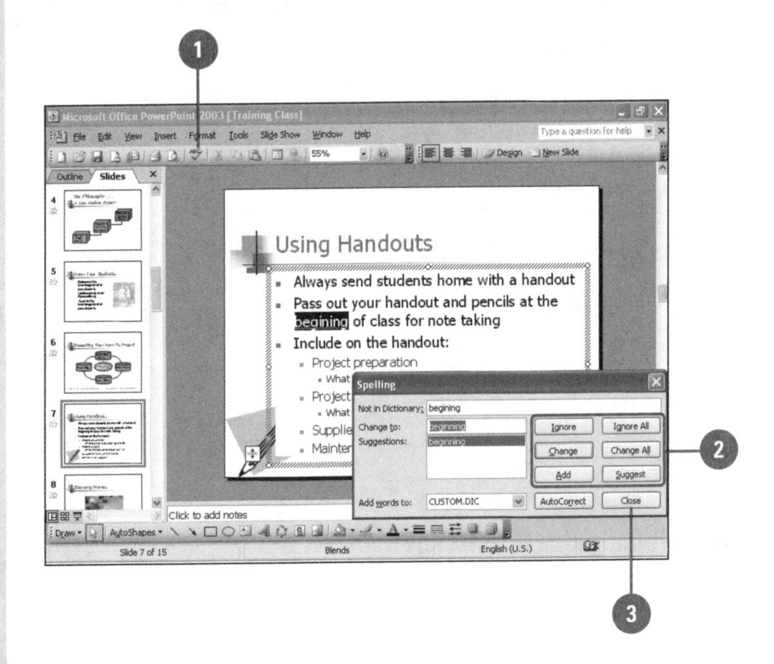

Did You Know?

You can mark a word as a foreign language word. Select the foreign word or phrase that you want to mark. Click the Tools menu, click Language, click the foreign language, and then click OK.

You can add a word to the custom dictionary. When the spelling checker stops on the word you want to add to your custom dictionary, click Add.

Correct Spelling as You Type

1. Click the Tools menu, and then click Options.
2. Click the Spelling And Style tab.
3. Select the Check Spelling As You Type check box.
4. Click OK.
5. If a red wavy line appears under a word as you type, right click it and then click the correct spelling.

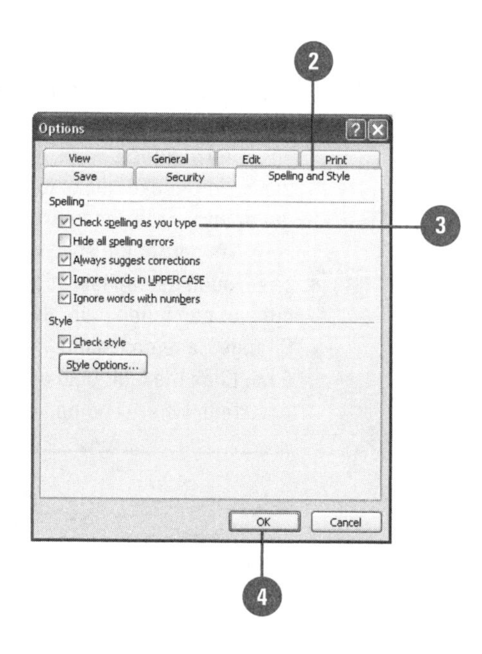

Click the light bulb to correct style.

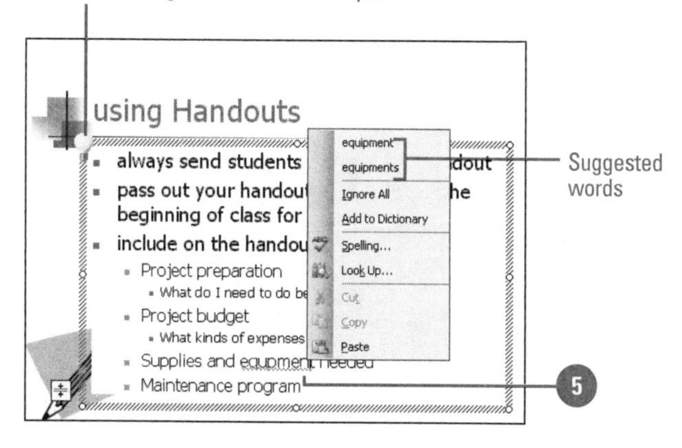

Checking Presentation Styles

PowerPoint's style checker works with the Office Assistant to help you correct common presentation style design mistakes so that your audience focuses on content, not visual mistakes. When the Office Assistant is visible, the style checker reviews the presentation for typical mistakes, and then suggests ways to improve the presentation. Typical mistakes the Style Checker looks for include incorrect font size, too many fonts, too many words, inconsistent punctuation, and other readability problems. As part of the style checking process, PowerPoint checks the text case, such as capitalization, of sentences and titles in the presentation, but you can independently change text case for selected text with the Change Case command. A light bulb appears when the style checker has a tip. Click the light bulb and a dialog balloon will appear over the Office Assistant, where you can use or ignore the tips.

Set the Style Options

1. Click the Tools menu, and then click Options.
2. Click the Spelling And Style tab.
3. Select the Check Style check box.
4. Click Style Options.

   If PowerPoint prompts you to enable the Office Assistant, click Enable Assistant.
5. Click the appropriate tab, and then set the style options you want the style checker to check.
6. Click OK.
7. Click OK.

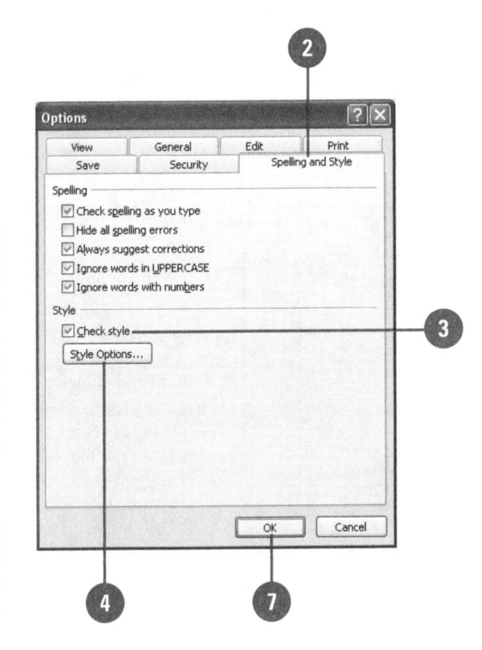

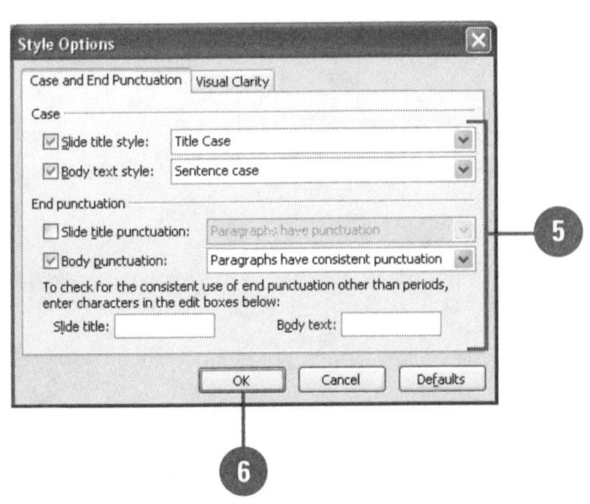

Did You Know?

You can reset the Style Checker Tips. If you make a decision on a tip and then change your mind, you may need to display the tip again. To do this, you need to reset your tips so that the Office Assistant will display all of them again. To reset your tips, right-click the Office Assistant, click Options, click Reset My Tips, and then click OK.

Change the Text Case

1. Select the text that you want to change.
2. Click the Format menu, and then click Change Case.

   The Change Case dialog box appears with the Sentence Case option set as the default.
3. Click the change case option that you want to apply to the selected text.
4. Click OK to apply the change option to the presentation.

Did You Know?

You can select a text case to apply. The Change Case command allows you to change text to sentence case, title case, uppercase, lowercase, or toggle case, which is a mixture of cases.

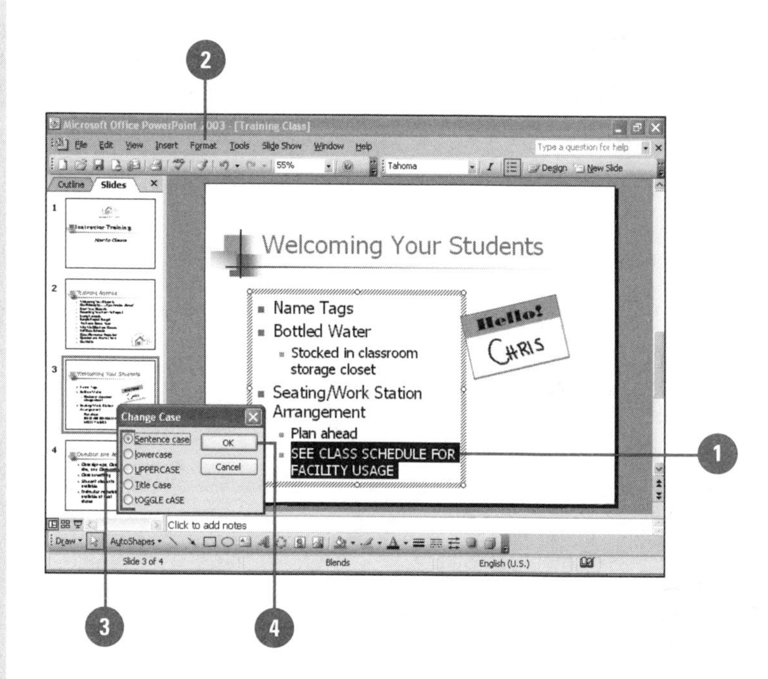

Documenting Presentation Properties

You can get feedback on your presentation before you present it by using PowerPoint's **File Properties** feature. PowerPoint allows you to document your presentation by entering information about the presentation and describing its contents so your feedback team has all the information it needs to evaluate it. You can also create custom file properties to help you manage and track files. If you associate a file property to an item in the document, the file property updates when you change the item. When you enter information for a property, you can use the Search command on the Tools menu in the Open dialog box or the Advanced File Search task pane to find a presentation with the desired property.

Display and Enter Presentation Properties

1. Click the File menu, and then click Properties.
2. Click the tabs (General, Summary, Statistics, or Contents) to view and add information:
   - **General.** To find out file location or size.
   - **Summary.** To add title and author information for the presentation.
   - **Statistics.** To display the number of slides, paragraphs, words and other details about the presentation.
   - **Contents.** To display slide titles and information about fonts and design templates used in the presentation.
3. Click OK.

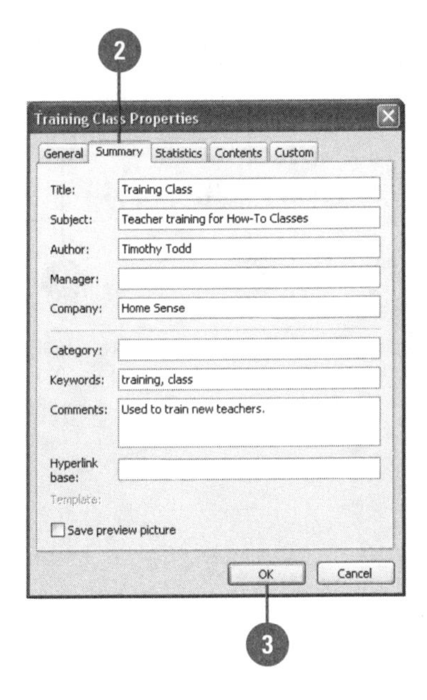

Did You Know?

You can automatically display the Properties dialog box when saving for the first time. Click the Tools menu, click Options, click the Save tab, select the Prompt For File Properties check box, and then click OK.

Customize Properties

1. Click the File menu, and then click Properties.
2. Click the Custom tab.
3. Type a name for the custom property or select a name from the list.
4. Select the data type for the property you want to add.
5. Type a value for the property that matches the type you selected in the Type box.
6. Click Add.
7. Click OK.

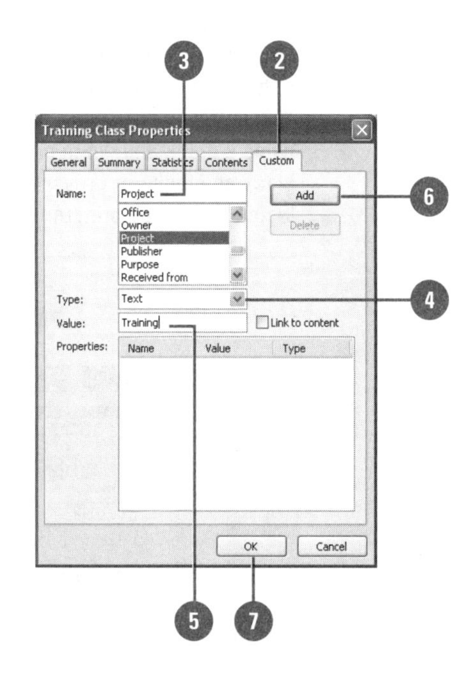

Link to Properties

1. Select the text or object in which you want to link the property.
2. Click the File menu, and then click Properties.
3. Click the Custom tab.
4. Type the name for the custom property.
5. Select the Link To Content check box.
6. Select the source to which you want to link.
7. Click Add.
8. Click OK.

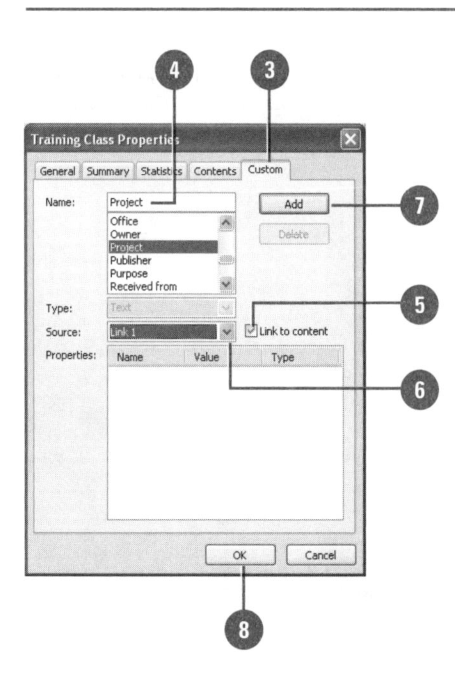

Previewing a Presentation

PP03S-4-7

Print preview allows you to see how your presentation will look before you print it. While in print preview, you have the option of switching between various views, such as notes, slides, outlines, and handouts. You can even view your presentation in landscape or portrait. If you are using a black and white printer, you can preview your color slides in pure black and white or grayscale in print preview to verify that they will be legible when you print them.

Preview Your Presentation

1. Click the Print Preview button on the Standard toolbar.

   If you are printing to a grayscale printer, your slides are shown in grayscale using print preview.

2. Click the Print What list arrow on the Print Preview toolbar, and then click an option in the list.

3. Click the Close button to close Print Preview.

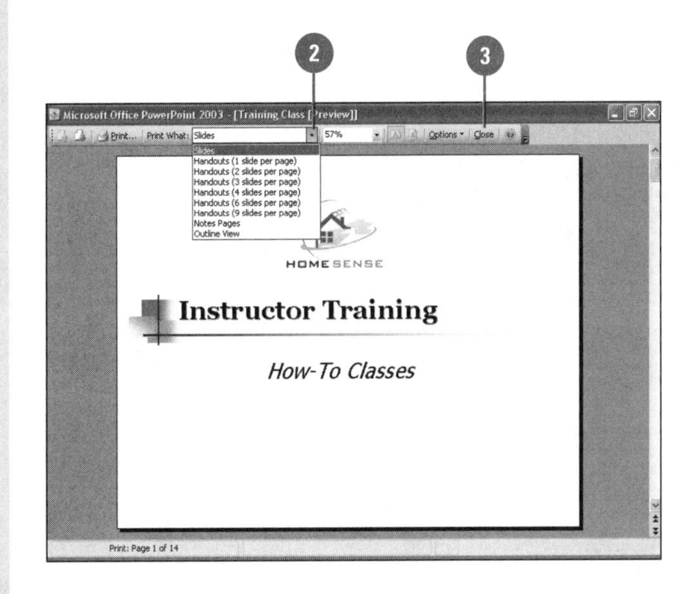

See Also

See "Printing a Presentation" on page 206 for information on printing a presentation.

Preview Slides in Pure Black and White or Grayscale

1. Click the Color/Grayscale button on the Standard toolbar. Or, if in Print Preview, click the Options list arrow, and then point to Color/Grayscale.
2. Click Pure Black And White or Grayscale.
3. Click the Setting button list arrow on the Grayscale View toolbar, and then click a Setting.
4. Click the Close Grayscale View button or the Close Black A nd White View button on the toolbar.

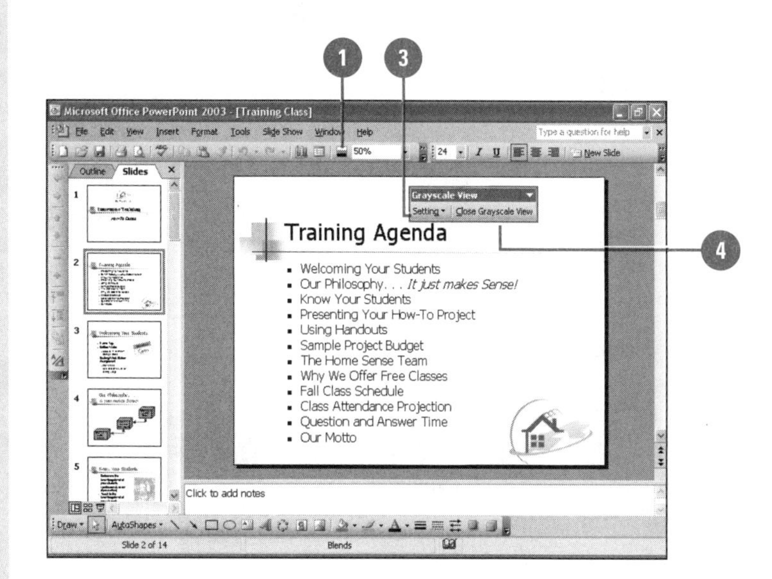

Printing a Presentation

PP03S-4-7

You can print all the elements of your presentation—the slides, outline, notes, and handouts—in either color or black and white. PowerPoint makes it easy to print your presentation; it detects the type of printer that you choose—either color or black and white—and then prints the appropriate version of the presentation. For example, if you select a black and white printer, your presentation will be set to print in shades of gray (grayscale). The Print dialog box also offers standard Windows features, giving you the option to print multiple copies, specify ranges, access printer properties, and print to a file.

Print a Presentation

1. Click the File menu, and then click Print.
2. Click the Name list arrow, and then select a printer.
3. Click the Print What list arrow, and then click what you want to print.
4. Change settings in the Print dialog box as necessary.
5. Click OK.

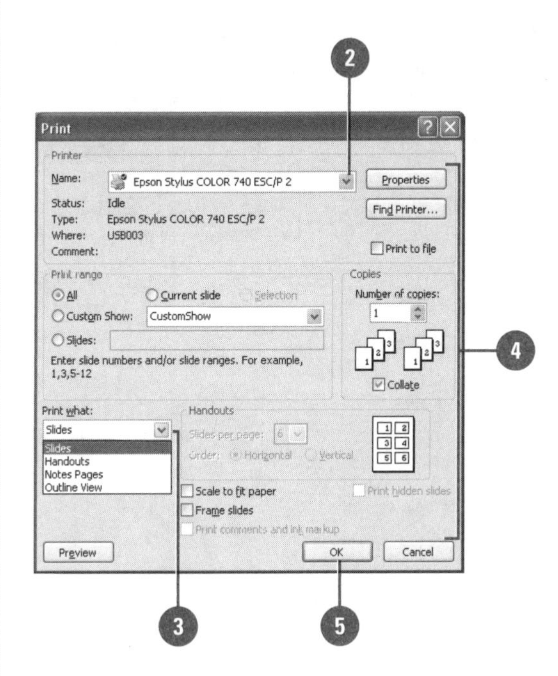

Did You Know?

You can print a presentation quickly. Use the Print button on the Standard toolbar only when you want to bypass the Print dialog box. If you need to make selections in the Print dialog box, use the Print command on the File menu.

Print a Custom Show

1. Click the File menu, and then click Print.
2. Click the Custom Show list arrow.
3. Click the custom show you want to print.
4. Change settings in the Print dialog box as necessary.
5. Click OK.

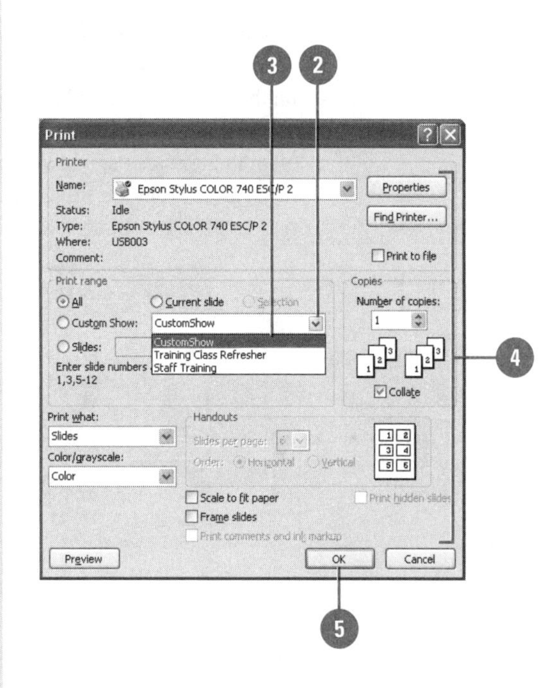

Print a Single Slide or a Range of Slides

1. Click the File menu, and then click Print.
2. If necessary, click the Print What list arrow, and then click Slides.
3. Select the range of slides you want to print.
4. Click OK.

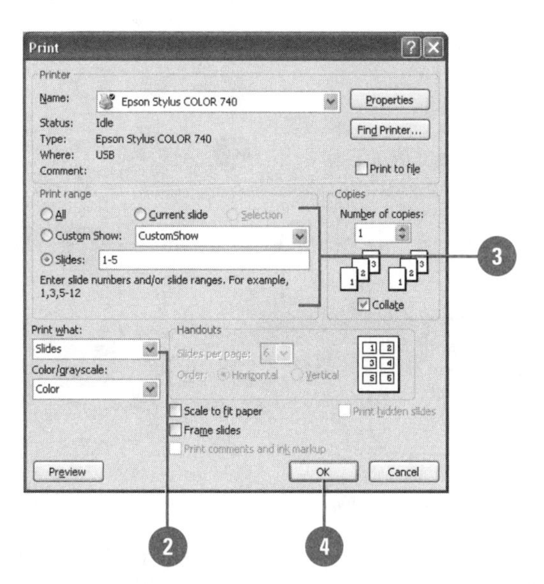

Printing an Outline

PP03S-4-7

When you print an outline, PowerPoint prints the presentation outline as shown in Outline view. What you see in the Outline pane is what you get on the printout. PowerPoint prints an outline with formatting according to the current view setting. Set your formatting to display only slide titles or all of the text levels, and choose to display the outline with or without formatting. From the Print dialog box you can choose to preview your outline before printing.

Print an Outline

1. In Outline pane, format your outline the way you want it to be printed.
   - Display only slide titles or all text levels
   - Display with or without formatting
2. Click the File menu, and then click Print.
3. Click the Print What list arrow, and then click Outline View.
4. Click the Preview button to view your outline before printing and access more print options, and then click Close.
5. Click OK.

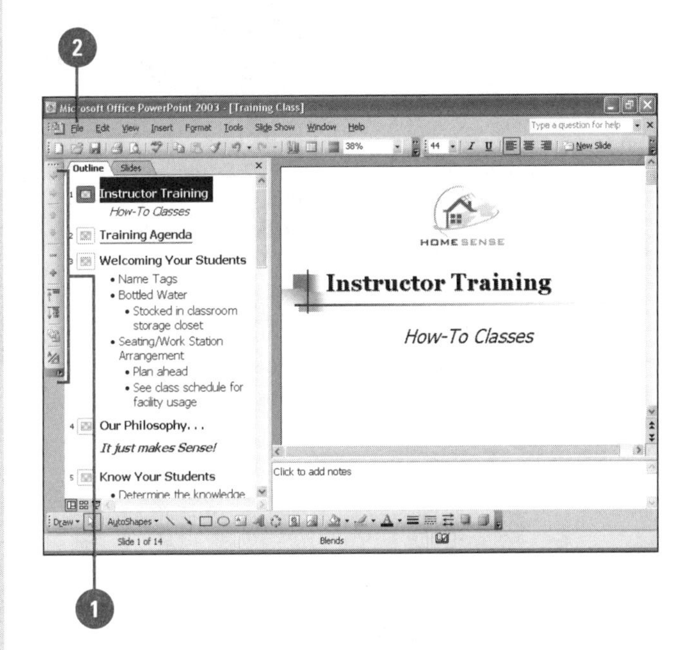

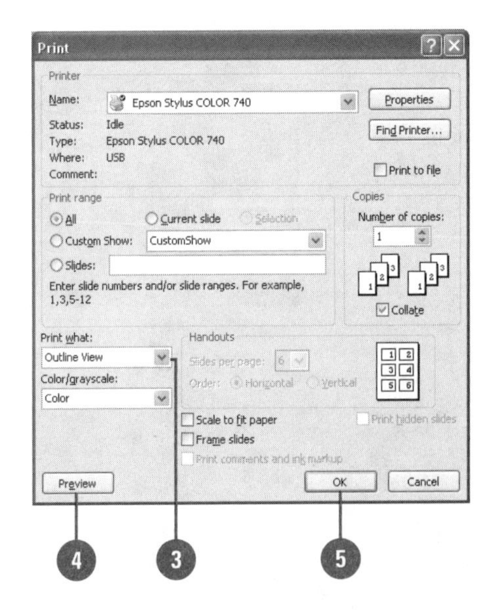

Did You Know?

You can scale slides to fit your paper when you print. Click the File menu, click Print, select the Scale To Fit Paper check box, and then click OK.

See Also

See "Working with Outlines" on page 196 for more information on saving a presentation as an outline.

Creating a Web Presentation

8

Introduction

Microsoft Office PowerPoint 2003 provides you with the tools you need to create and save your presentation as a Web page and to publish it on the World Wide Web. The Save As Web Page feature formats your presentation in **Hypertext Markup Language** (**HTML**), a simple coding system used to format documents for an intranet or the Internet. Saving your presentation in HTML format means you can use most Web browsers to view your presentation. Any presentation can easily be saved as a Web document and viewed in a Web browser. By saving your PowerPoint presentations as Web pages, you can share your data with others via the Web.

To assist you in creating Web pages, PowerPoint includes several Web templates that you can edit to fit your needs. Incorporating action buttons and hyperlinks within your presentation adds an element of connectivity to your work. If you add action buttons to your slides, you can click a button in a slide show to jump instantly to another slide, presentation, or program file. If you add hyperlinks to objects, you can jump to Internet and intranet locations. You can also customize your hyperlink by adding sound to it.

A digital signature adds authentification to your presentation. When customers, clients, employees or others see the digital stamp, it is a sign that the information is valid. When you have a presentation, the signature is assigned to the file. If the presentation has been converted to a Web page, the signature is assigned to a macro project.

Microsoft Office Online offers tips, software updates, tools, and general information to help you work with your PowerPoint presentation.

What You'll Do

Use Web Templates

Add Action Buttons

Add Hyperlinks to Objects

Create Hyperlinks to External Objects

Insert Hyperlinks

Use and Remove Hyperlinks

Create a Web Page

Change Web Page Options

Open a Web Page

Preview a Web Page

Use the Web Toolbar

Add a Digital Signature

Access Office Information on the Web

Using Web Templates

If you intend to use PowerPoint to create Web pages, you might want to take advantage of PowerPoint's specially designed Internet templates. The AutoContent Wizard lets you add hyperlinks between the slides in your presentation or hyperlinks to your e-mail address. The Group Home Page template helps you create a customized home page for your corporate or personal Web site.

Create a Web Presentation with the AutoContent Wizard

1. Click the File menu, and then click New.
2. In the New Presentation task pane, click From AutoContent Wizard.
3. Click Next to continue.
4. Click the button with the type of presentation you want.
5. Click a presentation, and then click Next to continue.
6. Click the Web Presentation option to specify how the presentation will be used, and then click Next to continue.
7. Enter the presentation title and any footer information, and then click Next to continue.
8. Click Finish.

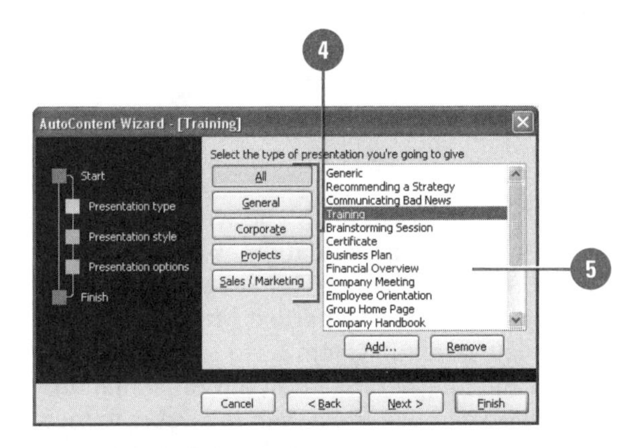

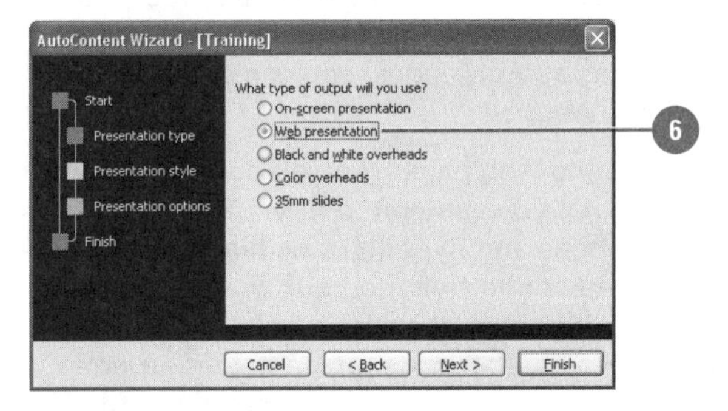

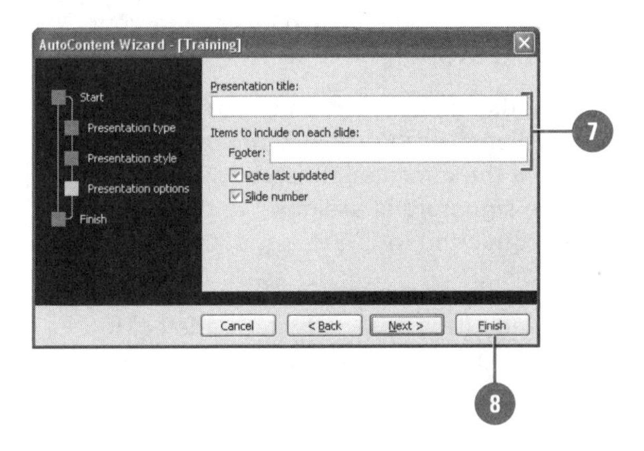

Create a Home Page

1. Click the File menu, and then click New.
2. In the New Presentation task pane, click From AutoContent Wizard.
3. Click Next to continue.
4. Click the All button, click Group Home Page, and then click Next to continue.
5. Click the Web Presentation option to specify how the presentation will be used, and then click Next to continue.
6. Enter the presentation title and any footer information, and then click Next to continue.
7. Click Finish.
8. Edit the presentation.
9. Click the File menu, click Save As Web Page, specify a filename and location, and then click Save.

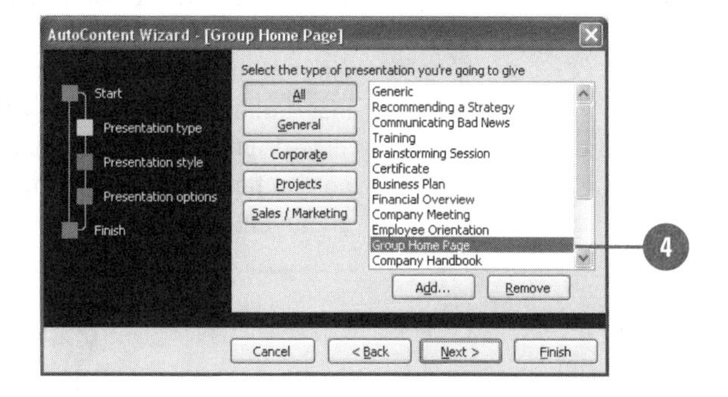

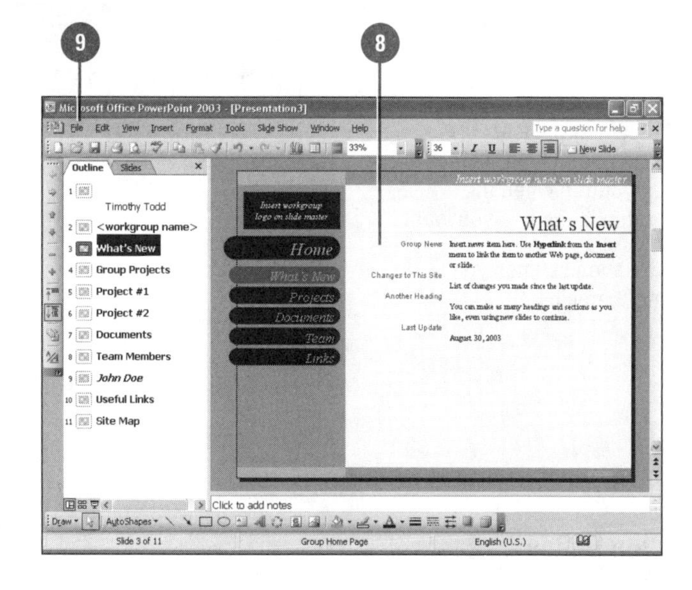

Adding Action Buttons

PP03S-4-2

When you create a self-running presentation to show at a kiosk, you might want a user to be able to move easily to specific slides or to a different presentation altogether. To give an audience this capability, insert **action buttons,** which a user can click to jump to a different slide or presentation. Clicking an action button activates a **hyperlink**, a connection between two locations in the same document or in different documents.

Insert an Action Button

1. Click the Slide Show menu.
2. Point to Action Buttons, and then choose the action button you want.
3. Drag the pointer to insert the action button, and then release the mouse button when the action button is the size you want.
4. Fill in the action settings you want, and then click OK.

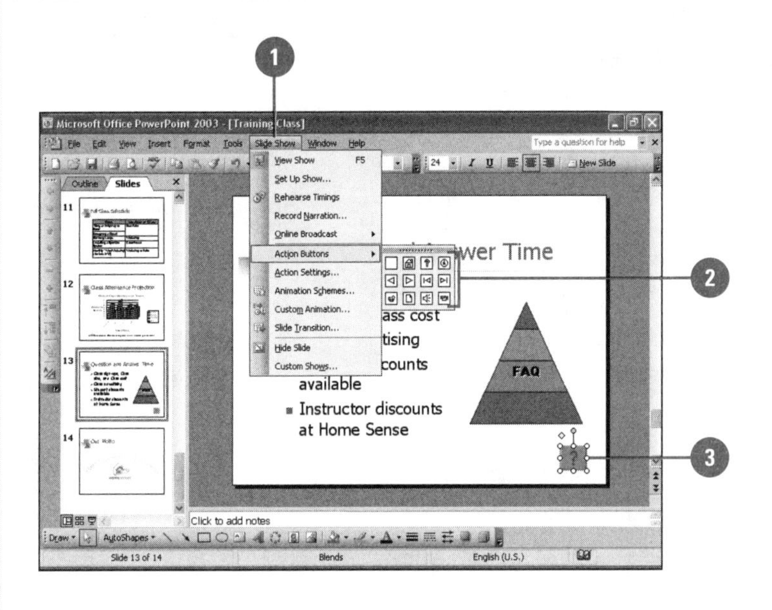

Test an Action Button

1. Click the Slide Show View button.
2. Display the slide containing the action button.
3. Click the action button.

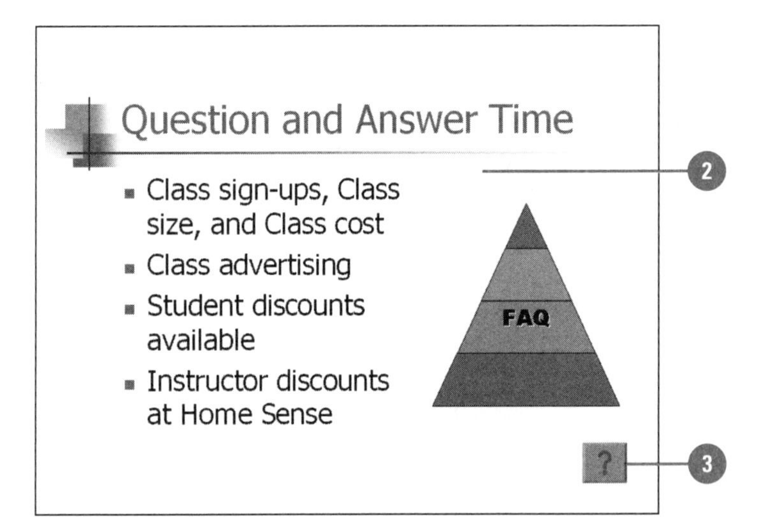

Create an Action Button to Go to a Specific Slide

1. Click the Slide Show menu, point to Action Buttons, and then click the Custom action button.
2. Drag the pointer to insert the action button on the slide.
3. Click the Hyperlink To option, click the list arrow, and then click Slide from the list of hyperlink destinations.
4. Select the slide you want the action button to jump to.
5. Click OK.
6. Click OK.
7. Right-click the action button, and click Add Text.
8. Type the name of the slide the action button points to.
9. Click outside the action button to deselect it.
10. Run the slide show and test the action button.

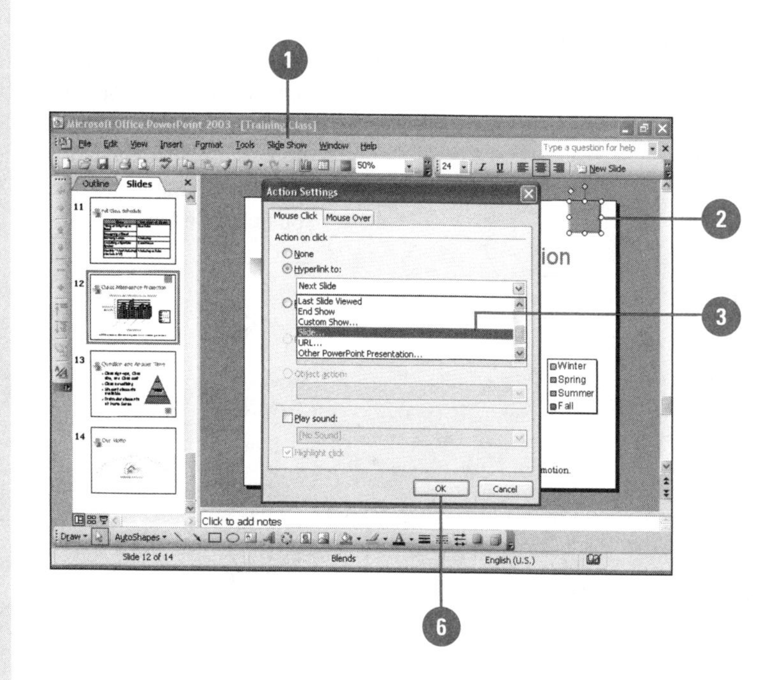

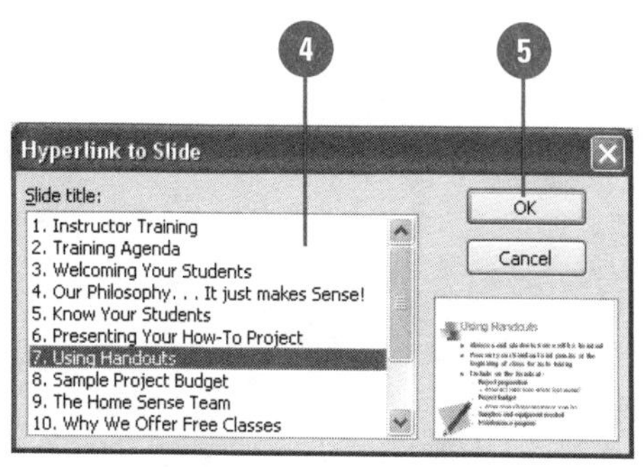

Did You Know?

You can insert an action button. Click the AutoShapes button on the Drawing toolbar, point to Action Buttons, and then click the action button you want to insert on your slide.

You can insert the Return action button to help navigate the slide show. If you want to return to the slide you were previously viewing, regardless of its location in the presentation, insert the Return action button.

You can create a square action button. Press and hold Shift as you drag to create a square action button.

Adding Hyperlinks to Objects

PP03S-4-1

You can turn one of the objects on your slide into an action button so that when you click or move over it, you activate a hyperlink and jump to the new location. You can point hyperlinks to almost any destination, including slides in a presentation and Web pages on the World Wide Web. Use the Action Settings dialog box to add sound to a hyperlink. You can add a default sound such as Chime, Click, or Drum Roll, or select a custom sound from a file.

Add a Hyperlink to a Slide Object

1. Right-click an object on the slide, and then click Action Settings.
2. Click the Mouse Click or Mouse Over tab.
3. Click the Hyperlink To option.
4. Click the Hyperlink To list arrow.
5. Click a destination for the hyperlink.
6. Click OK.
7. Run the slide show and test the hyperlink by pointing to or clicking the object in the slide show.

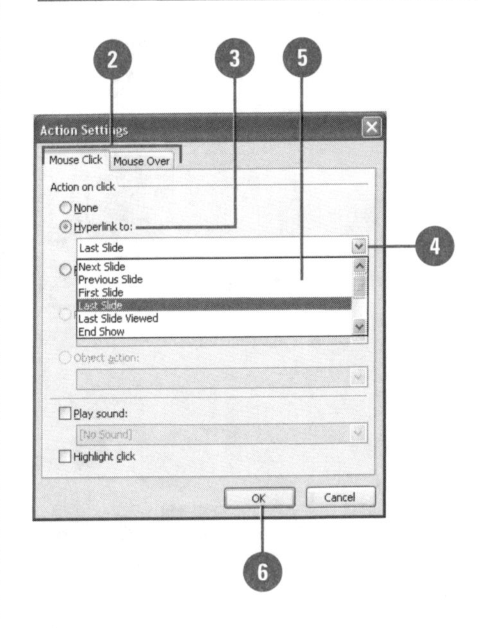

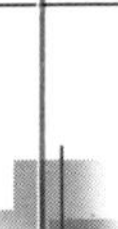

Using Handouts

- Always send students home with a handout
- Pass out your handout and pencils at the beginning of class for note taking
- Include on the handout:
  - Project preparation
    - What do I need to do before I get started?
  - Project budget
    - What kinds of expenses should I plan for?
  - Supplies and equipment needed
  - Maintenance program

Did You Know?

You can edit a hyperlink quickly. Right-click the object with the hyperlink, and then click Edit Hyperlink.

You can highlight a click or mouse over. When you click or move over a hyperlink, you can highlight the object. In the Action Settings dialog box, select the Highlight Click or Highlight When Mouse Over check box.

Add a Default Sound to a Hyperlink

1. In Normal view, right-click the object with the hyperlink, and then click Action Settings.
2. Select the Play Sound check box.
3. Click the Play Sound list arrow.
4. Click the sound you want to play when the object is clicked during the show.
5. Click OK.

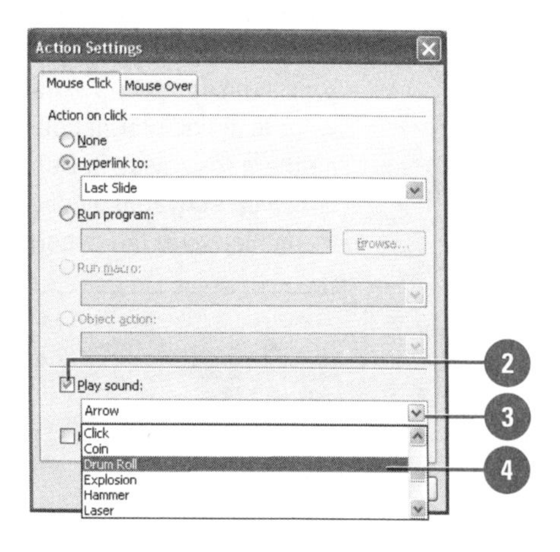

Add a Custom Sound to a Hyperlink

1. Right-click the hyperlinked object, and then click Action Settings.
2. Select the Play Sound check box, and then click the Play Sound list arrow.
3. Scroll to the bottom of the Play Sound list, and then click Other Sound.
4. Locate and select the sound you want to use.
5. Click OK, and then click OK again.

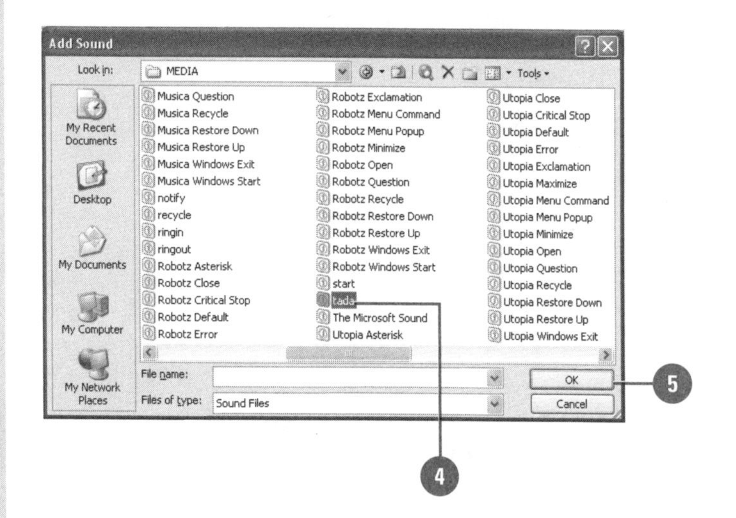

Did You Know?

You can create an action button to a sound. Click the Slide Show menu, point to Action Buttons, click the Sound action button, drag to create the sound action button, click the Play Sound list arrow, select the sound you want, and then click OK.

Creating Hyperlinks to External Objects

PP03S-4-1

You can create hyperlinks in your presentation that access other sources, such as another presentation, a file, a Web site, or even a program. This feature is especially useful for kiosk presentations, where you want to make information available to your audience, even if you can't be there to provide it. Depending on your audience, you can set a hyperlink to be activated by clicking the hyperlink with the mouse or by moving the mouse over the hyperlink.

Create a Hyperlink to Another Presentation

1. Right-click an object on your slide, and then click Action Settings.
2. Click the Hyperlink To option, click the list arrow, and then click Other PowerPoint Presentation from the list of hyperlinks.
3. Locate and select the presentation you want, and then click OK.
4. Select the slide that you want to link to.
5. Click OK.
6. Click OK again to save the hyperlink.

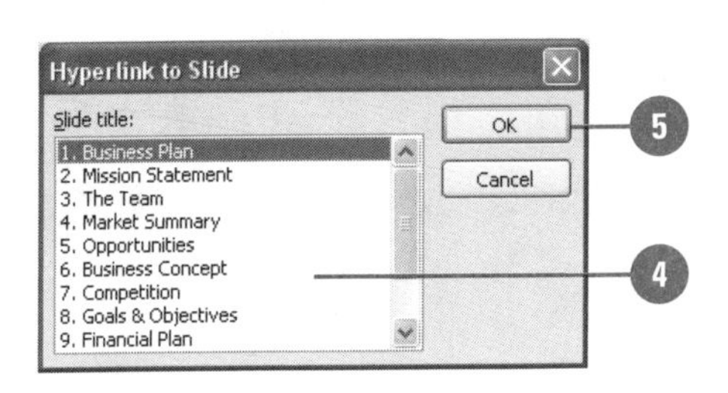

Create a Hyperlink to an External File

1. Right-click an object on your slide, and then click Action Settings.
2. Click the Hyperlink To option, click the list arrow, and then click Other File in the list of hyperlinks.
3. Locate and select the file on your computer.
4. Click OK, and then click OK again.

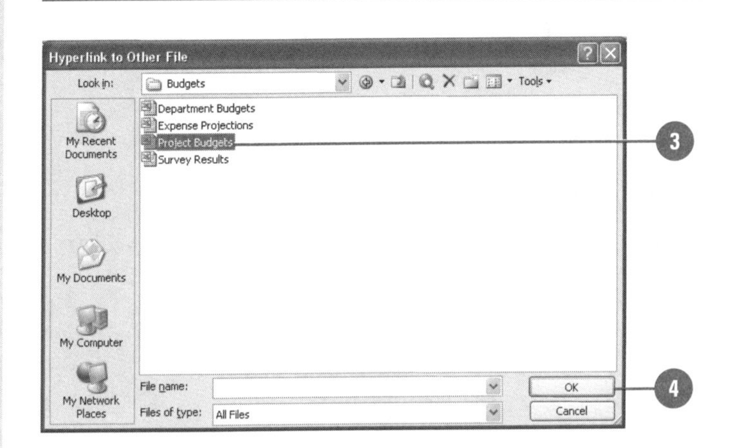

Create a Hyperlink to a Web Page

1. Right-click an object on your slide, click Action Settings, and then click the Hyperlink To option.
2. Click the Hyperlinks To list arrow, and then click URL.
3. Enter the URL of the Web page.
4. Click OK.
5. Click OK again to save the hyperlink.

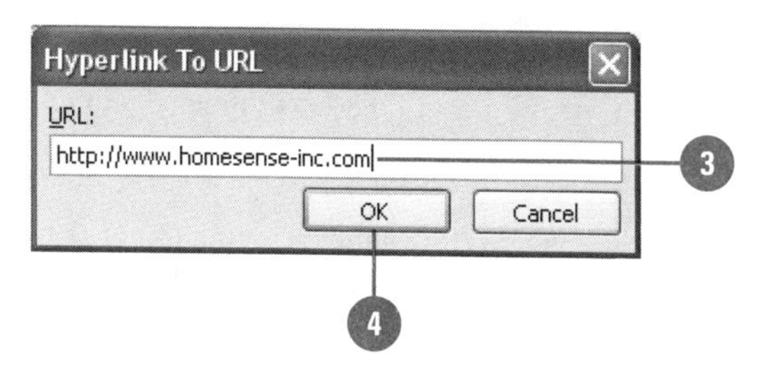

Create a Hyperlink to a Program

1. Right-click an object on your slide, and click Action Settings.
2. Click the Run Program option.
3. Click the Browse button, and then locate and select the program on your computer or network.
4. Click OK.
5. Click OK to save the hyperlink that runs the program.

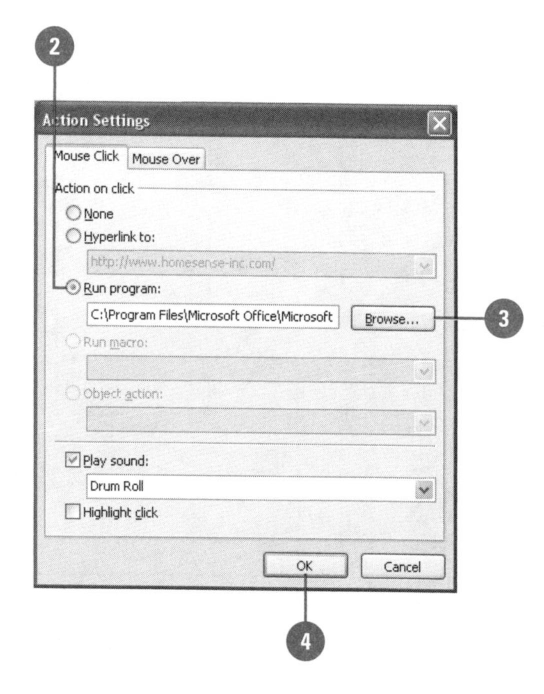

Did You Know?

You can use Mouse Over instead of Mouse Click. Set a hyperlink to be activated by clicking the hyperlink with the mouse or by moving the mouse over the hyperlink. To set a hyperlink to be activated by moving the mouse over it, click the Mouse Over tab in the Action Settings dialog box.

Inserting Hyperlinks

PP03S-4-1

When you reference information included earlier in a presentation, you had to duplicate material or add a footnote. Now you can create a **hyperlink**—a graphic object or colored, underlined text that you click to move (or **jump**) to a new location (or **destination**). The destination can be in the same presentation, another file on your computer or network, or a Web page on your intranet or the Internet. PowerPoint inserts an absolute link—a hyperlink that jumps to a fixed location—to an Internet destination. Office inserts a relative link—a hyperlink that changes when the hyperlink and destination paths change—between documents. You must move the hyperlink and destination together to keep the link intact.

Insert a Hyperlink Within a Presentation

1. Click where you want to insert the hyperlink, or select the text or object you want to use as the hyperlink.
2. Click the Insert Hyperlink button on the Standard toolbar.
3. Click Place In This Document.
4. Click a destination in the document.

   The destination can be a PowerPoint slide, slide title, or custom show.
5. Type the text you want to appear as the hyperlink.
6. Click ScreenTip.
7. Type the text you want to appear when someone points to the hyperlink.
8. Click OK.
9. Click OK.

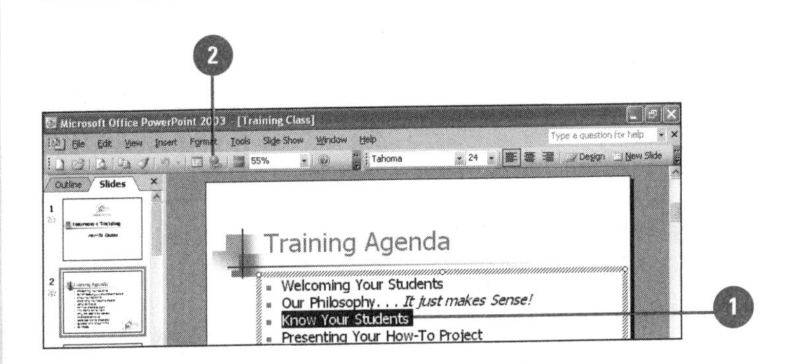

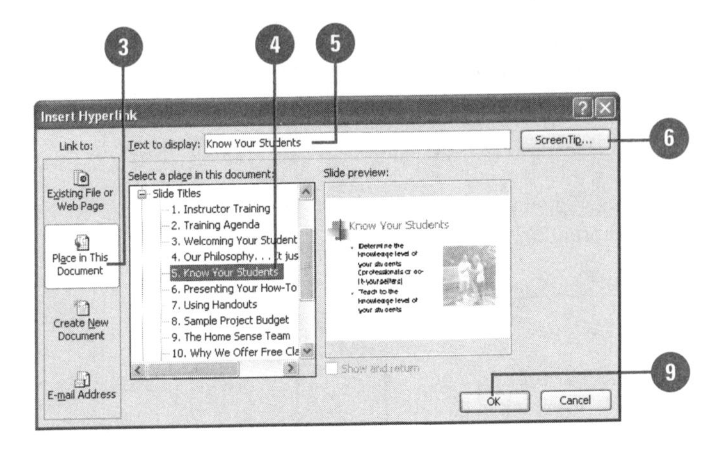

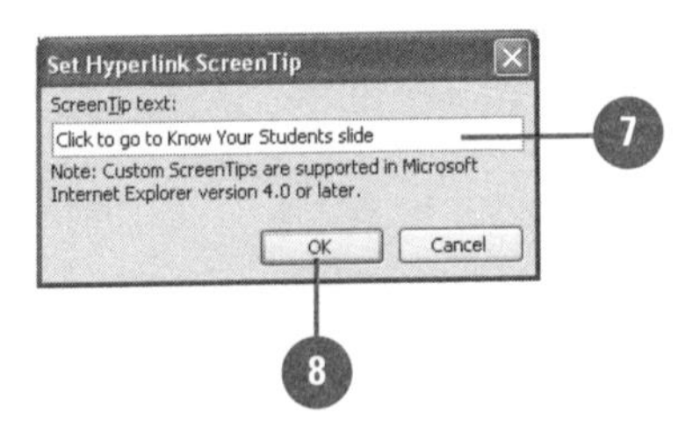

Insert a Hyperlink Between Documents

1. Click where you want to insert the hyperlink, or select the text or object you want to use as the hyperlink.
2. Click the Insert Hyperlink button on the Standard toolbar.
3. Click Existing File Or Web Page.
4. Enter the name and path of the destination file or Web page.
   - Or click the Bookmark button; select the bookmark, and then click OK.
5. Type the text you want to appear as the hyperlink, if available.
6. Click ScreenTip.
7. Type the text you want to appear when someone points to the hyperlink.
8. Click OK.
9. Click OK.

Did You Know?

You can create a hyperlink to send e-mail messages. Click where you want to insert the hyperlink, click the Insert Hyperlink button on the Standard toolbar, click E-Mail Address, enter the recipients e-mail address, enter a subject, enter the hyperlink display text, and then click OK.

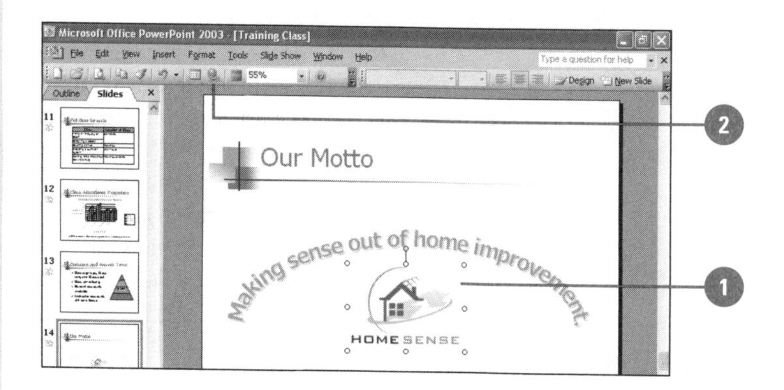

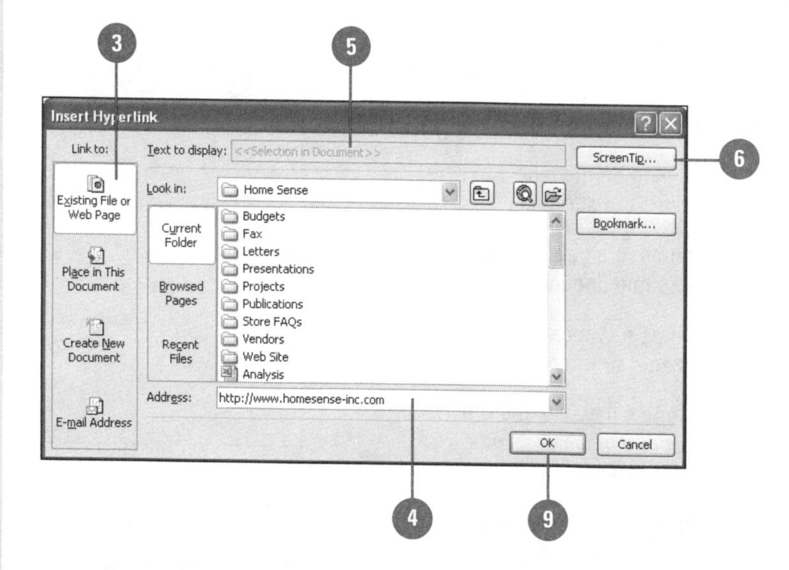

For Your Information

Understanding Web Addresses and URLs

Every Web page has a uniform resource locator (URL), a Web address in a form your browser program can decipher. Like postal addresses and e-mail addresses, each URL contains specific parts that identify where a Web page is located. For example, the URL for Perspection's Web page is http://www.perspection.com where "http://" shows the address is on the Web and "www.perspection.com" shows the computer that stores the Web page. As you browse various pages, the URL includes their folders and filenames.

Using and Removing Hyperlinks

Hyperlinks connect you to information in other documents. Rather than duplicating the important information stored in other documents, you can create hyperlinks to the relevant material. When you click a hyperlink for the first time (during a session), the color of the hyperlink changes, indicating that you have accessed the hyperlink. If a link becomes outdated or unnecessary, you can easily revise or remove it. PowerPoint repairs broken links. Whenever you save a presentation with hyperlinks, PowerPoint checks the links and repairs any that aren't working. For example, if a file was moved, PowerPoint updates the location.

Use a Hyperlink

1. In Slide Show view, position the mouse pointer (which changes to a hand pointer) over any hyperlink.
2. Click the hyperlink.

   Depending on the type of hyperlink, the screen

   - Jumps to a new location within the same document.
   - Jumps to a location on an intranet or Internet Web site.
   - Opens a new file and the program in which it was created.
   - Opens Outlook and displays a new e-mail message.
3. Navigate between open hyperlinked documents with the Web toolbar.
   - Click the Back or Forward button to move between documents.
   - Click the Start Page button to go to your home page.
   - Click the Search The Web button to go to a search page.

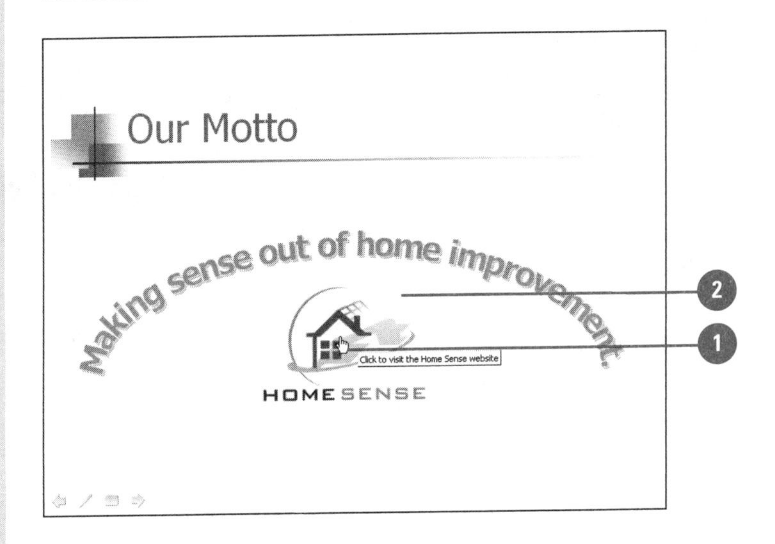

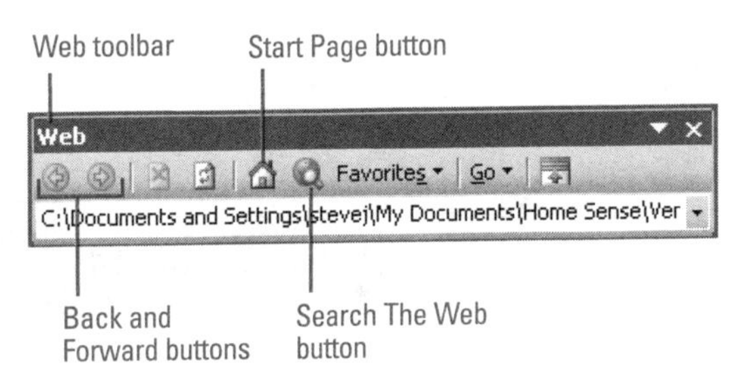

Edit a Hyperlink

1. Right-click the hyperlink you want to edit, and then click Edit Hyperlink.
2. If you want, change the display text.
3. If you want, click ScreenTip, edit the custom text, and then click OK.
4. If necessary, change the destination.
5. Click OK.

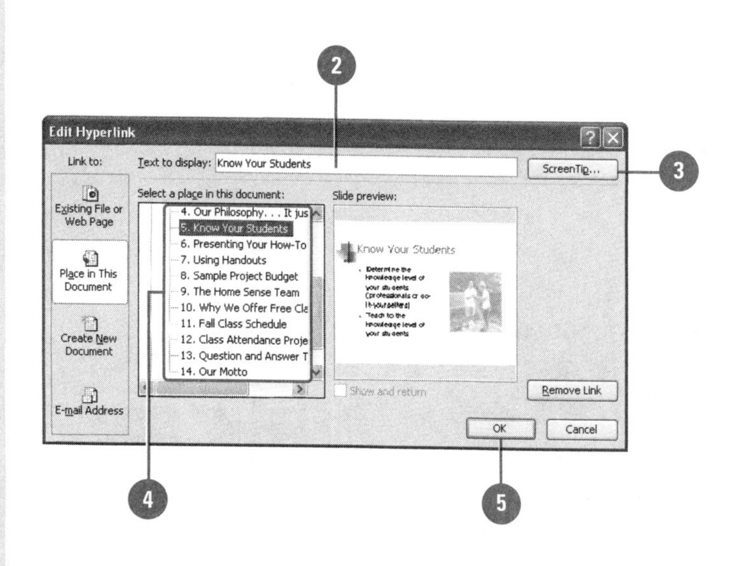

Remove a Hyperlink

1. Right-click the hyperlink you want to remove.
2. Click Remove Hyperlink.

TIMESAVER *Drag the I-beam pointer across the hyperlink to select it, and then press Ctrl+Shift+F9 to delete a hyperlink.*

3. If necessary, delete the text or object.

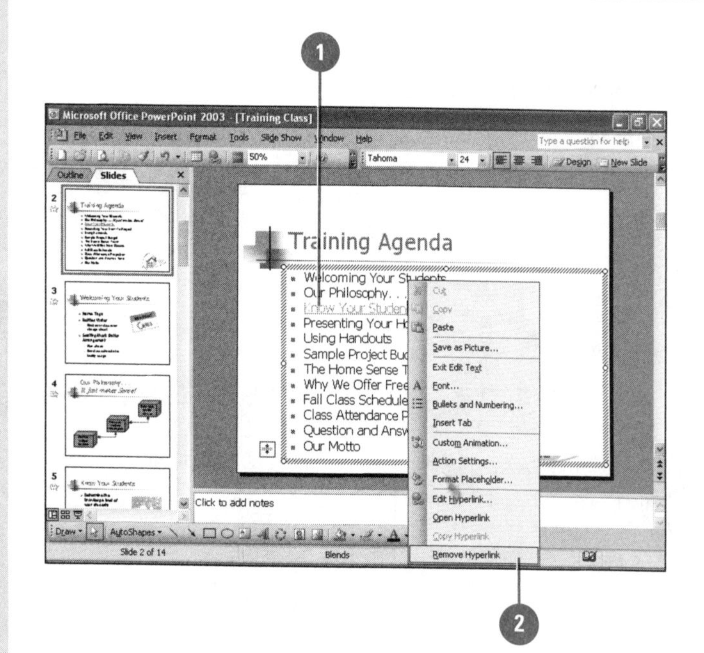

Did You Know?

You can display the Web toolbar. Click the View menu, point to Toolbars, and then click Web.

You can format a hyperlink. You can change the look of a hyperlink just as you do other text—select it and apply attributes. Right-click the hyperlink, click Select Hyperlink, and then use the Bold, Italic, Underline, Font, and Font Size buttons on the Formatting toolbar.

8

Creating a Web Page

PP03S-4-6

PowerPoint allows you to save any presentation as a Web page, written in HTML, the language used by Internet browsers to interpret and display Web pages. You can save a file as an HTML file by using the Save As command or the Save As Web Page command. Once you save the file in HTML format, you can preview and then publish the Web page. To publish a Web page means to place a copy of the presentation in HTML format on the Web. You can publish a complete presentation, a custom show, a single slide, or a range of slides.

Save a Presentation as a Web Page

1. Click the File menu, and then click Save As Web Page.
2. Click one of the icons on the Places bar for quick access to frequently used folders.
3. If you want to save the file in another folder, click the Save In list arrow, and then select a location for your Web page.
4. Click Change Title to change the title of your Web page.
5. Type the new title in the Set Page Title box.
6. Click OK.
7. Click Save.

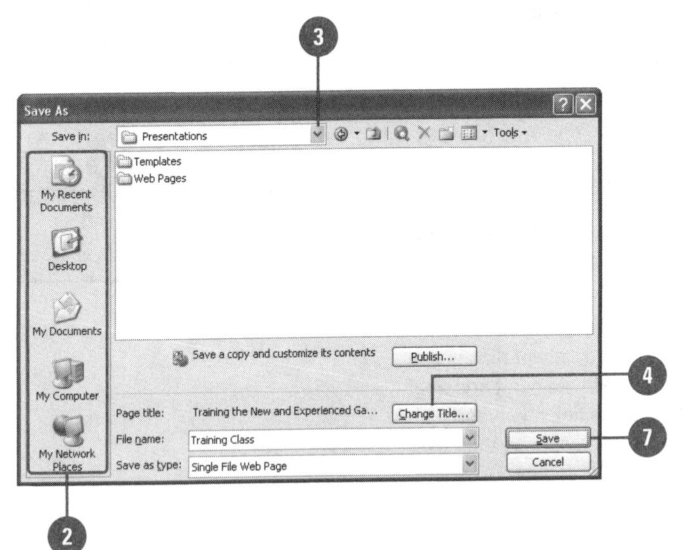

Did You Know?

You can save a presentation to an FTP server. Click the File menu, and then click Save As. Click the Save In list arrow, and then click FTP Locations. Double-click Add/Modify FTP locations. Type the address of the FTP server and any user information, and then click Add. Click OK. Choose the FTP server from the list in the Save As dialog box, and then click Open.

What is a Web server? A Web server is a computer on the Internet or intranet that stores Web pages.

Save and Publish a Presentation as a Web Page

1. Click the File menu, and then click Save As Web Page.
2. Click one of the icons on the Places bar for quick access to frequently used folders.
3. If you want to save the file in another folder, click the Save In list arrow, and then select a location for your Web page.
4. Click Change Title to change the title of your Web page.
5. Type the new title in the Page Title box, and then click OK.
6. Click Publish.
7. Select the publishing options you want.
8. Select the Open Published Web Page In Browser check box.
9. Click Publish.

Did You Know?

You can use Microsoft.Net Passport. When you click the Publish button in the Save As Web Page dialog box, you may be prompted to sign-in for Microsoft.Net Passport.

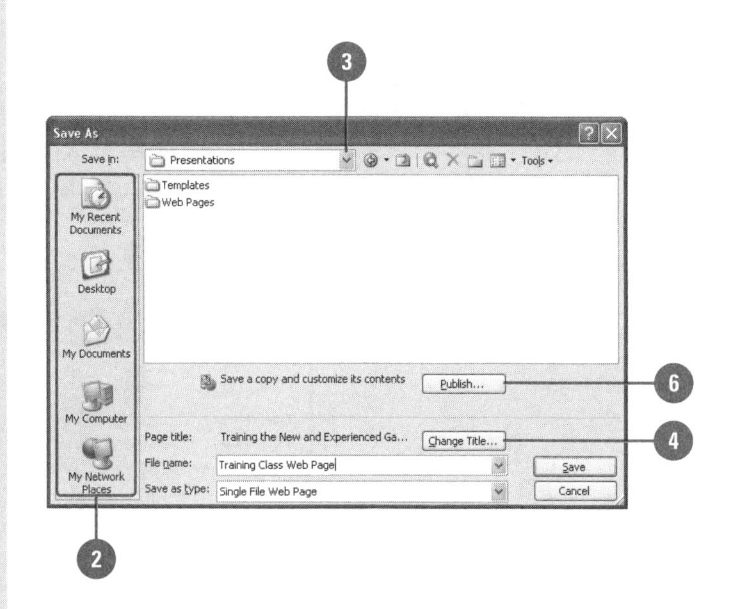

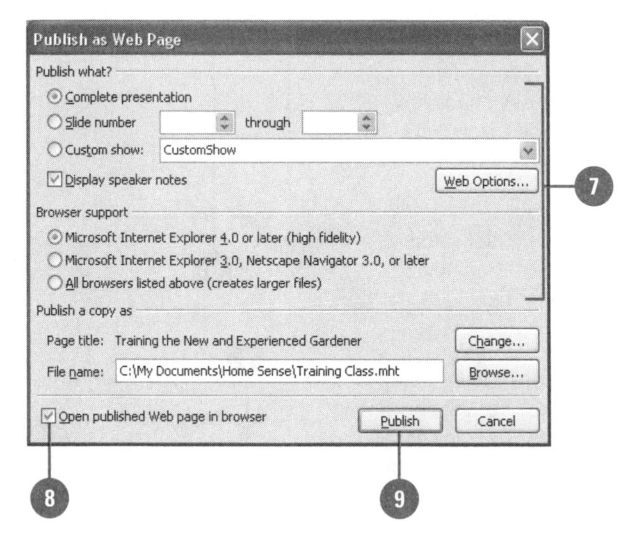

8

Changing Web Page Options

When you save or publish a presentation as a Web page, you can change the appearance of the Web page by changing PowerPoint's Web options. You can set Web options to add slide navigation buttons, change Web page colors, show slide transitions and animations in the browser window, and resize graphics to fit the display of the browser window.

Change Web Page Options

1. Click the Tools menu, and then click Options.
2. Click the General tab.
3. Click Web Options.
4. Click the General tab.
5. Click the options you want to use when you save or publish a Web page.
   - To add slide navigation controls and change the Web page colors, select the Add Slide Navigation Controls check box, and then click the Colors list arrow and select a color scheme.
   - To show slide transitions and animations, select the Show Slide Animation While Browsing check box.
   - To allow graphics to fit in different size browser windows, select the Resize Graphics To Fit Browser Window check box.
6. Click OK.
7. Click OK.

Did You Know?

You can view Web pages internationally? Web pages are saved using the appropriate international text encoding so users on any language system are able to view the correct characters.

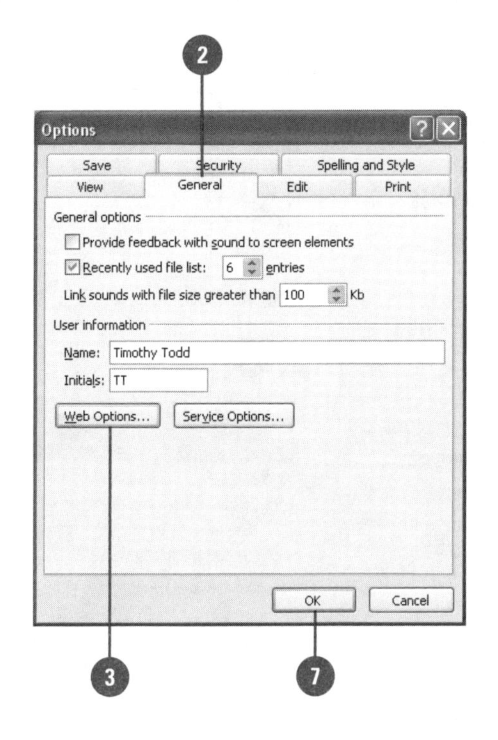

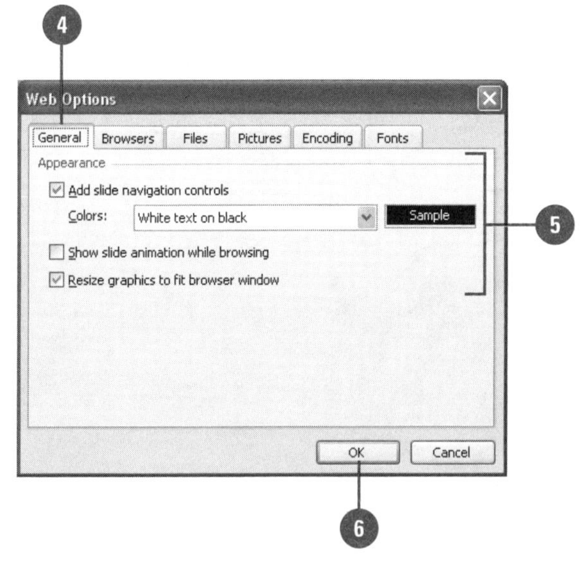

Opening a Web Page

After saving a presentation as a Web page, you can open the Web page, an HTML file, in PowerPoint. This allows you to quickly and easily switch from HTML to the standard PowerPoint format and back again without losing any formatting or functionality. For example, if you create a formatted chart in a PowerPoint presentation, save the presentation file as a Web page, and then reopen the Web page in PowerPoint, the chart will look the same as the original chart in PowerPoint. PowerPoint preserves the original formatting and functionality of the presentation.

Open a Presentation as a Web Page in PowerPoint

1. Click the Open button on the Standard toolbar.
2. Click the Files Of Type list arrow, and then click All Web Pages.
3. Click one of the icons on the Places bar for quick access to often-used folders.
4. If the file is located in another folder, click the Look In list arrow, and select the folder where the file is located.
5. Click the name of the presentation file.
6. Click Open.

   To open the Web page in your browser, click the Open button list arrow, and then click Open In Browser.

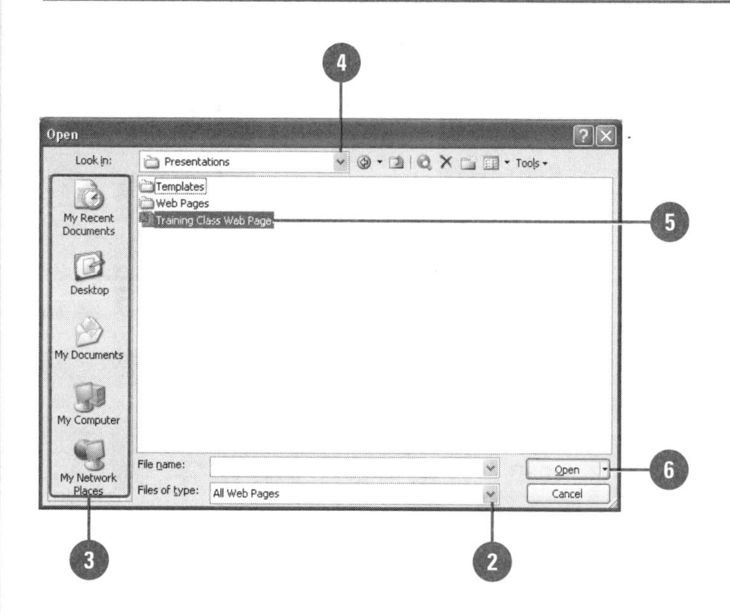

8

Previewing a Web Page

It is a good idea to preview your page before you publish it to the Web. Previewing a Web page shows you what the page will look like once it's posted on the Internet. When you display a Web presentation in a Web browser, a **navigation bar** appears with toolbar buttons to make it easy to navigate through the Web presentation. You can also view your presentation as a Web page one slide at a time, in full-screen mode, as an outline, or as the slide master.

Preview a Web Page

1. Open the presentation file you want to view as a Web page.
2. Click the File menu, and then click Web Page Preview.

   Your Web browser opens, displaying your Web page.
3. Click the Next Slide or Previous Slide button on the navigation bar to move from slide to slide.
4. Click the Full Screen Slide Show button on the navigation bar to display the presentation in slide show, and then click Escape to exit Full Screen Slide Show.
5. Click the Expand/Collapse Outline button on the navigation bar to display more or less outline detail.
6. Click the Close button to quit the browser and return to PowerPoint.

Did You Know?

You can show animation and transition effects while viewing your presentation in a browser. Click the Tools menu, click Options, and then click the General tab. Click Web Options, click the Show Slide Animation While Browsing check box, and then click OK. Click OK again to close the Options dialog box.

View an Individual Slide

1. Start your Web browser.
2. Click the File menu, and then click Open.

   If necessary, click Browse to help you locate your Web presentation.
3. Locate and open the folder containing your Web presentation files.

   Be sure you are opening the presentation folder, not the presentation itself.
4. Double-click the file slide000X, where "X" is the number of the slide.
5. Click OK.

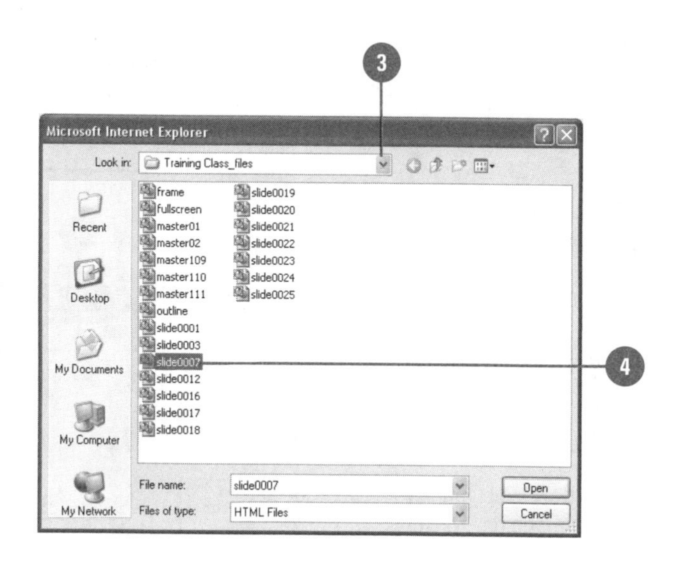

View a Presentation in Full-Screen Mode

1. Start your Web browser.
2. Click the File menu, and then click Open.
3. Locate and open the folder containing your Web presentation.
4. Double-click the file FULLSCREEN.
5. Click OK.

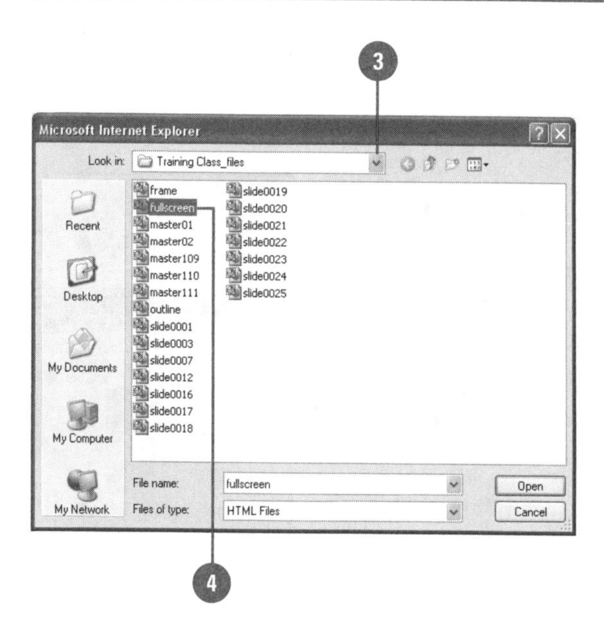

Did You Know?

You can view a Web presentation outline in a browser. Start your Web browser, click the File menu, click Open, locate and open the folder containing your Web presentation, double-click the file OUTLINE, and then click OK.

Using the Web Toolbar

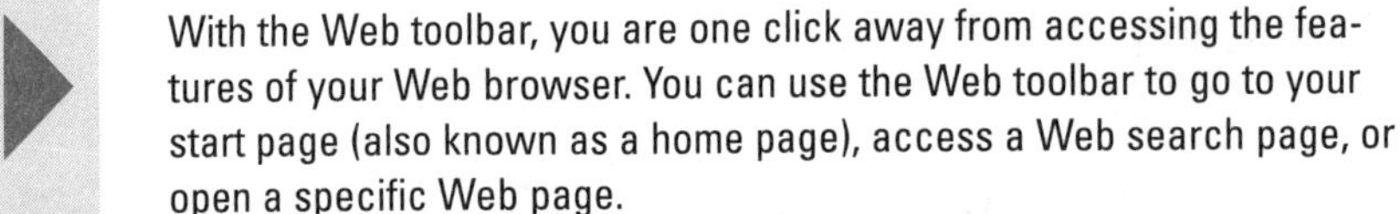

With the Web toolbar, you are one click away from accessing the features of your Web browser. You can use the Web toolbar to go to your start page (also known as a home page), access a Web search page, or open a specific Web page.

Display and Hide the Web Toolbar

1. Click the View menu, point to Toolbars, and then click Web.

   TIMESAVER *To display or hide the Web toolbar, right-click any toolbar, and then click Web.*

2. Click the Show Only Web Toolbar button on the Web toolbar to hide the rest of the toolbars.
3. Click the Show Only Web Toolbar button on the Web toolbar again to restore the hidden toolbars.
4. Click the View menu, point to Toolbars, and then click Web again to hide the Web toolbar.

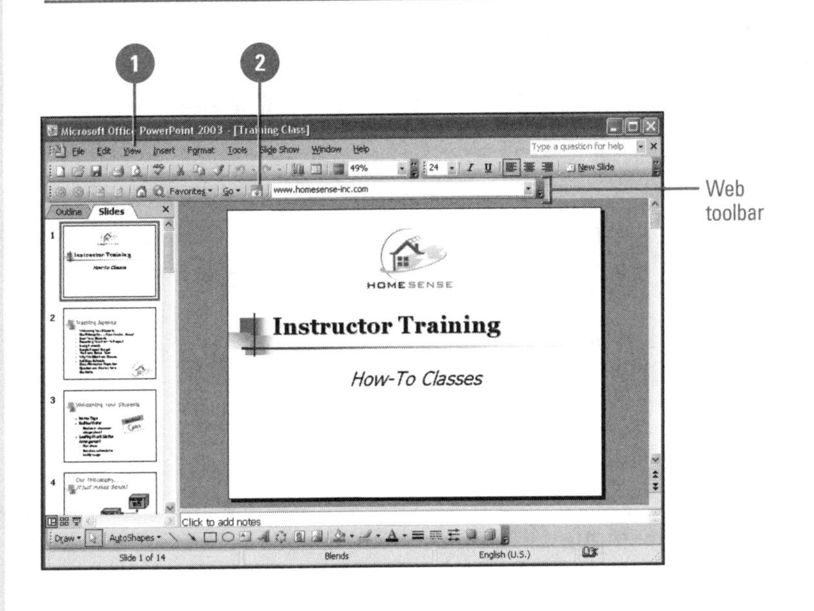

Create and View a Start Page

1. Display the Web toolbar.
2. Display the presentation you want to set as your Start Page.
3. Click the Go list arrow on the Web toolbar, and then click Set Start Page.
4. Click Yes.
5. Close the current presentation.
6. Click the Start Page button on the Web toolbar.
7. Click Yes to continue.

   Your browser opens, displaying your start or home page.

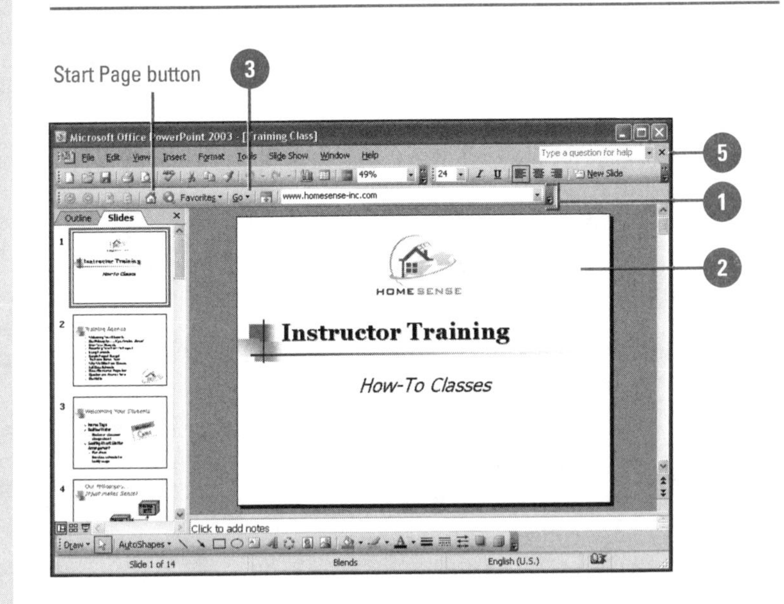

Open a Specific Web Page or File

1. Display the Web toolbar.
2. Click the Go button on the Web toolbar, and then click Open Hyperlink.
3. Type the URL of the Web page or location of the file that you want to open.
4. Select the Open In New Window check box.
5. Click OK.

   Your browser opens, displaying your Web page or file.

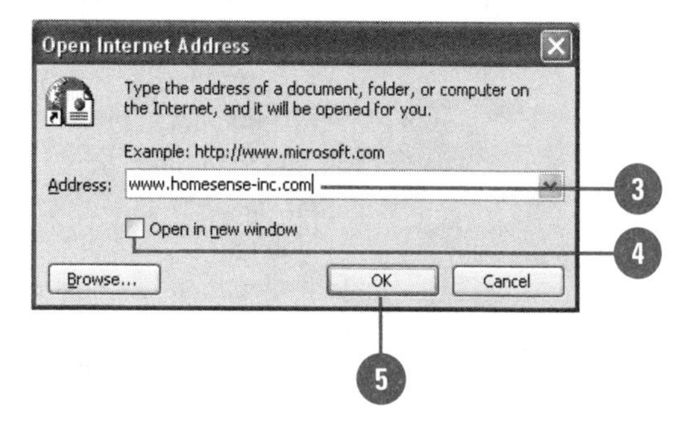

Search the Web

1. Display the Web toolbar.
2. Click the Search The Web button on the Web toolbar.

   Your browser opens, displaying your Web search page.
3. Follow the directions to search the Web for information.

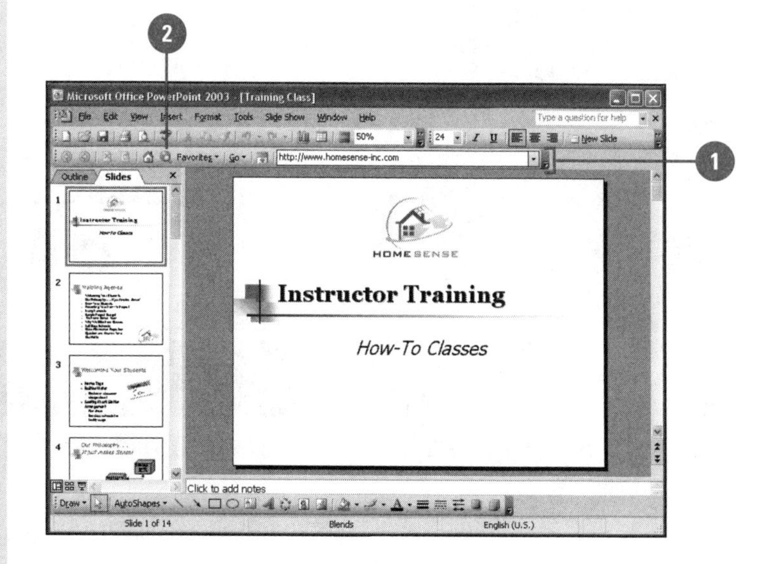

8

Adding a Digital Signature

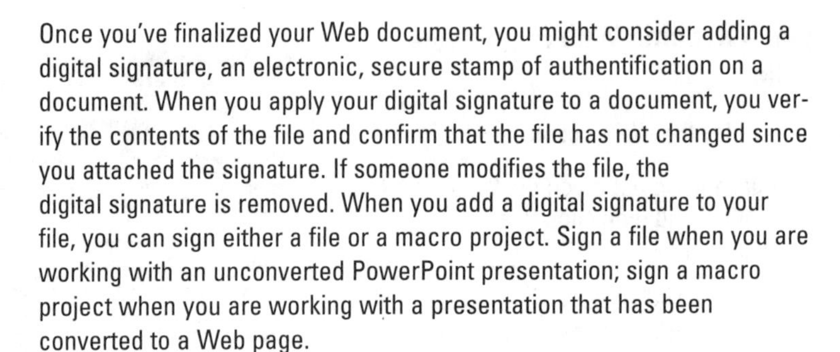

Once you've finalized your Web document, you might consider adding a digital signature, an electronic, secure stamp of authentification on a document. When you apply your digital signature to a document, you verify the contents of the file and confirm that the file has not changed since you attached the signature. If someone modifies the file, the digital signature is removed. When you add a digital signature to your file, you can sign either a file or a macro project. Sign a file when you are working with an unconverted PowerPoint presentation; sign a macro project when you are working with a presentation that has been converted to a Web page.

Sign a File

1. Click the Tools menu, and then click Options.
2. Click the Security tab, and then click Digital Signatures.
3. Click Add.
4. Click a certificate in the Select Certificate dialog box, and then click OK.
5. Click OK.

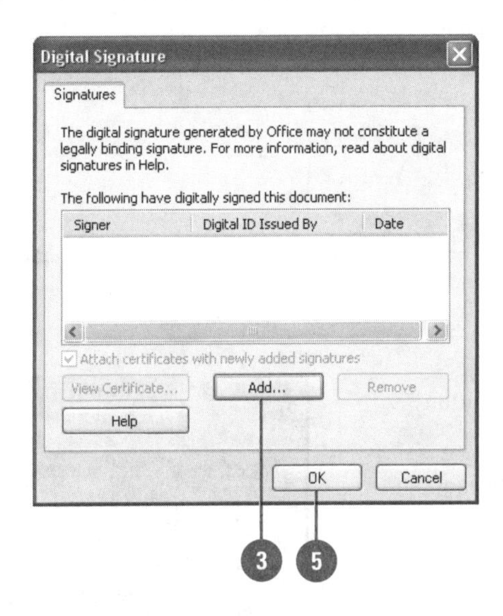

Important Information

Before You Add a Digital Signature

Before you can add a digital signature, you must install and run the Selfcert.exe file. This file enables you to create a digital signature that you will apply to your Web document. To install the file, insert your Office CD into your CD-ROM drive, run the Setup program, click the Add Or Remove Features option, if necessary, click Next, click the plus sign (+) next to Office Shared Features to expand the option, click the Digital Signatures for VBA Projects list arrow, and then click Update. To run the Selfcert.exe file, start Windows Explorer, and then double-click the Selfcert.exe file. The program is typically located in the Program Files\Microsoft Office\Office folder. In the Create Digital Certification dialog box, type your name, and then click OK.

Sign a Macro Project

1. Click the Tools menu, point to Macro, and then click Visual Basic Editor.
2. Verify that the the name of your file is in the left pane of the Visual Basic window.
3. Click the Tools menu in the Microsoft Visual Basic window, and then click Digital Signature.

   The Digital Signature dialog box appears, indicating that no certificate is assigned to the document.
4. Click Choose.
5. Select a certificate in the list, and then click View Certificate.
6. Click OK.
7. Click OK.
8. Click OK.
9. Click the Close button in the Microsoft Visual Basic window.
10. Click the Save button to save the presentation.

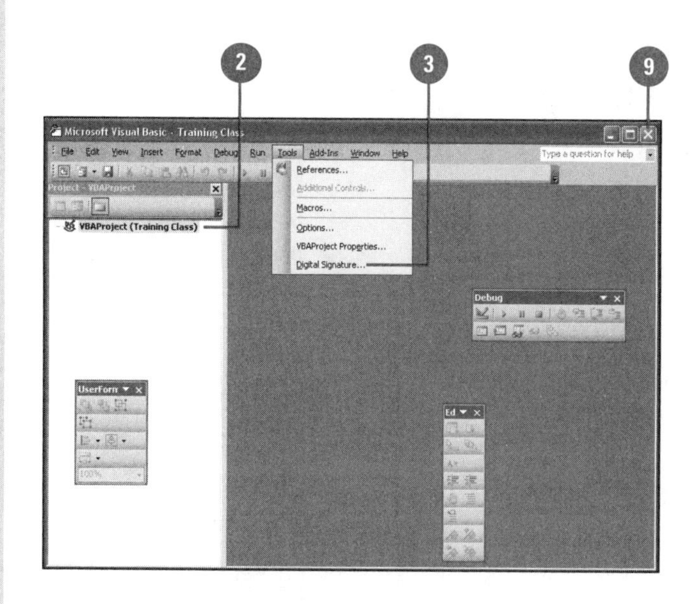

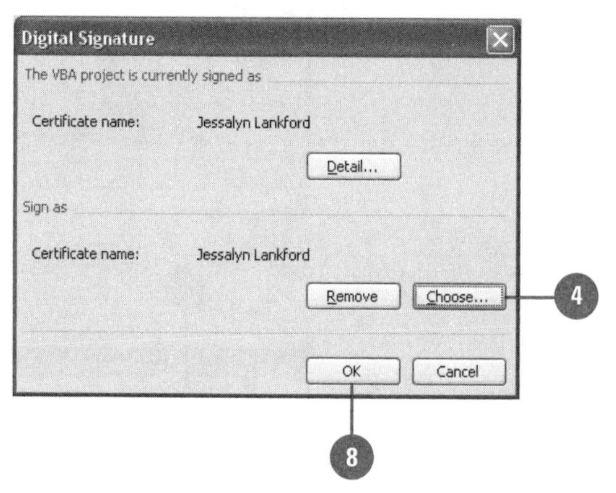

8

Accessing Office Information on the Web

New information about programs comes out with great frequency. You have access to an abundance of information about PowerPoint and other programs in the Office Suite from Microsoft. This information is constantly being updated. Answers to frequently asked questions, user forums, and update offers are some of the types of information you can find about Microsoft Office. You can also find out about conferences, books, and other products that help you learn just how much you can do with your Office software.

Find Online Office Information

1. Click the Help menu, and then click Microsoft Office Online.
2. Establish an Internet connection if prompted.

   Your Web browser opens, displaying the Microsoft Office Online Web page.
3. Click a hyperlink of interest.
4. Click the Close button to quit the browser and return to PowerPoint.

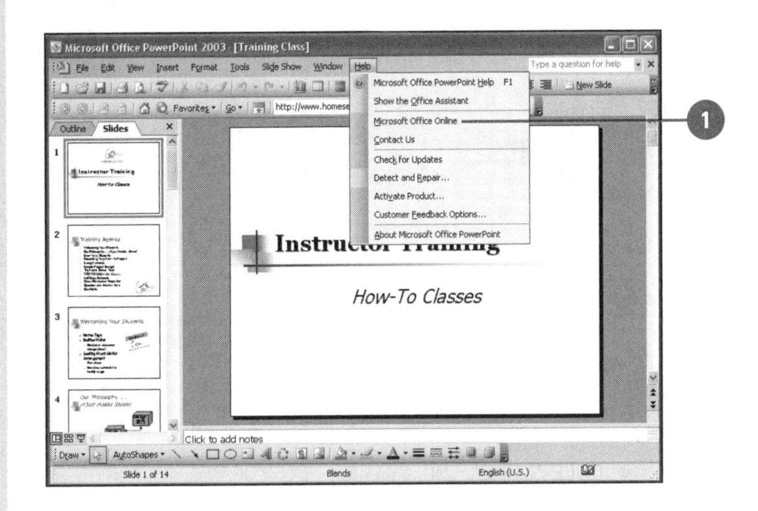

Preparing a Slide Show

9

Introduction

Microsoft Office PowerPoint 2003 provides many tools to help you coordinate your slide show as a complete multimedia production. After all your effort to create your presentation, the final details could be the lasting memory of your slide show.

Before you can deliver a slide show, you need to select the type of show you want. Will your show be presented by a speaker, or be self running? Will your show include narration or animation? These are some of the questions you will need to set up for your slide show. Some presentations include slides that are appropriate for one audience but not for another. PowerPoint lets you create custom slide shows that include only a selection of slides, in whatever order you want, intended for a given audience.

After setting up your slide show requirements, you can add other special features to customize your show. Elements such as creating transitions between slides, adding special visual, sound, and animation effects. Using animations—effects that animate your slide elements, such as text flying in from the right or fading text after it's been shown, can increase the interest in your slide show.

PowerPoint includes tools that let you time your presentation to make sure that it is neither too long nor too short. You can set the timing of your slides as you rehearse your slide show. You can see if each slide has enough time on the screen. You might want to add a narration to your slide show or a music clip to play during a planned coffee break in your presentation. You can also create a self-running presentation to package for off-site clients or to run at a trade show.

What You'll Do

Set Up a Slide Show

Create a Custom Slide Show

Create Slide Transitions

Add Animation

Use Specialized Animations

Coordinate Multiple Animations

Add Slide Timings

Record a Narration

Create a Self-Running Presentation

Setting Up a Slide Show

PP03S-4-2

PowerPoint offers several types of slide shows appropriate for a variety of presentation situations, from a traditional big-screen slide show to a show that runs automatically on a computer screen at a conference kiosk. When you don't want to show all of the slides in a PowerPoint presentation to a particular audience, you can specify only a range of slides to show, or you can hide individual slides. You can also save a presentation to open directly into Slide Show view or run continuously.

Set Up a Show

1. Click the Slide Show menu, and then click Set Up Show.
2. Choose the show type you want.
   - Click the Presented By A Speaker option to run a traditional full screen slide show, where you can advance the slides manually or automatically.
   - Click the Browsed By An Individual option to run a slide show in a window and allow access to some PowerPoint commands.
   - Click the Browsed At A Kiosk option to create a self-running, unattended slide show for a booth or kiosk. The slides will advance automatically, or a user can advance the slides or activate hyperlinks.
3. Select additional show setting check boxes as appropriate.
4. Click OK.

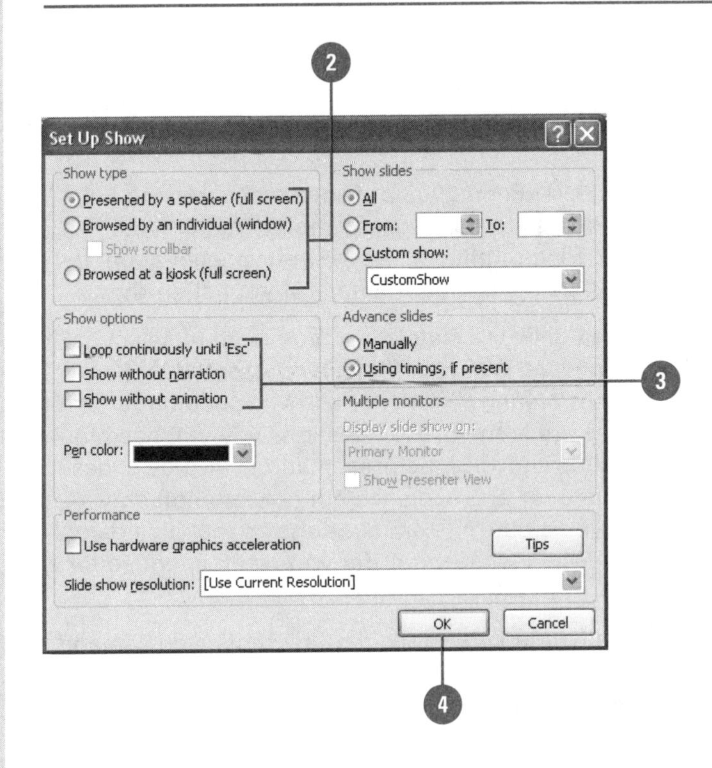

Show a Range of Slides

1. Click the Slide Show menu, and then click Set Up Show.
2. Click the From option.
3. Enter the first and last slide numbers of the range you want to show.
4. Click OK.

Hide Slides

1. In Slide Sorter view, or Normal view select or display the slide you want to hide.
2. Click the Slide Show menu, and then click Hide Slide.
3. To show a hidden slide, click it, click the Slide Show menu, and then click Hide Slide again.

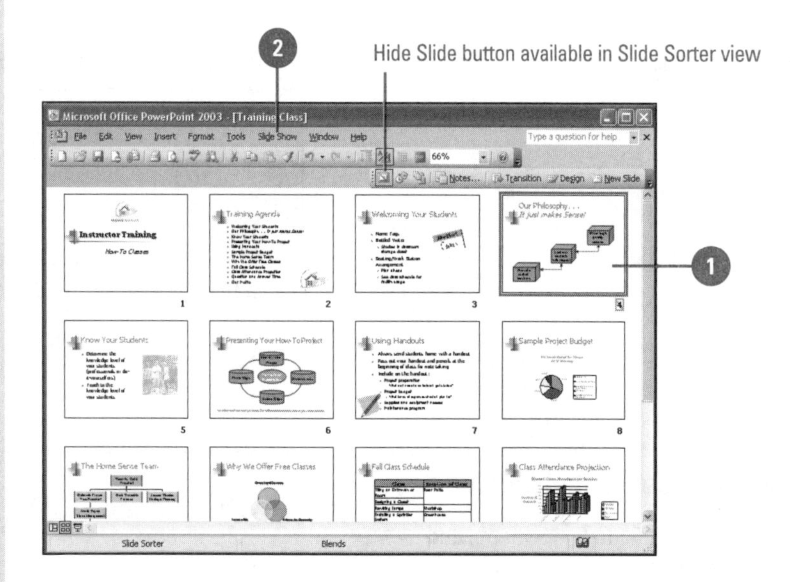

Did You Know?

You can open a presentation directly into Slide Show view. Click the File menu, click Save As, click the Save As Type list arrow, and then click PowerPoint Show.

You can run a slide show continuously. Open the presentation you want to run, click the Slide Show menu, click Set Up Show, select the Loop Continuously Until 'Esc' check box, and then click OK.

Creating a Custom Slide Show

PP03S-4-2

If you plan to present a slide show to more than one audience, you don't have to create a separate slide show for each audience. Instead, you can create a custom slide show that allows you to specify which slides from the presentation you will use and the order in which they will appear. You can also edit a custom show which you've already created. Add, remove, and rearrange slides in a custom show to fit your various needs.

Create a Custom Slide Show

1. Click the Slide Show menu, and then click Custom Shows.
2. Click New.
3. Type a name for the show.
4. Double-click the slides you want to include in the show in the order you want to present them.
5. Click OK.
6. Click Close.

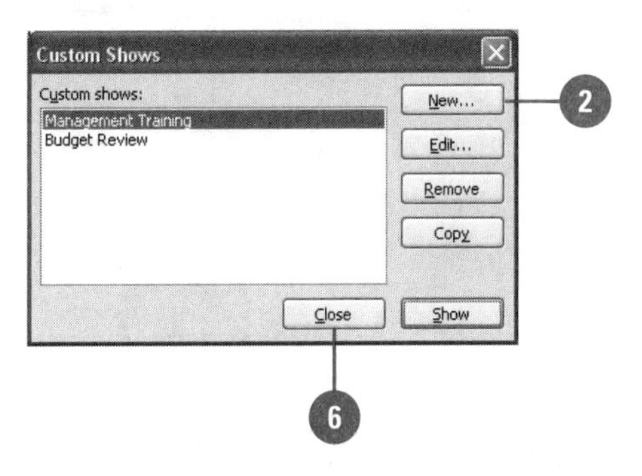

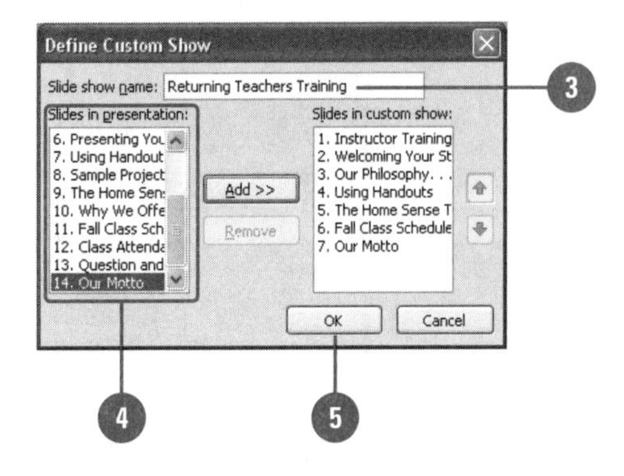

Show a Custom Slide Show

1. Click the Slide Show menu, and then click Custom Shows.
2. Click the custom slide show you want to run.
3. Click Show.

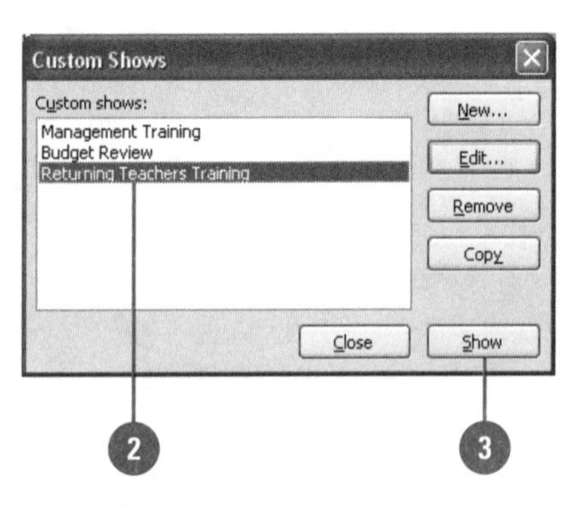

Edit a Custom Slide Show

1. Click the Slide Show menu, and then click Custom Shows.
2. Click the show you want to edit.
3. Click Edit.
4. To add a slide, click the slide in the Slides In Presentation list and then click the Add button. The slide appears at the end of the Slides In Custom Show list.
5. To remove a slide from the show, click the slide in the Slides In Custom Show list, and then click Remove.
6. To move a slide up or down in the show, click the slide in the Slides In Custom Show list, and then click the up or down arrow button.
7. Click OK.
8. Click Close.

Did You Know?

You can delete a custom slide show. Click the Slide Show menu, click Custom Shows, click the show you want to delete, click Remove, and then click Close.

You can use the Set Up Show command to display a custom slide show. Click the Slide Show menu, click Set Up Show, click the Custom Show option, click the Custom Show list arrow, select the custom slide show, and then click OK.

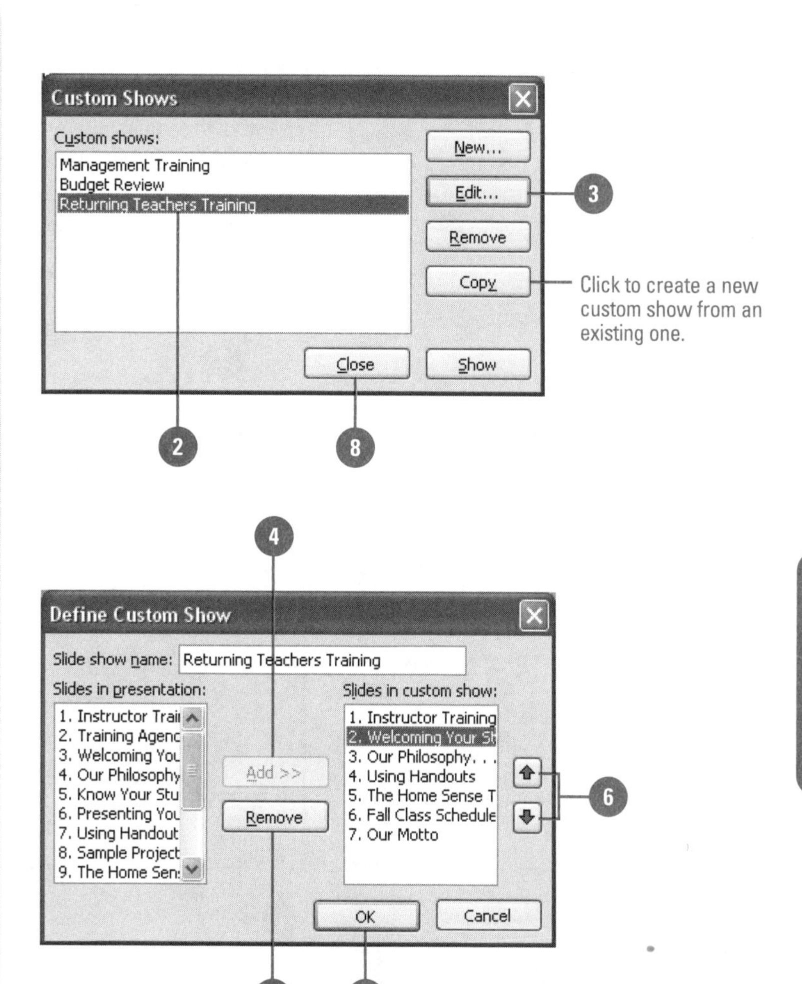

9

Creating Slide Transitions

PP03S-2-5

If you want to give your presentation more visual interest, you can add transitions between slides. For example, you can create a fading out effect so that one slide fades out as it is replaced by a new slide, or you can have one slide appear to push another slide out of the way. You can also add sound effects to your transitions, though you need a sound card and speakers to play them. When you add a transition effect to a slide, the effect takes place between the previous slide and the selected slide.

Specify a Transition

1. Click the Slide Sorter View button.
2. Click the slide to which you want to add a transition effect.
3. Click the Slide Transition button.
4. Click the transition effect you want.

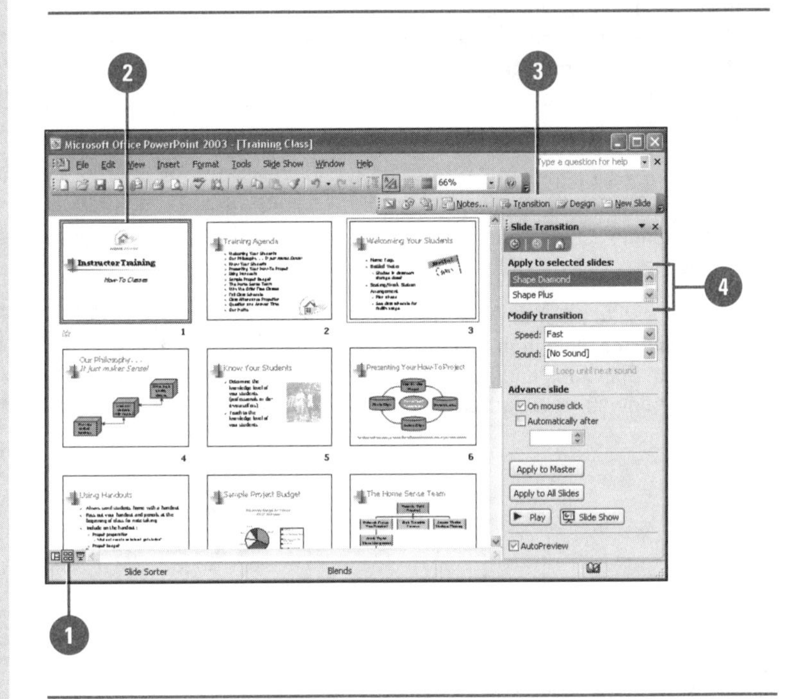

Did You Know?

You can view a slide's transition quickly in Slide Sorter view. In Slide Sorter view, click a slide's transition icon to view the transition effect.

Apply a Transition to All Slides in a Presentation

1. Click the Slide Show menu, and then click Slide Transition.
2. Click the transition you want.
3. Click Apply To All Slides.

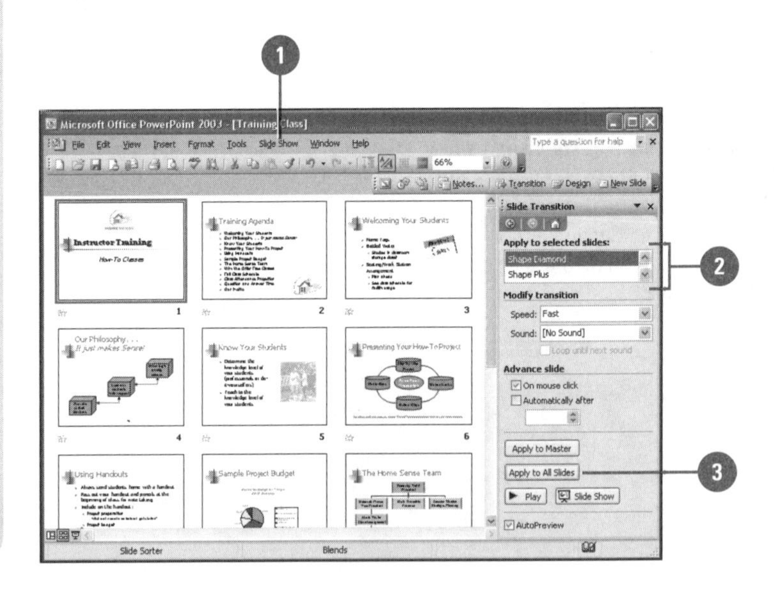

Set Transition Effect Speeds

1. In Normal or Slide Sorter view, click or display the slide whose transition effect you want to edit.
2. Click the Slide Show menu, and then click Slide Transition.
3. Click the Speed list arrow, and then click Slow, Medium, or Fast.
4. To apply the settings to all slides, click Apply To All Slides.

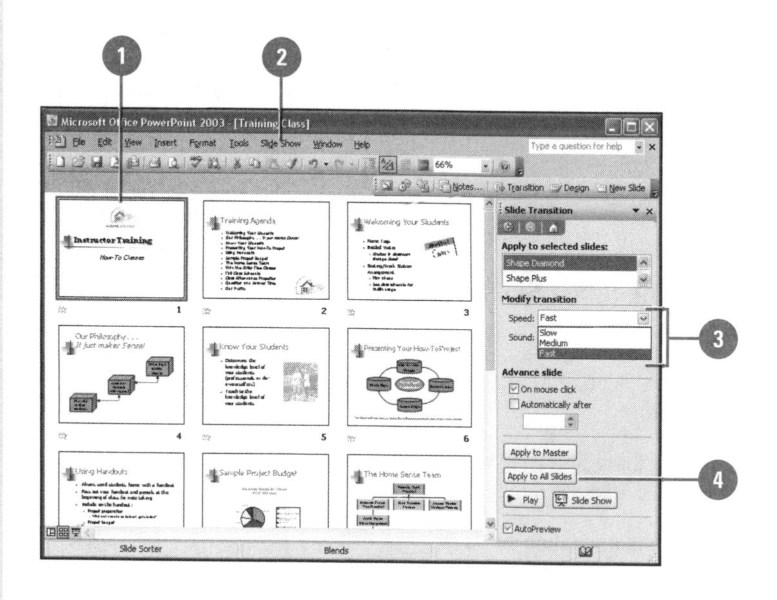

Add Sound to a Transition

1. In Normal or Slide Sorter view, click or display the slide to which you want to add a transition sound.
2. Click the Slide Show menu, and then click Slide Transition.
3. Click the Sound list arrow, and then click the sound you want.
4. To apply the settings to all slides, click Apply To All Slides.

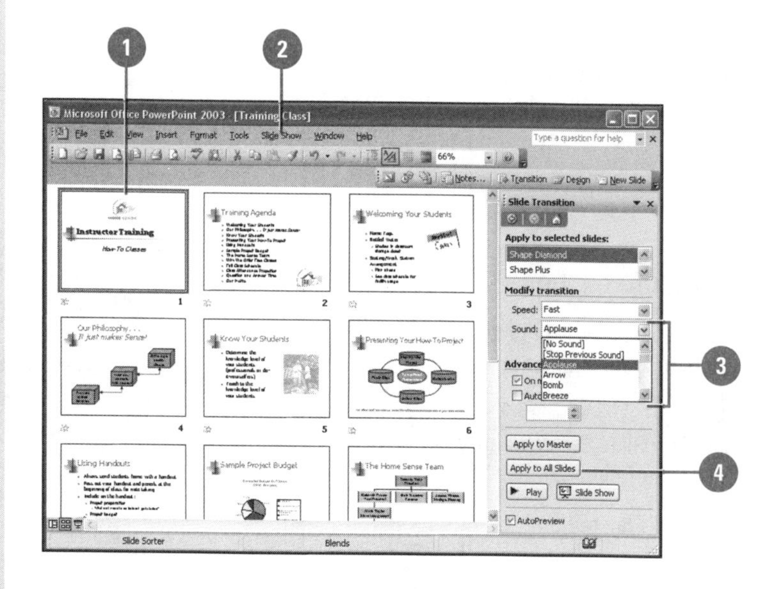

Did You Know?

You can use the Slide Transition button in Slide Sorter view. In Slide Sorter view, click the Slide Transition button on the Slide Sorter toolbar to quickly open the Slide Transition task pane.

Adding Animation

PP03S-2-4

You can use animation to introduce objects onto a slide one at a time or with special animation effects. For example, a bulleted list can appear one bulleted item at a time, or a picture or chart can fade gradually into the slide's foreground. The easiest way to apply animation effects to a slide show is to use Animation Schemes in the Slide Design task pane. You can also design your own **customized animations**, including those with your own special effects and sound elements.

Apply an Animation Scheme to a Slide

1. Select the slide or object you want to animate.
2. Click the Slide Show menu, and then click Animation Schemes.
3. Review the animation schemes which are divided into three categories: Subtle, Moderate, and Exciting.
4. Click the animation you want.
5. To apply the settings to all slides, click Apply To All Slides.

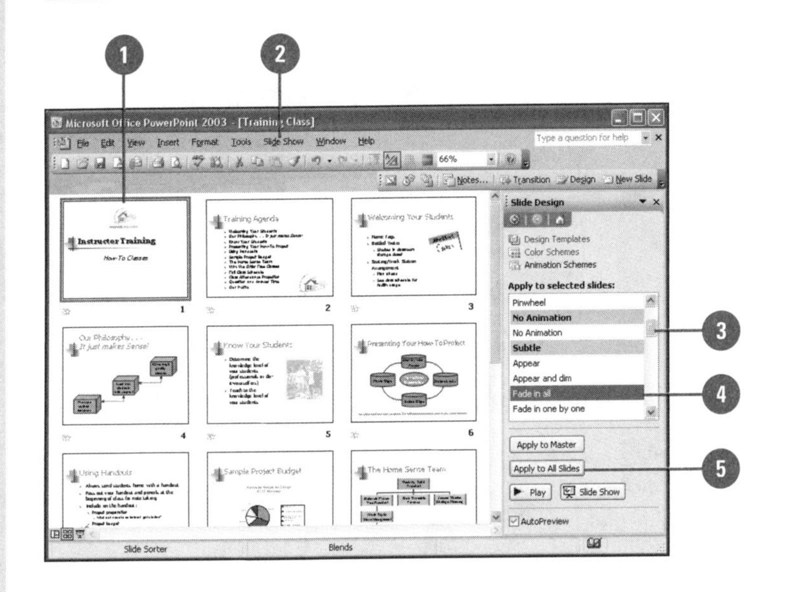

Preview an Animation

1. In Normal view, display the slide containing the animation you want to preview.
2. Click the Slide Show menu, and then click Animation Schemes.
3. Click the Play button.

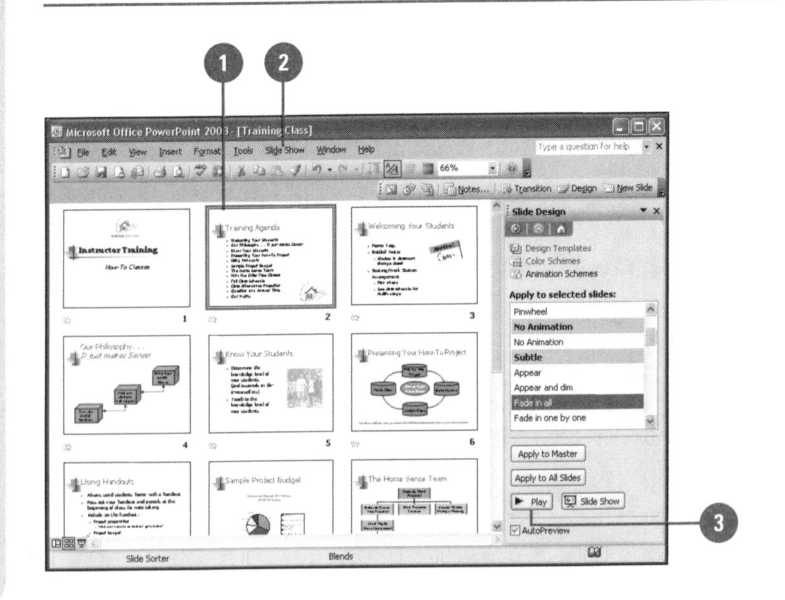

Did You Know?

You can view a slide's animation quickly in Slide Sorter view. In Slide Sorter view, click a slide's animation icon to view the animation.

Apply a Customized Animation

1. In Normal view, right-click the object you want to animate, and then click Custom Animation.
2. In the Custom Animation task pane, click Add Effect, select a category from the list menu, and then click the effect you want.
3. Use the Modify Effect options in the Custom Animation task pane to further modify the effect.
4. Click the Play button to see the animation effect.

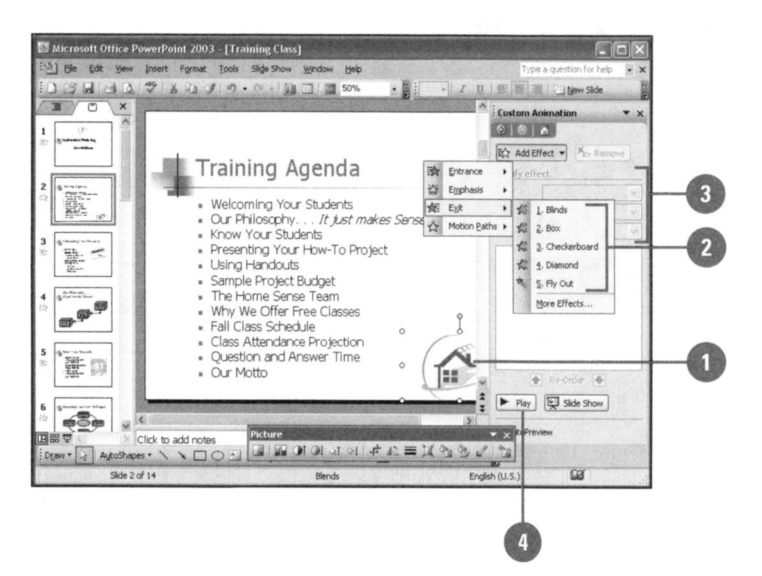

Add Sound to an Animation

1. In Normal view, right-click the object, and then click Custom Animation.
2. In the Animation Order list, click the list arrow of the animation to which you want to add a sound, and then click Effect Options.
3. Click the Sound list arrow, and then click the sound effect you want.

   To add your own sound, click Other Sound from the list, select the sound you want, and then click OK.
4. Click OK.
5. Click the Play button to hear the animation effect.

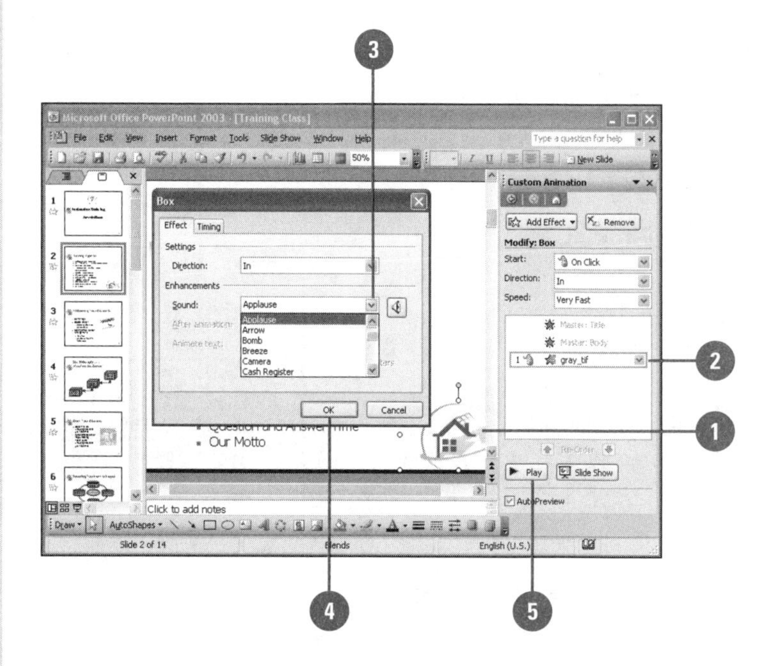

9

Using Specialized Animations

PP03S-2-4

Using specialized animations, you can apply animations specific to certain objects. For example, for a text object, you can introduce the text on your slide all at once or by word or letter. Similarly, you can introduce bulleted lists one bullet item at a time and apply different effects to older items, such as graying the items out as they are replaced by new ones. You can animate charts by introducing chart series or chart categories one at a time.

Animate Text

1. In Normal view, right-click the selected text object, and then click Custom Animation.
2. In the Custom Animation task pane, click Add Effect, point to an effect category, and then choose an effect from the list of animation effects.
3. In the Animation Order list, click the list arrow of the animation, and then click Effect Options.
4. Click the Animate Text list arrow, and then click the effect you want.
5. Click OK.

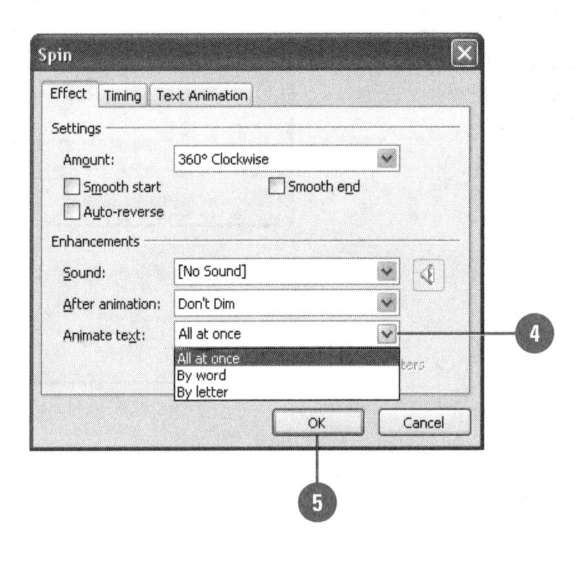

Animate Bulleted Lists

1. In Normal view, right-click the bulleted text, and then click Custom Animation.
2. In the Custom Animation task pane, click Add Effect, point to an effect category, and then choose an effect from the list of animation effects.
3. In the Animation Order list, click the list arrow of the animation, and then click Effect Options.
4. Click the Text Animation tab, click the Group Text list arrow, and then click at what paragraph level bulleted text will be animated.
5. Click OK, and then click Play.

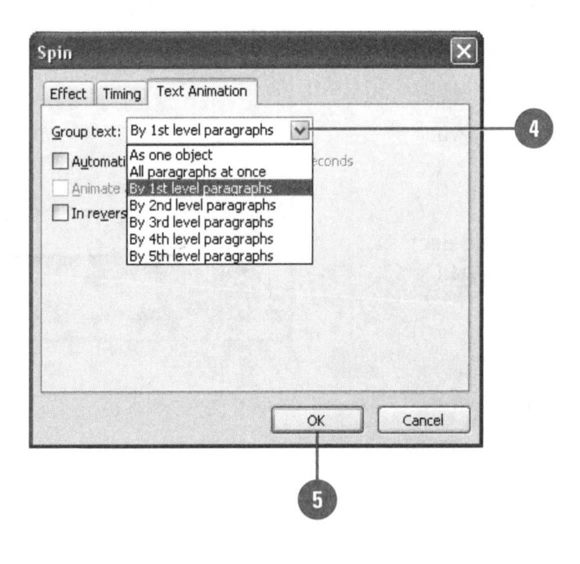

Dim Text After Its Animated

1. In Normal view, right-click the text, and then click Custom Animation.
2. In the Custom Animation task pane, click Add Effect, point to an effect category, and then choose an effect from the list of animation effects.
3. In the Animation Order list, click the list arrow of the animation, and then click Effect Options.
4. Click the After Animation list arrow, and then click the dim text color or option you want.
5. Click OK, and then click Play to see the animation effect.

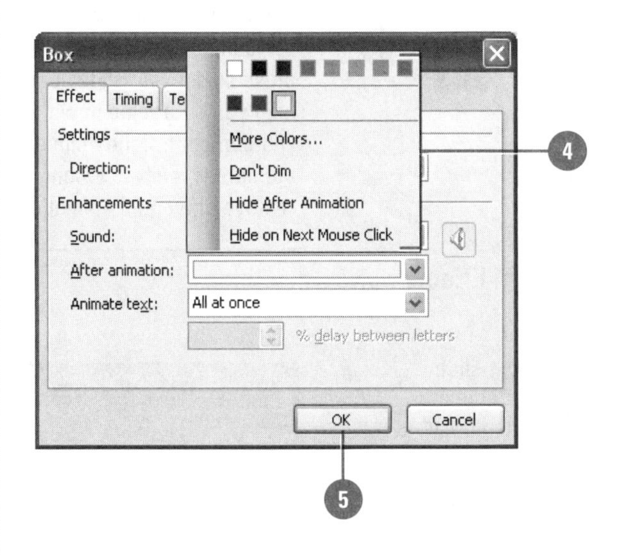

Animate Chart Elements

1. In Normal view, right-click the chart, and then click Custom Animation.
2. In the Custom Animation task pane, click Add Effect, point to an effect category, and then choose an effect from the list of animation effects.
3. In the Animation Order list, click the list arrow of the animation, and then click Effect Options.
4. On the Chart Animation tab, click the Group Chart list arrow, and then click the order in which chart elements should be introduced.
5. Select the Animate Grid And Legend check box to animate the chart grid and legend.
6. Click OK, and then click Play to see the animation effect.

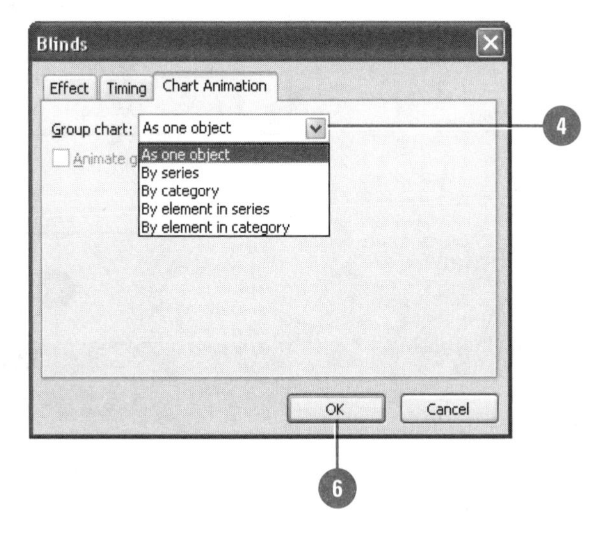

Coordinating Multiple Animations

PP03S-2-4

The Custom Animation task pane helps you keep track of your presentation's animations by listing all animated objects in a single location. Use these lists if your slides contain more than one animation, because they help you determine how the animations will work together. For example, you can control the animation of each object, in what order each object appears, specify how long to wait between animation effects, and remove unwanted animations.

Add Multiple Animation Effects to Slide Objects

1. In Normal view, click the slide object that you want to animate, click the Slide Show menu, and then click Custom Animation.
2. Click the Add Effect button, point to an effect category, and then choose an animation effect and any additional animation options.
3. Repeat Steps 1 and 2 to create multiple animation effects on a single slide.

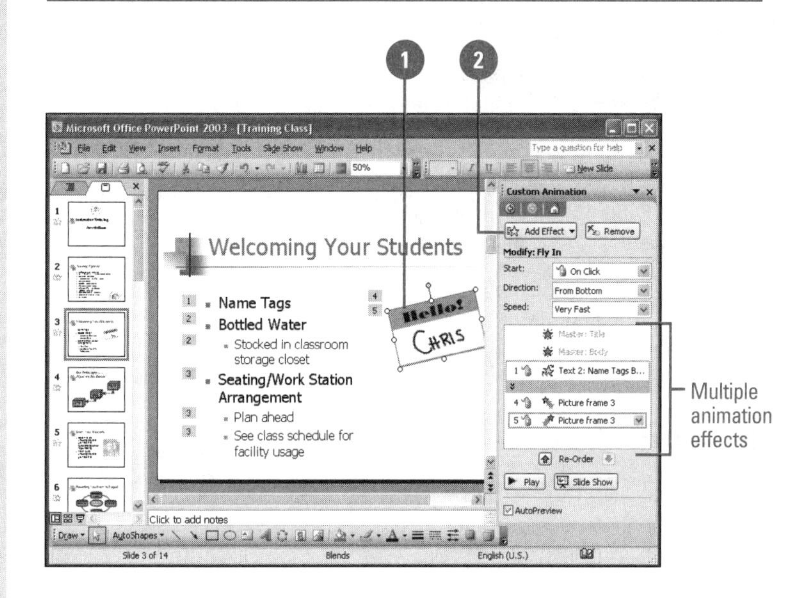

Modify the Animation Order

1. In Normal view, click the Slide Show menu, and then click Custom Animation.
2. In the Animation Order list, click an animation.
3. Click the Re-Order Up or Down arrow button.
4. Click the Play button.

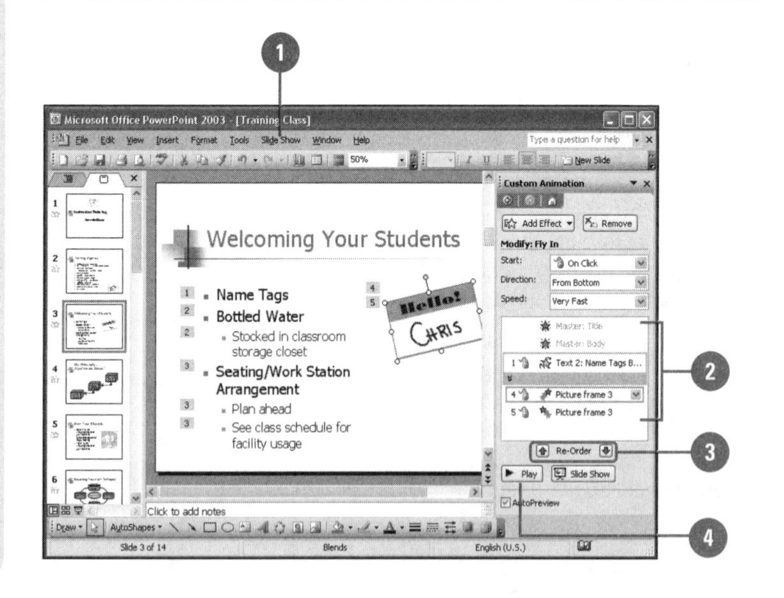

Set Time Between Animations

1. In Normal view, click the Slide Show menu, and then click Custom Animation.
2. In the Animation Order list, click the list arrow of an animation, and then click Timing.
3. Click the Start list arrow, and then click After Previous.
4. Use the Delay arrows to select the number of seconds between this animation and the previous event.
5. Click OK.

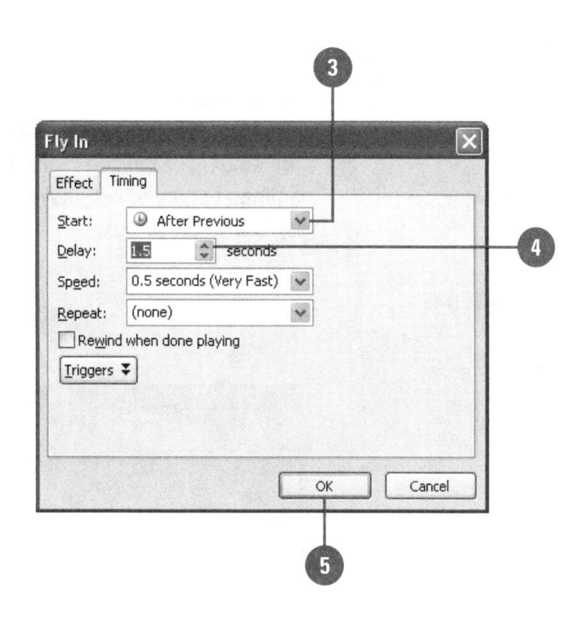

Remove an Animation

1. In Normal view, click the Slide Show menu, and then click Custom Animation.
2. Click the animation you want to remove from the Animation Order list, and then click the list arrow.
3. Click Remove.

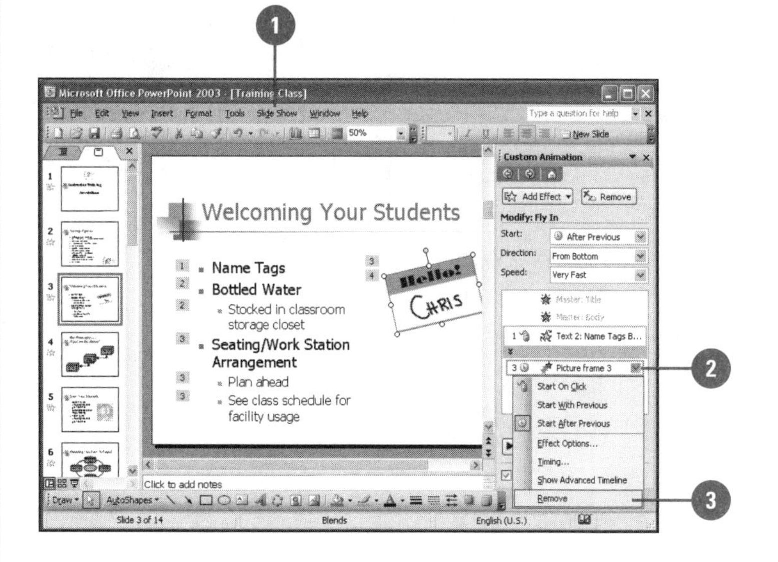

Did You Know?

You can show animation and transition effects while viewing your presentation in a browser. Click the Tools menu, click Options, and then click the General tab. Click Web Options, click the Show Slide Animation While Browsing check box, and then click OK. Click OK again to close the Options dialog box.

9

Adding Slide Timings

PP03S-4-3

Use PowerPoint's timing features to make sure that your presentation is not taking too long or going too fast. You can specify the amount of time given to each slide or use Rehearse Timings, which ensures that your timings are legitimate and workable. By rehearsing timings, you can vary the amount of time each slide appears on the screen. If you want the timings to take effect, make sure the show is set to use timings in the Set Up Show dialog box.

Set Timings Between Slides

1. Click the Slide Show menu, and then click Slide Transition.
2. Select the Automatically After check box.
3. Enter the time (in seconds) before the presentation automatically advances to the next slide after displaying the entire slide.
4. To apply the settings to all slides, click Apply To All Slides.

Did You Know?

You can use the mouse to control slide timings. In Slide Show View, a mouse click always advances a slide, even if the set timing has not elapsed, and holding down the mouse button prevents a timed transition from occurring until you release the mouse button.

Create Timings Through Rehearsal

1. Click the Slide Show menu, and then click Rehearse Timings.
2. As the slide show runs, rehearse your presentation by clicking or pressing Enter to go to the next slide.
3. When you're done, click Yes to accept the timings.
4. To test timings, start the slide show and note when the slides advance too quickly or too slowly.
5. Review and edit individual timings in Slide Sorter view.

Time spent on this slide

Time for the entire presentation

Rehearsal

0:00:06

0:00:06

HOME SENSE

Instructor Training

How-To Classes

Edit Timings

1. Click the Slide Sorter View button.
2. Click the slide whose timing you want to change.
3. Click the Slide Show menu, and then click Slide Transition.
4. Enter a new value in the Seconds box.
5. Click anywhere in the presentation to save the new timing.

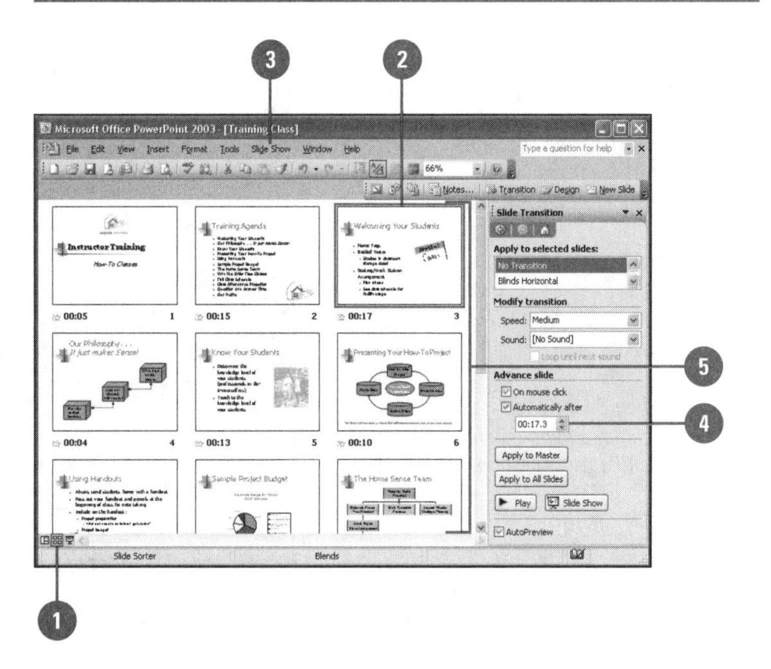

Did You Know?

You can control slide show timings. To control whether your presentation uses timings you set or advances manually, click the Slide Show menu, click Set Up Show, click the Manually or Using Timings, If Present option, and then click OK.

Recording a Narration

PP03S-4-3

If you are creating a self-running presentation, you might want to add a narration to emphasize the points you make. PowerPoint lets you record your own narration as you rehearse your slide show. You can record a narration before you run a slide show, or you can record it during the presentation and include audience comments. As you record the narration, you can pause or stop the narration at any time. When you play back a narration, the recording is synchronized with the presentation, including all slide transitions and animations. You can also delete a voice narration, as with any other PowerPoint object. You will need a microphone and a computer with a sound card to record the narration.

Record a Narration

1. Click the Slide Show menu, and then click Record Narration.
2. Click Set Microphone Level, set the microphone level you want, and then click OK.
3. Click Change Quality.
4. Click the Name list arrow, and then click the recording quality you want.
5. Click OK.
6. If necessary, select the Link Narrations In check box to insert the narration as a linked object.
7. Click OK.

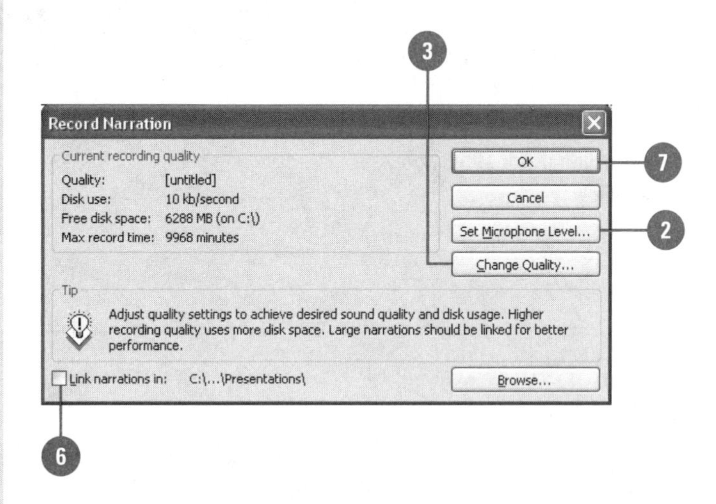

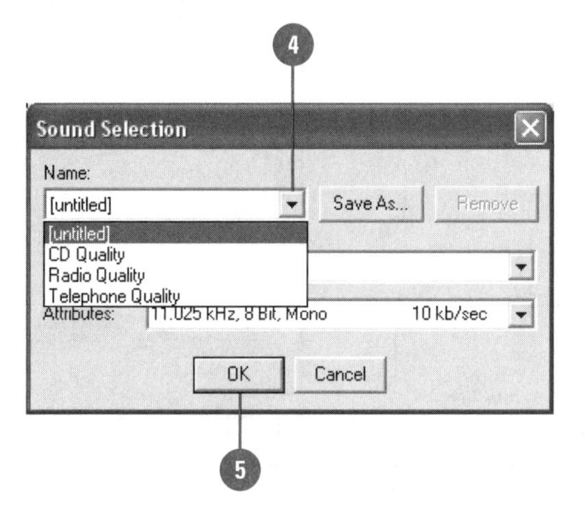

See Also

See "Recording Sounds" on page 144 for information on adding music or other sounds to a presentation.

8. If necessary, click Current Slide or First Slide.
9. Speak clearly into the microphone attached to your computer and record your narration for each slide.
10. Click Save when prompted to save slide timings along with your narration.
11. Rerun the slide show and verify that your narration has been recorded along with the automatic timings.

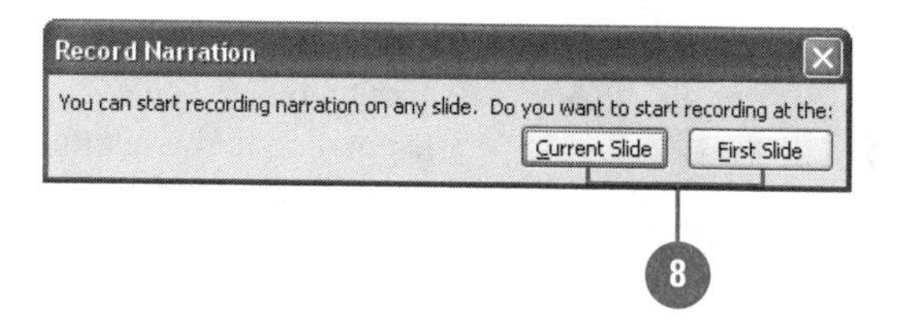

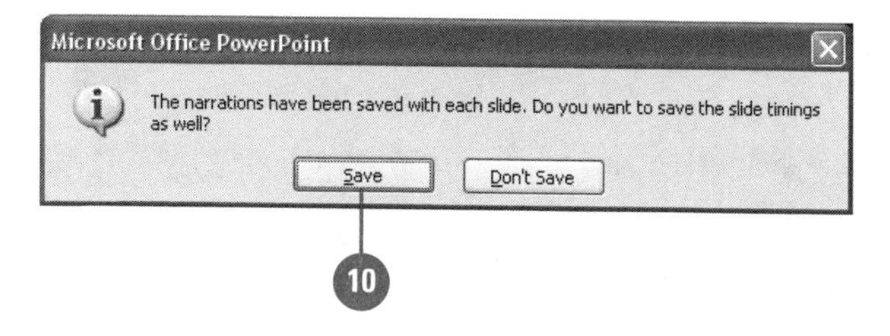

Did You Know?

You can pause Narration. Right-click anywhere on the screen, and then click Pause Narration.

You can resume Narration. Right-click anywhere on the screen, and then click Resume Narration.

You can show a Presentation without Narration. To show a presentation with narration on a computer without sound hardware installed, click Set Up Show on the Slide Show menu, and then select the Show Without Narration check box to avoid problems running the presentation.

Creating a Self-Running Presentation

Self-running slide shows are a great way to communicate information without needing someone to run the show. You might want to set up a presentation to run unattended in a kiosk at a trade show or place it on your company's Intranet to run at the user's convenience. When you save a presentation as a PowerPoint Show, it will launch directly into a slide show when opened.

Set Up a Self-Running Slide Show

1. Click the Slide Show menu, and then click Set Up Show.
2. Click the Browsed at a Kiosk (Full Screen) option.
3. Click OK.

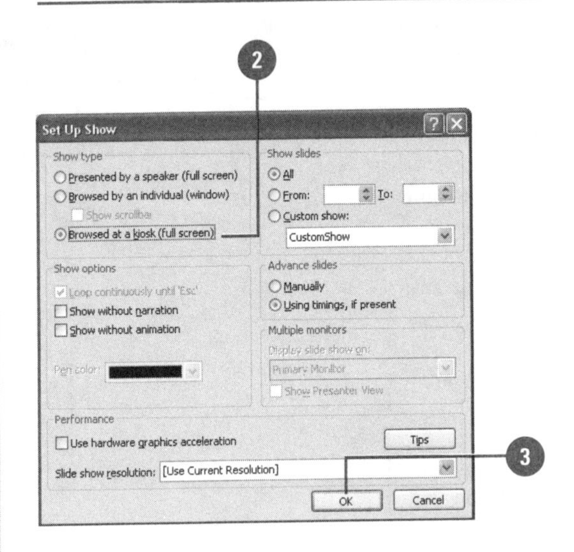

Save a Presentation as a PowerPoint Show

1. Click the File menu, and then click Save As.
2. Click the Save As Type list arrow, and then click PowerPoint Show.
3. Click Save.

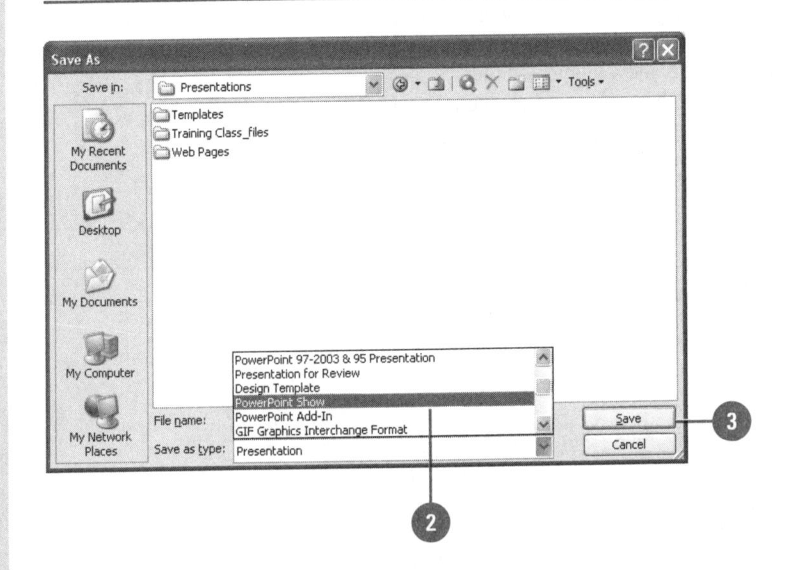

Did You Know?

What tools are active in a self-navigating show? A self-navigating show turns off all navigation tools except action buttons and other action settings available to the user.

Presenting a Slide Show

10

Introduction

When you're done preparing your slide show, it's time to consider how to show it to your audience. Microsoft Office PowerPoint 2003 gives you several ways to give and share your presentations.

When you're ready to give a slide show, PowerPoint provides many tools for presenting your show to audiences everywhere. When you are presenting the show in person, you can use PowerPoint's slide navigation tools to move around your presentation. You can move forward and backward or move to a specific slide. By using the various navigation keys on the keyboard, you can jump to any part of the presentation.

As you're presenting your slide show, you can highlight key ideas by using the mouse as a pointer or pen/highlighter. By annotating your slide show, you can give extra emphasis on a topic or goal for your audience. You can save your annotations as enhancements to your presentation later. If you are presenting a slide show using a second monitor or projection screen, PowerPoint includes the tools you need to properly navigate the display equipment.

If you are taking your presentation to another site, you might not need the entire PowerPoint package. Rather than installing PowerPoint on the sites' computer, you can pack your presentation into one compressed file, storing it on a CD. Once you reach your destination, you can expand the compressed file onto your client's computer and play it, regardless of whether that computer has PowerPoint installed.

What You'll Do

Start a Slide Show

Navigate a Slide Show

Annotate a Slide Show

Use Presenter View with Multiple Monitors

Package a Presentation on CD

Use the PowerPoint Viewer

Starting a Slide Show

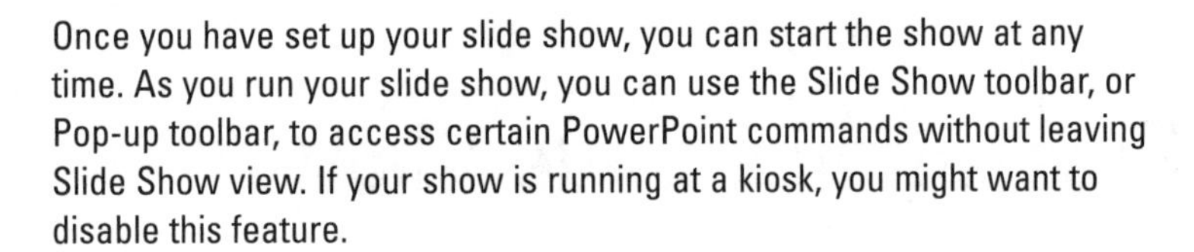

Once you have set up your slide show, you can start the show at any time. As you run your slide show, you can use the Slide Show toolbar, or Pop-up toolbar, to access certain PowerPoint commands without leaving Slide Show view. If your show is running at a kiosk, you might want to disable this feature.

Start a Slide Show and Display the Slide Show Toolbar

1. Click the Slide Show menu, and then click View Show.
2. Move the mouse pointer to display the Slide Show toolbar.
3. Click a button on the Slide Show toolbar to move to the next or previous slide, or navigate the slide show, or end the show.

Did You Know?

You can start a slide show quickly from the current slide. Click the Slide Show button.

See Also

See "Setting Up a Slide Show" on page 234 for information on preparing a slide show.

Set Slide Show Options

1. Click the Tools menu, and then click Options.
2. Click the View tab.
3. Select the slide show and pop-up toolbar check box options you want.
   - Prompt To Keep Ink Annotations When Exiting
   - Show Menu On Right Mouse Click
   - Show Popup Toolbar
   - End With Black Slide
4. Click OK.

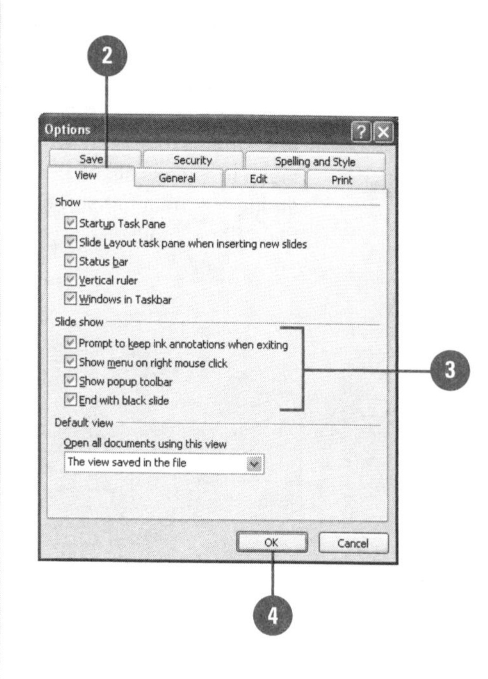

10

Navigating a Slide Show

PP03S-4-4

In Slide Show view, you advance to the next slide by clicking the mouse button, pressing the Spacebar, or pressing Enter. In addition to those basic navigational techniques, PowerPoint provides keyboard shortcuts that can take you to the beginning, the end, or any particular slide in your presentation. You can also use the navigation commands on the shortcut menu to access slides in custom slide shows. After a period of inactivity during a normal full-screen slide show, PowerPoint hides the pointer and Slide Show toolbar.

Go to a Specific Slide

1. In Slide Show view, move the mouse to display the Slide Show toolbar, and then click the Slide button.

   TIMESAVER *Right-click a slide to display a shortcut menu.*

2. Point to Go To Slide, and then click the title of the slide you want to go to.

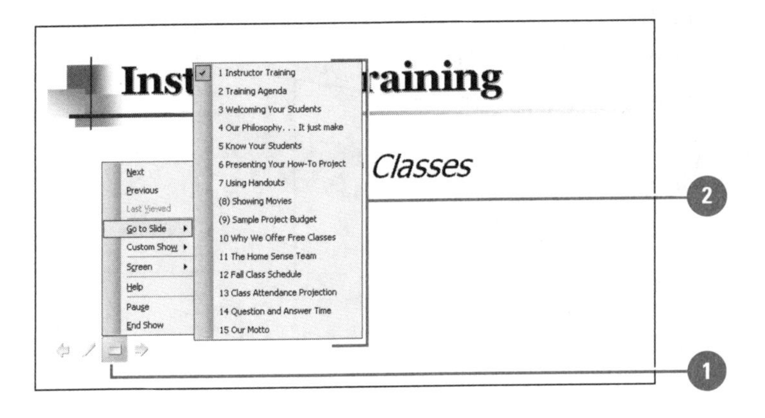

Use Slide Show View Navigation Shortcuts

1. Refer to the adjacent table for information on Slide Show view navigation shortcuts.

Slide Show View Shortcuts

Action	Result
Mouse click	Moves to the next slide
Right-mouse click	Moves to the previous slide (only if the Short-cut Menu On Right-Click option is disabled)
Press Enter	Moves to the next slide
Press Home	Moves to the first slide in the show
Press End	Moves to the last slide in the show
Press Page Up	Moves to the previous slide
Press Page Down	Moves to the next slide
Enter a slide number and press Enter	Moves to the slide number you specified when you press Enter
Press B	Displays a black screen; press again to return
Press W	Displays a white screen; press again to return
Press Esc	Exits Slide Show view

Did You Know?

You can add speaker notes in Slide Show. In Slide Show view, right-click a blank area on the slide, point to Screen, click Speaker Notes, type your notes, and then click Close.

Go to a Custom Slide Show

1. In Slide Show view, right-click a slide.
2. Point to Custom Show.
3. Click the custom slide show that you want to go to.

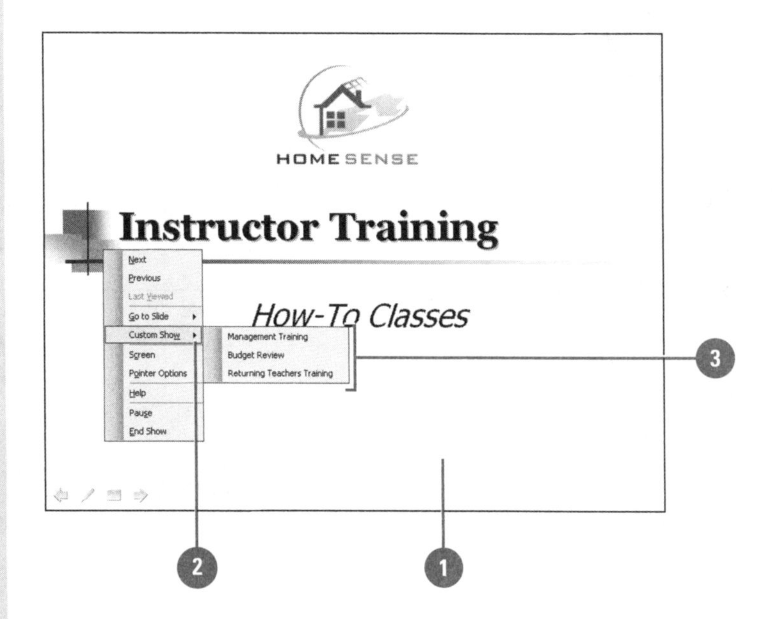

Did You Know?

You can switch to another program in Slide Show. In Slide Show view, right-click a blank area on the slide, point to Screen, and then click Switch Programs. Use the taskbar to switch between programs.

See Also

See "Creating a Custom Slide Show" on page 236 for information on creating a custom slide show.

10

Annotating a Slide Show

PP03S-4-4

When you are presenting your slide show, you can turn your mouse pointer into a pen tool to highlight and circle your key points. If you decide to use a pen tool, you might want to set its color to match the colors in your presentation. When you are finished, you can turn the pen back to the normal mouse pointer. Markups you make on a slide with the pen tool during a slide show can be saved with the presentation, and then turned on or off when you re-open the presentation for editing.

Change Pointer Options

1. In Slide Show view, move the mouse to display the Slide Show toolbar.
2. Click the Pen button, point to Arrow Options, and then click a pointer option.
   - **Automatic** hides the pointer until you move the mouse.
   - **Visible** makes the pointer visible.
   - **Hidden** makes the pointer invisible throughout the presentation.

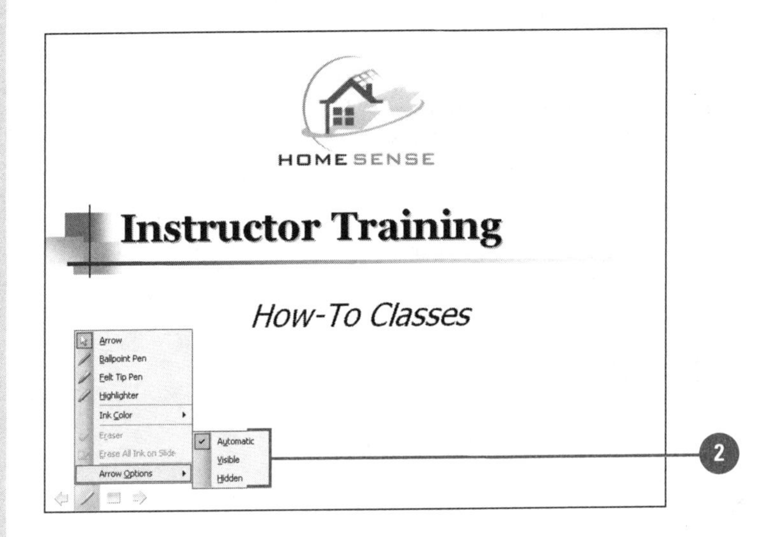

Use a Pen During the Slide Show

1. In Slide Show view, move the mouse to display the Slide Show toolbar.
2. Click the Pen button, and then click or point to an option.
   - A writing tool (Ballpoint Pen, Felt Tip Pen, or Highlighter).
   - Ink Color to select an ink color.
3. Drag the mouse pointer to draw on your slide presentation with the pen or highlighter.
4. Click the Pen button, and then click Eraser, to remove individual ink, or Erase All Ink On Slide.

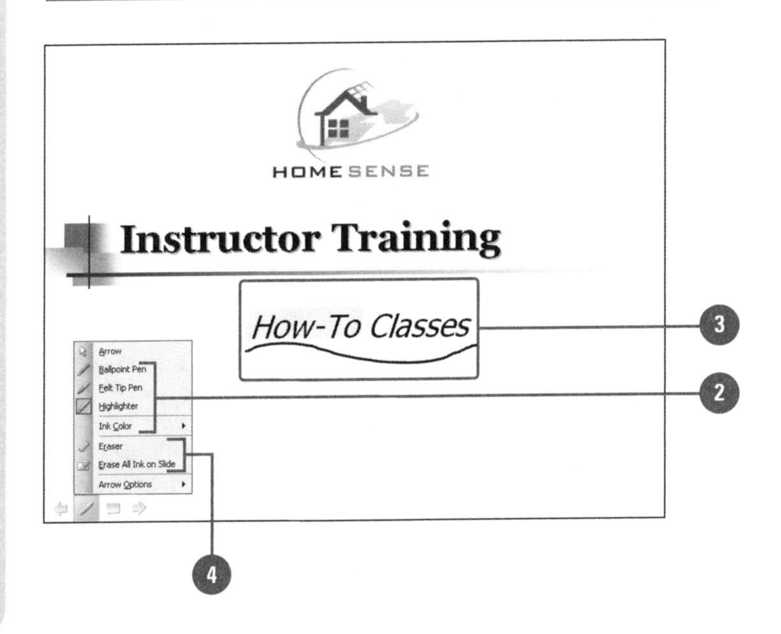

Save Annotations and Turn Them On and Off

1. In Slide Show view, right-click a slide.
2. Point to Pointer Options.
3. Click a pen or highlighter, and then make an annotation on a slide.
4. Right-click the slide, and then click End Show.
5. Click Keep when asked if you want to keep your ink annotations for editing.
6. In Normal view, click the View menu, and then click Markup.

   The annotations disappear from the slide.
7. Click the Close button, and then click Yes to save the changes.

   When you re-open this presentation, you can view the Markups in Normal or Slide Sorter view, and then turn them off or on.

Did You Know?

You can turn the pen back to the mouse pointer quickly. To turn the pen back to the normal mouse pointer, right-click a slide in Slide Show view, point to Pointer Options, and then click Arrow.

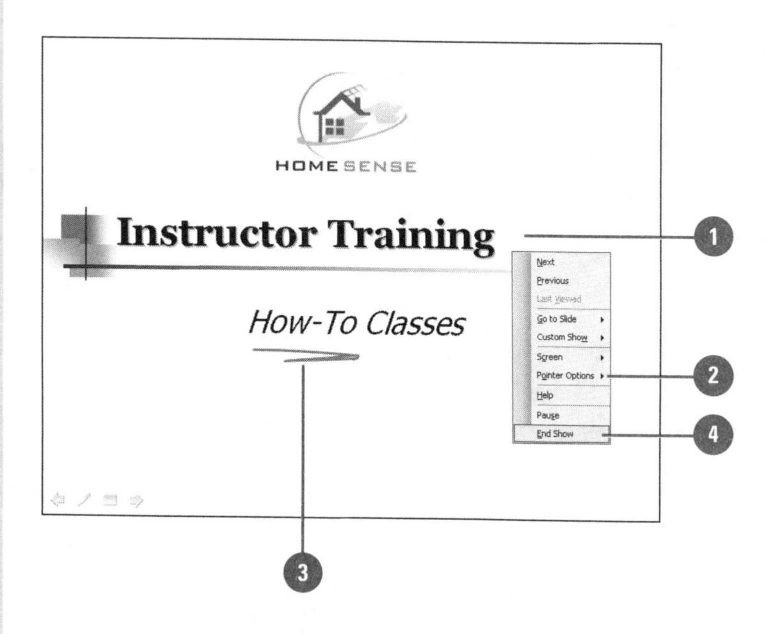

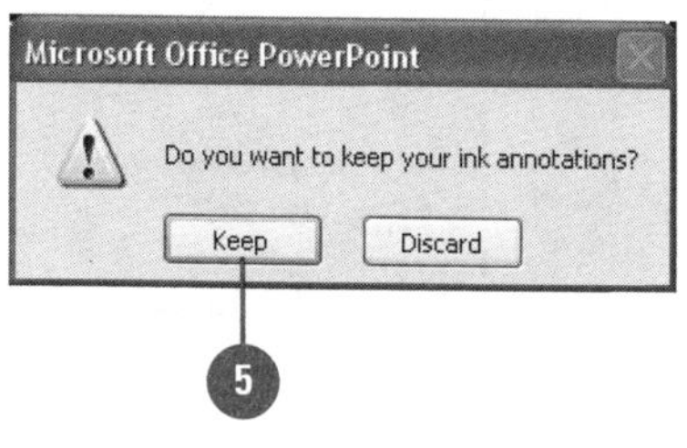

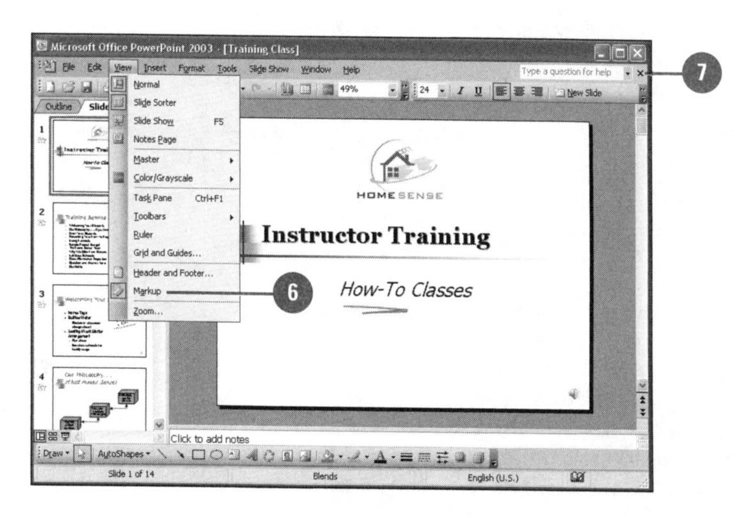

10

Using Presenter View with Multiple Monitors

If your computer is connected to two monitors, you can view a slide show on one monitor while you control it from another. This is useful when you want to control a slide show and run other programs that you don't want the audience to see. When you display your slide show on multiple monitors, you can present it using PowerPoint's Presenter Tools in the Presenter view, which allows presenters to have their own view not visible to the audience. In addition to including details about what bullet or slide is coming next, this view also enables you to see your speaker notes and lets you jump directly to any slide. You can only use Presenter view and run the presentation from one monitor.

Present a Slide Show On Two Monitors

1. Click the Slide Show menu, and then click Set Up Show.
2. Click the Display Slide Show On list arrow, and then click the name of the monitor on which you want to project the slide show.
3. Select the Show Presenter View check box.
4. Click OK.
5. Click the Slide Show button to start the slide show.
6. In Presenter view, use the navigation tools to deliver the presentation on multiple monitors.
7. If necessary, click the Close button to exit Presenter View.

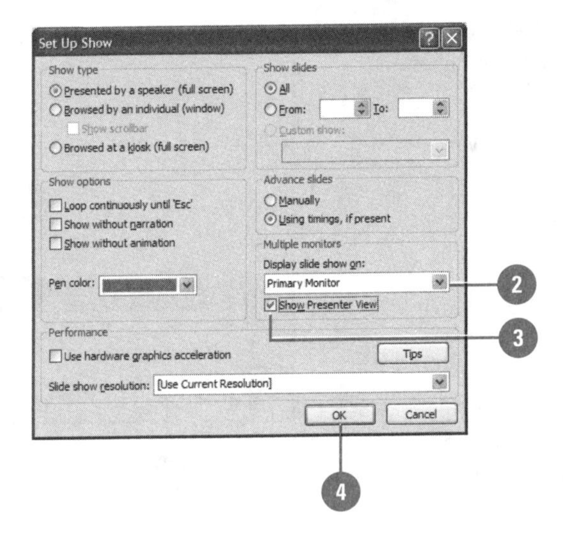

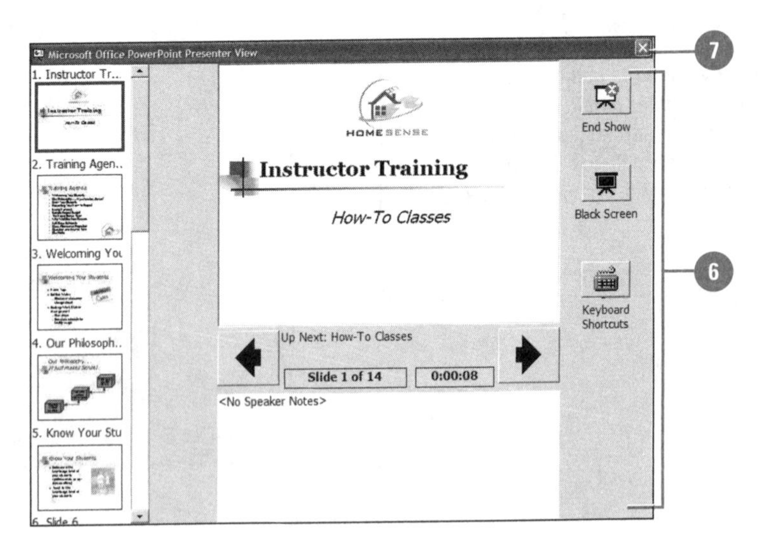

Did You Know?

What you need to run on a second monitor? To run a slide show on one monitor and view slides, notes, and the presentation outline on another, you must have dual-monitor hardware installed and be using Microsoft Windows 2000 with Service Pack 3 (or later) or Microsoft Windows XP.

Packaging a Presentation on CD

PP03S-4-5

The Package for CD feature allows you to copy on CD one or more presentations and all of the supporting files, including linked files. The feature also automatically runs your presentations. The updated PowerPoint Viewer is included on the CD when you package your presentations. The PowerPoint Viewer is a program used to run presentations on computers that don't have Microsoft PowerPoint installed. If you are packaging your presentation for use on your laptop computer or a network, you can use Package for CD to package your presentation to a folder or a network.

Package a Presentation on CD

1. Click the File menu, and then click Package For CD.
2. Type a name for the CD.
3. To add additional files to the CD, click Add Files, select the files you want, and then click Add.
4. Click Options.
5. To include the PowerPoint Viewer, select the PowerPoint Viewer check box, and then select a play option from the list arrow.
6. To link any external files (such as movies), select the Linked Files check box.
7. To make sure fonts are available on the play back computer, select the Embedded TrueType Fonts check box.
8. If you want, type a password to open or modify the presentation.
9. Click OK.
10. To copy to a folder, click Copy To Folder, specify a folder location, and then click OK.
11. Click Copy To CD, and then follow the CD writer instructions for your operating system.

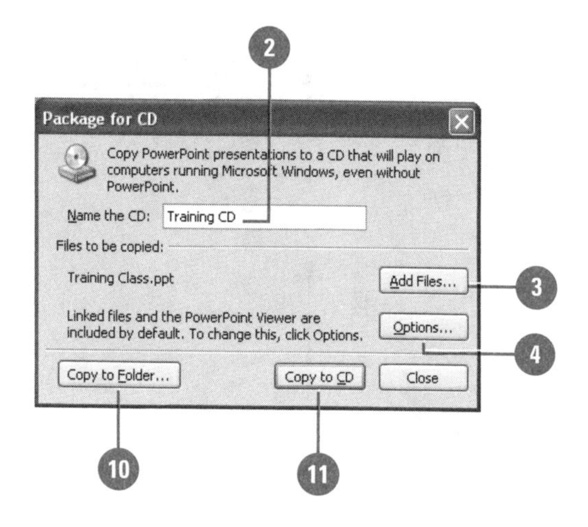

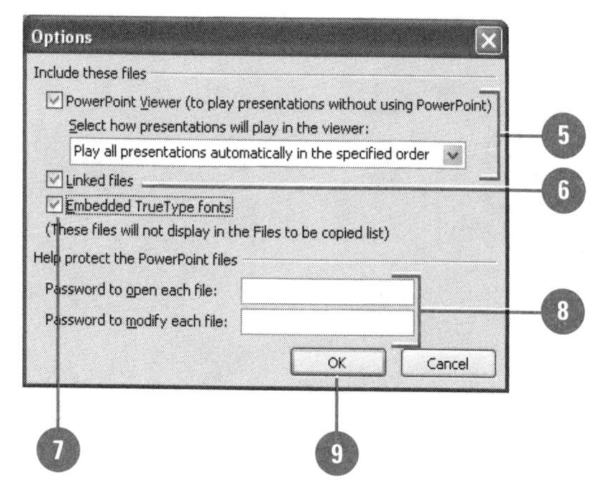

10

Using the PowerPoint Viewer

The PowerPoint Viewer is a program used to run presentations on computers that don't have Microsoft PowerPoint installed. This Viewer is used as part of the Package for CD feature, but you can also use the Viewer independently, which you can download from the Microsoft Office Online Web site. Use the Microsoft Office Online command on the Help menu to go to the Web site, and then follow Microsoft PowerPoint links that direct you to downloads. If a presentation contains password protection, the PowerPoint Viewer prompts you for a password. The Viewer supports all presentations created using PowerPoint 97 or later.

Run a Presentation with the PowerPoint Viewer

1. Click the Start button, point to All Programs, and then click Microsoft Office PowerPoint Viewer 2003.

   TROUBLE? *If the viewer is not available on the Start menu, open Windows Explorer, and then search for the pptview.exe file, which you can double-click to start the program.*

2. Locate and select the presentation you want to show.
3. Click Open.
4. Navigate the slide show.
5. Click Cancel to close the PowerPoint Viewer.

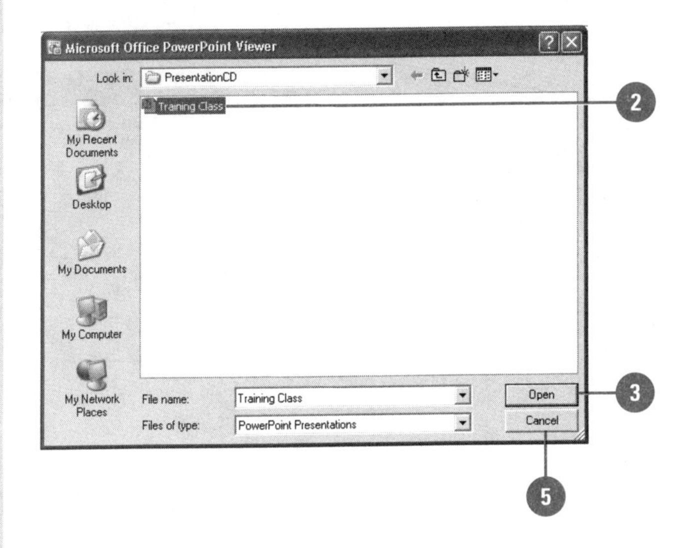

Reviewing and Sharing a Presentation

11

Introduction

When you've developed your content in your presentation and want feedback, you can send a PowerPoint presentation to reviewers electronically so that they can read, revise, and comment on the presentation without having to print it. With Microsoft Office PowerPoint 2003, others can add comments to your presentation and you can view them. Instead of reading handwritten text, or sticky notes on your printout, you can get clear and concise feedback.

When reviewers return the edited presentations to you, you can track all of the revisions and comments, accept or reject them, and merge them into the original presentation. You can track reviewer changes in two ways—by using the Reviewing toolbar, which contains buttons that let you accept and reject comments, or by using the Revisions pane, which shows information related to the changes and comments in your presentation.

Adding a password to protect your presentation is not only a good idea for security purposes, it's an added feature to make sure that changes to your presentation aren't accidentally made by unauthorized people. Not only can you guard who sees your presentation, you can set rights on who can actually add changes and comments to your presentation. You can also add restricted access known as Information Rights Access (IRM). IRM is a tool that is available with all Microsoft Office applications that restricts a file being sent through e-mail to other users.

If your computer is on a network or if you have access to the Internet, you can give a slide show on any other computer on the network by using PowerPoint's online broadcasting feature. You can also collaborate in an online meeting, and show your presentation online through your network.

What You'll Do

Add Comments to a Presentation

Add Password Protection to a Presentation

Restrict Presentation Access

Send a Presentation for Review Using E-Mail

Track Changes in a Presentation

Compare and Merge Presentations

Broadcast a Presentation

Collaborate in an Online Meeting

Adding Comments to a Presentation

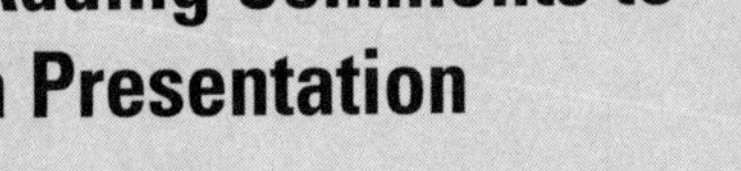

PP03S-3-2

When you review an Office document, you can insert comments to the author or other reviewers. **Comments** are like electronic adhesive notes tagged with your name. They typically appear in yellow boxes in PowerPoint. You can use comments to get feedback from others or to remind yourself of revisions you plan to make. A comment is visible only when you show comments and place the mouse pointer over the comment indicator. You can review comments in Normal view or by opening the Revisions pane.

Insert, Edit, and Delete a Comment

1. Click where you want to insert a comment.
2. Click the Insert menu, and then click Comment.
3. Type your comment in the comment box or pane.
4. Click outside the comment box.
5. To edit or delete a comment, right-click the comment, and then click Edit Comment or Delete Comment.

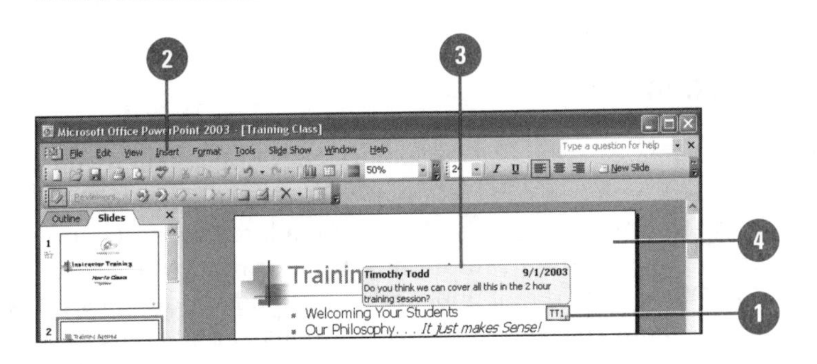

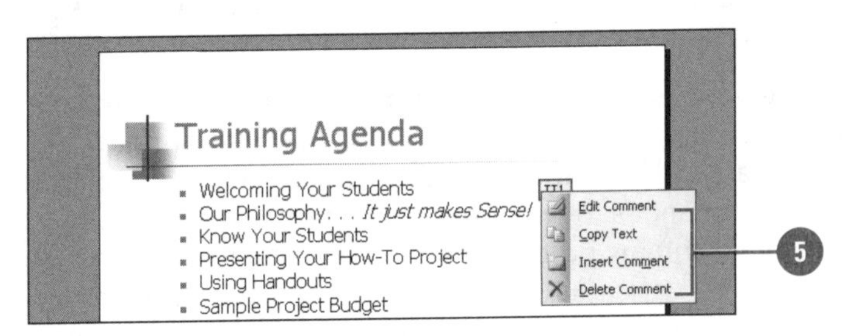

Did You Know?

You can insert a comment quickly. Click the Insert Comment button on the Reviewing toolbar to quickly add a comment. Right-click any toolbar, and then click Reviewing to display the toolbar.

Read a Comment

1. Click the View menu, point to Toolbars, and then click Reviewing to display the toolbar.
2. On the Reviewing toolbar, click the Show/Hide Markup button.
3. Point to the comment box.
4. Read the comment.
5. Click the Previous Item or Next Item button on the Reviewing toolbar to read another comment.

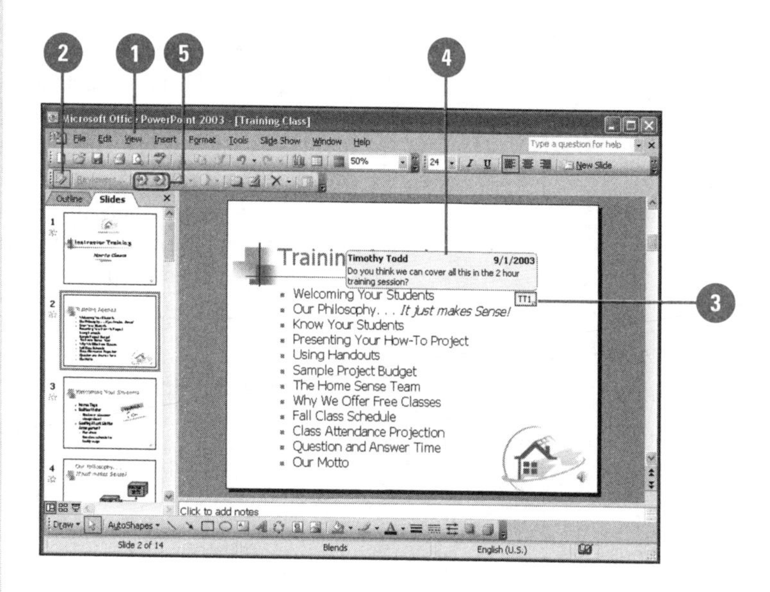

Open the Revisions Pane

1. Right-click any toolbar, and then click Revisions.
2. Click a comment in the Revisions task pane to read it.

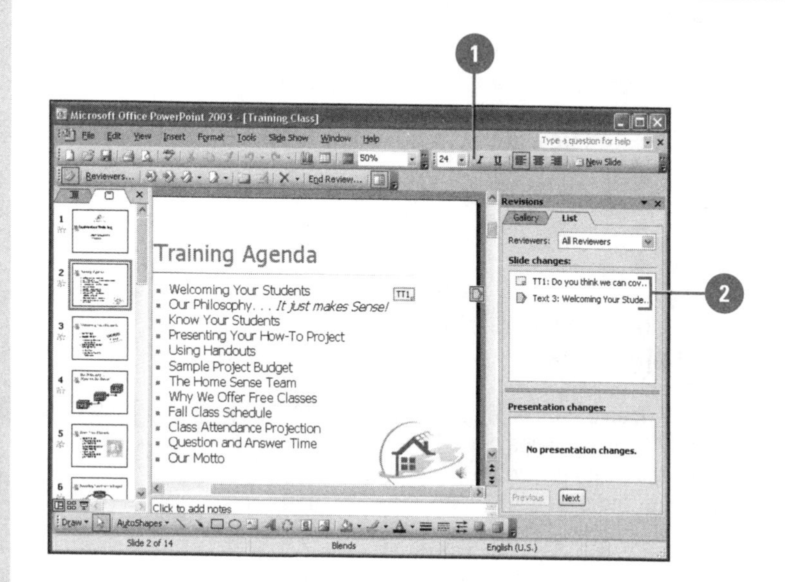

Did You Know?

You can display the Reviewing toolbar to access comment commands. Reviewers might find it handy to display the Reviewing toolbar, which provides buttons for adding, viewing, deleting, and editing comments. Click the View menu, point to Toolbars, and then click Reviewing to display the Reviewing toolbar.

You can review all the comments in a presentation. Click the Previous and Next Item buttons on the Reviewing toolbar to read all of the comments in a presentation.

Adding Password Protection to a Presentation

You can assign a password and other security options so that only those who know the password can open the presentation, or to protect the integrity of your presentation as it moves from person to person. At times, you will want the information to be used but not changed; at other times, you will want only specific people in your office to be able to view the presentation. Setting a presentation as read-only is useful when you want a presentation, such as a company-wide bulletin, to be distributed and read, but not changed. Password protection takes effect the next time you open the presentation.

Add Password Protection to a Presentation

1. Open the presentation you want to protect.
2. Click the Tools menu, and then click Options.
3. Click the Security tab, and then type a password in the Password To Modify box or the Password To Open box.
4. Click OK.
5. Type your password again.
6. Click OK.

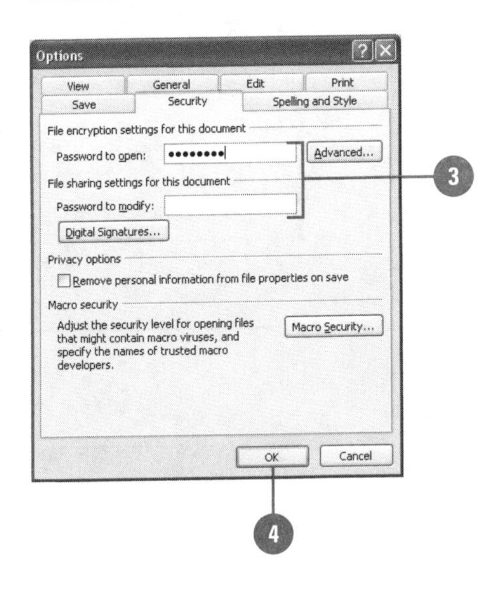

Open a Presentation with Password Protection

1. Click the Open button on the Standard toolbar, navigate to a presentation with password protection, and then click Open.
2. Click Read Only if you do not wish to modify the presentation, or type the password in the Password dialog box.
3. Click OK.

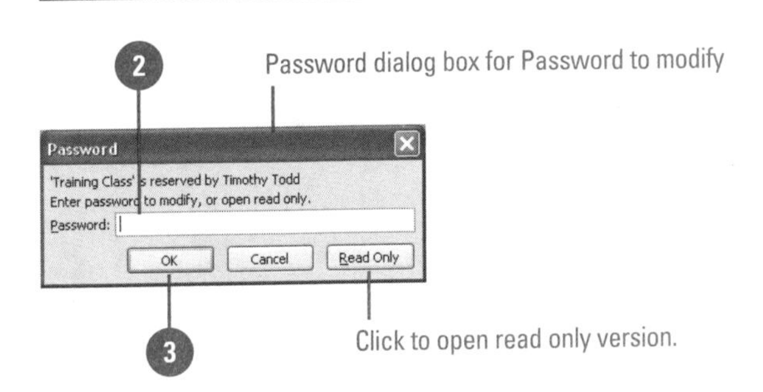

Change the Password Protection

1. Click the Open button on the Standard toolbar, navigate to a presentation with password protection, and then click Open.
2. Type the password in the Password dialog box, and then click OK.
3. Click the Tools menu, and then click Options.
4. Click the Security tab, and then select the contents in the Password To Modify box or the Password To Open box.
5. Type in a new password, and then click OK. The Confirm Password dialog box appears.
6. Type your new password again.
7. Click OK.

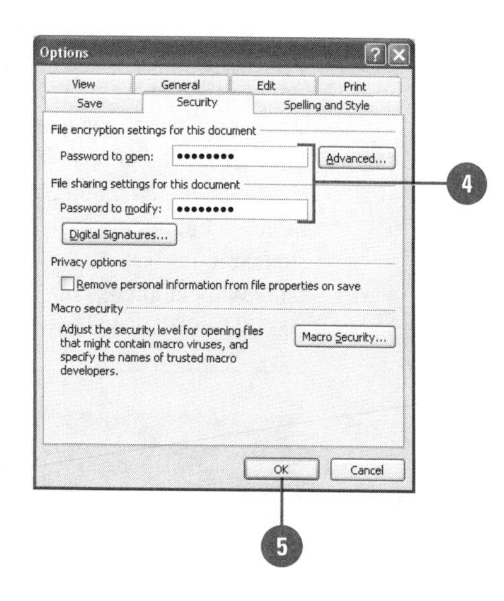

Remove the Password Protection

1. Click the Open button on the Standard toolbar, navigate to a presentation with password protection, and then click Open.
2. Type the password in the Password dialog box, and then click OK.
3. Click the Tools menu, and then click Options.
4. Click the Security tab, and then select the contents in the Password To Modify box or the Password To Open box.
5. Press Delete, and then click OK.

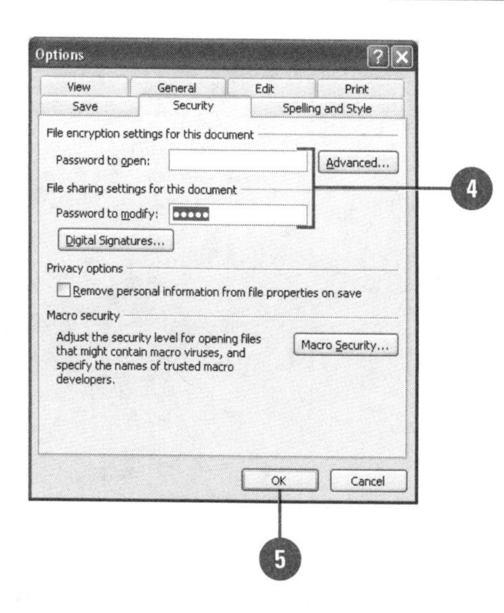

Restricting Presentation Access

You can use Information Rights Management (IRM) in Office 2003 programs to provide restricted access to Office documents. In Outlook, you can use IRM to create messages with restricted permission to help prevent presentations from being forwarded, printed, copied, or edited by unauthorized people. If you attach a presentation to an Outlook message, the presentation also contains the restriction. IRM uses a server to authenticate the credentials of people who create or receive presentations or e-mail with restricted permission. For Microsoft Office users without access to one of these servers, Microsoft provides a free trial IRM service, which requires a .NET Passport.

Set Up Information Rights Management

1. Click the File menu, point to Permission, and then click Restrict Permission As.
2. Click Yes to download and install IRM. Follow the wizard instructions.

   Upon completion, the Service Sign-Up Wizard opens.
3. Click the Yes, I Want To Sign Up For This Free Trial Service From Microsoft option.
4. Click Next, and then follow the remaining instructions to create a .NET Passport and complete the service sign-up.
5. Click Cancel.

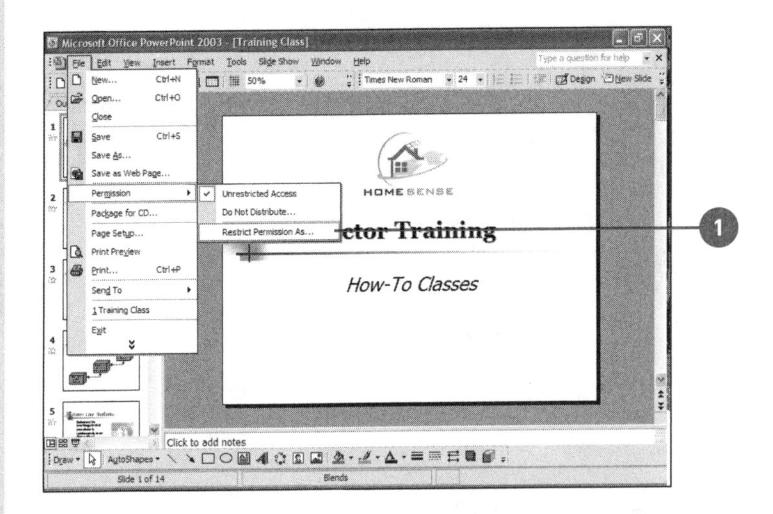

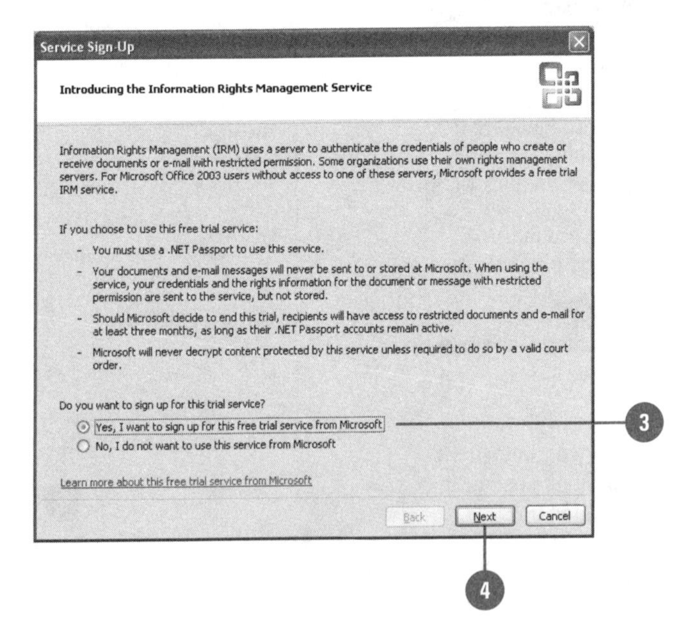

Create a Presentation with Restricted Permission

1. Open the presentation you want to restrict permission.
2. Click the File menu, point to Permission, and then click Restrict Permission As.
3. Click the user with the permissions to create or open restricted content.
4. Click OK.
5. Select the Restrict Permission To This Presentation check box.
6. Enter e-mail addresses of users in the Read and Change boxes or click the Read or Change button to select users from your Address Book.
7. Click More Options.
8. Select the check boxes with the specific permissions you want.
9. Click OK.

A restricted message appears above the address name.

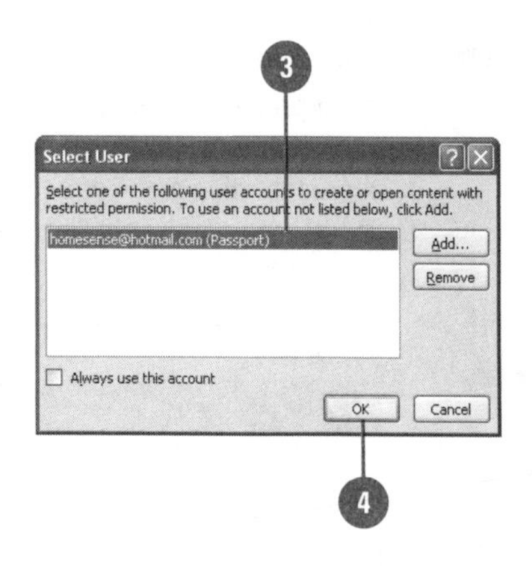

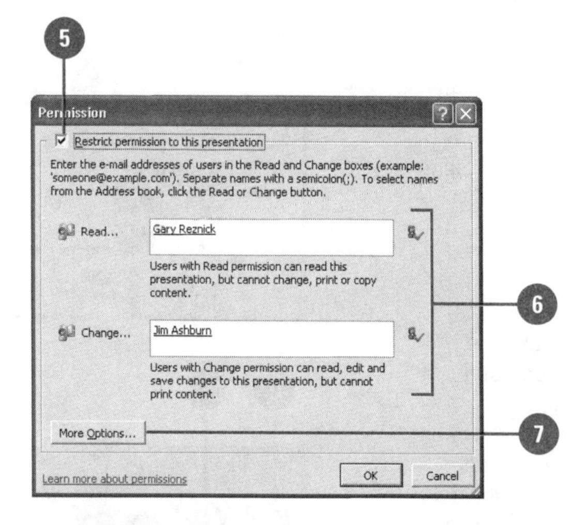

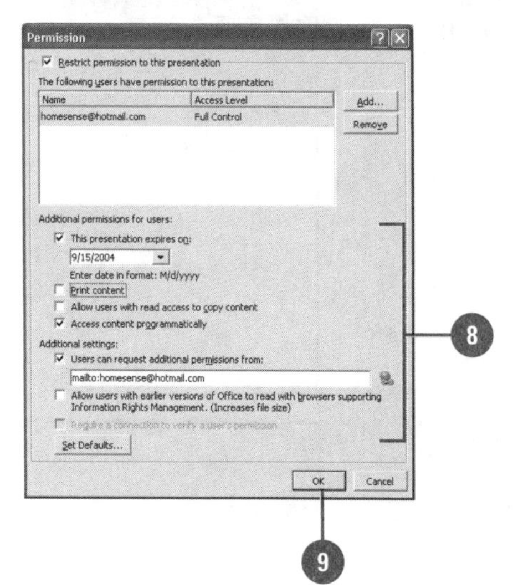

Did You Know?

You can unrestrict a presentation. Click the File menu, point to Permission, and then click Unrestricted Access.

11

Sending a Presentation for Review Using E-Mail

After you finish making changes to a presentation, you can quickly send it to another person for review using e-mail. PowerPoint allows you to send presentations out for review using e-mail from within the program so that you do not have to open your e-mail program. You can also send a presentation as an attachment using the Mail Recipient (As Attachment) option or by clicking the E-mail (as Attachment) button on the Standard toolbar.

Send a Presentation for Review Using E-Mail

1. Click the File menu, point to Send To, and then click Mail Recipient (For Review).
2. Click To, click the recipient names, and then click To, Cc, or Bcc.
3. Click OK, and then click the Send button on the toolbar.

   The message includes the text "Please review the attached document". The subject line of the e-mail will contain the file name of the presentation that you are sending.

   IMPORTANT *To complete these steps, you need to have an e-mail program installed on your computer and an e-mail account set-up.*

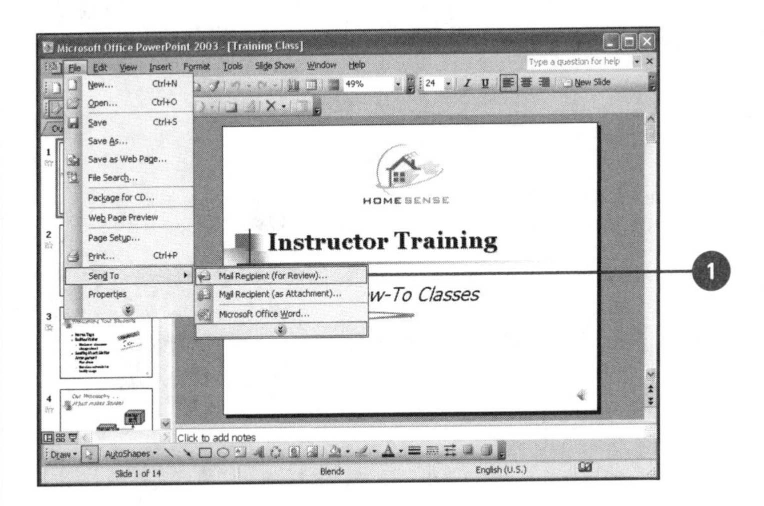

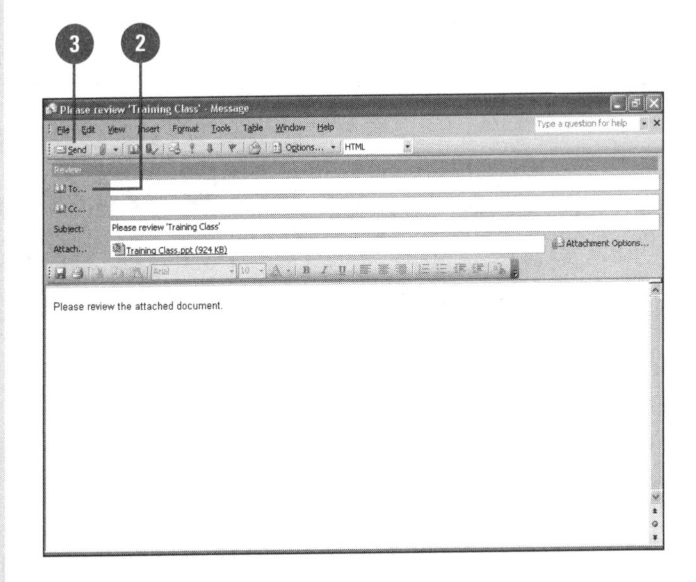

Send a Presentation in an E-Mail Message

1. Open the presentation you want to send.
2. Click the E-Mail (as Attachment) button on the Standard toolbar.

   Your default e-mail program opens.
3. Click To, click the recipient names, and then click To, Cc, or Bcc.
4. Click OK, and then click the Send button on the toolbar.

   The subject line of the e-mail will contain the file name of the presentation that you are sending.

Did You Know?

You can select names from your address book or contacts list. To select names from your address book or contacts list, click the To button, click recipient names in the Name list, and then click To, Cc, or Bcc.

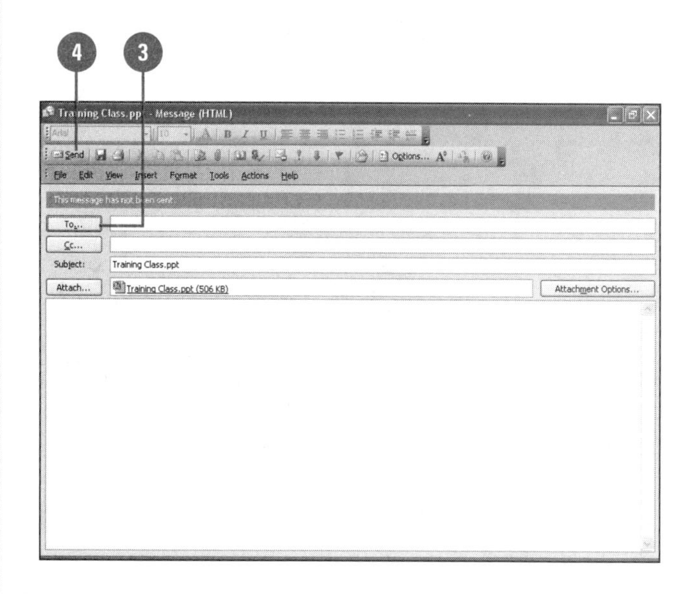

11

Tracking Changes in a Presentation

PP03S-3-1, PP03S-3-3

Once you send your presentation out for review, reviewers edit it using the markup feature so that you can see what they've changed.

After you receive the edited presentations back from reviewers, you have the ability to compare the various versions of the presentation and merge all of the revisions and comments into the original presentation.

When you compare and merge presentations, PowerPoint shows the differences between them as markups. You can accept and reject one or all markups or revisions. The Markup command on the View menu allows you to track changes made to your presentation by using call-outs within the presentation. These call-outs show changes in detail without obscuring the presentation or affecting its layout. They also give you a more visible and comprehensive view of the changes that have been made.

Each change made in PowerPoint is marked with a call-out box that contains the reviewer's name/initials, the date (on comments only), and the details of the actual comment or change. PowerPoint uses a different color call-out box for each reviewer, so you can quickly identify who made the change.

You can use the Reviewing toolbar to track, accept, and reject revisions. The Reviewing toolbar gives you a variety of views and options when reviewing presentations. The table on the right lists the Reviewing toolbar buttons and a brief description of each.

As you review the comments and changes, you can accept or reject them one at a time or all at once. When you accept a change, PowerPoint deletes the text or inserts it into the presentation, as appropriate. When you reject a change, PowerPoint restores the original text.

When you are comparing and merging changes, you can also open the Revisions task pane to easily identify the changes a reviewer has made to a presentation. You can see a list of the changes made by a given reviewer or get a graphical representation of the changes via the Gallery tab. A list menu makes it simple to apply or unapply changes that the reviewer has made.

Reviewing Toolbar

Button Name	Icon	Description
Markup		Allows you to track changes made to your presentation by using call outs within the presentation.
Reviewers	Reviewers...	Allows you to view changes by specific reviewers or all reviewers.
Previous Item		Allows you to move to the previous comment or tracked change.
Next Item		Allows you to move to the next comment or tracked change.
Apply		Allows you to apply a change in a presentation, all changes to a slide, or all changes to the presentation.
Unapply		Allows you to unapply a change in a presentation, all changes to a slide, or all changes to the presentation.
Insert Comment		Allows you to insert a comment into a presentation.
Edit Comment		Allows you to edit a comment within a presentation.
Delete Comment/Marker		Allows you to delete a comment or marker within a presentation or to delete all comments or markers in a presentation.
Revisions Pane		Allows you to show or hide the Revisions Pane.

11

Comparing and Merging Presentations

PP03S-3-1, PP03S-3-3

You can compare presentations to graphically indicate changes between different versions of a document. The changes can be merged into one document or viewed for comparison. For example, you can compare a newer version of a document with an older one to view the differences. When you compare or merge documents, the text that differs between the two versions will be highlighted in a different color or with track reviewing marks. When multiple people are involved in the editing and preparation of a presentation, the Track Changes feature will note who made any particular correction and save a record of all such changes for everyone who works on the presentation later. Each change can be either accepted or rejected by the person who has authority over the final form of the presentation. If you compare and merge two presentations, you can review the changes and accept or reject the results.

Compare and Merge Presentations

1. Open your original presentation.
2. If necessary, click the View menu, point to Toolbars, and then click Reviewing.
3. Click the Tools menu, and then click Compare And Merge Presentations.
4. Locate and select the presentation that you want to compare and merge with the currently opened presentation.
5. If necessary, click Merge, and then click Continue.
6. If necessary, click the Markup button on the Reviewing toolbar to display any comments and changes.

Continue on the next page to review changes from a compare and merge.

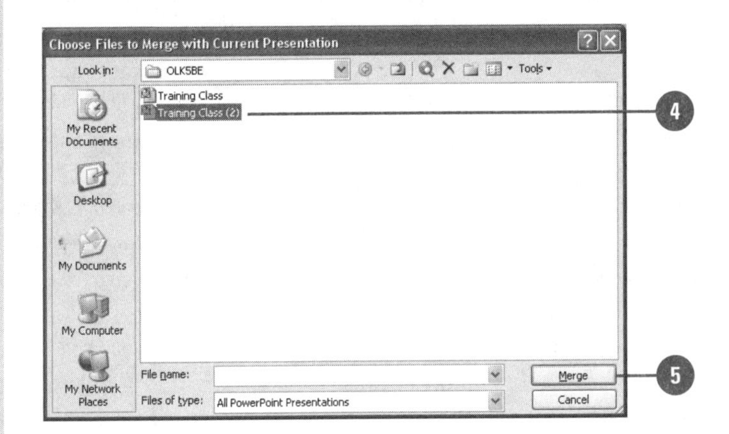

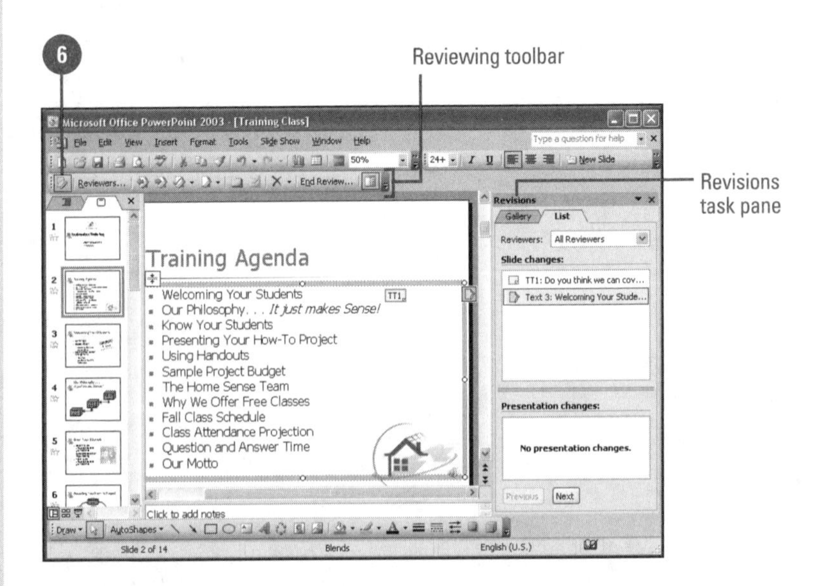

Review Changes from a Compare and Merge

1. If necessary, open the merged presentation.
2. If necessary, click the View menu, point to Toolbars, and then click Reviewing to display the toolbar.
3. Click the Markup button on the Reviewing toolbar, to display any comments and changes.
4. Click a comment or change on a slide or in the Revisions task pane to view it.
5. Select or clear the check boxes for the changes, or click the Apply or Unapply button on the Reviewing toolbar.
6. Click the Previous or Next Item button on the Reviewing toolbar.
7. When you're done, click the Close button on the Revisions task pane, and hide the Reviewing toolbar.

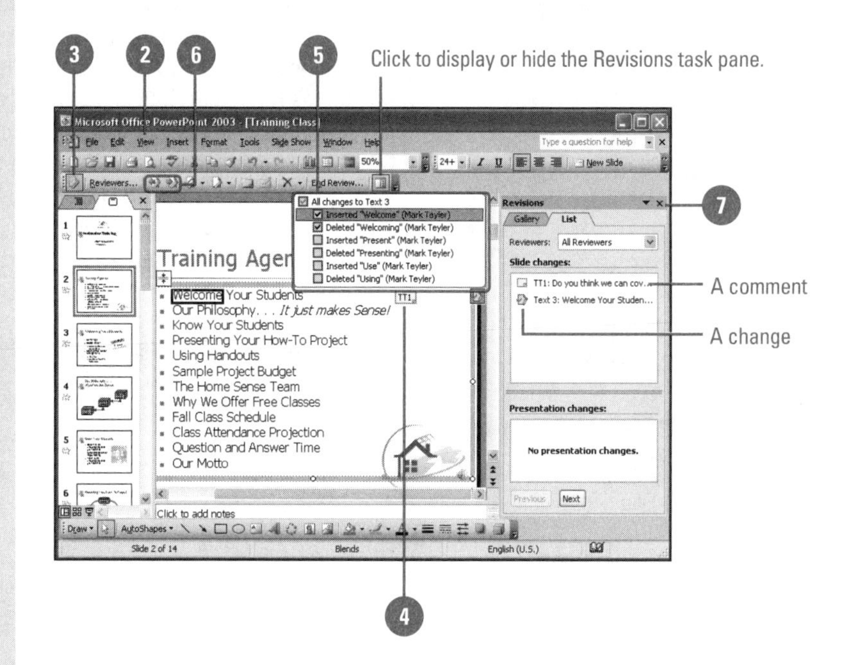

Did You Know?

You can apply or unapply all change to a slide or presentation. On the Reviewing toolbar, click the Apply button list arrow or the Unapply button list arrow, and then click the change command you want.

You can view changes by reviewer. On the Reviewing toolbar, click the Reviewers button, and then select All Reviewers or the individual reviewers you want.

You can view images or a list of revisions. In the Revisions task pane, click the Gallery tab to display slide thumbnails with changes, or click the List tab to display a list of changes.

Broadcasting a Presentation

PP03S-4-5

With online broadcasting, you can give or view a slide show over a computer network or on the Internet. Broadcasting is useful when your audience is large or at remote locations. Using an e-mail program, such as Microsoft Outlook 2003, you can schedule the broadcast just like any other meeting. The presentation saves as a Web page so that all your audience needs is a Web page browser to see the presentation. After the presenter starts the broadcast, each member of the audience needs to join the broadcast. After joining, each member sees a lobby page that contains information about the broadcast before it starts.

Set up and Schedule a New Broadcast

1. Open the presentation you want to broadcast.
2. Click the Slide Show menu, point to Online Broadcast, and then click Schedule A Live Broadcast.
3. Click Settings.
4. Click Browse, navigate to a shared folder, and then click Select.
5. Click OK.
6. Type your description.
7. Click Schedule.
8. Enter schedule information.
9. Enter e-mail addresses for the participants you want to invite to the online broadcast.
10. Click the Send button, and then click Yes to continue.

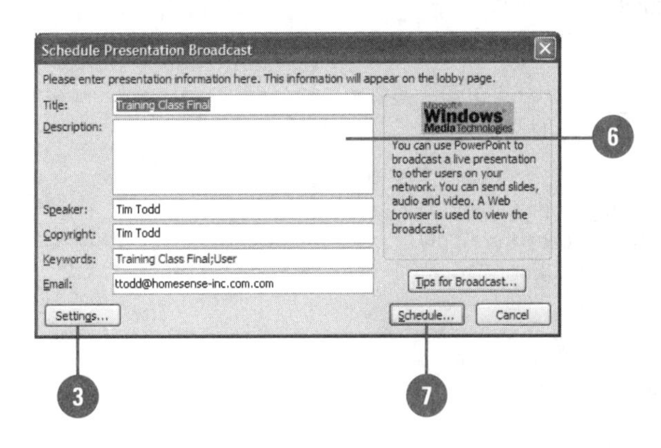

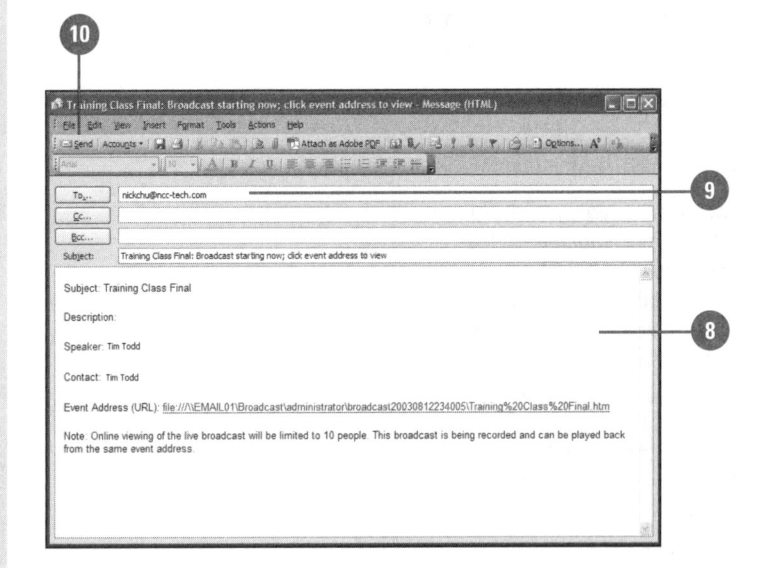

See Also

See "Collaborating in an Online Meeting" on page 276 for more information on using an e-mail program to schedule a broadcast.

Start a Broadcast

1. Open and save the presentation that you want to broadcast.
2. Click the Slide Show menu, point to Online Broadcast, and then click Start Live Broadcast Now.
3. Select the broadcast presentation you want to present.
4. Click Broadcast.

   Your presentation saves as a Web page at the location that you designated.
5. When you're ready to begin, click Start.

Did You Know?

You can join a broadcast. You need Internet Explorer 5.01 or later to join a broadcast. Open the e-mail message that contains the broadcast invitation, and then click the URL for the broadcast.

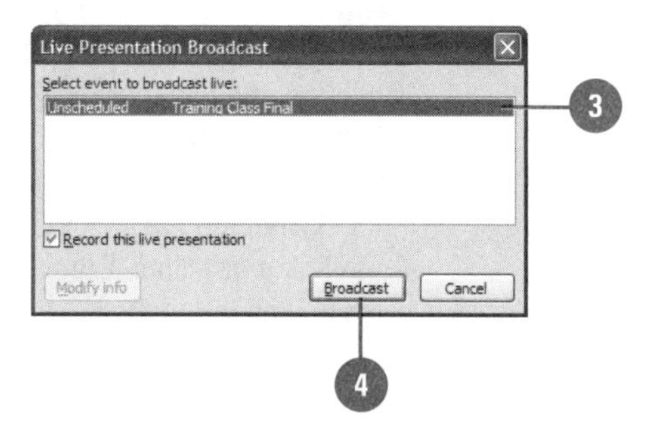

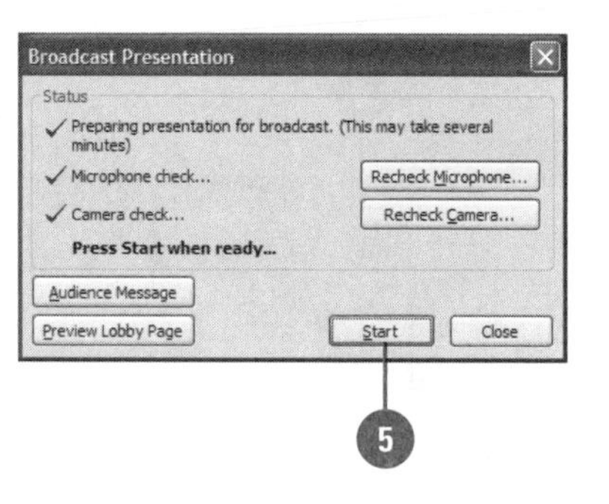

Online broadcast for the audience

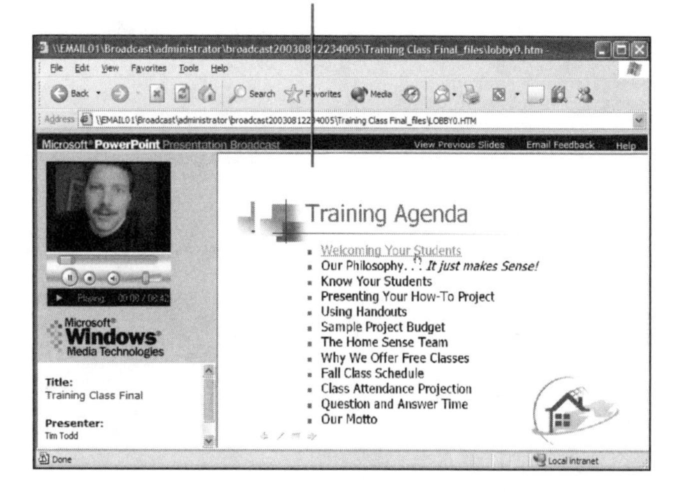

11

Collaborating in an Online Meeting

What's the most convenient way to work together on a presentation with others around the world? **NetMeeting**—a conferencing program for meeting and collaborating over the Internet or a corporate intranet. Participants share and exchange information as if they were in one room. The **host** starts the meeting and controls access to the presentation. When the host allows editing, participants can work on the presentation one at a time. Otherwise, they cannot make changes, but they can see any changes the host makes. All participants can talk to each other, video conference, share programs, collaborate on documents, send files, exchange messages in Chat, transfer files, and draw in the Whiteboard.

Schedule a Meeting

1. Click the Tools menu, point to Online Collaboration, and then click Schedule Meeting.
2. Enter participants' names or e-mail addresses, a subject, and the meeting location.
3. Click Browse, and then double-click a document you want to send.
4. Select a start and end date and time.
5. Type a message.
6. Click the Send button.

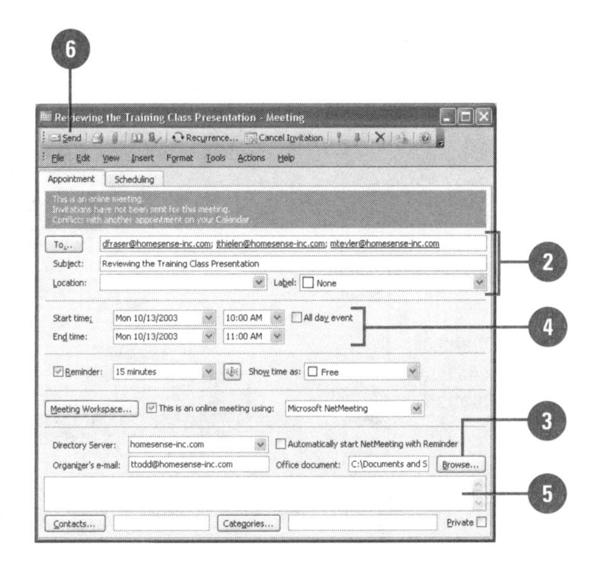

Hold a Meeting

1. Open the document you want to share.
2. Click the Tools menu, point to Online Collaboration, and then click Meet Now.
3. If this is your first meeting, enter your personal information, select a server, and then click OK.
4. Select the participants for the meeting, and then click Call.

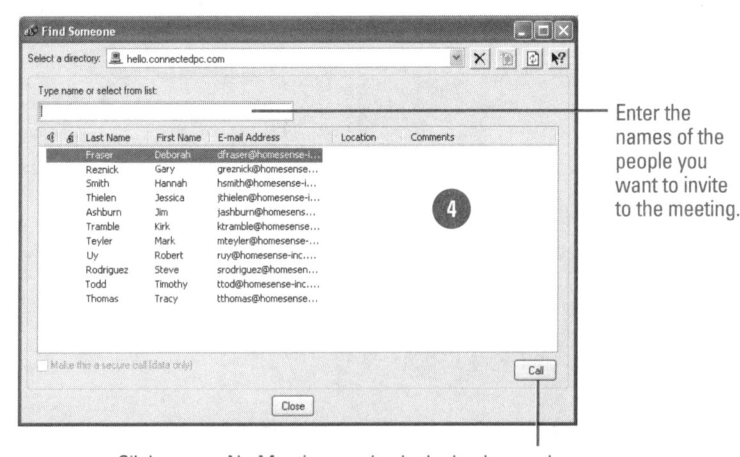

Click to start NetMeeting running in the background.

Collaborate in an Online Meeting

1. As the host, click the Allow Others To Edit button on the Online Meeting toolbar.
2. When collaboration is turned on, click anywhere in the document to gain control. If you are a participant, double-click anywhere in the document to gain control.
3. Click the Allow Others To Edit button again to turn off the collaboration, or press Esc if you don't have control of the document.

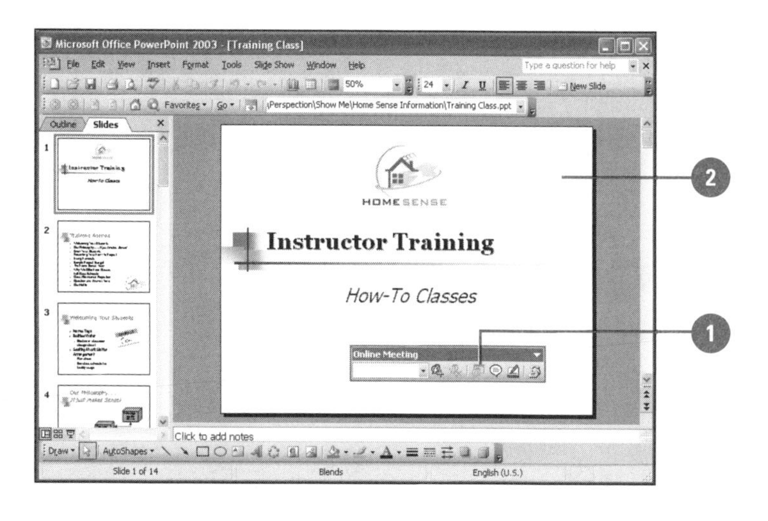

Participate in an Online Meeting

- Use the buttons on the Online Meeting toolbar to participate in an online meeting.

Did You Know?

You can receive an online meeting call. You must have NetMeeting running on your computer to receive an online meeting call.

You can start NetMeeting using the Start menu. Click the Start menu, point to All Programs, point to Accessories, point to Communications, and then click NetMeeting.

Online Meeting Toolbar

Button	Description
[Invite]	Allows the host to invite additional participants to the online meeting
[Remove]	Allows the host to remove a participant from the online meeting
[Allow Others To Edit]	Allows participants to edit and control the presentation during the online meeting
[Chat]	Allows participants to send messages in a Chat session during the online meeting
[Whiteboard]	Allows participants to draw or type on the Whiteboard during the online meeting
[End Meeting]	Allows either the host to end the online meeting for the group or a participant to disconnect

11

Working Together on Office Documents

12

Introduction

Microsoft SharePoint technology, known as SharePoint Team Services, is a collection of products and services which provide the ability for people to engage in communication, document and file sharing, calendar events, sending alerts, tasks planning, and collaborative discussions in a single community solution. SharePoint enables companies to develop an intelligent application which connects their employees, teams, and information so that users can be part of a Knowledge Community.

Before you can use SharePoint Team Services, SharePoint needs to be set up and configured on a Windows 2003 Server by your network administrator or Internet service provider.

SharePoint is integrated into Office 2003 and enables you to share data and documents using the Shared Workspace task pane directly from Office PowerPoint 2003, Office Word 2003, or Office Excel 2003. The Shared Workspace task pane allows you to see the list of team members collaborating on the current project, find out who is online, send an instant message, and review tasks and other resources. You can use the Shared Workspace task pane to create one or more document workspaces where you can collect, organize, modify, share, and discuss Office documents. The Shared Workspace task pane displays information related to the document workspaces stored on SharePoint Team Services.

What You'll Do

View SharePoint Team Services

Administer SharePoint Team Services

Store Documents in the Library

View Team Members

Set Up Alerts

Assign Project Tasks

Create an Event

Create Contacts

Hold Web Discussions

Work with Shared Workspace

Install Windows 2003 and SharePoint Server 2003

Viewing SharePoint Team Services

Microsoft SharePoint displays the contents of its home page so you can work efficiently with your site. The available pages are: The Home Page, Manage Content Page, Manage Users Page, Change Portal Site Navigation Page, Change Settings Page, and Site Settings Page. You can navigate within the site by clicking on each of the links within the home page. Certain Administrative Access rights are needed in order to view these pages.

Home Page view is the first page your users see when they access the URL for Microsoft SharePoint Server. If you are within a Windows 2003 Active Domain and have a Domain Account, you will not be prompted to type in your user credentials and password. If you do not have an account you will be asked to type in your credentials to have the page display your SharePoint Site. Please contact your Systems Administrator if you do not have access to the SharePoint Server.

Documents and Lists Page view allows you to manage content to your SharePoint Site. You can create Portal sites, a Document Library, Upload Graphic Images in an Image Library Site, Create Calender Events, Create an Address Book of Contents, setup Project Events, Create a Web Discussion site, and setup Surveys. Within your Document and Lists page you will be able to administer your content to provide users with content management capabilities.

Manage Users Page view allows you to add users to your SharePoint Site. If their e-mail address is located within their Domain Account on Windows 2003, SharePoint will e-mail the users you created, and then invite them to join in to the SharePoint Server. From the Manage Users page you can add, delete, and change the permissions of a user for your site.

Home Page

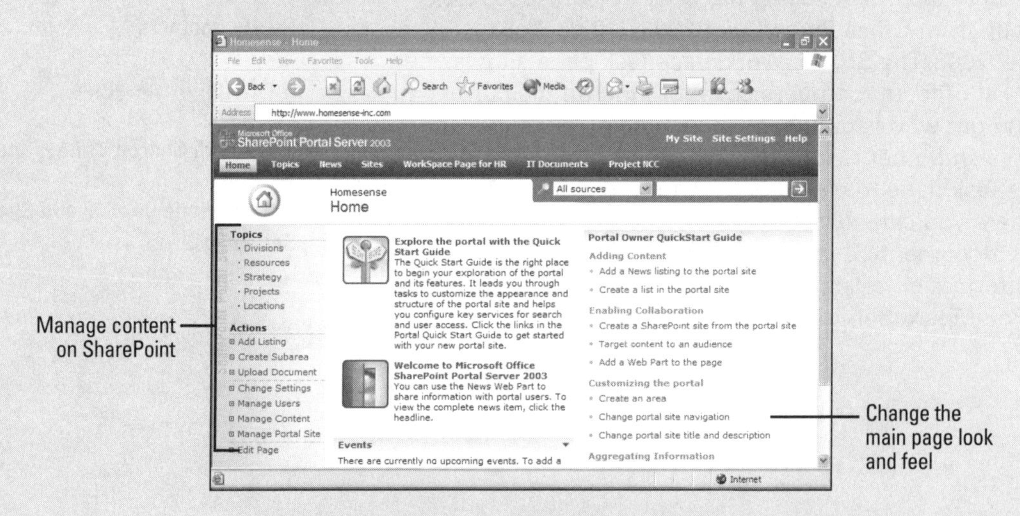

Documents and Lists Page

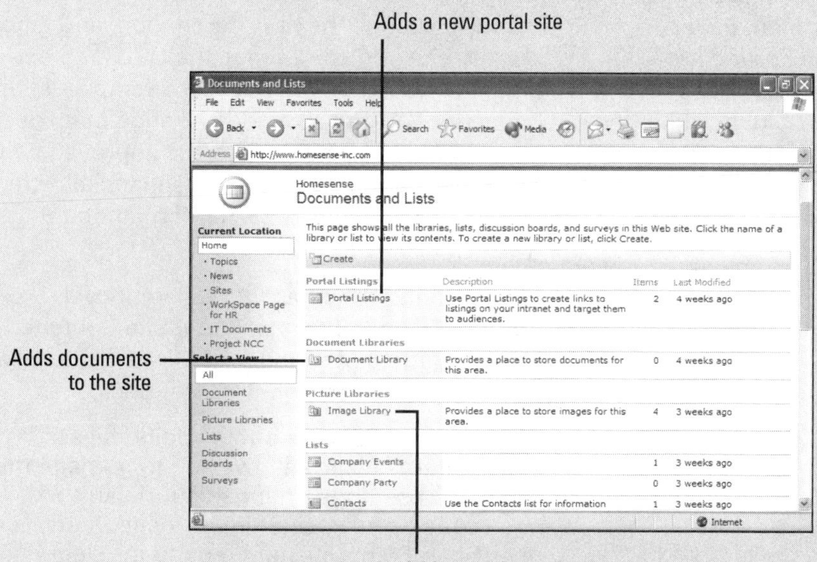

Manage Users Page

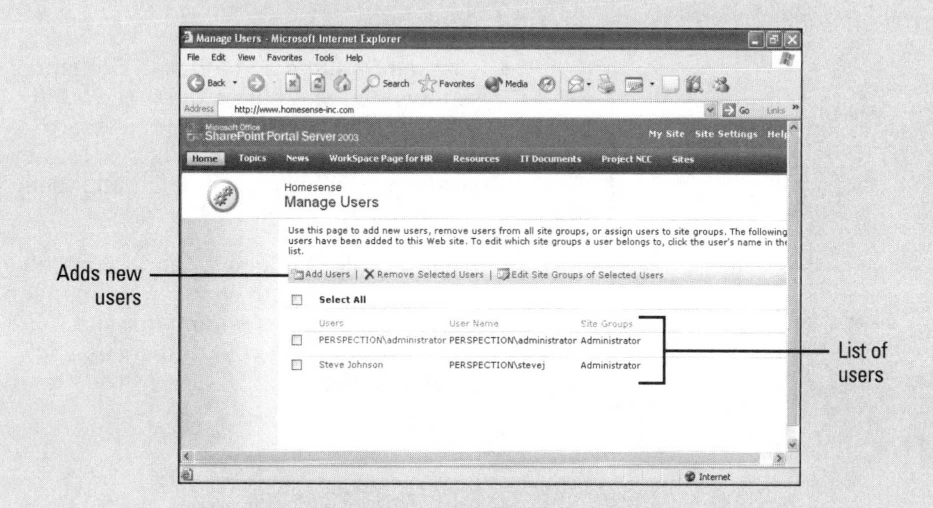

Administering SharePoint Team Services

Administering Microsoft SharePoint is easy within the site settings. The available pages are: The Home Page, Manage Content Page, Manage Users Page, Change Portal Site Navigation Page, Change Settings Page, and Site Settings Page. You can navigate within the site by clicking on each of the links within the home page. Certain Administrative Access rights are needed in order to view these pages.

Change Portal Site Navigation Page gives you a hierarchy structure to make changes to other portal sites within SharePoint. If you want to move your site to the top-level within SharePoint or modify your sub-level pages, you can do so with the SharePoint Portal Site Navigation Page.

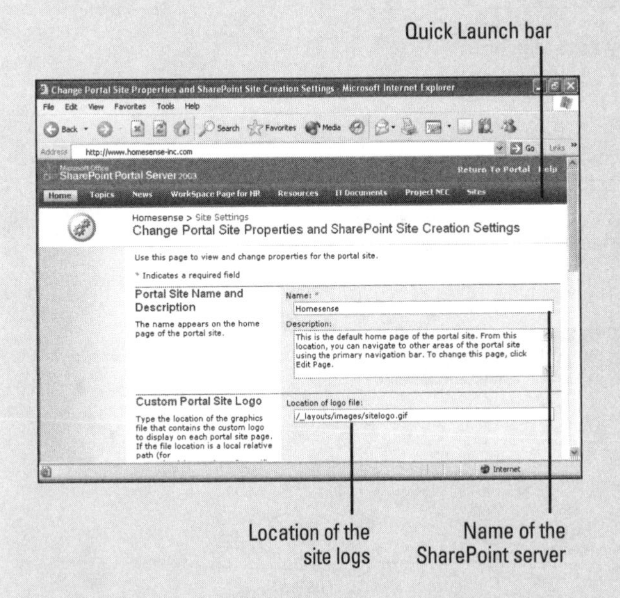

Change Settings Page allows you to swiftly customize the look and feel of your portal site. You can change the title, description, and logo for the site. You can change the URL for creating sites based on the published templates for your site. You can also add a change management process by having the site approved by a manager before being published, and allowing you to change your contact information for your site.

Site Settings Page has four different categories: General Settings, Portal Site Content, Search Settings and Indexed Content, and User Profile, Audiences, and Personal Sites.

- **General Settings** offers additional security features, which allows you to manage the alerts settings, change your default SMTP e-mail server, change the location of your SharePoint Site, and modify the Regional Language Settings to your site.
- **Portal Site Content** allows you to manage the site structure, view your site lists and document libraries, import data into your SharePoint Server, and add link listings to your site.
- **Search Settings and Indexed Content** allows you to create Meta tags within your SharePoint Server, create search crawlers to investigate your site for new key words which will create better search results within your site.
- **User Profile, Audiences, and Personal Sites** allows you to change and manage your user profiles within your site. You can also manage your audiences and personal settings.

Change Settings Page

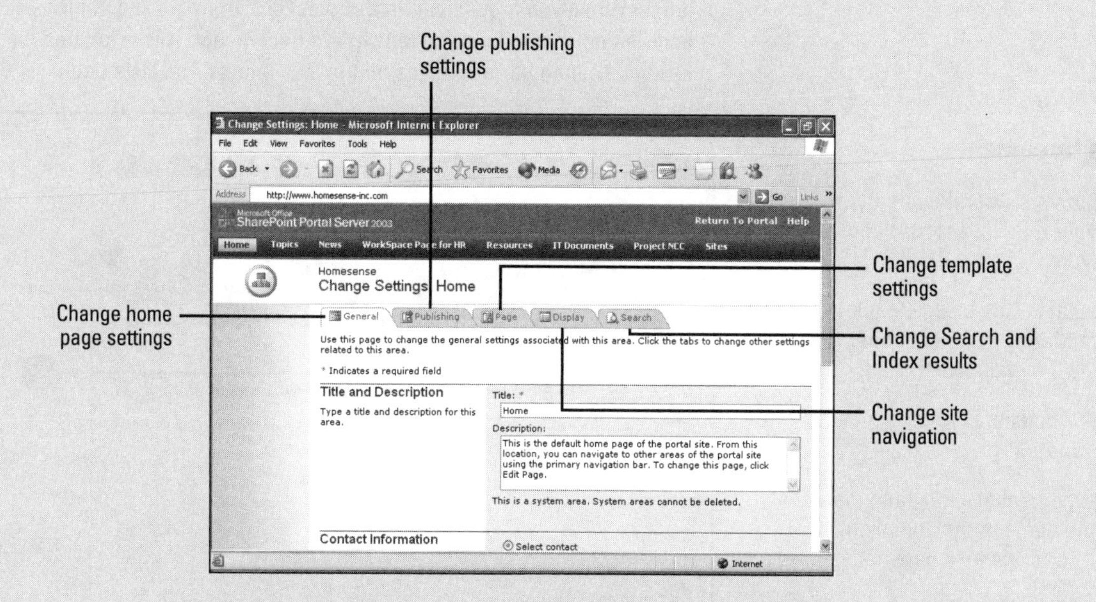

Site Settings Page

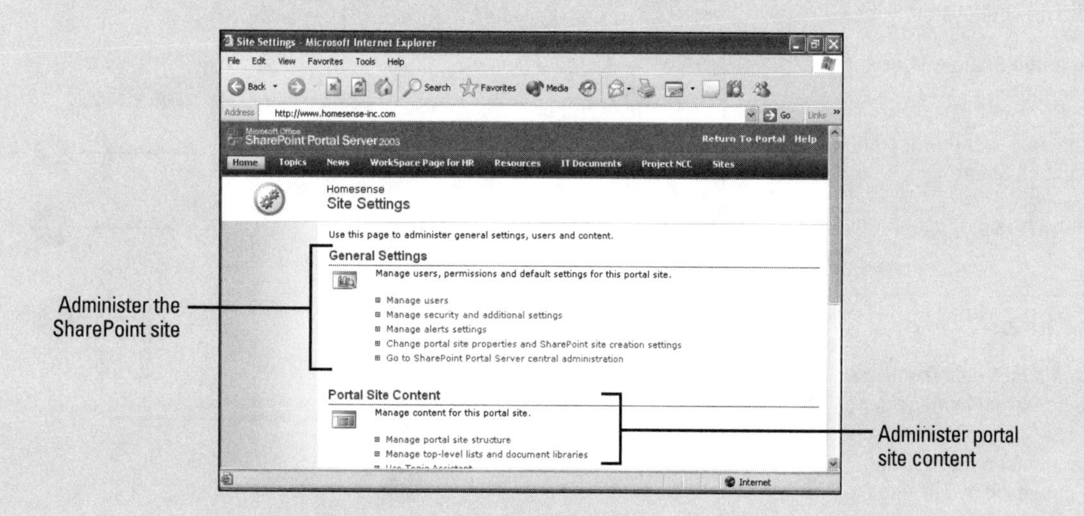

Storing Documents in the Library

A SharePoint **Document Library** is a central depository of files you can share with company employees, team members and permissible members with access. Within the Document Library you can create a list of common documents for a project, documented procedures, and company wide documents for departments such as human resources or finance. When you first install SharePoint 2003, the Web site comes with a built-in document library called **shared documents**. This is located on the Quick Launch bar as well as on the Documents And Lists page.

Upload a Document

1. Log into your SharePoint server with your domain account and password.
2. On the main Home page, click Create Manage Content under the Actions Sidebar.
3. On the Documents And Lists page, click Create.
4. Click Document Library, and then type the name of the document library for creating a new page.
5. Click Upload Document.
6. Type the location of the document, or click Browse to search for the document on your system.
7. Type the name of the owner and a brief description.
8. Select the status of the document, and then click Save.
9. Click the Save And Close button.

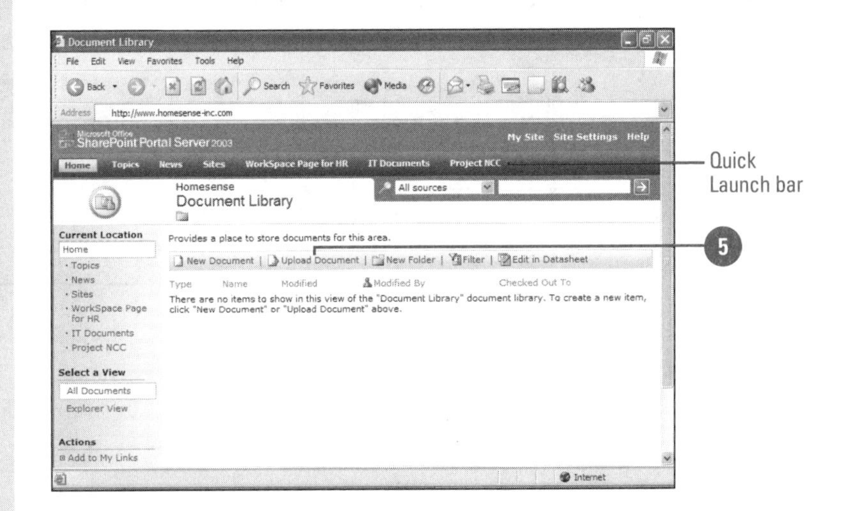

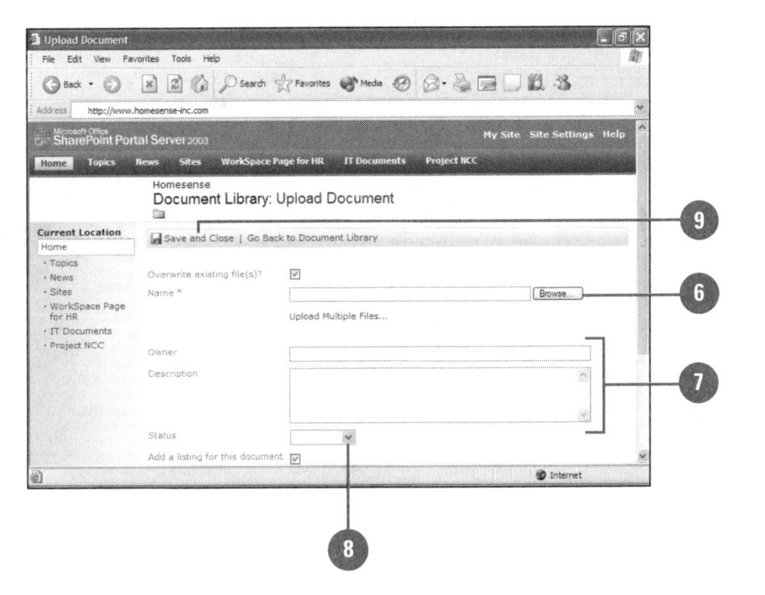

Did You Know?

You can check documents in and out. SharePoint's document management system ensures that only one person at a time can access a file. You can check out a document by clicking the Content menu in the document library, and then clicking Check Out.

Viewing Team Members

After you have setup a portal page, you need to specify a user access list to the site. Specifying a user access list controls who can access the site, as well as who has administrative privileges. With integration to Microsoft Active Directory, users can be managed with the same groups as your domain. The access will allow your users to perform a specific action in your site by assigning them to the appropriate groups.

Add New Members to the Site

1. Log into your SharePoint server with your domain account and password.
2. On the main Home page, click Give User Access To The Portal.
3. On the Manage Users page, click Add Users.
4. Type the name of their domain account.
5. Click the type of permissions you want to give this user:
   - **Reader.** Gives the user read-only access to the portal site.
   - **Contributor.** Gives the user write access to the document libraries and lists.
   - **Web Designer.** Gives the user the ability to create lists and document libraries and customize the overall look and feel of the site.
   - **Administrator.** Gives the user full access of the portal site.
   - **Content Manager.** Gives the user the ability to manage lists, libraries, sites and moderate the discussions.
   - **Member.** Gives the user the ability to personalize the portal site content and create lists.
6. Click Next, fill out any additional information, and then click Finish.

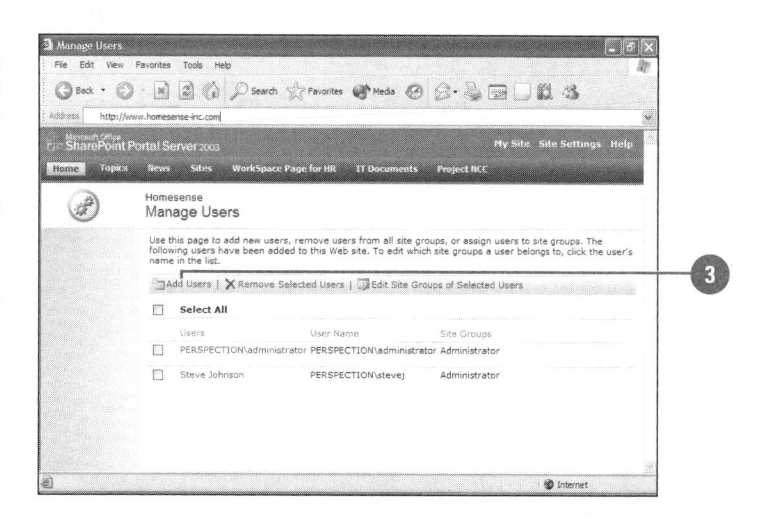

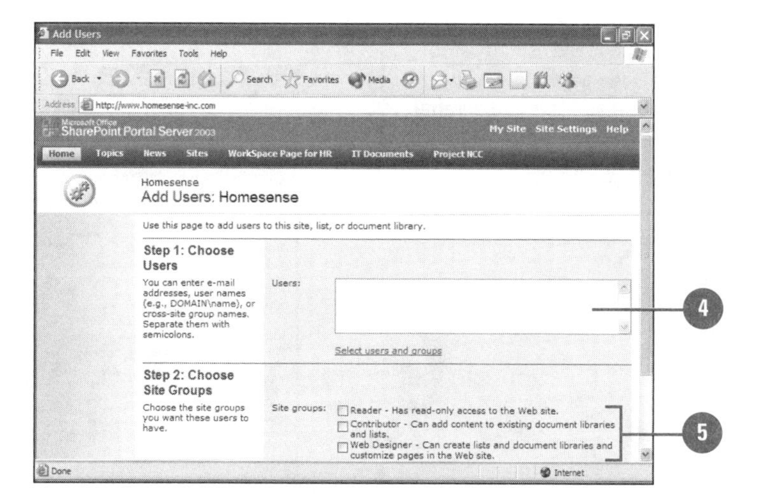

Setting Up Alerts

An Alert notifies you when there is new information which has been changed on the portal site. You can customize your areas of interests and define when you want to be notified after the site has been updated. You can define an alert to track new matches to a search query, changes to the site page, or a new site addition.

Create Your E-Mail Alert

1. Log into your SharePoint server with your domain account and password.
2. In a Portal Site, click Alert Me.
3. Define your delivery options, and then click Next.
4. Click Advanced Options if you want to set up filters.
5. Click OK.

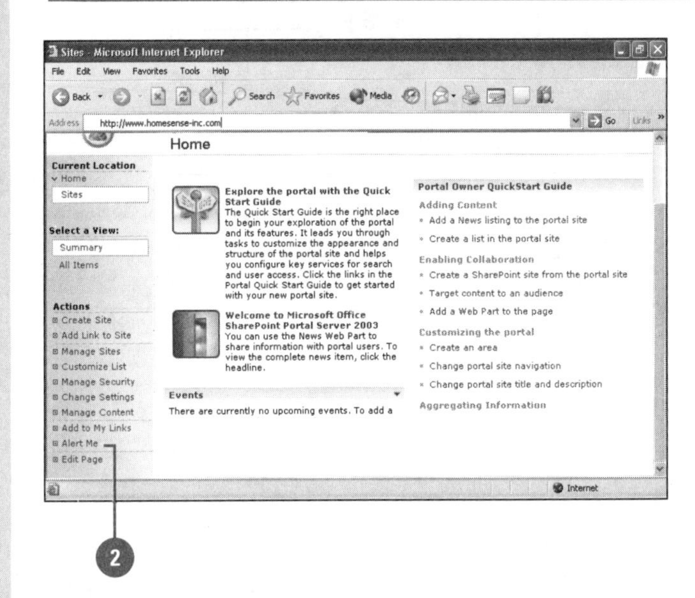

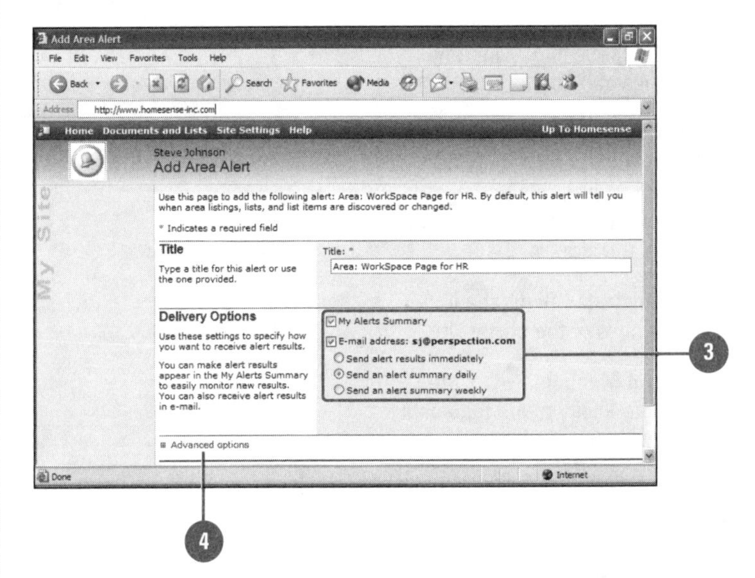

Did You Know?

You can use the following filter categories to be alerted with: Search queries, document and listings, areas, new listings, sites added to the site directory, sharepoint lists and libraries, list items, portal site users, and backward compatible document library folders.

Assigning Project Tasks

Assigning a project task is another way you can use SharePoint to collaborate on the site. By creating a task, you can manage your team with status updates. You can also provide a central way to manage the effectiveness of a project. Since this is a Web based system, everyone can access this with a simple Web browser.

Add a Task Item to Your Site

1. Log into your SharePoint server with your domain account and password.
2. On the main home page, click Create Manage Content under the Actions Sidebar.
3. Click Create, and then click Tasks.
4. Type the name of the task, add in an optional description, click Yes if you want to add the task to the menu bar, and then click Create.
5. Click New Item.
6. Type the title, set the priority, status, and completion percentage, assign your resource, add a description, and then set your due date.
7. Click the Save And Close button.

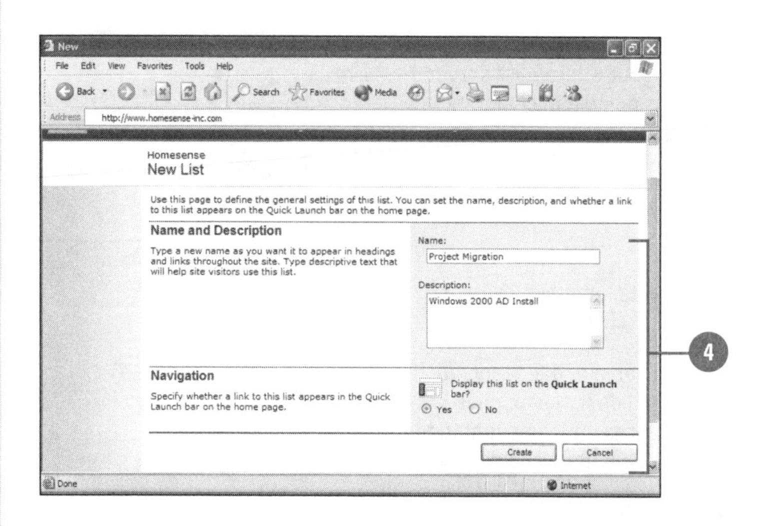

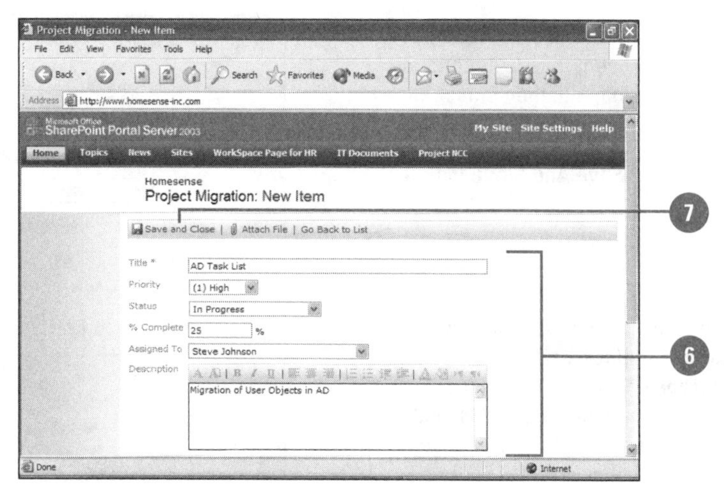

Did You Know?

You can use the Upload button to add an attachment. A general rule of thumb would be to keep your attachments under 1 MB, however, unless your administrator has set rights on your site, you are free to upload as much as you want.

Creating an Event

Creating an event allows you to send out notices on upcoming meetings, deadlines, and other important events. This is helpful if you need to send out information to a wide range of people or in a project you are working on. If you are looking to set up a meeting to a large group of people, you may want to set up an event which is seen by everyone who logs in.

Setup New Events

1. Log into your SharePoint server with your domain account and password.
2. On the main Home page, click Create Manage Content under the Actions Sidebar.
3. Click Create, and then click Events.
4. Type the name of the event, add in an optional description, click Yes , if you want to add the event to the menu bar, and then click Create.
5. Click New Item.
6. Type the event title, select a begin and end event time, a description, the location, and then select an recurrence option.
7. Click the Save And Close button.

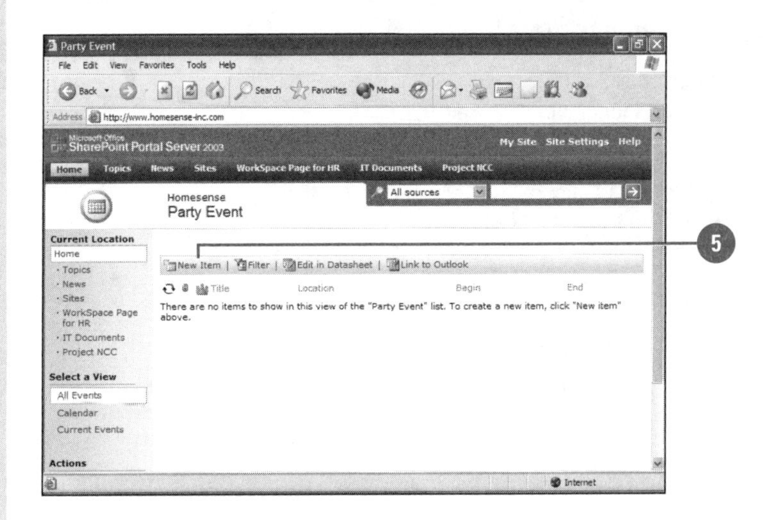

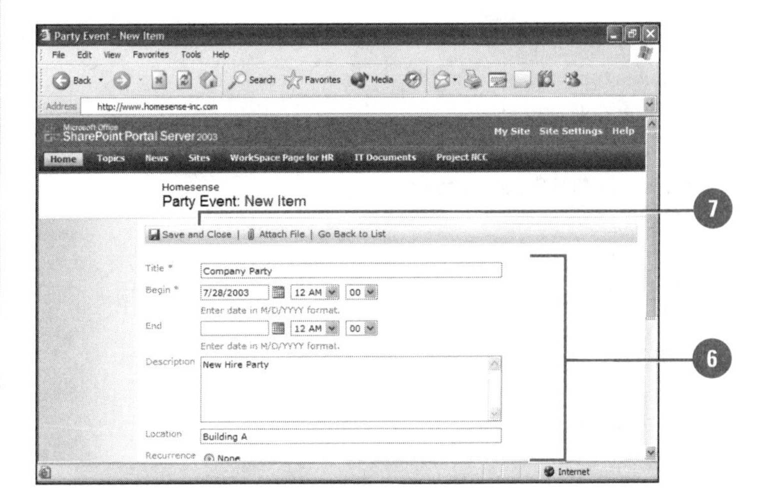

Did You Know?

You can use a new collaboration feature in Outlook 2003 called Meeting Workspace. Meeting Workspace allows you to gather information and organize everyone when you create a scheduled meeting event. To create a Meeting Workspace in Outlook 2003, prepare a calender event and set up your attendees for the event. Then click Meeting Workspace to link this to your SharePoint Server. You may need to type in the URL of your SharePoint server. Please get this from your System Administrator.

Link to Events in Outlook

1. On the Events page, click Link To Outlook.
2. If a security dialog box appears asking for your approval prior to adding a folder, click Yes.

   You will be prompted to type in the credentials of your user account.
3. Type in your Domain User credentials and password, and then click OK.
4. Click Other Calendars to view your SharePoint calendar.

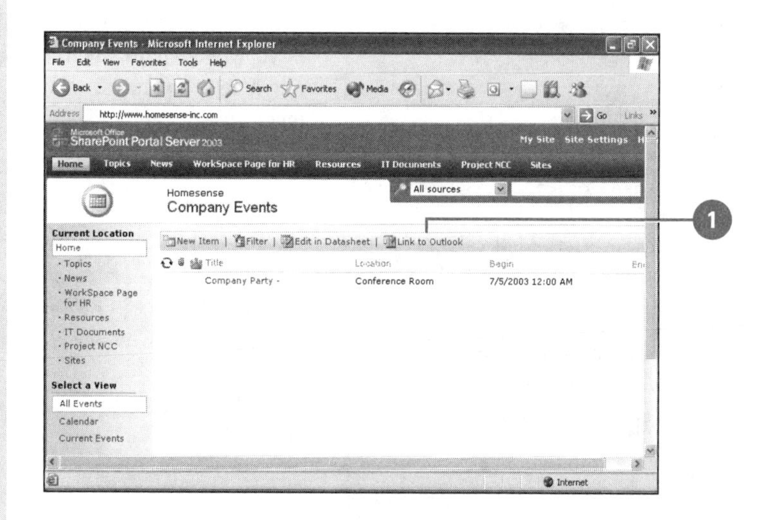

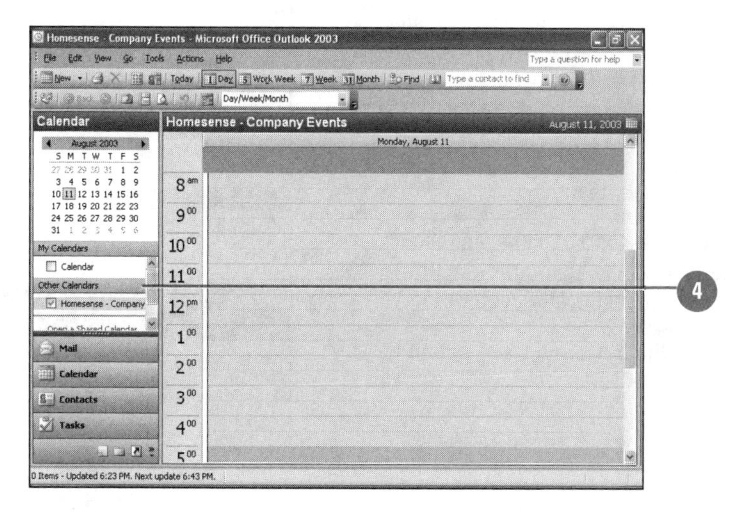

Did You Know?

You will not be able to change the events in your SharePoint calendar folder within Outlook 2003. You will only have read access rights within Outlook 2003. To change the SharePoint calendar information, return to your SharePoint Site, and then modify the information under your Events Site.

Creating Contacts

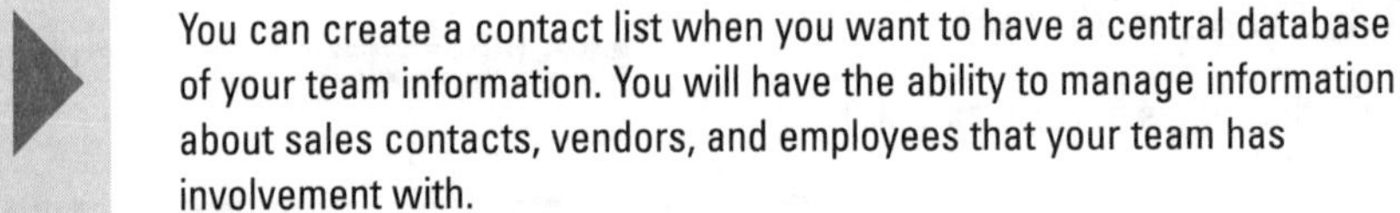

You can create a contact list when you want to have a central database of your team information. You will have the ability to manage information about sales contacts, vendors, and employees that your team has involvement with.

Create a Contact List

1. Log into your SharePoint server with your domain account and password.
2. On the main Home page, click Create Manage Content under the Actions Sidebar.
3. Click Create, and then click Contacts.
4. Type the name of the contact, add an optional description, click Yes if you want to add the contacts list to the menu bar, and then click Create.
5. Click New Item.
6. Type the contact name, and then add in all the appropriate information on your contact.
7. Click the Save And Close button.

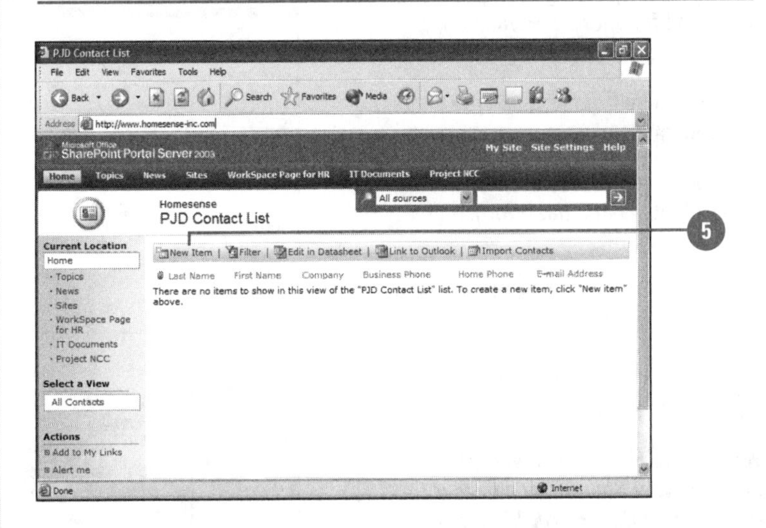

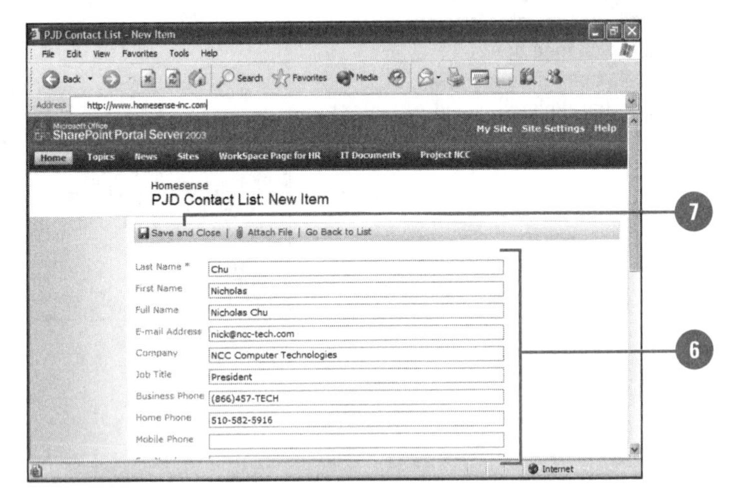

Link to Contacts in Outlook

1. On the Contacts page, click Link To Outlook.
2. If a security dialog box appears asking for your approval prior to adding a folder, click Yes.

   You will be prompted to type in the credentials of your user account.
3. Type your Domain User credentials and password, and then click OK.
4. Click Other Contacts to view your SharePoint contacts.

Did You Know?

You will not be able to change the contact information in your SharePoint contacts folder within Outlook 2003. You will only have read access rights within Outlook 2003. To change the SharePoint contacts information, return to your SharePoint Site, and then modify the information under your Contacts Site.

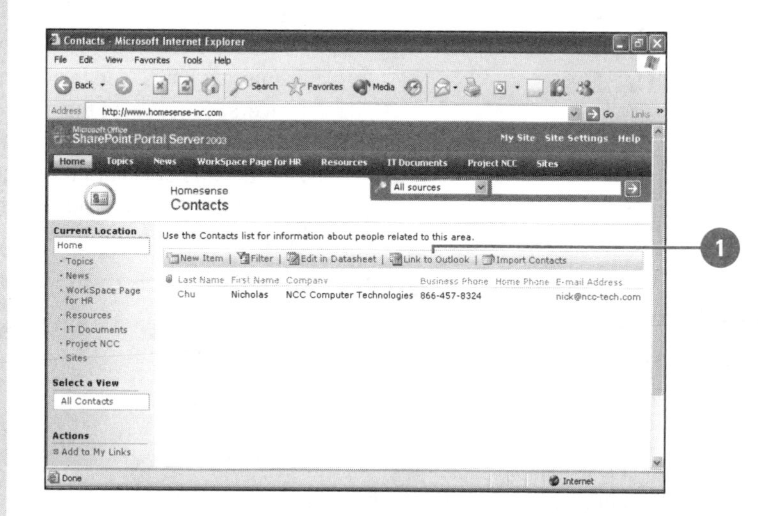

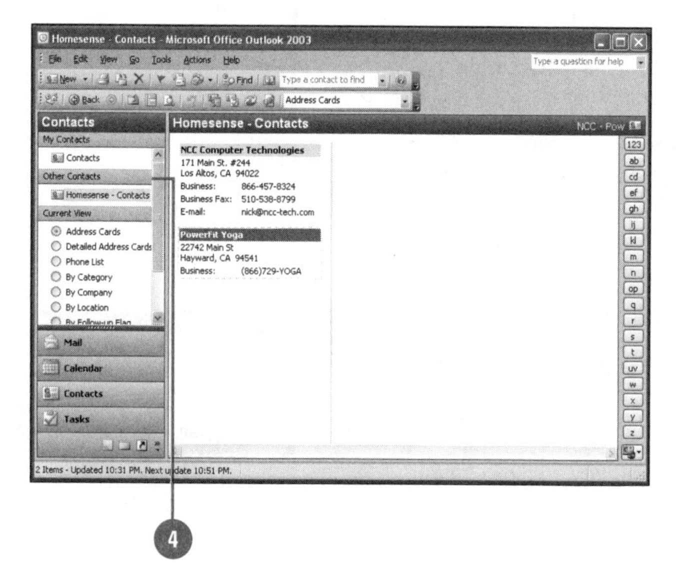

Holding Web Discussions

Web discussions are threaded discussions which allow users to collaborate together in a Web environment. Users can add and view discussion items, add in documents during the discussion and carry on conversations. Since the discussions are entered into a different area than the shared document, users can modify the document without effecting the collaborative discussion. Users can add changes to read-only documents and allow multiple users to create and edit discussion items simultaneously.

Hold a Web Discussion

1. Log into your SharePoint server with your domain account and password.
2. On the main Home page, click Create Manage Content under the Actions Sidebar.
3. Click Create, and then click Discussion Boards.
4. Type the name of the Discussion Board, add an optional description, click Yes, if you want to add this to the menu bar, and then click Create.
5. Click New Discussion.
6. Type the subject name, and then add in all the appropriate information on your discussion.
7. Click the Save And Close button.

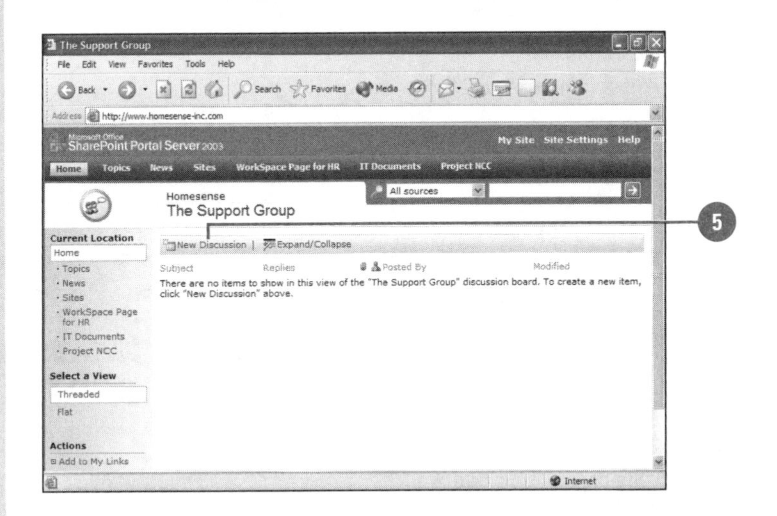

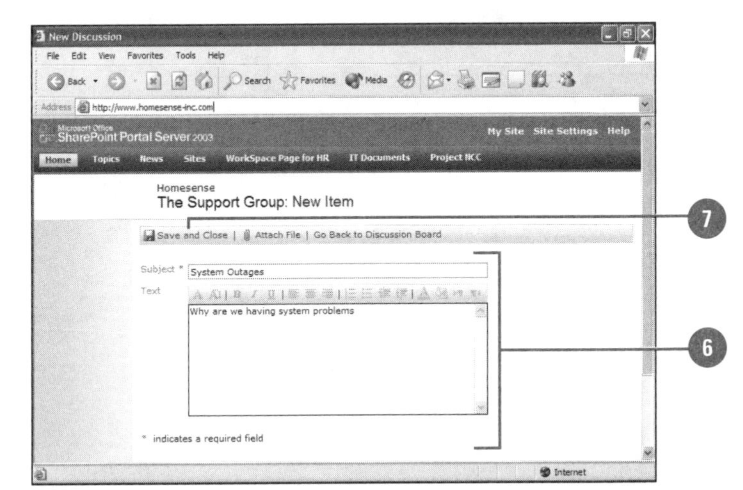

Working with Shared Workspace

Using Shared Workspace icons allow you to connect to your SharePoint Server in an Office 2003 program: Word, Excel and PowerPoint. Each icon displays different information on your document. Users can view the status of a document, see the availability of a document, display properties of a document, and list additional resources, folders, and access rights of a document. You can also show the current tasks which are assigned for your document, display the online team members of your group, and display the workspace information.

Use Shared Workspace in an Office 2003 Program

1. Log into your SharePoint server with your domain account and password.
2. In an Office 2003 program (Word, Excel and PowerPoint), click on the Tools menu, and then click Shared Workspace.

   If you open Shared Workspace for the first time you may be prompted to create a new workspace area.
3. Use the Shared Workspace Navigation bar tools.
   - **Status.** Displays the checked-in/checked-out status of your current document.
   - **Members**. Shows you who is online from your Team Members Group.
   - **Tasks**. Shows you the current tasks assigned for this current document and the completion status.
   - **Documents**. Displays the name and workspace of the selected document.
   - **Links**. Displays additional resources, folders, and lists the access of files.
   - **Document Info**. Displays the author of the document and the properties of the document.

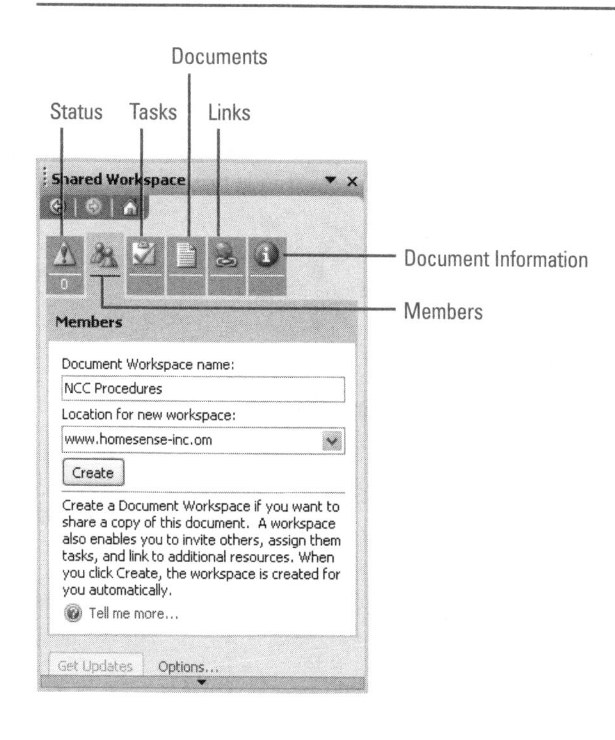

Installing Windows 2003 and SharePoint Server 2003

In order for you to install the new version of SharePoint, you must Install Windows 2003 Server. Windows 2003 Server uses the new .NET Architecture Internet Information Server (IIS) 6.0, Microsoft SMTP (Simple Mail Transport Protocol) Service and Microsoft SQL Server 2000 Desktop Engine (MSDE 2000) or Microsoft SQL Server 2000 Enterprise or Standard Edition (64-bit), with Microsoft SQL Server 2000 SP3 or later.

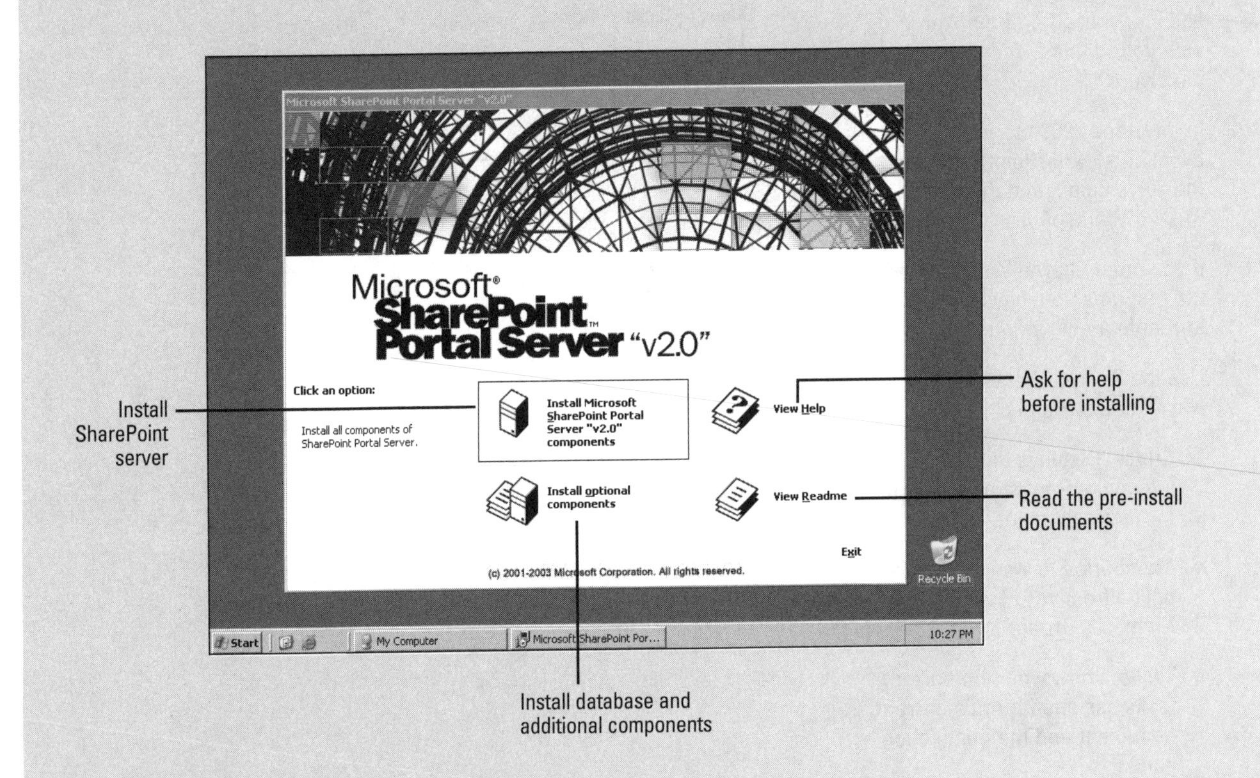

Customizing the Way You Work

13

Introduction

Once you've become familiar with Microsoft Office PowerPoint 2003 and all the features it contains, you might want to customize the way you work with PowerPoint. You can change your view settings so that your PowerPoint window looks the way you want it to. PowerPoint comes with set defaults, such as viewing the startup task pane or vertical ruler, how many files you've recently opened, which you can change to a new default.

You can change the configuration of the menus and toolbars that you use. You can also create your own toolbar for just the commands that you use when creating your presentations. Smart Tags can be activated to link data between your Office programs. Macros can simplify common repetitive tasks that you use regularly in PowerPoint. Macros can reside on PowerPoint toolbars for easy access. If a macro has a problem executing a task, PowerPoint can help you debug, or fix the error in your macro.

Some of the other PowerPoint customization features allow you to set a default font and related attributes to use when you are typing text in text boxes. Other defaults might be the color or line style of an AutoShape that you create.

You can also use the Language bar to perform a variety of functions in PowerPoint. The Language bar allows you to control your slide show presentation with your voice, or execute various commands without having to use the keyboard. PowerPoint will need to be trained to your voice in order to perform the voice recognition. You can also dictate text directly into your slides with the speech recognition feature. Or maybe, you want to add handwritten notes to a slide in your presentation.

What You'll Do

Set PowerPoint Options

Customize the Way You Perform Commands

Simplify Tasks with Macros

Control a Macro

Assign a Macro to a Toolbar or Menu

Customize the Way You Create Objects

Control PowerPoint with Your Voice

Execute Voice Commands

Dictate Text

Handwrite Your Text

Use Smart Tags

Use Multiple Languages

Setting PowerPoint Options

You can customize the performance of many PowerPoint features including its editing, saving, spelling, viewing, and printing procedures. The initial settings for these procedures are called the **defaults**. If you change a default setting, PowerPoint will use the new setting for all subsequent PowerPoint sessions until you change the setting again.

Change View Defaults

1. Click the Tools menu, and then click Options.
2. Click the View tab.
3. Change the View settings as necessary.
4. Click OK.

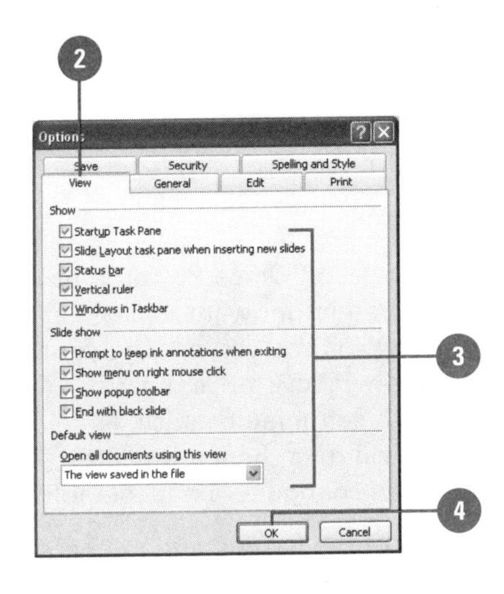

Change General Defaults

1. Click the Tools menu, and then click Options.
2. Click the General tab.
3. Change the General settings as necessary.
4. Click OK.

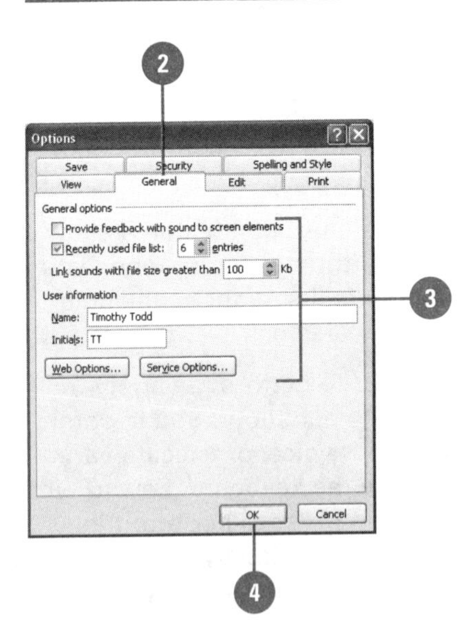

Did You Know?

You can control viruses. To help reduce the risk of macro infection, set the macro security level to High or Medium. Click the Tools menu, click Options, click the Security tab, click Macro Security, click a Security Level, and then click OK twice.

Change Edit Defaults

1. Click the Tools menu, and then click Options.
2. Click the Edit tab.
3. Change the Edit settings as necessary.
4. Click OK.

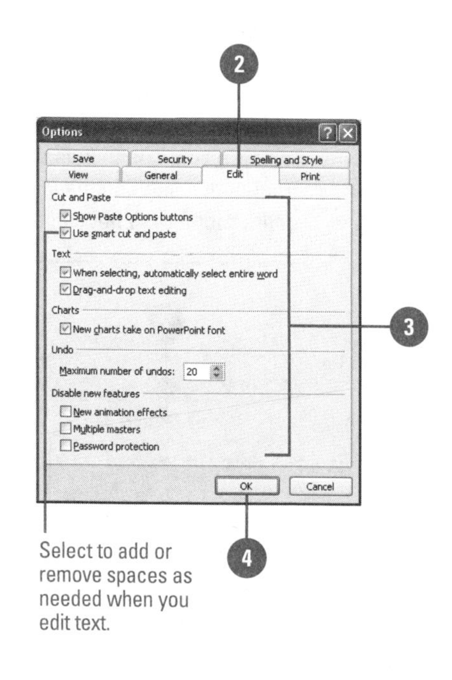

Select to add or remove spaces as needed when you edit text.

Change Spelling and Style Defaults

1. Click the Tools menu, and then click Options.
2. Click the Spelling And Style tab.
3. Change the Spelling and Style settings as necessary.
4. Click OK.

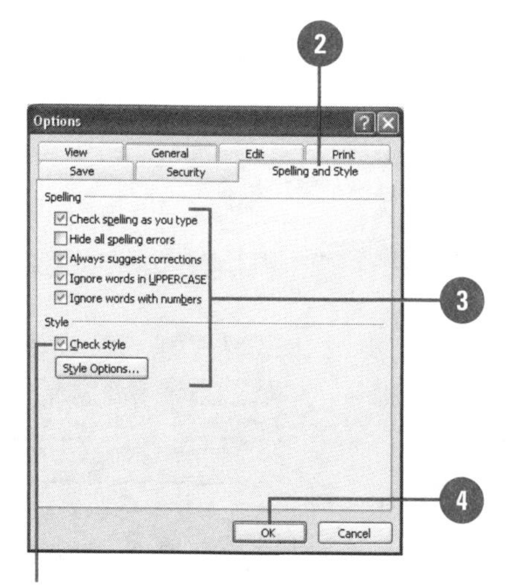

Select to have PowerPoint review the style in your presentation.

Did You Know?

You can set default print settings for a specific presentation. Click the Tools menu, click Options, click the Print tab, click the Use The Following Print Settings option, click the print settings you want, and then click OK.

Customizing the Way You Perform Commands

You can change the default toolbar options, such as having the Standard and Formatting toolbars share one row, or you can create new toolbars and customize the existing ones to maximize your efficiency. Toolbars are self-adjusting. That is, commands that you use more often stay on the toolbars, and commands that you use less often are replaced with more frequently used commands. Toolbars are also movable; you can drag entire toolbars to new locations on the screen.

Change Menu and Toolbar Options

1. Click the Tools menu, and then click Customize.
2. Click the Options tab.
3. Change the Options settings as necessary.
4. Click Close.

Add a Toolbar

1. Click the Tools menu, and then click Customize.
2. Click the Toolbars tab, click New, type a toolbar name, and then click OK.
3. Click the Commands tab, click a category, and then click a command.
4. Drag the command to a toolbar to add it to the toolbar or drag a button off the toolbar to remove it from the toolbar, and then click Close.

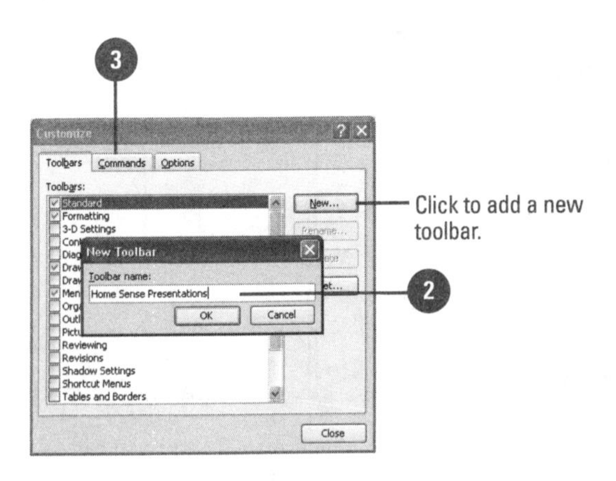

Click to add a new toolbar.

Add Buttons to a Toolbar

1. Click the Tools menu, and then click Customize.
2. Click the Toolbars tab, and then double-click the toolbar to which you want to add buttons.

   The toolbar is displayed.
3. Click the Commands tab.
4. Click a category, and then click a command.
5. Drag the command to a toolbar to add it to the toolbar or drag a button off the toolbar to remove it from the toolbar, and then click Close.

   If the command has a button icon associated with it, that icon appears. If it doesn't, the name of the command appears.
6. Repeat steps 4 and 5 to add all the buttons you want to the toolbar.
7. Click Close.

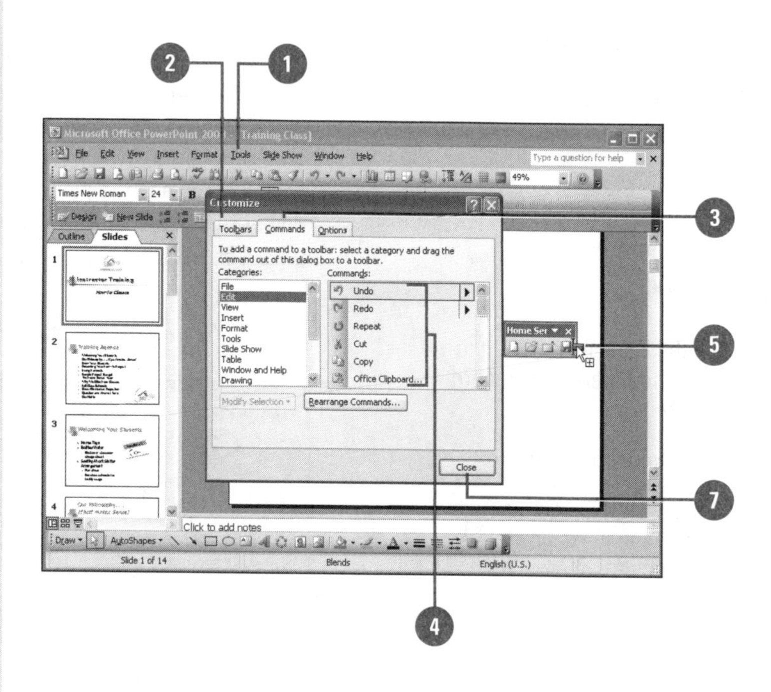

Reposition a Toolbar

1. Position the pointer over the vertical bar at the left edge of the Formatting toolbar.

   The pointer changes to the four-headed arrow pointer.
2. Drag the toolbar to the middle of the screen.

   The floating toolbar now has a title bar, a Toolbar Options list arrow, and a Close button.

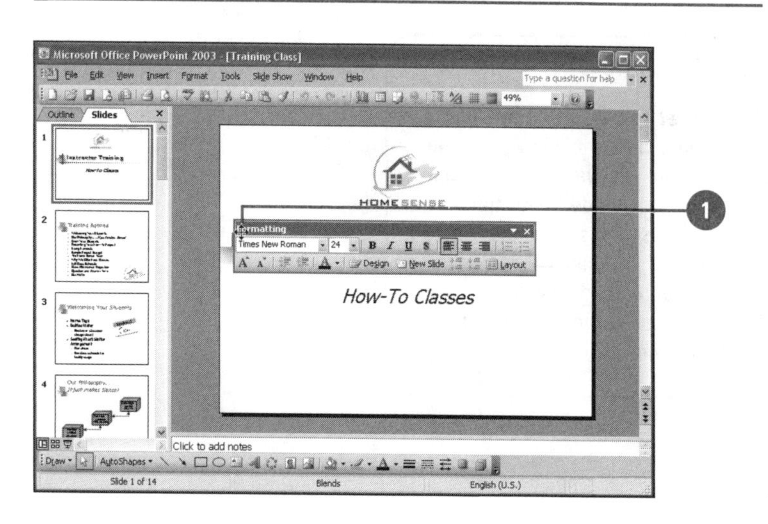

Simplifying Tasks with Macros

If you find yourself repeating the same set of steps over and over or if you need to add new functionality to PowerPoint, you could create a macro. PowerPoint macros can run several tasks for you at the click of a button. You can easily create your own macros using PowerPoint's Macro Recorder, which records your actions, and then replays them. You can then add the macro to the PowerPoint toolbars or to the PowerPoint menus for easy access.

Record a Macro

1. Click the Tools menu, point to Macro, and then click Record New Macro.
2. Type a name for the macro.
3. If necessary, type the name of the presentation in which you want to place the macro.
4. If you want, add to the description of the macro in the Description box.
5. Click OK.
6. Perform the actions you intend to place in the macro. Any action you perform in PowerPoint is recorded in the macro.
7. Click the Stop Recording button on the Macro toolbar.

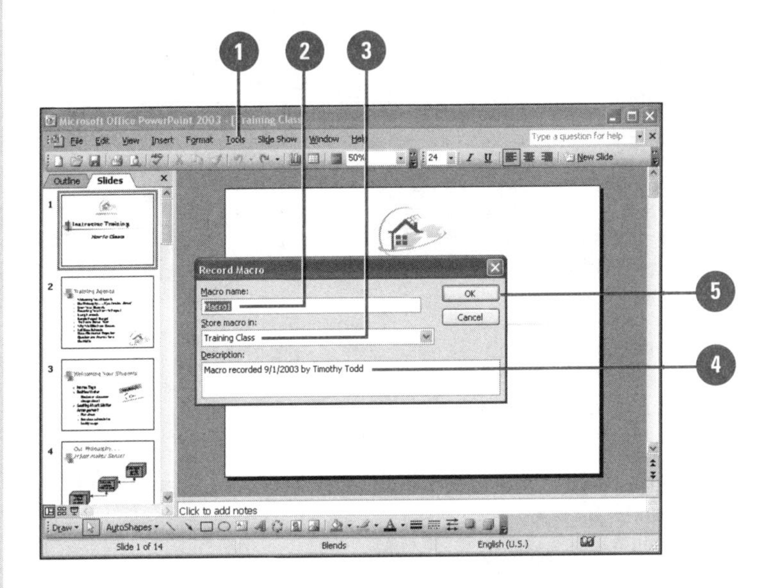

Did You Know?

You can set up a macro to run during a slide show. In Normal view, click the text or object you want to use to run a macro, click the Slide Show menu, click Action Settings, click the Mouse Click tab or the Mouse Over tab, click the Run Macro option, click the list arrow, select the macro you want, and then click OK.

Run a Macro

1. Click the Tools menu, point to Macro, and then click Macros.
2. Click the name of the macro you want to run.
3. Click Run.

Did You Know?

You can stop a macro. Press Ctrl+Break to stop a macro before it completes its actions.

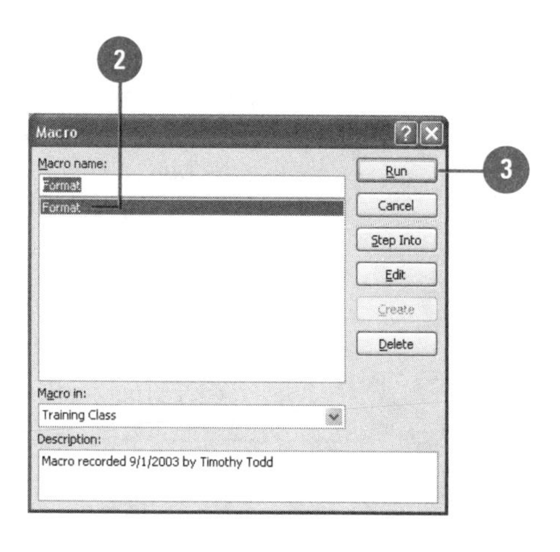

Delete a Macro

1. Click the Tools menu, point to Macro, and then click Macros.
2. Click the macro name.
3. Click Delete.
4. Click Delete to confirm the macro deletion.

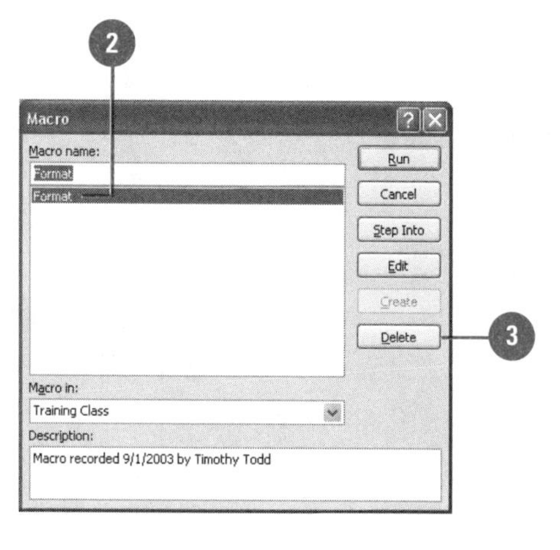

Controlling a Macro

If a macro doesn't work exactly the way you want it to, you can fix the problem without re-creating the macro. Instead of recording the macro over again, PowerPoint allows you to **debug**, or repair, an existing macro so that you change only the actions that aren't working correctly. When you use the Macro Recorder, you are actually writing a program in a programming language called Microsoft Visual Basic. All macros for a particular presentation are stored in a macro module, a collection of Visual Basic programming codes that you can copy to other presentation files. You can view and edit your Visual Basic modules using the Visual Basic editor. By learning Visual Basic you can greatly increase the scope and power of your programs.

Debug a Macro Using Step Mode

1. Click the Tools menu, point to Macro, and then click Macros.
2. Click the name of the macro you want to debug.
3. Click Step Into.
4. Click the Debug menu, and then click Step Into to proceed through each action.
5. When you're done, click the File menu, and then click Close And Return To [Program name].
6. Click OK to stop the debugger.

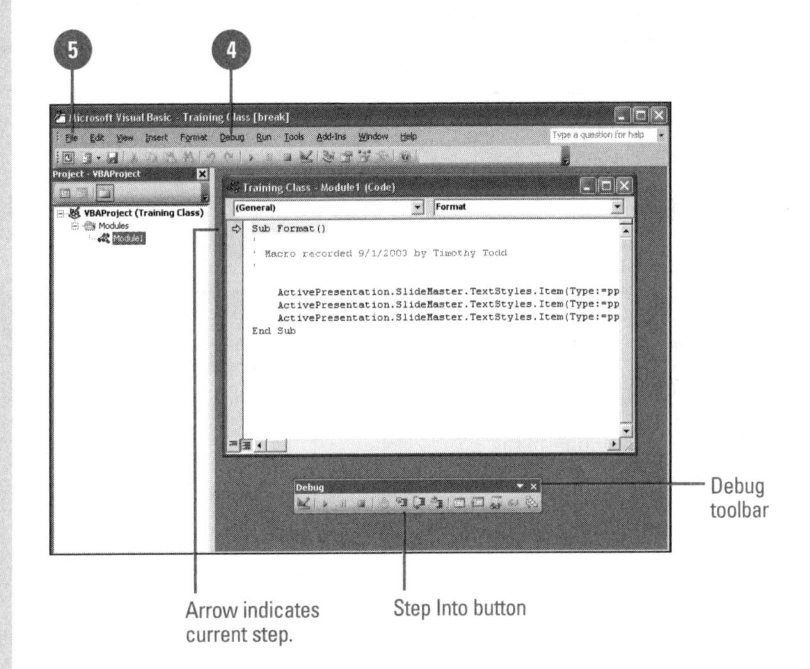

Did You Know?

You can display the Debug toolbar. Click the View menu, point to Toolbars, and then click Debug.

You can use the Visual Basic editor to help correct macro problems. If a problem occurs while you step through a macro, you have probably discovered why your macro isn't working. You can correct the problem using the Visual Basic editor.

Edit a Macro

1. Click the Tools menu, point to Macro, and then click Macros.
2. Click the name of the macro you want to edit, and then click Edit.
3. Click the Module window containing the Visual Basic code for your macro.
4. Type new Visual Basic commands, or edit the commands already present.
5. Click the File menu, and then click Close And Return To Microsoft PowerPoint.

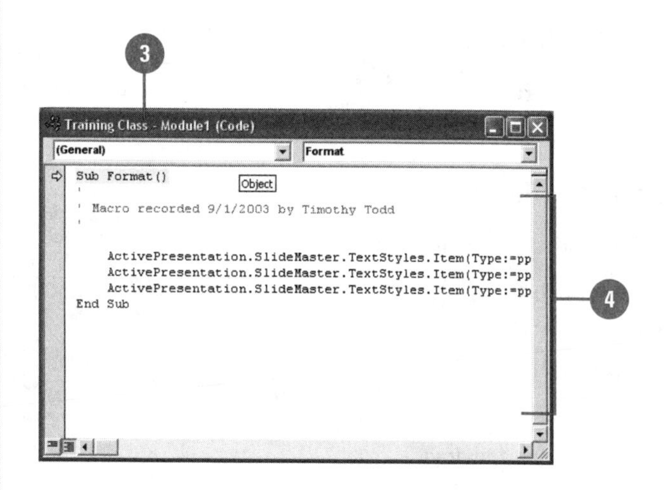

Copy a Macro Module to Another Presentation

1. Open the presentation files you want to copy the macro from and to.
2. Click the Tools menu, point to Macro, and then click Visual Basic Editor.
3. Click the View menu, and then click Project Explorer.
4. Drag the module you want to copy from the source presentation to the destination presentation.
5. Click the File menu, and then click Close And Return To Microsoft PowerPoint.

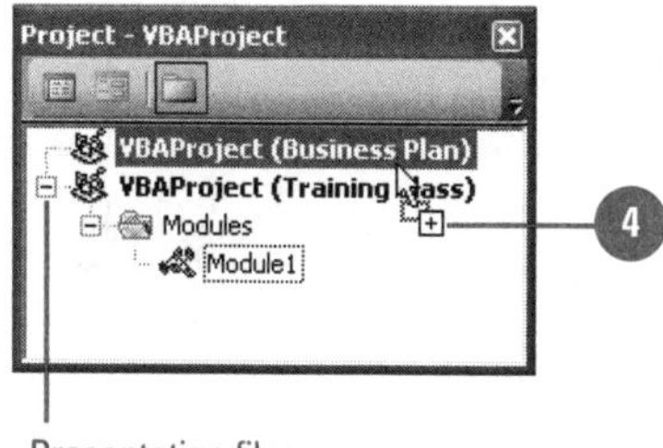

Presentation files currently open.

Did You Know?

You can get help with Visual Basic. To learn more about Visual Basic, place your macro in Edit mode, click the Help menu, and then click Microsoft Visual Basic Help.

Assigning a Macro to a Toolbar or Menu

Once you create a macro, you can then add the macro to the PowerPoint toolbars or to the PowerPoint menus for easy access. Modify your new button or menu entry by adding text or styling it. You can also remove the macro from a toolbar or menu at any time.

Assign a Macro to a Toolbar

1. Click the Tools menu, and then click Customize.
2. Click the Commands tab.
3. Click Macros in the Categories box.
4. Click the macro name, and drag it to the toolbar.

   To remove a macro button, select the button and drag it off the toolbar.
5. Click Modify Selection, and then select a style and button image for your macro button.
6. Click Close.

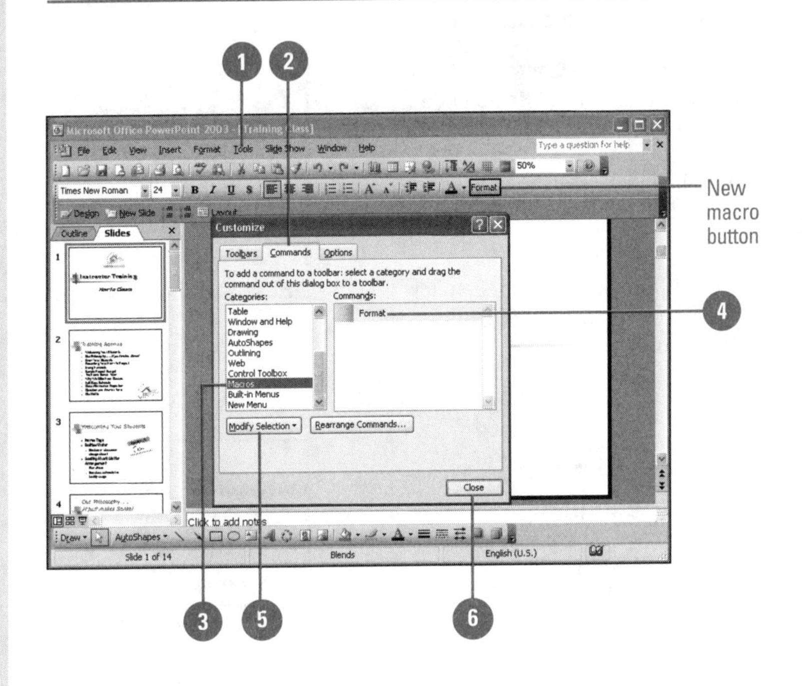

Assign a Macro to a Menu

1. Click the Tools menu, click Customize, and then click the Commands tab.
2. Click Macros in the Categories box.
3. Click the macro name, and drag it to the menu bar.

   To remove a macro from a menu bar, select the macro name and drag it off the menu.
4. Click Modify Selection, and then select a style and text for your menu entry, and then click Close.

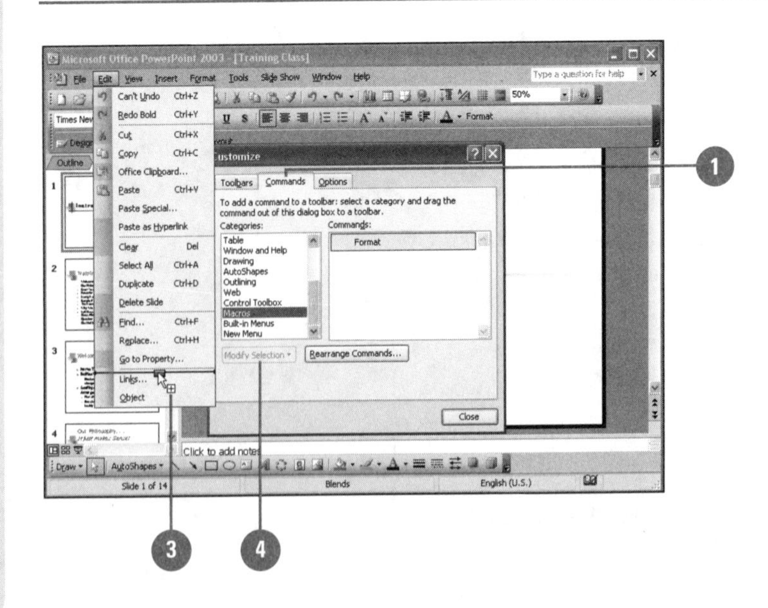

Customizing the Way You Create Objects

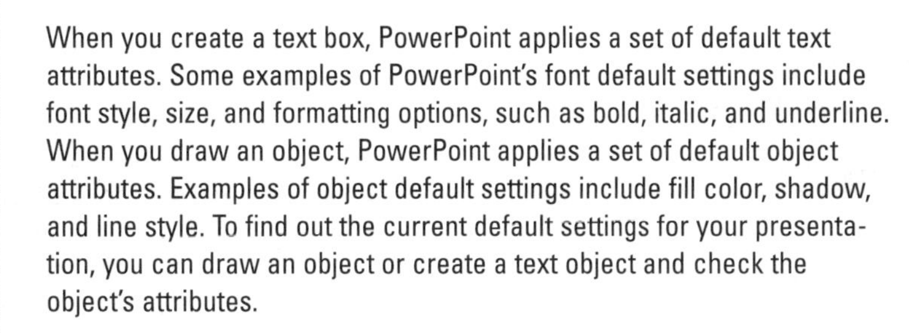

When you create a text box, PowerPoint applies a set of default text attributes. Some examples of PowerPoint's font default settings include font style, size, and formatting options, such as bold, italic, and underline. When you draw an object, PowerPoint applies a set of default object attributes. Examples of object default settings include fill color, shadow, and line style. To find out the current default settings for your presentation, you can draw an object or create a text object and check the object's attributes.

Customize the Way You Create Text Objects

1. Create a text box.
2. Click the Format menu, and then click Font.
3. Change the font options in which you want to be the default.
4. Select the Default For New Objects check box.
5. Click OK.

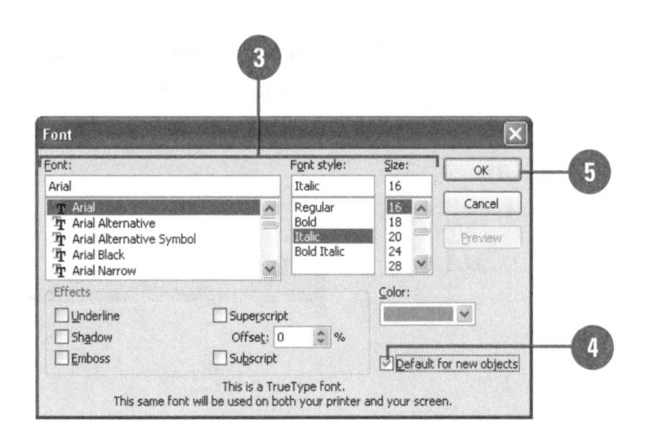

Customize the Way You Create Shape Objects

1. Create a shape, and then change the shape attributes.
2. Click the Draw button on the Drawing toolbar, and then click Set AutoShape Default .

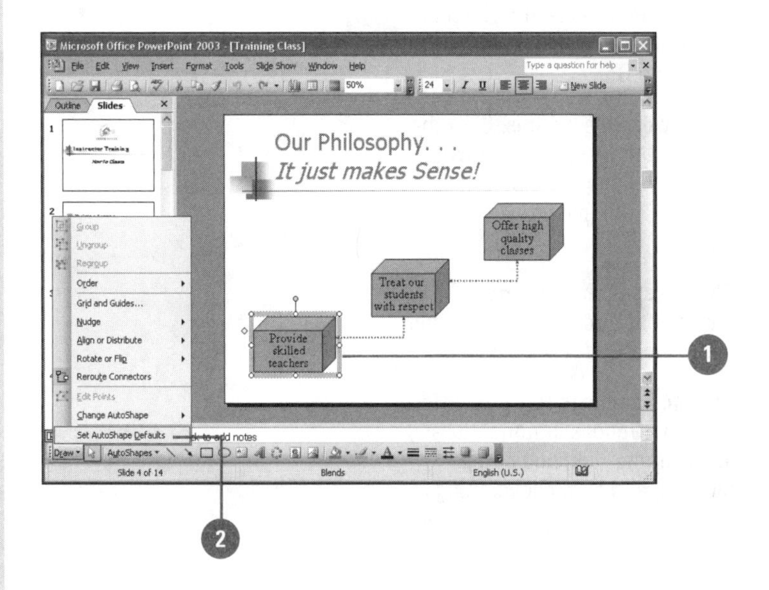

Controlling PowerPoint with Your Voice

The Language bar allows you to dictate text directly into your presentation and also to control buttons, menus, and toolbar functions by using the Voice Command option. When you first install PowerPoint, the Language bar appears at the top of your screen. If you are using English as a default language, the toolbar is denoted by the letters EN. (Other languages have appropriate abbreviations as well.) Before you can use speech recognition, you need to install it first. You can use Add Or Remove Programs in the Control Panel to change the Office 2003 installation. Before you can use the Language bar for either dictation or voice commands, you need to connect a microphone to your computer, and you must train your computer to your voice using the Speech Recognition Wizard.

Work with the Language Bar

- **Open.** Right-click a blank area on the taskbar, point to Toolbars, and then click Language Bar.
- **Minimize.** Right-click the Language bar, and then click Minimize. The Language bar docks in the taskbar at the bottom right of the screen, near the system clock.
- **Restore.** Right-click the Language bar, and then click Restore The Language Bar.
- **Display or hide options.** Click the Options button (the list arrow at the right end of the toolbar), and then click an option to display or hide.
- **Change speech properties.** Click the Speech Tools button, and then click Options.
- **Change Language Bar properties.** Click the Options button (the list arrow at the right end of the toolbar), and then click Settings.

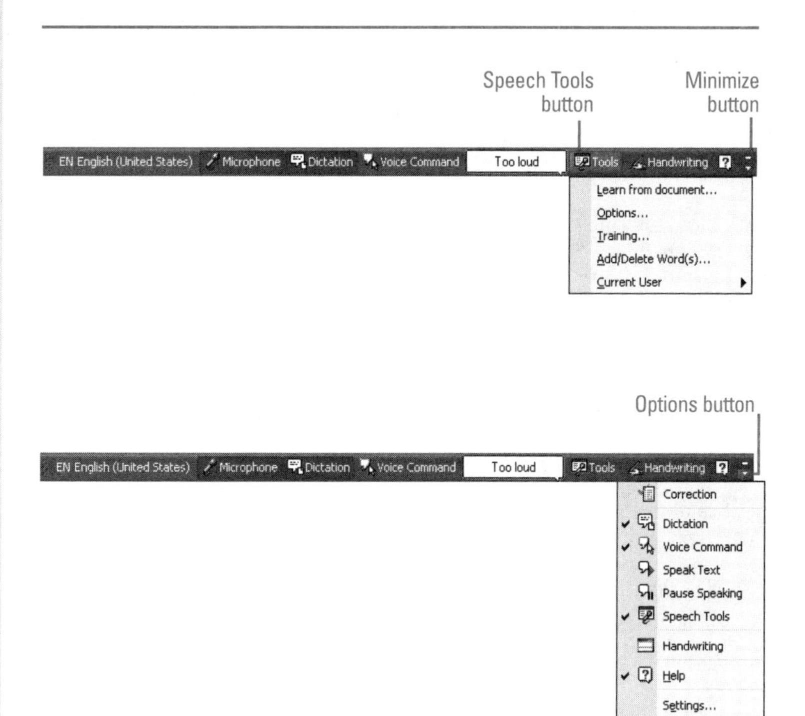

Train Your Computer to Your Voice

1. Click the Speech Tools button on the Language bar, and then click Training.
2. Click Next, read the instructions, ensure you are in a quiet place, and then click Next again.
3. Read the sentence provided to automatically set the proper volume of the microphone, and then click Next.
4. Read the text with hard consonants to help determine whether or not the microphone is positioned too closely to your mouth. Repeat the process until you have a clear, distinct audio playback, and then click Next.
5. After you are reminded to ensure that your environment is suitable for recording again, read the instructions, and then click Next.
6. Read the following series of dialog boxes. The words on the screen are highlighted as the computer recognizes them. As each dialog box is completed, the program will automatically move to the next one, and the process meter will update accordingly.
7. At the end of the training session, click Finish and your voice profile is updated and saved automatically.

Did You Know?

You can create additional speech profiles. Click the Speech Tools button on the Language bar, click Options, click New, and then follow the Profile Wizard instructions.

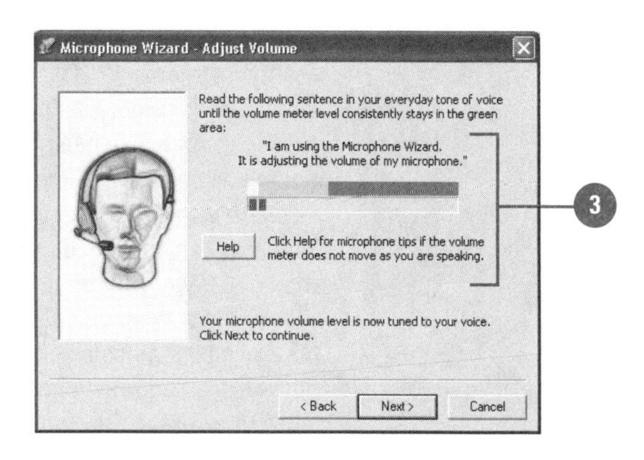

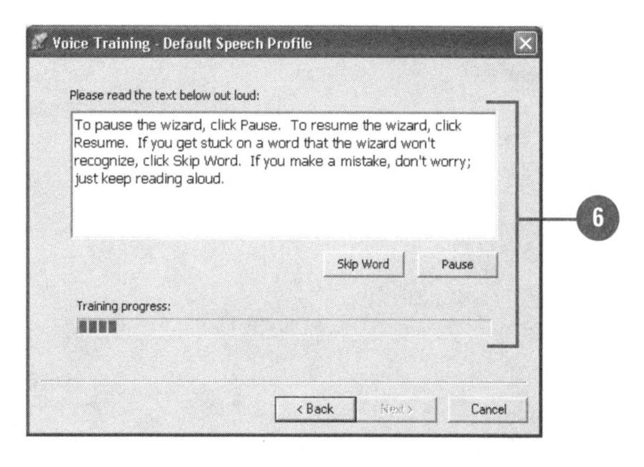

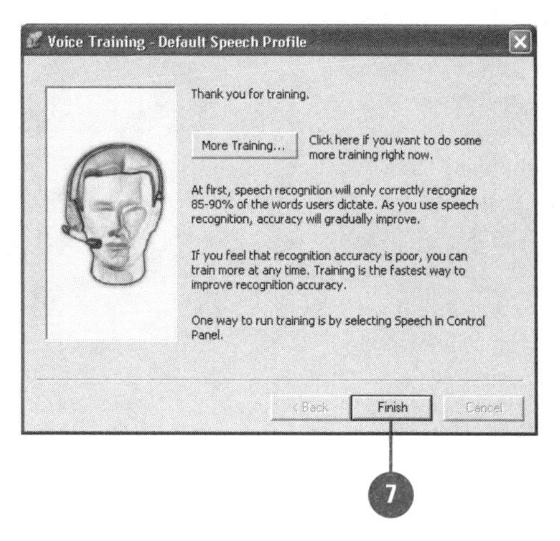

Executing Voice Commands

The two modes, Dictation and Voice Command, are mutually exclusive of one another. You do not want the word File typed, for example, when you are trying to open the File menu. Neither do you want the menu to open instead of the word File being typed when you are in the middle of a sentence. As such, you must manually click either mode on the Language bar to switch between them. The Voice Command mode allows you to talk your way through any sequence of menus or toolbar commands, simply by reading aloud the appropriate text instead of clicking it. For example, if you wanted to print the current slide of the presentation you are working on, you would simply say File, Print, Current Slide, OK (without saying the commands between the words as written here). You need not worry about remembering every command sequence because as you say each word in the sequence, the corresponding menu or submenu appears onscreen for your reference.

Execute Voice Commands

1. If necessary, display the Language bar.
2. Click the Microphone button on the Language bar. The toolbar expands so that the Voice Command button becomes available on the toolbar.
3. Click the Voice Command button to shift into that mode.
4. Work with your presentation normally. When you are ready to issue a command, simply speak the sequence just as you would click through it if you were using the menus or toolbar normally (i.e. with the mouse or via keyboard shortcuts).

Say "File" to display the menu.

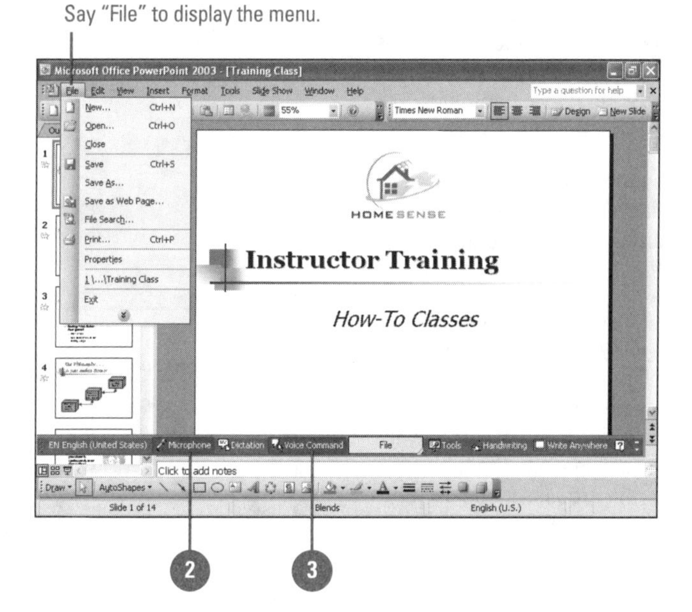

Did You Know?

You can have text read back to you. Display the Speak Text button on the Language bar. Select the text you want read back to you, and then click Speak Text.

Dictating Text

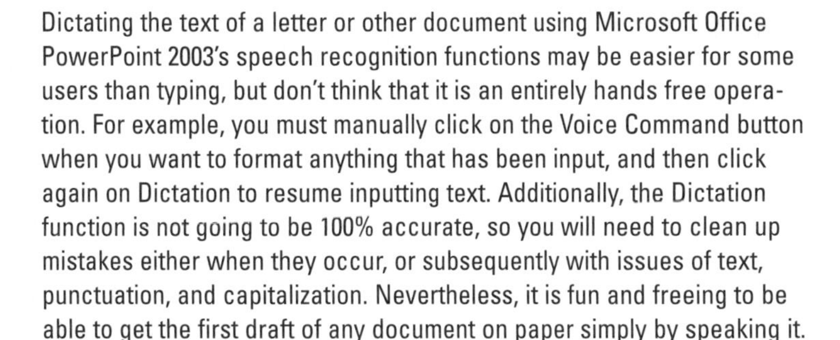

Dictating the text of a letter or other document using Microsoft Office PowerPoint 2003's speech recognition functions may be easier for some users than typing, but don't think that it is an entirely hands free operation. For example, you must manually click on the Voice Command button when you want to format anything that has been input, and then click again on Dictation to resume inputting text. Additionally, the Dictation function is not going to be 100% accurate, so you will need to clean up mistakes either when they occur, or subsequently with issues of text, punctuation, and capitalization. Nevertheless, it is fun and freeing to be able to get the first draft of any document on paper simply by speaking it.

13

Dictate Text

1. If necessary, display the Language bar.
2. Click the Microphone button on the Language bar. The toolbar expands so that the Dictation button becomes available on the toolbar.
3. Click to position the insertion point inside the presentation where you want the dictated text to appear, and then begin speaking normally into your microphone. As you speak, the words will appear on the page.
4. When you have finished dictating your text, click the Microphone button again to make the speech recognition functions inactive.

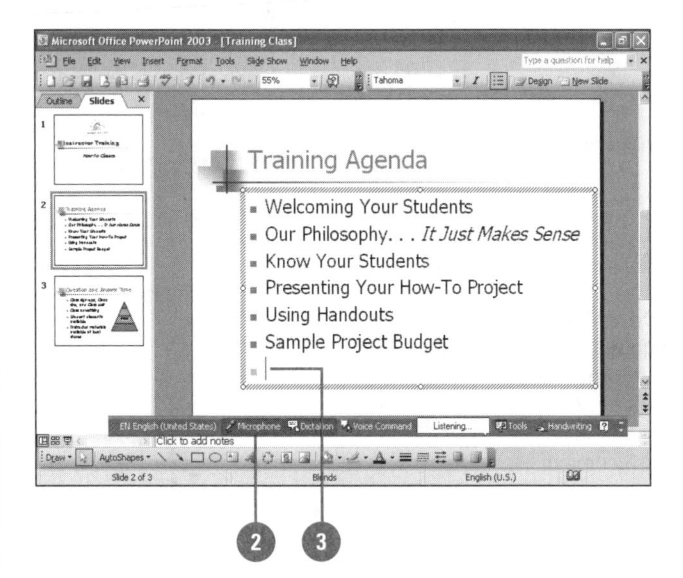

WARNING!

Turn off the Language toolbar functions when not in use. If you fail to turn off the Language toolbar functions while continuing to work in PowerPoint, distractions in the room like phone calls, even the sound of your keyboard clicking as you type, can introduce errors into your document.

Handwriting Your Text

Although entering information into a presentation through the keyboard is fast and efficient, you may find that you need to enter information in handwritten form. PowerPoint provides handwriting recognition to help you convert handwriting into text. Before you can insert handwritten text into a document, you need to have a mouse, a third party electronic stylus, an ink device, or a handwriting tablet, such as Tablet PC attached to your computer. Although you can use the mouse, for best results you should use a handwriting input device. When you insert handwritten text into a document that already contains typed text, the handwritten text is converted to typed text and then inserted in line with the existing text at the point of the cursor. The program recognizes the handwriting when there is enough text for it to do so, when you reach the end of the line, or if you pause for approximately two seconds. In addition, the converted text will take on the same typeface attributes as the existing text.

Insert Handwritten Text in a Document

1. Open the document in which you want to insert handwritten text.
2. Click the Handwriting button on the Language toolbar, and then click Write Anywhere. The Write Anywhere bar opens on your screen, and the Text button is selected by default.
3. Click where you want to insert text.
4. Write your text anywhere on the presentation. The handwritten words are converted to text on your screen.

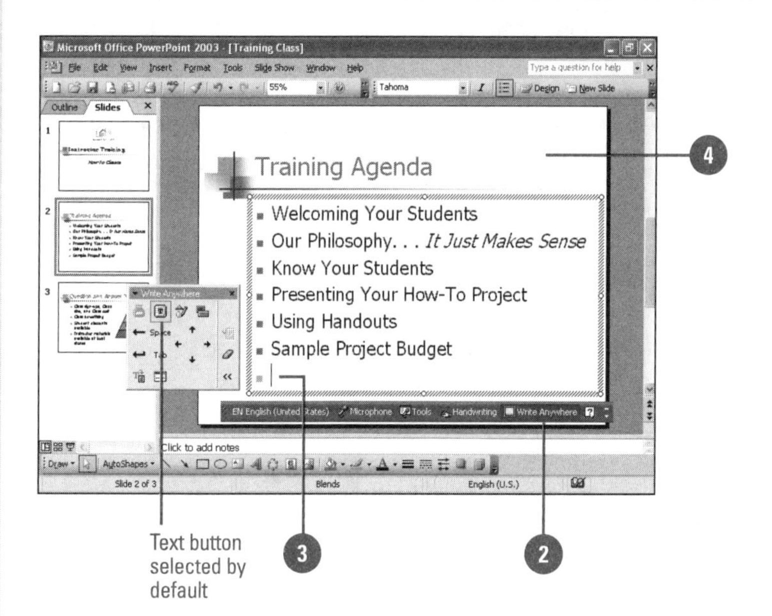

Insert Handwritten Text on a Writing Pad

1. Open the document you want to insert handwritten text.
2. Click the Handwriting button on the Language toolbar, and then click Writing Pad. The Writing Pad dialog box opens on your screen.
3. Click where you want to insert text.
4. Move the mouse cursor over the writing area of the Writing Pad dialog box, write your text. The new text is inserted into the document.

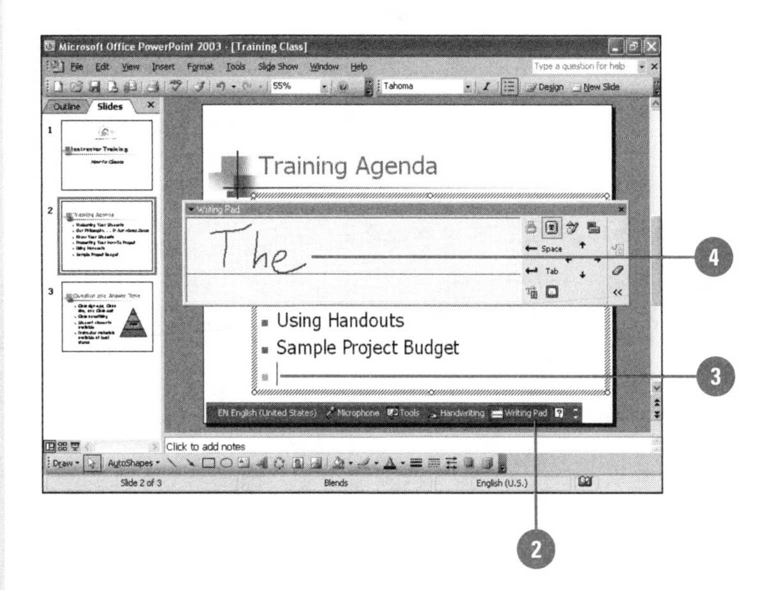

For Your Information

Using Additional Handwriting Tools

When you click the Handwriting button on the Language bar and then click the Writing Pad or Write Anywhere option, a dialog box opens on your screen with another toolbar. It has the same options that are available through the Handwriting button on the Language bar. In addition, the toolbar has the following buttons: Ink, Text, Backspace, Space, directional cursors, Enter, Tab, Recognize Now, and Write Anywhere. You use these buttons to control the input.

Using Smart Tags

Smart Tags help you integrate actions typically performed in other programs directly in PowerPoint. For example, you can insert a financial symbol to get a stock quote, add a person's name and address in a presentation to the contacts list in Microsoft Outlook, or copy and paste information with added control. PowerPoint analyzes the data you type and recognizes certain types that it marks with Smart Tags. The types of actions you can take depend on the type of data with the Smart Tag.

Change Smart Tag Options

1. Click the Tools menu, and then click AutoCorrect options.
2. Click the Smart Tags tab.
3. Select the Label Text With Smart Tags check box.
4. Select the check boxes with the Smart Tags you want.
5. To check the presentation for new Smart Tags, click Check Presentation.
6. To add more Smart Tags, click More Smart Tags, and then follow the online instructions.
7. Click OK.

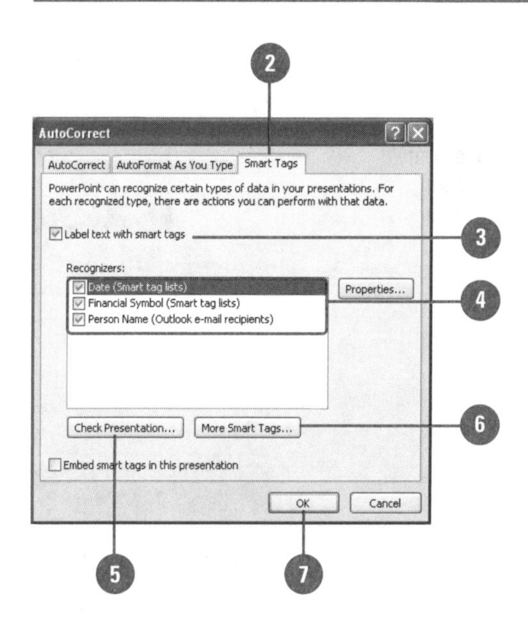

Did You Know?

You can save a smart tag in a presentation. Smart tags are not automatically saved when you close your presentation. To save smart tags, click the Tools menu, click AutoCorrect Options, click the Smart Tags tab, select the Embed Smart Tags In This Presentation check box, and then click OK.

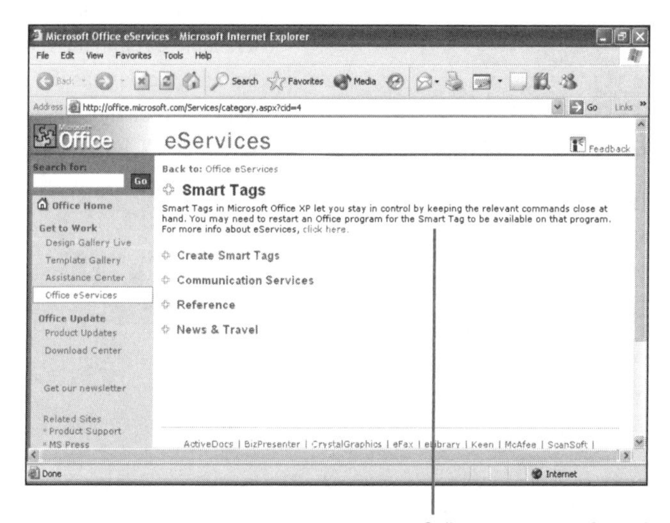

Online resource for Smart Tags; your screen might differ

Access Information Using a Smart Tag

1. Click a text box where you want to insert information using a smart tag.
2. Type the information needed for the smart tag, such as the date, a recognized financial symbol in capital letters, or a person's name from you contacts list, and then press Spacebar.
3. Point to the text with the purple dotted line underneath to display the Smart Tag button.

   The purple dotted line indicates a smart tag is available for the text.
4. Click the Smart Tag button, and then click the list arrow next to the button.
5. Click the smart tag option you want; options vary depending on the smart tag.

Did You Know?

You can remove a smart tag from text. Point to the text with the smart tag, click the Smart Tag button, and then click Remove This Smart Tag.

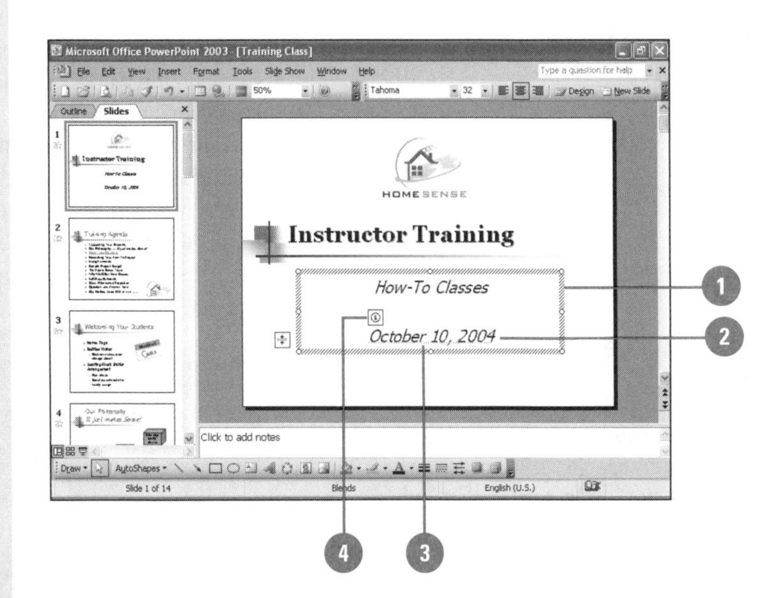

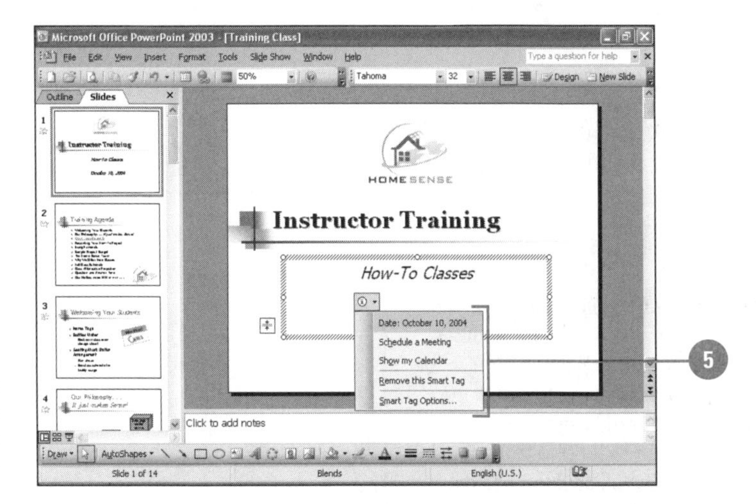

Using Multiple Languages

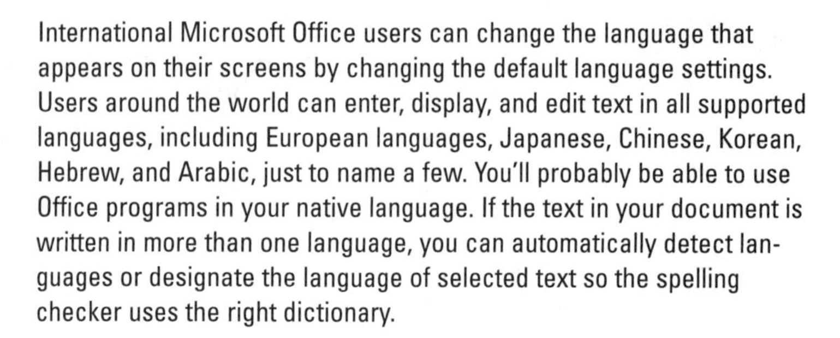

International Microsoft Office users can change the language that appears on their screens by changing the default language settings. Users around the world can enter, display, and edit text in all supported languages, including European languages, Japanese, Chinese, Korean, Hebrew, and Arabic, just to name a few. You'll probably be able to use Office programs in your native language. If the text in your document is written in more than one language, you can automatically detect languages or designate the language of selected text so the spelling checker uses the right dictionary.

Add a Language to Office Programs

1. Click Start on the taskbar, point to All Programs, point to Microsoft Office, point to Microsoft Office Tools, and then click Microsoft Office 2003 Language Settings.
2. Select the language you want to enable.
3. Click Add.
4. Click OK, and then click Yes to quit and restart Office.

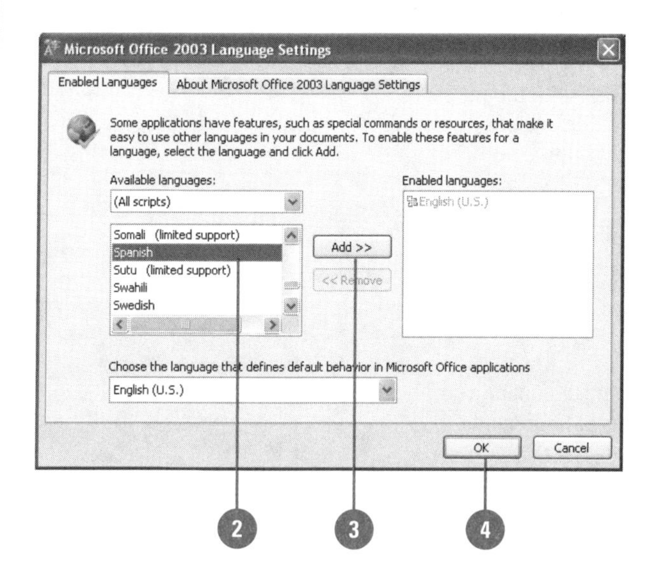

Did You Know?

You can check your keyboard layout. After you enable editing for another language, such as Hebrew, Cyrillic, or Greek, you might need to install the correct keyboard layout so you can enter characters for that language. In the Control Panel, double-click the Regional And Language icon, click the Language tab, and then click Details to check your keyboard.

Microsoft Office Specialist

About the Microsoft Office Specialist Program

The Microsoft Office Specialist certification is the globally recognized standard for validating expertise with the Microsoft Office suite of business productivity programs. Earning an Microsoft Office Specialist certificate acknowledges you have the expertise to work with Microsoft Office programs. To earn the Microsoft Office Specialist certification, you must pass one or more certification exams for the Microsoft Office desktop applications of Microsoft Office Word, Microsoft Office Excel, Microsoft Office PowerPoint, Microsoft Office Outlook, or Microsoft Office Access. The Microsoft Office Specialist program typically offers certification exams at the "specialist" and "expert" skill levels. (The availability of Microsoft Office Specialist certification exams varies by program, program version, and language. Visit *www.microsoft.com/officespecialist* for exam availability and more information about the program.) The Microsoft Office Specialist program is the only Microsoft-approved program in the world for certifying proficiency with Microsoft Office programs.

What Does This Logo Mean?

It means this book has been approved by the Microsoft Office Specialist program to be certified courseware for learning Microsoft Office PowerPoint 2003 and preparing for the certification exam. This book will prepare you fully for the Microsoft Office Specialist exam at the specialist level for Microsoft Office PowerPoint 2003. Each certification level has a set of objectives, which are organized into broader skill sets. Throughout this book, content that pertains to a Microsoft Office Specialist objective is identified with the Microsoft Office Specialist logo and objective number below the title of the topic:

PP03S-1-1
PP03S-2-2

PowerPoint 2003 Specialist Objectives

Objective	Skill	Page
PP03S-1	**Creating Content**	
PP03S-1-1	Create new presentations from templates	11-12
PP03S-1-2	Insert and edit text-based content	38-39, 42-43, 46-48, 198-199
PP03S-1-3	Insert tables, charts and diagrams	149, 165, 173, 182
PP03S-1-4	Insert pictures, shapes and graphics	88, 90, 121, 136
PP03S-1-5	Insert objects	128, 142-143, 170-172
PP03S-2	**Formatting Content**	
PP03S-2-1	Format text-based content	44-45, 50-51, 54-55
PP03S-2-2	Format pictures, shapes and graphics	34, 92-93, 100-105, 106-113, 114-115, 130-133
PP03S-2-3	Format slides	12, 32, 66, 83, 186-187
PP03S-2-4	Apply animation schemes	240-245
PP03S-2-5	Apply slide transitions	238-239
PP03S-2-6	Customize slide templates	84-85
PP03S-2-7	Work with masters	67, 70, 72-73, 76, 188-191
PP03S-3	**Collaborating**	
PP03S-3-1	Track, accept and reject changes in a presentation	270-272
PP03S-3-2	Add, edit and delete comments in a presentation	262-263
PP03S-3-3	Compare and merge presentations	270-271, 273
PP03S-4	**Managing and Delivering Presentations**	
PP03S-4-1	Organize a presentation	16-17, 32, 62-64, 106-107, 190, 192, 214-219
PP03S-4-2	Set up slide shows for delivery	212-213, 234-237
PP03S-4-3	Rehearse timing	246-249
PP03S-4-4	Deliver presentations	254-257
PP03S-4-5	Prepare presentations for remote delivery	259, 274-275
PP03S-4-6	Save and publish presentations	24, 197, 22-223
PP03S-4-7	Print slides, outlines, handouts, and speaker notes	204-208
PP03S-4-8	Export a presentation to another Microsoft Office program	195

Preparing for a Microsoft Office Specialist Exam

Every Microsoft Office Specialist certification exam is developed from a list of objectives, which are based on studies of how Microsoft Office programs are actually used in the workplace. The list of objectives determine the scope of each exam, so they provide you with the information you need to prepare for Microsoft Office Specialist certification. Microsoft Office Specialist Approved Courseware, including the Show Me series, is reviewed and approved on the basis of its coverage of the objectives. To prepare for the certification exam, you should review and perform each task identified with a Microsoft Office Specialist objective to confirm that you can meet the requirements for the exam.

Taking a Microsoft Office Specialist Exam

The Microsoft Office Specialist certification exams are not written exams. Instead, the exams are performance-based examinations that allow you to interact with a "live" Office program as you complete a series of objective-based tasks. All the standard menus, toolbars, and keyboard shortcuts are available during the exam. Microsoft Office Specialist exams for Office 2003 programs consist of 25 to 35 questions, each of which requires you to complete one or more tasks using the Office program for which you are seeking certification. A typical exam takes from 45 to 60 minutes. Passing percentages range from 70 to 80 percent correct.

The Exam Experience

After you fill out a series of information screens, the testing software starts the exam and the Office program. The test questions appear in the exam dialog box in the lower right corner of the screen.

- The timer starts when the first question appears and displays the remaining exam time at the top of the exam dialog box. If the timer and the counter are distracting, you can click the timer to remove the display.
- The counter at the top of the exam dialog box tracks how many questions you have completed and how many remain.
- If you think you have made a mistake, you can click the Reset button to restart the question. The Reset button does not restart the entire exam or extend the exam time limit.
- When you complete a question, click the Next button to move to the next question. It is not possible to move back to a previous question on the exam.
- If the exam dialog box gets in your way, you can click the Minimize button in the upper right corner of the exam dialog box to hide it, or you can drag the title bar to another part of the screen to move it.

Tips for Taking an Exam

- Carefully read and follow all instructions provided in each question.
- Make sure all steps in a task are completed before proceeding to the next exam question.
- Enter requested information as it appears in the instructions without formatting unless you are explicitly requested otherwise.
- Close all dialog boxes before proceeding to the next exam question unless you are specifically instructed otherwise.
- Do not leave tables, boxes, or cells "active" unless instructed otherwise.
- Do not cut and paste information from the exam interface into the program.
- When you print a document from an Office program during the exam, nothing actually gets printed.
- Errant keystrokes or mouse clicks do not count against your score as long as you achieve the correct end result. You are scored based on the end result, not the method you use to achieve it. However, if a specific method is explicitly requested, you need to use it to get credit for the results.
- The overall exam is timed, so taking too long on individual questions may leave you without enough time to complete the entire exam.
- If you experience computer problems during the exam, notify a testing center administrator immediately to restart your exam where you were interrupted.

Exam Results

At the end of the exam, a score report appears indicating whether you passed or failed the exam. An official certificate is mailed to successful candidates in approximately two to three weeks.

Getting More Information

To learn more about the Microsoft Office Specialist program, read a list of frequently asked questions, and locate the nearest testing center, visit:

www.microsoft.com/officespecialist

n

New! Features

Microsoft Office PowerPoint 2003

Microsoft Office PowerPoint 2003 is the presentation graphics program that helps you create lasting visual impact either in person or online. With enhanced multimedia support, save your presentations to a CD-ROM and play streaming audio and video within a slide show. With enhancements to the user interface and support for SmartTags, view and create high-impact presentations more easily.

- **Research task pane (p. 46)** The new Research task pane offers a wide variety of reference information and expanded resources if you have an Internet connection. You can conduct research on topics using an encyclopedia, Web search, or by accessing third-party content. Also available from the Research task pane, and new to PowerPoint, is support for the thesaurus. This feature is an outstanding tool for finding synonyms to enhance the quality of your presentation.
- **Enhancements to media playback (p. 145)** View and play your movies in full screen presentation with PowerPoint. Right-click the movie, click Edit Movie Object on the shortcut menu, and then select the Zoom to full screen check box. When Microsoft Windows Media Player version 8 or later is installed, improvements in media playback in PowerPoint support additional media formats, including ASX, WMX, M3U, WVX, WAX, and WMA. If a required media codec isn't present, PowerPoint will attempt to download it by using Windows Media Player technology.
- **Enhanced bitmap export (p. 197)** Export bitmaps that are larger and have better resolution.
- **New slide show navigation tools (p. 254-255)** The new Slide Show toolbar provides easy access to slide show navigation while you are making a presentation. In addition, common slide show tasks are simplified when the options are at your fingertips. The Slide Show toolbar puts ink annotation tools, pen and highlighter options, and the Slide Show menu within easy reach during a presentation, but the toolbar is never obtrusive or obvious to your audience.
- **Enhanced slide show ink annotations (p. 256-257)** Use ink to mark up your slides while giving a presentation, or draft slides for review by using the ink features in PowerPoint. Not only can you keep the ink that you used in your slide show presentation, but you can turn on or off the slide show markup after you have saved the ink markup in your presentation. Some aspects of the ink feature require that you run PowerPoint on a Tablet PC.

- **Package for CD (p. 259)** Package for CD is the new PowerPoint way to efficiently distribute your presentations. Make CDs of your presentations for viewing on computers running a Microsoft Windows operating system. Package for CD allows you to package your presentations and all of the supporting files, including linked files, and automatically run your presentations from the CD. The updated PowerPoint Viewer is included on the CD when you package your presentations. Therefore, no installation of the Viewer is required on a computer that doesn't have PowerPoint installed. Package for CD also gives you the option of packaging your presentations to a folder instead of a CD for archiving or posting to a network share.

- **Updated Viewer (p. 260)** The Microsoft Office PowerPoint Viewer has been improved with high fidelity output, including support of PowerPoint graphics, animations, and media. No installation is required for the new Viewer. Your presentation files, packaged with the new Package for CD feature, include the Viewer by default, or you can download the new Viewer from the Web. In addition, the Viewer supports viewing and printing. The updated Viewer runs on Microsoft Windows® 98 Second Edition or later.

- **Information Rights Management (p. 266-267)** Create or view content with restricted permission using Information Rights Management (IRM). IRM allows individual authors to specify permission for who can access and use documents or e-mail messages, and helps prevent sensitive information from being printed, forwarded, or copied by unauthorized people.

- **Document Workspaces (p. 279-293)** Create a Document Workspace to simplify the process of co-writing, editing, and reviewing documents with others in real time. A Document Workspace site is a Microsoft Windows SharePoint™ Services site that is centered around one or more documents and is typically created when you use e-mail to send a document as a shared attachment.

- **Support for ink devices, such as the Tablet PC (p. 310)** Quickly provide input by adding your own handwriting to Office documents on a Tablet PC as you would using a pen and a printout. Additionally, view task panes horizontally to help you do your work on the Tablet PC.instead.

- **New smart tag support (p. 312-313)** Smart tag support has been added to PowerPoint. By selecting AutoCorrect Options on the Tools menu, and then clicking the Smart Tags tab, you can choose to label text in your presentation with smart tags. Dates, financial symbols, and person names are included in the list of smart tag recognizers that ship with PowerPoint.

Troubleshooting

Aligning and arranging objects

I need to line up my text and objects is there a tool to help me measure 50
Can I change the indent amount for my outline 51
Is there a tool that can help me align all of my objects 106
What are these horizontal and vertical dashed lines on my screen 107
I inserted several objects, but they overlap each other 108
I want to connect two shapes with a line 110
My objects are stacked on each other can I change the order 111
An object on my slide is upside down! 114

AutoContent Wizard

I don't know how to start making my presentation, can PowerPoint help 11
Are there certain templates that work well with the Web 210
I need to create a Home Page and don't know where to start 211
There is a small button that appears on my presentation when I type a date 313

AutoRecover and file repair

A screen comes up saying Document Recovery, what does this mean 27
My Office program is having problems 29
How can I install additional features not installed with the typical installation 29

Charts and Graphs

Can I pull in a chart from Excel into my presentation 149
I always get the x-axis and y-axis confused 150
Can I change a chart type once it's in my presentation 160
Now that I have my chart just the way I want it, can I make it 3-D 163
I need to show an Organization chart in my slide show 165-169
Can I insert a Venn diagram into my presentation 182

Clip art

Can I delete the piece of ClipArt or other objects I have in my presentation 35
I found a piece of Clip Art that could work, is there something else out there 91
Is there an easy way to find a piece of Clip Art 122
Can I have my own category of Clip Art somewhere 124
I really like a piece of Clip Art that I like, but the colors just won't work 132
The WordArt title that I inserted looks too crowded 141

Colors, fill effects, and shadows

Can I put color on my AutoShape 100
I want my arrow line to be bright blue 101
What's a gradient fill 102
I need to distinguish some objects, is there a certain pattern I can put on them 103
Are there some suggestions for shadow angles on objects 104
I need the shadow on my object to be in same color family as my object 105

Copying, pasting, and moving

I need to move a section of text 40
I try and copy an object, but all the objects around it come too 117
Is there a way I can move an object I created to the Clip Organizer 118
How can I move my WordArt title 139
Can I copy an object to another part of my presentation 176

Customize PowerPoint

I want to use our company colors on all of our presentations 81
How can I get the right view defaults 296
All of these toolbars are confusing, can I make one just for me 298
There are certain tasks I do all the time can I create something to simplify my keystrokes 300
Now that I have a macro, is there a way I can put it on my toolbar 304

Drawing objects and pictures

What is an object 31
My slide looks too busy with all the objects on it, can I hide them on it 33
How do I select an object 34
My object is too big, can I make it smaller 34
Is there a way I can get a Flowchart shape on my presentation 88
Now that I have some objects on my presentation, can I make them a different size 89
How can I draw a line on my slides to call something out 92
Can I change a freeform vertex 97
I need to move an object on my presentation according to exact measurements 99

Editing

The text I entered looks too close together, can I spread it out 39
As I enter my text, PowerPoint is making it smaller to fit 41
Is there a way to undo something 43
I'd like to change the standard bullet that appears on my outline to a checkbox 57
Can I resize my picture 130
The piece of Clip Art I am using looks a little faded, can it be fixed 131
I think I cropped my object too much 134
Is there a way that I can enter data for my chart in Microsoft Graph 154

Help

How can i get the help I need 20
What is this paper clip thing that keeps popping up 22
Can I turn off the Assistant, it's getting in the way 23

Importing and Exporting

Can I bring in an outline that I created in Word 49
I'm having a hard time bringing in my digital picture that I took 128
My chart doesn't look updated 152
I have all the data I need on a Word table, can I insert it 172
How can I export my outline to Word 196
I need to save my slides in a different format 197

Languages and voice options

How can I use multiple languages in one presentation 194
I want to control my presentation with my voice so I don't have to use the keyboard 306
How does PowerPoint recognize my voice 307
Do I need to turn something on to dictate any text 309
Can I translate a presentation for some of our clients 312

Links and embedded objects

I'm not quite sure what the difference is between pasting, embedding, and linking 148

I'd like to insert a file and embed it into my presentation 178

Can I past a link to another file 179

My Excel worksheet has changed, do I need to update any links to my presentation 180

Masters

What exactly are masters 67

How can I include our company logo on every presentation 70

Can I have the current date and time show on every slide 74

I'd like to change the look of my footer 76

I would like to change the background color on my master 83

Menus, toolbars, and task panes

I can't find the task pane I want to use 4

How do I open a button on a toolbar 6

Sometimes there are just too many toolbars on my screen 7

I'm not sure what all my options are on a Dialog Box 8

A toolbar with peoples faces showed up on my screen, what does this mean 277

Microsoft Office Specialist

What are the list of requirements for the specialist certification 316

How do I get certified in Microsoft Office PowerPoint 2003 317

How do you take the exam 317

Are there any tips for taking the exam 318

Multimedia

What type of multimedia items can I insert into my presentation 120

How can I insert my favorite movie clip into my slide show 143

Is there a way that I can add narration to my presentation 144

Navigation

I'm viewing the PowerPoint window for the first time, how do I move around 3

Can I move between two PowerPoint windows 15

I don't understand all the different views in PowerPoint 16

How do I browse my presentation 18

How do I move around the presentation using my keyboard 254

Notes and handouts

I need to develop the vocabulary on my handouts 47

I'd like to add a header and footer on my handouts 189

I'm getting ready to give a presentation but need some notes 190

To develop some interest, how can I add color to my background on my notes 193

During our meeting, some great handwritten notes were taken, can I use these in PowerPoint 310

Outlines

How do I know when to use an outline 37

The font on my outline seems small 54

Can I stop bullets from appearing on my outline 56

Printing

Is there a way to preview my presentation before printing it 204

My clients don't have a color printer, can I format my presentation in black and white for them 205

Can I print just some of my slides 207

I need to print out my outline 208

Reviewing changes

Is there a way I can track changes to my presentation 270

How do I compare two presentations at once 272

I want to review the changes from my compare and merge 273

Running a show

I'd like to give my audience a summary of what will be covered in the presentation 184
How do I set up a slide show 234
There are some slides that I want to "hide" from my audience 235
Is there a way to highlight certain areas of my slide as i talk through my presentation 256
I like some of the notes I wrote on my presentation, is there a way to save those comments 257
I need to run a show from one computer and have my audience view it on another 258

Searching

I just realized I spelled a clients name wrong throughout my presentation can I find it and fix it 45
I need to look up some information to add to my presentation 46

SharePoint

I've heard that SharePoint would help our office 279
What are all the various page views 280
How do I administer my portal site 282
Is there a way to maximize all of our company documents 284
How can I control who views what documents on our site 285
Is there a way to know if changes have been made to the portal site 286
I'd like to notify our company about a large client presentation 288
I'm having a tough time setting up a new web discussion 292
What are the system requirements for using SharePoint 2003 294

Sharing data

I made some changes to an existing presentation, can I save it with a new name so I can share it with others 25
How can I put my entire presentation on a CD to send to our clients 259
I'd like to secure my presentation with a password 264
What exactly is IRM 266
Now that I'm sending my presentation all over the world, how does everyone know it's really from me 230

Slide design and layout

I just finished my presentation and left out a slide, can I add a new one 32
I need some help with designing my presentation, is there any advice 36
Can I make a copy of a slide 49
Can I view my presentation in different formats 62
Once my slide show is complete, am I able to change the order of my slides 63
Can I add a 3-D element to an object in my presentation 112
I'd like to add some jazz to my title 136
I want to change the page orientation of my presentation 187
Is there a way to have a button bring me to a specific slide 213

Spelling

Is there a way to add my company name to the Spelling feature so it's not recognized as an error 42
Can I check spelling in my slide 198
I need to make my slides uppercase 201

Templates and styles

I'm having a hard time finding a presentation I did a while ago 13
I created a slide, but I like an AutoLayout better, can I use it 32
Are there some pre-designed templates available from PowerPoint 66
I just created a great presentation, can I save it to use again for another presentation 84

Text boxes and text in objects

Can I put some text on an AutoShape 60
How can I add some comments in my presentation 262

Timing

I want to be able to have the slides show at a measured time 246

The time I set for my slide show is too fast for some slides, can I change the timing 247

Is there a way to set up a self-running show so I don't have to do anything 250

Transitions and animations

What are some special features that I can add to my presentation 233

How can I apply a transition to my presentation 238

I'd like to alert my viewers that the next slide will be shown 239

How can I make presenting a bulleted list interesting 242

There's just too much going on in my presentation, how can I remove some of my animations 245

Web and Web publishing

Is there a way to get any updates to PowerPoint from the Web 26

I'm running low on Clip Art ideas, is there anyway to get it from the Web 126

I've heard the term HTML, what is it 209

I need to set up a hyperlink in my presentation 217

What does all this URLs stuff mean 219

Is there a way to publish my presentation as a Web page 223

Can I view my presentation over the Web in full screen size 227

Should I check the Web for updates 232

Is there a way that I can set up an online broadcast 274

I need to have a meeting over the internet to discuss our presentation 276

Index

A

abbreviations, AutoCorrect for, 42
accent colors, 77
action buttons. *See* Web presentations
Action Settings dialog box, 214-215
Additional design templates, 12
address book, sending presentation to contacts in, 269
adjustment handles
  for AutoShapes, 88-89
  connecting two objects with, 110
Adobe PhotoShop, 120
  image editing with, 132
advertisement-sized slides, 186
agenda slides, summary slides as, 184
alerts in SharePoint Team Services, setting up, 286
Align Center button, 44
Align Left button, 44
alignments
  AutoShape, text in, 91
  changing text alignment, 44
  chart box, aligning text in, 168
  with Formatting toolbar, 44, 55
  grids or guides, aligning objects to, 106-107
  other objects, aligning objects to, 108-109
  setting, 36
  tab alignments, 52
  table cells, aligning text in, 174
  WordArt objects, aligning, 139
Align or Distribute command, 108-109
Align Right button, 44
angle of vertex, modifying, 97
animations, 233
  adding to slides, 240
  browsers, viewing presentations in, 245
  bulleted lists, animating, 242
  chart elements, animating, 164, 242-243
  customized animations, designing, 240-241
  deleting animations, 245
  dimming text after animation, 242-243
  multiple animations, coordinating, 244-245
  order for animations, modifying, 244
  previewing, 240
  sounds, adding, 241
  specialized animations, using, 242-243
  text, animating, 242-243
  time between animations, setting, 244-245
  in Web page presentations, 226
Animation Schemes, using, 240
annotations
  Pen tool, using, 256
  pointer options, changing, 256
  saving, 257
  text boxes for, 60
  turning on/off, 257
Apply button, 8
Apply button, Reviewing toolbar, 271, 273
archiving, voice narrations for, 144
arranging windows, 15
arrows
  charts, adding to, 164
  default size, changing, 93
  in dialog box, 8
  drawing, 92-93
  editing, 93
Arrow tool, 92
assistant-to place, 166
asterisk (*) wildcard, 14
.ASX file format support, 145
attachments
  presentations as, 268-269
  Upload button to add, 287
AutoContent Wizard, 9
  outlines, generation of, 48

AutoContent Wizard *(continued)*
suggested content, creating presentation with, 11
templates, adding, 85
templates from, 65
for Web presentations, 210-211
AutoCorrect
for abbreviations or codes, 42
adding entries to, 42
for foreign languages, 194
in Microsoft Graph, 154
numbers, recognition of, 58
for text, 42-43
undoing action, 43
AutoCorrect Options button, 42
AutoFit Text
text, resizing, 41
turning off, 41
AutoFormat
for organization charts, 168
text as you type, 58-59
AutoLayout
bulleted lists with, 56
clips, adding, 122-123
placeholders, list of, 33
for slides, 32
automatic save feature, 25
AutoNumber, 59
AutoRecover, 27
AutoShapes, 87, 88-89
action buttons, inserting, 213
adjusting, 88-89
adjustment handles, 88-89
aligning text in, 91
categories for, 88
Clip Art Gallery, inserting from, 90-91
connecting two objects, 110
defaults, setting, 101
editing text in, 91
groups for, 116
orientation of text, changing, 61
replacing, 89
resizing, 88-89
stacking order, changing, 111
text, adding, 61, 91
for text boxes, 60-61

B

background colors
See also color schemes
notes pages, customizing colors on, 193
preset, 83
Slide Master controlling, 67
suggestions for, 79
backgrounds
See also background colors
fills
match backgrounds, changing fills to, 103
selecting, 83
hiding master background objects on slide, 72
masters, controlling with, 72-73
transparent backgrounds, 132-133
washout coloring for, 132
Ballpoint Pen tool option, 256
banner-sized slides, 186
bars for chart elements, 164
Bcc for presentations, 269
bitmaps
See also pictures
colors, editing, 132
cropping, 134
transparent color with, 132-133
black and white
as picture color, 132
previewing color slides in, 204-205
blank presentations, 9
outlines with, 48
starting, 10
Blank Presentation template, 84
.BMP files. *See* bitmaps
boldfacing
hyperlinks, 221
text, 54
WordArt text, 136, 138
borders
in organization charts, 168
table cell borders, modifying, 175
bottom edge, aligning objects to, 109
breaking links, 181
brightness of pictures, changing, 131
Bring Forward for objects, 111

Bring to Front for objects, 111
broadcasting presentations, 274-275
joining broadcast, 274
scheduling presentation, 274
starting broadcast, 274
browsers
See also Web presentations
animations, viewing, 245
transitions, viewing, 245
browsing
with keyboard, 18
in outline, 19
in presentations, 18-19
in slides, 19
bulleted lists
adding or removing bullets, 56
animations, adding, 242
character of bullet, changing, 57
distance between bullets and text, changing, 56
modifying, 56-57
numbered bullets, creating, 56
objects, 36
for outlines, 48
placeholders, 33
selecting text in, 59
with summary slides, 184
text, entering, 36, 39
buttons
See also specific buttons
adding buttons to toolbar, 299
in dialog box, 8
on Master toolbar, 67
on Slide Master View toolbar, 70
Web presentations, action buttons for, 212-213

C

call-out boxes, 270
cameras, inserting pictures from, 128
Cancel button, 8
case of text, changing, 201
categories
for AutoShapes, 88
for clip art, 124-125
for SharePoint Team Services alerts, 286
Cc for presentations, 269
CD, packaging presentation on, 259
Cell Drag and Drop option, 153
cells, 149
See also tables
Cell Drag and Drop option, 153
deleting cells, 157
editing cell contents, 156
inserting cells in datasheets, 157
range of cells
editing, 156
selecting, 151
selecting, 151
center alignment
for objects, 109
of text, 44
certification as Microsoft Office Specialist. *See* Microsoft Office Specialist
Change Case command, 201
character spacing in WordArt, adjusting, 141
chart area, 162
chart objects, 162-163
chart area, 162
customizing, 163
defined, 162
enlarging, 162
formatting, 162
placement, changing, 163
plot area, 162
charts
See also cells; columns and rows; datasheets; legends for charts; organization charts
animating chart elements, 164, 242-243
applying custom chart types, 161
creating, 149
customized settings for, 160-161
drawing objects, adding, 164
elements of, 150
error bars, adding, 164
existing charts, opening, 150
fills for chart elements, 164
inserting, 149
Microsoft Excel charts, inserting, 170-171
moving average, creating, 164
placeholder, 33
saving customized settings for, 160

charts *(continued)*
selecting and deselecting chart boxes, 165
standard types, 160
Subordinate chart boxes, adding, 166
3-D charts, 160, 163
titles, adding, 161
trendlines, adding, 164
2-D effects for, 160
type of chart, selecting, 160-161
Chart Type button, 160
Chat rooms for meetings, 276
check boxes, 8
chime sound to hyperlinks, 214
circles, drawing, 89
click sound to hyperlinks, 214
clip art
See also Clip Organizer
AutoLayout, inserting image with, 122-123
categories for, 124-125
corner sizing handle, using, 34
cropping, 134-135
drag and drop pictures, 123
with Insert Clip Art task pane, 122-123
inserting, 120, 122-123
locating, 122-123
placeholder, 33
precisely cropping clips, 135
recoloring, 132-133
resizing, 130
transparent backgrounds, 132-133
on Web, 126-127
Clip Art Gallery
AutoShapes, inserting, 90-91
similar AutoShapes, finding, 91
Clip Art task pane
AutoShapes, inserting, 88
properties for clips, changing, 125
sounds, inserting, 142-143
videos, inserting, 142-143
Clipboard. *See* Office Clipboard
Clip Organizer
adding and removing clips, 120
categories for clip art, 124-125
shapes, adding, 118
Clippit feature, 22, 23
clips
See also clip art; sounds; videos
adding clips, 121
categories, organization into, 124-125
defined, 90
deleting clips, 121
downloading, 127
groups of clips, adding, 121
Internet, accessing, 126-127
previewing, 90
properties for clips, changing, 125
searching Web for, 127
similar clips, finding, 122
Clips Online, 126-127
Close button in windows, 15
Close Master View button, 67
closing
presentations, 30
task panes, 4
codes, AutoCorrect for, 42
collapsing slides, 63
Color Model, choosing, 81
colors
See also background colors; drawing objects; fonts/font size; shadows; templates; transparent colors
adding colors to presentation, 82
of bullets or numbers, 57
for curves, 95
defaults, setting, 103
fill colors, 77, 82
to freeforms, 95
of hyperlinks, 77, 220
for organization charts, 168
properties of, 80
recoloring pictures, 132-133
remembering colors with PowerPoint, 82
Slide Master creating, 67
of table cell borders, 175
WordArt colors, changing, 138-139
color schemes, 65, 77
choosing, 78
copying from slide to slide, 79
custom schemes, creating, 80-81
default schemes, 77
deleting, 78
design templates featuring, 66
previewing, 78
saving, 81

suggestions for, 79
viewing, 78
columns and rows
See also tables
Best Fit for columns, 158
excluding, 157
as labels, 153
precise column width, entering, 159
width of columns
datasheet columns, changing width of, 158-159
table columns, adjusting width of, 175
Column Width command, 158
commands
See also specific commands
default options, changing, 298
menu commands, choosing, 5
shortcut menu, choosing commands from, 5
toolbar button, choosing with, 6
comments
adding to presentation, 262-263
all comments, reviewing, 263
deleting, 144, 262
editing, 262
reading, 262
recording, 144
Revisions pane, reviewing in, 262-263
company name, masters containing, 67
comparing and merging presentations, 272-273
compressing pictures, 130
Confirm Password dialog box, 265
connecting two objects, 110
connection sites, 110
consistent presentations, creating, 67
contacts
in SharePoint Team Services, 290-291
with Smart Tags, 312
Content templates, 65
contrast of pictures, changing, 131
converting linked objects, 181
copying
See also Office Clipboard
CD, packaging presentation on, 259
color schemes, 79
drawing objects, 98-99
existing presentations, 9
macro modules to other presentations, 302-303
Microsoft Excel charts, 171
objects, 176-177
paste linking copied objects, 178-179
shortcut keys for, 35
with Smart Tags, 312
text, 40
windows, information in, 15
coworker-to place shape, 166
Create an Address Book of Contents, SharePoint Team Services, 280
Create a Web Discussion site, SharePoint Team Services, 280
Create Calendar Events, SharePoint Team Services, 280
Create Digital Certification dialog box, 230
cropping pictures, 134-135
Ctrl key
for commands, 5
drawing objects, copying, 98
curves
See also vertices
drawing curves, 94
formatting, 95
straight lines and curves, objects with, 94
WordArt curves, changing, 138
Custom Animation task pane, 244-245
customized slide proportions, 187
custom slide shows. *See* slide shows
cutting
moving slides, 62-63
shortcut keys for, 35
cycle diagrams, 182
Cyrillic, keyboard layout for, 314

D

Dash Style tool, 92
data markers, 150
dragging, editing by, 156
data series, 149
display, changing, 158
datasheets, 149
See also cells; columns and rows; data markers
AutoCorrect feature for, 154

datasheets *(continued)*
editing graph data, 156-157
entering data in, 154-155
fonts, changing, 154-155
formatting graph data in, 154-155
importing data into, 152-153
numbers, formatting, 154-155
pasting data into, 153
selecting data in, 151
Selection After Enter option for, 153
width of column, changing, 158-159
date and time
inserting date and time in presentation, 74
master placeholders for, 67
notes pages, adding to, 192
debugging macros, 302
Debug toolbar, 302
Decrease Paragraph Spacing button, 44
defaults
editing defaults, changing, 297
general defaults, changing, 296
menu options, changing, 298
spell checking defaults, changing, 297
Style Checker defaults, changing, 297
toolbar options, changing, 298-299
view defaults, changing, 296
Delete Comment/Marker button, Reviewing toolbar, 271
deleting
animations, 245
AutoShapes, 90
bullets from text, 56
cells from datasheets, 157
chart boxes, 166
clips, 121
color schemes, 78
comments, 144, 262
custom slide shows, 237
guides, 107
hyperlinks, 221
macros, 301
masters, 67
notes page, placeholders from, 192-193
objects, 35
password protection, 265
restrictions on presentations, 267
slides, 33, 48
sounds, 144
tables, columns and rows from, 174
text, 40
vertices, 97
Demote button, 50
demoting text, 50-51
deselecting objects, 34
design templates, 12, 65
applying, 66, 71
existing presentations, applying design from, 66
existing template, changing, 85
master, applying to, 71
destinations in OLE, 148
Detect and Repair command, 28
detecting problems, 28
diagrams
creating, 182
drawing, 110
formatting, 182
placeholder, 33
Diagram toolbar, 182
dialog boxes, 8
choosing options in, 8
help in dialog box, getting, 21
dictating text, 309
dictionaries
See also spell checking
custom words, adding, 199
for foreign languages, 314
Research task pane feature for, 46
digital cameras, inserting pictures from, 128
digital signatures
adding, 230-231
on macro projects, 230-231
dimming text after animation, 242-243
displaying/hiding. *See* showing/hiding
display view size, changing, 49
distributing objects, 108
docked toolbars, moving, 7
Document Library, 280
storing documents in, 284
Document Recovery task pane, 27
Documents and Lists Page, SharePoint Team Services, 280-281
downloading
clips, 127

updates to PowerPoint, 26
drag anddrop
Cell Drag and Drop option, 153
clip art, 123
connection end points, 110
data markers, dragging, 156
drawing objects, moving, 98
Excel charts to PowerPoint, 170
rearranging slides in, 62-63
text, moving, 40
toolbars, dragging, 7
drawing objects, 87
See also AutoShapes; freeforms; lines; 3-D effects
aligning, 108-109
charts, adding to, 164
Clip Organizer, adding shapes to, 118
colors, 87
changing fill colors, 100
connecting two objects, 110
fills for, 100-101
fixed point, rotating object around, 115
flipping, 114-115
Format dialog box, changing colors and lines in, 101
grouping and ungrouping, 116-117
hidden objects, viewing, 111
moving, 98-99
multiple objects, copying, 98-99
nudging, 98
precision
moving objects with, 99
rotating objects precisely, 115
regrouping objects, 116-117
rotating, 114-115
stacking order, changing, 111
text objects, 305
Drawing toolbar, 6, 88
for handouts, 188
for organization charts, 168
WordArt, formatting, 138
Draw Table button, 174
drum roll sound to hyperlinks, 214
dual-monitor hardware, 258
Duplicate command for copying drawing objects, 98
duplicating slides, 49

E

Edit Comment button, Reviewing toolbar, 271
editing, 40-45
See also slide shows
arrows, 93
AutoShape, text in, 91
cell contents, 156
comments, 262
custom slide shows, 237
data markers, 156
datasheets, graph data in, 156-157
defaults, changing, 297
embedded object in source program, 180
foreign language text, 194, 314
freeforms, 94
hyperlinks, 214, 221
lines, 92
macros, 302-303
notes, 190
organization charts, 165
text boxes, 60
timings for slides, 247
WordArt text, 137
Edit Points command for freeforms, 94
Edit WordArt Text dialog box, 137
elements of slide show, 1
ellipsis (...), 8
e-mail
See also attachments; SharePoint Team Services
alerts, setting up, 286
broadcasting presentations, 274-275
hyperlinks sending messages, 219
for restricted permission presentations, 267
review via e-mail, sending presentation for, 268-269
embedding, 148
Excel charts as objects, 170
Microsoft Word tables, 172
TrueType fonts, 185
working with embedded objects, 179
em-dashes, recognition of, 58
en-dashes, recognition of, 58
Eraser button, Draw Table button, 174
European languages. *See* languages
events. *See* SharePoint Team Services

excluding columns and rows from datasheets, 157
existing presentations
copying, 9
designs, applying, 66
opening, 13
saving, 25
expanding slides, 63

F

fading out effect, 238
Favorites list, slide presentations on, 65
Felt Tip Pen option, 256
File Properties feature, 202-203
files
datasheets, instant messaging porting into, 152
default location to save files, setting, 297
digital signatures, adding, 230-231
finding files, 14
hyperlinks to, 216
objects, inserting files in, 178
pictures from files, inserting, 128
Selfcert.exe file, installing, 230
wildcards, finding files with, 14
Fill Colors, adding, 82
Fill Effects dialog box, 102-103
fills, 101, 102-103
See also backgrounds; gradient fills; WordArt
applying effects, 102-103
for chart elements, 164
colors, 77, 82
for drawing objects, 100-101
patterns, creating, 101
removing fills, 100
financial symbols, inserting, 312
Find command, 45
finding
clip art, 122
Clip Art Gallery, AutoShapes in, 91
files or file contents, 14
presentations, 13
research information, 46
in task panes, 4
text, 45
Web toolbar, searching the Web with, 228-229
wildcards for finding files, 14
flipping
drawing objects, 114
freeforms, 95
imported objects, 115
floating toolbars, reshaping, 7
flow charts, drawing, 110
folders, saving presentation to, 24
Font Color button menu, 82
fonts/font size, 36
applying fonts, 54
in datasheets, 154-155
Formatting toolbar, changing font with, 55
for headers and footers, 76
for hyperlinks, 221
replacing fonts, 185
Slide Master creating, 67
Style Checker for, 200
TrueType fonts, embedding, 185
for WordArt, 136
working with, 185
footers. *See* headers and footers
foreign languages. *See* languages
Format command for resizing AutoShapes, 88
Format dialog box for drawing objects, 101
Format Painter, 55
color schemes, applying, 79
Format Picture dialog box, cropping with, 134-135
formatting, 36, 54-55
See also AutoFormat; fonts/font size; templates
chart objects, 162
curves, 95
datasheets, data in, 154-155
dates and times, 74
diagrams, 182
with Format Painter, 55
freeforms, 95
hyperlinks, 221
organization charts, 168-169
showing/hiding, 50
tables, 174-175
WordArt text, 138

Formatting toolbar, 6
aligning text with, 44, 55
default options, changing, 298
fonts, changing, 55
for handouts, 188
for hyperlinks, 221
moving text with, 50
for organization charts, 168
using, 54
fractions
recognition of, 58
undoing automatic formatting, 58
frames around printed slides, adding, 189
freeforms, 87
See also curves; vertices
creating, 94-95
formatting, 95
freehand drawing, 95
From AutoContent Wizard. *See* AutoContent Wizard
From Design Template option, 9
From Existing Presentation option, 9
FTP server, saving presentation to, 222
full-screen mode
slide shows, viewing, 234
Web presentations, viewing, 226-227
Full Screen Slide Show button, 226-227

G

Getting Started task pane, 13
.GIF format
modifying files, 132
slide as .GIF file, saving, 197
gradient fills
applying, 102
for chart elements, 164
colors for, 101
graph charts. *See* charts
Graph commands, 150
graphics
See also clip art; pictures
selecting, 34
slide as graphic image, saving, 197
for Web pages, 224
grayscale
pictures in, 132
previewing color slides in, 204-205
Greek, keyboard layout for, 314
Grid and Guides dialog box, 106-107
grids and guides
adding guides, 107
aligning objects to, 106-107
animating legends, 243
moving guides, 107
overriding grid settings, 107
removing guides, 107
snap into place, setting objects to, 106
Group Home Page template, 210-211
groups
clips, adding groups of, 121
shapes, grouping and ungrouping, 116-117
guides. *See* grids and guides

H

Handout Master, 67
viewing, 69
handouts, 1, 183
customizing, 188
headers and footers for, 188-189
masters, preparing, 188
Microsoft Word, creating in, 183, 195
orientation for, 187
placeholders in master, 188
printing, 189
spell checking, 198-199
with Web presentations, 214
handwriting input devices, 310-311
handwritten text
document, inserting in, 310
Writing Pad, inserting on, 311
headers and footers
adding, 76
for handouts, 188-189
master placeholders for, 67
to notes master, 190
to notes pages, 192
Hebrew, keyboard layout for, 314
height
rows in tables, adjusting height of, 175
WordArt letters, changing height of, 140

help, 20-21
  See also Office Assistant
  dialog box, getting help in, 21
  with Microsoft Graph, 151
  online help, 20-21
  with Visual Basic, 303
  working, getting help while, 21
hidden objects, viewing, 111
hiding. *See* showing/hiding
Highlighter option, 256
highlighting hyperlinks, 214
Home Page, SharePoint Team Services, 280
home page for Web presentations, creating, 210-211
hosts for online meetings, 276
HTML (Hypertext Markup Language), 209, 222
  opening HTML files, 225
hue, defined, 80
hyperlinks, 184
  action buttons activating, 212
  activation of, 217
  colors for, 77, 220
  deleting, 221
  between documents, 219
  editing, 214, 221
  e-mail messages, hyperlinks sending, 219
  to external objects, 216-217
  to files, 216
  formatting, 221
  highlighting with click or mouse over, 214
  inserting, 218-219
  jumping with, 218
  mouse
    activation with, 217
    highlighting with, 214
  navigating between hyperlinked documents, 220
  to other presentations, 216
  to programs, 216-217
  same presentation, hyperlinks within, 218
  saving presentations with, 220
  slide objects, adding to, 214-215
  sounds, adding, 214-215
  using hyperlinks, 220
  to Web pages, 216-217

I

icons
  objects inserted as, 179
  Shared Workspace icons, 293
importing and exporting
  datasheets, importing data into, 152-153
  flipping imported objects, 115
  Microsoft Excel worksheets or charts, 171
  Microsoft Word, notes and slides to, 195
  rotating imported objects, 115
Increase Paragraph Spacing button, 44
indents
  changing indents, 51
  level of indent, changing, 50
  setting, 36
Information Rights Management (IRM), setting up, 266-267
ink color for Pen tool, setting, 256
Insert Clip Art button, 121
Insert Clip Art task pane, 122-123
Insert Comment button, Reviewing toolbar, 271
Insert Diagram or Organization Chart button, 182
insertion point
  location of text, determining, 39
  in tables, 173
  for text, 38
Insert Object command, 178-179
installing
  Selfcert.exe file, 230
  SharePoint Server 2003, 294
  Windows 2003, 294
international paper sized slides, 186
Internet
  See also Microsoft Office Online; Web presentations
  broadcasting presentations, 274-275
  clip art, accessing, 126-127
  for multimedia clips, 119
  sharing presentations on, 1
  updates to PowerPoint on, 26
  Web addresses, understanding, 219
intranet, self-running presentations on, 250
italicizing
  hyperlinks, 221

with Slide Master, 67
text, 54
WordArt text, 136, 138

J

joining broadcast presentation, 274
joining two objects, 110
.JPEG format
modifying files in, 132
slide as .JPEG file, saving, 197

K

Kern Character Pairs option, 141
keyboard
See also shortcuts
browsing slides with, 18
drawing objects, nudging, 98
foreign languages, layout for, 314
grid settings, overriding, 107
objects, moving, 35
keyword, finding clip art by, 122
kiosk presentations
hyperlinks in, 216
popup menus with, 252
as self-running presentations, 250
setting up slide shows, 234

L

labels
columns and rows as, 153
rotating chart axis labels, 163
landscape orientation, 187
viewing presentations in, 204
Language bar, 306-307
dictating text, 309
properties, changing, 306
Voice commands, executing, 308
languages
AutoCorrect for, 194
multiple languages, using, 314
spelling, marking foreign words for, 199
text to language, changing, 194
thesauruses for foreign languages, 47
for Web pages, 224
laptop computer, packaging presentation for, 258
ledger paper sized slides, 186
left alignment
for objects, 109
tables, text in, 174
of text, 44
legends for charts, 150
animating, 243
letter paper sized slides, 186
lighting for 3-D objects, 113
Line Colors, adding, 82
lines, 87
connecting line, joining objects with, 110
connecting two lines, 110
editing lines, 92
fill effects, applying, 103
in organization charts, 168
straight lines, drawing, 92
WordArt line style, changing, 140
line spacing, adjusting, 39, 44
Line Style tool, 92
linking objects, 148
See also hyperlinks
breaking links, 181
converting linked objects, 181
Excel chart objects, 170
modifying linked objects, 180-181
paste linking copied objects, 178-179
to presentation properties, 203
reconnecting broken links, 181
source of linked object, changing, 180
task panes, links in, 4
updating links, 180
list boxes, 8
lists. *See* bulleted lists; numbered lists
locking master, 71
logos
Blank Presentation template including, 84
Clip Organizer for, 118, 120
masters containing, 67
Microsoft Office Specialist logo, 315
looping option for slide shows, 235
lowercase, changing text to, 201
luminosity, defined, 80

M

macro projects, digital signature on, 230-231
Macro Recorder, 300
  debugging macros with, 302
macros
  copying to other presentations, 302-303
  debugging macros, 302
  deleting macros, 301
  editing, 302-303
  menus, assigning macros to, 304
  recording macros, 300-301
  running macros, 301
  Step mode, debugging macros with, 302
  stopping macros, 301
  toolbar, assigning macro to, 304
macro security levels, 296
Mc SharePoint Server. *See* SharePoint Team Services
maintenance for Office programs, 28
management tools, 1
Manage Users Page, SharePoint Team Services, 280-281
Markup button, Reviewing toolbar, 271, 273
markups
  See also annotations
  on merging presentations, 270
masters, 65
  See also Slide Master; Title Master
  appearance of slide, controlling, 70-71
  for consistent presentations, 67
  deleting, 67
  design templates, applying, 66, 71
  handout master, formatting, 188
  headers and footers, adding, 76
  locking master, 71
  multiple masters, creating, 67
  notes master, formatting, 190-191
  placeholders in, 67
  preserving masters, 71
  viewing masters, 68-69
Master toolbar, 67
matte surface to 3-D objects, 112
Maximum button in windows, 15
media clips
  My Collections for, 124
  placeholder, 33
meetings
  See also online meetings; SharePoint Team Services
Meeting Workspace feature, 288
  Meeting Workspace feature, 288
menus, 5
  default options, changing, 298
  macros, assigning, 304
merging presentations
  comparing and, 272-273
  markups on, 270
merging table cells, 175
metal surface to 3-D objects, 112
microphones, 119
  Language bar requiring, 306
  for narrations, 248
Microsoft Excel
  See also charts; OLE (object linking and embedding); SharePoint Team Services
  copying existing charts, 171
  importing worksheets or charts, 171
  inserting charts, 170-171
  pasting existing charts, 171
  Shared Workspace, working with, 293
Microsoft Graph
  See also charts
  advanced techniques, 164
  help with, 151
  starting, 149
Microsoft.Net Passport
  Information Rights Management (IRM), setting up, 266
  using, 223
Microsoft Office Application Recovery feature, 28
Microsoft Office Online, 20-21
  accessing, 232
  templates from, 12
  updates from, 26
Microsoft Office Specialist, 315-318
  objectives for, 316
  preparing for exam, xvi, 317
  taking exam, 317-318
  tips for taking exam, 318
Microsoft Outlook 2003, 274
  See also SharePoint Team Services
  events, links to, 289

Meeting Workspace feature, 288
Microsoft Paint, 120
image editing with, 132
Microsoft SMTP (Simple Mail Transport Protocol) Service, 294
Microsoft SQL Server 2000 Desktop Engine (MSDE 2000), 294
Microsoft SQL Server 2000 Enterprise or Standard Edition, 294
Microsoft SQL Server 2000 SP3, 294
Microsoft Visual Basic
help with, 303
macros with, 302
Microsoft Windows 2000 for dual-monitor shows, 258
Microsoft Windows 2003, installing, 294
Microsoft Windows XP for dual-monitor shows, 258
Microsoft Word
See also SharePoint Team Services; tables
handouts, creating, 183, 195
linking notes to, 195
outlines created in Word, inserting, 48-49
Shared Workspace, working with, 293
middle, aligning objects to, 109
Minimize button in windows, 15
minimizing Language bar, 306
More Colors, adding, 82
More Related Words, searching for, 47
mouse
See also hyperlinks
objects, moving, 35
promoting/demoting text with, 51
slide timings, controlling, 246
movies. *See* videos
moving
See also objects
drawing objects, 98-99
group, object in, 116
guides, 107
in tables, 173
text, 40, 50
toolbars, 7
vertex in freeform, 96
windows, information in, 15
moving average, creating, 164
.M3U file format support, 145
multimedia objects
See also clip art; sounds; videos
inserting, 120
multiple languages, using, 314
My Collections for media files, 124

N

names
company name, masters containing, 67
saving presentation with different name, 25
for sounds, 144
narrations
pausing and resuming narration, 249
recording, 144
for self-running presentations, 248-249
for slide shows, 248-249
navigating
in dialog boxes, 8
in self-running presentations, 250
in Shared Workspace, 293
slide shows, 254
Web pages, navigation buttons for, 224
.NET Architecture Internet Information Server (IIS) 6.0, 294
NetMetting, 276-277
networks
online broadcasting feature, 261
packaging presentation for, 258
New icon, xiii
New on the File menu for AutoContent Wizard, 11
new presentation, starting, 9
New Presentation task pane, 9
displaying, 10
New Slide button, 32
new slides
sounds, inserting, 143
videos, inserting, 143
Next Item button, Reviewing toolbar, 271
Next Slide button, 18
Normal view, 16
See also Outline pane
comments, reviewing, 262
diagrams, creating, 182
notes, entering, 190
objects, manipulating, 34

Normal view *(continued)*
- sounds, playing, 145
- tables, inserting, 173
- text, viewing, 36
- videos, playing, 145

notes, 1
- *See also* notes pages
- editing, 190
- headers and footers to master, 190
- linking notes to Microsoft Word, 195
- master, formatting, 190-191
- Microsoft Word, exporting notes to, 195
- Normal view, entering in, 190
- Notes Page view, entering in, 190
- orientation for, 187
- placeholders on notes master, 192-193
- in Slide Show view, 254

Notes Master, 67
- viewing, 69

notes pages, 190
- background colors, customizing, 193
- customizing, 192-193
- dates and times, adding, 192
- deleting placeholders from, 192
- headers and footers to, 192
- numbering, adding, 192
- reinserting placeholders, 192-193
- spell checking, 198-199

Notes Page view, 17
- handouts, creating, 183
- notes, entering, 190

nudging
- drawing objects, 98
- shadows, 104

numbered lists
- AutoNumber feature, 59
- character of number, changing, 57
- selecting text in, 59
- undoing automatic numbering, 58

numbers
- *See also* numbered lists; slide numbers
- bullets, creating numbered, 56
- datasheets, formatting numbers in, 154-155
- notes pages, adding numbering to, 192

Number Slides From box, 186

O

objects
- *See also* chart objects; drawing objects; OLE (object linking and embedding)
- aligning objects to other objects, 108-109
- all objects, selecting, 35
- bulleted list objects, 36
- copying, 176-177
- customizing creation methods, 305
- defined, 31
- deleting, 35
- files, inserting, 178
- grids or guides, aligning objects to, 106-107
- icons, inserting objects as, 179
- independently moving objects, 108
- linking objects, 148
- masters containing, 67
- moving, 35, 177
  - independently moving objects, 108
- multiple objects, copying, 177
- to notes master, 190
- paste linking copied objects, 178-179
- pasting, 176-177
- resizing, 34
- snap into place, setting objects to, 106
- Tab key, selecting with, 35
- text box objects, 36
- text objects, 36
  - customizing creation method, 305
- title text objects, 36
- working with, 34-35

Office Assistant, 22-23
- character, changing, 22-23
- presentation style design, checking, 200-201
- showing/hiding, 23
- turning on/off, 23

Office Clipboard
- drawing objects, copying, 98-99
- multiple objects, copying, 177
- objects, copying and pasting, 176-177
- options, changing, 177
- viewing, 99

Office programs. *See* programs

OLE (object linking and embedding), 147
- methods for embedding and linking objects, 178-179

terms, definitions of, 148
online meetings, 276-277
collaborating in, 276-277
holding, 276
participating in, 277
receive meeting calls, 277
scheduling, 276
Online Meeting toolbar, 277
Open dialog box Search feature, 14
opening
Language bar, 306
password-protected presentations, 264
presentations, 13
Revisions pane, 263
task panes, 4
Web page, presentation as, 225
Open on the File menu, 13
Options button in dialog box, 8
ordinals, recognition of, 58
organization charts
adding chart boxes, 166
aligning text in, 168
creating, 165-167
default styles, 169
deleting chart boxes, 166
diagrams with, 182
editing, 165
formatting, 168-169
Insert Shape list for, 166
layout, changing, 167
rearranging chart boxes, 167
structuring for, 166-167
styles, changing, 169
Organization Chart Style Gallery, 169
Outline pane
collapsing slides in, 63
deleting slides in, 33
duplicating slides in, 49
expanding slides in, 63
other programs, inserting outlines from, 48-49
printing in, 208
rearranging slides in, 62
reorganizing presentation content with, 37
slides, adding, 48
text
entering, 37, 48
viewing, 36
outlines
See also Outline pane
with AutoContent Wizard, 48
browsing in, 19
entering text on, 37
Microsoft Word, sending outline to, 196
orientation for, 187
other programs, inserting outlines from, 48-49
printing, 208
in RTF (Rich Text Format), 196
saving presentation as, 196
spell checking, 198-199
text, entering, 48
Web presentations, viewing, 226-227
Outlining toolbar, 50
ovals, drawing, 88
overlapping objects, 111

P

Package for CD feature, 259
PowerPoint Viewer in, 260
Page Setup dialog box, 186
page setup options, changing, 186-187
Page Up/Page Down keys, 18
Paint Shop Pro, 120
image editing with, 132
paragraph line spacing, adjusting, 39, 44
passwords
See also SharePoint Team Services
changing passwords, 265
deleting password protection, 265
opening presentations with, 264
for PowerPoint Viewer, 260
for presentations, 264-265
paste linking
copied objects, 178-179
notes to Microsoft Word, linking, 195
Paste Special command, 178-179
pasting
See also paste linking
datasheets, data into, 153
Microsoft Excel charts, 171
objects, 176-177

pasting *(continued)*
in OLE (object linking and embedding), 148
shortcut keys for, 35
slides, 62-63
with SmartTags, 312
patterns
in backgrounds, 83
fill patterns, creating, 101, 103
to freeforms, 95
in WordArt, 140
pencil pointer, Draw Table button, 174
Pen tool
changing to mouse pointer, 257
using, 256
photo albums, creating, 129
pictures
See also Clip Organizer
applying picture fills, 102
backgrounds with pictures, creating, 83
brightness, changing, 131
charts, adding to, 164
compressing pictures, 130
contrast, changing, 131
cropping, 134-135
files, inserting pictures from, 128
for fills, 101, 102
inserting, 120, 128-129
modifying, 130-131
photo albums, creating, 129
placeholder, 33
precisely cropping pictures, 135
recoloring, 132-133
redisplaying cropped pictures, 134
resizing, 130
restoring settings for, 131
scanners, inserting pictures from, 128
Picture submenu, 128
placeholders
See also Slide Master
AutoFit Text feature, 41
in handout master, 188
list of AutoLayout placeholders, 33
in masters, 67
modifying, 73
notes placeholders on notes master, 192-193
text placeholders, 33, 38
in Title Master, 67
plastic surface to 3-D objects, 112
playing videos or sounds, 145
plot area for charts, 162
.PNG files, modifying, 132
pointer options, changing, 256
polygons, creating, 94
Popup toolbar, 252
portrait orientation, 187
viewing presentations in, 204
power failures, automatic save feature and, 25
PowerPoint Viewer
packaging presentation for, 259
using, 260
presentation graphics program, 1
presentation properties, 202-203
customizing, 203
displaying, 202
linking to, 203
presentations
See also existing presentations; reviewing presentations; slide shows; Web presentations
FTP server, saving presentation to, 222
previewing, 204-205
printing, 206-207
with restricted permissions, 267
style design, checking, 200-201
templates
creating presentations with, 12
saving presentation as, 84-85
Presented By A Speaker option, 234
Presenter view, slide shows in, 258
presenting slide shows, 251
preview box, 8
previewing
animations, 240
in black and white, 204-205
clips, 90
color schemes, 78
in grayscale, 204-205
presentations, 204-205
print preview for presentations, 204-205
Web presentations, 222, 226-227
Previous Item button, Reviewing toolbar, 271
Previous Slide button, 18
Print dialog box

features of, 206
handouts, preparing, 188
outline, previewing, 208
printers, selecting, 206
printing
custom presentations, 207
defaults, setting, 297
handouts, 189
outlines, 208
presentations, 206-207
range of slides, 207
single slides, 207
Print preview for presentations, 204-205
problems, detecting and repairing, 28-29
product name, masters containing, 67
Profile Wizard, 307
programs
hyperlinks to, 216-217
maintenance on, 28
recovering Office programs, 28
shortcuts, creating, 2
Promote button, 50
promoting/demoting text, 50-51
Properties dialog box, 202-203
proprietary company information, researching, 46
Publish As Web Page dialog box, 223
publishing Web pages, 222-223
punctuation, Style Checker for, 200
pyramid diagrams, 182

Q

question mark (?) wildcard, 14
quitting PowerPoint, 30

R

radial diagrams, 182
range of cells. *See* cells
range of slides
printing, 207
setting up for, 234-235
reading comments, 262
read-only presentations, creating, 264
real world examples, xiv
recoloring pictures, 132-133
recording
comments, 144
macros, 300-301
narrations, 144
sounds, 144
recovery
of Office program, 28
of presentations, 27
rectangles, drawing, 88
redoing undone actions, 43
Regroup command, 116-117
regrouping objects, 116-117
Rehearse Timings, using, 246-247
repairing problems, 28
Replace command, 45
replacing
AutoShapes, 89
fonts, 185
text, 45
research material, inserting, 46
Research task pane, 46
Reset Picture button, 131
reshaping toolbars, 7
resizing
arrows, 93
AutoShapes, 88-89
clip art, 130
embedded objects, 179
objects, 34
pictures, 130
text while you type, 41
views, 19
Web pages, graphics for, 224
windows, 15
WordArt text, 141
Restore Down button in windows, 15
restoring
Language bar, 306
picture settings, 131
restricted permission presentations, 267
Return action buttons, inserting, 213
Reviewers button, Reviewing toolbar, 271
reviewing presentations, 261
See also tracking reviewer changes
accepting or rejecting revisions, 270
call-out boxes, 270
comments, 262-263

reviewing presentations *(continued)*
- e-mail review, sending presentation for, 268-269
- thumbnails of slides with changes, viewing, 273

Reviewing toolbar, 261, 263
- buttons on, 271
- tracking revisions with, 270

Revisions pane
- comments, reviewing, 262-263
- tracking reviewer changes with, 270

Revisions pane button, Reviewing toolbar, 271

right alignment
- for objects, 109
- of text, 44

rotating
- chart axis labels, 163
- drawing objects, 87, 114-115
- 15-degree increments, constraining rotation to, 115
- fixed point, rotating object around, 115
- freeforms, 95
- imported objects, 115
- precisely rotating objects, 115
- WordArt text, 138

rows. *See* columns and rows

RTF (Rich Text Format)
- outline text, saving, 196
- presentation, saving, 197

ruler
- *See also* indents; tabs
- quick operation of, 51
- showing/hiding, 50

S

saturation, defined, 80

Save As command, 24
- HTML file, saving as, 222

Save As Web Page command, 222

Save command, shortcut key for, 5

saving
- annotations, 257
- automatic save feature, 25
- with AutoRecover feature, 27
- changing save options, 25
- charts, customized settings for, 160
- on closing presentation, 30
- color schemes, 81
- default location to save files, setting, 297
- different name, saving presentation with, 25
- existing presentation, 25
- first time, saving presentation for, 24
- FTP server, saving presentation to, 222
- hyperlinks, presentation with, 220
- new folder, saving presentation to, 24
- outline, presentation as, 196
- RTF (Rich Text Format), saving text in, 196
- self-running presentations, 250
- slides, formats for saving, 197
- template, presentation, 84-85

scaling slides to fit paper, 208

scanners, inserting pictures from, 128

scheduling
- broadcast presentation, 274
- online meetings, 276

ScreenTips for undoing actions, 43

scribbles, drawing, 95

scrolling
- master views, switching between, 68
- in presentations, 18

searching. *See* finding

Search Results task pane, 20

Search task pane, 14
- *See also* finding

security
- *See also* passwords
- macro security levels, 296

selecting
- chart boxes, 165
- drawing objects, 99
- objects, 34
- text, 40

Selection After Enter option for datasheets, 153

Select Picture dialog box, 122

Selfcert.exe file, 230

self-running presentations
- creating, 250
- narrations for, 248-249
- saving, 250

Send Backward for objects, 111

Send to Back for objects, 111

Send To Microsoft Word feature, 196

sentence case, changing text to, 201
Set Transparent Color button, 133
Set Up Show command, 234
  for custom slide shows, 237
  slide timings, setting, 246
shaded backgrounds, creating, 83
shadows
  colors, 77
    changing color of, 105
  creating shadows, 104-105
  to freeforms, 95
  location, changing, 104
  nudging, 104
  preset shadows, using, 104
  removing shadows, 104
  on text, 54
  text, adding to, 105
Shadow Style button, 104-105
shapes. *See* AutoShapes; drawing objects
Shared Workspace, working with, 293
Shared Workspace task pane, 279
SharePoint Team Services, 279-283
  administering, 282-283
  alerts, setting up, 286
  categories for alerts, 286
  Change Portal Site Navigation Page, 282
  Change Settings Page, 282-283
  checking documents in and out, 284
  contacts, creating, 290-291
  Document Library, storing documents in, 280, 284
  Documents and Lists Page, 280-281
  e-mail
    addresses of users, 280
    alerts, setting up, 286
  events
    Outlook, link to events in, 289
    setting up, 288
  Home Page, 280
  installing SharePoint Server 2003, 294
  Manage Users Page, 280-281
  Microsoft Outlook
    contacts, links to, 291
    events, links to, 289
  new members, adding, 285
  passwords
    for contact links, 291
    for Shared Workspace, 293
  permissions for users, 285
  Portal sites on Documents and Lists Page, 280
  shared documents with, 284
  Shared Workspace, working with, 293
  Site Settings Page, 282-283
  surveys, setting up, 280
  tasks, assigning, 287
  team members, viewing, 284
  uploading documents to library, 284
  user access list controls, specifying, 285
  viewing, 280-281
  Web discussions, holding, 292
sharing information
  See also OLE (object linking and embedding); pasting; SharePoint Team Services
  embedding objects, 148
  presentations, 1
shortcut menus, 5
  commands, choosing, 5
  for Grouping command, 116
  for Order command, 116
shortcuts
  for commands, 5
  dialog boxes, navigating, 8
  objects, working with, 35
  program shortcuts, creating, 2
  slide show view shortcuts, 254
showing/hiding
  Debug toolbar, 302
  formatting, 50
  Language bar, 306
  master background objects on slide, 72
  New Presentation task pane, 10
  Office Assistant, 23
  presentation properties, 202
  ruler, 50
  slides in show, 235
  toolbars, 7
  Web toolbar, 221, 228
  WordArt toolbar, 137
Show Me Live software, xv
signatures, digital, 230-231
size of slides, controlling, 186

sizing handles
AutoShapes, resizing, 88
for clip art, 34
of pictures, 130
text boxes, adjusting, 60
Slide design button, 66
Slide Design task pane for Animation Schemes, 240
Slide Finder feature, 65
Slide Layout button, 32
Slide Layout task pane, 9
new slides, inserting, 32
Slide Master, 67
backgrounds of slides, controlling, 72-73
design templates, applying, 71
every slide, including object on, 70
hiding objects with, 72
master layout, changing, 73
new master, inserting, 70
placeholders, 67
modifying, 73
preserving masters, 71
viewing, 68
Web presentations, viewing, 226
Slide Master View toolbar, 70
slide numbers
controlling, 186
different number, starting with, 75
inserting slide numbering, 74
master placeholders for, 67
Slide pane, rearranging slides in, 62
slides. *See also* range of slides; text
action buttons to specific slides, creating, 213
browsing in, 19
collapsing slides, 63
customized slide proportions, 187
deleting, 48
duplicating slides, 49
expanding slides, 63
formats for saving slides, 197
frames, adding, 189
graphic image, saving as, 197
Microsoft Word, exporting slides to, 195
new slides, creating, 32
orientation, changing, 187
other presentations, inserting slides from, 64
Outline pane, adding slide in, 48
pasting, 62-63
printing slides in presentation, 207
scaling slides to fit paper, 208
size of slides, controlling, 186
Slide Finder feature, 65
spell checking, 198-199
text, entering, 37-39
slide shows, 233
See also animations; annotations; presentations; transitions
continuously running shows, setting up, 235
current slide, starting from, 253
custom slide shows
creating, 236-237
navigation in, 255
deleting custom slide shows, 237
editing
custom slide shows, 237
timings, 247
hiding slides in, 235
looping option for, 235
macros running during, 300
narrations, recording, 248-249
navigating in, 254
options, setting, 253
Pen tool, using, 256
in Presenter view, 258
range of slides, showing, 234-235
Rehearse Timings, using, 246-247
setting up, 234-235
shortcuts for viewing, 254
specific slide, going to, 254
timings, settings for, 246-247
on two monitors, 258
view navigation shortcuts, 254
Slide Show view
notes, adding, 254
opening presentations in, 235
other program, switching to, 255
slide timings, setting, 246
sounds, playing, 145
videos, playing, 145

Slide Sorter view, 17
    deleting slides in, 33
    rearranging slides in, 62
    summary slides, creating, 184
    transitions, viewing, 239
Slides pane, deleting slides in, 33
slide-title master pair, 67
Slide Transition button, 239
Smart Tags, 312-313
    accessing information with, 313
    options, changing, 312
snap into place, setting objects to, 106
software, Show Me Live, xv
sound cards, 119, 145
    for narrations, 248
sounds, 1, 119
    See also Clip Organizer; Web presentations
    for action buttons, 215
    animations, adding to, 241
    hyperlinks, adding to, 214-215
    inserting, 120, 142-143
    new slides, inserting on, 143
    playing sounds, 145
    recording sounds, 144
    transitions, adding to, 238-239
source file object in OLE, 148
source of linked object, changing, 180
source program
    editing embedded object in, 180
    in OLE, 148
speakers, 119, 145
speaker's notes. *See* notes
Speak Text button, 308
specific Web page, opening, 228-229
Speech commands. *See* Voice commands
speech profiles, creating, 307
Speech Recognition Wizard, 306
Speech Tools button, 307
speed of transition effects, setting, 239
spell checking, 198-199
    with AutoCorrect feature, 42
    defaults, changing, 297
    turning off as you type feature, 199
    as you type option, 199
splitting table cells, 175
squares
    action buttons as squares, creating, 213
    colors for, 100
    drawing, 89
stacking order of shapes, changing, 111
Standard toolbar, 6
    default options, changing, 298
    Save button on, 24
    Undo button, 43
starting
    Microsoft Graph, 149
    PowerPoint, 2
    slide shows, 252
    Windows Explorer, starting PowerPoint from, 2
Start menu, 2
step-by-step instructions, xiv
Step mode, debugging macros with, 302
stock quotes, obtaining, 312
straight lines
    curves and lines, objects with, 94
    drawing, 92
Style Checker, 200
    defaults, changing, 297
    resetting tips, 200
    text case, changing, 201
Subordinate chart boxes, adding, 166
subordinate-to place, 166
subtitles
    for outlines, 48
    with Title Master, 67
suggested content, creating presentation with, 11
summary slides, creating, 184
supplements, 1, 183
    See also handouts
surfaces for chart elements, 164
switching
    between closed and open curves, 94
    between master views, 68
    in Slide Show view, 255
    between task panes, 4
    between windows, 15
synonyms. *See* thesauruses

T

Tab key, 52
    drawing objects, selecting, 116
    objects, selecting, 35

tables
- aligning text in cells, 174
- borders of cells, modifying, 175
- cells, 173
  - aligning text in, 174
  - borders, modifying, 175
  - merging, 175
  - splitting, 175
- columns and rows, 173
  - height and width, adjusting, 175
  - inserting and deleting, 174
- defined, 173
- deleting columns and rows from, 174
- entering text in, 173
- eraser tool with, 174
- formatting for, 174-175
- inserting
  - created tables, 173
  - Word tables, 172
- merging cells in, 175
- moving in tables, 173
- pencil tool with, 174
- placeholder, 33
- splitting cells in, 175

Tablet PC, 310

tabs
- alignments, 52
- clearing tabs, 53
- default tabs, changing, 53
- distance between stops, changing, 53
- setting, 36, 52-53

Tabs option in dialog box, 8

task panes
- new presentation options, 9
- opening and closing, 4
- using, 3

tasks with SharePoint Team Services, assigning, 287

templates
- *See also* design templates; presentations
- AutoContent Wizard, adding to, 85
- creating templates, 84-85
- existing presentations, applying templates to, 12
- Group Home Page template, 210-211
- types of, 65
- for Web presentations, 210-211

Templates folder, storing templates in, 84

text, 1
- *See also* alignments; editing; fonts/font size; formatting; handwritten text; indents; objects; Outline pane; WordArt
- animating text, 242-243
- AutoFormat text as you type, 58
- AutoShapes, adding text to, 61, 91
- bulleted list, entering text in, 36, 39
- case, changing, 201
- colors of, 77
- copying, 40
- correcting text while typing, 42-43
- date and time as, 74
- deleting, 40
- developing text, 36-37
- dimming text after animation, 242-243
- entering text, 37-39
- finding, 45
- inserting text, 38
- language, marking text as, 194
- location of text, determining, 39
- moving text, 40, 50
- organization charts, aligning text in, 168
- paragraph line spacing, adjusting, 39
- placeholders, 33, 38
- promoting/demoting text, 50-51
- replacing, 45
- resizing while you type, 41
- RTF (Rich Text Format) , saving text in, 196
- selecting text, 40
- shadows, adding, 105
- Style Checker for, 200
- in table cells, 173

text boxes, 8
- AutoShapes for, 60-61
- charts, adding to, 164
- creating, 60-61
- editing, 60
- objects, 36
- orientation of text, changing, 61
- sizing handles for adjusting, 60

Text Import Wizard, 152

textures
- for backgrounds, 83
- for chart elements, 164

for fills, 101
thesauruses
Research task pane feature for, 46
using, 47
3-D effects
for charts, 160, 163
depth, setting, 113
direction of object, changing, 113
for freeforms, 95
lighting, setting, 113
preset styles, applying, 112
shapes
adding to, 112-113
transforming, 87
surfaces, adding, 112
tilting 3-D objects, 112
3-D settings toolbar, 112
thumbnails
pictures, viewing, 128
slides with changes, viewing, 273
tick marks in charts, 150
tilting 3-D objects, 112
time. *See* date and time
timings between slides, setting, 246-247
title case, changing text to, 201
Title Master, 67, 70
viewing, 68
titles
for charts, 161
for outlines, 48
text colors, 77
text objects, 36
Web page, presentations as, 223
toggle case, changing text to, 201
Toolbar Options list, 6
toolbars, 6-7
adding toolbars, 298
commands, choosing, 6
default options, changing, 298-299
macros, assigning, 304
moving, 7
repositioning, 299
reshaping, 7
showing/hiding, 7
top edge, aligning objects to, 109
Track Changes feature, 272-273
tracking reviewer changes, 261, 270-271
on comparing and merging presentations, 272-273
transitions, 233
all slides in presentation, applying to, 238
browsers, viewing presentations in, 245
sounds, adding, 238-239
specifying transitions, 238
speed of effects, setting, 239
viewing, 239
in Web page presentations, 226
Web pages showing, 224
transparencies, 1
creating slides sized for, 186
transparent colors
for backgrounds, 132-133
WordArt, transparency settings for, 141
trendlines, 164
troubleshooting
drawing objects, arrangement of, 117
guide, xv
TrueType fonts, embedding, 185
turning on/off
annotations, 257
AutoCorrect feature, 42
AutoFit Text feature, 41
guides, 107
Language bar, 309
Office Assistant, 23
Office Clipboard preferences, 177
spell checking as you type feature, 199
2-D effects
for charts, 160
shapes, transforming, 87
two monitors, slide shows on, 258
Type A Question For Help box, 20

U

Unapply button, Reviewing toolbar, 271, 273
underlining
hyperlinks, 221
text, 54
undoing
AutoCorrect action, 43
automatic numbering, 58
redoing undone actions, 43

updating
links, 180
PowerPoint online, 26
Upload button to add attachments, 287
Upload Graphic Images in an Image Library Site, SharePoint Team Services, 280
uppercase, changing text to, 201
URLs (uniform resource locators), 219
with Meeting Workspace feature, 288

V

vector image technology, 134
Venn diagrams, 182
vertically formatting WordArt text, 140
vertices, 96-97
angles, modifying, 97
inserting, 96
moving, 96
video conferencing, 276
videos, 1, 119
See also Clip Organizer
changing settings for, 145
inserting, 120, 142-143
new slides, inserting on, 143
playing videos, 145
View Datasheet button, 154
views and viewing
See also Normal view; Notes Page view; Slide Show view; Slide Sorter view
clips on Web, 126
color schemes, 78
defaults, changing, 296
display view size, changing, 49
Handout Master, 69
masters, viewing, 68-69
Notes Master, 69
Office Clipboard, 99
PowerPoint window, 3
SharePoint Team Services, 280-281
size of view, changing, 19
for text, 36
transitions, 239
two monitors, viewing slide shows on, 258
Web presentations, 226
viruses, controlling, 296
Visual Basic
help with, 303
macros with, 302
Visual Basic Editor, 231
Voice Command option, 306-309
Voice commands, 306-309
dictating text, 309
executing, 308
training computer to your voice, 307
voice narrations. *See* narrations

W

washout coloring for pictures, 132
.WAX file format support, 145
Web. *See* Internet
Web discussions with SharePoint Team Services, 292
Web presentations, 209
See also hyperlinks
action buttons, 212-213
sounds for, 215
specific slides, action buttons to, 213
testing, 212
addresses of, 219
animations in presentations, 226
AutoContent Wizard for, 210-211
broadcasting presentations, 274-275
creating, 222-223
digital signatures, adding, 230-231
full-screen mode, viewing in, 226-227
Group Home Page template, 210-211
handouts with, 214
home page, creating, 210-211
hyperlinks to, 216-217
individual slides, viewing, 227
languages for, 224
Microsoft.Net Passport, using, 223
navigation bar for, 226
navigation buttons, creating, 224
opening presentation as, 225
options, changing, 224
outlines, viewing as, 226-227
previewing, 226-227
publishing, 222-223
Return action buttons, inserting, 213
saving presentation as Web page, 197
sounds

for action buttons, 215
for hyperlinks, 214-215
specific Web page, opening, 228-229
square action buttons, creating, 213
start page, creating, 228
templates, using, 210-211
transitions in presentations, 226
Web servers, defined, 222
Web toolbar
displaying, 221
navigating with, 220
searching the Web with, 228-229
showing/hiding, 228
specific Web page, opening, 228-229
start page, creating, 228
Whiteboard for online meetings, 276
width of columns. *See* columns and rows
wildcards, searching with, 14
windows
arranging windows, 15
resizing, 15
viewing PowerPoint window, 3
Windows Explorer
Selfcert.exe file, running, 230
starting PowerPoint from, 2
Windows Media Player, 120
playing videos or sounds with, 145-146
wire frame surface to 3-D objects, 112
wizards
See also AutoContent Wizard
Profile Wizard, 307
Speech Recognition Wizard, 306
Text Import Wizard, 152
.WMA file format support, 145
.WMX file format support, 145
WordArt, 147
aligning objects, 139
character spacing, adjusting, 141
colors, changing, 138-139
creating text, 136-137
editing text, 137
existing WordArt, applying different style to, 137
fills, 103, 140
colors, changing, 139
formatting text, 136, 138
height of letters, changing, 140
line style, changing, 140
modifying text styles, 138-139
rotating text, 138
shape, changing, 138
size or position, changing, 141
text effects, applying, 140-141
transparency settings for, 141
vertically formatting text, 140
WordArt toolbar, 136-137
Writing Pad
features of, 311
inserting text on, 311
.WVX file format support, 145

X

x-axis, 150
labels for, 153
rotating chart axis labels, 163

Y

y-axis, 150
labels for, 153
rotating chart axis labels, 163

Z

zooming on chart objects, 162